D1467645

Councils and Synods with other documents relating to the English Church, volume II, edited by the late Sir Maurice Powicke and by Professor C. R. Cheney, was published by the Clarendon Press in 1964, and was immediately recognized throughout the scholarly world as a fundamental collection of documents relating to the conciliar and legislative activities of the English Church in the 13th and early 14th centuries (1205–1313); it comprises canons of provincial and legatine councils, synodal statutes, notes on other meetings, legations, etc., with magisterial commentary.

Volume I is designed to fill the gap between the conclusion of the English section of Haddan and Stubbs's *Councils and Ecclesiastical Documents* (1869–78), and volume II. It is published in two parts: 871–1066 (edited by Dorothy Whitelock), for which *acta* of councils are exceedingly rare, and a picture of the pastoral organization and legislative activity of the Church is built up from royal codes, bishops' pastoral letters, narratives of important meetings and a variety of other ecclesiastical documents; and 1066–1204 (edited by Martin Brett and C. N. L. Brooke), for which a number of conciliar *acta* and narratives of ecclesiastical councils, and royal councils in which important ecclesiastical business was conducted, form the nucleus, to which are added notes on legations, on the English participation in papal councils, on negotiations for crusading taxes and other matters related to the central themes of the book. Critical texts, full details of surviving manuscripts, and historical commentary are provided throughout.

Dorothy Whitelock is Elrington and Bosworth Professor Emerita of Anglo-Saxon at Cambridge University.
Martin Brett is Fellow of Robinson College, Cambridge University.
Christopher N. L. Brooke is Dixie Professor of Ecclesiastical History, Cambridge University, and Fellow of Gonville and Caius College.

COUNCILS & SYNODS

WITH OTHER DOCUMENTS
RELATING TO
THE ENGLISH CHURCH

Planned under the General Editorship of
F. M. POWICKE
in continuation of the
'Councils and Ecclesiastical Documents'
of Arthur West Haddan and
William Stubbs

COUNCILS & SYNODS

WITH OTHER DOCUMENTS
RELATING TO

THE ENGLISH CHURCH

I

A.D. 871–1204

EDITED BY

D. WHITELOCK, M. BRETT
AND C. N. L. BROOKE

PART II · 1066–1204

ST. JOSEPH'S UNIVERSITY

3 9353 00238 8898

BR
741
.C68
Vol. 1
Pt. 2

CLARENDON PRESS · OXFORD

Oxford University Press, Walton Street, Oxford OX2 6DP

Oxford New York Toronto
Delhi Bombay Calcutta Madras Karachi
Kuala Lumpur Singapore Hong Kong Tokyo
Nairobi Dar es Salaam Cape Town
Melbourne Auckland

and associated companies in
Beirut Berlin Ibadan Nicosia

Published in the United States by
Oxford University Press, New York

© *Oxford University Press 1981*

First published 1981
Reprinted 1986

All rights reserved. No part of this publication may be reproduced,
stored in a retrieval system, or transmitted, in any form or by any means,
electronic, mechanical, photocopying, recording, or otherwise, without
the prior permission of Oxford University Press

British Library Cataloguing in Publication Data
Councils & synods with other documents
relating to the English church.
1: 871–1204
1. Great Britain—Church history—Sources
I. Whitelock, Dorothy   II. Brett, Martin
III. Brook, Christopher N. L.
274.2   BR741
ISBN 0-19-822394-3

Printed in Great Britain by
Antony Rowe Ltd,
Chippenham

TABLE OF CONTENTS

TEXTS

85

1070. LEGATION OF THE CARDINALS JOHN AND PETER WITH BISHOP ERMENFRID OF SION

See Tillmann, pp. 12-15, Freeman, *Norman Conquest,* iv
(1876), 329-45, esp. 329-30, Böhmer, *Kirche und Staat,*
pp. 79-88, Z.N. Brooke, *The English Church and the
Papacy,* pp. 132-43, H.E.J. Cowdrey, 'Pope Gregory VII
and the Anglo-Norman church and kingdom', *Studi Gregoriani,* ix (1972), 77-114, C. Morton, 'Pope Alexander II and
the Norman Conquest', *Latomus,* xxxiv (1975), 362-82.

On the death of Edward the Confessor the duke of Normandy sent
an ambassador to Rome, probably Archdeacon Gilbert of Lisieux,
to seek papal support for his proposed invasion of England.
Archdeacon Hildebrand gave his cause powerful backing, but
some doubt attaches to the success of the mission.[1] No direct
evidence of the arguments of the duke's adherents survives,
though much later Orderic Vitalis spoke of the pope regarding
William as the legitimate heir and Harold as a usurper. An undated fragment of a letter from Alexander to William written
after the success of the invasion suggests that the pope considered it as having restored England to a former posture 'sub
apostolorum principis manu et tutela', whatever the precise
content of that phrase.[2]

By the end of 1067 Ermenfrid bishop of Sion (Canton Valais,
Switzerland) was at Rouen as papal legate, possibly engaged in
the promulgation of the penitential articles printed below,
and certainly involved in the negotiations surrounding the
translation of John of Avranches to Rouen. Papal approval of
this move was transmitted to Normandy by further unnamed

---

[1] Against William of Poitiers, *Gesta Guillelmi Conquestoris,* p. 154, OV
ii.142 and one view of *Gregorii VII Registrum,* vii.23 compare Morton,
Latomus, xxxiv (1975), 362-82.

[2] *Die Kanonessammlung des Kardinals Deusdedit,* ed. Wolf von Glanvell,
p. 378 (JL 4757); T. Schmidt, *Alexander II. (1061-1073) und die römische
Reformgruppe seiner Zeit,* pp. 220-4 and the references below, p. 625.

legates.[1] The need to take urgent action for the reorganization
of the English church, and particularly to deal with the ambiguous position of Archbishop Stigand may have become manifest
after the death of Ealdred of York on 11 September 1069 and
the general rising of the English during which it occurred.[2]
In any case the cardinal priests John and Peter arrived in
England before Easter in 1070 with Bishop Ermenfrid. If, as
seems most probable, these legates are the same as the cardinals Peter and John Minutus whom Gregory VII later mentions as
counselling King William on the endowments of Caen, then John
may be identified as the cardinal priest of S. Maria in
Trastevere. The identity of Peter is apparently clarified by
the appearance at the foot of a genuine or largely genuine
charter of William for St. Martin-le-Grand of the attestations
of Peter, there styled cardinal priest and chancellor 'ab ...
papa in Angliam delegatus', and John 'per Gallias et Angliam
... vices apostolicas gerens'.[3] According to Orderic the
legates spent almost a year with the king, though this cannot
be true of Peter at least.[4] The chronicles agree in associat-
ing Bishop Ermenfrid with them; while he alone celebrated the
council of May, after their departure, the summons to that of
April was issued only in their names and a later letter from
Alexander II described an action of the May council as taken
'a suppositis legatorum nostrorum', so suggesting that Ermenfrid's was only a subordinate role.[5]

---

[1] J. Mabillon, *Vetera Analecta* (1675-85), ii.442-4, JL 4643, Schieffer,
Die päpstlichen Legaten in Frankreich, pp. 79-80, H.E.J. Cowdrey, *JEH* xx
(1969), 225-42, Schmidt, *Alexander II*, p. 154 and n.

[2] Stenton, *Anglo-Saxon England*, p. 659 n. 1.

[3] *Gregorii VII Registrum*, i.70, *Reg.* i, no. 22 (on which see W.H. Ste-
venson, 'An Old-English charter of William the Conqueror', *EHR* xi (1896),
744 and J.H. Round, *The Commune of London*, pp. 28-35). If the whole witness-
list is genuine the cardinals' attestations must have been added later.
Peter became cardinal-priest of St. Chrysogonus before 13 Jan. 1070 when
he appeared at Rome with that title (JL 4670, and see more generally Hüls,
p. 170, L. Santifaller, *Bullettino dell'Istituto Storico Italiano*, lvi
(1940), 185-6). For John see Hüls, p. 187.

[4] See references in previous note and JL 4677, which shows that Peter
was at Lucca with the pope on 16 August.

[5] Below, pp. 577-9.

86

7 OR 11 APRIL 1070. LEGATINE COUNCIL AT WINCHESTER

In the earliest surviving text of its kind from England (no. I) the cardinal priests John and Peter summoned Wulfstan of Worcester and the abbots of his diocese to a council to be held on the third day after Easter, 7 April. The Worcester *Chronicon ex Chronicis* (no. II) places it on 11 April, and distinguishes clearly between this and the later council at Windsor, but the common source of the narratives of the *Vita Lanfranci* and Orderic (nos. III, IV) had already confused them.[1]

The chief business of this council was the deposition of a number of Anglo-Saxon prelates, headed by the archbishop of Canterbury. The list of charges against Stigand in the Worcester account is substantially repeated in the profession of Remigius of Dorchester to Lanfranc (no. VIII), necessary because he had been consecrated by Stigand, and no doubt comes near the indictment which the archbishop faced at the council.[2] Nothing is known of the charges against Stigand's brother Æthelmær of East Anglia, and not even the names have survived of any abbots deposed at the council. However, some Anglo-Saxons had abandoned their houses or been expelled in the period since the Conquest, and it may well be that a formal sentence of deposition was delivered against them on this occasion.[3] Leofwine, bishop of Lichfield, was summoned to answer charges relating to his notorious marriage, but refused to appear and was condemned as contumacious in his absence. Not until a year later did he appear at the royal court to resign his see.[4]

---

[1] On the relation between the texts see OV ed. Chibnall, ii.xix-xxi, xxxiv-xxxv. The common source may well be the lost conclusion of the *Gesta Guillelmi* of William of Poitiers. The letter of summons may be compared with that of the two cardinals for the Poitevin council of 1100 in Mansi, xx.1125.

[2] On these and the difficulty in accepting the charges entirely at their face value see Barlow, *The English Church 1000-1066*, pp. 302-10.

[3] Compare *Heads*, pp. 28, 36, 66, 79.

[4] See below nos. II n. and VII. The 13th-cent. Ann. Burton (*Ann. Mon.* i.185) place the consecration of Peter, Leofwine's successor, in 1067; the texts used here agree with the *Acta Lanfranci* (ASC ed. Plummer, i.289), which places his consecration after 29 August, 1072; he does not appear among the bishops who attest below no. I(B) of May, 1072. See further Tait in *Essays in History presented to R.L. Poole*, pp. 154-6; curiously there is no profession for Peter among the Canterbury archives.

Other business is more obscurely attached to this council. The decision to imprison Æthelric, the former bishop of Durham, at Westminster, and to outlaw his brother Æthelwine, to whom he had resigned his see, was taken according to the D Chronicle (no. VI) at Easter in this year, and so may have been discussed if not taken in the council, though the charges of theft and perhaps treason were at least as appropriate to the king's court under a more general aspect. Æthelwine was among those who fled with Edgar Atheling to Scotland, and was captured the next year at the fall of Ely.[1] After the deposition of Æthelric of Selsey in the May council eight of the fifteen English sees had fallen vacant either by death or deprivation since the Conquest, and William's control of the episcopate was assured.

If one interprets strictly the words of the Conqueror's writ recording the transfer of the see of Dorchester to Lincoln, according to which the change was made 'auctoritate et consilio Alexandri pape et legatorum eius', this too must have been brought before the legates, possibly at Winchester; the first direct evidence that the move was in contemplation belongs to 1073.[2]

The *capitula* printed below (no. IX) were first attributed to this council by Böhmer on the grounds that the first canon, which has few contemporary parallels, was specially appropriate to the deposition of Stigand. Further grounds for accepting this conclusion derive from the manuscript tradition, for they are associated with the penitential articles of Ermenfrid in all three of the earliest copies, and one at least is very

---

[1] For the charges against Æthelric see Symeon, i.92 and WMGP, p. 271; the career and end of Æthelwine are covered in Symeon, i.94, 100, 105, ii.189-95, ASC 1069E and *Chronicon Monasterii de Abingdon*, i.485-6. These accounts are consistent; the passage in *Flor. Wig.* ii.8 is a misplaced interpolation from Symeon, i.105. The account taken from Wendover in Paris, *Chron. Maj.* ii.6 and amplified in *Flores Historiarum*, ii.4 probably refers to his conduct at Peterborough, not in this council.

[2] *Reg.* i, no. 283; a facsimile and commentary in *Reg. Lincoln*, i, no. 2 and *Facsimiles of English Royal Writs to 1100*, pl. xiii. If the consenting legates were in England and at the same time this is the only recorded multiple legation of the reign in which it could have occurred; see also Brooke in *Studia Gratiana*, xii (1967), 51 n.

likely to have been completed before the meeting of the next
known council at Winchester, that of Easter, 1072.[1]

The abbreviated form in which the canons survive precludes
any exact pursuit of their sources; in general they bear a
family resemblance to those pronounced earlier at Coyanza and
Gerona and a little later in Normandy.[2]

The manuscripts are these:

A Cambridge, Corpus Christi Coll. ms. 190, p. 292 (Ker,
   Catalogue, no. 45). Probably among the manuscripts
   presented to Exeter cathedral by Bishop Leofric before
   his death in February, 1072. However the canons, which
   are followed by those attributed below to Whitsun 1070,
   and the penitential articles, are an addition to the
   main text made possibly after it reached the cathedral,
   though still before c.1100; see above, p. 191 and
   Exeter Book, pp. 15-27.

B London, BL ms. Cotton Tib. C. i, fo. 202^{r-v}, among the
   earliest additions to the Rhenish pontifical used at
   Sherborne under Bishop Herman, who died in 1078 (Ker,
   in *Catalogue*, no. 197). There is a partial facsimile
   in Ker, *English Manuscripts in the Century after the
   Norman Conquest*, pl. 1a.[3]

C Bodl. ms. Junius 121, fos. 2^{v}-3, a late 11th-cent. entry
   on the flyleaf of a volume of canons written for Bishop
   Wulfstan, following the penitential articles (Ker, *Catalogue*, no. 338 and above, p. 191).[4]

D Montpellier, École de Médecine, ms. 304, fo. 24^{r-v}, in

[1]Böhmer, *Kirche und Staat*, pp. 62-4 n.; Tillmann, p. 14 n. 8; Brooke,
art. cit., pp. 58-9.
[2]For the councils of Coyanza and Compostella (1056), which both exist
in two forms, one certainly interpolated, see A. García Gallo in *Anuario
de Historia del Derecho Español*, xx (1950), esp. 286-302, and G. Martínez
Díez, *Anuario de Estudios Medievales*, i (1964), 121-38.
[3]Also N.R. Ker, in *The Anglo-Saxons: studies presented to Bruce Dickins*,
ed. P. Clemoes, pp. 262-79.
[4]A 17th-cent. transcript of these canons, with those of Winchester (1076)
and Ermenfrid's penitential articles, presumably from this ms., is bound
into the end of Dublin, Trinity Coll. ms. 526, pp. 175-6.

a short late 12th-cent. collection of councils in
England and Normandy under William.[1]

It is remarkable that A, B, and C are closely associated with
bishops who presumably attended the council. Though none appears
a copy of any other, the fact that all contain the same corrupt
reading in the last canon suggests that they all derive from a
single ancestor. B was the basis of Sp. ii.12 and so Labbe,
x.351-2, W. i.365, Mansi, xx.460. A transcript of D was printed
in Labbe, x.311-12 and thence Mansi, xx.400-2.

I. *Summons to a council at Winchester*

> Bodl. ms. Hatton 113, fo. ii (the first of two companion
> volumes to Junius 121, for which see above). Printed in
> W. i.323, Wake, *State of the Church*, p. 161, *Vita Wulf-
> stani*, pp. 189-90, and (from a late transcript) Hoveden,
> i.123-4 n.

Epistola cardinalium urbis Romae ad Wlstanum episcopum.

I. et P. presbiteri cardinales sancti Petri Wlstano de Wihra-
ceastre episcopo salutem. Licet R(omana) ęcclesia circa correctionem omnium Christianorum invigilare debeat, specialius tamen
eam conversationis vestrę mores convenit inquirere et Christianam religionem qua vos primitus instruxit diligentia suę
visitationis reparare. Huius itaque sollicitudinis debito nos
qualescumque beati Petri apostoli ministros et vice atque
auctoritate domini nostri pape Alexandri fultos ad partes
vestras direxit ut concilium vobiscum cęlebraturi quę in vinea
Domini Sabaoth male pululant resecemus et animarum et corporum
utilitati profutura plantemus. Vestram igitur fraternitatem in
partem tantę sollicitudinis apostolica auctoritate invitamus ut
tertia die post proximum Pascha, remota omni occasione, ad
Wincestram conveniatis, et omnes abbates diocesis vestrę ostensis his litteris nostris vobiscum venire commoneatis.

---

[1] For this ms. see Brett in *JEH* xxvi (1975), 301-8.

II. *Worcester Chronicon ex chronicis s.a. 1070*

> Oxford, Corpus Christi Coll. ms. 157, p. 347 (= C), a ver-
> sion partially the autograph of John of Worcester. Select
> variants from Dublin, Trinity Coll. mss. 502 (E. 5.23),
> fo. 227^{r-v} (= H) and 503 (E. 6.4), fo. 96^{r-v} (= G), a
> very early abbreviation from Worcester; printed *Flor. Wig.*
> ii.5-6. Later versions appear in Symeon, ii.192-3, Hove-
> den, i.122-3 and their derivatives. Sp. ii.3, W. i.322
> and Mansi, xx.5-6 draw on Hoveden.

Concilium magnum in octavis Pascę[d] Wintonie celebratum est,
iubente et presente rege Willelmo, domno Alexandro papa consentiente et per suos legatos Hearmenfredum Sedunensem episcopum et presbiteros Iohannem et Petrum, cardinales sedis
apostolicę, suam auctoritatem exhibente. In quo concilio
Stigandus Dorubernię archiepiscopus degradatur tribus ex causis, scilicet quia episcopatum Wintonię cum archiepiscopatu
iniuste possidebat, et quia vivente archiepiscopo Rotberto non
solum archiepiscopatum sumpsit sed etiam eius pallio, quod
Cantuuarie remansit dum vi iniuste ab Anglia pulsus est, in
missarum celebratione aliquandiu usus est, et post a Benedicto
quem sancta Romana ęcclesia excommunicavit, eo quod pecuniis
sedem apostolicam invasit, pallium accepit. Eius quoque frater
Agelmarus East-Anglorum episcopus est degradatus. Abbates etiam
aliqui ibi degradati sunt, operam dante rege ut quamplures ex
Anglis suo honore privarentur, in quorum locum suę gentis personas subrogaret, ob confirmationem scilicet sui quod noviter
adquisierat regni.[b] Hinc et nonnullos tam episcopos quam abbates, quos nulla evidenti causa nec concilia nec leges seculi
damnabant, suis honoribus privavit et usque ad finem vitę
custodię mancipatos detinuit, suspitione ut diximus tantum
inductus novi regni. In hoc itaque concilio, dum ceteri trepidi

---

[a] iii id' Apr' (11 April) *add* G.   [b] In hoc concilio degradatus est de
sede episcopali abbas Leofwinus et reversus est ad abbatiam suam, scilicet
Covintr', unde prius assumptus fuerat. H² *in margin; see above p. 565
n. 4.*

utpote regis agnoscentes animum ne suis honoribus privarentur
timerent, venerandus vir Wulstanus Wigornensis episcopus[a] possessiones quamplures sui episcopatus, ab Aldredo arciepiscopo
dum a Wigornensi ęcclesia ad Eboracensem transferretur, sua
potentia retentos, qui tunc eo defuncto in regiam potestatem
devenerant, constanter proclamabat, expetebat, iustitiamque
inde fieri tam ab ipsis qui concilio pręerant quam a rege
flagitabat.[1] At, quia Eboracensis ęcclesia non habens pastorem
qui pro ea loqueretur muta erat, iudicatum est ut ipsa querela
sic remaneret quousque, arciepiscopo ibi constituto qui
ęcclesiam defenderet, dum esset qui eius querelę responderet,
ex obiectis et responsis posset evidentius ac iustius iudicium
fieri. Sicque tunc ea querela ad tempus remansit.

III. *Vita Lanfranci c. VI (part)*

>   *Lanfranci Opera Omnia,* ed. D'Achery, p. 7 (= A), from a
>   lost ms. of Bec (ed. Giles, i.292-3, *PL* cl.40); Vatican,
>   ms. Reg. Lat. 499, fo. 56 (= B), a 15th-cent. collection
>   of lives of the abbots of Bec.

Post hæc venerunt ad regem in Angliam tres legati simul,
Ermenfredus Sedunorum episcopus et duo clerici cardinales,
missi ad petitionem ipsius a papa Alexandro, qui eum in Pascha
coronam regni capiti eius imponentes in regem Anglicum confirmaverunt. Congregata est ergo synodus magna Windresoris in qua,
præsidente rege, ab ipsis legatis deiecti sunt quidam episcopi
indigni episcopatu propter vitam criminosam et inscitiam curæ[b]
pastoralis. Inter quos deposuerunt Stigandum cum anathemate
reprobatum, multis criminibus coinquinatum, qui cum duobus
episcopiis infanda ambitione Cantuariensem archiepiscopatum
invaserat.

---

[a]ut leo confidens et absque terrore solus *add* G *(compare Prov. 28, 1).*
[b]insitiam curam B.

---

[1]York's claims are discussed in *Vita Wulfstani,* pp. xxv-xxxi.

IV. *Orderic Vitalis, Historia Ecclesiastica*

> Printed from Paris, BN ms. lat. 5506, vol. ii, fos. 65^V-
> 66 (the autograph), in OV ed. Chibnall, ii.236-8 (used
> here); also ed. Duchesne, *Historiae Normannorum Scriptores
> Antiqui*, p. 516, OV ed. Le Prévost, ii.199-200.

Post hæc Guillelmus rex Dominicam Resurrectionem in urbe Guenta
celebravit, ubi cardinales Romanæ æcclesiæ coronam ei solenniter
imposuerunt. Nam ex petitione ipsius Alexander papa tres idoneos
ei ut karissimo filio legaverat vicarios, Ermenfredum pontificem Sedunorum et duos canonicos cardinales. Quos apud se ferme
annuo spacio retinuit, audiens et honorans eos tanquam angelos
Dei. In diversis locis in plurimis negociis sic egere, sicut
indigas canonicæ examinationis et ordinationis regiones illas
dinovere. Maxima vero ac ùtillima sinodus Windresoris celebrata
est, anno millesimo septuagesimo ab incarnatione Domini. Rex et
cardinales eidem concilio præsiderunt, et illic Stigandum
pridem reprobatum anathemate deposuerunt. Periuriis enim et
homicidiis coinquinatus erat, nec per hostium in archipræsulatum
introierat. Nam a duobus episcopiis, Norfulcano et Guentano,[1]
infanda gradatione ambitionis ac supplantationis ascenderat.
Suffraganei quoque aliquot deiecti sunt, indigni pontificatu
propter criminosam vitam et curæ pastoralis inscitiam.

V. *William of Malmesbury, Gesta Pontificum*

> Oxford, Magdalen Coll. ms. Lat. 172, fo. 12 (the auto-
> graph); printed in WMGP, p. 37.

Sed quicquid his tegebatur involucris erupit in clarum veniente
Angliam Ermenfredo, Sedunense episcopo legato Alexandri papę.
Qui ad voluntatem regis coacto concilio Stigandum deposuit
fidem Willemi appellantem et violentiam reclamantem. Et quanvis
ille se blande excusans preceptum papę obiectaret, non tamen
opinionem affectatę depositionis exclusit quod eum toto ęvo in
vinculis Wintonię habuerit.

---

[1]Stigand was translated from Elmham to Winchester in 1047.

VI. *Anglo-Saxon Chronicle D*

> BL ms. Cotton Tiberius B. iv, fo. 83; printed in *ASC* ed.
> Thorpe, i.342, ed. Plummer, i.204, ed. Classen and
> Harmer, p. 90; trans. Thorpe, ii.175, Whitelock *et al.*,
> p. 150 (used here).[1]

And se kyng wæs þone midwintres dæig on Eoferwic, 7 swa ealne þone winter on þam lande, 7 com to Wincestre on þa ilcan Eastron. 7 Ægelric biscop wæs forwreged, þe wæs on Burh, 7 hine man lædde to Westmynstre, 7 utlagode his broðor Ægelwine biscop.

And the king was in York on Christmas Day, and so was in the country all the winter. And he came to Winchester that same Easter. And Bishop Æthelric, who was at Peterborough, had an accusation brought against him, and was taken to Westminster, and his brother Bishop Æthelwine was outlawed.

VII. *Letter of Lanfranc to Pope Alexander II (part)*

> BL ms. Cotton Nero A. vii, fo. 3^{r-v} (= N); Vatican, ms.
> Reg. Lat. 285, fos. 1^{V}-2 (= V); printed in *Lanf. Letters,*
> ed. Clover and Gibson, no. 2, ed. Giles, no. 4.[2]

Licifeldensis vero episcopus qui apud legatos vestros de incontinentia carnis, cui uxor publice habita filiique procreati testimonium perhibebant, aliisque criminibus accusatus ad sinodum tamen eorum venire noluit, unde et predicti legati vestri eum excommunicaverunt, regique substituendi successorem ut dicitur licentiam concesserunt. In Paschali solennitate ad curiam venit, de illatis culpis causam inire noluit, regi in conventu episcoporum atque laicorum episcopatum reddidit, se

---

[1]These events are put under 1068, but D begins this annal with an event late in 1068 and continues without a break until William's return to Winchester in 1070.

[2]From the context this letter was written between Easter (24 April) 1071, when Leofwine resigned his see, and October, when Lanfranc was in Rome himself. A post-medieval copy of JL 4695, Alexander's letter to the Conqueror, written either during Lanfranc's journey or just after it, includes as a marginal addition a plea on behalf of one Tedald 'communem fidelem nostrum' for the vacant see of Chester; for details of Lanfranc's journey and this letter see below.

amplius non habiturum nec successori calumniam aut damnum illaturum iureiurando spontanea voluntate firmavit. Dehinc ad monasterium in quo ab infantia nutritus monachus fuerat repedavit.[1] Ego tamen novus Anglus rerumque Anglicarum nisi quantum ab aliis accipio adhuc pene inscius in locum eius non presumpsi vel episcopum consecrare vel consecrandi licentiam aliis episcopis dare quoadusque preceptio vestra veniat, quę in tanto [fo. 3^v] negotio quid oporteat fieri informare nos debeat. Nec id^a quoque differat amanda paternitas vestra, quia diu est ex quo illa miserrima aecclesia pastore est destituta. Omnipotens Dominus det nobis semper audire de vobis quod audire coepimus et audire desideramus, diligende, colende, reverende pater.

VIII. *Profession of Remigius, bishop of Dorchester*

> BL ms. Cotton Cleopatra E. i, fo. 26^{r-v}, an early 12th-cent. copy of a (presumed) lost original; printed in *Canterbury Professions,* no. 32, Giraldus, *Opera,* vii.151-2. The 15th-cent. copy in Canterbury, D & C Reg. A, fo. 224 contributes only errors.

Tempore quo ego Remigius, Dorcacensis et Legoracensis et Lincolinę provincię cęterarumque provinciarum quibus antecessores mei prefuerunt, sum electus antistes, sanctę Cantuariensi ęcclesię Stigandus pręsumptor pręsidebat. Cum enim contempta Helmeanensis ęcclesię mediocritate translatus esset ad Wentanę civitatis episcopium, stimulante adhuc maioris honoris ambitu, post paucos annos Robertum archiepiscopum partim vi partim insidiis expulit, metropolem invasit, pallium, quod a sede apostolica ipse detulerat, cum cęteris ablatum usurpare non metuit. Qua temeritate Rome audita a Romanis pontificibus sepe vocatus, tandem damnatus et excommunicatus est. Ipse tamen decem et novem annis in sui cordis obstinatione permansit, quo tanti temporis intervallo pręfatę Romanę ęcclesię pontifices,

---

^{a}Ne id *superscript* V[1].

---

[1]Coventry; see above, p. 569 n. a.

Leo, Victor, Stephanus, Nicholaus, Alexander[1] legatos suos suis
quisque temporibus in Anglicam terram transmiserunt, et ne
aliquis ad eum ordinandus accederet apostolica auctoritate
prohibuerunt. Ego vero, huius negotii nec ex toto gnarus nec
usquequaque ignarus, ordinandus ad eum veni,[2] professionem sibi
suisque successoribus feci, curamque episcopalem de manu ipsius
me consecrantis accepi. Post paucos dies prefatus domnus
Alexander papa legatos suos in terram Anglorum transmisit,
eumque deponi omnesque qui ab eo ordinati sunt aut abici aut
ab officiis suspendi precepit. Verum te, eiusdem sanctę metro-
politanę sedis antistes Lanfrance, Romam petente, prefatum
papam adii, teque [fo. 26[v]] mediante indulgentiam petii et
impetravi.[3] Cognoscens igitur ex auctoritate predicti papę nec
eum antecessorem tuum fuisse nec te successorem ipsius existere,
tibi quidem de obędientia mea scriptam professionem porrigo,
meque tuis omniumque qui tibi successuri sunt iussionibus
obtemperaturum esse promitto.

IX. *Capitula of canons pronounced at a council at Winchester*

> Based on A, collated throughout with B, C, and D, whose
> common readings are preferred.

---

[1]Leo IX (1048-54), Victor II (1054-7), Stephen IX (1057-8), Nicholas II
(1058-61), and Alexander II (1061-73), but see above, p. 565 n. 2.

[2]In 1067; the *Acta Lanfranci* (*ASC* ed. Plummer, i.288) speak of Lanfranc
receiving professions from all the bishops consecrated by the pope or other
archbishops in the time of Stigand between his first dispute with Thomas
of York and their departure for Rome; this document, however, belongs after
their return, perhaps to 1072. Remigius was the only bishop still in office
to have been consecrated by Stigand, but his profession may be compared
with those of Wulfstan, who had been consecrated by Ealdred, and Herfast
of Elmham, who was consecrated in the vacancy between Stigand and Lanfranc
(*Canterbury Professions,* nos. 31, 33).

[3]On this journey see also Eadmer, pp. 10-11 and Herman's 'Miracles of
St. Edmund' in *UGQ,* pp. 249-50. The *Acta Lanfranci* place it in the second
year of Lanfranc's pontificate, i.e. after 29 Aug. 1071; Abbot Baldwin
of Bury was in Rome with the two archbishops, and the privilege he secured,
JL 4692, is dated 27 Oct. 1071. See further T. Schmidt, *Alexander* II,
pp. 39-41.

Celebrati Capitula Concilii apud Wintoniam[a]

[1] Quod nulli liceat duobus episcopatibus presidere.[1]

[2] Quod nullus per symoniacam heresim ordinetur.[2]

[3] Quod extranei clerici sine commendaticiis litteris non recipiantur.[3]

[4] Quod ordinationes certis[b] temporibus fiant.

[5] De altaribus quod lapidea[c] sint.[4]

[6] Quod sacrificium de cervisia vel sola aqua non fiat, sed solummodo de[d] vino aqua mixto.[e][5]

[7] De baptismate quod in Pascha[f] et[g] Pentecosten solummodo celebretur[h], nisi periculum mortis fuerit.[6]

[8] Quod[i] in ecclesiis nisi ab episcopis consecratis misse non celebrentur.[7]

---

[a]Cap. Conc. apud Wint. cel. BD; Cap. Conc. apud Winceastram cel. C.
[b]certius C.   [c]ut lapidea BD; quod lapidei C.   [d]de *om*. BD.   [e]aqua vino mixto BD; vino aqua mixtum C.   [f]Pasca B.   [g]in *add* A.   [h]celebretur B[2] *margin*.   [i]ut BD.

---

[1]CC. of Chalcedon, c. 10 (Hinschius, p. 286), Rome (1059), c. 8, Tours (1060), c. 5; compare CC. of Nantes, c. 8 in Burchard, iii.47 and Rouen ('1050'), c. 3 (this council is dated *c*.1045 by R. Foreville, in *Church and Government in the Middle Ages*, pp. 22, 27).
[2]CC. of Rouen ('1050'), c. 6, Rome (1059), c. 9, Tours (1060), cc. 1, 2, Gerona (1068), c. 1.
[3]CC. of Chalcedon (451), c. 13 in Hinschius, p. 286, Rouen ('1050'), c. 9, Gerona (1068), c. 9.
[4]CC. of Epaone (517), c. '10' in Burchard, iii.25, Coyanza (1050), c. 3; compare *Vita Wulfstani*, p. 54.
[5]CC. of Braga III (613), c. 1 in Hinschius, p. 434, and Worms, c. 2 in Burchard, v. 2.
[6]Compare *Decreta Siricii*, c. 1, *Decreta Leonis*, cc. 4-6, *Decreta Gelasii*, c. 12 (Hinschius, pp. 520-1, 613, 652); contrast *NPL* 10.
[7]*Ex gestis Silvestri*, c. 9 (Hinschius, pp. 450-1), Can. Ps.-Edg. 15, *NPL* 13. An example of such an unconsecrated church in use is recorded in an extract from the lost cartulary of Plympton in Bodl. ms. James 23, pp. 164-5; a more graphic case is found in the Life of S. Wolfhelm (*MGH Scriptores*, xii.

[9] Quod^a in ęcclesiis^b corpora defunctorum hominum^c non sepeliantur.[1]

[10] Quod tintinnabula non pulsentur quando missa celebratur tempore secretę.^d

[11] Quod de criminibus soli episcopi pęnitentiam tribuant.[2]

[12] Quod monachi qui habitum dimiserint^e neque in militia neque in conventu clericorum^f recipiantur, sed excommunicati habeantur.[3]

[13] Quod quisque episcopus omni anno^g synodum celebret.[4]

[14] Quod^a decimę ab omnibus reddantur.[5]

[15] Quod^a clerici aut caste vivant aut ab officiis^h recedant.[6]

[16] Quod calices non sint cerei.ⁱ[7]

---

^aUt BD.   ^beclesiis BC.   ^c*om.* BD.   ^dsecreti BD.   ^edimiserint BD; dimiser't C; dimiser' A.   ^fnon *add* A.   ^gbis *add* A.   ^hofficio BD. ⁱ*Sic* ABCD; *recte* aerei; erei D²; vel lignei *add* BD.

---

[1] CC. of Braga I (559), c. 18 (Hinschius, p. 423), and Nantes, c. 11 in Burchard, iii.159; compare above, *Can. Ps.-Edg.* 29.

[2] C. of Carthage III (435), cc. 31-2 in Hinschius, p. 299.

[3] CC. of Chalcedon (451), c. 7 in Hinschius, p. 286 and Burchard, viii.4, Tours (1060), c. 7.

[4] The reading of A — 'omni anno bis' — has been rejected as peculiar to this ms.; however Windsor (1070) (to which A is the sole witness), c. 4 also requires two synods a year, as do many earlier canonical texts (e.g. Leo I, ep. xiv, c. 6, CC. of Nicaea (325), c. 5, Antioch (341), c. 20 in Hinschius, pp. 619, 258, 272). English practice later varied, but the reading of A here may well be correct.

[5] C. of Rome (1059), c. 5; compare e.g. VI Æthelred Lat. 16.

[6] Tillmann, p. 14 n. 8, sees this as an assertion of the strict doctrine on celibacy, for which see below, p. 616. Compare also Barlow (1979), p. 124.

[7] Read evidently *aerei*, as in Labbe, x.312, but this is a later emendation in D; all the mss. apparently stem from a copy in which the diphthong had been misread. A condemnation of the use of wooden chalices as in B and D is found in CC. of Rheims, c. 5 in Burchard, iii.96 and Coyanza (1050), c. 3; compare *NPL* 15.

87

24 MAY 1070. LEGATINE COUNCIL AT WINDSOR

The second council of the year was held at Whitsun by Bishop
Ermenfrid, after the return of the legates John and Peter.[1]
Apart from the confused narratives of the *Vita Lanfranci* and
Orderic, printed earlier, the sole direct evidence for it comes
from the Worcester *Chronicon*, but the deposition of Bishop Æthelric of Selsey is also mentioned in a letter of Alexander II to
the king (no. II). The difficulties to which this deposition gave
rise dragged on until 1076, but its grounds are unknown.[2]

The *capitula* printed below as no. III have also been attributed to this council. They are found in only one surviving
early copy:

> Cambridge, Corpus Christi Coll. ms. 190, p. 292, from
> Exeter, which is described above on p. 567. The canons
> follow directly upon those attributed to the council of
> April.

Spelman's claim that his text came not only from an Exeter
book, almost certainly Corpus 190, but also 'e libro Saxonico
Wigornensis ecclesiae' (Sp. ii.12) rests upon an error, and
his text contains no variants to support such a claim.[3]

The attribution of these canons to the Windsor council is

---

[1] Those who directed the council are spoken of by Alexander in no. II as
the legates' 'suppositi', which suggests that here, as at Easter, the
Worcester account exaggerates the part of Ermenfrid.

[2] In *Anglia Sacra*, i.322 (JL 4762) of 1072-3, since clearly later than
no. II below, Alexander wrote to Lanfranc: '... de liberatione capti episcopi
quod experientie tue commisimus valde miramur an hoc tua pretermiserit negligentia an regis penam adiciens contempserit inobedientia'. Æthelric's
deposition was not finally settled until the Winchester council of 1076.
The consecration of his successor within a week of his original deposition
adds a good deal of force to the suggestion that the council of 1070 acted
with precipitate haste.

[3] Spelman's notes to this text are rather incoherent; the reason appears
to be that his source is the volume of Joscelyn's collections, now BL ms.
Cotton Vitellius D. vii, fo. 117, where Corpus 190 is transcribed; Joscelyn
had used both this and Junius 121 for his copy of the Winchester canons
and was noting that only the Corpus ms. had these Windsor ones.

far from certain; it rests upon their association in the ms.
with two texts, one certainly and the other probably the work
of Ermenfrid, and also on the likelihood that the ms. was
largely complete before the death of Leofric of Exeter in
January 1072, who gave the book to his cathedral library. The
suggestion that the caption should be modified to fit the
council of 1072 appears weak, and other canons have a stronger
claim to that date.[1] The canons were first printed in Sp. ii.12
and thence in Labbe, x.351, W. i.365, Mansi, xx.459-60.

I. *Worcester Chronicon ex chronicis s.a. 1070*

> Oxford, Corpus Christi Coll. ms. 157, p. 347 (= C), Dub-
> lin, Trinity Coll. ms. 502 (E. 5.23), fo. 227^V (= H). C
> has here been altered; H represents the original reading,
> as does London, Lambeth Palace, ms. 42, fo. 138^V. The
> later state of C is followed by Bodl. ms. Bodl. 297,
> p. 381 and Cambridge, Corpus Christi Coll. ms. 92, fo.
> 151^V. Printed in *Flor. Wig.* ii.6-7 immediately after the
> passage printed above, pp. 569-70, where later deriva-
> tives are noticed.

Die autem Pentecostes rex apud Windesoram venerando Baiocensi
canonico Thomę Eboracensis ęcclesię arciepiscopatum et Walcelino
suo capellano Wintoniensis ęcclesię dedit presulatum. Cuius
iussu mox in crastino predictus Sedunensis episcopus Armen-
fridus sinodum tenuit, Iohanne et Petro prefatis cardinalibus
Romam reversis. In qua sinodo Agelricus Suthsaxonum pontifex

---

[1]Böhmer, *Kirche und Staat*, pp. 62-4 n., argued that these canons were
incompatible with those of Winchester above in the matter of synods (c. 4),
and that the meeting at Windsor was a royal court, not a church council. He
wished therefore to amend Windsor to Winchester, Whitsun to Easter, and
place the canons in 1072, seeing c. 9 as a reference to the career of Æthelwine of Durham. For c. 4 see the note above, p. 576 n. 4; if we are to believe
our only ms., 1070 provides the only known occasion on which a church council met at Whitsun at Windsor during the Conqueror's reign. Böhmer's arguments were accepted by Stenton in *Anglo-Saxon England*, p. 665 and n. 4 but
rejected by Brooke in *Studia Gratiana*, xii (1967), 58-9 n. Barlow (1979),
pp. 124-5, argued for Lanfranc holding a second council at Windsor in 1072,
to which these canons could be attributed. There is no evidence for this, and
the manuscript associations are against it.

non canonice degradatur, quem rex sine culpa mox apud Mearles-
beorge in ᵃcustodiam posuit; abbates etiam quamplures degradan-
tur.ᵇ¹ Quibus degradatis rex suis capellanis Arfasto East-
anglorumᶜ et Stigando Suðsaxonum dedit episcopatum,ᵈ qui
Stigandus mutavit sedem in Cicestram, diocesis suę civitatem.ᵈ
Nonnullis etiam Normannicis monachisᵉ dedit abbatias.² Et quia
Dorubernięᶠ archipresul depositus et Eboracensis erat defunctus, iussu regis in octavis Pentecostes ab eodem Armenfrido
Sedunensi episcopoᵍ ordinatus est Walcelinus.ᵃ

II. *Letter of Alexander II to King William (part)*; late 1071.³

> BL ms. Cotton Nero A. vii, fos. 9ᵛ-10ᵛ, Vatican ms. Reg.
> Lat. 285, fo. 5ʳ⁻ᵛ. Printed in *Lanf. Letters*, ed. Clover
> and Gibson, no. 7, ed. Giles, no. 9. Also Mansi, xix.950-1,
> W. i.326, JL 4695.

Pręterea eminentię vestrę notum esse volumus quod causa Alricii,
qui olim Cicestrensis ęcclesię presul dictus a suppositis
legatorum nostrorum depositus est, non ad plenum nobis tractata
videtur. Ideoque, sicut in canonibus cautum est, in pristinum

---

ᵃ⁻ᵃ*written over an erasure* C.   ᵇquam plures degradantur C; degradati
sunt quamplures H.   ᶜEastanglorum C; Orientalium presulatum H.   ᵈQui
Stigandus ... civitatem C *(cf. WMGP, p. 205)*; *om.* H.   ᵉmonachis H; modo C.
ᶠDorubernie C; Dorubernensis H.   ᵍsedis apostolice legato *add* H.

---

¹As for the Easter council, no names of such abbots are known.
²Though no abbots can now be proved to have been appointed at this council, it is possible that Scotland, abbot of St. Augustine's at Canterbury,
and (more remotely) Frederick of St. Albans were chosen at this time. Turold
was transferred from Malmesbury to Peterborough this year though the sources
say nothing of conciliar activity intervening (*Heads,* pp. 36, 55, 60, 66).
³For the date of Lanfranc's journey to Rome, and so of this letter, see
above, p. 574. This letter is found in many other mss. which have been
collated, but provide no variants of substance in this passage. BL ms.
Cotton Cleop. E. i, fo. 50ᵛ (12th cent.), Canterbury, D.& C., Reg. A, fo. 8
(15th cent.), and Cambridge, Trinity Coll. O. 10.16, p. 232 (17th cent.),
derive at one or more removes from Lanfranc's letters. BL mss. Cotton Claud.
E. v, fo. 244 (12th cent.) and Vitellius A. xx, fo. 72 (13th-cent. partial
text) and Cambridge, Corpus Christi Coll. 298 (iv), fo. 53ᵛ (16th-cent.
transcript from an apparently lost Passional of Christ Church) may represent an independent transmission. See above p. 572 n. 2 for a substantial
insertion in the Trinity copy.

locum debere restitui iudicavimus, deinde causam eius iuxta
censuram canonicę traditionis diligenter retractandam et diffi-
niendam predicto fratri nostro archiepiscopo Lanfranco commisimus. Item sibi negotium de discernenda lite quę inter archiepiscopum Eboracensem et episcopum Dorcacestrensem de
pertinentia diocesis eorum est firmiter iniungendo commendavi-
mus, ut hanc causam diligentissima perquisitione pertractet et
iusto fine determinet.[1] In causis autem [fo. 10^v] pertractandis
et diffiniendis ita sibi nostrę et apostolicę auctoritatis
vicem dedimus ut quicquid in eis, iusticia dictante, determina-
verit quasi in nostra presentia definitum deinceps firmum et
indissolubile teneatur.

III. *Capitula of canons pronounced at a council at Windsor*

Capitula concilii apud Windlesora celebrati in Pentecosten
[1] De introitu episcoporum et abbatum per symoniacam heresim.[2]

[2] De ordinationibus passim factis et per pretium.[3]

[3] De vita et conversatione eorundem.[4]

[4] Quod episcopi bis concilia [a]celebrant[b] per annum.[5]

[5] Ut episcopi archidiaconos et ceteros sacri ordinis ministros
in ęcclesiis suis ordinent.

[6] Ut episcopi liberam facultatem habeant per diocesim tam de
clericis quam de laicis.[6]

---

[a]*A lacuna here caused by the erasure of one or two letters.*   [b]*Later
partially corrected to* celebrent.

---

[1]See above, pp. 539, 550.   [2]C. of Winchester (1070), c. 2.
[3]Compare Leo I in Hinschius, p. 627.
[4]See the suggested interpretation in Barlow (1979), p. 125 n. 110.
[5]C. of Winchester (1070), c. 13 and note there.
[6]CC. of Coyanza (1050), c. 3 and Nicholas II, *Synodica generalis* (1059),
c. 5.

[7] Ut episcopi et sacerdotes laicos invitent ad penitentiam.

[8] De apostaticis clericis et monachis.[1]

[9] De episcopis ut certas sedes habeant. Et ut nullus conspirationem faciat contra principem.[2]

[10] Ut laïci decimas reddant sicut scriptum est.[3]

[11] Ut nullus invadat ecclesiastica[a] bona.

[12] Ut nullus clericus secularia arma ferat.[4]

[13] Ut clericis et monachis digna reverentia exhibeatur. Qui hec non fecerit anathema sit.[b]

88

1067 x 1070. PENITENTIAL ARTICLES ISSUED AFTER THE BATTLE OF
   HASTINGS

   See Cowdrey in *JEH* xx (1969), 225-42, Stenton, *Anglo-
   Saxon England,* pp. 661-2, Morton in *Latomus,* xxxiv (1975),
   362-82.

The penitential articles printed below are not referred to by
any contemporary chronicler, and there can be no certainty on

---

[a]aliena *erased*; vel ecclesiastica *superscript.*   [b]Qui hec − sit *written apparently later than the rest.*

---

[1]C. of Winchester (1070), c. 12; compare c. 3 of the canons attributed
to Rheims (1049) by U.-R. Blumenthal, *Deutsches Archiv* xxxii (1976), 23-48.
   [2]The ms. appears to run these clauses together, and so the traditional
if apparently irrational grouping has been preserved. See above, p. 566 for
some suggestion that the later widespread movement of bishops' sees was
already being contemplated; an alternative interpretation in Barlow (1979),
p. 48 n. 103 sees the first part of the canon as an attack on those bishops
who fled their sees.
   [3]CC. of Winchester (1070), c. 14 and Gerona (1068), c. 2.
   [4]CC. of Rheims (1049), c. 2 (ed. Blumenthal), Coyanza (1050), c. 3, Tours
(1060), c. 7, Gerona (1068), c. 5.

the circumstances in which they were published. According to
the text they were issued by the Norman bishops and confirmed
by Ermenfrid as legate, though not necessarily at the time of
their original issue. The confirmation at least occurred most
probably either in 1067, when Ermenfrid was in Rouen, or in
1070 when he presided over the Norman council at which Lanfranc
accepted election to Canterbury.[1] Since it is difficult to
believe that such penances were imposed long after the event,
the earlier date is preferable.

The manuscript tradition, however, is entirely English; the
articles are found in the three early manuscripts which also
include the canons of the legatine council at Winchester in
1070:

A. Cambridge, Corpus Christi Coll. ms. 190, pp. 293-4.
B. BL ms. Cotton Tib. C. i, fos. 111^V-12^V.
C. Bodl. ms. Junius 121, fos. 3-4.

As with the canons, all three copies share a corrupt text,
and hence all derive from a lost source, perhaps the legate's
own copy. The articles were first printed in Sp. ii.12-13,
based on A and C, followed by Mansi, xx.460-2. W. i.366 incorporated a conjectural emendation of the corrupt passage in the
prologue which had been proposed by Somner.[2] The text was
printed from A, B, and C in *Latomus*, xxxiv.381-2; translated in
EHD ii.606-7. The version below is based on A.

Although no precise parallel to this text is known to exist,
imposing as it does a heavy penance on only one side in a
battle, and that the victorious one, its authenticity is
guaranteed both by the manuscript tradition and by the agreement of its provisions with the principles set out in such
current guides to penance as the *Corrector* of Burchard of

---

[1]Above p. 563, below p. 585.
[2]Below p. 583 n. c; Spelman's sources are clear in Bodl. e Mus. ms. 49,
fos. 17-18. Somner's emendation is among those he suggested for Spelman's
second volume in Bodl. ms. Jones 13, fo. 1, where he prefaces it 'Lege ut
opinor rectius sic:'. It was printed in the Addenda to J. Johnson, *A Collection of all the Ecclesiastical Laws ... of the Church of England,* s.a. 1072.

Worms, or the penitential ordinances of Archbishop John of
Rouen.[1]

De pęnitentia in bello homines occidentium[a]
Hec est pęnitentię institutio secundum decreta Normannorum
presulum, auctoritate summi pontificis confirmata per legatum
suum Ermenfredum episcopum Sedunensem, imponenda illis hominibus quos W. Normannorum dux suo iussu, et qui ante hunc iussu[b]
sui erant,[c] et ex debito ei militiam debebant.[d]

[1] Qui in magno prelio scit hominem se occidisse, secundum
numerum hominum, pro unoquoque uno anno pęniteat. Pro unoquoque
quem percussit si nescit eum inde mortuum fuisse, si numerum
retinet, pro unoquoque quadraginta diebus pęniteat, sive continue sive per intervalla. Si autem numerum percussorum vel
occisorum[e] ignorat ad arbitrium episcopi sui quoad vivit uno
die in ebdomada pęniteat aut, si potest, vel ęcclesiam faciendo
vel ęcclesię largiendo perpetua elemosina redimat.

[2] Qui autem neminem percusserit, si percutere voluerit,
triduo pęniteat.[f]

[3] De clericis qui pugnaverunt aut pugnandi gratia armati
fuerunt, quia pugnare eis illicitum erat, secundum instituta
canonum acsi in patria sua peccassent pęniteant.

[4] Pęnitentia monachorum secundum regulam suam et abbatum

---

[a]*heading in A only.*   [b]hunc iussu AC; nunc iussum B.   [c]et qui ... sui
erant, *where all have a point after* suo iussu ABC; armavit, et qui absque
iussu suo erant armati, *Wilkins, following Sommer. For some alternative
emendations see* Latomus *xxxiv (1975), 381 n. If the other half of the contrast implied here is found in c. 5, then a single word such as* summonuit
may have dropped out after the first iussu.   [d]debebant AC; debeant B.
[e]vel *add* B.   [f]percusser' ... voluer' ... peniteat A; percusserunt ...
voluerunt ... penit' B; percusser' ... voluer' ... penit' C.

---

[1]Against the doubts expressed in Freeman, *Norman Conquest*, iv (1876),
810-2 and D.C. Douglas, *William the Conqueror*, p. 192 n. 1 see Stenton,
Anglo-Saxon England, p. 661 n. 4 and Cowdrey, *JEH* xx (1969), 233-40. Archbishop John's ordinances are found in Bodl. ms. Barlow 37, fo. 50r-v.

iudicia statuantur.[a]

[5] Qui autem tantum premio adducti pugnaverunt cognoscant se[b]
sicut pro homicidio penitere debere. Sed quia in publico bello
pugnaverunt pro misericordia tres annos penitentie eis episcopi
statuerunt.

[6] De sagittariis qui ignoranter aliquos occiderunt,[c] vel
absque homicidio vulneraverunt, tribus quadragesimis[d] peniteant.

[7] Quicumque excepto hoc prelio ante regis consecrationem
victus querendi[e] causa per regnum discurrerunt, hostibus repug-
nantibus aliquos occiderunt pro singulis uno anno peniteant.

[8] Qui autem non necessitate victus sed predandi[f] causa discurrerunt et aliquos occiderunt[g] tres annos peniteant.

[9] Qui autem post consecrationem regis hominem occiderunt[c]
sicut de homicidiis sponte commissis,[h] hoc excepto ut si quis
de illis quemquam qui [p. 294] adhuc repugnabant regi occidit
vel percussit sicut supra peniteat.

[10] De adulteriis et raptibus et fornicationibus quibuscumque
acsi in patria sua pecassent peniteant.

[11] De violatione ecclesiarum similiter.

[12] Res quas de ecclesia abstulerunt, si reddere[i] eidem cui
abstulerunt[j] possunt, reddant. Si hoc non possunt alii ecclesie
reddant. Si autem reddere noluerint statuerunt episcopi ut
neque ipsi vendant neque alii emant.[k]

---

[a]B *underlines the* n.   [b]se *superscript* A.   [c]occider' A; occiderunt B;
occidunt C.   [d]quadragesimas C *only*.   [e]querendi AB; querenda C.   [f]predandi
AC; preliandi B.   [g]occider' AC; occidunt B.   [h]penit' *add* B.   [i]reddere AB;
redde C.   [j]abstulerunt *om*. B.   [k]FINIT *add* C.

89

APRIL—AUGUST 1070. ELECTION OF LANFRANC AS ARCHBISHOP OF CANTERBURY

The chief sources are OV (ed. Chibnall), ii.248-54, Milo's *Vita Lanfranci* (*Lanfranci Opera*, ed. Giles, i.292-5), *Flor. Wig.* ii.7, *Acta Lanfranci* (*ASC* ed. Plummer, i.287-8), *Lanf. Letters*, ed. Clover and Gibson, no. 1, ed. Giles, no. 3, *Intravit* (below pp. 588-91).

The fullest account of the negotiations surrounding Lanfranc's appointment to Canterbury is found in the narratives of Orderic and Milo, who follow a common source;[1] part of their version is confirmed by Lanfranc's letter to the pope. For events in England the English sources are much fuller.

As soon as Stigand had been deposed in April King William tried to persuade Lanfranc, abbot of Caen, to accept the archbishopric, as he had earlier attempted to appoint him to Rouen. Again he refused, and to overcome his objections it was necessary for the legate Ermenfrid to cross the Channel after the Whitsun council at Windsor and summon a meeting of the Norman bishops and abbots.[2] Lanfranc continued to resist his promotion, but eventually gave way when urged by the queen, her son, and his own former abbot, Herluin of Bec.

On 15 August he was formally elected at a royal council in England; a fortnight later he was consecrated at Canterbury in the presence of most of his suffragans.[3]

---

[1] See above p. 565; the uncharacteristic passage in OV ii.254 suggests that he may also have used a text similar to *Intravit*.

[2] Lanfranc's letter to the pope speaks of this council as being held by Ermenfrid and the legate Hubert; Orderic mentions only Ermenfrid, while Milo appears to assert that he was accompanied by the cardinals Peter and John who had been in England earlier. Morton in *Latomus*, xxxiv (1975), 379-80, suggests that Lanfranc may have been imposed on William by the pope.

[3] According to *Flor. Wig.* ii.7, he was consecrated by Giso of Wells and Walter of Hereford, both of whom had been consecrated by Nicholas II during the rule of Stigand (above nos. 76-8). *Intravit*, by listing all those who were present, implies that Walter (like Leofric of Exeter and Wulfstan of Worcester) was absent. The last Anglo-Saxon annal in ASC A is seriously confused, and may itself depend on *Intravit*. For the general circumstances see M. Gibson, *Lanfranc of Bec*, pp. 114-15.

90

1070-1072. PRIMACY DISPUTE BETWEEN CANTERBURY AND YORK

> See H. Böhmer, *Die Fälschungen Erzbischof Lanfranks von
> Canterbury*, pp. 17-31; Dueball, *Suprematstreit*, pp. 19-
> 35; Z.N. Brooke, *The English Church and the Papacy*, pp.
> 118-26; Stenton, *Anglo-Saxon England*, pp. 664-5; R.W.
> Southern, 'The Canterbury Forgeries', *EHR* lxxiii (1958),
> 193-207; *Canterbury Professions*, pp. lix-lxviii; M. Gib-
> son, *Lanfranc of Bec*, pp. 116-31.

Thomas, treasurer of Bayeux cathedral, was nominated to the
archbishopric of York at the Council of Windsor on May 24,
1070; his consecration however was delayed until after that of
Lanfranc on 29 August. When Thomas arrived at Canterbury
Lanfranc required of him a profession of obedience reinforced
by an oath, demands which were asserted to rest upon ancient
custom, but for which there are no known parallels either in
England or France.[1]

For the events that followed the chief sources are a letter
of Lanfranc to the pope[2] and a narrative very probably also
written by Lanfranc, *Intravit,* which was composed after the
death of Alexander II. This may perhaps have been intended as
a preface to evidence for use at Rome in an unsuccessful effort
to secure papal confirmation of the decision of the councils of
1072.[3] The narrative is found in both early copies of Lanfranc's
letters, where it is followed by a number of related texts,
which include the profession made by Thomas, a copy of the
judgement in 1072, and the acts of the Council of 1075. The
collection was used by a number of later writers, including

---

[1]These events presumably took place late in 1070, but the exact date is
unknown.

[2]Printed below, pp. 597-601.

[3]Since Alexander II is spoken of in the text as 'felicis memorie',
Intravit was presumably written in or after 1073; since the associated texts
in all the early copies include the council of 1075, and *Intravit* speaks of
several bishops by both their original titles and those they took after the
movement of sees generally associated with that council, it may well have
been written some time after 1075. For Lanfranc's authorship see Eadmer,
p. 13, WMGP, pp. 38-9.

Milo in his *Vita Lanfranci*, William of Malmesbury in both the
Gesta Regum and *Gesta Pontificum* and the author of the *Acta
Lanfranci*. In Malmesbury and BL ms. Cotton Cleopatra E. i these
texts are associated with copies of the forged papal privileges
confirming Canterbury's primacy, but there is no convincing
reason for supposing that these were known in Lanfranc's life-
time.[1]

Further details of the negotiations at Rome when both archbishops went to seek their pallia late in 1071 are supplied by
Eadmer in the *Historia Novorum* (followed by Malmesbury's *Gesta
Pontificum*), who describes charges levelled against Thomas of
York as the son of a priest, and Remigius, bishop of Dorchester,
accused of simony for his active part in the Norman Conquest.
These charges were referred to Lanfranc by the pope, and remitted at the archbishop's request; the account is, however,
too late to deserve unquestioned acceptance.[2]

The only surviving account of the primacy dispute from the
point of view of York is even later; it occurs in the *History
of the Church of York* by Hugh the Chanter which was written
after 1127 to celebrate the success of Archbishop Thurstan in
defeating the Canterbury claim, and is demonstrably unreliable
for the earlier period.[3]

In accordance with the papal decision both questions at issue
between Lanfranc and Thomas, the profession and the dependence
of the sees of Dorchester, Worcester, and Lichfield, were referred to a decision of a council to be held in England in 1072,
the acts of which are discussed and printed below.[4]

---

[1]See Southern, *EHR* lxxiii.193-226, H. Clover in *La Normandie Bénédictine*,
pp. 417-42, Gibson, *Lanfranc*, pp. 231-7.

[2]Eadmer, pp. 10-12, WMGP, pp. 65-6; compare OV iii.10, *EA* 283 (JL 5930).
On the ancestry of Thomas see *Liber Vitæ Ecclesiæ Dunelmensis* (Surtees
Soc., xiii, 1841), pp. 139-40; for Remigius at the conquest the *Second
General Report from the Commissioners of Public Records* (1800-19), i.488
and Giraldus, *Opera*, vii.14-15. According to his profession, while at Rome
Remigius was excused by Lanfranc from the general condemnation of Stigand's
ordinations.

[3]See below, pp. 591 n. 1, 641.

[4]For Dorchester see above, pp. 539, 580, for Worcester compare *Vita Wulfstani*, pp. xxv-xxxi, 24-6, *Flor. Wig.* ii.8, and *Chronicon Abbatiae de Evesham*,
pp. 89-90.

Lanfranc's account of the preliminaries to the council of 1072
  (Intravit)

BL ms. Cotton Nero A. vii, fos. 3^V-5 (= N) ed. Böhmer,
Die Fälschungen Lanfranks, pp. 165-7; also in Vatican,
ms. Reg. Lat. 285, fos. 2-4^V (= V) and BL ms. Cotton
Cleopatra E. i, fos. 45^V-7 (= E). Largely incorporated
by Malmesbury in his *Gesta Pontificum*, printed from
Oxford, Magdalen Coll. ms. Lat. 172 fos. 12^V-14 (= P)
in WMGP, pp. 39-42, and by Milo Crispin in his *Vita Lanfranci*, printed from a lost ms. from Bec by D'Achery in
Lanfranci Opera Omnia, pp. 11-13 (= Mi), and also found
in Vatican, ms. Reg. Lat. 499, fos. 62-63^V (= Mv). Edited
from all these sources in *Lanf. Letters*, ed. Clover and
Gibson, no. 3.

[a]Anno dominicę incarnationis millesimo septuagesimo intravit
Anglicam terram Lanfrancus Cadomensis coenobii abbas, monenti-
bus atque precipientibus Willelmo glorioso Anglorum rege[b] et
felicis memorię Alexandro totius sanctae aecclesię summo
pontifice. Is post paucos sui introitus dies Dorobernensem
aecclesiam regendam suscepit. Consecratus est autem quarto
kalendas Septembris in sede metropoli a suffraganeis ipsius
sedis Willelmo Londoniensi episcopo, Walchelino Wentano,
Remigio Dorcensi sive Lincholiensi, Siwardo Rofensi, Herfasto
Helmeanensi sive Tehfordensi,[c] Stigando Selengensi, Hermanno
Siraburnensi, Gisone Wellensi. Ceteri qui absentes fuerunt
causas suę absentię tam legatis quam litteris ostenderunt. Ipso
anno Thomas Eboracensis aecclesię electus antistes Cantuar-
beriam ex prisca consuetudine ab eo sacrandus advenit. A quo
cum Lanfrancus scriptam de obędientia sua cum adiectione iuris
iurandi professionem custodito antecessorum more exposceret,
respondit Thomas se id numquam facturum nisi prius scriptas de

---

[a]*The heading* Qualiter Thomas archiepiscopus Eboracensis sacrandus
antistes Cantuariam venit, et nolens professionem facere Lanfranco et successoribus eius non sacratus abscessit, et quod postea rediit, profitetur
et sacratus est, et de calumniis eius et eorum diffinitione E *only.*
[b]Anglorum rege NVMiMv; rege Angl. EP.   [c]Tehf. N; Tetf. V; Tedf. E; Thesf.
Mi; Theff. Mv; Tehtf. P.

hac re auctoritates legeret, nisi testes huius antiquitatis
assertores cerneret, postremo nisi congruas super hac [fo. 4]
re rationes audiret, quibus id iuste et rationabiliter sine
suę aecclesię preiudicio facere deberet. Hoc autem ignorantia
magis quam spiritus elati pertinatia agebat.[a] Novus enim homo
et Anglicę consuetudinis penitus expers verbis adulatorum plus
ęquo et bono fidem exhibebat. Lanfrancus tamen in presentia
paucorum episcoporum qui ad eum pro hac consecratione convenerant[b] quod postulavit ostendit, at ille aspernatus omnia
non sacratus abscessit. Quod rex audiens graviter accepit
existimans Lanfrancum iniusta petere, et scientia litterarum
magis quam ratione et veritate confidere, quamvis nec ipsi
Thomę deesset scripturarum peritia, multo ingenio multoque
studio comparata.[1] Paucorum dierum spacio evoluto Lanfrancus
ad curiam venit, a rege audientiam postulavit, redditis rationibus eius animum mitigavit, transmarinis qui aderant suę parti
iusticiam adesse suasit et persuasit. Angli enim[c] qui rem
noverant assertionibus eius per omnia constantissime testimonium
perhibebant. Itaque regio edicto communique omnium decreto
statutum est ad praesens debere Thomam ad matrem totius regni
aecclesiam redire, professionem scribere, scriptam legere,
lectam inter examinandum in presentia episcoporum aecclesiastico
more[d] Lanfranco porrigere, in qua preceptis quidem eius in
omnibus quę ad Christianę religionis cultum pertinent se obtemperaturum absolute nulla interposita conditione promitteret,
successoribus vero eius non ita nisi prius vel coram rege[e] vel
in episcopali concilio competens ei ratio redderetur qua antecessores suos Dorobernensis aecclesię primatibus id fecisse et
facere debuisse evidentissime ostenderetur. [fo. 4^V] Igitur
rediit, quę iussa sunt implevit, sacratus abscessit. Non post
multos dies Lanfrancus ab universis Anglici regni episcopis
qui diversis temporibus diversis in locis ab aliis archiepiscopis

---

[a]agebat NVMiMv; aiebat E; fatiebat P.   [b]convenerant NE; advenerant V;
venerant MiMvP.   [c]enim NEMiMvP; autem V.   [d]aeccl. more NEVMv; tsp. Mi;
om. P.   [e]rege NE; om. VMiMvP.

---

[1]Thomas was one of the clerks educated at the cost of Odo of Bayeux (OV
iv.118).

vel a papa tempore Stigandi sacrati sunt professiones petiit et
accepit.[1] Sequenti anno cum prefato[a] archiepiscopo Romam ivit,
et honorifice a sede apostolica susceptus unum quidem pallium[b 2]
de altari Romano more accepit, alterum vero in[c] indicium videlicet sui amoris cum quo missam celebrare solebat Alexander ei
papa sua manu porrexit. In cuius presentia Thomas calumniam
movit de primatu Dorobernensis aecclesię, et de subiectione
trium episcoporum, Dorcensis sive Lincoliensis, Wigorniensis,
Licifeldensis qui nunc est Cestrensis, dicens Cantuariensem
aecclesiam atque Eboracensem parem ad se invicem honorem habere,
nec alteram alteri secundum beati Gregorii constitutionem
debere ullatenus subiacere, excepto quod alterutrius archiepiscopum priorem et digniorem oporteat esse eo quem constiterit
fuisse posterius ordinatum,[3] prędictos vero tres episcopos suę
sedi suisque antecessoribus ab antiquis temporibus extitisse
subiectos. Lanfrancus hoc audiens etsi moleste tulit modesta
tamen discretione verba illius veritate penitus carere respondit, asseverans Gregorianam illam constitutionem non de
Cantuariensi et Eboracensi aecclesia sed de Londoniensi et
Eboracensi esse promulgatam. De qua re et de tribus episcopis
multis hinc inde verbis prolatis decrevit Alexander papa
oportere hanc causam in [fo. 5] Anglica terra audiri et illic
totius regni episcoporum et abbatum testimonio et iudicio
definiri. Lanfrancus quamvis alligatum illum[d] suo tempore facta
ab eo professione teneret, maluit tamen pro successoribus[e]
laborare quam eis in posterum indiscussam hanc tantam calumniam

---

[a]Eboracensi *add* E.   [b]unum quidem pallium NVEP; MiMv *here read* est.
Siquidem venienti papa assurrexisse dicitur, tum pro sua magna religione et
eminenti scientia, tum quia dum esset in Normannia venientes Romane ecclesiæ
ministros honorifice suscipiebat, et quosdam papæ consanguineos studiose
docuerat. Fertur etiam papa dixisse, Non ideo assurrexi ei quia archiepiscopus Cantuariæ est, sed quia Becci ad scholam eius fui, et ad pedes eius
cum aliis auditor consedi. Itaque duo pallia illi dedit, unum quod...
[c]in VMiMvPN²; *om.* NE.   [d]eum E.   [e]suis *add* MiMv.

---

[1]Compare above p. 573 (no. VIII) and the texts printed in *Canterbury
Professions,* nos. 31-33.
[2]Compare below, p. 601. For the interpolation by Mi here and its un-
reliability see T. Schmidt, *Alexander II*, pp. 10-24.
[3]JE 1829, Bede, *HE* i.29.

discutiendam reservare. Uterque igitur in Paschali solennitate
ad regem venit, ibique prolatis in medium partium rationibus
sententiam de negotio regalis curia^a dedit. Iussum tunc est
fieri scriptum totius causę continens finem. Lanfrancus
Alexandro papae epistolam^b direxit in qua ei totius negotii
gestionem breviter et veraciter enarravit. Utraque scripta
subter annexa sunt, praemissa professione quam Thomas Lanfranco
coram rege et eius curia manu in manum porrexit.

(There follow the texts printed below, pp. 597-605.)

91

*c.*8 APRIL 1072. COUNCIL AT WINCHESTER

In accordance with the pope's decision, a council was held at
Winchester at Easter, 1072, after the return of the two archbishops from Rome. Our knowledge of these events is drawn
chiefly from *Intravit* (above, p. 586), from Lanfranc's letter
to Alexander (no. II), from the record of the judgement reached
in the course of the year (no. III), and from the garbled version of events preserved at York in the twelfth century.[1]

These texts raise a number of problems; according to Lanfranc's letter and a note added to one version of the judgement
the matter of the primacy was discussed in the king's court
sitting in the royal chapel, though in the presence of the
legate Hubert, and this may distinguish the occasion from the
council proper, whose acts and legislation are mentioned by the
Acta Lanfranci (no. I).

Secondly the two versions of the judgement itself present
some difficulty. Both exist in apparently contemporary single

---

^{a}ut per concilium finiretur *add* E. ^{b}ecclesiam *subsequently cancelled
but not corrected* V.

---

[1]Printed in Hugh the Chanter, pp. 2-6 (*Hist. York,* ii.99-103). According
to this account Thomas made only one profession, that at his consecration,
which was absolute to Lanfranc but not to his successors. The subsequent
events of this council, and the record of it printed below, Hugh dismisses
as a Canterbury fabrication.

sheets which have always belonged to the archives of Canterbury. However, while the shorter one is authenticated by what appear to be the autograph crosses of the king and queen, and by autograph subscriptions of the legate, both archbishops, and four bishops, the longer had formerly an impression of the genuine great seal attached *en placard*, and the witnesses, whose subscriptions are not autograph, are far more numerous. Here those who attest the first version are said to have subscribed, while the rest are said to have consented. In a note added by the original hand in a smaller script the case is said to have been first ventilated at Winchester, but to have reached a final settlement at a second royal court held at Windsor at Pentecost (27 May). The witnesses to this version are consistent with Pentecost but not Easter.[1]

While the short version is known only from the original and the text which seems to lie behind most existing copies of Lanfranc's correspondence, the longer is widespread. There was a copy probably on a single sheet in the archbishop's own archives late in the thirteenth century, and another was kept among the royal charters at Peterborough. There appears to have been yet another among the muniments of St. Augustine, Canterbury. Copied by William of Malmesbury into his *Gesta Regum*, it also circulated in other later chronicles.[2] According to Lanfranc's letter, copies of the judgement were sent to the principal churches of England, and both the manuscript tradition and the form of authentication of the longer version, capable of indefinite multiplication, support the view that the 'published' version was that produced at Pentecost.

The date at which the shorter version was drawn up is far more doubtful. Lanfranc describes the hearing at Winchester as

---

[1] Osbern of Exeter and Riwallon of New Minster both took office between Easter and Whitsun. It is noteworthy that Osbern was the first bishop-elect to make his profession to Lanfranc as 'totius Britannice regionis primas', *Canterbury Professions,* no. 35.

[2] The version of the council in Pseudo-Ingulf, ed. Fulman in *Rerum Anglicarum Scriptorum Veterum Tom. I,* pp. 92-3 is certainly copied from Malmesbury's *Gesta Regum*; that in Diceto, i.205-6 may well be. William made extensive use of materials from Canterbury, and there is no good reason to suppose his copy came from his own abbey's archives.

ending with Thomas submitting and the king asking Lanfranc to
come to an amicable settlement. The short version certainly
represents this agreement, by which Lanfranc remitted the oath
of obedience while securing every other point at issue. Whether
it was drawn up at the council at Winchester, or by the parties
involved between Easter and Pentecost, or actually at Windsor,
is quite unknown. Although the text found in the better copies
of Lanfranc's letters is more closely related to the short
version than the long, the collection itself was put together
well after the event, and Lanfranc claimed to be sending the
pope a version of the text as it was circulated. He cannot then
have written until the long version had been produced, and may
well have sent a copy of that to Rome.[1]

The main text is printed from

> A. Canterbury, D. & C. muniments, Chartae antiquae A. 2,
> late 11th cent., a document which has never long been
> absent from the cathedral archives to judge from the
> press marks on its dorse. A facsimile appears in
> Palaeographical Society, iii, part x (1880), pl. 170.

For the additional matter in the long version the text is
that of

> B. Canterbury, D. & C. muniments, Chartae antiquae A. 1,
> late 11th cent., formerly bearing an impression of
> the great seal of William I; similarly identified as
> in the unbroken possession of Christ Church. It was
> printed, with a photograph of the seal, in *Facsimiles
> of English Royal Writs to A.D. 1100,* pl. xxix and
> notes.

These single sheets are clearly the most authoritative to
survive. Of the numerous other copies which have been collated
for this edition select variants are printed from representatives

---

[1] A contrary view is advanced in Böhmer, *Die Fälschungen,* p. 21 and
Southern in *EHR* lxxiii.200. See also below, p. 594 n. 1.

of two classes of text. Firstly

    N. BL Cotton Nero A. vii, fos. 5^v-6,

    V. Vatican, Reg. Lat. 285, fo. 3^{r-v},

    P. Oxford, Magdalen Coll. Lat. 172, fo. 14^{r-v} (printed
       in WMGP, pp. 42-3),

represent a text nearer A than B which gained currency as part
of Lanfranc's correspondence and was incorporated by Milo in
his *Vita Lanfranci* (ed. D'Achery, pp. 12-13).[1] A version in
which the main text is very similar, but where the witnesses
of the long version have been added, is found in

    E. BL Cotton Cleopatra E. i, fos. 47-8^v, the source for
      the 15th-cent. Canterbury, D & C, Reg. A, fos.
      6^v-7.

    R. BL Arundel 35, fos. 108-9, a good and early example
      of the 'A' version of Malmesbury's *Gesta Regum*, chosen
      as a representative copy of this widespread text
      (WMGR i.lxvii, ii.349-52).

Secondly, select variants have been noted from copies possibly taken from other exemplars of B, now lost, in:

    L. Lambeth Palace 1212, pp. 186-7, from a fragmentary
      13th-cent. register of the archbishop's archives
      (Davis, *Medieval Cartularies,* no. 159). From the in-
      ventory on pp. 1-7 it appears that a copy of the
      council's acts was kept in the archbishop's treasury
      among his royal privileges in the reign of Edward I,
      and this may well have been distinct from B, kept at
      the priory.[2] There is another copy from the same

---

[1]The text in Lanfranc's letter collection has undergone some later re-
touching, for at p. 602 n. k it calls Hubert a subdeacon; he subscribes both
versions of the judgement as only a lector. See further below, p. 626 n. 1.

[2]The evidence of L's readings is indecisive. The text does not occur in
the inventory of 1330 printed by I. Churchill, 'Table of Canterbury Archbishopric charters', *Camden Miscellany XV,* Camden 3rd Ser. xli, 1929. When
Archbishop Ralph wished to consult the document in 1119 he sent for the
copy kept at Christ Church — Eadmer, p. 251.

source on pp. 14-15. The text found in Lambeth, Archbishop Arundel's Register, i, fos. 13^V-14 is virtually
indistinguishable.

D. BL Cotton Domitian v, fos. 13-14, from a collection of documents on the primacy written at Canterbury *c*.1200.[1] Though this has the full witness list of
B the text is intermediate between that and A.

X. BL Cotton Vitellius A. xx, fos. 72-3, a much shorter
thirteenth-century collection on the primacy. The
text is close to that of D, but the attestations are
in the version of Malmesbury in the *Gesta Regum*.

S. London, Society of Antiquaries, 60, fos. 56^V-8 (*olim*
51^V-3), the only twelfth-century register of Peterborough, described in Davis, *Medieval Cartularies,* no.
754. Here, as in the later cartularies of the house,
the council is entered among 'transcripta quarundam
cartarum Burg' ecclesie'.

C. London, P.R.O. Exchequer K.R. Misc. Books i (E 164).
27, fos. 29-30, in a composite 13th/14th-cent. register
of St. Augustine's, Canterbury (Davis, *Medieval Cartularies*, no. 195). Here the council is preceded by
Anglo-Saxon royal charters and followed by an account
of the quarrel between the abbey and Christ Church
priory. There is a copy of this in the Baker transcripts
(17th cent.) in Oxford, Jesus Coll. ms. 75^A, fo. 36^{r-v}.

W. BL Cotton Vitellius C. viii, fos. 10^V-11, in a chronicle
made at Worcester *c*.1140 by conflating passages from
the local *Chronicon ex Chronicis* with others from
Malmesbury's *Gesta Pontificum*. In a partial edition
of the chronicle Liebermann (*UGQ*, p. 21) believed this
version of the council to be derived from Malmesbury's
Gesta Regum, but its readings differ from his at important points, and it is at least as likely that its
source was a Worcester exemplar of B since lost.

---

[1]The manuscript is described by Böhmer, *Die Fälschungen,* pp. 14-16.

The text was printed in Sp. ii.5-6 from the *Gesta Pontificum*
and D.[1] W. i.324-5 also used Arundel's Register and Canterbury
Cathedral Reg. A. Of the numerous other printed versions see
particularly D'Achery, *Lanfranci Opera Omnia,* pp. 12-13,
Labbe, ix.1211-2, Mansi, xx.19-22, *Literæ Cantuarienses,* ed.
J.B. Sheppard (RS), 1887-9, iii.351-2 (from A), Eadmer, pp. 252-
4 (whose version rests on B), Böhmer, *Die Fälschungen,* pp. 167-
9, *Hist. York,* iii.10-13 (from D), and *Lanf. Letters,* ed. Clover
and Gibson, no. 3.

The canons (no. V) which are here printed as the acts of
Lanfranc's Winchester council, mentioned in the *Acta Lanfranci,*
are found in only one manuscript:

> Montpellier, École de Médecine, 304, fos. 26^V-7. Late
> 12th-cent. from the Cistercian house of St. Mary,
> Fontenay, at the end of a small collection of English
> and Norman councils.

They are attributed to this council chiefly on the strength of
the eleventh and fourteenth canons. The feast of St. Bartholomew was generally celebrated on August 25 in England before
1066, while it was observed in Normandy on August 24. By the
death of Lanfranc English practice had been widely accommo-
dated to that of Normandy. The feast of St. Augustine of
Canterbury falls on the Vigil of Whitsun only rarely; it
occurred in 1067, 1072, and 1078, but not after that until
1151. Canon 11 is therefore unlikely to have been issued
after 1078, and the only councils, for which no acts survive,
known to have been held in England between 1070 and 1078 are
those of 1072 and 1077/8. Such indications as there are favour
the earlier date, and it is therefore printed here, though the
attribution remains conjectural.[2] The canons survive only as

---

[1]Sp. ii.11 also prints a summary of the decisions of this council as
part of those of 1075; it derives from a manuscript once at Cambridge and
first printed in W. Dugdale, *History of St. Paul's Cathedral* (London,
1658), p. 195. For this and the related manuscripts which survive see
below, p. 611.

[2]The other councils in this manuscript are described, and the arguments
for dating this to 1072 are set out more fully, by Brett, *JEH* xxvi (1975),
303-5.

capitula, as with the councils of 1070, but even in this form they show a clear relation to the legislation of earlier Norman councils.

I. *Acta Lanfranci*

> Cambridge, Corpus Christi Coll. ms. 173, fo. 32. Printed in *ASC*, ed. Plummer, i.288, and, in facsimile, in *The Parker Chronicle and Laws*.

Hoc quoque anno generale concilium Wentonie celebravit, in quo Wluricum Novi Monasterii abbatem deposuit, multaque de Christianę religionis cultu servanda instituit. Post dies paucos in Lundonia Osbernum Essecistrensi episcopum et Cantuarie Scotlandum ęcclesię Sancti Augusti abbatem sacravit.[1]

II. *Letter of Lanfranc to Alexander II*

> BL Cotton ms. Nero A. vii, fos. 6-8^V (= N), Vatican ms. Reg. Lat. 285, fos. 3^V-4^V (= V). Used in Milo's *Vita Lanfranci* in Vatican ms. Reg. Lat. 499, fos. 64-6 (= M), and, abbreviated, in Malmesbury's *Gesta Pontificum*, printed from Oxford, Magdalen Coll. ms. Lat. 172, fos. 14^V-15^V (= P) in WMGP, pp. 44-6. Also in BL Cotton ms. Cleopatra E. i, fos. 48^V-50 (= E). Printed from these sources in *Lanf. Letters*, ed. Clover and Gibson, no. 4, ed. Giles, no. 5.

Domino totius Christianę religionis summo speculatori A. papę L.[a] sanctę Dorobernensis ęcclesię antistes, debitam cum omni servitute oboedientiam. Meminisse debet humiliter excellens excellenterque humilis beatitudo vestra quia quo tempore apud vos fuimus Eboracensis aecclesię antistes adversum me palam murmuravit, clam detraxit, in praesentia celsitudinis vestrę

---

[a]indignus *add* E.

---

[1]The date and manner of the departure of Scotland's predecessor, Abbot Ælfsige, subsequently abbot at Ramsey, are extremely obscure. See *Heads*, pp. 35-6, 62.

calumniam suscitavit, dicens me iniuste velle agere, eo quod
super se suamque aecclesiam [fo. 6^v] iure nostrę ęcclesię
primatum niterer obtinere. De quorundam quoque subiectione
episcoporum quos ęcclesię suę conatus est aggregare antiquam
sua querela non est veritus consuetudinem temerare. Quibus de
rebus vos sicut sanctam prudentemque pastorem decuit et oportuit per scriptum sententiam promulgastis quatinus conventus
Anglicę terrę episcoporum, abbatum, ceterarumque religiosi
ordinis personarum utriusque partis rationes audiret, discuteret,
definiret. Factumque est ita. Convenerunt enim ad regalem curiam
apud Wentanam civitatem in Pascali solennitate episcopi, abbates
ceterique ex sacro ac laicali ordine quos fide et actione
morumque probitate par fuerat convenisse. In primis adiurati
sunt a nobis ex vestra auctoritate per sanctam obędientiam,
deinde regia potestas per semetipsam contestata est eos per
fidem et sacramentum quibus sibi colligati erant quatinus hanc
causam intentissime audirent, auditam ad certum rectumque finem
sine parcium favore perducerent. Utrumque omnes concorditer
susceperunt, seseque ita facturos sub prefata obligatione
spoponderunt. Allata est igitur ęcclesiastica gentis Anglorum
ystoria^a quam Eboracensis ęcclesię presbiter et Anglorum doctor
Beda composuit, lectę sententię quibus pace omnium demonstratum
est a tempore beati Augustini primi Dorobernensis archiepiscopi
usque ad ipsius Bedę ultimam senectutem, quod fere centum et
quadraginta annorum spatio [fo. 7] terminatur, antecessores meos
super Eboracensem ęcclesiam totamque insulam quam Britanniam
vocant necnon et Hiberniam primatum gessisse, curam pastoralem
omnibus impendisse, in ipsa Eboracensi urbe persepe locisque
finitimis ubi eis visum fuit episcopales ordinationes atque
concilia celebrasse, Eboracenses antistites ad ipsa concilia
vocasse,^{b} et cum res poposcisset de suis eos actibus rationem
reddere compulisse. Episcopos quoque quorum subiectionem in
questionem^c adduxerat infra illud centum et quadraginta annorum
spacium per Dorobernenses archiepiscopos fuisse sacratos, ad

---

^{a}ystoria N; historia VMP; hystoria E. ^{b}Eboracenses ... vocasse VMPE;
om. N, *with a mark of omission. The passage is supplied in a post-medieval
hand in the margin.* ^{c}T. add P; Thomas *add a post medieval hand in the
margin of* N.

concilia vocatos, quosdam quoque exigentibus culpis ab eis cum
Romanę sedis auctoritate depositos, multaque in hunc modum,
quę epistolaris modestia per singula explicare non potest.
Diversa ad legendum porrecta concilia quę diversis temporibus
diversis de causis a meis sunt antecessoribus celebrata, quę
tametsi non eandem suę institutionis habere materiam, eandem
tamen de primatu et subiectionibus episcoporum tenuere sententiam. Recitatę eorumdem de quibus questio versabatur episcoporum
ante predecessores meos factę electiones et per eos ordinationes,
qui Dorobernensi ęcclesię de sua obędientia scriptas reliquerunt
professiones. Urbs nanque que nunc Cantuarberia nominatur antiquis temporibus ab ipsius terrę incolis Dorobernia vocabatur.
Accesserunt omnium testimonia qui omnia quę scripta sonuerunt
se suis quisque temporibus vidisse et audisse constantissime
firmaverunt. [fo. 7^v] Nec defuere gesta quibus reseratum est,
cum Anglia per plures esset regulos divisa, Nordanymbrorum[a]
regem, ubi sita est civitas Eboraca, accepto precio cuidam
simoniaco episcopium vendidisse, pro qua culpa a Dorobernensi
archiepiscopo ad concilium vocatum fuisse, nolentemque venire
pro sua inoboedientia excommunicationis sententiam pertulisse.
Cuius communionis atque consortii omnis illarum parcium ęcclesia tamdiu abstinuit quoadusque concilio seipsum exhibuit, cul-
pam dixit, quod male gestum est correxit, de reliquo emenda-
turum se fore spopondit.[1] Quę res non mediocre tulit indicium
antecessores meos super illam[b] terram illamque aecclesiam
habuisse primatum. Ultimum quasi robur totiusque causę firmamentum prolata sunt antecessorum vestrorum Gregorii, Bonefacii,
Honorii, Vitaliani, Sergii, item Gregorii, Leonis, item ultimi
Leonis[c] privilegia atque scripta, quę Dorobernensis ęcclesię
presulibus Anglorumque regibus aliis atque aliis temporibus
variis de causis sunt data aut transmissa. Reliqua enim reli-
quorum tam autentica quam eorum exemplaria in ea combustione

---

[a]Nordanhymbrorum N; Nordanimbrorum VMP; Northanhimbrorum E.   [b]ipsam V.
[c]item ultimi Leonis NVME; Iohannis P.

---

[1]No trace of the origins of this story has been found by modern
scholars.

atque abolitione quam ęcclesia nostra ante quadriennium per-
pessa est penitus sunt absumpta.[1] His atque aliis quę particu-
latim breviterque explicari non possunt ex parte nostrę
ęcclesię in causa peroratis, contra tantam tantarum auctorita-
tum evidentiam paucissimas contradictiones opposuit, epistolam
illam precipue ferens in medium qua beatus Gregorius Londonien-
sem atque Eboracensem ęcclesiam pares esse, nec alteram alteri
subiacere instituit. [fo. 8] Quam scripturam cum in rem nichil
facere concordi sententia cuncti protinus definissent, pro eo
quod nec ego Londoniensis episcopus essem, nec de Londoniensi
ęcclesia esset quęstio instituta, vertit se ad alia egena
atque infirma argumenta, quę post paucam moram Christo revelante
paucis sunt obiectionibus[a] aboleta.[b] Quem cum rex dulci pater-
naque reprehensione argueret,[c] quod contra tantam argumentorum
copiam tam inops rationum venire presumpsisset, respondit se
antea ignorasse Dorobernensem ęcclesiam tot tantisque auctoritatibus tamque perspicuis rationibus esse munitam. Versus
itaque ad preces est. Rogavit enim regem ut me rogaret quatinus
omnem mentis rancorem adversus eum pro hac causa conceptum
omitterem, pacem diligerem, concordiam facerem, aliqua quę mei
essent iuris studio ei caritatis concederem. Cui peticioni ego
libenter et cum gratiarum actione assensum prebui, quia miserante
Deo non ego sed ille prisce consuetudinis violator causa erat
istius scandali. Facta est igitur communi omnium astipulatione
de hac re quędam scriptura, cuius exemplaria per principales
Anglorum ęcclesias distributa futuris semper temporibus testimonium ferant ad quem finem causa ista fuerit perducta. Cuius
exemplar vobis quoque quibus sanctam totius mundi ęcclesiam
constat esse commissam transmittendum curavi, ut ex hoc atque
aliis quę transmissa sunt perspicue cognoscatis ex more antecessorum quid mihi Christique ęcclesię quam regendam suscepi
concedere debeatis. [d]Quod [fo. 8[v]] peto honeste et sine

---

[a]obiectionibus sunt E.　　[b]aboleta N[2]EVM; abolita NP; P *ends.*　　[c]argue-
ret NME; augueret V.　　[d]Quod peto ... transmittere curavi *(below,　p. 601
l. 17)* NMV; *om.* E.

---

[1]In 1067; see particularly *ASC* E (ed. Plummer, i.200) and *Anglia Sacra,*
ii.187-8.

dilatione per indultum sedis apostolicę privilegium fieri,
quatinus ex hoc quoque quantum me diligatis evidenter possit
ostendi. De me autem revera estimate quod de fideli ac servo
beati Petri ac vestro sanctęque ęcclesię Romanę. Nunquam enim
res quęlibet de archa mei pectoris eicere quavis occasione
poterit inauditam illam humilitatem quam mihi extremo hominum
tantis indigno honoribus Romę exhibuistis, quodque duo pallia,
unum de altari ex more, et alterum quo sanctitas vestra missas
celebrare consueverat, ad ostendendam circa me benivolentiam
vestram mihi impendistis, illud quoque quod omnibus quorum
mediator extiti quicquid iuste ac salubriter petierunt me
interveniente protinus concessistis, ut taceam alia plura quę
in hac parte ab his minime discrepant, quęque mihi memoriam
vestri nominis siquid boni[a] bonifacio dulciter representant.
Epistolam quam Berigerio scismatico dum adhuc Cadomensi
cenobio preessem transmisi, paternitati vestrę sicut precepistis
transmittere curavi.[b][1] Omnipotens Dominus vitam vestram ad
honorem sanctę aecclesię vestris dispositionibus divinitus
commissę in tempore prolixam faciat, quatinus post tempus quę
sine tempore sunt prolixa aeternitatis spacia vobis concedat.

III. *Judgement of a Council on the Primacy*

Anno ab incarnatione Domini nostri Iesu Christi[c] millesimo
septuagesimo secundo, pontificatus autem domni Alexandri papę
undecimo, regni vero Wilelmi gloriosi regis Anglorum et ducis
Northmannorum[d] sexto, ex pręcepto eiusdem Alexandri papę, annuente eodem rege, in pręsentia ipsius et episcoporum atque abbatum
ventilata est causa de primatu quem LANFRANCUS Dorobernensis
archiepiscopus super Eboracensem ęcclesiam iure suę aecclesię
proclamabat, et de ordinationibus quorundam episcoporum de quibus ad quem specialiter pertinerent certum minime constabat.

    Et tandem aliquando diversis diversarum scripturarum auctori-
tatibus probatum atque ostensum est quod Eboracensis ęcclesia
Canturiensi debeat subiacere, eiusque archiepiscopi ut primatis

---

[a]boni N; *om.* VM.   [b]Quod peto ... transmittere curavi NMV; *om.* E.
[c]Iesu Christi *om.* C.   [d]Northmannorum ABN; Normannorum VERSLCWDX; N. P.

---

[1]Gibson, *Lanfranc of Bec,* pp. 81-91.

totius Britannię dispositionibus in iis[a] quę ad Christianam
religionem pertinent in omnibus oboedire. Subiectionem vero
Dunelmensis, hoc est Lindisfarnensis, episcopi atque omnium
regionum a terminis Licifeldensis episcopii[b] et Humbrę magni
fluvii usque ad extremos Scotię fines, et quicquid ex hac parte
prędicti fluminis ad parochiam Eboracensis aecclesię iure
competit, Canturiensis metropolitanus Eboracensi archiepiscopo
eiusque successoribus in perpetuum[c] obtinere concessit. Ita ut
si Canturiensis archiepiscopus concilium cogere voluerit
ubicunque visum ei[d] fuerit, Eboracensis archiepiscopus sui
pręsentiam cum omnibus sibi subiectis episcopis[e] ad nutum eius
exhibeat, et eius canonicis dispositionibus oboediens existat.

Quod autem Eboracensis archiepiscopus professionem Canturiensi archiepiscopo facere etiam cum sacramento debeat LANFRAN-
CUS Dorobernensis archiepiscopus ex antiqua antecessorum consuetudine ostendit, sed ob amorem regis Thomę Eboracensi
archiepiscopo sacramentum relaxavit, scriptamque tantum professionem recepit, non pręiudicans successoribus suis qui sacramentum cum professione a successoribus Thomę exigere voluerint.

Si archiepiscopus Canturiensis vitam finierit, Eboracensis
archiepiscopus Doroberniam veniet, et eum qui electus fuerit
cum cęteris pręfatę aecclesię episcopis ut primatem proprium
iure consecrabit. Quodsi Eboracensis archiepiscopus[f] obierit,
is qui ei successurus eligitur, accepto a rege archiepiscopatus
dono, Canturiam vel ubi Canturiensi archiepiscopo[g] placuerit[h]
accedet, et ab ipso ordinationem canonico more suscipiet.[i]

Huic constitutioni consenserunt pręfatus rex et archiepiscopi,[j] LANFRANCUS Canturiensis et Thomas Eboracensis[k] et
cęteri qui interfuerunt episcopi.[l]

---

[a]iis ABNVERSPL; hiis CDX; his W.   [b]episcopi CL *p. 14.*   [c]in perpetuum
om. RX.   [d]visum ei ABERSLC; ei visum NVPWDX.   [e]episcopis ANVPE[2]; *om.*
BERSLCWDX.   [f]Ebor. arch. ABERSLCWDX; arch. Ebor. NVP.   [g]obierit...Cant.
archiepiscopo *om.* C.   [h]placuerit ABERSLCWDX; visum fuerit NVP.   [i]P *ends.*
[j]archiepiscopi: ipse archiepiscopus W.   [k]et Hubertus sancte Romane ecclesie subdiaconus et prefati Alexandri pape legatus *add* NVERX.   [l]et abbates
add NVERX; NV *end.*

A

Signum | Wilelmi regis

        Sig|num Mathildis
           reginę   + Ego Hubertus sanctę Romanę
                            ecclesię lector et domni
                            Alexandri pape legatus sub-
                            scripsi

+ Ego Lanfrancus Dorobernensis + Ego Thomas Eboracensis archi-
  archiepiscopus subscripsi   episcopus concedo

  + Ego Walchelinus Wentanus   + Ego Remigius Dorcacestren-
    episcopus subscripsi   sis[a] episcopus subscrisi

                        + Ego Erfastus Tetfortensis
                        episcopus subscripsi

  + Ego Wlstanus Wigornensis episcopus subscripsi

BERSLCWDX

Ventilata est autem hęc causa prius apud Wentanam civitatem
in Pascali solemnitate in capella regia quę sita est in castello,
postea in villa regia quę vocatur Windisor, ubi et finem accepit
in pręsentia regis, episcoporum, abbatum, diversorum ordinum,
qui congregati erant apud curiam in festivitate Pentecostes.[b]

+ Signum Willelmi + Signum Mathildis + Ego Hubertus sanctę
  regis   reginę[c]   Romanę ęcclesię lector
                                et domni Alexandri
                                [pa]pę legatus sub-
                                scripsi[d]

+ Ego Lanfrancus Dorobernensis + Ego Odo Baiocensis episcopus
  archiepiscopus subscripsi   et comes Cantię consensi

+ Ego Thomas Eboracensis archi- + Ego Goisfridus Constantiensis[e]
  episcopus subscripsi   episcopus et unus de primati-
                          bus Anglorum consensi

+ Ego Willelmus Lundoniensis   + Ego Scollandus abbas cenobii[f]
  episcopus consensi   sancti Augustini consensi

+ Ego Herimannus Siraburnensis + Ego Elfwinus abbas cenobii
  episcopus subscripsi[1]   quod Rammesei dicitur consensi

---

[a]Written either side of an erasure.   [b]C *adds* Rege Willelmo et Matilda
regina cum duobus archiepiscopis et xiii episcopis et H. legato et xi abbatibus consencientibus et conscribentibus *and ends.*   [c]W *adds* Subscripsit autem
Hubertus sancte Romane ecclesie lector, Alexandri pape legatus. Subscrip-
serunt et prefati archiepiscopi, subscribentibus et eidem dispositioni con-
sentientibus omnibus tam episcopis quam abbatibus Anglie *and ends.*   [d]SL
*p. 15 place the subscription of the legate after that of Osbern of Exeter
below;* B *is damaged at* pape.   [e]Constantiensis BERDX; Constantiniensis SL.
[f]cenobii *om.* S.

---

[1]*Subscripsi* is probably an error for *consensi*; Herman is the only witness
who is said to have subscribed B without having set his hand to A.

+ Ego Wlstanus[a] Wigornensis
episcopus subscripsi

+ Ego Walterus Herefordensis
episcopus consensi

+ Ego Giso Wellensis episcopus
consensi[d]

+ Ego Remigius Dorchacensis
episcopus subscripsi

+ Ego Walchelinus Wentanus
episcopus subscripsi

+ Ego Herfastus Helmeanensis
episcopus subscripsi

+ Ego Stigandus Cicestrensis
episcopus consensi

+ Ego Siwardus Hrofensis[g]
episcopus consensi

+ Ego Osbernus Exoniensis
episcopus consensi

+ Ego Elnodus[b] Glestoniensis
abbas consensi[c]

+ Ego Thurstanus abbas cenobii
quod in insula quę dicitur
Heli situm est consensi

+ Ego Ulwoldus abbas cenobii
quod Certisei dicitur consensi

+ Ego Elwius abbas cenobii
Hevesandi consensi

+ Ego Fredericus abbas cenobii[e]
sancti Albani consensi

+ Ego Goisfridus abbas cenobii
sancti Petri[f] quod non longe
a Lundonia situm est consensi

+ Ego Balduinus abbas cenobii
sancti Eadmundi consensi

+ Ego Toroldus   + Ego Adelelmus
abbas de Bur-   abbas Abben-
go consensi   donię consensi

+ Ego Rualodus[h] abbas Novi
Monasterii Wentonię consensi

IV. *Profession of obedience to Canterbury made by Archbishop
Thomas of York*

Printed in *Canterbury Professions*, no. 34 from BL Cotton
ms. Cleopatra E. i, fo. 47 (= E) (which was the source
for Canterbury, D & C, Reg. A), Domitian v, fo. 14
(= D) and Nero A. vii, fo. 5 (= N); also in Vatican ms.
Reg. Lat. 285, fo. 3 (= V), Milo's *Vita Lanfranci*, ed.
D'Achery, p. 12 (= Mi), and in Vatican ms. Reg. Lat. 499,
fo. 63[v] (= Mv), Malmesbury's *Gesta Regum*, here cited from
BL Arundel ms. 35, fo. 109 (= R) and *Gesta Pontificum,*
Oxford, Magdalen Coll. ms. Lat. 172, fo. 14 (= P); BL
Cotton ms. Vitellius A. xx, fo. 73 is probably a copy
of the *Gesta Regum* text. Further printed in WMGP, p. 42,
WMGR ii.352 §299, *Hist. York*, iii.13-14, Böhmer, *Die*

---

[a]Wlstanus BERLD; Wltannus S; Willelmus X.   [b]Elnodus BEDX; Elnothus RS;
Eilnothus L (L p. 15 *as* B).   [c]S *places this subscription after that of
Baldwin of Bury.*   [d]Ego Giso — consensi *om.* S.   [e]*om.* ER.   [f]sancti
Petri *om.* L.   [g]Hrof. BSD; Rof. ERL.   [h]Rualodus B *(written either side of
a space)* LSED; Rualdus RXL *p.15.*

Fälschungen, p. 167, *Lanf. Letters,* ed. Clover and Gibson, no. 3 (iii). Our text is based on N.

[a]Decet Christianum quenque Christianis legibus subiacere, nec his[b] quae a sanctis patribus salubriter instituta sunt quibuslibet rationibus contraire.[c] Hinc nanque irę, dissensiones, invidię, contentiones ceteraque procedunt quę amatores suos in poenas aeternas demergunt, et quanto quisque altioris est ordinis, tanto impensius divinis debet obtemperare preceptis. Propterea ego Thomas, ordinatus iam Eboracensis ęcclesię metropolitanus antistes, auditis cognitisque rationibus, absolutam tibi, Lanfrance Dorobernensis archiepiscope, tuisque successoribus de canonica oboedientia professionem facio, et quicquid a te vel ab eis iuste et canonice iniunctum mihi fuerit servaturum me esse promitto. De hac autem re dum[d] a te adhuc[e] ordinandus essem dubius fui, ideoque tibi quidem sine conditione, successoribus vero tuis conditionaliter obtemperaturum me esse promisi.

V. *Canons of the council*

[1] De infantibus ut liceat quocumque tempore baptizari propter mortis[f] periculum.[1]

[2] Ut pannum habeant unde totum corpus albati involvatur, propter sacrum crisma quod in baptisterio mittitur, et non laventur ante septimum diem, ut tunc in ecclesia laventur super fontes et pannus non sit ad aliut ministerium quam ad opus ecclesie, et candela remaneat in ęcclesia.[2]

[3] Ut nemo postulet pretium pro accipiendo corpore Christi ut Iudas venditor.

---

[a]Professio Thome Eboracensis Archiepiscopi ERD; quam fecit Lanfranco Cant' archiepiscopo D *only*.   [b]iis E.   [c]Decet — contraire *was added at the foot of the leaf by* N, *with a note to show where it belongs*.   [d]re dum NEVDRP; antea cum MiMv.   [e]*om*. Mi.   [f]i mostis *ms*.

---

[1]CC. of Winchester (1070), c. 7, Rouen (1072), c. 24.
[2]C. of Rouen ('1050'), c. 19. Compare *Manuale ... insignis ecclesiæ Eboracensis,* ed. W.G. Henderson (Surtees Soc. lxiii for 1874), pp. 133*, 136*, 147*.

[4] Ut nullum ministerium sacri ordinis aut vendatur aut ematur, et nemo monasterium emat aut vendat, quia omnis nego-tiator sacrorum periculum excommunicationis incurrit, et quicumque emit peniteat.[1]

[5] Ut nemo mittat presbiterum in aeclesia sine autoritate episcopi[a] qui sibi commendet curam animarum, et quicumque sine episcopo miserit irritum sit.[2]

[6] Ut nemo episcopus clericum, nemo abbas monachum, ex aliis monasteriis sine testimonio litterarum vel cognoscibili indicio recipiat, et qui probabiliter non sunt de terra exeant.[3]

[7] Ut clerici non sunt aleatores neque venatores.[4]

[8] Ut nemo cẹlet episcopo vel ministro episcopi criminale peccatum qui scierit.

[9] Ut nemo contra regem vel contra terram in qua conversatur proditionem faciat. Et unusquisque episcopus vel presbiter tales excommunicet in parrochia sua. Et unusquisque presbiter cantet tres missas pro rege et cæteri ordines unum psalterium, et laici septem elemosinas faciant ut pauperibus omnes sub-veniant suis elemosinis.[5]

[10] Ut presbiter nullius sit prepositus nisi episcopi.[6]

[11] Ut festivitas sancti Agustini que erit in vigilia Pente-fostes [fo. 27] celebretur[b] uno die ante idem[c] in sexta feria.[7]

---

[a]episcopo *ms.*   [b]caele/celebretur *ms.*   [c]*Recte* id est?

---

[1]C. of Winchester (1070), c. 2; compare CC. of Windsor (1070), c. 2. Rheims (1049), c. 2, Rouen (1072), c. 13.
[2]C. of Tours (1060), c. 4; compare C. of Rome (1059), c. 6.
[3]C. of Winchester (1070), c. 3.   [4]C. of Gerona (1068), c. 11.
[5]C. of Windsor (1070), c. 9; compare the council of 779/80 in *MGH Conc.*, ii.108-9, and above, VII Æthelred 1-3.
[6]C. of Lisieux (1064), c. 8 printed by Delisle in *Journal des Savants* (1901), 516-21; compare Hinschius, p. 248.
[7]Just such arrangements are forbidden in C. of Rouen (1072), c. 23.

[12] Ut in ebdomada Pentecostes non agantur ieiunia quattuor
temporum nisi tunc ex necessitate quando festivitas sancti.
Iohannis occurrerit in proxima ebdomada post Pentecosten.[1]

[13] Ut quattuor dies Pentecostes celebrentur omnino sicut in
Pasca.

[14] Ut festivitas sancti Bartholomei celebretur in die festivi-
tatis sancti Audoeni transmarino more, hoc est nono kl' Septembris.

92
25 DECEMBER 1074 x 28 AUGUST 1075. COUNCIL AT LONDON

See C.N.L. Brooke, 'Archbishop Lanfranc, the English
bishops, and the Council of London of 1075', *Studia
Gratiana*, xii (1967), 39-59, Stenton, *Anglo-Saxon England*, pp. 666-7, McDonald, *Lanfranc*, pp. 97-103, Böhmer,
Kirche und Staat, p. 92, Z.N. Brooke, *English Church and
the Papacy*, p. 59, D.J.A. Matthew, *The Norman Conquest*,
pp. 174-6, Gibson, *Lanfranc of Bec*, pp. 143-5.

According to the *Acta Lanfranci* the archbishop 'Quinto anno
generale concilium Lundonie celebravit, cuius gestionem rogatu
multorum litteris commendavit.'[2] This is the only external
evidence to illustrate the canons, which survive in a number of
copies. The date of the council cannot be fixed within close
limits. The ninth year of King William in the text began on
25 December 1074; the fifth year of the rule of Lanfranc of the
Acta ended on 28 August 1075. The councils of 1070, 1072, and
1076 were all held either at Easter or Whitsun, and although
the king was overseas in 1075 and this council was not therefore

---

[1]The feast of St. John the Baptist very rarely falls in the week after
Whitsun week. It did so, however, in 1071, and again in 1082. See further
Gibson, *Lanfranc of Bec*, pp. 143, 241, and compare VI Æthelred Lat. 23.
[2]*ASC* ed. Plummer, i.289; compare W. i.369 from BL ms. Cotton Domitian
v, fo. 14, and the late note in *Ann. Mon.* iv.372.

associated with a crown-wearing, the weeks following 5 April or 24 May of 1075 remain the most likely occasions for its meeting.

Its *acta* were 'signed' by all the English bishops then in office except Walcher of Durham,[1] by Geoffrey of Coutances, by the archdeacon of Canterbury, and by twenty-one abbots. Of the twelve houses whose heads had attested the judgement of 1072, ten were represented in 1075, but the abbots from the west and south-west appeared in much greater numbers. Of the heads of larger houses who might have appeared in 1075 only the abbots of Peterborough, St. Benet of Holme, and Crowland seem to have been absent, and these houses were all in areas much affected by the rising of 1075.[2]

The text of these canons is the first since the Conquest, and the only one attributable to Lanfranc, which appears to survive in its full form, including references to the authorities upon which the canons rest. The sources quoted are all to be found either in the abbreviated Pseudo-Isidore which Lanfranc was responsible for introducing into England or in the Rule of St. Benedict. Apart from the unusually detailed monastic provisions, however, several of the canons renew decrees made at the councils of 1070 and 1072.

The two major new decisions deal with the precedence of the bishops and with the moving of episcopal sees to larger centres. The matter of precedence had clearly already been thought over at the council of 1072, for the signatories to the longer version of the judgement there follow the same order as those of 1075 except for Walkelin of Winchester, who attests 1072 in

---

[1] The see of Rochester is said (p. 612) to be vacant. In the Rochester annals in BL ms. Cotton Vespasian A. xxii, fo. 27ᵛ (followed by *Flores Historiarum*, ii.8) Siward's death is placed in 1075, after that of Queen Edith, which occurred in December. His obit was later celebrated on 14 or 30 October (Le Neve, ii.75, *Custumale Roffense*, ed. J. Thorpe (London, 1788), p. 37), and his successor was appointed between 29 Aug. 1075 and 28 Aug. 1076 (*ASC*, ed. Plummer, i.289). Since Siward was alive at Whitsun 1072 (above, p. 604) but dead at the time of this council, either he died in October 1072-4 or his obit was not celebrated in the month of his death. The entry in *Flor. Wig.* ii.2 appears to be an erroneous afterthought.

[2] On Archdeacon Anschetill see Le Neve, ii.12; Westminster was probably vacant at the time of the council (*Heads*, p. 76).

order of consecration but here follows the bishop of London
(who already took precedence over Herman of Sherborne in 1072,
though consecrated six years later). Correspondingly in this
matter the precedence of Winchester may be the only wholly new
provision of 1075.[1]

The moving of sees was not in itself a novelty; similar
general principles had been enunciated by Leo IX in authoriz-
ing the move from Crediton to Exeter in 1050 (above, no. 70),
and may also have been canvassed in Normandy before the Conquest,[2] but the number of sees which were moved in England,
and the absence of direct papal assent, were without recent
parallel. The first suggestion of an intention to move the
sees of Selsey and Lichfield, which are mentioned in the text,
and of Elmham and Dorchester, which are not, antedate the council by several years. However, most of the proposed new sites
for sees have this in common, that they place the cathedral
near or even within defensible walls. It is therefore possible
that the threat of rebellion in 1075, or indeed its outbreak,
may have hastened these decisions on.[3]

The most important manuscript of the canons is clearly

> J. Cambridge, St. John's Coll. ms. L. 9 (236), late 11th
> cent., a single sheet where the main text was written
> by a member of Lanfranc's household.[4] The *signa* are
> probably not autograph, but the several scribes who
> wrote the attestations seem to have made some effort

---

[1] See *Studia Gratiana*, xii.47-51. The confused passage in WMGR ii.352-4
§§300-2 appears to describe a discussion on the issue in 1072, but in terms
which paraphrase the text of 1075.

[2] The French text printed in G. Du Moulin, *Histoire Générale de Normandie*
(Rouen, 1631), p. 160 and translated in *Sanctae Rothomagensis Ecclesiae
Concilia*, pp. 71-2, seems to refer to a synod at Caen before the Conquest
which dealt with this issue; see further a similar but briefer account in
C. de Bourgeville, *Les recherches et antiquitez de la ville et Université
de Caen* (Caen, 1588), pp. 18-19 and Foreville in *Church and Government in
the Middle Ages*, pp. 22, 26.

[3] Brooke, *Studia Gratiana*, xii.51-5. While the movement of Dorchester to
Lincoln may have received the assent of papal legates as early as 1070
(above, p. 566), formal papal confirmation of most of these moves had to
wait until the reign of Henry I (below, p. 657). The merits of Exeter's
defensive position were emphasised explicitly by King Edward in no. 71 above.

[4] See the note by T.A.M. Bishop in Brooke, *Studia Gratiana*, xii.57.

to copy the features of original attestations in their
exemplar. The endorsements show that this copy was
kept among the archives of Christ Church, at least in
the twelfth and thirteenth centuries. This, or a virtually indistinguishable text, was apparently the
source for Lambeth Palace ms. 1212, pp. 398-9. Similarly Cambridge UL ms. Ee 5.31, fo. 239^{r-v}, where an
incomplete version of the council is among the documents inspected by Prior J. of Canterbury in a text
itself inspected by Prior Henry in letters dated 12
November 1324, shows no clear sign of an independent
transmission.[1]

A version without the *signa* circulated among the letters of
Lanfranc, where it is represented in

N. BL ms. Cotton Nero A. vii, fos. 13-15
V. Vatican, ms. Reg. Lat. 285, fo. 7^{r-v}
E. BL ms. Cotton Cleopatra E. i, fos. 51-2, the source
  for the 15th-cent. Canterbury D & C Reg. A, fos. 8^{v}-9.

Slightly modified texts of the same tradition are found in
Malmesbury's *Gesta Pontificum* and Milo's *Vita Lanfranci*.[2]

Spelman claimed to print his version in Sp. ii.7-9 from an
ancient register of the church of Worcester. An examination
of Bodl. ms. e Mus. 49, fos. 9-11^{v}, the text which he prepared
but Dugdale subsequently revised for the press, shows that
here, as for May 1070 (above, p. 577 n. 3), he was using a
transcript by Joscelyn, who was here copying a lost book from
Worcester. In several minute respects the readings of this
version appear to represent an ancient tradition. All but the
most trivial variants therefore have been recorded from

---

[1] In the surviving copy the inspeximus by Prior J. is undated. It is
probably the document referred to in *The Great Register of Lichfield Cathedral*, ed. H.E. Savage (William Salt Archaeol. Soc., *Collections*, 1926 for
1924), p. 201 no. 413 of October 1226. A 13th/14th-cent. French translation of
a text in the same tradition is in Canterbury Cath. Library, ms. Add. 17, p. 17.
  [2] *Lanf. Letters*, ed. Clover and Gibson, no. 11, ed. Giles, i.305-7; WMGP,
pp. 66-8.

Joscelyn's copy 'e veteri libro Wigornensis ecclesiae'

    S. BL ms. Cotton Vitellius D. vii, fos. 118-19^V.

Some of these readings are confirmed in four abbreviations, three of which also derive from Worcester:

    D. Dugdale, *History of St. Paul's* (London, 1658), p. 195, reprinted in Sp. ii.10-11, from a manuscript once at Cambridge but now apparently lost

    M. London, Lambeth Palace ms. 171, fo. 6^V

    R. Oxford, Bodl. ms. Rawlinson C.428, fo. 101.

M and R are virtually identical copies of a canonical collection made at Worcester in the fourteenth century (below, p. 697), and are very close to D. An earlier and independent copy of the prologue and canon 1 is found in another Worcester manuscript of the mid-twelfth century

    W. BL ms. Cotton Vitellius C. viii, fo. 11^{r-v} (above, p. 595).

The importance of these abbreviations is that they support some of the variants of Joscelyn's transcript, and confirm its point of diffusion as Worcester.[1]

The text printed below is that of J, which is probably not more than one remove from an 'original' text produced at the council, collated throughout with S. Select variants only of the other manuscripts are noticed. Sp. ii.7-11 printed from S and D; Labbe, x.346-50; W. i.363-4 from Sp. collated with Canterbury, D & C Reg. A; Mansi, xx.449-56.

---

[1] In J the *signa* are arranged with the bishops and Archdeacon Anschetill in the left-hand column, the abbots of St. Augustine and New Minster at the head of the right-hand column and below them the remaining abbots in two columns. S or its original transcribed the whole as a single sequence with some slight variation of order.

Anno incarnationis dominicę MLXX^{mo}v^{to}, regnante glorioso
Anglorum rege Willelmo, anno regni eius nono, congregatum est
Lundonię[a] in ecclesia beati Pauli apostoli concilium totius[b]
Anglicę[c] regionis, episcoporum videlicet,[d] abbatum necnon et
multarum religiosi ordinis personarum, iubente atque eidem concilio pręsidente Lanfranco sanctę Dorobernensis ecclesię archi-
pręsule totiusque Britannicę[e] insulę primate, considentibus
secum viris venerabilibus Thoma Eboracensi archiepiscopo, Willelmo Lundoniensi episcopo, Goisfredo[f] Constantiensi, qui cum
transmarinus esset episcopus in Anglia multas possessiones
habens cum ceteris in concilio residebat, Walchelino Wintoniensi,
Herimanno[g] Siraburnensi, Wlfstano[h] Wiricestrensi, Waltero Herefordensi, Gisone Willensi, Remigio Dorcacensi seu Linconiensi,[i]
Herfasto Helmeanensi seu Norwicensi,[j] Stigando Selemgensi,
Osberno Exoniensi, Petro Licifeldensi.[k] Roffensis ecclesia per
idem tempus pastore carebat. Lindisfarnensis qui et Dunelmensis
episcopus, canonicam excusationem habens, concilio interesse non
poterat. Et quia multis retro[l] annis in Anglico regno usus
conciliorum obsoleverat, renovata sunt nonnulla quę antiquis
etiam noscuntur canonibus[m] definita.

[1] Ex concilio igitur Toletano quarto, Milevitano atque
Bracharensi[n] statutum est ut singuli secundum ordinationis suę
tempora sedeant,[1] preter eos qui ex antiqua consuetudine sive
suarum ecclesiarum privilegiis digniores sedes habent. De qua
re interrogati sunt senes et etate provecti quid vel ipsi
vidissent vel a maioribus atque antiquioribus veraciter ac
probabiliter accepissent. Super quo responso petitę sunt
inducię ac concessę usque in crastinum. Crastina autem die
concorditer perhibuere quod Eboracensis archiepiscopus ad

---

[a]Lundonie JSWE; Lundoniis D; Londonie NV.   [b]totius *om.* DMR.   [c]Anglice
JS[2]NEVDMR; Anglie SW.   [d]DMRW *add* et.   [e]Brittanice JSN[1]V[1]MR[1]D; Britannie
NEVR.   [f]Goisfredo JV; Goisfrido SNEV; Gosfrido W.   [g]Herimanno JVS; Hermanno NE; Heremanno W.   [h]Wlfstano JV; Wlstano SNER; Wulstano WMD.   [i]Lin-
coniensi JNV; Lincoliensi SE; Lincolliensi W.   [j]Norwicensi JNEVW; Norhwi-
censi S.   [k]Licifeldensi JNEV; Licedfeldensi S; Lichesfeldensi W.   [l]multis
retro *transp.* DMR.   [m]noscuntur canonibus *transp.* SDMRW.   [n]Bracharensi
JNEVW; Bracarensi SDMR.

---

[1]Hinschius, pp. 364 c. 3, 318 cc. 13-14, 423 c. 6.

dexteram Dorobernensis sedere debeat, Lundoniensis episcopus
ad sinistram, Wentanus[a] iuxta Eboracensem. Si vero Eboracensis
desit, Lundoniensis ad dexteram, Wentanus ad sinistram.[b]

[2] Ex regula beati Benedicti, dialogo Gregorii, et antiqua
regularium locorum consuetudine,[1] ut monachi ordinem debitum
teneant, infantes preçipue et iuvenes in omnibus locis deputa-
tis sibi idoneis magistris custodiam habeant, nocte luminaria
ferant, generaliter omnes nisi a prelatis concessa proprietate
careant. Si quis vero aliquid proprii sine prefata licentia
habere in morte fuerit deprehensus, nec ante mortem id reddiderit, cum penitentia et dolore peccatum suum confessus, nec
signa pro eo pulsentur, nec salutaris pro eius absolutione
hostia immoletur, nec in cimiterio sepeliatur.

[3] Ex decretis summorum pontificum, Damasi videlicet et
Leonis, necnon ex conciliis Sardicensi atque Laodicensi,[2] in
quibus prohibetur episcopales sedes in villis existere, con-
cessum est regia munificentia et sinodali auctoritate prefatis
tribus episcopis de villis ad civitates transire, Herimanno[c]
de Siraburna[d] ad Serisberiam, Stigando de Selemgeo ad Cicestrum,
Petro de Licifelde ad Cestrum. De quibusdam qui in villis seu
vicis adhuc degebant dilatum est usque ad regis audientiam, qui
in transmarinis partibus tunc temporis bella gerebat.

[4] Ex multis Romanorum presulum decretis diversisque sacrorum
canonum auctoritatibus, ne quis alienum clericum vel monacum
sine commendaticiis litteris retineat vel ordinet.[3]

[5] Ad comprimendam quorundam indiscretorum insolentiam, ex

---

[a]Wentanus JNEVW; Ventanus S.   [b]W ends.   [c]Herimanno JNV; Hermanno SE.
[d]Siraburna JNE; Syraburna V; Sciraburna S.

[1]*Benedicti Regula,* cc. 33, 70; *Lanfranc's Monastic Constitutions,* ed.
Knowles, pp. 8, 94; *Gregorii Magni Dialogi Libri IV,* ed. U. Moricca, pp.
317-20.
[2]Hinschius, pp. 512, 624, 267 c. 6, 276 c. 57.
[3]CC. of Winchester (1070), c. 3, Winchester (1072), c. 6, Rouen (1074),
c. 3.

communi decreto sanccitum est ne quis in concilio loquatur
preter licentiam a metropolitano sumptam, exceptis episcopis
et abbatibus.

[6] Ex decretis Gregorii maioris necnon et[a] minoris, ut nullus
de propria cognatione vel uxoris defunctę seu quam cognatus
habuit uxorem accipiat quoadusque parentela ex alterutra parte
ad septimum gradum perveniat.[1]

[7] Ut nullus sacros ordines seu officium ecclesiasticum quod
ad curam animarum pertineat emat vel vendat. Hoc enim scelus
a Petro apostolo in Simone mago primitus damnatum est,[b] postea
a sanctis patribus vetitum et excommunicatum.[2]

[8] Ne ossa mortuorum animalium quasi pro vitanda animalium
peste alicubi suspendantur, nec sortes vel aruspicia seu divi-
nationes vel aliqua huiusmodi opera diaboli ab aliquo exerceantur. Hęc enim omnia sacri canones prohibuerunt, et eos qui
talia exercent data sententia excommunicaverunt.[3]

[9] Ex conciliis Eliberritano et Toletano undecimo, ut nullus
episcopus vel abbas seu quilibet ex clero hominem occidendum
vel menbris truncandum iudicet, vel iudicantibus suę auctoritatis favorem commodet.[c4]

+ Ego Lanfrancus Dorobernensis   [d]+ Ego Scollandus abbas sancti
  archiepiscopus subscripsi   Augustini subscripsi

-----

[a]et JNEV; *om.* SDMR.   [b]est *interlined* J.   [c]Hoc sancitum atque con-
firmatum est coram duobus archiepiscopis et xii episcopis et Aschenillo
archidiacono Dorobernensis ecclesie et xxi (xi R) abbatibus *and end* DMR.
[d]*The second, right-hand, column of witnesses begins in* J.

-----

[1]Hinschius, pp. 751, 754 c. 9.
[2]CC. of Winchester (1070), c. 2, Windsor (1070), cc. 1-2, Winchester
(1072), c. 3, Rouen (1074), c. 1.
[3]CC. of Neocaesarea, c. 24, Carthage IV, c. 89, Toledo IV, c. 28 (Hinschius, pp. 263, 306, 369); compare VI Æthelred 7.
[4]C. of Toledo XI, c. 6 (Hinschius, p. 409). The reference to the C. of
Elvira is a mistake (Brooke, *English Church and the Papacy,* p. 67 n.).

+ Ego Thomas Eburacensis ęcclesię
archiepiscopus subscripsi[a]

+ Ego Willelmus Lundoni-
ensis ęcclesię episco-
pus[d]

+ Ego Walchelinus Winto-
niensis[i] episcopus sub-
scripsi

+ Ego Gaufridus Constan-
tiniensis[l] episcopus et
unus de Anglicę[m] terrę
primatibus subscripsi

+ Ego Herimannus[p] Seri-
beriensis episcopus
subscripsi

+ Ego Wlfstanus[s] Wigor-
nensis episcopus sub-
scripsi

+ Ego Walterus Herefor-
densis episcopus sub-
scripsi

+ Ego Giso Wellensis
episcopus subscripsi

+ Ego Remigius Lincholi-
ensis episcopus sub-
scripsi

+ Ego Erfastus[y] Norwi-
censis[z] episcopus
subscripsi

+ Ego Stigandus Cices-
trensis episcopus
subscripsi

+ Ego Osbernus Exoniensis episcopus subscripsi

+ Ego Riwallonus[b] abbas
sancti Petri Wintoniensis[c]
subscripsi

+ Ego Adelelmus[e]
abbas Abbendone[f]
subscripsi

+ Ego Balduinus[j]
abbas sancti Ed-
mundi subscripsi

+ Ego Eluinus ab-
bas de Evessam[n]
subscripsi

+ Ego Alwinus ab-
bas de Ramisei[q]
subscripsi

+ Ego Sarlo[t] abbas
Glaucestrensis
subscripsi

+ Ego Fredericus
abbas Verolamii
subscripsi

+ Ego Leuwardus
abbas Muchelanie
subscripsi

+ Ego Lewinus ab-
bas de Coventre[w]
subscripsi

+ Ego Æswerdus ab-
bas Abbetis-
berię[aa] subscrip-
si

+ Ego Osirich[cc] de Hortuna subscripsi

+ Ego Ulwoldus ab-
bas Certesei[g]
subscripsi[h]

+ Ego Teduinus ab-
bas Eliensis[k]
subscripsi[h]

+ Ego Elnaldus ab-
bas de Glastinge-
berie[o] subscrip-
si

+ Ego Galannus ab-
bas Wicelcomę[r]
subscripsi

+ Ego Warinus ab-
bas Meldunnensis
subscripsi

+ Ego Edmundus
Personę[u] sub-
scripsi

+ Ego Ælsi[v] de
Bada subscripsi

+ Ego Elduinus de
Mildeltuna[x] sub-
scripsi

+ Ego Edwardus[bb]
abbas de Cernel
subscripsi

---

[a]Subscripserunt et alii episcopi vel abbates qui interfuerunt *and end*
NEV.   [b]Riwalo S.   [c]Wintoniae S.   [d]S *adds* subscripsi.   [e]Athelelmus S.
[f]Abandoniae S.   [g]Certieseig S.   [h]*The entries for Ulwold and Teduin are*
transposed in S.   [i]S *adds* ecclesiæ.   [j]Baldwinus S.   [k]Eligensis S.
[l]Constantiensis S.   [m]Angliae S.   [n]Elwinus abbas de Evesam S *(ms. damaged;*
partially supplied from Spelman).   [o]Elnodus abbas de Gleastinberie S.
[p]Hermannus S.   [q]Rameseig S.   [r]abb. Wic. J; de Wincelcumbe S.   [s]Wlstanus
SJ; Wlfstanus J[1].   [t]Serlo S.   [u]Eadmundus abbas Persorae S.   [v]S *adds*
abbas.   [w]Covantr' S.   [x]Eldwinus abbas de Middeltune (de *subsequently*
cancelled) S.   [y]Herfastus S.   [z]Norhwicensis S.   [aa]Abbatisberiae S.
[bb]J *has a stroke above the E;* Edwardus S.   [cc]S *adds* abbas.

✝ Ego Petrus Cestrensis episcopus subscripsi

✝ Ego Anschitillus sanctę Dorobernensis ecclesię archidiaconus[a] subscripsi

93

1 APRIL 1076. PRIMATIAL COUNCIL AT WINCHESTER

On this council see Böhmer, *Kirche und Staat*, pp. 92-4, Stenton, *Anglo-Saxon England*, pp. 667-71, McDonald, *Lanfranc*, pp. 103-9.

According to the *Acta Lanfranci* the archbishop 'Sexto anno ... Wentonie concilium celebravit'.[1] According to the acts of the council, which again survive only imperfectly, it met on the Friday after Easter, presumably during the crown-wearing.

The only recorded judicial act of the council was a final decision on the case of Æthelric, deposed from the see of Selsey in 1070. Although the bishop must have been very old, this deposition had aroused grave concern at Rome before April 1073, for Pope Alexander had complained to the king of the long delay in dealing with irregularities in the case, evidently without effect.[2]

The canons are divided between those which follow the pattern of the previous post-Conquest councils and new matter. Of the new legislation the most striking is found in the first canon, dealing with clerical celibacy. This was one of the chief preoccupations of contemporary councils elsewhere in Europe, but it had been notably absent from canons of English councils between 1070 and 1075. In Normandy a married clergy had been condemned at a council at Rouen whose acts are lost, but whose provisions were renewed at Lisieux in 1064, where all priests and deacons who had married since the earlier council

---

[a]Anschit. archid. s. Dorob. eccl. S (*and see note c, p. 614 above*).

---

[1]*ASC*, ed. Plummer, i.289; cf. BL ms. Cotton Domitian v, fo. 14 in W. i.369.

[2]Above, p. 579; Stubbs, *Memorials*, p. 164, Textus Roffensis, fo. 169[v] (no. 84).

were required to abandon their wives; canons in lesser orders
were not to marry in future, but might keep the wives they
already had. This seems to suggest that the provisions of
Rouen had been not unlike those of 1076. At Lisieux as at Winchester subdeacons had been allowed to marry.[1] However, the
Council of Rouen of 1072 had withdrawn this concession, so
bringing Norman theory into line with the papal legislation of
1059 (which was incorporated into Lanfranc's canonical collection).[2] In 1074 and 1075 Gregory VII renewed the decrees of
1059 with increased emphasis. This programme of reform had
provoked a very lively resistance, in Normandy as elsewhere,
and the measure propounded by Lanfranc was much more re-
strained.[3] To judge by the astonished reaction to the decree
of Anselm in 1102 it was also almost certainly ineffective. It
is notable, however, that Bishop Wulfstan of Worcester, from
whose archives the sole early copy of these canons comes,
sought to enforce celibacy even more strictly than the council
required.[4]

Canon 3, prohibiting the public ministrations of monks, deals
with a matter then much debated, but is remarkable for its
condemnation of such action even with the consent of the
bishop.[5] Here the text from a late Worcester collection in mss.
M and R below ends, being followed without a break by the forged
decree attributed to Boniface IV (JE 1996), *Sunt nonnulli,* defending the monks' rights to exercise priestly functions.[6]

---

[1] Ed. Delisle in *Journal des Savants* (1901), p. 517. Lanfranc refers this
canon to Norman precedent in *Lanf. Letters,* ed. Clover and Gibson, no. 41,
ed. Giles, no. 25, though Barlow (1979), pp. 125-6 n. 111, sees some difficulty; his alternative suggestion depends on his arguments for dating our
C. of Windsor (1070), for which see above, p. 578 n. 1.

[2] CC. of Rouen (1072), c. 15, Rome (1059), c. 3, Brooke, *English Church
and the Papacy,* pp. 65-6.

[3] *Reg. Greg. VII,* ii.62, 66, ed. Caspar, i.217, 221; *The* Epistolae Vagantes
of Pope Gregory VII, ed. H.E.J. Cowdrey, nos. 6-11 and pp. 160-1; OV ii.200;
A. Fliche, *Revue des Sciences Religieuses,* v (1925), 14-34.

[4] Below, pp. 670, 683 ff.; *Vita Wulfstani,* pp. 53-4; *Reg.* i, nos. 121, 342.

[5] U. Berlière, *Revue Bénédictine,* xxxix (1927), 246-50, 341-5.

[6] This canon is first found in Italian collections *c.*1050, and seems to
have been known in England well before 1100. It was printed from an early addition to Cambridge, Trinity Coll. ms. B. 16. 44 (405) in Böhmer, *Die Fälschungen,* pp. 161-3; it occurs widely elsewhere. For the background see particularly
C. Dereine in *Studia Gratiana* ii (1954), 307-18 and S. Kuttner and R. Somerville in *Tijdschrift voor Rechtsgeschiedenis,* xxxviii (1970), 175-89.

Canon 5 lays down the procedure for enforcing a layman's obedience to episcopal judgement. Although the penalty for the contumacious is set out in the traditional terms of Anglo-Saxon law, the process laid down is closely related to that in the king's writ on church and lay courts (below no. 94), and may represent a recent reform.

Effectively there is only one manuscript of importance for this council,

A. Bodl. ms. Junius 121, fo. 4^{r-v}, late 11th cent.

This was almost certainly the source for all the late medieval or post-medieval transcripts of the complete text.[1] It was probably also the source of the truncated text in

M. Lambeth Palace ms. 171, fos. 6^v-7, 14th cent.

and

R. Bodl. ms. Rawlinson C 428, fo. 101^{r-v}, 14th cent.[2]

The text was first printed in M. Parker, *De Antiquitate Britannicae Ecclesiae,* London, 1572, p. 98; Parker's text was at first that of R, corrected and expanded from A. In some copies of the first edition and all later ones 'overseuuenesse seu laxelit' has been rendered into Anglo-Saxon script.[3] This was the version that was printed in Sp. ii.13-14 from the second edition of 1605, Labbe, x.353, Mansi, xx.462. In W. i.367 from the third edition of 1729.

The text below is that of A, with a few variants from M and R.

---

[1] The 15/16th-cent. BL ms. Add. 49366 (formerly Holkham 228), fo. 123^{r-v}, the 16th-cent. Cambridge, Corpus Coll. mss. 117, fo. 167, 298 (iv), fo. 55^v and BL ms. Cotton Vitellius D. vii, fo. 116 (Joscelyn's copy of A) and the 17th-cent. Dublin, Trinity Coll. ms. 526, p. 176 (above, p. 567 n. 4) have been collated, but reveal no signs of an independent transmission.

[2] See below, p. 697.

[3] The list of corrections in later copies of the first edition emends to 'oferhyrnesse seu lahslite'.

Canons of the Council

Anno ab incarnatione Domini millesimo lxxvi, indictione xiiii, regnante in Brittannia gloriosissimo rege Willelmo, presidente Cantuarię Lanfranco totius Brittannię primate, in Eboraco vero Thoma archiepiscopo, eo inquam anno in kalendis Aprilis habita est sinodus Wintonie, convocata ab eodem Cantuariensis ecclesię primate. In qua fratris nostri[a] Ailrici Cicestrensis quondam episcopi causa canonicę definita et ad certum finem perducta est.

[1] Decretumque est ut nullus canonicus uxorem habeat. Sacerdotum vero in castellis vel in vicis habitantium habentes uxores non cogantur ut dimittant, non habentes interdicantur ut habeant.[b] Et deinceps caveant episcopi ut sacerdotes vel diacones [fo. 4^V] non presumant ordinare nisi prius profiteantur ut uxores non habeant.[1]

[2] Nullusque clericus aut monachus in episcopatu alicuius suscipiatur absque episcopi sui litteris.[2]

[3] Si quis vero monachus etiam canonice susceptus fuerit, non permittatur ęcclesiis publice deservire.[c][3]

[4] Statutum est etiam ne aliquis clericus civilis vel rusticus de beneficio ęcclesie aliquid servitium reddat preter illud quod fec(erit) tempore regis Edwardi.[4]

[5] Laici vero si de crimine suo accusati fuerint, et episcopo

---

[a]nostris A; *om.* MR.   [b]Sacerdotum ... habeant A; Sacerdotes vero habentes uxores non cogantur ut dimittant, non habentes uxores non (ut R) cogantur MR. [c]etc. *add* MR *and end.*

---

[1]Compare C. of Winchester (1070), c. 15 and VI Æthelred Lat. 4-5 with the references above, p. 617 nn. 1 and 2.
[2]C. of London (1075), c. 4.
[3]Compare Mansi, xx.400 c. 5, an unidentified Anglo-Norman council on which see *JEH* xxvi.301-2.
[4]V Æthelred 10.2, VI Æthelred Lat. 15.

suo obedire noluerint, vocentur semel et iterum et tertio. Si post tertiam vocationem emendari noluerint, excommunicentur. Si autem post excommunicationem ad satisfactionem venerint, forisfacturam suam quę anglice vocatur overseuuenesse seu laxelit pro unaquaque vocatione episcopo suo reddant.[1]

[6] Preterea statutum est ut nullus filiam suam vel cognatam det alicui absque benedictione sacerdotali. Si aliter fecerit non ut legitimum coniugium sed ut fornicatorium iudicabitur.[2]

[7] Supplantationes vero ęcclesiarum omnibus modis interdicimus.[3] Finit.

94

1072 x 1085. ORDINANCE OF WILLIAM I ON CHURCH COURTS

See Liebermann, iii.274-5, Barlow, *English Church 1000-1066*, pp. 274-6, Barlow (1979), pp. 150-4, 159, C. Morris, 'William I and the Church Courts', *EHR* lxxxii (1967), 449-63, Matthew, *Norman Conquest*, pp. 193-5.

The charter printed below exists in two versions. One is addressed to all who hold lands in the bishopric of Lincoln, and was carefully preserved among the privileges of that see. The other is addressed to the sheriffs of Essex, Hertfordshire, and Middlesex, which cover the bishopric of London. Although this version is earliest recorded among the archives of St. Paul's it was also copied at Canterbury and Durham; although only a Latin text now survives, several manuscripts refer also to an English translation. There is no trace of a version

---

[1]See above, p. 305 n. 3, VI Æthelred 50-1 and *NPL* 2-45, 51-4, and in general Liebermann, ii.130, 169, 624-5, 642-4.

[2]C. of Rouen (1072), c. 14; Hinschius, pp. 87, 140; A. Esmein, *Le mariage en droit canonique*, i.25-6, 115-9; J.-B. Molin and P. Mutembe, *Le rituel du mariage en France du XIIe au XVIe siècle*, pp. 28-37; A. Nocent, 'Contribution à l'étude du rituel du mariage', *Studia Anselmiana*, lxviii (1979), 243-65, esp. 244-9; compare above no. 58 c. 8.

[3]For the use of *supplantatio* to mean usurpation of rights see C. of Rouen ('1050'), cc. 5, 11; compare VI Æthelred Lat. 13, 15.

addressed to any other see.

The purpose of the document remains controversial; its apparent object is the creation of separate tribunals in which the bishop will hear all ecclesiastical cases according to canon law, calling upon the secular arm only to coerce the obdurate. However, in neither version is there any mention of the shire courts in which the earlier Anglo-Saxon laws assumed that such cases would often be heard, nor does it seem probable that ecclesiastical courts of some kind were altogether a novelty in England. It has therefore been suggested that the actual purpose of the ordinance was to attack the secular usurpation of church jurisdiction or to enforce the right of the bishop's agents to collect the penalties for offences against church law. Very similar motives dominate the provisions of the Council of Lillebonne of 1080.[1] Whatever its object it seems to have attracted little attention before the beginning of the fourteenth century, when Archbishop Winchelsey cited it in his *Gravamina* of 1309,[2] and there is no direct contemporary reference to any reforms with which it may have been associated.

The date of the document is correspondingly difficult to determine. Canon 5 of the Council of Winchester of 1076 assumes that the bishop has jurisdiction over the offences of laymen without specifying the court in which they are to answer, and lays down traditional Anglo-Saxon penalties for the guilty. Although the similarity of wording between canon and ordinance is too close to be coincidental it does not follow that they must be contemporary.[3] The Lincoln version can only be dated to the pontificate of Remigius, but the address of the London version allows rather greater precision. Although Geoffrey de Mandeville was probably sheriff of Middlesex from soon after

---

[1]See further Foreville in *Church and Government in the Middle Ages*, pp. 26-7.

[2]*Councils*, ii (2), 1269-70; this reference led Liebermann to suggest a lost version at Canterbury, but see ms. C below. Sir Robert Cotton in *Cottoni Posthuma* (London, 1651), pp. 213-14, cited the writ from Cartae Antiquae BB; this is probably a mistaken reference to one of the later royal confirmations of the Lincoln version.

[3]Böhmer, *Kirche und Staat*, pp. 93-4 n. argued for a date of *c.*1076 for the writ on these grounds.

1066 until after the compilation of Domesday Book,[1] Robert fitz Wymarc remained sheriff of Essex for a while after the Conquest, and was succeeded by his son Swein and he by Ralph Bainard, though at unknown dates.[2] Peter de Valognes became sheriff of Hertfordshire after Ilbert, who was still in office in February 1072, and probably also after Ralph Taillebois.[3]

The text printed below is based upon the London version, as the more widespread. The following manuscripts have been used:

> A. London, St. Paul's D.& C. mun. W.D. 1, fo. 1, the
>   mid-13th-cent. Liber A (*Pilosus*).[4]
> B. London, St. Paul's D.& C. mun. A/69, no. 10, where it
>   is copied among the early charters of the see in a
>   roll written in the late 13th cent.
> C. Lambeth Palace, 1212 (cartulary of the archbishopric
>   of Canterbury), p. 15. A 14th-cent. addition at the
>   foot of the page, transcribed in the early 16th-cent.
>   Bodl. ms. Tanner 223, fo. 23[v].
> D. PRO Durham 3/1 (Bishop Kellawe's Register), fo. 247
>   (*olim* 282). Early 14th cent.

For the Lincoln version:

> E. Lincoln, D.& C. mun. A/1/5 (*Registrum Antiquissimum*),
>   fo. 1. Early 13th cent.

---

[1]J.H. Round, *Geoffrey de Mandeville*, pp. 37 n, 354, 439; *Reg.* i, nos. 15, 265; C.W. Hollister, *History*, lviii (1973), 19. See however the cautionary note struck in C.N.L. Brooke and G. Keir, *London 800-1216*, p. 372.

[2]*KCD* 859; *DB* ii.1, 98; *Reg.* i, nos. 84-6, 209; Freeman, *Norman Conquest*, iv (1876), 734-6. Ralph Bainard occurs, apparently as sheriff, in the dubious *Reg.* i, no. 181 as well as *DB* ii.1. By 1085 Peter de Valognes was also sheriff of Essex (*Reg.* i, no. 214).

[3]Peter became sheriff of Herts. certainly after February 1072, but possibly before 1077 (Walker, *EHR* xxxix (1924), 399-400, *Reg.* ii.396, no. 218a). Ralph Taillebois appears to be mentioned as a former sheriff in *DB* i.132[v], and compare 142[v]; to judge by *Reg.* ii, no. 218a he remained sheriff of Beds. after Peter had succeeded him in Herts.

[4]This, rather than the lost 'Liber B', was the source for Dugdale, *The History of St. Paul's Cathedral* (1658), p. 196.

The text has often been printed, most notably in *Early Charters ... of St. Paul*, ed. Gibbs, no. 4 (from A and B), *Registrum
Palatinum Dunelmense*, iii.82-83 (from D), *Reg. Lincoln*, i, no.
1 (and 63), citing E and many other Lincoln copies, Liebermann
i.485 (from A, E, and a variety of later texts),[1] Stubbs,
Select Charters, pp. 99-100, *PL* cxlix.1291-2, Sp. ii.14-15
(from A), W. i.368-9 (from A and E), and (in translation) *EHD*
ii.604-5, no. 79; calendared in *Reg.* i, no. 93.

ABCD	E
W. Dei gratia rex Anglorum	W. gracia Dei rex Angl' comi-
R. Bainardo et G. de Magna	tibus, vicecomitibus et
Villa, P. de Valoines,	omnibus Francigenis et Anglis
ceterisque meis fidelibus de	qui in episcopatu Remegii
Essex' et de Hertfordschir'	episcopi terras habent,
et de Middelsex',	

salutem. Sciatis vos omnes et ceteri mei fideles qui in Anglia
manent quod episcopales leges, que non bene nec secundum
sanctorum canonum precepta usque ad mea tempora in regno
Anglorum fuerunt, communi concilio et consilio archiepiscoporum[a] et[b] episcoporum et abbatum et omnium principum regni
mei emendandas iudicavi. Propterea mando et regia auctoritate
precipio ut nullus episcopus vel archidiaconus de legibus
episcopalibus amplius in hundret placita teneant, nec causam
que ad regimen animarum pertinet ad iudicium secularium hominum
adducant. Sed quicunque secundum episcopales leges de quacumque
causa vel culpa interpellatus fuerit ad locum quem ad hoc episcopus elegerit et nominaverit veniat, ibique de causa vel
culpa[c] sua respondeat, et non secundum hundret sed secundum
canones et episcopales leges rectum Deo et episcopo suo faciat.
Si vero aliquis per superbiam elatus ad iusticiam episcopalem venire

---

[a] meorum *add* E.   [b] ceterorum *add* E.   [c] vel culpa *om.* E.

---

[1] A text printed in Rymer (1816), i.3 as from the Red Book of the Exchequer, fo. 143, was collated by Liebermann. Rymer's reference is a misunderstanding of Wilkins, *Leges*, p. 230, which itself depends on Spelman's
copy of the writ in Bodl. ms. e Mus. 89, fos. 46^{r-v}, 49, from an Inspeximus
of the Lincoln version, collated with ms. C.

contempserit vel^a noluerit, vocetur semel et^b secundo et tercio,
quod si nec sic ad emendationem venerit, excommunicetur, et si
opus fuerit ad hoc vindicandum^c fortitudo et iusticia regis vel
vicecomitis adhibeatur. Ille autem qui vocatus ad iusticiam
episcopi venire noluerit pro unaquaque vocatione legem episcopalem emendabit. Hoc etiam defendo et mea auctoritate interdico,
ne ullus vicecomes aut prepositus seu^d minister regis nec
aliquis laicus homo de legibus que ad episcopum pertinent se
intromittat, nec aliquis laicus homo alium hominem sine
iustitia episcopi ad iudicium adducat. Iudicium vero in nullo
loco portetur nisi in episcopali sede aut in illo loco quem
episcopus ad hoc^e constituerit.

In hac eadem carta ponuntur eadem verba Anglico sermone
verbo ad verbum.^{f}

B *only*

Willeam kyng gret Rauf Bainard 7 Gosfregd of Magna villa

95

29 AUGUST 1077 x 28 AUGUST 1078. COUNCIL AT LONDON

The existence of this council is known directly only from an
entry in the *Acta Lanfranci*: 'Octavo anno concilium Lundonie
celebravit, in quo Ailnodum Glastingensis cenobii abbatem
deposuit'.[1] No other surviving acta are known which may

---

^{a}contempserit vel ABD (*partially expuncted in* B); *om.* CE. ^{b}et *om.* D.
^{c}et *add.* D. ^{d}seu ABCD; aut E. ^{e}ep. ad hoc ABC; ad hoc episcopus DE.
^{f}In hac ... verbum AB; Tenor istius carte est in Anglico de verbo ad verbum
in eadem carta et continetur in registro episcopi Lundoniens' C; Item alia
carta Anglice scripta continetur in eadem E (*marginal note*); *om.* D.

---

[1]*ASC* ed. Plummer, i.289; this council is omitted from the list in BL ms.
Cotton Domitian v, fo. 14 (W. i.369). Sp. ii.14 (W. i.367) prints as from
Diceto the end of a charter for Westminster dated 1077. After noticing the
presence of a great number of witnesses it continues 'Hæc pro authoritate
Regis ad causas ecclesiasticas tractandas inseritur, Ego Robertus de Oleyo
confirmavi, Ego Hamo dapifer signavi, multis preterea illustrium virorum
personis et regni principibus diversi ordinis omissis, qui similiter suæ
confirmationi, piissimo affectu testes et fautores fuerunt; hii etiam illo
tempore a Regia potestate e diversis provinciis et urbibus, ad universalem

plausibly be attributed to this council. For reasons similar to
those advanced for the date of the council of 1075 it is perhaps
most likely that this one met at Whitsun 1078, which fell on
27 May.

Æthelnoth of Glastonbury had been one of the hostages whom
King William took with him to Normandy in 1067. Of those whose
names are recorded he was the only one who had retained his
office up to 1078.[1] His house remembered him as one who wasted
its resources, but no direct record survives of the charges on
which he was removed.[2] After his deposition 'per beate memorie
Lanfrancum ... in generali totius Anglie synodo' he lived in
dignified confinement at Canterbury cathedral priory.[3]

96

AFTER 8 MAY 1080.[4] LEGATION OF THE SUB-DEACON HUBERT

> See Z.N. Brooke, 'Pope Gregory VII's Demand for Fealty
> from William the Conqueror', *EHR* xxvi (1911), 225-38 and
> *English Church and the Papacy,* pp. 138-46; Böhmer, *Kirche
> und Staat,* pp. 131-8; McDonald, *Lanfranc,* pp. 220-7;
> Tillmann, pp. 15-17; H.E.J. Cowdrey, *Studi Gregoriani,*
> ix (1972), 89-96. On the background see A. Fliche, *La
> Réforme grégorienne*, ii.317-50.

---

synodum, pro causis cuiuslibet sanctæ ecclesiæ audiendis et tractandis, ad
præscriptum celeberrimum Cœnobium, quod Westmonasteriense dicitur convocati.'
The reference to Diceto has not been identified, but the text clearly resembles that of *Reg.* i, nos. 34 (1070), 144 (1081, compare below, p. 630
n. 2) and 216. All are almost certainly forgeries; see P. Chaplais in *Misc.
D.M. Stenton,* pp. 89-110.

[1]ASC D, ed. Plummer, i.200, trans. Whitelock *et al.*, p. 145.
[2]'De Antiquitate Glastoniensis Ecclesiae', ed. T. Hearne in *Adami de
Domerham Historia de rebus gestis Glastoniensibus,* i.90, 110; compare WMGP,
pp. 196-7 and *DB* i.90^V-1.
[3]Stubbs, *Memorials,* p. 420.
[4]The letters which Hubert carried were dated 8 May, but if the king's
letter printed below represents his answer it was written in England after
a three-year absence in France. William was in Normandy as late as 14 July
1080 (*Reg.* i, no. 125) and probably held his Christmas feast at Gloucester
(below, no. 97, and *Reg.* i, no. 128). The king's itinerary is uncertain, but
there is nothing to show that he had not been out of the country for almost
three years late in 1080.

Between his appearance at the primacy council of 1072 and 1080 Hubert was the chief agent of Gregory VII in his dealings with King William. He had played a leading part in the negotiations around the see of Dol in 1078 and again in 1079, and on this second visit he was entrusted with other business also, for the pope had several grievances against the king. At Rouen the new archbishop was said to be the son of a priest, at Le Mans the abbot of La Couture installed by William was being denounced by the pope's chief partisans in France and more generally Gregory believed that William had made it a deliberate policy to prevent the bishops and abbots of his dominions from visiting Rome.[1] On 23 September 1079 Gregory recalled Hubert from France to Rome, instructing him to summon the English and Norman clergy, or two bishops from each province, to the Lent council of 1080, or after Easter if there was insufficient time for their journey.[2]

By 24 April 1080 William had sent an embassy to Rome, though it probably contained none of the Norman bishops.[3] Evidently the ambassadors conveyed a conciliatory message, for in the matter of Le Mans Gregory overrode the action of his legates and his letter to the king is friendly in tone, although it refers to further messages which he has entrusted to the ambassadors.[4] A second letter written on May 8 contains an unusually full treatment of the relation between the papacy and a king, in which he cites the celebrated letter of Gelasius to illustrate the subordination of Christian kings to apostolic direction. The companion letter to the queen of the same date mentions further messages which Hubert would deliver in person.[5]

No external evidence survives on the legate's action, but the two letters printed below have generally been associated

---

[1] Hubert was still a lector in 1072 (above, p. 603). At Canossa in January 1077 he was described as sub-deacon (*Reg. Greg. VII*, ed. Caspar, i, p. 315 n.). For his other activities see particularly ib. iv. 10, 17, v. 19, 22, vii.16 and *The* Epistolae Vagantes *of Pope Gregory VII*, nos. 23, 34.
[2] *Reg. Greg. VII*, vii.1.   [3] Ibid., vii.23; compare ix.1.   [4] Ibid., vii.22.
[5] Ibid., vii.25, 26. Gregory is only otherwise known to have cited Gelasius' letter (JK 632) in his second letter to Hermann of Metz, when defending his right to excommunicate Henry IV and absolve subjects from their allegiance — *Reg. Greg. VII*, viii.21.

with it. They are copied consecutively in both manuscripts of
Lanfranc's letters and read naturally together. If they are
rightly dated they reveal a good deal of Gregory's purposes.
Lanfranc was chiefly concerned to clear himself of the charge
that his persistent refusal to come to Rome was evidence of
cooling affection and deliberate disobedience. Such charges had
been levelled by Gregory in surviving letters of March 1079,
and were to be repeated in 1082.[1] The king's letter concerns
two demands brought by Hubert, the first that Peter's Pence
should be paid according to ancient custom,[2] the second that
he should do fealty for England to the papacy. A similar demand
had been made by Alexander II according to the fragments of a
letter incorporated by Cardinal Deusdedit in his first sketch
of a *Liber Censuum*,[3] and it is likely that Gregory's demands
were modelled upon those of his predecessor.

There is no trace of a direct response by Gregory to the
king's letter, and it is quite likely that it never reached
Rome. Ten years later Urban II wrote to Anselm of Bec to ask if
any of the possessions of Hubert were still there; he wished
them to be sent on to Rome as he understood that Hubert had
died at Bec while returning from a legation in England from
Gregory, and laden with the proceeds of Peter's Pence.[4] This
must have occurred between 1080 and 1085, but there is no evidence of Hubert's continued activity after 8 May 1080 in
Gregory's correspondence or anywhere else.

---

[1] Ibid., vi.30, ix.20.

[2] W.E. Lunt, *Financial Relations of the Papacy with England*, pp. 31-3, 45-7.

[3] Above p. 563; Brooke, *English Church and the Papacy*, pp. 141-3; Cowdrey, *Studi Gregoriani*, ix.90-2. For the general background see K. Jordan, 'Das Eindringen des Lehnswesens in das Rechtsleben der römischen Kurie', *Archiv für Urkundenforschung*, xii (1932), 64-83.

[4] *EA* 125; Stiernon in *Rivista di storia della Chiesa in Italia*, xix (1965), 11, cites Paris, BN ms. lat. 12884, fo. 73^V for D. Thibault's *Chronicon Beccense auctum et illustratum* s.a. 1088 'Eodem anno Hubertus subdiaconus Romane ecclesie Becci defunctus est. Hic Gregorii septimi et Victoris tertii legatus in Angliam missus, ut censum beati Petri colligeret, coactam pecuniam maluit Becci reponere quam in Anglia relinquere donec daretur opportunitas in urbem transportandi ...'; this, however, appears to be simply a mistaken elaboration of *EA* 125. *Reg.* i, no. 187 is valuable evidence for the collection of Peter's Pence in the reign, but is not necessarily connected with Hubert's mission.

I. *Letter of Lanfranc to Gregory VII*

> BL ms. Cotton Nero A. vii, fos. 27^V-28 (= N), Vatican
> ms. Reg. Lat. 285, fo. 13^V (= V). Printed in *Lanf.*
> *Letters,* ed. Clover and Gibson, no. 38, ed. Giles, no.
> 11. Translated from Giles in *EHD* ii.647-8. The text
> below is based on N.

Reverendo sanctę universalis aecclesię summo pastori Gregorio
peccator et indignus antistes L. servitium cum debita subiectione. Litteras excellentię vestrę per Hubertum sacri palatii
vestri subdiaconum porrectas qua decuit humilitate suscepi. In
quarum fere omni contextu paterna me dulcedine reprehendere
studuistis quod in episcopali honore positus sanctam Romanam
ęcclesiam vosque ob eius reverentiam minus diligam quam ante
ipsius honoris susceptionem diligere quondam solebam, presertim cum apostolicę sedis auctoritate ad ipsius apicem honoris
me pervenisse non dubitem, nec quenquam dubitare existimem.
Et quidem, venerande pater, verbis tuis calumniam ingerere nec
volo nec debeo. Ego tamen teste conscientia mea in memetipso
intelligere non possum quod vel corporalis absentia vel locorum
tanta intercapedo aut ipsa qualiscunque honorum sullimitas in
hac parte vindicare sibi quicquam prevaleat quin mens mea
preceptis vestris in omnibus et per omnia secundum canonum
precepta subiaceat. Et si praestante Deo praesens presenti
loqui quandoque valerem, me amando crevisse, vos vero, quod
pace vestra dictum sit, a pristino amore nonnulla ex parte
defecisse, non tam verbis quam rebus ipsis ostenderem. Verba
legationis vestrę cum prefato legato vestro prout melius potui
domino meo regi suggessi, suasi sed non persuasi. Cur autem
voluntati vestrę omnifariam non assenserit [fo. 28] ipsemet[a]
vobis tam verbis quam litteris innotescit.

II. *Letter of King William to Gregory VII*

> N, fo. 28, V, fo. 13^V; printed in *Lanf. Letters*, ed.
> Clover and Gibson, no. 39, ed. Giles, no. 10, S. Baluze,

---

[a] ipsimet V.

Miscellaneorum libri i-vii (Paris, 1678-1715), vii.127-8.[1] Translated from Giles in *EHD* ii.646-7.

Excellentissimo sanctę aecclesię pastori GR. gratia Dei Anglorum rex et dux Normannorum W. salutem cum amicicia. Hubertus legatus tuus, religiose pater, ad me veniens ex tua parte me admonuit quatinus tibi et successoribus tuis fidelitatem facerem, et de pecunia quam antecessores mei ad Romanam ęcclesiam mittere[a] solebant melius cogitarem. Unum admisi, alterum non admisi. Fidelitatem facere nolui nec volo, quia nec ego promisi nec antecessores meos antecessoribus tuis id fecisse comperio. Pecunia tribus ferme annis in Galliis me agente neglegenter collecta est. Nunc vero divina misericordia me in regnum meum reverso quod collectum est per prefatum legatum mittitur, et quod reliquum est per legatos Lanfranci archiepiscopi fidelis nostri cum opportunum fuerit transmittetur. Orate pro nobis et pro statu regni nostri, quia antecessores vestros dileximus et vos prę omnibus sincere diligere et obędienter audire desideramus.

97

CHRISTMAS 1080. COUNCIL AT GLOUCESTER

This council was held at the king's first crown-wearing after his long absence in Normandy. Its approximate date is fixed by the consecration of William of St. Carilef as bishop of Durham by Archbishop Thomas on 3 January 1081.[2] The participation of suffragans of Canterbury was necessary as there was

---

[a] *add* N[1].

---

[1] Baluze printed from the collections of Duchesne; his immediate source has not been identified, but his text contains no important variant and probably derives ultimately from V.

[2] Symeon, i.119 and 170 agree that William was consecrated on 3 Jan. 1081, which was a Sunday. *Flor. Wig.* ii.16 gives 5 Jan. and Symeon, ii.211, with Liège, UL ms. 369c, fo. 95[v], give 2 Jan., neither of which was a Sunday. The late 12th-cent. Durham Cathedral Library ms. B. II.35, fo. 277 gives 27 Dec. 1080, which was, but 3 Jan. is preferable. See Le Neve, ii.29.

only one other bishop in the province of York who acknowledged
Thomas's authority, Ralph of Orkney, whom Lanfranc had allowed
the bishops of Worcester and Chester to assist Thomas in consecrating seven years earlier.[1]

It is likely that some of those who attended this council
appear as witnesses to *Reg.* i, no. 144, a charter purporting to
have been granted to Westminster at this council. Although the
main text is clearly not authentic as it stands, the witness-
list is consonant with the alleged date, and the precedence of
the first few bishops (though not the later ones) conforms to
the principles set out in 1075.[2] Both the texts printed below
require that Giso of Wells was also present at the council.

Giso is represented as a leading figure in the only other
known business which is likely to have been transacted at this
council. The proceedings are described in the thirteenth-
century manuscript of William of Malmesbury's *De Antiquitate
Glastoniensis Ecclesiae,* a text which has certainly undergone
extensive modification from its original form. Although the
claim of Glastonbury to such extensive rights over Athelney
and Muchelney is not recorded elsewhere the stylistic evidence
is in favour of the substantial authenticity of this passage.
If, as it appears, the occasion described is a church council
under the presidency of Lanfranc, that of Christmas 1080 is
the only one known to have met between the deposition of Abbot
Æthelnoth of Glastonbury in 1077/8 and the ejection of Abbot
Thurstan in 1083.[3]

I. *Acta Lanfranci*

Cambridge, Corpus Christi Coll. ms. 173, fo. 32[v]. Printed

---

[1]*Lanf. Letters,* ed. Clover and Gibson, nos. 12, 13, ed. Giles, nos. 14,
15. For the date see also H.& S. ii(1), 162 n against *Acta Lanfranci* in
ASC ed. Plummer, i.289 and J. Tait in *Essays in History presented to Reginald Lane Poole,* p. 159.

[2]Brooke, *Studia Gratiana,* xii.46. However, the appearance of Abbot Æthelnoth (presumably of Glastonbury), who had been deprived in 1077/8, is
suspicious; compare above, pp. 624-5 n.

[3]On this text see J.A. Robinson, *Somerset Historical Essays,* pp. 1-25,
esp. 2-3. The passage is translated and discussed in *Two Cartularies of
Muchelney and Athelney* (Somerset Record Soc., xiv, 1899), pp. 7-9. See
above p. 624 and *ASC* E, ed. Plummer, i.214-15, Gibson, *Lanfranc of Bec,*
p. 142.

in *ASC*, ed. Plummer, i.289-90 and (in facs.) *The Parker
Chronicle and Laws,* fo. 32b.

Anno xi. celebravit concilium apud Claudiam civitatem, ubi et
Thomas archiepiscopus Eboracensis, iubente rege et Lanfranco
consentiente, sacravit Willelmum Dunelmensi episcopum, eo quod
a Scottorum episcopis qui sibi subiecti sunt habere adiutorium
non potuit.[1] Huius ministerii cooperatores fuerunt, Lanfranco
precipiente, Wlstanus, Osbernus, Giso, Rotbertus episcopi.

II. *De antiquitate Glastoniensis ecclesiae of William of
Malmesbury*

> Cambridge, Trinity Coll. ms. R. 5. 33 (724), fo. 17
> (= A), late 13th cent.; BL ms. Add. 22934, fo. 18 (= B),
> early 14th cent. Printed from A in *Historiae Britannicae
> Scriptores XV,* ed. Gale, p. 331, and from both by Hearne
> in *Adami de Domerham Historia de rebus gestis Glastonien-
> sibus,* i.111-13.[2]

De Abbatibus de Muchelnie et Athelingie.
Hiis igitur ad instanciam abbatis Turstini sic patratis, etiam
illud prosequamur, qua efficacia vicinos abbates Muchalniensem
et Ethilingensem sui iuris asseruit. Nam cum eos, falsa dela-
cione Gisonis Wellensis episcopi, Lanfrancus archiepiscopus in
generali concilio Anglie mordaciter impeteret, Muchaniensis,[3]
qui exercitatior esset in seculi rebus, respondit se in capitulo Glaston' iussu eiusdem loci abbatis et[a] sui responsurum,
ceterum extraordinarias accusaciones non timere. Ethelingensis
autem ioculariter eludens questionem minanti archiepiscopo
baculum ei auferendum: 'Non curo, inquit, quia meliorem habeo,
nec tamen istum tibi trado.' Tum iussus abbas Turstinus ut si
sibi competere sciret causam ageret, surrexit loco sentencie
dicende, egitque multa et constanti facundia, memoriter retexens

---

[a] et abbatis B.

---

[1] Above, p. 602.
[2] BL ms. Cotton Vit. D. vii, fos. 159[v]-60 is Joscelyn's 16th-cent. copy of A.
[3] Probably the Leofweard who attested the judgement of 1075 (above, p.
615); see *Heads,* p. 57. The name of the abbot of Athelney is unknown.

privilegia regum a Kentuino et Ina regibus usque ad Edwardum,[1]
quibus allegavit in eos abbates nullam iurisdictionem aliquem
nisi Glastoniensem abbatem habere, adeo ut in predictas ecclesias nullus debeat abbas intrare nisi fuerit electus a conventu
Glastonie. Tum cum archiepiscopus in regem conversus dixisset
se beati Dunstani nutriculam nolle minuere, illeque retulisset
nec se velle matrem Domini contristare, set pro caucione futurorum episcopum Wellensem debere in Glastonie capitulo rem diffinire, resumpsit abbas sermonem, privilegia ecclesie sue autentica
esse, nullam cuiuslibet dignitatis personam causa iudicii
Glastoniam debere venire, sua ibi esse omnia, et in ecclesiasticis et in secularibus rebus iudicia,[2] facile fore ut invictus
princeps et sanctus archiepiscopus in re nova constituenda
perpetua pulsarentur invidia. Ceterum quod antecessores sui
habuissent integrum se qui in defensanda dignitate ecclesie
eodem vigilaret spiritu, nequaquam omissurum. Quocirca episcopus
Wellensis si quid allegandum putaret suo, non regis vel archiepiscopi, iussu Glastoniam veniret. Quid plura? Optinuit causam
abbas. Et quidem episcopus in capitulum venit, sed purgantibus
se abbatibus victoria excidit, et inglorius dicessit.

98

CHRISTMAS 1085. COUNCIL AT GLOUCESTER

According to the *Acta Lanfranci* the archbishop held his last
recorded council in his sixteenth year (August 1085/6): 'Hoc
quoque anno apud Cleucestram concilium celebravit, in quo

---

[1]None of the surviving Anglo-Saxon charters of Glastonbury, however unreliable, mentions this right, and there is no known charter of a King
Edward for the house to which this might refer. However, Centwine of Wessex
is cited as an earlier grantor of liberties by Ine (Sawyer, *Anglo-Saxon
Charters*, no. 250), Cuthred (Sawyer, no. 257), Edmund (Sawyer, no. 499), and
Cnut (Sawyer, no. 966). All these are spurious, but they suggest the existence by the twelfth century of a lost grant in Centwine's name. The surviving grant (Sawyer, no. 237) attributed to him contains no such rights.
[2]This immunity is asserted in the charters of Ine, Cuthred, Edmund, and
Cnut cited in the previous note, and most fully in that of Edgar (Sawyer,
no. 783). All are spurious, and all are found first in Malmesbury's WMGR
or *De Antiquitate*.

Wlfketelum Crulandensis cęnobii abbatem deposuit.'[1] The Anglo-Saxon Chronicle (below, no. I) mentions this alone of all the councils under the Conqueror, and shows that it was held during the Christmas feast at which the king and his counsellors determined upon the Domesday survey. According to the Thorney annals (below, no. II) Folcard of St. Bertin was also deposed as *vice-abbas* of Thorney at this time. No canons are recorded and none may have been issued. In the late summer the king sailed for Normandy, never to return.

I. *Anglo-Saxon Chronicle 1085 (E)*

> Bodl. ms. Laud Misc. 636, fo. 62[v], facsimile ed. Whitelock in *Early English Manuscripts in Facsimile*, iv.124. Printed *ASC*, ed. Thorpe, i.352-3, ed. Plummer i.216, ed. Clark p. 8, W. i.368. Translated *ASC*, ed. Thorpe, ii.186, ed. Whitelock *et al.*, p. 161 (used here), *EHD* ii.161.

Ða to þam midewintre wæs se cyng on Gleaweceastre mid his witan, 7 heold þær his hired .v. dagas, 7 syððan þe arcebiscop 7 gehadode men hæfden sinoð þreo dagas. Ðær wæs Mauricius gecoren to biscope on Lundene, 7 Willelm to Norðfolce, 7 Rodbeard to Ceasterscire, hi wæron ealle þæs cynges clerecas.

Then at Christmas, the king was at Gloucester with his council, and held his court there for five days, and then the archbishop and clerics had a synod for three days. There Maurice was elected bishop of London, and William for Norfolk, and Robert for Cheshire — they were all clerics of the king.

II. *Annals of Thorney s.a. 1085*

> Oxford, St. John's Coll. ms. 17, fo. 29, an early 12th-cent. marginal note referred to this year in an Easter table by a pen-stroke. Printed C. Hart, 'The Ramsey *Computus*', *EHR* lxxxv (1970), 44.

---

[1] *ASC*, ed. Plummer, i.290.

Hoc anno fuit concilium apud Gloecestre in Natale Domini in
quo Fulcardus viceabbas Thorneiam perdidit, et abbas de Cruland
Ulketel depositus est. Et abbas Gunterius directus a rege Willelmo seniore Thorneiam venit feria secunda post dominice [*sic*] ramis
palmarum, fecitque Pascha non' Aprilis Thorneie sine baculo.[1]

99
1085-1093. RELATIONS BETWEEN ENGLAND AND THE PAPACY

> For these years see particularly F. Liebermann, 'Lanfranc
> and the anti-pope', *EHR* xvi (1901), 328-32 and 'Anselm
> von Canterbury und Hugo von Lyons' in *Historische Auf-
> sätze dem Andenken an Georg Waitz gewidmet*, pp. 159 ff.,
> P. Kehr, 'Zur Geschichte Wiberts von Ravenna (Clemens
> III.)', *Sitzungsberichte der preußischen Akademie der
> Wissenschaften* (1921), pp. 355-68, Southern, *St. Anselm,*
> pp. 154-5, A. Becker, *Papst Urban II. (1088-1099)*, pp.
> 169-80.

At the outbreak of schism with the election of the anti-pope
Clement III in 1080 relations between England and Gregory VII
were already under some strain. Yet although Clement and Cardinal Hugh Candidus, a leading supporter of his cause, made
serious attempts to attract the allegiance of Lanfranc and the
Conqueror, England remained no more than neutral.[2] After the
Conqueror's death the two halves of his inheritance went

---

[1]These chronological indications fit Easter, 1086. For the Crowland tradition on Wulfketel see also OV ii.344-6, according to whom the abbot was
imprisoned at Glastonbury, but subsequently allowed to return to his original house at Peterborough. The Pseudo-Ingulf in *Rerum Anglicarum Scriptorum
Veterum Tom. I*, ed. Fulman, p. 73, has a circumstantial but inaccurate
account of his fall, which is attributed to his devotion to the memory of
Earl Waltheof. The later Thorney traditions differ on the date of Folcard's
removal, but agree with the substance of the annals printed above. Compare
Cambridge UL ms. Add. 3021, fo. 416 (14th cent.) with BL ms. Add. 40000, fo.
11 (15th cent., printed in *Vita Ædwardi*, p. lii n. 1); see further *Heads,*
pp. 42, 74. In BL ms. Add. 40000, fo. 10 a hand of *c.*1100 enters Folcard
immediately after Abbot Gunter among the brethren.

[2]*Lanf. Letters*, ed. Clover and Gibson no. 52, ed. Giles no. 65, *PL* cl.
548-9, *EHR* xvi (1901), 330-2. Compare further Eadmer, p. 52, *EA* 192, Becker,
Papst Urban II, pp. 169-78, Gibson, *Lanfranc*, pp. 136-9, F. Lerner, *Kardinal
Hugo Candidus* (1931), p. 58.

different ways. By 1088 Normandy almost certainly recognized
Urban, for the sub-deacon Roger was in the duchy as legate of
a legitimate pope, but there is no reason to suppose that his
letters for England were ever delivered.[1] However the Norman
decision for Urban clearly had its effect; when Bishop William
of Durham was exiled for his part in the rising of 1088 he
appealed to Urban, though with little if any result.[2] Similarly,
when the simoniac Herbert of Thetford repented of the methods
he had used to secure his promotion, it was to Urban that he
turned for absolution.[3] After 1091, when King William secured
a substantial foothold in Normandy,[4] his recognition of Urban
could hardly be avoided, but there were tactical advantages in
delay. After the election of Anselm to Canterbury in 1093 the
problems of the schism merged with the more general issues at
stake between king and archbishop, and it was not until the
summer of 1095 that England finally accepted Urban as pope.

100

1092. BISHOP WULFSTAN'S SYNOD AT WORCESTER

The document printed below is the earliest authentic record of
the holding of a bishop's synod in England,[5] and that is the

---

[1]JL 5351, Schieffer, *Die päpstlichen Legaten in Frankreich*, pp. 141-2,
D. Stiernon, 'Le cardinal-diacre Roger et les archevêques Rangier et Roger
de Reggio Calabria', *Rivista di storia della Chiesa in Italia*, xix (1965),
10-11.

[2]*De iniusta vexatione Willelmi episcopi* in Symeon, i.170-95. The authority
of this account, attacked by Offler in *EHR* lxvi (1951), 321-41, was defended
by Hoffmann, *Deutsches Archiv* xv (1959), 438-40, Southern, *St. Anselm*, p. 148 n. 1,
A. Gransden, *Historical writing in England* c.550-c.1307, p. 122n., Gibson,
Lanfranc, pp. 220-1, and Barlow (1979), pp. 281-7. It is certainly strange
that a contemporary account should lay so much stress on the bishop's appeal
to Rome without anyone on either side referring to the schism. Urban's
letter on William's behalf was printed from the 'Collectio Britannica' in
S. Loewenfeld, *Epistolae pontificum Romanorum ineditae*, p. 63 (no. 129, JL
5397), but there is no proof of its ever being delivered to the king.

[3]Below, p. 624.

[4]OV iv.220-36, 250-2. The fullest modern account of these events is in
C.W. David, *Robert Curthose, duke of Normandy*, pp. 58-61.

[5]We assume that it is genuine, though this is perhaps not beyond doubt.
For some inauthentic early evidence at Durham see *Durham Episcopal Charters,
1071-1152*, ed. H.S. Offler, p. 45.

chief reason for its inclusion. It also gives more indications
of procedure than the majority of similar later texts. The
dependence of all the city churches on the cathedral, with
which the record is concerned, was not the chief business of the
meeting, which was summoned to deal with larger issues of canonical discipline when the bishop thought himself near death, though
he did not die until three years later.

Since this gathering had so specific an origin, it cannot be
claimed as evidence for the routine celebration of synods in
the diocese so early, and it is not until the pontificate of
Bishop Simon (1125-50) that we hear of such meetings as an
established custom at Worcester; however, there is good reason
to suppose that they were held regularly elsewhere even before
1092.[1]

The only surviving medieval copy is now the 13th-cent. Worcester Cathedral Lib. ms. Reg. 1 (A.4), fos. 7^V-8 (= A), from
a transcript of which it was printed in *Hemingi chartularium
ecclesiæ Wigornensis*, ed. T. Hearne, ii.527-31. It was also
found in an early single sheet which was seen at Worcester by
Dugdale in 1643, but may already have gone by 1705.[2] Meanwhile
it had been printed in *Anglia Sacra*, i.542-3 (= B). Our text
is adapted from that of R.R. Darlington in *The Cartulary of
Worcester cathedral priory*, no. 52, and based on A with the
more substantial variants of B.

Ego Wlstanus Dei gratia[a] Wigorn' episcopus decrevi sinodum
congregare in monasterio sancte Marie in criptis quas ego a
fundamentis edificavi et per misericordiam Dei postea dedicavi.[3]
Hec sinodus habita est anno dominice incarnationis M^O.XC^O.II°.

---

[a]gratia Dei B.

---

[1]Brett, *English Church*, pp. 156-9.
[2]Dugdale's list was printed by Wanley in Hickes, *Thesaurus*, ii.299-301,
but with the note 'haud ita pridem'. Hearne reprinted Wanley in *Hemingi
chartularium*, ii.579-85.
[3]*Vita Wulfstani*, pp. 21, 52-3; a late entry in *Ann. Mon.* iv.373 places
the beginning of the new work in 1084, but as a charter of Wulfstan of 1089
(*Cartulary of Worcester*, no. 3) is dated in the first year of the monks'
entry into the new monastery, this is almost certainly too late.

indictione XV. Ad hanc sinodum invitati convenerunt omnes
sapientissime persone de tribus comitatibus nostre dioceseos,
Wigracestrie,[a] Glaucestrie, Warewiccie, eo quod ego, longevus
dierum, imbecillitatem mei corporis[b] sentiens et finem vite
mee iam[c] instare intelligens, cupiebam res ecclesiasticas nostre
cure commissas canonice tractare et queque emendanda forent
illorum sapienti consilio corrigere et emendare. Nostra itaque
humilitate in hac sinodo presidente, orta est questio inter duos
presbyteros, Ælfnothum scilicet presbyterum sancte Elene et
Alam presbyterum sancti Albani, de parrochiis et consuetudinibus
ecclesiarum suarum. Horum presbyterorum altercatio sanctam sinodum multum detinuit. Hanc litem ego canonice discindere cupiens,
iussi seniores quosque et quibus notissime essent antique insti-
tutiones ecclesiarum seu parrochiarum Wigracestrie veritatem
edicere, tam de supradictarum quam de omnium ecclesiarum urbis
Wigrac' antiquissimis institutionibus et parrochiis earum.[d] Et
quoniam[e] inter supradictorum presbyterorum disceptationem auditus est a sancta synodo clamor filiorum ecclesie monachorum,
videlicet quod ipsi dampna paterentur suorum reddituum quos
iuste habere debuissent de sua ecclesia, sancte Elene scilicet,
propter tam diuturnam presbyterorum discordiam, iussi ut[f] sicut
de institutionibus ceterarum ecclesiarum sic eciam de huius
matris ecclesie institutione dicerent. Ad harum rerum scrutinium
ex nostro precepto fuerunt Thomas prior, Ælfer secretarius,
Godricus Wirl[g] camerarius, Uhtred cantor, Ægelric archidiaconus,
Edwine frater eius, Frideric, Ægelmer presbyter, cum aliis
quamplurimis quos ad hoc elegi.[1] Hii omnes igitur, communi

---

[a]videlicet *add* B.   [b]corporis mei B.   [c]iam *om.* B.   [d]earum *om.* B.
[e]cum B.   [f]ut *om.* B.   [g]Godricpirl B.

---

[1]For Wulfstan's household see *Vita Wulfstani*, pp. xxxv-xxxix; Thomas is
usually said to have been prior from before 1080 until 1113 (*Cartulary of
Worcester*, pp. lvi-lvii, Le Neve, ii.102, *Heads*, p. 83), but his first dated
occurrence is in 1089, and *Cartulary of Worcester*, no. 304 can only be dated
by the occurrence of Wulfstan (d. 1095) and Abbot 'Alwinus' of Ramsey. If
this is Ælfwine it belongs before 1080, if it is Aldwin it belongs after
1092. After Wulfstan's death the monks made Fritheric priest of St. Helen's,
and his 'Testament' gives a good account of the endowments of the church
(*Cartulary of Worcester*, no. 53, Brett, *English Church*, pp. 180-1). For
Archdeacon Ailric see now Le Neve, ii.104.

habito consilio, reversi in sanctam synodum affirmaverunt nullam
esse parrochiam in tota urbe Wigrac' nisi tantum matris ecclesie. Ecclesiam vero sancte Elene vicariam huius matris ecclesie
extitisse[a] a temporibus Æthelredi regis[1] et Theodori archiepiscopi[2] qui locum hunc[b] fundaverunt, et ibi Boselum primum episcopum constituerunt, anno incarnationis Domini DCLXXX, indictione VII.[3] Hec institutio a tempore supradicti Boseli per
tempora omnium episcoporum huius sancte ecclesie per manus
clericorum in hac sede servientium inconvulsa servata est usque
ad tempora beati Oswaldi archiepiscopi[4] qui, opitulatione
Ædgari regis et auctoritate pii patris Dunstani Cantuariensis
archiepiscopi,[5] de irregulari conversatione clericorum in regularem conversationem et habitum monachorum transtulit et mutavit
huius ecclesie congregationem anno dominice incarnationis
DCCCC.LX.IX, indictione XII.[6] Huius pii patris Oswaldi temporibus Winsius, [fo. 8] sancte Elene presbyter, vicarius huius
sancte matris ecclesie extitit. Hic idem monitis sancti Oswaldi,
cum ceteris qui in clericali habitu huic ecclesie ut cumque
serviebant, mundo posthabito monastice religionis habitum suscepit, et claves ecclesie sancte Elene, quarum ipse sicut vicarius
custos extiterat, cum terris, decimis ceterisque redditibus ad
communem usum monachorum reddidit. Winsio proinde monacho facto
cum ceteris qui secum sponte elegerunt converti,[c] tam supradicta[d] ecclesia quam cetere que nunc usque monachorum sunt ecclesie, terre, decime,[e] sepulture vel quelibet alie consuetudines
seu dignitates ecclesiastice que clericorum quasi propria
hactenus extiterant in ius monachorum tunc[f] transierunt et in

---

[a]extitiste A.   [b]tunc B.   [c]converti elegerunt B.   [d]praedicta B.
[e]decime *om.* B.   [f]tunc *om.* B.

---

[1]King of Mercia 674-704.   [2]Archbishop of Canterbury 668-90.
[3]The date is that of the Council of Hatfield, Bede, *HE* v.24, *Flor. Wig.*
i.36, though ibid., i.239, gives 679.
[4]Bishop of Worcester 961-92, archbishop of York 972-92.
[5]960-88.
[6]This is the earliest occurrence of this date for the introduction of
monks at Worcester, followed in *Flor. Wig.* i.141, which gives a different
but not irreconcilable account of the career of Wynsige. The year is much
disputed; see the arguments of E. John, summarized in *TRHS* 5th Ser., xxvii
(1977), 192-3, above p. 115 n. 1, and *Cartulary of Worcester*, pp. xliv-xlv.

communem usum illorum redacte sunt, assensu regis Eadgari et
beati Dunstani sanctique Oswaldi archiepiscoporum. Anno tercio
ꝗonversionis Winsii presbyteri beatus Oswaldus prioratum ei super
monachos huius ecclesie concessit, assensu eiusdem regis. Concessit eciam illi omnibusque suis successoribus prioribus huius
ecclesie decanos esse super omnes ecclesias suas et presbyteros,
ita videlicet quod nullus decanus, nullus archidiaconus de monachorum ecclesiis seu clericis se intromittat nisi per priorem
ecclesie, omnes ecclesiasticas consuetudines prior sicut summus
decanus episcopi pro suis ecclesiis episcopo persolvat.[1] Harum
rerum sicut ab antecessoribus nostris didicimus et hiis nostris
temporibus sub antecessore vestro[a] Aldredo[2] et vobis[b] hactenus
servatas vidimus, testes sumus. Horum[c] igitur testimonium ego
Wlstanus verum comprobans, litem presbyterorum sedavi, et veram
comprobationem testimonio huius sancte synodi litteris nostris
et sigillo corroboravi, cavens ne amodo de hiis rebus in hac
sancta et matre ecclesia inter monachos et alias quaslibet personas dissensio sive scandalum oriatur. Servantibus hec vita
eterna donetur in celestibus, qui autem fregerit, vel in peius
mutaverit, cum diabolo et angelis eius perpetuis dampnetur
cruciatibus. Amen.

B

Titulus in dorso: Privilegium sancti Wlstani de ecclesia sancte
Elenae et sancti Wlfstani[3]

101

6 MARCH - 4 DECEMBER 1093. ELECTION OF ANSELM AS ARCHBISHOP
OF CANTERBURY

Sources: Eadmer, pp. 27-43, *Life of St. Anselm*, ed.

---

[a]nostro A vestro B.   [b]nobis A vobis B.   [c]Hoc B.

---

[1]The phrasing here need not be taken to indicate that the monks thought
that such officers were actually at work in Oswald's time; compare *Vita
Wulfstani*, p. xxxv n. 2.
[2]Bishop of Worcester 1047-62, archbishop of York 1061-9.
[3]This is clearly an error for St. Alban, which retained its dedication.

Southern, pp. 63-7, *EA* 147-59, ed. Schmitt, Hugh the
Chanter, pp. 7-9 (*Hist. York*, ii.104-6). See further
Southern in *Mediaeval and Renaissance Studies*, iii (1954),
78-92 and *St. Anselm and his Biographer*, pp. 150-3.

After the death of Archbishop Lanfranc on 28 May 1089 the see
of Canterbury remained in the king's hand until Lent, 1093. By
then it was already rumoured that Anselm, abbot of Bec, was a
possible successor, and for this reason he long delayed a visit
to England to which he was urged by the business of his house
and the importunity of Hugh of Avranches, earl of Chester. At
length he crossed the sea, spent the night of 7/8 September
1092 at Canterbury, had an interview with the king, and then
went on to Chester, where the earl was engaged in replacing the
canons of St. Werburgh with monks from Bec. Prevented from returning to Normandy he probably settled at Westminster around
Christmas for a prolonged stay. During the Christmas feast the
king was again urged to fill the vacant see of Canterbury, and
prayers were said in many churches for the king's heart to be
moved. These prayers were composed by the bishops with the
advice of Anselm.

At the beginning of March 1093 he was staying near Gloucester when the king fell ill and was carried there, apparently at
the point of death. Among the many acts of penitence which William then performed the appointment of an archbishop took a
large part, and on 6 March he chose Anselm; the choice was
acclaimed by the bishops, who joined the king in forcing a
pastoral staff on the resisting abbot and carried him bodily to
the nearby church to sing a Te Deum. Anselm continued to protest, alleging not only his own unfitness but his duty to Duke
Robert of Normandy, the archbishop of Rouen, and his own monks
at Bec. While their consent was being obtained (before 15 August,
except for the monks, who finally agreed in chapter that day[1]),
Anselm was maintained on the archiepiscopal manors. He had a
number of interviews with the king, at which he sought guarantees on his free enjoyment of all the estates of Canterbury with

---

[1] *Lanfranci Opera*, ed. Giles, i.316.

all the prerogatives of his office, and on his liberty to continue to recognize Urban II as legitimate pope. Although he
received no decisive answer to these demands he did homage for
the archbishopric at Winchester and was seised of the estates.
On Sunday 25 September he was enthroned at Canterbury, and on
4 December all the bishops of England except those of Worcester
and Exeter, who were ill, were at Canterbury for his consecration. The rite was performed by Archbishop Thomas of York, and
was interrupted by a dispute over Anselm's primatial title, which
was rapidly if temporarily resolved.[1]

102
1093 x 1094. LEGATION OF ROGER THE SUBDEACON AND BISHOP HERBERT
   OF THETFORD

See Tillmann, p. 19, Schieffer, *Die päpstlichen Legaten
in Frankreich*, pp. 142-3, B. Dodwell, *TRHS* 5th Ser., vii
(1957), 3-6, D. Stiernon, *Rivista di storia della Chiesa
in Italia*, xix (1965), 15-17, J.W. Alexander, 'Herbert of
Norwich,1091-1119', pp. 127-30, 150-2, 164-5, Hüls,
p. 253.

Two documents record legatine duties entrusted by Urban II to
Roger and Bishop Herbert. The first is an account of their
mediation in the dispute between Fécamp and Archbishop William
of Rouen over the abbey's exemption from an archiepiscopal
interdict. The second is a bull rebuking Thomas I of York for
his submission to Canterbury and summoning him to the pope the

---

[1]According to Eadmer, pp. 42-3, Canterbury was first described as 'ecclesia totius Britanniae metropolitana', but York objected and 'metropolitana'
was altered to 'primas'. Hugh the Chanter, pp. 7-9, claims that 'primas
totius Britannie' was replaced by 'metropolita Cantuariensis'. All the
professions made to Anselm call him 'totius Britanniae primas', and the
late garbled reference from the Winchester ms. BL Cott. Vespasian E. iv
copied into the Worcester Annals in *Ann. Mon.* iv.373 may also support
Eadmer. See further Southern, *St. Anselm,* pp. 136, 303, *Canterbury Professions,* pp. lxix, 34-7, and H. Clover, in *La Normandie bénédictine au temps
de Guillaume le Conquérant*, pp. 434-5.

following Easter if he is not excused by the same legates, to
whom are entrusted 'in Anglie regno vices nostras'. Both are
undated.[1] Roger appears as a witness to a charter issued in
Normandy after 11 December 1093, though there is no reason to
suppose that he reached England on this occasion any more than
in 1088.[2] The appearance of Bishop Herbert has generally been
associated with his repentance after buying his bishopric, his
submission to the pope and absolution, for which he was apparently deprived of his staff by King William at Hastings in
February 1094.[3] Herbert was in England at Anselm's consecration
on 4 December 1093, and attests a royal charter at Christmas,
but does not appear in office again before the end of 1094, so
that his negotiations with Urban and deprivation presumably
fall in the later year.[4] Since England had still not recognized

---

[1]*Gallia Christiana*, xi (1759), Instr. 18-19, also, and perhaps independently, *Annales Ordinis Sancti Benedicti*, ed. J. Mabillon, v (1713), 263-4;
Hugh the Chanter, ed. Johnson, pp. 6-7 (*Hist. York*, ii.103-4). The Fécamp
text, from a lost manuscript, was dated in Böhmer, *Kirche und Staat*, p. 146
n. 1, to 1093 by analogy with his interpretation of the English evidence,
and he has been followed by all subsequent writers without further proof,
including J.-F. Lemarignier, *Etude sur les privilèges d'exemption et de
juridiction ecclésiastique des abbayes normandes*, p. 194. Urban's bull for
York has been dismissed as a forgery by Tillmann and Alexander, but on
inadequate grounds; Hugh the Chanter does not offer any date for it, but
inserts it in his text at that point on thematic, not chronological, grounds.
If the text has been tampered with, the likelihood of the address and some
of the conclusion being a York invention is slight. See further Becker,
Papst Urban II, pp. 176-7.
[2]*Reg*. i, no. 342, P. Marchegay, 'Chartes normandes de l'abbaye de Saint-
Florent près Saumur', *Mém. de la Soc. des antiquaires de Normandie*, xxx
(1880), 682-5. The Council of Bonneville occurred an uncertain time after
the dedication of Briouze on 11 Dec.
[3]*ASC*, ed. Plummer, i.229, ed. Clark, p. 21, trans. Whitelock *et al.*,
p. 171, simply records Herbert's deprivation. The manuscripts of the Worcester chronicle here diverge widely; the original reading is best preserved
in ms. L (*Flor. Wig.* ii.34n), and the source of Symeon, ii.223, where Herbert is said to have been deprived because 'Latenter enim Urbanum adire, et
ab eo pro episcopatu quem sibi ... emerat, absolutionem quaerere voluit.'
Two of the other mss. here have an erasure, and in most Malmesbury's passage
from WMGP, p. 151 has been substituted for the original reading. William's
authority for precise chronology as early as this is relatively slight, for
there is no reason to suppose that he was using more than common report or
trying to do more than summarize the character of the origins of Norwich.
See further Freeman, *The Reign of William Rufus*, ii.568-70 (Appendix, Note X).
[4]*Memorials of St. Edmund's Abbey*, i.87 shows Herbert back in office by
April 1095; *Reg*. ii.401 (no. 348a) where Herbert attests a royal charter
dated 11 Feb. 1094 is a forgery (*Facsimiles of English Royal Writs to 1100*,

Urban it is extremely unlikely that Herbert even attempted to
exert his authority.

103

1093-1100. RELATIONS BETWEEN ANSELM AND WILLIAM RUFUS

> See particularly Southern, *St. Anselm*, pp. 150-63, Lieber-
> mann, *Historische Aufsätze dem Andenken an Georg Waitz
> gewidmet*, pp. 162-84, Becker, *Papst Urban II*, pp. 169-87,
> Barlow (1979), pp. 287-97. The chief sources are Eadmer,
> pp. 38-117, *Life of St. Anselm*, pp. 66-124, *EA* 176-210.

Even before his consecration, Anselm was aware that there were
serious differences between him and the king, over the lands of
Canterbury alienated during the long vacancy and those which
Lanfranc had not been able to recover, as well as over his preeminent right to advise the king in spiritual matters and over
his earlier recognition of Pope Urban while abbot of Bec.[1] None
of these was resolved before his consecration in December 1093.
At the Christmas court Rufus, anxious for money for his expedition to Normandy, demanded £1,000 from the archbishopric, which
Anselm refused, instead distributing to the poor the £500 he
had offered earlier. While the king was waiting to cross the
Channel in February 1094, Anselm raised again the matter of the
new fees created by the king on the estates of Canterbury and
further occasions of dispute: the need to celebrate a council
for the correction of vice, and to supply abbots to the increas-
ing number of vacant abbeys. The king and the archbishop were
now openly divided, and William demanded in vain a substantial
sum for the recovery of his grace.[2]

---

pp. xxi-xxii). Dodwell in *TRHS* 5th Ser., vii.6 and n. attributes *Reg.* ii.403,
nos. 385a-c, to the period of Herbert's restoration.

[1] Anselm's conduct is examined further in two detailed studies which need
to be used with caution, N.F. Cantor, *Church, Kingship and Lay Investiture in
England*, pp. 42-130 and S. Vaughn, in *Journal of Medieval History*, i (1975),
279-305.

[2] On the knights of Canterbury see in general F.R.H. Du Boulay, *The Lord-
ship of Canterbury*, pp. 75-83. Eadmer's account of these events is largely

When the king returned from Normandy late in December 1094
Anselm had been archbishop for more than a year, and believed
that he could no longer exercise a legitimate metropolitan
authority without a pallium.[1] The issue of the recognition of
Urban II had therefore become central for him. However, at an
interview at Gillingham the king made it clear that he required
an absolute submission to his will on the matter. When Anselm
required a public judgement a council was summoned at Rockingham for Sunday 25 February. In the course of a stormy meeting
the bishops, led by William of Durham, urged him to submit, and,
when he refused, withdrew their obedience. Perhaps because the
archbishop retained the support of many of the magnates, the
king then put the dispute in respite until Whitsun. Without
Anselm's knowledge he also sent two of his clerks to Urban with
an offer of recognition and a request for a pallium for an unspecified archbishop. Shortly before Whitsun the messengers
returned to England, accompanied by Walter, cardinal bishop of
Albano. At a meeting with the legate William agreed to publish
his adherence to Urban, and is said to have secured an undertaking in return that no further legate should be sent except
at his request. He failed, however, in an attempt to have
Anselm deposed. Shortly after the Whitsun court the king restored
the archbishop to favour at Windsor and without payment. It may
well have been then that Anselm promised to observe the customs
and laws of the realm if 'secundum Deum', for according to Hugh
of Flavigny he also swore obedience to the pope 'salva fidelitate domini sui regis', and that with the legate's assent.[2]
Though the open breach between king and archbishop was now

---

confirmed by *EA* 176. By 1094 the abbeys of St. Augustine, Canterbury, Chertsey, Ely, and St. Albans were certainly vacant, while several more, notably
in the south-west, may well have been (*Heads*, pp. 36, 38, 45, 66).

[1]*Flor. Wig.* ii.35, *EA* 176, C.-B. von Hacke, *Die Palliumverleihungen bis
1143*, esp. pp. 109-15. Gregory VII in *Reg.*, ix.1 (ed. Caspar, ii.568-9) of
1081 had told Archbishop William of Rouen that he was required to secure his
pallium within three months.
[2]*MGH Scriptores*, viii.474-5, for which see below, p. 649. Anselm's promise
is treated as occurring at Rockingham in *Life of St. Anselm*, p. 85n. but
Eadmer, pp. 83-4, places it after the council, and attributes it to the
period of reconciliation rather than open conflict.

apparently healed, and those of his supporters who had been
exiled after the council at Rockingham were allowed to return,
the issues of the estates of Canterbury, the vacant abbeys,
and the subjection of the church to 'voluntarie consuetudines'
remained untouched.[1]

For the rest of the year and until the return of the king
from Normandy by Whitsun 1097 no new cause of conflict is mentioned. Anselm helped in the maintenance of order in the south
during the king's Scottish campaign in 1095, and contributed
two hundred marks from the cathedral treasury towards the
'mortgage' of Normandy by Duke Robert in 1096. William's return
from the duchy in 1097, and his bitter complaints at the quality
of the Canterbury contingent of knights for his Welsh campaign
that summer showed Anselm that he could no longer hope for the
king's goodwill, without which no effective measure of reform
in the church could be possible. Similarly the ignominious
failure of the mission of Abbot Jarento in 1096 had revealed
the impotence of papal legates before the king's wealth and
intransigence. Accordingly he determined to go to Rome himself.
At frequent royal courts through the summer and autumn of 1097
he renewed his request; in October the king finally agreed to
his departure, though he had already shown that he would seize
the estates of Canterbury and did not intend to allow him to
return should he leave.

In November Anselm crossed from Dover to Wissant; on 23
December he was at Cluny, and moved thence to Lyons, where he
wrote to the pope giving a formal account of the reasons for
his exile and seeking leave to resign his office. On 16 March
1098 he set out for Rome, where Urban welcomed him, and both
wrote to the king demanding the restoration of the Canterbury
estates. Anselm accompanied the pope south to the siege of
Capua, and while they were at or near Aversa Urban declared
that he was determined that the archbishop should not resign,
and summoned him to a council at Bari in October 1098 to hear
his judgement on the king's conduct.

After the council at Rome in 1099 Anselm retired to Lyons.

---

[1]The phrase is from *EA* 206, but compare the earlier *EA* 176.

At the end of the year he wrote to the new pope, Paschal II, outlining the causes for his exile again, and summarizing the king's misdeeds in words which Eadmer was later to adapt to describe the usages of the Conqueror.[1] It was not, however, papal pressure but the king's death which brought the archbishop back to England.

104

MAY-JUNE 1095. LEGATION OF WALTER, CARDINAL BISHOP OF ALBANO

> For the legation see Tillmann, pp. 19-21, Southern, *St. Anselm*, pp. 130-1, 155; for the legate see Hüls, pp. 91-92.

King William sent his agents to Urban to negotiate for a recognition of the pope in England and the sending of a pallium probably immediately after the council at Rockingham at the end of February 1095. Before Whitsun they had returned with Bishop Walter, travelled through Canterbury, and held a meeting with the king. According to Hugh of Flavigny William agreed to accept Urban in return for an undertaking that no further legate should be sent except at his request: Eadmer believed in more general terms that the king thought he had secured a free hand in the kingdom free from papal challenge.[2] Since the legate would not agree to Anselm's deposition it was at last revealed to the archbishop that the pallium had arrived. On 27 May Walter was received at Canterbury by a procession led by the monks of Christ Church and St. Augustine and placed the pallium on the high altar of the cathedral. Anselm then took it up and

---

[1] *EA* 210, compared with Eadmer, p. 10. The bearing of Eadmer's summary on earlier conditions is uncertain. J.P. Gilson printed a long letter from Hugh of Lyons to Rufus on Anselm's behalf, which was written at about the same time, in 'Two letters addressed to William Rufus', *EHR* xii (1897), 290-3.

[2] The king's agents were William Warelwast, his chaplain and later bishop of Exeter, and Gerard, possibly still chancellor (later bishop of Hereford before his translation to York in 1100). Compare *MGH Scriptores*, viii.475 with Eadmer, pp. 68-70, 83-4.

celebrated a solemn mass.[1]

It is clear that the archbishop felt slighted by the whole manner of the legate's conduct, and particularly by his willingness to listen to his detractors. Shortly after the reception of the pallium the king marched against Scotland, and Walter suggested that they should hold a council for the reform of the church; Anselm's reply was firm. Behind the immediate excuse of the king's absence and his own duty to watch the coasts seems to lie a determination to preserve the rights of the archbishopric against the legate's claim to intervene. This was a constant theme of his pontificate, but this first hint of it was clearly associated with a well-grounded sense that he had not received from Walter the treatment he deserved.[2] Hugh of Flavigny attributed the legate's willingness to fall in with the king's wishes to lavish bribes, and his conduct was later criticized by the pope, but England's adherence to Urban may well have been a sufficient cause for his complaisance.

105

18 NOVEMBER 1095. PAPAL COUNCIL AT CLERMONT

The studies of R. Somerville, *The Councils of Urban II*, i (*Decreta Claromontensia*), 'The Council of Clermont (1095), and Latin Christian society', *Archivum Historiae Pontificiae,* xii (1974), 55-90, and 'The Council of Clermont and the First Crusade', *Studia Gratiana,* xx (1976), 323-37 discuss and largely supersede the very extensive earlier literature, including Mansi, xx.815-920 and Hefele—Leclercq, v (1).396-425; Becker, *Papst Urban II*, pp. 213-24, provides a modern account of the general issues.

The council at Clermont was the first held by Urban II after his journey across the Alps in 1095; the only surviving summons

---

[1]Eadmer, pp. 71-3; compare *Pontifical of Magdalen College,* pp. 250-1 and below, p. 709 n. 1.
 [2]*EA* 191-2.

was issued at Le Puy on 15 August. As at the earlier council at
Piacenza in March[1] there was a very large attendance; the three
Norman bishops of Bayeux, Evreux, and Séez were present, and
Anselm at least knew of its summoning, since he sent Boso of
Bec as his agent,[2] but no English prelate is known to have
been at either council. Clermont is chiefly remembered for the
preaching of the first crusade, but this was far from its only
purpose, and it produced a great deal of legislation. This does
not survive in any complete and authoritative form, but versions
of it were early found in English manuscripts; a text very close
to that known in Normandy was collected by William of Malmesbury[3] while other and distinct forms are found in BL ms. Cotton
Claudius E. v (an addition made at Canterbury ultimately from
the type of text known at Arras) and Oxford, Bodl. ms. Selden
Supra 90, a unique summary version.[4]

In Normandy the council was given wide publicity; in February
1096 Archbishop William summoned a council at Rouen and read
out the Clermont decrees before himself publishing seven canons.
Though the first six share some of the preoccupations of the
papal council, they are closer in phrasing and detail to earlier
Norman legislation.[5] However, the last forbids any priest to do
homage to a layman, here following a provision first made at
Clermont but not found in the 'Anglo-Norman' version.

For the history of Anglo-papal relations the council clearly
had some importance. Anselm may have had its provisions in mind

---

[1]For the council at Piacenza see Hefele—Leclercq, v (1), 388-96, G. Tangl,
Die Teilnehmer an den allgemeinen Konzilien des Mittelalters, pp.172-6. The
canons are best edited by Weiland in *MGH Constitutiones*, i.560-3 using
inter alia BL ms. Harley 3001, fos. 80^V-2, which is not of English origin.
Similarly Oxford, Bodl. mss. Selden supra 90, fos. 24^V-25^V and Canon. Pat.
Lat. 39, fo. 86 may well not be.

[2]*Vita Bosonis* in *Lanfranci Opera*, ed. Giles, i.328-9: 'Eodem tempore
audiens Anselmus Urbanum papam convocasse concilium generale apud Clarummon-
tem in Alvernia provincia, quia ipse non potuit ire, misit ... Bosonem ad
idem concilium'; compare OV v.18.

[3]See Somerville, *Councils of Urban II*, i.83-98. His mss. C and L can now
be shown to be copies of a text collected by William (R. Thomson, 'William
of Malmesbury's edition of the *Liber Pontificalis*', *Archivum Historiae Pontificiae*, xvi (1978), 93-112). There seems no good reason to treat William's
text as dependent on any surviving Norman copy. See also OV v.10-15.

[4]Somerville, *Councils of Urban II*, i.53-4, 112-17, above n. 1.

[5]OV v.18-22.

when dealing with clerical would-be crusaders soon afterwards,[1]
and the legislation of 1102 shows some traces of its effect,
but potentially the most important was the condemnation of
homage as well as investiture; however, this was not ever cited
by the participants in later disputes in England[2] and Anselm
invariably referred to the later council of Rome in 1099, which
he had attended in person, for his authority to refuse homage
to King Henry. More strikingly, in spite of the wide publication of the Clermont decrees in Normandy, Anselm's refusal in
1100 seems to have found the English king and bishops quite
unprepared.[3] The crusade preaching caught the attention of
English chroniclers and English crusaders, but the legislation
had little direct effect.

106

c.JANUARY—MAY 1096. LEGATION OF ABBOT JARENTO OF ST. BÉNIGNE DE DIJON

> See Tillmann, pp. 21-2; *Chartes et documents de Saint-
> Bénigne de Dijon*, ii.255-6 and nos. 386, 390.

This legation is not mentioned in English sources and is known
directly only from the chronicle of Hugh of Flavigny, who
accompanied his abbot. Jarento was sent soon after the Council
of Clermont, which he had attended, to deal with three matters:
the quarrel between King William and Duke Robert, which would
have to be resolved before the duke could set out on crusade,
the prevalence of simony, clerical incontinence and long

---

[1]Somerville, *Studia Gratiana*, xx (1976), 330-1, H.E.J. Cowdrey, *History*,
lv (1970), 183-5, *EA* 195.

[2]It was, however, presumably Abbot Boso's authority for refusing homage
to Henry I in 1124, since he had been at Clermont but not at the later
councils (*Lanfranci Opera*, ed. Giles, i.328-9, 330-1).

[3]See below. However, about this time several canons of Gregory VII's
council of November 1078, including c. 3 prohibiting lay investiture, were
entered at Exeter on the flyleaves of Oxford, Bodl. ms. Bodley 718, fos.
ii^v-iii^v, 180 (Cowdrey, *Studi Gregoriani*, ix (1972), 105); c. 6 is also
found in Lambeth Palace ms. 351, fo. 94. There is no proof that either these
or the English copies of Clermont were written before 1100.

vacancies at several English abbeys, and the agreement made
between Walter of Albano and the king the previous year.[1]
Jarento was detained by the king over Easter (13 April) until
the embassy which he had sent earlier to the pope could return.
When it did it was accompanied by a nephew of the pope, who
allowed the king a further respite till Christmas on the ecclesiastical issues. Late in May the legate was in Normandy, where
he arranged for an agreement between the two brothers, and
escorted Duke Robert as far as Pontarlier on his road to the
Holy Land, where they parted about the beginning of October.[2]

107

3 OCTOBER 1098, *c.*24 APRIL 1099. PAPAL COUNCILS AT BARI AND ROME

> In general see Mansi, xx.947-52, 961-6, Hefele—Leclercq,
> v (1), 458-64, JL i, pp. 694, 700, and for Bari the
> references collected in P. Palazzini, *Dizionario dei
> concili,* i.146-8. For Anselm's action there see particu-
> larly Eadmer, pp. 104-14; *Life of St. Anselm,* pp. 112-
> 16; Southern, *St. Anselm,* pp. 164-7.

Urban II summoned the Council of Bari for 1 October, but it
seems to have opened two days later.[3] The recorded business of
the council is almost wholly concerned with relations with the
churches of the East, in which Anselm played a leading part as
a defender of the Latin view of the Incarnation.[4] However, his
later correspondence shows that other business was conducted
there. Although no canons have been preserved, it is very
likely that Urban rehearsed here the legislation of earlier

---

[1]The list is Hugh's in *MGH Scriptores,* viii.474-5, but it is unlikely
that Robert took the cross until *c.*Feb. 1096, well after the council (David,
Robert Curthose, p. 90).

[2]David, *Robert Curthose,* pp. 89, 96; compare C.H. Haskins, *Norman Institutions,* pp. 66-7, 69-70, 75-6, 286.

[3]Eadmer, p. 104, *Rerum Italicarum Scriptores* ed. L.A. Muratori, v (1724),
48, 155.

[4]Eadmer, pp. 104-6, *EA* 239, and in general B. Leib, *Rome, Kiev et Byzance
à la fin du XI*[e] *siècle,* 287-96.

councils,[1] but the substance of only one decision is recorded.
In 1102 Paschal II reminded Anselm of the sentence pronounced
against investiture at Bari; Eadmer does not mention this
canon, and Anselm himself referred always to the judgement of
the council at Rome the next year.[2] Again according to Eadmer
the pope threatened to excommunicate King William for his
oppression of the church and maltreatment of the archbishop,
and was only dissuaded from this by Anselm, and that with difficulty.[3] After the council he returned to Rome with the pope.

Messengers from the king arrived there at Christmas, and
secured a further respite until Michaelmas, which convinced
Anselm that no further help could be looked for at Rome, but
Urban prevailed upon him to remain until the council which he
had summoned for April. The council met in the third week after
Easter, though the exact date is uncertain.[4] The surviving
canons are an amalgamation of earlier legislation from Piacenza and Melfi, with two additions, and none mentions homage
or investiture.[5] However, according to Eadmer, after the
decrees had been read out a sentence of excommunication was
pronounced against all who gave or received investiture of
churches and all who exacted or performed homage for them. Although no source outside Anselm's circle confirms this,[6] there

---

[1]He did this at Rome in 1099 and probably at Clermont in 1095; it is
correspondingly possible that some of the canons found in numerous canon
law collections without an attribution might in fact have been collected at
Bari, though indistinguishable from earlier decrees; see below, n. 5,
Somerville, *Annuarium Historiae Conciliorum*, ii (1970), 61-3, and *Councils
of Urban II*, i.125-6, F. Gossman, *Pope Urban II and Canon Law*, pp. 104-8.

[2]*EA* 282 (JL 5929), below, p. 652 n. 1.

[3]It is difficult to take this literally; see Southern, *St. Anselm*,
p. 304n.

[4]The date is given as 24-30 Apr. (*Flor. Wig.* ii.43, followed by many
dependent compilations, and Bernold of Constance in *MGH Scriptores*, v.466);
25 Apr. (*Chroniques des églises d'Anjou*, ed. P. Marchegay and É. Mabille
(Paris, 1869), pp. 418-9); 26 Apr. (Sdralek, *Wolfenbüttler Fragmente*,
p. 39, possibly the source for the notes in the Collection in Ten Parts
cited by Gossman, *Urban II and Canon Law*, pp. 93-102 and Sirmond's notes
cited in Mansi from Cossart). Lambert of Arras also gives 24 Apr. (*PL*
clxii.644), which is the conventional date.

[5]At least three versions of the canons are known, though none is English,
but so far no marked differences between them, or aberrant texts, have been
reported. Compare Sdralek, *Wolfenbüttler Fragmente*, pp. 39-41; Somerville,
Councils of Urban II, i.64.

[6]WMGP and *Flor. Wig.* here depend on Eadmer, except for the date, which
Flor. Wig. provides from an unidentified source.

can be little doubt that Eadmer is right, for Anselm's letters make frequent reference to this judgement as his authority for refusing to do homage to Henry I.[1]

The bishop of Lucca, with whom Anselm was associated in delivering a judgement at the council,[2] broke off his reading of the decrees to lament the failure to offer any redress for the archbishop's wrongs, and justly so, for the pope's negotiations with the king were evidently coming to no conclusion.[3] Anselm left Rome the day after the council closed, and it seems clear that his supporters at least were thoroughly dissatisfied with its outcome.

108
5 AUGUST 1100. CORONATION CHARTER OF HENRY I

> For the text of the charter see particularly Liebermann, i.lx (citing earlier editions), 521-3 and iii.293-9 and most fully in *TRHS* New Ser., viii (1894), 21-48, also *Statutes of the Realm*, i.1-2. See further C. Bémont, *Chartes des libertés anglaises (1100-1305)*, pp. vii-xii, R.L. Poole, 'The publication of Great Charters by the English kings', *Studies in Chronology and History*, pp. 308 ff., Stubbs, *Select Charters* (9th ed.), pp. 116-19. The manuscripts are calendared in *Reg.* ii, no. 488 and the text best translated in *EHD* ii.400-2 (no. 19).

On 2 August William II was killed while hunting in the New Forest. His brother Henry secured the treasury at Winchester and then rode for London. On 5 August he was crowned at Westminster, where, in addition to his coronation oath, he issued the first surviving charter of liberties, granting his subjects relief from a variety of exactions common under his father and

---

[1] *EA* 214, 217-19, 280, 327, 329, 388.
[2] *Cartulaires du chapitre de l'église métropolitaine Sainte-Marie d'Auch*, pp. 55-7, no. 56.
[3] Southern, *St. Anselm*, pp. 161-8.

brother.[1] The majority of its clauses deal with the abuse of
feudal custom and right or secular extortion, but c. 1 declares
that he makes the church free, particularly from the heavy
demands earlier made on vacant churches. As at the time the
archbishopric of Canterbury was in the king's hand, Winchester
and Salisbury were vacant, and numerous abbeys were also in
royal custody, this was an urgent matter.[2] It seems likely,
however, that he conceived this as a renunciation of such extreme measures as the taking of reliefs from vacant churches or
the creation of new fees on their estates, widely practised by
Flambard in his brother's reign, rather than of all regalian
right, which he certainly retained throughout his reign.[3]
According to Eadmer Henry made general promises to observe the
liberties of the church to Anselm in 1101 during the crisis
caused by Duke Robert's landing, and in 1106 before the archbishop's return from exile, when again he laid particular stress
on his conduct during vacancies. It is even possible that the
charter was formally reissued in 1101, though precise evidence
is lacking.[4]

Clause 7 of the charter is also printed below, as it deals
with the right of a tenant-in-chief to dispose of his chattels
at death, a subject of evident interest to the church and one
which gave rise to frequent ecclesiastical litigation.[5]

No original of the charter survives, and only one can be
traced in any known medieval archive,[6] but later copies abound.
The text therefore presents complex problems, which are

---

[1]*Flor. Wig.* ii.46-7 (incorporating quotations from the charter), Eadmer,
p. 119, Malmesbury in WMGR ii.470, §393, *ASC* ed. Plummer, i.236, ed. Clark,
p. 28, tr. Whitelock *et al.*, p. 176.

[2]*Heads*, s.nn., *Chronicon Monasterii de Abingdon*, ii.42-4 appear to
provide under Abingdon, Bury, St. Augustine at Canterbury, Cerne, Chertsey,
Ely, Glastonbury, Milton, Muchelney, Peterborough, and the New Minster at
Winchester the eleven houses mentioned by *ASC*.

[3]M. Howell, *Regalian Right in Medieval England*, pp. 6-29, Brett, *English
Church*, pp. 105-6.

[4]Eadmer, pp. 127, 181-3; compare *Reg.* ii, no. 531. The arguments of
L. Riess in *EHR* xli (1926), 321-31, rest on no adequate foundation.

[5]See below p. 695 and Brett, *English Church*, p. 227.

[6]In the inventories of charters in the treasury of the archbishop of
Canterbury *c.*1277 in London, Lambeth Palace ms. 1212, p. 2 and 1330 in
I. Churchill, *Camden Miscellany XV*, 1-2. This is the text copied in Lambeth
ms. 1212, pp. 187-8 (*c.*1225) and 17-18 (*c.*1277).

increased rather than clarified by the number of thirteenth-
century versions; these testify more to a widespread interest
in it during the period of Magna Carta than to its earlier
importance. A version addressed to the bishop and men of Worcestershire was copied into the Red Book of the Exchequer
towards the end of the thirteenth century, another to the men
of Hertfordshire into the chronicle of Roger of Wendover. All
the rest, beginning with the earliest known copy, in the Textus
Roffensis, have a general address. The Worcester version has
the longest witness list, though others add the names of Henry
de Port or Abbot Gilbert Crispin, while that of the *Quadripartitus* group has a generalized list with no specific names.
The extracts below are taken from the Worcester version, which
contains relatively few idiosyncratic readings. It is found in
London, PRO KR Misc. Book i (E. 164) 2, fo. 266[V] (formerly fo.
163[V]).

[a](H)enricus rex Anglorum Samsoni episcopo et Ursoni de Abetot
et omnibus baronibus et fidelibus suis tam francigenis quam
angligenis de Wirecestrescira salutem.

[1] Sciatis me Dei misericordia et communi consilio baronum
regni Anglie eiusdem regni regem coronatum esse; et quia regnum
oppressum erat iniustis exactionibus ego, respectu Dei et amore
quem erga vos omnes[b] habeo, sanctam Dei ecclesiam imprimis
liberam facio, ita quod nec vendam nec ad firmam ponam nec,
mortuo archiepiscopo seu episcopo sive abbate, aliquid accipiam
de dominio ecclesie vel de hominibus eius donec successor in
eam ingrediatur. Et omnes malas consuetudines quibus regnum
Anglie iniuste opprimebatur inde aufero; quas malas consuetudines ex parte hic pono.

[7] Et si quis baronum vel hominum meorum infirmabitur, sicut
ipse dabit vel dare disponet pecuniam suam, ita datam esse

---

[a]*Heading* Carta r(egis) H. primi filii r(egis) W. de libertatibus concessis Anglis, et habuit quilibet comitatus talem *added in a later hand, following an earlier note at the head of the leaf.*   [b]omnes *om.* ms. *and
Textus Roffensis. In all other versions.*

concedo. Quod si ipse preventus vel armis vel infirmitate pecuniam suam non dederit nec dare disposuerit, uxor sua sive liberi
aut parentes aut legittimi homines eius eam pro anima eius
dividant sicut melius eis visum fuerit.

109
? BEFORE 23 SEPTEMBER 1100. LEGATION OF GUY, ARCHBISHOP OF
VIENNE

   See Tillmann, p. 22, Brett, *English Church*, pp. 35-6.

Guy of Vienne, the later Calixtus II, was appointed legate over
all Britain by Paschal II at the beginning of his pontificate.
The only evidence of his activity comes from Eadmer, who refers
to a brief and fruitless visit in 1100, and from a letter of
Anselm protesting at such an appointment as a breach of the
privileges of Canterbury.[1] Since Anselm appears to have known
of the legation only by hearsay it is most likely that Guy's
visit took place before Anselm's return to England on 23 September 1100,[2] and possibly even before the death of William II.
He seems to have made no further effort to exercise his powers
in England.

110
1100-1105. RELATIONS OF ANSELM WITH HENRY I

        See the literature cited above, p. 643. The chief
        sources are Eadmer, pp. 118-75, *EA* 212 ff., *Life of St.
        Anselm*, pp. 126-34.

Anselm first heard of King William's death from monks of Bec
and Canterbury at La Chaise-Dieu. While staying at Cluny on

---

[1]Eadmer, p. 126 (his year begins either at Christmas or 1 January); *EA*
214 (which proves that Guy's appointment if not his visit occurred before
Anselm's return).
[2]Eadmer, p. 119.

the road north he received an invitation to return in the name
of the new king and his magnates, on the strength of which he
crossed the Channel and met Henry at Salisbury about the end
of September. When the king offered to re-invest him with the
archbishopric and Anselm refused on the grounds of the papal
prohibitions which he had heard at the councils of 1098/9, the
English investiture conflict had begun.

Uncertain of his throne, Henry suggested that the issue be
shelved until the next Easter, while an embassy to Rome could
seek a relaxation of such demands, to which Anselm agreed. The
messengers did not return until after Whitsun, by which time
Anselm was active in encouraging support for the king against
Duke Robert, whose army landed in England on 20 July.[1] In return, Henry promised the archbishop his entire obedience to the
papal decrees. After peace had been made between the brothers
Anselm was summoned to the royal court, probably that at Windsor on 3 September 1101,[2] to discuss the letters of Paschal in
which the pope required the king to surrender his claim to
elect and invest bishops.

This meeting produced no result, though the king threatened
to banish any who denied his rights. However, at a further
meeting at Winchester, probably in October, Henry and Anselm
agreed on a further embassy to Rome to urge the king's case.
The king's representatives were Gerard, recently translated
from Hereford to York and so anxious to secure his pallium,
Herbert of Norwich, and Robert of Chester. Anselm sent the
monks Baldwin of Bec and Alexander of Canterbury to report the
pope's reply and seek to convince him of the reality of Henry's
threats.[3]

The embassy reached Rome before 10 April 1102 but probably

---

[1]C.W. Hollister, *EHR* lxxxviii (1973), 315-34 gives the most recent detailed account. The source of his text is an abbreviation of the Durham
Historia Regum in an earlier state than any that now survives, best represented by Liège, UL ms. 369C, described by B. Meehan, *Bull. of the Board of
Celtic Studies*, xxviii (1978), 37-46. For the content of some of Paschal's
letters at this time see below p. 690.

[2]Compare *Reg.* ii, nos. 544-9. In no. 549 Anselm styles himself 'vicar
of Pope Paschal'; for the presence of papal legates see below no. 112.

[3]Anselm had also been distressed by the absence of any letter to him
after Warelwast's embassy of 1100/1 (*EA* 217-20).

after the Lent council. The king's agents each received a favourable answer to their requests on their own behalf, Gerard securing his pallium and Herbert and Robert bulls confirming the movement of their sees to Norwich and Coventry,[1] but the larger issues were attended by some confusion. Before Michaelmas 1102 the ambassadors had returned and the king had crushed the revolt of the house of Bellême. Anselm was therefore summoned to London to discuss the pope's messages. His letter to Anselm was clear; at the Lateran council of March he had denounced investiture, homage, and lay intervention in elections, and would change nothing.[2] His letter to the king, however, only specifies investiture as the necessary concession. The bishops further asserted that the pope had privately assured them that he would take no steps against Henry, even if he continued to invest, so long as he appointed suitable candidates, but that such a concession could not be made formally. This was at best a mistake,[3] but Anselm agreed to take no steps against any bishops the king might appoint until a further embassy could resolve these doubts, though he would not allow their consecration. With a temporary truce so concluded the archbishop proceeded to celebrate his Westminster council.

Early in 1103[4] the king sought to bring the dispute to a

---

[1]Eadmer, pp. 132-4, JL 5886 (*Hist. York*, iii, no. 11). *Hist. York*, iii, no. 12, another bull for Gerard, is printed defectively; in the ms. it is dated exactly as JL 5886 except for the day. For Coventry see JL 5912, for Norwich JL 6594 (dated in *PUE* ii, no. 3); for the chronology of these bulls and missions see Brett, *English Church*, pp. 234-6.

[2]*EA* 222 (JL 5908) is the only substantial evidence for legislation at this council, and was widely excerpted by French canonists; the council is fully discussed in U.-R. Blumenthal, *The Early Councils of Pope Paschal II*, pp. 11-23. *EA* 223 (JL 5909) also contains a denunciation of homage, though associated with a licence for the archbishop to dispense with the rigour of the canons in case of necessity.

[3]In view of Paschal's reluctance to discuss homage in his extant letters to the king (below, p. 690 n. 1), it is possible that the bishops, quite unused to the precise analysis of such questions in England, misunderstood a first tentative suggestion of the compromise reached finally in 1106/7. It is unlikely that they were simply lying.

[4]Reinhelm was not nominated to Hereford until after the death of Roger the larderer (who died some time after the Michaelmas council) and possibly not until after Christmas (*Reg.* ii, no. 613, Eadmer, p. 144). The most likely occasion for the abortive consecration is therefore the Ember Days 18-21 February 1103.

head by commanding Archbishop Gerard to consecrate the three
bishops-elect of Winchester, Hereford, and Salisbury. Reinhelm
of Hereford resigned his ring and staff, and was expelled from
court.[1] William of Winchester caused a greater scandal by refusing consecration just as the service was beginning, and was
stripped of office and banished. Frustrated here, in mid-Lent
(c.10 March) Henry came to Canterbury and demanded the submission of Anselm on all points, refusing to discuss the papal
letters which Anselm's messengers had brought back from Rome,
but he had not yet opened.[2] The king at last offered a further
compromise; Anselm himself should go to Rome to seek an accom-
modation with the pope. Though this seemed a hopeless course,
at the Easter court (29 March) he allowed himself to be persuaded. On 27 April Anselm landed at Wissant and travelled
south, reaching Rome before 10 November;[3] he had been preceded
by the king's agent, William Warelwast, and was accompanied by
William, the former elect of Winchester, and two abbots, Aldwin
of Ramsey and Richard of Ely, who had been deposed at the council of 1102.[4]

The pope's attitude remained relatively firm. Anselm secured
a confirmation of the rights of Canterbury to her estates and
primacy as they had been enjoyed since the time of St. Augustine, and letters for the king and queen, which were not

---

[1] In EA 343 of 1103/7 Anselm encouraged Reinhelm to constancy; he was
obviously wavering in his determination, and it is not impossible that he
was reconciled with the king before the agreement with Anselm was complete.

[2] EA 281-2 (JL 5928-9); these letters would have caused great embarrass-
ment, as Anselm had gathered from his messengers, for they excommunicated
any bishop who had been consecrated or invested in recent months. He did
not open them before leaving England at the end of Apr. (Eadmer, pp. 148-9).
JL 5928 circulated widely in canonical collections (Blumenthal, Early Councils of Pope Paschal II, p. 20). The source may well have been the appendix
to the Collection in IX Books, where a full text is found (M. Sdralek,
Wolfenbüttler Fragmente, p. 56). See further below, p. 660 n. 1.

[3] Abbot Arnald of St. Pierre-le-Vif secured a bull for his house on 10
November (JL 5953), and had found Anselm and William of Winchester there on
his arrival (Clarius of Sens in Bibliothèque historique de l'Yonne, ii.
514-15).

[4] Flor. Wig. ii.52; it is possible that this information, in part confirmed by Clarius, Diceto, i.234, and Quadripartitus in Liebermann, i.545,
was found by the Worcester chronicler in an earlier version of Eadmer's
Historia than the surviving text. See further Brett, English Church, p.
235n. and for Richard of Ely below, p. 690 n. 2.

delivered and may not have survived.[1] Paschal's extant letter
to Henry makes no concession on investiture and urges Anselm's
return, but on all other matters promises the king the most
favourable treatment.

As the English mission approached Lyons on the road home,
William Warelwast on the king's behalf required Anselm to maintain all the customs of the Conqueror and Rufus if he wished
to return to England in peace.[2] He therefore settled at Lyons
for a further stay, writing to the king to ask if Warelwast had
indeed conveyed the king's will accurately, and to assert his
obedience to the unshaken papal decision on investiture. The
king accordingly seized the estates of the archbishopric into
his hands, while continuing to urge Anselm to return and seeking further delays in his negotiations with the papacy. In this
way 1104 slipped past with little achieved; the king subjected
the church to heavy exactions and Anselm's apparent inactivity
was widely criticized. By 23 December Paschal was demanding a
satisfactory renunciation of the right to invest from the king
before the Lent council of 1105.[3] A second letter written
shortly afterwards made it clear that failure to renounce investiture and restore Anselm would ensure that the king and his
councillors would be excommunicated.[4] On 23 March 1105 Paschal
wrote to tell Anselm that Robert of Meulan and all who urged
the king to maintain his claims had been placed under a ban at
the Lent council, but that sentence on the king had been de-
ferred until his messengers, due at Easter (7 April), had

---

[1]*EA* 303 (JL 5955), 304. *EA* 305 (JL 5956), dated a week after the Canterbury privileges, appears to be the letter given to Warelwast; compare *EA*
315.
[2]The threat is explicit in *Life of St. Anselm*, p. 130; the fuller account
in Eadmer, p. 157, confirmed by *EA* 315, shows that William's message was more
oblique, in part explaining both such criticism as that met in *EA* 330,
ll. 12-13 and Anselm's desire to discover exactly what the king required.
[3]*EA* 348 (*PUE* i, no. 6).
[4]*EA* 351 (*PUE* i, no. 7) speaks of this as his third letter of warning,
presumably as the canonical preliminary to the threatened excommunication.
Compare further *EA* 352 (*PUE* i, no. 8). Although Eadmer copied *EA* 216 (JL
5868), 224 (JL 5910) and 305 (JL 5956), none of the pope's letters to the
king, including *EA* 348, 351-2, is found in the chief Canterbury letter
collection represented by Lambeth ms. 59 and its related copies.

arrived.[1] A letter to Gerard of York, written after Easter,
commanded him to publish the ban on the counsellors.

Anselm interpreted this hesitant progress towards decisive
action as a clear sign that no further or effective help could
be looked for at Rome, and determined to take his own steps. In
May he left Lyons and moved north, declaring his intention of
excommunicating the king for his seizure of the estates of
Canterbury. In part he may have been influenced by an ever-
growing volume of criticism of his conduct, while at least one
of his supporters, William of Winchester, had been reconciled
with the king and restored as bishop-elect by February 1105.[2]
On the king's side there had also been changes. Since the
crushing of the Bellême revolt in 1102 his position in England
had become steadily stronger, and by the summer of 1105 he was
ready to undertake a complete conquest of Normandy. At such a
time a final and open breach with archbishop and pope would be
peculiarly inconvenient, little though Paschal found to commend in Duke Robert's conduct towards the Norman church.[3] The
king's need for a formal reconciliation makes it hard to assess
how far a number of letters from Anselm's former opponents
among the English clergy represent a genuine change of heart
after the excommunication of Robert of Meulan.[4]

In these circumstances a message from the countess of Blois
that the sentence against the king was imminent produced rapid

---

[1]For the council see Blumenthal, *Early Councils of Pope Paschal II*,
pp. 23-31. *EA* 353 (JL 6028) in all the surviving versions which derive
ultimately from the Canterbury collection,says that sentence has been delayed on the king because his messengers, due 'in praeteriti Paschae tempore', had not yet arrived. The copy entered in the appendix to the Collection in IX Books seems to be independent and reads, clearly rightly,
praesenti for *praeteriti*. F.S. Schmitt, 'Zur Entstehungsgeschichte der
handschriftlichen Sammlungen der Briefe des hl. Anselm von Canterbury',
Revue Bénédictine, xlviii (1936), 300-17 discusses the Canterbury collection,
though his conclusions need some revision. For the Collection in IX Books,
see Sdralek, *Wolfenbüttler Fragmente*, pp. 55-9, Somerville, *Councils of
Urban II*, i.56-7, above p. 658 n. 2.
[2]Compare *EA* 322, 344 (which can only be dated approximately, and may not
have been written in that order), *Reg.* ii, nos. 684, 753, 790. According
to Eadmer, p. 164, Anselm had also formally required the king to restore
the Canterbury estates three times before preparing his excommunication.
[3]*Papsturkunden in Frankreich*, Neue Folge ii (1937), no. 4.
[4]*EA* 362-3, 369, 386-7; only Gerard's letter to the pope can have been
written before the meeting at Laigle.

results. At a meeting at Laigle on 21 July[1] Henry restored
Anselm to his bishopric and a joint embassy to Rome was
arranged to settle the larger issues.

111

23 SEPTEMBER x 11 NOVEMBER 1100. COUNCIL AT LAMBETH

> See Southern, *St. Anselm,* pp. 182-90 and Barlow (1979),
> pp. 169-70 for these events and their background.

Shortly after Anselm's return to England in 1100 and first interview
with the king at Salisbury[2] he found that Henry had determined
on a marriage with Matilda, daughter of Malcolm III of Scotland
and grand-daughter of Edward the Atheling. The match posed
serious problems, as Matilda had long lived apparently as a
nun at Wilton. Several years earlier Anselm had written to the
bishop of Salisbury to secure her return to the monastic habit
which she had abandoned, probably in connection with a projected
marriage to Count Alan of Richmond,[3] and there appears to have
been widespread murmuring at the king's proposal. Matilda
assured Anselm that she had been compelled to assume a veil
only in defence against Norman importunity, had resisted its
imposition, and cast it off as soon as possible, jumping on it
in her indignation. On all this she offered to submit herself
to the judgement of the whole church of the English. Accordingly
Anselm sent the archdeacons of Canterbury and Salisbury to
Wilton to collect evidence which was presented to a gathering

---

[1] Eadmer, p. 166 gives 22 July; Anselm himself in *EA* 364 says that the
agreement was made on the vigil of St. Mary Magdalene (21 July).

[2] Anselm landed at Dover on 23 Sept., and the king was at Salisbury on
29 Sept. (Eadmer, p. 119, *Reg.* ii, no. 494).

[3] *EA* 177. According to OV iv.272 Matilda (Edith) had been educated at
Romsey, where her aunt Christina was certainly for long a nun (*Heads,*
p. 219). Malmesbury in WMGR ii.493 §418 says that Matilda was educated at
both Romsey and Wilton, while Eadmer at p. 123 places her at Wilton, and
both in *EA* 177 and below at p. 662 her affairs are the concern of the
diocese of Salisbury, which fits Wilton but not Romsey (dioc. Winchester).
Eadmer, who was in an admirable position to know, is therefore presumably
right in placing her at Wilton, at least in the later years before her
marriage.

at Lambeth. Its composition is uncertain, but it is most unlikely to have contained any bishop from the province of York.[1]

Of the two surviving accounts that of Eadmer (no. I) is the
more reliable. The passage from Hermann of Tournai (no. II) may
depend originally on a report from Baldwin, the former advocate
of Tournai who became a monk of Bec and one of Anselm's closest
companions,[2] but was not written until 1142-7, which may explain several inaccuracies.[3]

I. *Eadmer, Historia Novorum in Anglia s.a. 1100*

> Cambridge, Corpus Christi Coll. ms. 452, pp. 139-43 (= A)
> and BL ms. Cotton Titus A. ix, fos. 55-56[v] (= B). Printed
> in Eadmer, pp. 122-5 and, from B only, in W. i.365-6 and
> *PL* clix.426-8, ultimately from the edition of Selden.

Differt Anselmus sententiam ferre, et causam iudicio re[p. 140]-
ligiosarum personarum regni determinandam pronuntiat. Statuto
itaque die coeunt ad nutum illius episcopi, abbates, nobiles
quique ac religiosi ordinis viri in villam[a] sancti Andreę de
Rovecestra quę Lamhetha[b][4] vocatur, quo et ipsum praesentis
negotii tunc tenor adduxerat. Causa igitur iuxta praescriptam
seriem in medium deducta est. Prodeunt hinc inde idonei testes,
verba puellę purę veritati subnixa protestantes. Accedunt istis
archidiaconi duo, Willelmus videlicet Cantuariensis et Hum-
baldus Serberiensis,[5] quos pater Anselmus Wiltuniam ubi illa

---

[a]villa B.   [b]Lambeta B.

---

[1]Ranulf Flambard of Durham was under arrest (Symeon, i.138, ii.232, *ASC*,
ed. Plummer, i.236, ed. Clark, p. 28, *Flor. Wig.* ii.47). According to Hugh
the Chanter, ed. Johnson, pp. 10, 12 (*Hist. York,* ii.107, 109) Archbishop
Thomas of York never saw King Henry again after their meeting in Sept.
(*Reg.* ii, no. 492); he died at Ripon on 18 Nov. (*Hist. York,* ii.364).
[2]*MGH Scriptores,* xiv.280, Southern, *St. Anselm,* pp. 184 n. 3, 195-8.
[3]Hermann probably died on the Second Crusade in 1147; he refers to
Stephen's recovery of the crown after the battle of Lincoln in *MGH Scrip-*
tores, xiv.282.
[4]Possibly the council met here rather than at London because St. Paul's
had not been rebuilt after the great fire of 1087 (*ASC*, ed. Plummer, i.218,
ed. Clark, p. 10, WMGP, pp. 145-6). See further C.N.L. Brooke, *Report of*
the Friends of Lambeth Palace Library for 1972, 14-16.
[5]Archdeacon William first occurs in *EA* 208 of 1099/1100 (Le Neve, ii.12).
Humbald had been appointed by St. Osmund (WMGP, pp. 429-31).

fuerat educata pro huius rei certitudine rimanda direxerat, qui
publica voce attestati[a] sunt se et rem a sororibus diligentissime perquisisse et nil quod relatę rationi obsisteret ab eis
capere potuisse. Monet ergo Anselmus et per christianam obędientiam omnibus imperat ut nullum a veritate favor aut timor
deflectat, sed sicut revera causę Dei quo iuste determinetur
unusquisque pro viribus opem ferat, ne, quod absit, aiens, talis
iudicii sententia prodeat cuius exemplo in superventuris
temporibus vel sua quilibet libertate non iure privetur, vel
Deus iis[b] quę sui iuris esse debent iniuria defrudetur. Accla-
mant omnes ita faciendum, et se non aliter facturos spondent.
Remoto itaque a conventu solo patre, ęcclesia Anglię quę convenerat in unum de proferenda sententia tractat. Deinde illo in
medium reverenter adducto, expositum est quid de negotio communis omnium sensus invenerit. Ratum aiunt perspecta re sibi
videri, et ad hoc comprobandum [p. 141] paratos se asserunt,
nulla sententia posse puellam pro causa sua iure constringi
quin libertate corporis sui quocunque modo legaliter velit
valeat uti. Quod licet inquiunt levi argumento probare possemus,
eo tamen cum opus non sit supersedemus, nostris argumentis
firmiorem tenentes parem iudicii huius sententiam a venerandę
memorię praedecessore vestro,[c] patre et magistro nostro Lanfranco
simili de causa promulgatam. Nam quando ille magnus Willelmus
hanc terram primo devicit, multi suorum sibi pro tanta victoria
applaudentes omniaque suis voluntatibus atque luxuriis obędire
ac subdi debere autumantes, non solum in possessiones victorum
sed et in ipsas matronas ac virgines ubi facultas eis[d] aspira-
bat nefanda libidine cęperunt insanire. Quod nonnullę praevi-
dentes et suo pudori metuentes, monasteria virginum petivere
acceptoque velo sese inter ipsas a tanta infamia protexere. Quę
clades cum postmodum sedata et pro temporis qualitate pax rebus
data fuisset, quęsitum ab eodem patre Lanfranco est quid de
iis[e] quę tali refugio suam pudicitiam servaverunt ipse sentiret,
essentne videlicet constringendę in monasterio velum tenere
quod acceperant necne? At ipse quęstionem ipsam consilio generalis concilii taliter solvit, ut eis pro castitate, quam se tam

---

[a] testati B.   [b] his B.   [c] et *add* B.   [d] eis fac. B.   [e] his B.

manifestę rei ostensione amare testatę fuerant, debitam magis
reverentiam iudicaret exhibendam quam ullam servandę religionis
continentiam, nisi propria illam [p. 142] voluntate appeterent,
violenter ingerendam.[1] Et adiunxerunt, 'His interfuimus, hęc
approbari a sapientibus viris audivimus, et hęc in praesenti
negotio valere volumus ac roborari postulamus. Licet enim scia-
mus causę illarum istius esse leviorem, dum illę sponte, ista
coacta pari de causa velum portaverit, tamen ne quis nos favore
cuiusvis duci existimet non ultra progredi in iudicio volumus,
hoc solo contenti, ut quod valuit in maiori valeat in minori.'
Tunc Anselmus ad hęc, 'Scitis quid monuerim, quid praeceperim,
quidque polliciti sitis. Cum igitur secundum quod vobis visum
est iustius in commune iudicaveritis sicut asseritis, ego
iudicium vestrum non abicio, sed eo securius illud suscipio quo
tanti patris auctoritate suffultum audio.' Illa dehinc in medium
ducitur, gesta comi vultu audit et amplectitur, auditum sibi
pręstari paucis precatur. Loquens ergo obtulit se vel sacramento
vel alia quam magis eligerent ęcclesiastica lege probaturam,
solidę veritati subnixam esse iam definitam rationem suam. Quod
non propterea facturam fatetur quasi sibi non creditum esse
putet, sed ut malivolis hominibus omnem deinceps blasphemandi
occasionem amputet. Respondetur nichil horum opus esse, quoniam
si malus homo de malo thesauro cordis sui protulerit mala dicto
citius opprimetur ipsa veritate iam tantarum personarum astipulatione probata et roborata. Allocutione post hęc et benedictione Anselmi potita abiit, et pauculis diebus evolutis fit, ut
dixi, regina et coniunx. Verum cum ipsa coniunctio iuxta ritum
[p. 143] ęcclesię fieri firmarique deberet, pater ipse totam
regni nobilitatem populumque minorem pro hoc ipso circumfluen-
tem necne pro foribus ęcclesię[2] regem et illam circumvallantem,
sullimius cęteris[a] stans in commune edocuit quo ordine causa

---

[a]eminentior *crossed out* B.

---

[1]No record of such a conciliar decision by Lanfranc survives, but *Lanf.*
Letters, ed. Clover and Gibson, no. 53, ed. Giles, no. 35, addressed to a
Bishop G., incorporates a similar ruling, issued with the king's assent.
[2]On Sunday 11 Nov. at St. Peter, Westminster (*ASC*, ed. Plummer, i.236,
ed. Clark, pp. 28-9; *Flor. Wig.* ii.47-8; WMGR ii.470 §393).

virginis quam fama vulgarat per episcopos et religiosas regni[a]
personas ventilata fuerit et determinata. Quo facto, monendo
auctoritate Dei praecepit quatinus si quis aliter de negotio
illo sentiret ac sententia tulerat, unde scilicet ipsam copu-
lam secundum legem christianam fieri non debere posset ostendi,
nichil hęsitans salva pace omnium coram proferret. Ad quę
cunctis una conclamantibus[b] rem iuste definitam, nec in ea quid
residere unde quis nisi forte malicia ductus iure aliquam posset
movere calumniam, legitime coniuncti sunt honore quo decuit
regem et reginam.

II. *Hermann, De restauratione ecclesiae Tornacensis*

> Brussels, Bibliothèque Royale de Belgique, ii.1020 (3791),
> fos. 5[v]-6 (formerly Cheltenham, Phillipps 11603); printed
> in *MGH Scriptores,* xiv.281, citing earlier editions, and
> *PL* clix.427-30.

Hic ergo confirmatus in regno voluit coniugem habere puellam
quandam, filiam David[1] regis Scotie, dixitque domno Anselmo,
tunc temporis Cantuariensis urbis venerabili archiepiscopo, ut
eam sibi benediceret et sollempnibus nuptiis benedictam in
coniugium sociaret. Respondit archiepiscopus se nolle eam bene-
dicere nec suo consilio regem in coniugium eam sibi sociaturum,
quoniam velum sanctimonialium, sicut ipse pro certo didicerat,
gestasset super caput suum, quo se celestis potius quam terreni
regis monstrasset fore sponsam. Rex econtra dixit se promisisse
et etiam iureiurando confirmasse patri eius regi David quod eam
coniugem duceret, ideoque pro conservando iuramento suo se non
eam dimissurum, nisi canonico iudicio fuisset determinatum,
precepitque ut ascito archiepiscopo Eburacensi[2] congregaretur
concilium episcoporum et abbatum totiusque Anglie ecclesiasticarum personarum ad diffiniendum ecclesiastica censura tantum

---

[a]regni *om.* B.   [b]clamantibus B.

---

[1]An error throughout for Malcolm III (1058-93). David was his son and
Matilda's brother, who ruled 1124-53.
[2]See above, p. 662 n. 1.

negotium. In generali ergo concilio requisita est abbatissa illa
in cuius monasterio puella illa fuerat nutrita,[1] utrumne re vera
more sanctimonialium velo capiti imposito benedictione episcopali fuisset consecrata. Respondit abbatissa publice coram
omnibus: 'Re vera rex David, pater eius, mihi eam commendavit
non ut sanctimonialis fieret, sed ut solummodo in ecclesia nostra
propter cautelam cum ceteris puellulis nostris coetaneis suis
nutriretur et litteris erudiretur. Cum autem iam adolevisset,
nuntiatum est mihi quadam die regem Guilelmum, domini mei regis
Henrici germanum, qui tunc vivebat, propter eam videndam venisse
iamque cum militibus suis ante ianuas ecclesie nostre descen-
disse utque ianue sibi orandi gratia aperirentur precepisse. Hoc
audiens nimiumque perterrita ne forte ille, ut iuvenis et rex
indomitus qui omne quod animo sibi occurrisset ilico facere
volebat, visa pulcritudine puelle aliquam ei illicitam violentiam faceret, qui tam improvisus et insperatus propter eam
videndam advenisset, in secretius cubiculum eam introduxi, rem
ei sicut erat aperui, eaque volente velum unum capiti eius impo-
sui quatinus eo viso rex ab illicito complexu revocaretur. Nec
me fefellit spes mea. Rex siquidem quasi propter inspiciendas
[fo. 6] rosas et alias florentes herbas claustrum nostrum ingressus, mox ut eam vidit cum ceteris puellis nostris velum
capite gestantem claustro exivit et ab ecclesia recessit, aperte
ostendens se nonnisi propter eam venisse. Cum autem rex David,
pater puelle, infra eamdem ebdomadam ad ecclesiam nostram venisset velumque super caput filie sue vidisset, iratus velum
conscidit et ad terram proiectum pedibus suis conculcavit filiam-
que suam secum reduxit.' Inquisita deinde abbatissa quot annorum
tunc fuisset puella, respondit duodennem esse potuisse. Tunc rege
monente archiepiscopum ut iuberet super hoc iudicium fieri,
episcopi et abbates, consilio accepto lectisque diversis capitu-
lis canonum, in commune iudicaverunt propter huiusmodi factum
non ei prohibendum coniugium quoniam, quamdiu infra legitimam
etatem sub tutela patris fuerat, nil ei sine eius assensu facere
licuerat. Finito iudicio, rex interrogavit archiepiscopum si

---

[1] If the abbey is Wilton this is probably Matilda, who occurs in 1093 x
1099 in *EA* 185 (*Heads,* p. 222), but see above p. 661 n. 3.

quid in eo vellet calumpniari. Respondit domnus Anselmus, se
non illud calumpniaturum, quoniam revera secundum canonum
decreta recte iudicassent. Tunc rex, 'Quandoquidem, inquit,
iudicium prolatum laudatis, volo ut puellam mihi desponsetis.'
Et domnus Anselmus, 'Iudicium, inquit, non reprehendo, sed si
maiestas vestra mihi credere vellet, ut eam non duceretis con-
sulerem quoniam, quomodocumque contigerit, tamen velum super
caput portavit, et sufficienter de filiabus regum aut comitum
vobis invenire possetis.' Rege vero in eo quod ceperat perse-
verante, subiunxit ille vir sanctissimus, 'Vos quidem, domne
rex, consilio meo pretermisso facietis quod vobis placuerit,
sed qui diutius vixerit, puto quod videbit non diu Angliam
gavisuram de prole que de ea nata fuerit.' Hec ego adolescens
eum dixisse audivi, nunc vero ex magna parte video iam contigisse.[a]

112

c.SEPTEMBER 1101. LEGATION OF JOHN, CARDINAL BISHOP OF TUSCULUM (FRASCATI), AND TIBERIUS, PAPAL CHAMBERLAIN

See Tillmann, pp. 22-3, Brett, *English Church*, pp. 48-9,
Hüls, pp. 141-2.

On 24 February, 1101, Paschal II informed Anselm that he was
sending John and Tiberius to England, and begged him to help
them, particularly it seems in composing the quarrel between
Duke Robert of Normandy and the king,[1] but also perhaps in
collecting Peter's Pence[2] and more general reform.

There is no proof that either of them reached England before

---

[a]*corr. from* contingisse.

---

[1]For John see further *Life of St. Anselm*, ed. Southern, p. 106n., Klewitz,
Reformpapsttum und Kardinalkolleg, p. 121, and W. Holtzmann in *Neues Archiv*
1 (1933), 277. For Tiberius and the recently created office of papal chamberlain see J. Sydow, *Deutsches Archiv* xi (1954/5), 41-62, summarizing
earlier literature. Paschal's letter is *EA* 213 (JL 5883).
[2]Hugh of Flavigny in *MGH Scriptores,* viii.494; compare *EA* 215.

Robert's invasion in July, and they first appear as witnesses
to charters granted at the royal court on 3 September at
Windsor, after the treaty of Alton.[1] The only evidence that may
cast light on their activities is an indulgence in the name of
Cardinal John for Bury St. Edmunds, an exempt house.[2]

113

c.29 SEPTEMBER 1102. COUNCIL AT WESTMINSTER

See Brett, *English Church*, pp. 76-9.

From the beginning of his rule Anselm had been anxious to celebrate a council for the reform of the church. In 1094 he had
urged on King William the need to condemn the spread of unnatural
vice and many infractions of the prohibited degrees of marriage,
but without success.[3] It was not until a truce had been patched
up with King Henry over investitures that he was at last able
to hold his council.

It opened at Westminster abbey about Michaelmas; according to
the Annals of Margam, which seem to have had access to a list of
councils with their duration which is otherwise unknown, the
council opened on 26 September and lasted two days,[4] an unusually short time. It is clear on other grounds that the business had to be hurried through. Contemporaries, little concerned
apparently with the conciliar statutes, were most struck by the
deposition of nine abbots or abbots-elect.[5] Of these nine two

---

[1]*Reg.* ii, nos. 544, 547-8. Tiberius attests no. 544 as *dapifer*, also a
novel title, discussed by Sydow, op. cit.

[2]Brett, *English Church*, p. 49 n. 4.   [3]Eadmer, pp. 48-9.

[4]*Ann. Mon.* i.7 (further ii.41, iv.374); see also *UGQ*, pp. 76 (Annals of
St. Augustine's) and 93 (Annals of Chichester) s.a. 1101, an error found in
some later annals including the Rochester series in BL ms. Cotton Vesp. A.
xxii, fo. 28, which may have been a source for the forger of *Registrum Roffense*, ed. J. Thorpe (London, 1769), p. 442 (*Mon.* i.175-6), a charter of
Anselm dated 1101 'in concilio prelatorum' with an impossible witness list.
Numerous similar entries under either 1101 or 1102 are found in later annals.

[5]Annals of Thorney in BL ms. Cotton Nero C. vii, fo. 81[V] s.a. 1102: 'Hoc
anno fuit concilium apud Lundon' ad festum S. Michaelis, Anselmo et Gerardo
archiepiscopis, rege Henrico, in quo multi abbates degradati sunt, et de
presbiteris constitutum ne uxores haberent'; below no. V. It may have been

of the three abbots already blessed who were deposed for simony
had been appointed by Rufus, and so perhaps had the third.[1]
Little is known of the three abbots-elect also deposed for
simony, but a circumstantial account of the election of the
abbot of Peterborough written at the abbey later in the century
explains that the monks proffered King Henry 300 marks for a
free election and then chose Godric.[2] Another Anglo-Saxon,
Ægelric of Milton, had also been appointed under Henry. Of the
remaining three, deposed on other grounds, Robert of Bury and
Richard of Ely had been given their abbeys by Henry at the very
beginning of his reign. While Anselm had given every support to
the monks of Bury in resisting the choice of Robert, the grounds
for the deposition of Richard are more obscure. The *Liber Eliensis* attributed his temporary fall to political rather than
ecclesiastical motives.[3] The anonymous abbot of Muchelney was
also probably appointed by Henry and deposed for irregular
appointment or defect of character.[4]

At this council Bishop Herbert of Norwich attempted again to
recover his authority over the abbey of Bury from which he had
been excluded by Alexander II and the repeated judgements of
the Conqueror and Lanfranc. It is said that one of the bishop's
objects in going on the royal embassy to Rome in 1101 had been
to secure the revocation of Alexander's grant, but although it
is quite likely that the matter was raised again in 1102 the
surviving account from Bury (no. IV) is unlikely to be wholly
reliable.[5] The *Quadripartitus* memorandum (no. V) recalls the

---

at this council that an attempt was made on the life of Vitalis of Savigny,
E. Sauvage, 'Vitae BB. Vitalis et Gaufridi', *Analecta Bollandiana,* i (1882),
373–4.

[1] *Heads,* pp. 59, 62, 72.
[2] *Chronicle of Hugh Candidus,* pp. 86–7; *Heads,* p. 60.
[3] For Milton see *Chronicon Monasterii de Abingdon,* ii.44, *Heads,* p. 56;
for Bury *UGQ,* pp. 130–1, *Mon.* iii.155, *EA* 251–2, 266–7, 269, 271, OV (ed.
Chibnall), v.296–8, *Memorials of St. Edmund's Abbey,* i.353–5, *Heads,* p. 32;
for Ely *Liber Eliensis,* pp. 226–7, 413, *Heads,* p. 45. Richard of Ely, Guy
of Pershore, and (ultimately) Aldwin of Ramsey later regained office.
[4] *EA* 228.
[5] Strictly the case could scarcely be opened during the vacancy consequent
on Robert's deposition. See further p. 682 n. 1 below. According to Eadmer,
pp. 132–3 and *Memorials of St. Edmund's Abbey,* i.353–4 Herbert of Norwich
had attempted to reopen the case at Rome in 1101.

last known judicial act of the council, the degradation of two monks for homicide.

The canons prepared in or for this gathering are the most extensive piece of legislation in England since the Conquest, but they suffered a curious fate, for there was insufficient time for a careful examination of the long list of provisions, and shortly after the council Anselm was contemplating a second council the following year in which to emend and perfect his text (no. IX). However, his departure for Rome at Easter in 1103 and subsequent exile prevented this, and so it is likely that no 'official' version of the full text ever circulated.[1] The archbishop's correspondence in the months following the council, which casts a most unusual measure of light on such activities,[2] shows that he was anxious that no complete text should circulate without revision. Accordingly he sent his archdeacon only 'nomina rerum de quibus ibi locuti sumus' and Archbishop Gerard a set of *capitula* (nos. VI, X). In form even the longest surviving draft of these canons is plainly incomplete compared with such texts as those of 1075 or 1125, and nos. VIII and X show that the canons as recited in the council were substantially fuller than this draft.

The limited circulation of the canons did not, however, prevent their being enforced. The decrees against married clergy and sodomy were pursued for a while with some zeal, though the canon against clerical marriage in particular provoked an active resistance, and even Eadmer remarked that the results were short-lived.[3]

The sources of this legislation are not easy to trace, not only because the text is abbreviated but also because the decrees of Urban's councils are still somewhat problematic. Those of Clermont and Piacenza in 1095 were known in England in one form

---

[1] But see *EA* 348.

[2] Somerville, *Councils of Urban II*, i.20-1; C.R. Cheney, in *Medieval Texts and Studies*, pp. 116-18.

[3] See particularly below nos. VII-X, *EA* 374, 391-2, Hunt., p. 234, who adds 'antea non prohibitas' to the condemnation of a married clergy in his source, and Symeon, ii.235: 'unde plures eorum ostia ecclesiarum obseraverunt, omittentes omnia officia ecclesiastica'. The provisions of c. 29 may be compared with the draconian legislation of C. of Naples (1120).

or another,[1] but there is little to show how canons of the two
papal councils which Anselm attended, Bari in 1098 and Rome in
1099, circulated; indeed no canons of Bari are known, and the
recorded canons of Rome simply restate decisions of Melfi in
1089 and Piacenza.[2] The more provocative canons concerning investiture and homage could scarcely find a place at Westminster
under the circumstances, but the surviving acts seem to show a
blend of Anglo-Norman tradition and recent papal influence of
a kind not seen in England since the Conquest.

The fullest text of the canons is that preserved in Eadmer's
Historia Novorum, which he describes as taken from the archbishop's own draft. It is found in:

A Cambridge, Corpus Christi Coll. ms. 452, pp. 162-6, the
autograph. The trivial variants in the later copy, BL
ms. Cotton Titus A. ix, fos. 65-6, have not been noted.
Similarly the versions in Malmesbury's *Gesta Pontificum*
and Oxford, Bodl. ms. Bodley 297, pp. 404-6 have no
independent value.[3]

B Lambeth Palace ms. 59, fos. 178[V]-9 (*c.*1125-30) has the
same form at the end of the Christ Church, Canterbury,
copy of the major collection of Anselm's letters as
archbishop.[4] There are early versions of this in Cambridge, Corpus Christi Coll. ms. 135 and Paris, BN ms.
lat. 2478. It is possible that the source was a draft
of the *Historia Novorum* (see below, p. 697), but it
might also be an independent copy of Eadmer's source,
and the text has been fully collated.

A quite independent version is found in:

---

[1]Somerville, *Councils of Urban II,* i.37-8, 54, 85 ff., 112 ff.; S. Wil-
liams, *Studia Gratiana,* xiii (1967), 27-43, above no. 105.
[2]Mansi, xx.961-4, above, no. 107.
[3]WMGP, pp. 118-21; Oxford, Bodl. ms. Bodley 297 is the only copy of *Flor.
Wig.* which here transcribes the whole of Eadmer's text; the rest follow
Flor. Wig. ii.51, a conflation of ASC and a very abbreviated Eadmer.
[4]Southern, *St. Anselm,* pp. 67-8n.

    C Paris, BN ms. lat. 13413, fos. 152^V-153^V, where it fol-
    lows immediately upon a copy of the 'Anglo-Norman'
    version of the canons of Clermont in a copy of Anselm's
    works once at Sées (early 12th cent.).[1]

In general it is much shorter than Eadmer's text, but the order
of the canons is slightly different, it includes one canon not
found elsewhere, and it supplies the full text of the excommunication which the council published.

    Another version was printed in Matthew Parker's *De Antiquitate
Britannicae Ecclesiae* (1572), pp. 104-5 'ex archivis'. Another
copy of this is found in the 16th-cent. BL ms. Cotton Titus
A. xiii, fos. 147-148^V. This gives every appearance of being an
abstract of Eadmer's text, from which it differs only by omission, and it has not been noted here.

    Eadmer's version was printed (ultimately from BL ms. Cotton
Titus A. ix) in W. i.382-3 and from A in Eadmer, pp. 141-4.
Malmesbury's copy is found in Sp. ii.23-5 and WMGP, pp. 118-21.
Also printed in Labbe, x.728-31, Mansi, xx.1229-32.

I. *Anglo-Saxon Chronicle 1102 E*

    Bodl. ms. Laud. Misc. 636, fo. 74^V, facsimile ed. White-
    lock in *Early English Manuscripts in Facsimile*, iv.148.
    Printed *ASC*, ed. Thorpe, i.366, ed. Plummer, i.238, ed.
    Clark, p. 30. Translated *ASC*, ed. Thorpe, ii.206, ed.
    Whitelock *et al.*, p. 178 (used here).

Ða þær æfter, to sancte	Then after that, at Michael-
Michaeles mæssen, wæs se cyng	mas, the king was at West-
æt Wæstmynstre, 7 ealle þa	minster, and all the chief
hæfod men on þis lande, geha-	men in this country, cleric
dode 7 læwede; 7 se arcebiscop	and lay; and Archbishop Anselm
Ansealm heold gehadodra manna	held a synod of clerics and
sinoð 7 hi ðær manega beboda	there they prepared many de-
setton þe to Christendome	crees pertaining to Christianity,

---

[1]Somerville, *Councils of Urban II*, i.85.

belimpað, 7 ægðer manige, Frencisce 7 Englisce, þær heora stafas 7 rice forluron, þe hi mid unrihte begeaton oððe[a] mid woge þær on lifedon.	and many, both French and English, lost their pastoral staffs and their authority, which they had obtained unjustly or lived in wrongfully.

II. *Eadmer, Historia Novorum in Anglia s.a. 1102*

> Cambridge, Corpus Christi Coll. ms. 452, pp. 161-6 (= A) and BL ms. Cotton Titus A. ix, fos. 64[v]-66[v] (= B). Printed from A and B in Eadmer, pp. 141-4 and from B in W. i.382-3 and *PL* clix.437-40, ultimately from the edition by Selden.

Per idem tempus celebratum est generale concilium episcoporum et abbatum totius regni in ęcclesia beati Petri apostolorum principis, quę in occidentali parte Lundonię sita est. Cui concilio pręsedit Anselmus archiepiscopus Dorobernensis, considentibus secum archiepiscopo Gerardo, [p. 162] Mauricio episcopo Lundoniensi, Willelmo electo episcopo Wintoniensi,[1] Roberto episcopo Lincoliensi, Sansone Wigornensi, Roberto Cestrensi, Iohanne Bathoniensi, Herberto Noruuicensi, Radulfo Cicestrensi, Gundulfo Rhofensi,[b] Herveo Pangorensi,[2] et duobus noviter investitis, Rogerio scilicet Serberiensi, et Rogerio Herefordensi. Osbernus autem Exoniensis infirmitate detentus interesse non potuit. In hoc concilio multa ęcclesiasticę disciplinę necessaria servari Anselmus instituit, quę postmodum sedis apostolicę pontifex sua auctoritate confirmavit.[3] Cuius concilii seriem sicut ab eodem patre Anselmo descripta est, huic operi inserere non incongruum existimavimus. Scribit itaque sic. (*There follows no. III*) ... [p. 165] Et hic quidem

---

[a] odde *ms.*   [b] Rofensi B.

---

[1] For the significance of the sequence of names here and in no. III see C. of London (1075), c. 1.

[2] This is the first clear case of a Welsh bishop attending an English church council since the Conquest, but Hervey had already been expelled from his diocese; see *Liber Eliensis*, p. 245, *EA* 282, Conway Davies, i.92-7.

[3] *EA* 348.

Lundoniensis concilii textus est, qui post non multos institutionis suę dies [p. 166] multos sui transgressores in omni hominum genere fecit. Sane quod ultimum de renovanda excommunicatione dominicis diebus statutum fuit, ipsemet Anselmus rationabili dispensatione usus postponi concessit. Finito concilio Anselmus Lundonia decessit.^a

III. *Canons of the council*

AB

Anno dominicę incarnationis millesimo centesimo secundo, quarto autem praesulatus Paschalis summi pontificis, tercio regni Henrici gloriosi regis Anglorum, ipso annuente, communi consensu episcoporum et abbatum et principum totius regni celebratum est concilium in ęcclesia beati Petri in occidentali parte iuxta Lundoniam^b sita. In quo praesedit Anselmus archiepiscopus Dorobernensis et primas totius Britannię, considentibus venerabilibus viris Gerardo Eboracensi archiepiscopo, Mauricio Lundoniensi episcopo,^c Guilielmo Wentonię^d electo episcopo, aliisque tam episcopis quam abbatibus. Huic conventui affuerunt, Anselmo archiepiscopo petente a rege, primates regni, quatinus quicquid eiusdem concilii auctoritate decerneretur, utriusque ordinis concordi cura et [p. 163] sollicitudine ratum servaretur. Sic enim necesse erat, quoniam multis retro annis sinodali cultura^e cessante, vitiorum vepribus succrescentibus, Christianę religionis fervor in Anglia nimis refrixerat.

[1] Primum itaque ex auctoritate sanctorum patrum symoniacę heresis surreptio in eodem concilio damnata est.¹ In qua culpa inventi depositi sunt Guido abbas de Perscore,^f et Wimundus de Tavestoc, et Ealdwinus de Rammesei,^g et alii nondum sacrati remoti ab abbatiis, scilicet Godricus de Burgo, Haimo de Cernel,

---

^adiscessit B.   ^biuxta Londoniam A; Lundonie B.   ^cepisc. *om.* B. ^dWillelmo Wintoniensi B.   ^ecura B.   ^fWido ... Perscole B.   ^get Eald. de Ramm. *om.* B.

---

¹CC. of Winchester (1070), c. 2, Windsor (1070), cc. 1, 2, Winchester (1072), c. 4, London (1075), c. 7, Rouen (1074), c. 1, Piacenza and Clermont (1095), *passim,* Rome (1099), c. 1.

Ægelricus de Middeltune. Absque simonia[a] vero remoti sunt ab abbatiis pro sua quisque causa[b] Ricardus de Heli et Robertus de Sancto Edmundo et qui erat[c] apud Micelenei.

[2] Statutum quoque est ne episcopi secularium placitorum officium suscipiant,[1] et ut non sicut laici, sed ut religiosas personas decet ordinatas vestes habeant, et ut semper et ubique honestas personas testes habeant suę conversationis.[2]

[3] Ut etiam archidiaconatus non dentur ad firmam.

[4] Ut archidiaconi sint diaconi.[3]

[5] Ut nullus archidiaconus, presbyter, diaconus, canonicus uxorem ducat, aut ductam retineat. Subdiaconus vero[d] quilibet qui canonicus non est, si post professionem castitatis uxorem duxit eadem regula constringatur.[4]

[6] Ut presbyter quamdiu illicitam conversationem mulieris habuerit, non sit legalis, nec missam celebret, nec si celebraverit eius missa audiatur.[5]

[7] Ut nullus ad subdiaconatum aut supra ordinetur sine professione [p. 164] castitatis.[6]

[8] Ut filii presbyterorum non sint heredes ęcclesiarum patrum suorum.[7]

---

[a]simonia A; his B.   [b]quisque pro sua causa B.   [c]qui erat *om.* B *leaving a space.*   [d]vero *om.* B.

[1]C. of London (1075), c. 9.
[2]C. of Windsor (1070), c. 3; C. of Toledo IV, c. 21, Gregory I, c. 2 in Hinschius, pp. 368, 746; compare above, p. 410 .
[3]CC. of Poitiers (1078), c. 7, Clermont (1095), cc. LL 1, VM 32 in Somerville, *Councils of Urban II,* i.75, 82.
[4]CC. of Rouen (1072), c. 15, Winchester (1076), c. 1, Lillebonne (1080), c. 3, Melfi (1089), cc. 2, 12, Clermont (1095), cc. LL 7, AN 5 in Somerville, *Councils of Urban II,* i.74, 91.
[5]Below nos. VIII, X, and previous n., C. of Clermont (1095), c. P 7 in Somerville, *Councils of Urban II,* i.111.
[6]C. of Rouen (1074), c. 5 and above pp. 616-17.
[7]CC. of Melfi (1089), c. 14, Clermont (1095), cc. LL 9, 23, AN 22 in Somerville, *Councils of Urban II,* i.76, 79-80, 95.

[9] Ne quilibet clerici sint secularium prępositi vel procuratores, aut iudices sanguinis.[1]

[10] Ut presbyteri non eant ad potationes, nec ad pinnas bibant.[2]

[11] Ut vestes clericorum sint unius coloris, et calciamenta ordinata.[3]

[12] Ut monachi vel clerici qui ordinem suum abiecerunt[a] aut redeant aut excommunicentur.[4]

[13] Ut clerici patentes coronas habeant.[5]

[14] Ut decimę nonnisi ęcclesiis dentur.[6]

[15] Ne ęcclesię aut prębendę emantur.[7]

[16] Ne novę capellę fiant sine consensu episcopi.[8]

[17] Ne ęcclesia sacretur donec provideantur necessaria et presbytero et ęcclesię.[9]

[18] Ne abbates faciant milites, et ut in eadem domo cum mona-

---

[a] abiecerint B.

---

[1] CC. of Winchester (1072), c. 10, London (1075), c. 9, above c. 2.
[2] CC. of Carthage III, c. 27, Laodicea, c. 24 in Hinschius, pp. 299, 275. For drinking 'to the pins' see WMGR, i.166 §149 and the note to Hardy's edition, i.237-8.
[3] CC. of Agde c. 20 (Hinschius, p. 333), Melfi (1089), c. 13, below no. X.
[4] CC. of Winchester (1070), c. 12, Windsor (1070), c. 8, Rouen (1072), cc. 11-12, Lillebonne (1080), c. 25.
[5] Compare Le De Officiis Ecclesiasticis *de Jean d'Avranches*, ed. R. Delamare (Paris, 1923), p. 4.
[6] CC. of Lillebonne (1080), c. 4, Clermont (1095), cc. LL 17, AN 26 in Somerville, *Councils of Urban II*, i.78, 96, Rouen (1096), c. 5.
[7] CC. of Rouen (1072), c. 13, (1074), c. 1, London (1075), c. 7, Clermont (1095), cc. LL 4, AN 7 in Somerville, *Councils of Urban II*, i.75, 92 (and compare ib. pp. 111, 114), Poitiers (1100), c. 7.
[8] C. of Winchester (1076), c. 7; compare Burchard, *Decretum,* iii, c. 7.
[9] Brett, *English Church,* p. 125 n. 6; compare C. of Lillebonne (1080) c. 14.

chis suis manducent et dormiant nisi necessitate aliqua prohibente.[1]

[19] Ne monachi pęnitentiam cuivis iniungant sine permissu abbatiṣ sui, et quod abbates eis licentiam de hoc dare non possunt, nisi de eis quorum animarum curam gerunt.[2]

[20] Ne monachi compatres vel monachę commatres fiant.[3]

[21] Ne monachi teneant villas ad firmam.[4]

[22] Ne monachi ęcclesias nisi per episcopos accipiant,[5] neque sibi datas ita exspolient suis redditibus, ut presbyteri ibi servientes in iis[a] quę sibi et ęcclesiis necessaria sunt penuriam patiantur.[6]

[23] Ut fides inter virum et mulierem occulte et sine testibus de coniugio data, si ab alterutro negata fuerit, irrita habeatur.[7]

[24] Ut criniti sic tondeantur ut pars aurium appareat, et

---

[a]his B.

---

[1]To elucidate this canon Selden cites numerous texts (*PL* clix.551-2), of which WMGR ii.360 §305, relating the knighting of Henry by Lanfranc, is the only solid reference to earlier practice. Compare also *Mon.*, iv.40-1, where Henry I provides that the abbot of Reading 'nec faciat milites nisi in sacra veste Christi', paralleled in later evidence from Battle, and Pseudo-Ingulf in *Rerum Anglicarum Scriptorum Veterum Tomus I*, ed. Fulman, p. 70, which is the most explicit and least reliable illustration of this.

[2]C. of Winchester (1076), c. 3, Poitiers (1100), c. 11, unidentified Anglo-Norman C. in Mansi, xx.400, c. 8.

[3]Ivo, *Decretum*, i, cc. 132-3; see Lynch, *American Ben. Review*, xxxi (1980), 108 ff.

[4]Possibly a reference to the obsolescent form of estate management described by G. Lambrick in *JEH* xvii (1966), 159-83.

[5]CC. of Winchester (1072), c. 5, Poitiers (1078), c. 6, Melfi (1089), c. 6, Clermont (1095), c. LL 5 in Somerville, *Councils of Urban II*, i.75 (also c. 9L 2), Rouen (1096), c. 6, Rome (1099), c. 16, Anglo-Norman council in Mansi, xx.400, c. 5. Compare Brett, *English Church*, pp. 141-4 and B. Kemp, 'Monastic Possession of Parish Churches in England in the Twelfth Century', *JEH* xxxi (1980), 137 ff.

[6]C. of Lillebonne (1080), c. 15.

[7]C. of Rouen (1072), c. 14; compare C. of Winchester (1076), c. 6.

oculi non tegantur.[1]

[25] Ne cognati usque ad septimam generationem [p. 165] ad
coniugium copulentur vel copulati simul permaneant, et si quis
huius incestus conscius[a] fuerit et non ostenderit, eiusdem
criminis se participem esse cognoscat.[2]

[26] Ne corpora defunctorum extra parochiam suam sepelienda
portentur, ut presbyter parochię perdat quod inde illi iuste
debetur.

[27] Ne quis temeraria novitate corporibus mortuorum aut fontibus aut aliis rebus, quod contigisse cognovimus, sine episcopali
auctoritate reverentiam sanctitatis exhibeat.[3]

[28] Ne quis illud nefarium negotium quo[b] hactenus homines in
Anglia[c] solebant velut bruta animalia venundari, deinceps ullatenus facere praesumat.[4]

[29] Sodomiticum flagitium[d] facientes, et eos in hoc voluntarie[e]
iuvantes, in eodem concilio gravi anathemate damnati sunt,
donec pęnitentia et confessione absolutionem mereantur.[5] Qui
vero in hoc crimine publicatus fuerit, statutum est si quidem

---

[a]conscius *interlined* B[1].   [b]quod B.   [c]in Anglia *om.* B.   [d]flagium B.
[e]voluntare B.

---

[1]C. of Rouen (1096), c. 6; compare Le De Officiis Ecclesiasticis *de Jean
d'Avranches*, p. 4, OV iv.188-92, *Vita Wulfstani*, p. 23, Eadmer, p. 48.
[2]CC. of Rouen (1072), c. 14, Winchester (1076), c. 6, Clermont (1095),
c. AN 20 in Somerville, *Councils of Urban II*, i.95 (a canon not found in
other versions).
[3]CC. of Lillebonne (1080), c. 34, London (1075), c. 8. Compare Anselm's
letters on the cult of Waltheof in *EA* 236-7.
[4]*Vita Wulfstani*, p. 43, V Æthelred 2, VI Æthelred Lat. 9, Liebermann,
i.488. The phrasing of this canon has no obvious source in law, but seems
to be something of a commonplace of the period. See for example *MGH Diplo-
mata*, iv, no. 130 (a diploma of Conrad II for Verden of 1027 x 9), Guibert
de Nogent, *Gesta Dei per Francos*, i.2 (*PL* clvi.688), and *Cosmae Pragensis
Chronica Boemorum* ed. B. Bretholz in *MGH Scriptores* (Octavo Ser., ii, 1923),
p. 92.
[5]For the prevalence of such vice see further OV iv.188, WMGR ii.369-70
§314, Hugh of Flavigny in *MGH Scriptores*, viii.496-7, *Epistolae Herberti
de Losinga*, no. 6. Compare C. of Rheims (1049), c. 11 in the edition of
Blumenthal.

fuerit persona religiosi ordinis, ut ad nullum amplius gradum promoveatur, et si quem habet ab illo deponatur. Si autem laicus, ut in toto regno Anglię legali suę conditionis dignitate[a] privetur. Et ne huius criminis absolutionem iis qui se sub regula vivere non voverunt aliquis nisi episcopus deinceps[b] facere praesumat. Statutum quoque est ut per totam Angliam in omnibus ęcclesiis et in omnibus dominicis diebus excommunicatio praefata renovetur.

C

Concilium Anselmi Cantuariensis Episcopi apud Lundonias

i. Ne episcopi officium accipiant placitandi. [fo. 153] (AB c. 2)

ii. De vestimentis episcoporum. (AB c. 2)

iii. De testimonio vitę eorum. (AB c. 2)

iv. Ut archidiaconatus non sint ad firmam. (AB c. 3)

v. Ut archidiaconi sint diaconi. (AB c. 4)

vi. De castitate archidiaconorum et canonicorum et presbiterorum et diaconorum et professorum subdiaconorum. (AB c. 5)

vii. Ut presbiter uxoratus non sit legalis. (AB c. 6)

viii. Ut filii presbiterorum non sint heredes ecclesiarum (AB c. 8)

ix. Ne presbiteri vel diaconi prepositi vel procuratores aut iudices sanguinis sint. (AB c. 9)

x. Ne ad potationes eant vel ad pinnas bibant. (AB c. 10)

---

[a] cond. dign. A; condignitate B.   [b] B *has a lacuna after* deinceps.

xi. Ut vestes eorum unius coloris sint. (AB c. 11)

xii. Ut nullus audiat missam presbiterorum uxoratorum. (AB c. 6)

xiii. Ut clerici vel monachi qui ordinem suum abiecerunt redeant aut excommunicentur. (AB c. 12)

xiv. Ut patenter coronas habeant. (AB c. 13)

xv. Ne ęcclesię emantur. (AB c. 15)

xvi. Ut decimę nisi ęcclesiis dentur. (AB c. 14)

xvii. Ne novę capellę fiant sine consensu episcopi. (AB c. 16)

xviii. Ne abbates adobbent aut faciant milites. (AB c. 18)

xviiii. Ne monachi cuivis penitenciam iniungant sine permissu abbatis sui, et quod abbates eis licentiam in hoc dare non possunt nisi super eos super quos ipsi inde potestatem habent. (AB c. 19)

xx. Ne monachi vel monachę compatres vel commatres fiant. (AB c. 20)

xxi. Ne monachi prepositi sint villarum. (AB c. 21)

xxii. Ne decimis ęcclesias despolient. (AB c. 22)

xxiii. Ne fides occulte detur. (AB c. 23)

xxiv. De his qui cognatas suas in coniugium habent. (AB c. 25)

xxv. Ut criniti tondeantur ita ut aures pareant. (AB c. 24)

xxvi. Ut longis tunicis vel talaribus non utantur.

xxvii.[a] Ne monachi vel clerici corpora alterius parrochię asportent. (AB c. 26)

xxviii. De noviter inventis sanctis et sacris ad fontes. (AB c. 27)

xxix.[b] Ne homines vendantur. (AB c. 28)

Excommunicatio sodomitarum. xxx. Ex auctoritate Dei Patris Omnipotentis et Filii et Spiritus Sancti et sanctorum apostolorum et sanctorum canonum excommunicamus et anathematizamus et a liminibus sanctę Dei [fo. 153^v] ęcclesię sequestramus N. et sicut candela ista extinguitur, ita lucerna eorum extinguatur ante tribunal domini nostri Ihesu Christi nisi resipuerint, et ad emendationem venerint Amen. Fiat, fiat.[1] (AB c. 29)

IV. *Bury St. Edmunds copy of the Worcester Chronicon ex chronicis*

> A passage added at the foot of Oxford, Bodl. ms. Bodley 297, pp. 406-7. Printed in *Memorials of St. Edmund's Abbey*, i.355. The addition appears to be contemporary with the main hand of *c.*1140, and a note indicates that it should follow *postponi concessit* at the end of no. II above.

Anno eodem et in eodem concilio, id est iii^o Henrici regis anno, Herebertus episcopus Norwicensis proposuit calumniam satis facunde de subiectione ecclesie[c] sancti Ædmundi multisque de causis iustam ac necessariam ibi fore suam praelationem. Sed causa diligenter ventilata, calumpniam ipsius irritam esse debere comprobavit ac decrevit universa sinodus, quia episcopi quamplures et abbates necnon duces regii considentes affirma-

---

[a]xxviii ms.   [b]xxviiiii *after* vendantur ms.   [c]ecclesia *ms.*

---

[1]Of the conveniently available formulae of excommunication this is closest to that in the Textus Roffensis (Liebermann, i.440 (ix)), but has distinctive features.

verunt se interfuisse causis Arfasti episcopi et Baldwini abbatis,[1] ipsumque Arfastum a causa cecidisse, abbatem vero Bald-
winum per legitimos testes comprobasse se ac suam abbatiam per
quinquaginta tres annos[2] liberam et quietam ac sine calumnia
fuisse ab omnibus antecessoribus ipsius Arfasti. Demonstrasse
quoque testati sunt praedictum abbatem suum monasterium dedica-
tum ab archiepiscopo Agethnotho Doroberensi[3] seque postea abbatem consecratum fuisse a metropolitano eiusdem sedis,[4] antecessorum etiam [p. 407] ipsius, alterum ab episcopo Lundoniensi,
alterum a presule Wintoniensi ordinatos,[5] monacos[a] quoque sui
monasterii a quibuslibet episcopis ad diversos ordines promo-
tos[b] sine contradictione Tetfordensis episcopi eleganti testimonio comprobasse. Discussa tandem causa calumniaque prefati
Herberti honestis rationibus refutata per decretum universalis
concilii, ne mutire quidem ausus est deinceps contra ecclesiam
sancti Eadmundi quoad vixerat.

V. *Quadripartitus*

> BL ms. Add. 49366 (formerly Holkham 228), fo. 103[v] (= H),
> Manchester, John Rylands Lib. ms. Lat. 420, fo. 38[v] (= G),
> and BL ms. Cotton Titus A. xxvii, fo. 155[v] (= T). Printed
> in *Quad.*, p. 154. For this text see also above p. 15
> n. 2.

Post reditum autem predictorum nuntiorum[6] habitum est Lundonie
famosum illud concilium de archidiaconis et canonicis et pres-
byteris in uxoribus abiurandis; ne monachi vel presbyteri sint

---

[a]monachos *corr. in another hand.*   [b]permotos *ms.*

---

[1]This is a summary of the account by Herman the archdeacon in *UGQ*, pp.
255-7 (*Memorials of St. Edmund's Abbey,* i.65-7); the session appears to have
occurred in 1081 (M. Gibson, *Lanfranc,* p. 149). No bishop or abbot then in
office is known to have survived to 1102, but possibly some of those present
had attended the earlier occasion before their promotion.
[2]Fifty-one years in Herman's account.   [3]1020-38.
[4]On 15 August 1065 (*UGQ,* p. 245), and therefore by Stigand, if Herman is
to be believed.
[5]Abbots Ufi (1020-44) and Leofstan (1044-65).
[6]Archbishop Gerard of York and the bishops of Chester and Norwich, Eadmer,
pp. 132-7.

prepositi laicorum, de superfluis crinibus et vestibus; ut
occulta vota pueri vel puelle sint irrita; de sodomitis publicę
excommunicandis. Depositi sunt ibi duo[a][1] abbates propter
simonie circumventionem.[b] Exordinati duo monachi propter homi-
cidium in ęcclesia.

VI. *Letter of Anselm to Archbishop Gerard (part)*

> Printed *EA*, ed. Schmitt, 253, citing earlier edns., espe-
> cially IV.15 in *PL* clix.209-10.

Capitula concilii solummodo mitto, quia sententiarum eorum ex-
positiones nulli volo transcribere, donec vestro et aliorum
episcoporum, qui in concilio affuerunt, approbentur iudicio.

VII. *Letter of Anselm to Bishop Herbert of Norwich*

> Printed *EA*, ed. Schmitt, 254, also IV.113 in *PL* clix.260-
> 1. Here based on Lambeth Palace, ms. 59, fo. 94.

Anselmus, servus ęcclesię Cantuariensis Herberto, episcopo
Thiotfordensi, salutem.

De presbiteris de quibus quęrit vestra prudentia consilium,
respondeo quia nichil relaxandum est de iis quę constituta sunt
in concilio. Quoniam autem ipsi malunt dimittere quicquid pertinet ad presbiteri officium quam feminas, si aliqui inveniuntur
casti, faciant pro illis. Si autem nullus aut paucissimi tales
inveniuntur, iubete ut interim monachi missas dicant populo,
ubi ipsi fuerint, et faciant corpus Domini, quod per clericos
portetur egrotis. Qui clerici vestra iussione vice vestra
accipiant confessionem et faciant absolutionem et sepeliant
corpora mortuorum. Quę omnia etiam monachis provectioris ętatis
precipere potestis, donec ista duricia presbiterorum Deo visi-
tante mollescat. Non enim diu durabit Deo propitiante, si in
incępto perseveraverimus. De baptismo vos scitis quia quicumque

---

[a]duo ibi G.   [b]et *add* T.

---

[1]See above, p. 674 n. g, but probably an error.

baptizet, Christus baptizat.

Laicis omnibus, maioribus et minoribus, ex parte Dei et ex parte omnium nostrum, qui hoc constituimus in concilio, rogando pręcipite ut, si Christianos se confitentur, adiuvent vos, quatinus expellatis presbiteros concilio inobędientes de ęcclesiis et rebus earum, et dignos pro illis constituatis. Et si expulsi contra illos qui in ęcclesiis caste servire voluerint, aut aliquo alio modo in aliquam superbie temeritatem proruperint, omnes Christiani sint contra illos, et non solum a societate sua, sed etiam a terris quas de illis habent, eos cum feminis suis excludant, donec resipiscant.

VIII. *Letter of Archbishop Gerard to Anselm*

> Printed *EA*, ed. Schmitt, 255, citing earlier edn. Here
> based on Lambeth Palace ms. 59, fo. 181^{r-v}.

Patri et domino vere dilecto et vere diligendo, Anselmo, Cantuariensi archiepiscopo Girardus, Eboracensis ęcclesię humilis servus, salutem.

Cervus sitiens ad fontem currit, et viator ex itinere fatigatus ubi requiescat attentus inquirit. Ego sitiens et lassus ad fontem sapientię vestrę et ad requiem consilii vestri confugio. Sitio clericorum meorum integritatem, et in ea requiescere volo. Sed preter in paucis admodum vel aspidis surditatem vel fabulosi cuiusdam Prothei mutabilitatem invenio. Arent ad verbum 'pudicitię', quia sancti spiritus carent unctione. Variis linguarum aculeis modo minas, modo convitia infligunt. Sed hoc facilius in iis qui remotiores sunt tolero. Illud autem difficile, illud omnino grave genus mali est, quod ii qui quasi in sinu meo sunt, qui canonicorum nomine gaudent, canones aspernantur, adversus concilii vestri statuta quasi sophistici disputatores argumentantur. Ecce dicunt: Iuxta concilium in domibus nostris fęminę non erunt.[1] Sed nulla concilii regula prohibet, quin in domibus vicinorum nostrorum cum fęminis soli et sine teste conversemur. Professiones vero mihi pęnitus abnegant canonici illi, qui sine

---

[1] Some such phrase was perhaps in the text of c. 5 or 6 in the form known at York, but is not in either surviving version.

professione ad sacros ordines inordinabiliter sunt provecti. Hi
etiam, qui in presbiterio vel diaconatu constituti, et uxores
sive concubinas in publico hactenus habuerunt, et ab altari
nulla se reverentia continuerunt. Sed quomodo eis sine professione castitatis corporis et sanguinis Domini consecrationem
vel ministerium credam, quorum praesumptio diutius inter ipsa
luxurię inquinamenta hęc tractavit, ut vicissim et publice a
thoro concubinarum ad altare, ab altari ad eundem nequitię
thorum reverterentur? Cum vero ad ordines aliquos invito, dura
cervice renituntur, ne in ordinando castitatem profiteantur,
miraque superbia et de beneficiis ęcclesiarum divites esse
presumunt et ad altaris officium ipsi dedignantur. Ita canonicis a longe stantibus et de divitiis ęcclesiarum superbientibus,
ad altaris servitium extranei conducuntur.

In his interim, pater sancte, me nutantem firma, lassum
recrea, sitientem refrigera, ut auctoritate litterarum tuarum
confir[fo. 181^V]matus, securius prelier prelium Domini, et
scuto protectionis tuę munitus, minus timeam iacula adversę
partis. Pręcipe, ut pari forma et a canonicorum domibus mulieres
et a mulierum domibus canonici abstineant. Pręcipe, ut qui
contra ordinem presbiteri vel diaconi sine professione[a] ordinati sunt, professionem ex integro faciant, si et ordine et
honore gaudere volunt. Pręcipe, ne pro canonico persona ad
altaris ministerium conducatur, dum canonicus, ut mundo liberius
vacet, ordinari dedignatur. Et qui archidiaconi infra diaconi
ordinem sunt constituti, si vice perversa maluerint archidiaconatus dimittere quam ordinari, nec adquieverint ut ordinem
honore dignum suscipiant, praebendarum amissione adquiescere
cogantur.

Quidam sacerdotis filius et archidiaconi donum prebendę
patris sui et decimarum quas pater tenuerat, patre adhuc, sicut
et modo est, superstite, precio interveniente a me suscepit.
Quod quia cum peccato factum, sine peccato durare posse non
video, pecuniam post concilium reddere volui et inhonestum
commercium destruere patrique sua, dum viveret, dimittere. Sed
et oblatam pecuniam recipere noluerunt, et ut res contra Deum

---

[a]sine professione *added in margin.*

facta firmitatem habeat ratiocinando contendunt. In hac causa
nullius preces, nullius vanę supplicationes sanctitatis tuę
veritatem emolliant. Sed te omnino annuente, adiuvante, praeci-
piente licet mihi rem malefactam destruere, ne totiens peccatum meum mihi occurrat, quotiens emptorem ęcclesię mecum in
ęcclesia videro, cui et pecuniam suam reddere volui et adhuc,
prout iustum fuerit, reddere volo.

Te, pater, culpa respiciet, si Eboracensis ęcclesia penuria
auxilii tui inordinata remanserit. Nescit enim, nescit sanctitas vestra quę patimur, cui felicem[a] primę ęcclesię statum
representat iocunda et Deo placens unitas monachorum.

Valete, et inter illa quę cotidie cum Deo habetis orationum
et pietatis[b] commercia, mei, precor, mementote. Litteras istas
rogo ne videant, qui in causa Dei et vobis et nobis adversan-
tur. Religiosi viri, qui vobis abundant, eas videant, et ut
mihi subveniatis ipsi quoque precatores accedant.

IX. *Letter of Anselm to Archbishop Gerard*

> Printed *EA* 256, ed. Schmitt, formerly IV.16 (*PL* clix.210).
> Here from Lambeth Palace, ms. 59, fo. 94[r-v].

Anselmus, servus ęcclesię Cantuariensis, reverendo archiepiscopo
Gerardo Eboracensi salutem.

Lętor de vestro bono et religioso studio circa clericorum
vestrorum integritatem. Ad ea vero de quibus vestra prudentia
nostrum petit consilium, respondeo quia de iis quę in concilio
nostro et coepiscoporum nostrorum communi consensu statuta sunt,
nichil relaxandum consulo. De illis autem de quibus in eodem
concilio non tractavimus, non enim simul omnia necessaria
potuimus, ut de ablatione prębendarum ante idem con[fo. 94^v]ci-
lium venditarum et de similibus, quoniam non solum ad meam et
vestram personam et ęcclesias nostras pertinent, sed etiam ad
multas ęcclesias et personas, et in his multi dissentiunt,[c]
conveniens mihi videtur ut in proxima Nativitate Domini[1] nostro

---

[a]*added at head of leaf.*   [b]et pietatis *interlined.*   [c]sed etiam ...
dissentiunt *added at head of leaf.*

---

[1]Probably Christmas, 1103, since the letters suppose the passage of some
time since the council.

et coepiscoporum nostrorum communi consilio, Deo dictante,
sententiam certam statuamus.

X. *Letter of Anselm to Archdeacon William of Canterbury*

Printed *EA* 257, ed. Schmitt, formerly III.62 (*PL* clix.
94-7). Here from Lambeth Palace, ms. 59, fos. 94^V-95.

Anselmus archiepiscopus Willelmo archidiacono,[1] dilecto suo,
salutem et benedictionem.

Sententias capitulorum concilii expositas nolo vobis aut
alicui ad pręsens mittere, quia, quando in ipso concilio expositę sunt, non potuerunt ad plenum et perfecte recitari, propterea quia subito sine pręmeditatione ac competenti tractatione,
sicut oportuerat, sunt prolatę. Unde quędam videntur addenda
et forsitan quędam^a mutanda, quod non nisi communi consensu
coepiscoporum nostrorum volo facere. Volo ergo eas dictare et
prius eisdem episcopis ostendere, cum convenerimus, prius quam^b
per ęcclesias Anglię dictatę et expositę mittantur. Nomina
tamen rerum, de quibus ibi locuti sumus, vobis mittimus, ut
secundum quod recordari poteritis nos de illis decrevisse,
faciatis.

De illis qui ante excommunicationem, vel post excommunicationem nescientes eam factam, sodomitico peccato peccaverunt,
par et similis erit sententia, si confitentes pęnitentiam
petierint. Quam secundum discretionem vestram dabitis, consi-
derantes ętatem, peccati diuturnitatem, et utrum habeant uxores
an non, et secundum quod videritis eos ex corde pęnitere et
deinceps integram correctionem promittere. Considerandum etiam
est quia actenus ita fuit publicum hoc peccatum, ut vix aliquis
pro eo erubesceret, et ideo multi magnitudinem eius nescientes
in illud se precipitabant. Illi vero, qui post excommunicationem cognitam eodem se peccato contaminaverunt, graviori sunt
multandi pęnitentia. Quam etiam in vestra discretione secundum

---

^{a}videntur ... quedam *interlined.* ^{b}convenerimus prius quam *over an*
erasure; primo convenerimus, quam *Schmitt.*

---

[1]Above, p. 662 n. 5.

prędictas causas ponimus. De iis qui tonderi nolunt, dictum
est, ut ęcclesiam non ingrederentur;[1] non tamen pręceptum est,
ut, si ingrederentur, cessarent sacerdotes, sed tantum annun-
tiarent illis quia contra Deum et ad damnationem suam ingrediun-
tur. De calciamentis laicorum nichil decrevimus, sed tantum
clericorum.

De archidiaconibus et canonicis, qui uxores suas derelictas
extra domos suas in maneriis suis ponunt, existimo interim,
donec aliud statuatur, tolerandum, si certam promissionem
fecerint se nullam conversationem cum illis habituros nec sine
legitimis testibus locuturos.[2] De presbiteris, qui timore non
audent feminas suas relinquere, quod statutum est in concilio
servabitur, [fo. 95] quia quamdiu eas aliqua occasione tene-
bunt, nec missas celebrabunt nec legales erunt, sed tantum
usque ad initium Quadragesimę si habuerint qui pro illis caste
in ęcclesiis serviant, beneficiis ęcclesię non privabuntur.
Illos autem qui presbiteros propinquas suas dimittere prohibent,
sicut eos qui contra Deum et contra Christianitatem agunt ar-
guite, et totum peccatum fornicationis presbiterorum illis
imputandum ostendite, et nostram et omnium coepiscoporum nostrorum excommunicationem illis certam promittite.

114

*c.*1102-1106. MINOR LEGATIONS

It is possible that Oddo II, cardinal bishop of Ostia, was in
England soon after the translation of St. Milburga on 2 February 1102, for the unique late twelfth-century manuscript of an
account of her invention has the rubric 'Incipit prologus
domni Atonis Ostiensis episcopi cardinalis ...' The author was
clearly a Cluniac monk who had visited Wenlock in person, and
he describes himself as a citizen of Milan. Atto is a frequent
name in north Italy, and none of this information is clearly
inconsistent with what little is known of Oddo's career from

---

[1] See c. 24, which lacks this detail.
[2] Compare cc. 5, 6 with C. of London (1108), c. 2.

other sources; no later bishop of Ostia before 1200 bore a name
which could be credibly represented as Ato. However, the author
seems to be writing after 1109, for he speaks of Anselm as
'then archbishop';[1] mystery attends the later years of Oddo,
whose last probable occurrence is on 31 March 1102 in Rome, but
whose successor does not appear before 1106/7.[2] It remains
difficult to believe that a visit from so eminent a legate could
have passed entirely unnoticed in the comparatively abundant
sources for the years 1102/7.

Tiberius, already a legate in 1101, was the bearer of papal
letters again in the summer of 1103, when he met Anselm, probably at Bec. He had been ordered to look to the collection of
Peter's Pence, which Gundulf of Rochester was then gathering on
the archbishop's behalf, but there is now no proof that he ever
reached England.[3] A number of other papal messengers are implied by Paschal's correspondence with England and the king
between Anselm's exile and his return in 1106, but their names
are not recorded.

115
1-*c*.4 AUGUST 1107. COUNCIL AT WESTMINSTER

> See Southern, *St. Anselm*, pp. 174-9, Eadmer, pp. 163-88,
> *Life of St. Anselm*, pp. 134-40, *EA* 355-423. For the
> events of 1100-1105 see above no. 110.

Considerable delays attended the embassy to Rome upon which
Anselm and the king had agreed at their interview at Laigle in
July 1105, and it was not until late in March that Baldwin of
Bec and William Warelwast received their answer. No extant

---

[1] A.J.M. Edwards, *Trans. of the Shropshire Archaeological Soc.*, lvii
(1961-4), 134-51 describes and translates the text, of which she gave a full
account in 'Odo of Ostia's history of the translation of St. Milburga and
its connection with the early history of Wenlock Abbey'. Of her printed
text see particularly pp. 143-4, 146, 151.
[2] On Oddo II see the references collected by Klewitz, *Reformpapsttum und
Kardinalkolleg*, pp. 115, 119 and Hüls, pp. 57, 103-4.
[3] *EA* 299, 301.

letter of Paschal to the king had ever formally required him to
abandon the homage of ecclesiastics, though his earlier letters
laid great stress on canonical election, whatever the content
of the verbal messages which had been sent. By the end of 1102
he was no longer mentioning homage even in his letters to Anselm, and election was also passed over.[1] Since Henry was already prepared to abandon investitures by late 1105 in order to
secure a settlement it is unremarkable that Paschal's letter
of 23 March 1106 empowered Anselm to restore to communion all
those who had formerly received investiture and done homage.
Henceforward any candidate for preferment who had done homage
might be consecrated, provided that he had not received investiture. Anselm's urgings, it was hoped, might later induce Henry
to abandon homage also. Only Richard, abbot-elect of Ely, who
had been deposed at the council of 1102, had travelled to Rome
with Anselm in 1103, and then returned to be reconciled with
the king before February 1105, was exempted from the general
settlement.[2]

The chief consequences of this agreement were discussed at a
meeting between king and archbishop at Bec on 15 August, and
by 28 September Anselm was back in England, though Henry remained in Normandy after his victory at Tinchebrai and did not

---

[1] The letters of Paschal to Henry *EA* 216 (JL 5868) of 1101/2 and 224 (JL
5910) of Apr. 1102 deal with both election and investiture, while all later
letters deal explicitly only with investiture. Of his letters to Anselm
EA 222 (JL 5908) of Apr. 1102, on which see now Blumenthal, *Early Councils
of Pope Paschal II*, pp. 17-18, deals with homage, investiture and election,
EA 281 (JL 5928) of Dec. 1102 deals with investiture and election only, and
no subsequent letter makes any specific demands about homage. Compare the
judgement of Hugh the Chanter, ed. Johnson, p. 14 (*Hist. York*, ii.110-11)
and the discussion by Hoffmann, *Deutsches Archiv* xv (1959), 409-23, supplemented by R. Sprandel, *Ivo von Chartres und seine Stellung in der Kirchen-
geschichte*, pp. 161-9.
[2] For Henry's position after the meeting at Laigle see *EA* 389; *EA* 397
(JL 6073) is the decisive letter of Paschal informing Anselm rather obliquely
of the compromise. At the Council of Guastalla in October 1106 no surviving
canon contains a denunciation of homage, and much attention was devoted to
the canonical authority for remitting the penalties for those German bishops
who had repented of their improper consecration; similarly at Troyes in May
1107 (c. 5) the pope condemned only investiture (Blumenthal, *Early Councils
of Pope Paschal II*, pp. 32-101). For the career of Abbot Richard of Ely in
these years see *Liber Eliensis*, pp. 227-35, 413, *Heads*, p. 45, *Reg.* ii,
nos. 684-5.

cross the Channel until the spring of 1107. A formal end to the
dispute was then further delayed by news of Paschal's intention
to hold a council at Troyes and by Anselm's illness, which
delayed him at Bury until after 2 June.[1]

At last a great council of prelates and magnates met at
Westminster on 1 August, 1107.[2] After three days of debate the
settlement was finally confirmed, though no formal act survives
to record it, and none may have been issued. The way was now
open for a good deal of business which had been suspended for
the last five years. The most pressing was the filling of a number of vacancies; new abbots were certainly chosen for Peterborough and Battle in this assembly, and the Anglo-Saxon chronicl
refers to others in England and Normandy in general terms.[3]
The first known meeting of Anselm and Gerard of York since the
issue of Paschal's bull of 1103 with its cautious confirmation
of the primacy of Canterbury[4] was the natural occasion for a
demand for a profession from Gerard, but the king persuaded
·Anselm to settle for an undertaking that Gerard would maintain
the obedience he had already professed as bishop-elect of

---

[1]Eadmer, pp. 182-5.
[2]Eadmer gives London but 'in palatio regis'; ASC has Westminster, and
the writs probably associated with this council are dated, if at all, there
also: *Reg.* ii, nos. 827, 831, 833. The suspicious text *Reg.* ii, no. 828 has
a long witness-list consistent with its supposed date which is probably
authentic, and so casts light on the attendance at the council. It is noteworthy that the bishops attest in the order of precedence laid down in C. of
London (1075) c. 1, with the exception of Bishop Robert, of Chester or Lincoln.
[3]Compare no. II below with *Chronicle of Hugh Candidus*, p. 90: 'Post hec
factum est grande concilium apud Lundoniam, ibique dati sunt multi episcopatus et abbatie, oblatusque est monachis de Burch prior de archiepiscopatu
Cancie, Ernulfus nomine' and *Chron. Battle*, p. 116: '... rex Henricus, con-
gregato universali concilio, cum multis orbatis ecclesiis pastores secundum
canones delegasset ... quendam suorum consilio asciscens ... Radulfum ...
prefecit abbatem ecclesie. Qui in die sancti Petri ad vincula (1 Aug.) elec-
tus· ...' Both Eadmer and ASC mention many other abbots in England and Normandy. The English abbots probably included Hugh at St. Augustine, Canterbury (Eadmer, p. 188), Hugh of Chertsey and Peter of Gloucester, and there
were possibly others (*Heads*, pp. 36, 38, 52 and compare ibid. pp. 32, 72,
82). A number of Norman abbots had been appointed by Henry in Normandy after
Tinchebrai; none is explicitly said to have been chosen at the August council,
but perhaps some earlier nominations were then confirmed.
[4]*EA* 283 (JL 5930), ordering Gerard to make a profession, was issued on
12 Dec. 1102, but may have been one of those Anselm did not open until he
left England in 1103 (above, p. 658 n. 2); the primacy was confirmed by
Paschal in *EA* 303 (JL 5955) of 16 Nov. 1103.

Hereford in 1096. A week later five bishops-elect presented themselves at Canterbury for consecration by Anselm, assisted by five of his suffragans with Archbishop Gerard and Ranulf of Durham. The last stage of the reconciliation was marked at the same time by the restoration of Abbot Aldwin of Ramsey, deposed with Richard of Ely in 1102 and like him reinstated by papal favour.[1]

Although the events of this council were of great importance the account by Eadmer, printed below, is the only one which treats them at any length; the chronicle of Worcester follows it very closely, while the brief notices elsewhere deal only with the appointments which were made in such remarkable numbers.[2]

I. *Eadmer, Historia Novorum in Anglia s.a. 1107*

> Cambridge, Corpus Christi Coll. ms. 452, pp. 220-2 (= A) and BL ms. Cotton Titus A. ix, fos. 86[v]-87 (= B). Printed in Eadmer, pp. 186-7, from A and B, and from B in W. i.386-7 and *PL* clix.465-6, ultimately from the edition of Selden.

In kalendis ergo Augusti conventus episcoporum, abbatum et[a] procerum regni Lundonię in palatio[b] regis factus est, et per tres continuos dies absente Anselmo inter regem et episcopos satis a[p. 221]ctum de ęcclesiarum investituris, quibusdam ad-hoc nitentibus ut rex eas faceret more patris et[c] fratris sui, non iuxta preceptum et obędientiam apostolici. Nam papa in sententia quę exinde promulgata fuerat firmus stans concesserat hominia quę Urbanus papa ęque ut investituras interdixerat, ac per hoc regem sibi de investituris consentaneum fecerat, ut ex

---

[a]*om.* B.   [b]palatium B.   [c]ac B.

---

[1]Richard was restored to papal grace by *EA* 422 (JL 6152) of 30 May, but died on 16 June (*Liber Eliensis*, p. 413).

[2]Compare no. II below with the passages cited above p. 691 n. 3 and the quite unreliable passage printed from a ms. of the Crowland chronicle in Sp. ii.28 (W. i.387). The passage in the *Life of St. Anselm*, pp. 139-40 in general follows no. I (below), but also asserts that the king promised not to choose prelates 'per se'.

epistola quam supra descripsimus colligi potest.[1] Dehinc praesente Anselmo, astante multitudine, annuit rex et statuit ut ab
eo tempore in reliquum nunquam per dationem baculi pastoralis
vel anuli quisquam episcopatu aut[a] abbatia per regem vel quamlibet laicam manum in Anglia investiretur,[b] concedente quoque
Anselmo ut nullus in praelationem electus pro hominio quod regi
faceret consecratione suscepti honoris privaretur. Quibus ita
dispositis, pene omnibus ęcclesiis Anglię quę suis erant pastoribus diu viduatę per consilium Anselmi ac procerum regni sine
omni virgę pastoralis aut anuli investitura patres a rege sunt
instituti. Instituti quoque sunt ibidem et eodem tempore ab
ipso rege quidam ad regimen quarundam ęcclesiarum Normannię,
quę similiter suis erant patribus destitutę. Inter ista cępit
Anselmus coram rege regnique episcopis atque principibus exigere
a Gerardo archiepiscopo Eboracensi professionem de sua[c] subiectione, quam non fecerat ex quo de episcopatu Herefor[p. 222]-
densi in archiepiscopatum Eboracensem ut supra meminimus translatus fuerat.[2] Ad quę cum rex ipse diceret sibi quidem non
videri necesse esse ut professioni quam ordinationis suę tempore Gerardus fecerat aliam superadderet, praesertim cum, licet
ęcclesiam mutaverit, idem tamen qui fuerat in persona perman-
serit nec a prima professione absolutus extiterit, Anselmus in
praesenti quidem regiis verbis adquievit, ea conditione ut
Gerardus in manum sibi daret se eandem subiectionem in archiepiscopatu ei servaturum quam in episcopatu professus fuerat.
Annuit Gerardus et, sua manu imposita manui Anselmi, interposita fide sua pollicitus est se eandem subiectionem et
obędientiam ipsi et successoribus eius[d] in archiepiscopatu
exhibiturum quam Herefordensi ęcclesię ab eo sacrandus antistes
illi[e] promiserat.[3]

---

[a]vel B.   [b]investiretur in Anglia B.   [c]obedientia et *add* B.   [d]suis B.
[e]om. B.

---

[1]*EA* 397 (JL 6073).
[2]6 January 1101 according to Hugh the Chanter, ed. Johnson, p. 12 (*Hist.
York*, ii.109).
[3]See the note attached to Gerard's profession as bishop of Hereford from
BL ms. Cotton Cleop. E. i, fo. 29 in *Canterbury Professions*, no. 53. Later
tradition at York attacked this account (*Hist. York*, ii.365-6).

II. *Anglo-Saxon Chronicle 1107 E*

> Bodl. ms. Laud. Misc. 636, fos. 76^V-77, facsimile ed.
> Whitelock in *Early English Manuscripts in Facsimile*,
> iv.152-3. Printed *ASC*, ed. Thorpe, i.368, ed. Plummer,
> i.241, ed. Clark, pp. 33-4. Trans., ed. Thorpe, ii.209,
> ed. Whitelock *et al.*, pp. 180-1 (used here).

On þisum geare ... se cýng Henri ... syððan eft to Augustes anginne on Westmýnstre wæs, 7 þær þa biscopricen 7 abbodricen geaf 7 sette þe on Englelande oððe on Normandige buton ealdre 7 hýrde wæron.[a] Ðera wæron swa fela swa nan man næs þe gemvnde þet æfre ær swa fela togædere gyfene wæron; 7 æt þes ýlcan [fo. 77] syðe,[b] onmang þa oðre[c] þe abbodrices underfengon, Ernulf, þe ær wæs prior on Cantwarbýrig,[1] feng to þam abbodrice on Burh.

In this year ... King Henry ... afterwards again at the beginning of August was at Westminster, and there he gave and disposed of the bishoprics and abbacies that there were in England or Normandy without ruler or pastor. These were so many that no man could remember that so many had ever been given together before; and at this same time, among the others who received abbacies, Ernulf, who had been prior at Canterbury,[1] succeeded to the abbacy of Peterborough.

116

c.28 MAY 1108. PRIMATIAL COUNCIL AT LONDON

See Brett, *English Church*, pp. 79-80, 98.

Anselm's second council was held during the royal court at Whitsun 1108, which fell that year on 24 May. All but one of

---

[a]wæron *om.* ms.; *suppl. edd.*   [b]syde ms.   [c]oðre ms.

---

[1]Prior of Christ Church *c*.1096-1107 (*Heads*, p. 33).

the versions of the canons agree in the presence of Thomas as archbishop-elect of York, chosen six days after the death of his predecessor Gerard, who died at Southwell on 21 May while on his way to the council.[1] This can scarcely have met therefore before 28 May, and may have begun later.

Anselm's correspondence after the council at Westminster in 1102 shows how widespread had been resistance to the decree on clerical celibacy.[2] In 1105-6 the king's efforts to enforce this legislation by secular power and to his own profit had been checked by Anselm, but the problem remained. The king now encouraged the bishops to renewed action.[3] The resulting statutes are most unusual for their date, being entirely devoted to the mechanics of enforcing a single principle. They derive rather from administrative experience than any specific earlier authority. However, there are some parallels with the provisions of the Council of Lillebonne of 1080, which may have affected the phrasing of canons 3 and 6.

Apart from the canons other ecclesiastical business was transacted at this time. Richard of Belmeis was promoted to the bishopric of London, for which, it is said, the king had intended to nominate Archbishop Thomas; there was some discussion on the creation of a new bishopric at Ely (no. I),[4] and a dispute over burial customs between the abbey of Gloucester and the bishop of Hereford was resolved (no. III).[5] As the council was held during a royal court it is neither possible nor useful to decide whether the assembly in which these measures were discussed was secular or ecclesiastical.

The manuscript tradition for the canons is very full, being based apparently upon a number of different exemplars in widely scattered houses. Four families may be distinguished:

---

[1] Hugh the Chanter, pp. 14-15, *Hist. York*, ii.111, 522.

[2] Above, pp. 683-8 , *EA* 365, 374.

[3] Eadmer, pp. 172-3, 175, *EA* 391-4.

[4] Hugh the Chanter, p. 15 (*Hist. York*, ii.111-2). For the creation of the see of Ely see particularly *EA* 441, 457-60 (JL 6210-13), *Liber Eliensis*, pp. 245 ff., 277-8, and in general E. Miller, *The Abbey and Bishopric of Ely* (Cambridge, 1951), pp. 75-7, 282-3.

[5] Such disputes were not uncommon at this time; see the references collected in Brett, *English Church*, pp. 93-4, 98-9, 227 and a later case at Gloucester in *Cart. Gloucester*, i.lxxv-lxxvii (*GFL* no. 372).

(a) i D Durham Cathedral Library, B. IV. 17, fo. 169^{r-v}, a
12th-cent. addition to a copy of Burchard's *Decretum*,
which has apparently always been at Durham.[1]

H Hereford Cathedral Library, O. ii. 7, fos. 150^{v}-151,
added in the 12th cent. on the flyleaves of a version
of the Collection in XVII Books.[2]

V Cambridge, Corpus Christi Coll. ms. 298 (iv), fos.
60^{v}-61, a 16th-cent. transcript 'e libro vetusto
ecclesie Cant.' in a collection of notes made for
Archbishop Parker. Its source cannot be traced.

(a) ii E Cambridge, Corpus Christi Coll. ms. 452, pp. 230-2,
Eadmer's autograph of the *Historia Novorum* (also
in the later BL ms. Cotton Titus A. ix, fo. 90^{r-v}).

L London, Lambeth Palace, ms. 59, fo. 179^{r-v}, a Canterbury collection of Anselm's letters of *c.*1125-30
(found also in several other early copies of the
same collection, for which see above pp. 660 n. 1, 671).

(b)   T BL ms. Cotton Titus A. xxvii, fos. 159^{v}-60, early
13th cent. from St. Augustine, Canterbury.

G Manchester, John Rylands Library, Lat. 420, fos. 38^{v}-
39, mid 12th cent.

K BL ms. Add. 49366, fos. 103^{v}-104^{v}, of *c.*1200.

Bc Cambridge, Corpus Christi Coll. ms. 96, not foliated,
s.a. 3 Henry I, 15th-cent. copy of the chronicle
given by Abbot Brompton to Jervaulx.

Bt BL ms. Cotton Tiberius C. xiii, fo. 106^{v}, a similar
copy.

(c)   J Oxford, Corpus Christi Coll. ms. 157, p. 367, an
early marginal addition to the Worcester chronicle;
hence it passed into the other manuscripts of the
work (though entered at varying points), into the
Durham *Historia Regum* (Symeon, ii.240-1), Hoveden's
Chronica (Hoveden, i.165-7) and, via the 'Intermediate

---

[1] The ms. is described briefly in Z.N. Brooke, *English Church and the Papacy*, p. 237.

[2] Ibid., pp. 238-9; compare further P. Fournier and G. Le Bras, *Histoire des collections canoniques en occident* (Paris, 1931-2), ii.230-5 with P. Brommer, *Jahrbuch für westdeutsche Landesgeschichte*, i (1975), 26, 32-3, 35-6.

Compilation', Walter of Coventry's *Memoriale*
(Coventry, i.126-7). None of these later versions
appears to have a text of clearly independent value,
but the *Historia Anglorum sive Saxonum post obitum
Bedae,* the basis of Hoveden's first section, has some
aberrant readings. Select variants are taken therefore from the earliest surviving copy (of *c*.1150):

F   BL ms. Royal 13. A. vi, fo. 87^{r-v}, where this departs
from the text of J.

(d)   C   Canterbury, D.& C., Cartae Antiquae L 138a, entered
in a mid-13th-cent. hand on the dorse of an early
copy of the acts of the Council of Lambeth of 1261
(see *Councils,* ii (1).663).

M   London, Lambeth Palace ms. 171, fo. 10, a 14th-cent.
collection of canons etc. made at Worcester.

R   Oxford, Bodl. ms. Rawlinson C. 428, fos. 101^v-102,
another copy of the same work, of similar date and
provenance. See further below, p. 734, *Councils,* ii (1).52.

Family (a) i contains three independent texts, from Hereford,
Durham, and Canterbury. Sub-group (a) ii contains Eadmer's
version as used in the *Historia Novorum.* Here the whole is cast
in narrative form, and all the tenses are correspondingly
altered to fit indirect speech. L follows this and every other
peculiarity of the *Historia,* and may therefore be treated as
derived from a copy of it, though not necessarily from E itself.
The chief peculiarity of this family is the inclusion of the
last canon, omitted in all other forms.

Family (b) contains the surviving copies of the *Quadripartitus,* and two manuscripts of Brompton's chronicle which have
much of the same text, though modified by consulting a version
close to that of Hoveden and perhaps by the caprice of the
compiler. The original version of this work was written between
1108 and 1114 by someone close to Archbishop Gerard of York,
and cannot be treated lightly.[1] It has several curious and

---

[1] On the date and composition of this work see above, p. 15 n. 2, *Quad.,*
pp. 16-43, *Leges Henrici Primi,* ed. Downer, pp. 34-45.

distinctive features. The council is said to have been held at
Winchester, not London, and by Anselm and Gerard, not Thomas;
canon 4 is much shorter and canons 2 and 6 much longer than
those of the other families; throughout, the clergy are said
to have 'wives' rather than the more consistent 'women' of
families (a) and (c). Like (c) it lacks the last canon, but in
other respects its readings are closer to those of (a). The
phrasing is generally rather unpolished, which is consistent
with the suggestion that it represents a first draft, prepared
for an earlier council at Winchester; the most likely occasion
is the royal court at Easter the same year, though there is no
direct evidence that such matters were discussed there.[1]

Family (c) contains the version added as an afterthought by
the compiler of the Worcester chronicle, which was to be widely
influential on later historians. Though the Canterbury text C
and the Worcester copies in M and R, family (d), are clearly
of the same type, they agree in sufficient minor variants to
suggest that they descend from another source than J. The
peculiarities of these families lie in the provision of a date
rather than a place for the council, an alteration in the number
of witnesses by whom deacons and subdeacons should clear themselves of charges, the abbreviation of canon 6, and the omission of the last canon, which attributes the profits of justice
in such cases to the bishops.

If then family (a), geographically the most widespread, may
represent the text as Anselm and Thomas published it at Whitsun,
1108, and family (b) a draft for the Easter council, family (c)
could indicate a reissue on royal authority when the king interested himself in the enforcement of these canons after
Anselm's death.[2]

The text has been printed often; see particularly Eadmer,
pp. 193-5, from E, *Quad.*, pp. 163-5, from the (b) mss., *Flor.
Wig.* ii.57-9 (partly from J), Sp. ii.29-(30), Labbe, x.75[6]-7,
W. i.387-8, Mansi, xx.1229-32. That below is based on H, fully
collated with D and V, and corrected where necessary; the

---

[1]*ASC*, ed. Plummer, i.242, ed. Clark, p. 34, tr. Whitelock *et al.*, p. 181.
[2]Eadmer, pp. 212-13.

peculiarities of tense from E and L are not noted, and 'Brompton' is used very sparingly.

I. *Eadmer, Historia Novorum in Anglia s.a. 1108*

    Cambridge, Corpus Christi Coll. ms. 452, pp. 230-3 (= A);
    BL ms. Cotton Titus A. ix, fos. 90-1 (= B). Printed from
    B in *PL* clix.470-2, ultimately from the edition by Sel-
    den, and from A and B in Eadmer, pp. 193-5. The text
    below is based on A.

Divina nichilominus officia quoniam indigne per quorundam sacerdotum manus eousque tractabantur, sollicitus institit [rex] ut
et ipsa suo ritu caste celebrarentur. Multi nempe presbiterorum,
statuta concilii Lundoniensis necne vindictam quam in eos rex
exercuerat, quorum superius mentionem fecimus,[1] postponentes,
suas feminas retinebant aut certe duxerant quas prius non habe-
bant. Quod incontinentię crimen rex subvertere cupiens, adunatis
ad curiam suam in solennitate Pentecostes apud Lundoniam cunctis
maioribus regni, de negotio cum Anselmo archiepiscopo et cęteris
episcopis Anglię tractavit, eosque ad malum illud extirpandum
regali auctoritate atque potentia fultos roboravit. Unde Anselmus archiepiscopus Cantuariensis et Thomas electus archiepiscopus
Eboracensis, nam Gerardus tunc nuper ad eandem curiam tendens
obierat, et omnes alii Anglię episcopi statuerunt in praesentia
eiusdem gloriosi regis Henrici, assensu omnium baronum suorum
ut presbiteri ...
        (*Then follow the canons, no. II below*)
[p. 232] ... His diebus sermo habitus est de parochia episcopi
Lincoliensis, quę in nimium tendebatur, eoque processit ut
quoniam ratio Christianitatis id utile fore suadebat regi et
archiepiscopo cęterisque principibus regni visum fuerit de ipsa
parochia sumendum quo fieret alter episcopatus, cuius cathedrę
principatus poneretur in abbatia de Heli. Sed Anselmus quem
ipsius negotii summa respiciebat sciens [p. 233] preter consensum et Romani pontificis auctoritatem novum episcopatum

---

[1]C. of Westminster (1102), c. 5, above p. 698 n. 2.

nusquam rite institui posse, scripsit ei sic: (*there follows*
EA 441).

II. *Canons of the council*

Hęc sunt statuta[a] de archidiaconibus, presbiteris, diaconibus,
subdiaconibus[b] et canonicis[c] in quocunque gradu constitutis[d]
quę Lundonię[e] statuerunt Anselmus archiepiscopus Cantuariensis
et cum eo Thomas electus archiepiscopus Eboracensis,[f] et omnes[g]
alii Anglię episcopi in presentia gloriosi regis Henrici[h]
assensu omnium[i] baronum suorum.

[1] Statutum est[j] ut presbiteri, diaconi, subdiaconi[k] caste
vivant, et feminas in domibus suis non habeant preter proxima
consanguinitate sibi iunctas,[l] secundum hoc[m] quod sancta Nicena
synodus definivit.[1]

[2] Illi vero presbiteri, diaconi sive[n] subdiaconi qui post
interdictum Lundoniensis concilii feminas suas [o]tenuerunt vel
alias duxerunt,[o]

HDVELJMRC	GKT(BcBt)
si amplius missam[p] celebrare voluerint eas a se omnino faciant sic[q] alienas ut nec	si elegerint in sacris ordinibus remanere, iurent quod cum eis carnale commercium non

---

[a]statuta HVGKJMRC; instituta DT.   [b]archidiaconibus ... subdiaconibus
HVJ; archidiaconibus, presbiteris DTGK; archidiaconis, presbiteris, diaconis,
subdiaconis MRC.   [c]*corr. from* canonibus H[1].   [d]*Symeon, but not Hoveden,
reads* secularibus *for* in quocunque gradu constitutis.   [e]Lundonie HDV;
Wintonie TGKB; anno Dominice Incarnationis MCVIII JMRC.   [f]cum eo ...
Eboracensis (H *om.* electus) HD; Thomas archiepiscopus Eboracensis cum eo V;
Thomas electus archiepiscopus Eboracensis cum eo JMRCF (F *with* electus *after*
Eboracensis); cum eo Girardus archiepiscopus Eboracensis TGKB.   [g]et omnes
HDVTGK; omnesque JMRC.   [h]Herrici H.   [i]omnium HDVTGK; *om.* JMRC; comitum
et F.   [j]*to this point* L *follows* E *as in no. I above.*   [k]subdiaconi
HVELTJMRC; et subdiaconi D; *om.* GK.   [l]coniunctas DB.   [m]hoc HDVJTGK;
om. ELMRCB.   [n]sive DVELTGKB; *om.* HJMRC.   [o]tenuerunt ... duxerunt HDVJMC;
tenuerint vel alias duxerint TGKBR.   [p]missam HELJ; missas DVMRCF.   [q]a se
omnino faciant (facient H, facerent EL) sic HDEL; a se omnino sic faciant
(facient J) JMRC; omnino a se facient sic V; omnino a se sic faciant F.

---

[1]C. of Westminster (1102), c. 5.

illę in domos eorum, nec
ipsi in domos earum intrent,
sed neque in aliqua domo[a]
scienter conveniant,

habebunt[b] amplius. Statutum
est etiam ut predicte femine
in [c]domos eorum vel ipsi in
domos earum non intrent sed
neque in aliqua[c] domo scienter
conveniant,

neque huiusmodi feminę in territorio ęcclesię habitent. Si autem
propter aliquam honestam causam eos[d] colloqui opporteat, cum
duobus ad minus[e] legittimis testibus extra domum colloquantur.

[3] Si vero in duobus aut in[f] tribus legittimis testibus vel
publica parrochianorum fama aliquis eorum accusatus fuerit quod
hoc[g] statutum violaverit[h] purgabit se adiunctis secum ordinis
sui idoneis[i] testibus, sex si presbiter, quinque si diacònus,
quatuor si subdiaconus fuerit.[j] Cui[k] autem hęc purgatio defecerit ut transgressor sacri statuti iudicabitur.[l] [fo. 151]

[4] Illi autem[l] presbiteri qui divini altaris et sacrorum
ordinum contemptores preelegerint cum mulieribus[m] habitare, a
divino officio remoti et omni ecclesiastico beneficio privati,[n]
extra chorum[o] ponantur, infames pronuntiati.[p] [q]Qui vero rebellis
et contemptor feminam suam[r] non reliquerit et missam celebrare
presumpserit, vocatus ad satisfactionem si neglexerit octavo[s]
die excommunicetur.[q2]

---

[a]domo aliqua D.   [b]habebunt B; habeb't T; habebat GK.   [c]domos ...
aliqua T; *om.* GK; domibus cum eis scienter non conveniant B.   [d]eos HDVEL
TGK; eas FJMRC; vel eos *add* F[1].   [e]ad minus HDVELTGKR[2]; om. JMRC.   [f]aut
in HDVEJTGK; aut L; vel in MC; vel R.   [g]hoc *om.* D.   [h]violaverit HDV
(EL violasset) JMRC; transieriṭ TGK; B *summarizes the passage:* statutum
violasse accusatus fuerit.   [i]*om.* V.   [j]quinque si diaconus, quatuor si
subdiaconus fuerit HDVELGKT; quatuor si diaconus, duo si subdiaconus fuerit
JMRC; fuerit, si autem diaconus quatuor, si subdiaconus duo F.   [k]Cui
HVELGKJMRC; Cum DT.   [l]autem *om.* H.   [m]mulieribus HDVELJMRC; uxoribus suis
TGKB.   [n]et omni ... privati (reprivati H) HDVEL; omnique ecclesiastico
beneficio privati JMRC; *om.* TGK.   [o]hortum GK.   [p]pronuntiati HDVELJR[2]GK;
nuntiati MRC; pronuntiari T.   [q]Qui vero ... excommunicetur HDVELJMRC;
om. TGK.   [r]suam HDELR[2]; *om.* VJMRC.   [s]octavo HELMR; octava DJ; viii VC;
octavo die *om.* F.

---

[1]C. of Lillebonne (1080), c. 3. The process of exculpation in c. 3 is
closely related to that in VIII Æthelred 20.1-21 (= I Cnut 5.1a-2), provided
for a priest or deacon charged with any offence by three accusers.
[2]C. of Troyes (1107), c. 3 in Blumenthal, *Early Councils of Pope Paschal
II*, pp. 91-2.

[5] Eadem sententia archidiacones[a] et canonicos omnes[b] complec-
titur et[c] de mulieribus relinquendis[d] et[c] de[e] vitanda earum[f]
conversatione, et de districtione censurę si statuta transgressi
fuerint.

[6] Iurabunt archidiacones omnes[g] quod pecuniam non accipient
pro toleranda transgressione huius statuti, nec[h] tolerabunt[i]
presbiteros quos scient feminas habere[j] cantare vel vicarios
habere, et si eos audierint calumpniari veritatem inde inquirent.[k] Similiter et decani hęc eadem per omnia iurabunt.[l]
Qui vero archidiaconus vel decanus[m] hęc[n] iurare noluerit archidiaconatum vel decaniam irrecuperabiliter[o] perdet.[1]

[7] Presbiteri vero qui relictis mulieribus[p] Deo et sacris
altaribus[q] servire elegerint[r] quadraginta dies[s] ab officio
cessantes pro se interim[t] vicarios habebunt, iniuncta eis penitentia secundum[u] quod episcopis eorum visum fuerit.[v]

[HDVEL *continue*]

[8] Omnia mobilia lapsorum[w] presbiterorum, diaconorum, sub-

---

[a]archidiacones HDVE; archidiaconos LTGKBJMRC.   [b]omn. arch. et can. D.
[c]et ... et HDVTGKJMRC; tam ... quam EL.   [d]mulieribus relinquendis HDVEL
JMRC; abiurandis uxoribus TGK.   [e]de *om.* L.   [f]earum HVELJMRC; eorum DTGK.
[g]archidiacones (-oni VJMRC) omnes HDVJMRC; insuper archidiaconi omnes EL;
etiam archidiaconi omnes GKTF.   [h]nec HDVELJMRC; sed neque ullo modo TGK.
[i]patientur F.   [j]quos scient feminas habere HVEL; quos scient habere feminas D; quos scient feminas habere missam JMRC; uxoratos TGK; quos sciunt
feminas habere vel missam F.   [k]et si ... veritatem inde (inde veritatem
H, veritatem in D) inquirent HDEL (requirerent L); et si eos audierint de
hoc crimine calumniari veritatem inde inquirent V; et quod ipsi non dissimula-
bunt per archidiaconatos (-tus T) suos hoc inquirere et fideliter episcopis
suis renuntiabunt, et attente et fideliter de exsequenda huius rei vindicta
episcopos suos adiuvabunt TGK; *om.* JMRC.   [l]et decani ... iurabunt VELTGK;
et decani hec omnia eadem iurabunt H; et decani hec omnia eadem per omnia
iurabunt D; decani facient JMRC; decani iurabunt F.   [m]Archidiaconus vero
vel decanus qui F.   [n]hec *om.* V.   [o]irrecuperabiliter HDVELTGK; *om.* JMRC.
[p]mulieribus HDVELJMRC; uxoribus TGK; relictis mulieribus *after* servire D.
[q]altaribus HDVELJMRC; ordinibus TGK.   [r]elegerint HVTGKJ; elerint D;
elegerunt MRC.   [s]pro transgressione prefati (pacti V) concilii *add* ELV.
[t]interim HDVELJMRC; *om.* TGK.   [u]hoc *add* VJ.   [v]GKTJMRC *end here.*
[w]mobilia lapsorum DV; mobilia H; vero mobilia lapsorum post hec EL.

---

[1]See above, p. 701, n. 1.

diaconorum et canonicorum[a] tradentur episcopis et[b] concubinę
cum rebus suis velut adulterę.[1]

III. *De prima fundacione monasterii sancti Petri Gloucestriae*

> Gloucester Cathedral Library, ms. 34, fo. 5 (= A), early
> 15th cent.; printed from Oxford, Queen's Coll. ms. 367,
> fo. 12[v] (= B), mid 15th cent., and BL ms. Cotton Domit.
> viii, fo. 129[v] (= C), a slightly later revision of B, in
> *Cart. Gloucester*, i.13-14.[2]

Istius [sc. Petri abbatis] tempore fuit grandis altercacio
inter domnum abbatem Petrum[3] et Remelinum episcopum Herefordensem[4] in presencia regis Henrici et dompni Anselmi archiepiscopi
et Roberti comitis de Mellent et multorum episcoporum, abbatum
et procerum in Pentecost' pro[c] ablacione corporis Radulphi
filii Askitilli,[5] quod ille episcopus Remelinus per vim abstulerat. Et fuit diracionatum[d] ut corpus defoderetur et redderetur, Roberto comite iudicium dictante, ut in posterum haberent
universi liberam potestatem se ubicunque vivi disposuerant post
mortem sepeliendi. Hoc universis episcopis qui adherant consencientibus, ipse Remelinus omnes calumpnias et querelas quas
habuit erga domnum abbatem Petrum pro ecclesia sancti Petri in

---

[a]et canonicorum *om.* D.   [b]eorum *add* D.   [c]pro AC[1]; *om.* BC.   [d]ordinatum *superscript* B.

---

[1]C. of Melfi (1089), c. 12; compare above p. 307 n.1 and Brett, *English Church*, p. 149.

[2]For the high authority of the early sections of this text, and its relation to the chronicle of Gregory of Caerwent see C.N.L. Brooke, in *Celt and Saxon*, pp. 260-77 and *GF*, p. 36 n. 1. Gregory's chronicle is now known only from the extracts by Laurence Nowell in BL ms. Cotton Vesp. A. v, fos. 195-203[v], where this passage is summarized on fo. 197.

[3]Abbot of Gloucester 1107-13 (*Heads*, p. 52).

[4]Reinhelm, formerly chancellor to the queen, was consecrated on 11 Aug. 1107 (Eadmer, p. 187) and died 27 October 1115 (*Flor. Wig.* ii.68). Since Anselm died before Whitsun 1109, the date of these events is fixed in 1108, under which year they are entered by Gregory of Caerwent.

[5]Ralph fitz Aschetill attests Hugh de Lacy's grant of St. Peter, Hereford to Gloucester abbey in 1100/1, and was probably buried at Gloucester as a benefactor of the dependency at Hereford.

Hereford' dimisit,[1] excepta duntaxat pulsacione signorum ante
canonicos, tantum corpus non defoderetur. Hac de causa remansit corpus indefossum.[2]

117
*c.*MAY 1108. LEGATION OF PETER THE CHAMBERLAIN

Two letters of Anselm appear to refer to a mission of Peter the
chamberlain in 1108. Shortly after the Whitsun council the archbishop sent letters to Pope Paschal by the hand of Bernard, the
chamberlain's servant. Although this does not in itself establish Peter's presence, in November the pope referred to some
preliminaries to the creation of the see of Ely, of which
Anselm had informed him through Bishop Hervey of Bangor and
Peter, so that one may well suppose that he had been in England
in the summer. He had been at the king's court at Rouen in late
1106 or early 1107, presumably on an earlier mission.[3] In
neither case is a purpose given; however, Peter, a monk of
Cluny, is the first known holder of the office of papal chamberlain, his responsibilities were financial, and it seems not
unlikely that he was sent to encourage or arrange the sending
of Peter's Pence. This may well have been suspended during the

---

[1]St. Peter was founded as a collegiate church by Walter de Lacy, who died
on 27 March 1085, while supervising its construction (*Cart. Gloucester*, i.73,
DB i.165^V, 184, Gregory of Caerwent, fo. 195^V), and was buried at Gloucester
the next day. He was also a benefactor of Gloucester as early as 1080 (*Cart.
Gloucester*, i.374-5). In 1100 or 1101 his son, Hugh de Lacy, gave the abbey
his house at Hereford (ibid. i.326, iii.256, though *Reg.* ii.410, no. 379a,
is a very doubtful charter of William II purporting to confirm this gift in
1096). Monks had already been established at Hereford early in Reinhelm's
pontificate, if one may trust the charters in Oxford, Balliol Coll. ms. 271,
fos. 93^V, 102^V. See further the account by W.E. Wightman, *The Lacy family
in England and Normandy 1066-1194*, pp. 168, 173-6, 182-3.
[2]For the importance of bell-ringing in disputes between neighbouring
houses see further Brett, *English Church*, pp. 60 n. 3, 94 n. 1. The decision
of 1108 did not end the dispute, which was still active in 1134 (*Cart.
Gloucester*, i.86-7; better in Oxford, Balliol Coll. ms. 271, fo. 97^V).
[3]*EA* 451, 460; Guibert of Nogent, *Histoire de sa vie*, ed. G. Bourgin,
p. 143. This encounter took place after the capture of Rouen in October
(*OV* vi.92) but before the visit of Paschal II to Dijon in mid-February
1107 (*JL* i, p. 729).

preceding years of tension, but was a constant preoccupation
of papal letters of the period.[1]

118

MAY-AUGUST 1109. LEGATION OF THE CARDINAL PRIEST ODALRIC

> On this legation see Tillmann, pp. 23-4, Dueball,
> *Suprematstreit*, pp. 55-67.

The appointment of Thomas II to the see of York at the Whitsun
council of 1108 naturally opened another round of the primacy
contest. Very shortly after his promotion the king urged Thomas
to send messengers to Rome to secure his pallium;[2] meanwhile
Anselm, whose health was failing steadily, began to put pressure on Thomas to set a date for his consecration at Canterbury,
with a profession of obedience. While the canons of York urged
Thomas to resistance, Anselm forbade him to seek a pallium before he had been consecrated, and wrote to Rome to forewarn the
pope of the danger, asking that no pallium be sent until Canterbury had reported Thomas's consecration. In letters dated 12
October 1108 Paschal assured Anselm of his goodwill, though he
offered no concrete guarantees.[3] Meanwhile Anselm was becoming
more pressing in his demands; when it became clear that Thomas
was turning to open resistance he sent the bishops of London
and Rochester to Southwell to urge Thomas to submission. The
archbishop-elect replied that he had sent messengers to the king
in Normandy and the pope, and would give his answer when they
returned. Shortly afterwards he sent Anselm a royal writ putting
the whole matter in respite until the king's return to England,

---

[1]*Life of St. Anselm*, p. 134 is the only good evidence that he was in
office before the death of Urban II; on the chamberlains, and Peter in particular, see J. Sydow, *Deutsches Archiv* xi (1954/5), 41-4, 56, 62 citing
earlier literature. Compare *EA* 213 (JL 5883) with the other references collected in Brett, *English Church*, pp. 47-9, 168-73.

[2]*EA* 444, Hugh the Chanter, p. 18 (*Hist. York*, ii.114). See in general
Southern, *St. Anselm and his Biographer*, pp. 138-41.

[3]Eadmer, pp. 199-203, Hugh the Chanter, pp. 18-21 (*Hist. York*, ii.114-7),
EA 443, 445, 451, 452 (JL 6206), 455.

which he expected about Easter 1109.[1] York's messenger to Rome
appears to have been the dean, who was entrusted with letters
seeking the pallium. In Normandy he secured the king's support
and royal letters asking for a legate to be sent with the
pallium and power to settle the dispute over the primacy.[2]

By the spring Anselm was clearly dying; it seems to have
been almost his last act to suspend Thomas from his priestly
office until he submitted, and copies of his letter were sent
to all the bishops; on 21 April 1109 he died at Canterbury.[3]
Shortly after his death the cardinal priest Odalric arrived in
Normandy with the pallium and some power to hear arguments over
the primacy; he was accompanied by Prior Geoffrey of St. Bénigne
of Dijon. After a short stay with the king in Normandy they
preceded him to England, and were summoned to the royal Whitsun court at Westminster, where the issue of the profession was
debated at length.[4] The king had now been won over to the cause
of Canterbury entirely; when the canons of York appealed to
the legate he replied that he had come to preside over a formal
action, but would not intervene unless compelled to do so. In
the event the whole body of the bishops stood firm by Anselm's
dying wishes, and Thomas submitted to informal pressure. On 27
June he made a profession with some reservations before being
consecrated by the bishop of London at St. Paul's.[5] The legate
accompanied the new archbishop to York, and there on Sunday 1
August handed over the pallium, immediately before Thomas

---

[1]Eadmer, pp. 204-5, Hugh the Chanter, pp. 21-2 (*Hist. York*, ii.117-8),
EA 464 (which alone refers so early to messengers sent to Rome), 470.

[2]Hugh the Chanter, pp. 22-3 (*Hist. York*, ii.118-19).

[3]Eadmer, pp. 205-6, *EA* 471-2.

[4]Eadmer, p. 207, Hugh the Chanter, pp. 23-4 (*Hist. York*, ii.119-20). Odalric,
formerly *scholasticus* of Rheims, was a cardinal of unknown title from *c.*1107
to before 1114 (Hüls, p. 215). Johnson followed Raine in reading *Dunonensis*
for Geoffrey's house; no priory of Dunois is known, and the ms. of Hugh
pretty clearly reads *Divionensis*. 'Odalrinus, cardinalis sancte Romane ecclesie, Gaufridus Divionensis ecclesie prior et Vitalis monachus eiusdem
ecclesie' appear in *Liber Vitae Ecclesiae Dunelmensis* (facs. ed.), fo. 42.
Geoffrey was prior of St. Bénigne from *c.*1100 to his death on 24 November
1112 (*Chartes et documents de Saint-Bénigne de Dijon*, ii.277). Possibly he
may have been considered as the representative of his abbot, Jarento, the
legate of 1096.

[5]Eadmer, pp. 207-11, Hugh the Chanter, pp. 23-31 (*Hist. York*, ii.119-26),
Canterbury Professions, pp. lxxi-lxxiii, 37 (no. 62), 116 (no. 10).

consecrated Turgot as bishop of St. Andrews. Three days later
the cardinal set off for Rome. According to Hugh the Chanter
he was barely persuaded not to summon Thomas to Rome for his
failure to maintain the provisions of Gregory the Great.[1]

Widely though Hugh and Eadmer differ in their accounts of
these events, in both the cardinal's conduct appears dis-
tinctly ineffective. It is uncertain whether this is to be
attributed more to the strength of opinion in England or to
the pope's reluctance to force a conflict with King Henry so
soon after his surrender on investitures and just as he was
forging a marriage alliance with Henry V, the new king of Germany, on whom Paschal might still hope to exercise some influence.[2]

119

26 APRIL 1114. ELECTION OF RALPH D'ESCURES AS ARCHBISHOP OF
CANTERBURY

Sources: Eadmer, pp. 221-3; Malmesbury in WMGP, pp. 125-8;
Chronicon Monasterii de Abingdon, ii.287; *Flor. Wig.*
ii.47 n.

King Henry returned from a two-year stay in Normandy in the summer of 1113, and shortly afterwards he began to fill a number of
ecclesiastical vacancies.[3] Few of these had lasted long, but it
was almost five years since the death of Anselm of Canterbury.
The pope, the monks of Christ Church, and others had all protested at the delay, and a month after Easter the king held his

---

[1]Hugh the Chanter, p. 31 (*Hist. York,* ii.126-7), Eadmer, p. 211, *Flor.
Wig.* ii.60, Symeon, ii.241 (where the date of 30 July is a misreading of
iii Kal. for *in Kal.*; the correct reading is found in Hoveden and Liège,
UL ms. 369C, fo. 98^V, for which see above, p. 656 n. 1). See also in
general Brett, *English Church,* pp. 17-18.

[2]German affairs, including Matilda's marriage presumably, were being
discussed before the end of 1108 and through the winter (*EA* 451-2, 461);
the Whitsun court of 1109 also saw the marriage arrangements confirmed —
ASC, ed. Plummer, i.242, ed. Clark, p. 34, tr. Whitelock *et al.*, p. 181;
in general see K. Leyser in *TRHS* 5th Ser., x (1960), 61-83.

[3]*ASC* (H), ed. Plummer, i.243-5, ed. Whitelock *et al.*, pp. 182-4.

court at Windsor to decide on a successor. Henry had already
shown a preference for his physician, the Italian Faricius,
abbot of Abingdon, who had been summoned to court, together
with Bishop Ralph of Rochester and the prior of Canterbury with
some of his monks. The bishops, however, who were all seculars
except Ralph and Herbert of Norwich, protested, and were joined
by some of the lay magnates in demanding either the translation
of one of the secular bishops or the choice of a clerk from the
royal chapel.[1] When others objected, citing the long tradition
of monastic archbishops and the unhappy precedent of Stigand,
the bishops offered Bishop Ralph as a compromise candidate,
whom the king and representatives of Canterbury soon accepted.[2]
On 16 May Ralph was enthroned at Canterbury, and shortly afterwards an embassy set off for Rome to secure the pallium, bearing letters from the king, archbishop, the monks of Canterbury,
and most of the bishops.

120

SUMMER 1115. LEGATION OF ANSELM, ABBOT OF ST. SABA

          See Tillmann, pp. 24-5, Brett, *English Church*, pp. 36-7.

The embassy which left England to seek the pallium for Archbishop Ralph was not well received at Rome, and it was only
with difficulty that Paschal was persuaded to approve Ralph's
translation in letters dated 18 February 1115.[3] The ambassadors
had been much assisted by Anselm, nephew of the late archbishop,
who was charged with the delivery of the pallium; he also carried two letters addressed to the king of 30 March and 1 April
in which the pope denounced England's lack of respect for the
authority of the Roman church, in translating a bishop without
her consent, in failing to bring matters of importance to Roman
judgement, and in negligent payment of Peter's Pence.[4] On all

---

[1]D. Bethell, *EHR* lxxxiv (1969), 675-6.   [2]Brett, *English Church*, p. 73.
[3]Eadmer, p. 231 (JL 6449).
[4]Eadmer, pp. 228-9 (JL 6450), and see below. A short biography of Anselm
from the Bury ms. BL Harl. 1005 is translated by H. Thurston in *The Month*,
no. 480 (1904). 571-2. See further the references in *Heads*, p. 32.

these points Anselm was to provide with the king for amendment.
The legate arrived in Normandy in the summer, and spent some
days with the king before crossing the Channel, accompanied by
the English embassy which had awaited his arrival. On 27 June
he delivered the pallium to Ralph at Canterbury before a large
assembly, and received his profession of obedience to Rome.[1]
Anselm remained in England for the council of September, described below, before returning to Rome.[2]

121

16 SEPTEMBER 1115. ROYAL COUNCIL AT WESTMINSTER

      See Nicholl, *Thurstan*, pp. 51-2; Dueball, *Die Supremat-
streit*, pp. 70-1, Conway Davies, i.133-5.

Although the accounts of Eadmer (no. I) and Hugh the Chanter
(no. II) leave no doubt that the council of September 1115 was
summoned on the king's authority, and held at the royal palace
at Westminster, churchmen were extremely numerous.[3] The witness
list of the royal grant of the bishopric of St. Davids to
Bernard the queen's chancellor records the presence of all the
bishops of England and Urban of Glamorgan with the archbishop
of Rouen and John of Lisieux. The presence of the two Normans
is confirmed by Hugh, while Bernard was consecrated in the
presence of Gilbert of Limerick. In one way or another more
churches were represented than in the majority of properly
ecclesiastical councils.[4] Further all its recorded business
concerned the church. Eadmer stresses the importance of the

---

[1]Eadmer, pp. 228-30; an *ordo* for the reception of the pallium from Rome
is found in the 12th-cent. pontifical from Canterbury, Dublin, Trin. Coll.
ms. B. 3. 6, printed in *Pontifical of Magdalen College*, pp. 250-1, to which
the ceremonies described by Eadmer conform very closely. A form of oath to
the papacy is printed in *Canterbury Professions*, p. 109 from an early 12th-
cent. pontifical.

[2]Eadmer, p. 239.

[3]The summary account in *Flor. Wig.* ii.68 adds nothing to Eadmer beyond
describing Bernard, accurately, as the queen's chancellor. ASC does not
notice the council.

[4]*Reg.* ii, no. 1091 survives only in a late copy, with a corrupt but
elaborate dating clause. It can scarcely have been drafted by a royal scribe,
but the content and witness list present no obvious difficulty.

legate's letters, which were certainly of remarkable asperity, and the king's anxiety at the conduct of Cono of Palestrina, who had excommunicated the body of Norman bishops for their failure to attend his legatine council at Châlons-sur-Marne in July,[1] and suggests that the debates over the consecration of Bishop Bernard occurred during the same meeting.

Thurstan, a royal chaplain and subdeacon, had been nominated as archbishop of York on 15 August 1114. He had been made deacon by William of Winchester in December and was then enthroned at York by the bishop of Chester. On Christmas Day 1114 he crossed to the king in Normandy, intending to proceed to Rome for consecration, and so frustrate the demand for a profession which Archbishop Ralph had already advanced. The king, however, detained him, but, on the advice of Cono, had him ordained priest by Ranulf of Durham at Whitsun. He then returned to England, shortly before the king, who had undertaken to compose the quarrel rather than send him to Rome as Cono had suggested. The council of September naturally therefore gave rise to the inconclusive debates reported by Hugh.[2]

I. *Eadmer, Historia Novorum in Anglia s.a. 1115*

> Cambridge, Corpus Christ Coll. 452, pp. 277-83 (= A), BL Cotton Titus A. ix, fos. 107-9 (= B), and Cambridge, Corpus Christi Coll. 341, a single leaf in Eadmer's hand[3] (= L). Printed in Eadmer, pp. 231-6, and from B only in *PL* clix.494-5, ultimately from the edition of Selden.

Eodem anno Henricus rex iussit omnes episcopos et principes totius regni ad curiam suam sub uno venire. Unde rumor per totam terram dispersus est pontificem Cantuariorum generale

---

[1]Schieffer, *Die päpstlichen Legaten in Frankreich*, pp. 198-203 notices the chief sources for Cono's legation; for events in Normandy see particularly Epp. 270, 273 of Ivo of Chartres (*PL* clxii.273-6), *Flor. Wig.* ii.68 and WMGP, p. 129. On the legate's councils see further R. Somerville, *Traditio*, xxiv (1968), 493-503 and Hüls, pp. 113-16.

[2]Hugh the Chanter, pp. 33-7 (*Hist. York*, ii.129-32).

[3]L is discussed in Brett, 'A note on the *Historia Novorum* of Eadmer', *Scriptorium*, xxxiii (1979), 56-8; in a brief extract *Flor. Wig.* ii.68, follows L against A.

concilium praesente legato domini papę cuius supra meminimus
celebraturum, et nova quędam tantoque conventui digna pro cor-
rectione Christianę religionis in omni ordine promulgaturum.
Itaque ut rex iusserat xvi kl' Octobris conventus omnium apud
Westmonasterium in palatio regis factus est, et quod de concilii celebratione et Christianitatis emendatione rumor [p.
278] disperserat nichil fuisse quę confluxerat multitudo tandem
advertit. Venit tamen illuc sepe nominatus Anselmus qui pallium
Cantuariam detulerat, deferens epistolam ex parte apostolici
regi et episcopis Anglię, hoc textum habentem:

[1]Paschalis episcopus servus servorum Dei dilecto filio Henrico illustri regi et episcopis Anglici regni salutem et
apostolicam benedictionem. Qualiter ęcclesia Christi[a] fundata
sit non est a nobis nunc temporis disserendum. Hoc enim plenius
evangelii textus et apostolorum litterę profitentur. Qualiter
vero ęcclesię status praestante Domino perseveret et referendum
nobis est et agendum. A Sancto siquidem Spiritu ęcclesię dictum est, 'Pro patribus tuis nati sunt tibi filii, constitues eos
principes super omnem terram.' Super qua constitutione Paulus
apostolus pręcepit, dicens, 'Manum cito nemini imposueris,
neque communicaveris peccatis alienis.'[2] Quam eiusdem apostoli
sententiam beatus Leo doctor exponens ait, 'Quid est cito manum
imponere, nisi ante ętatem maturitatis, ante tempus examinis,
ante meritum laboris, ante experientiam disciplinę sacerdotalem
honorem tribuere non probatis?'[3] Qua igitur ratione Anglici
regni episcopis sacerdotalis honoris confirmationem tribuere
possumus quorum vitam, quorum scientiam nulla probatione cognoscimus? Ipse caput ęcclesię dominus Iesus Christus cum pastori
primo apostolo Petro ęcclesiam commendaret dixit, 'Pasce oves
meas, pasce agnos meos.'[4] Oves quippe in ęcclesia ęcclesiarum

---

[a]Dei B.

---

[1]JL 6453. The letter is found in three 12th-cent. mss. connected with
Canterbury, BL mss. Cotton Claudius A. i, fo. 40 and Claudius E. v, fo. 249,
and Durham Cathedral Lib. ms. B. IV. 18, fo. 70[v]. In all essentials these
present a text identical to Eadmer's, and agree in no variant.
[2]Ps. 44, 17; I Tim. 5, 22.
[3]Hinschius, p. 622. The letter and its sources are discussed by U.-R.
Blumenthal in *Archivum Historiae Pontificiae*, xvi (1978), 76-9.
[4]Ioan. 21, 15-17.

praepositi sunt, qui Deo filios generare ipso donante consuerunt.
Quomodo ergo vel agnos vel oves [p. 279] pascere possumus, quos
neque novimus nec videmus? Quos neque audimus neque ab ipsis
audimur? Quomodo super eos illud Domini praeceptum implebimus
quo Petrum instruit, dicens, 'Confirma fratres tuos'?[1] Universum siquidem terrarum orbem Dominus et magister noster suis
discipulis dispertivit, sed Europę fines Petro singulariter
commisit et Paulo. Nec per eorum tantum sed per successorum
discipulos ac legatos Europę universitas conversa est et confirmata. Unde usque ad nos licet indignos eorum vicarios hęc
consuetudo pervenit, ut per nostrę sedis vicarios graviora
ęcclesiarum per provintias negotia pertractentur seu retracten-
tur.[a] Vos autem inconsultis nobis, etiam episcoporum negotia
definitis, cum martir Victor ęcclesię Romąnę pontifex dicat,
'Quanquam comprovintialibus episcopis accusati causam pontificis scrutari liceat, non tamen definire inconsulto Romano pontifice[b] permissum est.' Zepherinus quoque martir et pontifex,
'Iudicia', inquit, 'episcoporum maioresque causę a sede apostolica et non ab alia sunt terminandę.'[2] Vos oppressis apostolicę
sedis appellationem subtrahitis, cum sanctorum patrum conciliis
decretisque sancitum sit, ab omnibus oppressis ad Romanam
ęcclesiam appellandum. Vos praeter conscientiam nostram concilia
sinodalia celebratis, cum Athanasius Alexandrinę ęcclesię
scribat, 'Scimus in Nicea magna sinodo trecentorum decem et
octo episcoporum ab omnibus concorditer esse corroboratum non
debere absque Romani pontificis scientia concilia celebrari.'[3]
Quod ipsum scriptis suis sancti pontifices firmaverunt, et
aliter acta concilia [p. 280] irrita fieri statuerunt. Videtis
igitur et vos contra sedis apostolicę auctoritatem plurimum
excessisse, et dignitati plurimum subtraxisse, et nobis id pro
nostri officii debito imminere ut probatos habeamuş quibus
sacerdotalem conferimus dignitatem, ne contra apostolum manum

---

[a] pertractarentur seu retractarentur B.   [b] L begins here.

---

[1] Luc. 22. 32.
[2] Hinschius, pp. 128, 132, and see Blumenthal, ut sup.
[3] Hinschius, p. 479.

citius cuiquam imponentes communicemus peccatis alienis, quia
iuxta beati Leonis sententiam, 'gravi semetipsum afficit damno
qui ad suę dignitatis collegium sullimat indignum'.[1] Vos preter
auctoritatem nostram episcoporum quoque mutationes praesumitis,
quod sine sacrosanctę Romanę sedis auctoritate ac licentia fieri
novimus omnino prohibitum. Si ergo in his omnibus sedi apostolicę dignitatem ac reverentiam servare consentitis, nos vobis
ut fratribus ac filiis caritatem debitam conservamus, et quę
vobis ab apostolica ęcclesia concedenda sunt benigne ac dulciter Domino pręstante concedimus. Si vero adhuc in vestra
decernitis obstinacia permanere, nos[a] evangelicum dictum et
apostolicum exemplum pedum in vos pulverem excutiemus,[2] et tanquam ab ęcclesia catholica resilientes divino iudicio trademus,
dicente Domino, 'Qui non colligit mecum dispergit, et qui non
est mecum adversum me est.'[3] Deus autem omnipotens et nobiscum
vos in ipso esse, et nobiscum vos in ipso colligere ita concedat, ut ad ęternam eius unitatem quę idipsum permanet pervenire
concedat. Data Lateranis kl' Aprilis indictione octava.

Rex ad hęc consilio cum episcopis habito quid super his et
quibusdam aliis quę animum suum plurimum offendebant[b] papę
responderet, placuit in commune ut suos nuncios [p. 281] mitteret, per quos quę vellet securius papę mandaret. Nam ante hos
dies quidam[c] Romanę ęcclesię cardinalis functus legatione
apostolicę sedis, Cono nomine, Franciam venerat, et ibi iuxta
suę legationis officium generalia concilia celebrans episcopos
Normannię ab episcopali officio suspensos excommunicavit, eo
quod conciliis suis[d] tercio vocati interesse noluerant.[e] Quę
episcoporum excommunicatio animum regis valde reddidit conturbatum,[f] [g]et rationis esse duxit super his papam convenire,

---

[a]iuxta *add* Durham Cathedral Library, B. IV. 18.   [b]offendebant A; of-
fenderant L; offendedant(?) B.   [c]sanctę *add* L.   [d]*om.* B.   [e]interesse
noluerant AB; se presentare omiserant L.   [f]reddidit conturbatum AB; turba-
verat L.   [g]et rationis esse ... velle insistere AB; et hinc principum suorum
consilio usus nuncios Romam dirigere sicut diximus maxime disponebat. Videbatur etenim illi dominum papam eo ipso quod de suis episcopis factum erat
privilegia patri et fratri suo sibique a Romano sede collata scidisse et ea
re rationis vis ... (ms. *damaged*) esse ipsum super hoc opportere conveniri L.

---

[1]Hinschius, p. 622.
[2]Mat. 10, 14; Mar. 6, 11; Luc. 9, 5.
[3]Luc. 11, 23 (with the clauses reversed).

maxime quod in huiusmodi visus sit privilegia patri et fratri
suo sibique a Romana ęcclesia iam olim collata se non promerente
scidisse. Ad hęc itaque agenda directus est Willelmus antistes
Exoniensis, papę notissimus, utpote qui sepe ad eum tempore
gloriosi patris Anselmi pro negotiis quę tunc inter reges Anglię
et eundem patrem versabantur ab ipsis fuerat regibus destinatus.
Nec enim cęcitas quę visum ei tulerat ab ipso itinere illum
poterat excusare, quia praeterita gesta illius fiduciam regi
praebebant illum pro posse iuxta morem suum suę causę fideliter
velle insistere.[a]

Interea[b] clerici ęcclesię Meneuwensis,[c] quę sub patrocinio
beati Andreę et sancti David in Walis[d] fundata consistit, episcopum sibi defuncto Wilfrido episcopo suo[e] a rege Henrico
postulavere, et electus[f] in hoc opus Bernardus quidam capellanus reginę,[1] vir probus et multorum iudicio sacerdotio dignus.
Electus est autem Sabbato ieiunii septimi mensis [18 Sept.],
et eodem die ad presbiteratum[g] a Wentano pontifice[h] Willelmo
apud Suthwercham consecratus.[i] [p. 282] De promotione[j] vero
pontificatus, quam mox in crastino fieri et rex et alii plures
optabant,[k] cum ubi aptius fieri posset disquireretur, intulit
Robertus comes Mellenti[l] supervacue de loco dubitari, dum con-
staret episcopum tali eventu electum ex consuetudine in capella
regis debere consecrari,[m] et hoc se probaturum si opus esset[n]
pronunciat. Quod non ęquum hominis dictum pater Radulfus pacato
animo ferre non valens, dixit eum huiusmodi allegatione leviter
posse efficere ut nec ibi nec alibi nisi Cantuarię pro quavis
causa pontifex idem sacraretur. Sciret tamen comes ipse, quia
postquam de capella regis tantum[o] dixit, nulla[p] ratione se illum

---

[a]*See p. 713 n. g.*   [b]Interea AB; Inter hęc L.   [c]eccl. Meneuwensis A;
Men. eccl. B; [eccl. *ms. damaged*] Menevensis L.   [d]Walis AB; Gualis L.
[e]ep. suo Wilfr. B.   [f]est *add* L.   [g]presbiteratum AB; gradum presbiteratus
L (*and Flor. Wig.*).   [h]pontifice AL (*and Flor. Wig.*); episcopo B.   [i]con-
secratus AB; promotus L (*and Flor. Wig.*).   [j]promotione AB; consecratione L.
[k]optabant AB; praeoptabant L.   [l]Mellenti AL; de Mellento B.   [m]consecrari
AL; sacrari B.   [n]si opus esset AB; firma ratione L.   [o]regis tantum AL;
tantum regis B.   [p]unquam *add* L.

---

[1]The queen's chancellor, described as a priest of the diocese of Hereford
in the petition for his consecration drawn up at Canterbury, *Canterbury
Professions*, p. 117.

inibi consecraturum. Ad quę rex ad comitem versus, 'Nichil est', inquit, 'quod intendis. Nec enim ego aut quilibet alter potest archiepiscopum Cantuariensem aliquo modo constringere ut episcopos Britannię alibi consecret quam velit ipse. Quapropter viderit suum est; consecret[a] episcopum suum ubi voluerit.' Proposuit itaque illum in ęcclesia hospitii sui apud Lamhetham consecrare. Verum quoniam[b] ipsi officio regina interesse volebat, postulatus ab ea sacravit ipsum in ęcclesia beati Petri Westmonasterii xiii kal' Octobris [19 Sept.],[1] accepta ab eo solita professione de subiectione et obędientia ęcclesię Cantuariensi et episcopis eius exhibenda.[2] Huic consecrationi interfuerunt et cooperatores extiterunt suffraganei ęcclesię Cantuariensis, episcopi videlicet hi, Willelmus Wintoniensis, Robertus Lincoliensis, Rogerius Serberiensis, Iohannes Bathoniensis, Urbanus Glamorgatensis, [p. 283] Gislebertus Lumniensis de Hibernia.

II. *Hugh the Chanter, History of the Church of York*

> York Minster Library, Magnum Registrum Album, i. fo. 9[v]; printed in Hugh the Chanter, ed. Johnson, pp. 37-8 (*Hist. York*, ii.132-3).

Circa festum sancti Michaelis convocavit rex apud Londoniam episcopos et abbates, principes et primores regni sui, cum eis de pace, de statu regni, de negociis acturus,[c] inter quos diversi ordinis plurimi affuerunt. Ibi rex electo nostro de dilacione consecracionis sue conquerenti, astante comite de Mellent et Nigello de Albaneio, consilium dedit quatinus proborum virorum testimonio archiepiscopum conveniret, et ab eo consecrari humiliter[d] requireret. Quod si antequam faceret aliquid quod iniustum videatur exigeret, in sentenciam et

---

[a]L *ends.*   [b]quia B.   [c]acturis *ms.*   [d]humilite *ms.*

---

[1]The queen normally resided at Westminster, WMGR ii.494 §418, *Liber Monasterii de Hyda*, pp. 311-12.
[2]*Canterbury Professions*, no. 64. Subsequently this profession became of central importance in St. Davids' struggle for metropolitan status, on which see most recently M. Richter, *National Library of Wales Journal*, xv (1967/8), 197-214 and *JEH* xxii (1971), 177-89.

voluntatem domini[a] inde se[b] ponere diceret. Letus de consilio,
et secum adhibitis Gaufrido Rotomagensi archiepiscopo, Iohanne
Luxoviensi episcopo, Rannulfo Dunelmensi et multis clericis et
monachis et quibusdam laicis, archiepiscopum coram pluribus[c]
de suo numero cuiusque ordinis suppliciter requisivit ut eum
consecraret. Cui ille, 'Libenter', inquit, 'faciam, si feceritis quod debetis.' Et Eboracensis, 'Ex iure ecclesiarum nostrarum,
quarum archiepiscopi sese debent invicem consecrare, a vobis
consecrari postulo. Si quid deinde ecclesie vestre vel persone
me debere vel canonice monstrare poteritis, exhibere non recuso.
Tunc Rotomagensis archiepiscopus, 'Non est', inquit, 'tantarum
personarum uti duplicitate verborum. Quid ab alterutro exigat
vel alterutro deneget aperte uterque denunciet.' 'Non loquar
ambicione', ait Cantuariensis; 'nisi professione[d] prius tradita
nequaquam illi manus imponam.' Ad quod electus, 'De hoc in sentenciam et consilium domini pape paratus sum me ponere.' Et ille,
'Non ita iuvenis, non sum adeo levis, nec sic agilis, nec sic
apparatus ut modo tantum iter agrediar.' Et addidit,[e] 'Si dominus
papa michi ore ad os preciperet ut vos, seposita professione,
consecrarem, de hoc minime obedirem.' Quod multi qui aderant pen-
santes, nec canonice nec sapienter dictum reputaverunt.

122

1116. SECOND LEGATION OF ANSELM, ABBOT OF ST. SABA

See Tillmann, p. 25, Brett, *English Church*, pp. 37-40.

It is not known what success Bishop William of Exeter enjoyed
in attempting to defend the privileges of the Anglo-Norman
kingdom during his visit to Rome late in 1115, though nothing
further was heard of the banning of the Norman episcopate. It is,
however, clear that the pope's concern with the affairs of
England had not diminished, for on 24 May he commissioned Anselm
of St. Saba as legate in letters addressed to the English

---

[a]pape *add ed.*   [b]*om. ms.*   [c]pluris *ms.*   [d]professionem *ms.*   [e]adierunt
ms.

bishops. The purpose of the legation was twofold, the celebration of councils for the reform of the church and the collection
of Peter's Pence. Another letter to Archbishop Ralph urged him
to co-operate with the legate, and to send the monk Warner of
Christ Church as his representative to Rome.[1]

About August 1116 Anselm arrived in Normandy and met the
king, who detained him there while a message was sent to England
announcing his coming. At a meeting of churchmen and magnates
in London under the queen's presidency it was determined that
Archbishop Ralph should cross the sea, expound to the king
the threat such a legation offered to the customs and liberties
of the realm, and then proceed to the pope to seek its ending.[2]
Ralph was also doubtless moved by anxieties over the progress
of his dispute with Thurstan, elect of York. Immediately before
the council at Salisbury in March 1116 Thurstan had received
papal letters confirming him in his resolution to resist a profession to Canterbury and ordering Ralph to consecrate him without exacting one. Such pressure was brought to bear on Thurstan
at the council that he resigned his claim to the see and did
not deliver the pope's letter to Ralph. Since, however, the
canons of York announced their determination to accept no alternative candidate, since the king made no move to find one, and
since William of Exeter had told Ralph on his return from the
pope that only a personal appearance at the curia offered the
archbishop any chance of maintaining the primacy, this too may
have encouraged him to undertake the journey.[3]

Meanwhile the legate remained in Normandy, where he lingered
on in the hope at least of collecting the outstanding balance
of Peter's Pence. He finally abandoned his efforts early in
1120, by which time Paschal and Gelasius his successor were both
dead, and a new legate had already been appointed.[4]

---

[1]Eadmer, pp. 245-6 (JL 6525). Warner had been to Rome for Ralph's pallium
in 1114 (Eadmer, p. 226, *ASC*, ed. Plummer, i.246, ed. Whitelock *at al.*,
p. 184).   [2]Eadmer, p. 239.
[3]Eadmer, pp. 237-9, Hugh the Chanter, pp. 40-7 (*Hist. York*, ii.134-41),
WMGP, pp. 129-31. See further Dueball, *Suprematstreit*, pp. 71-6, Nicholl,
Thurstan, pp. 52-7, Bethell, *JEH* xix (1968), 151-4.
[4]Hugh the Chanter, p. 54 (*Hist. York*, ii.147), Eadmer, pp. 245, 259,
below p. 722. Anselm may well have long abandoned hope of exercising his,
powers, and we have no evidence that these had been renewed after Paschal's
death; in 1121 he became abbot of Bury St. Edmunds.

123

18 OCTOBER 1119. PAPAL COUNCIL AT RHEIMS

For this council see Hefele–Leclercq, v.569-91 and R.
Somerville, 'The Councils of Pope Calixtus II: Reims
1119', citing earlier literature. The canons are found
in Mansi, xxi.235-6 (and widely elsewhere); the attendance is most fully listed in the document from Tours in
coll. 255-6. The chief sources for the council's proceedings are Orderic in OV, ed. Chibnall, vi.252-76 and Hesso
'scholasticus' in *MGH Libelli de Lite,* iii.21-8.

As soon as the cardinals still in Rome heard of the election
of Archbishop Guy of Vienne as Pope Calixtus II on 2 February
1119 they wrote to their colleagues to confirm their choice and
to urge the need for a council. By 4 May Calixtus could write
to the archbishop of Magdeburg summoning him to a council at
Rheims on 18 October.[1] Similar letters were written to the
archbishops of Canterbury and York at about the same time, and
their substance was repeated on 17 May.[2]

A considerable body of the English clergy was then in Normandy with the king on various business, and accordingly an
unparalleled number of them attended the council. From an
English point of view the most remarkable events concerned the
dispute between Canterbury and York. Thurstan, archbishop-elect
of York, was allowed by the king to attend under certain conditions which cannot now be recovered with any confidence. By
22 September, accompanied by some of his clergy, he was with
the pope at Tours, and travelled with him to Rheims, where he
was joined by the bishop of Orkney. Meanwhile Seffrid, half-
brother of Archbishop Ralph, Archdeacon John of Canterbury,
and Bishop Urban of Glamorgan had arrived directly from the
king in Normandy in time for the events of Sunday, 19 October,
when Calixtus himself consecrated Thurstan in the cathedral,

---

[1] In JL 6688 of 16 Apr. Calixtus had already spoken of a council to be
held in the autumn; JL 6693 (U. Robert, *Bullaire du pape Calixte II*, i,
nos. 7, 12).

[2] Hugh the Chanter, pp. 66-8 (*Hist. York,* ii.158-61, JL 6722-4).

without a profession to Canterbury and in the teeth of their
protests.[1] The other English representatives, the bishops of
Durham, St. Davids, and Exeter, did not arrive until the next
day. The most obvious absentee was Archbishop Ralph; he appears
to have had a stroke on 11 July, from which he never wholly
recovered, but his long record of resistance to the mandates of
Paschal and Gelasius had already hopelessly prejudiced his
case, and on the closing day of the council Thurstan was given
his pallium.[2]

Bishop Urban may well have travelled to Rheims independently;
he had prepared a long memorandum on the grievances of his see,
on the basis of which he secured several bulls before the council opened and one, commending him to the king, issued during
its course.[3] No other bulls are known to have been issued to
English beneficiaries at the time, but other matters which
closely concerned the Anglo-Norman clergy were debated. At the
outset of the council King Louis appeared in person to demand
justice against Henry for his treatment of his nephew, William
Clito, and for his part in instigating the war of 1116. When
the archbishop of Rouen sought to reply he was shouted down,
but the pope promised that he would seek to mediate between the
two kings after the council in a general programme of reconciliation.[4]

On 30 October the canons of the council were read out in
their final form and the council dispersed. Not surprisingly
the five canons generally attributed to the council are found
widely in English manuscripts; apart from the version incorporated in the Durham *Historia Regum* and its derivatives,[5]
eight apparently independent copies survive in twelfth-century
books from England or Wales.

---

[1]Ibid., pp. 68-73 (*Hist. York*, ii.161-5); Eadmer, pp. 255-7.
[2]OV, ed. Chibnall, vi.318, but see there n. 4, Hugh the Chanter, p. 75
(*Hist. York*, ii.167); JL 6767 (Robert, *Bullaire du pape Calixte II*, i,
no. 86) is merely a fragment of JL 6831 of 11 March 1120.
[3]*Book of Llandaff*, pp. 89-94. The text cited in Brett, *English Church*,
p. 52 n. 2 is a mistranscription by Morice from Paris, BN ms. fr. 22322,
also the source of Mansi, xxi.255-6 (where the whole Canterbury delegation
is listed) and other copies; compare *Papsturkunden in Frankreich* (Neue Folge),
v.48.
[4]OV, ed. Chibnall, vi.256-8, 264.
[5]Symeon, ii.255-6, Hoveden, i.174-5, and see above pp. 696-7.

Aberystwyth, NLW, ms. 17110 E, coll. 109-10, *Book of Llan-daff*, pp. 95-6.

Cambridge, UL, Kk 4. 6, fos. 279^V-280, from a Worcester copy of a collection compiled originally at Malmesbury. See Levison in *Neues Archiv* xxxv (1910), 396-7, and above, p. 648 n. 3.

Cambridge, Trinity Coll. ms. 0. 7. 9, fo. 180, now bound with some slightly later material from Buildwas.

Hereford Cathedral Library, ms. P. i. 3, fo. ii^V, a cathedral ms. described by W. Holtzmann in *Neues Archiv* l (1933), 284-6.

BL ms. Cotton Cleopatra C. viii, fo. 163^V, entered without attribution at the end of a canonical collection briefly described by Z.N. Brooke in *English Church and the Papacy*, pp. 93-4. This copy has only faint claims to an English provenance.

BL ms. Harley 633, fo. 70^{r-v}, a late 12th-cent. northern copy of a collection similar to that in the Cambridge UL; for the Rheims canons its text differs widely in detail.

Oxford, Jesus Coll. ms. 26, fos. 191^V-192, among the additions to a copy of the *Pannormia* apparently given to Cirencester by Master Alured; see Ker, *Catalogue*, no. 355.

Oxford, St. John's Coll. ms. 149, fo. 192^{r-v}, with some important additional material printed by W. Holtzmann in *Neues Archiv* l (1933), 318-9.

What appears to have been another English text, added at the end of a copy of the Collection in IV Books, was destroyed in Warsaw in 1944.[1]

---

[1] The manuscript, once St. Petersburg ms. F.v.II. 13, was described by A. Halban-Blumenstok, *Deutsche Zeitschrift für Kirchenrecht*, v (1895), 226, 287-302, supplemented by A. Staerk, *Les manuscrits latins du Ve au XIIIe siècle conservés à la Bibliothèque Impériale de Saint-Pétersbourg*, i.253-60, no. xcix, who assigns it correctly to the Załuski collection, and to a date 1130-43. It is no longer at Leningrad, and cannot be traced at Warsaw, so it must be presumed to have been destroyed with the great bulk of the Załuski manuscripts in 1944, after their return to Poland under the terms of the Treaty of Riga. The text of Rheims was an addition, followed by a version of the Council of Westminster (1125), with which the manuscript ended.

No earlier papal council had been so promptly or so widely
recorded in English sources. Although many of its provisions
were taken into those of the Lateran council of 1123, which in
turn was the most powerful external influence on the English
legatine councils of 1125 and 1127, there are signs that the
canons of Rheims also had some effect.[1] If this may have been
slight, the consecration of Archbishop Thurstan and the presence
of an exceptionally large English delegation lend the council
a special interest in the history of Anglo-papal relations.

124

1119-1121. NEGOTIATIONS WITH CALIXTUS II

> For the background to these events see particularly
> U. Robert, *Histoire du pape Calixte II*, pp. 89-97 and
> Nicholl, *Thurstan*, pp. 66-74.

By the close of the Council of Rheims there were three substantial points at issue between the king and the pope. The council
had given considerable support to the charges made by Louis VI;
the consecration of Thurstan as archbishop of York in defiance
of the king's known wishes would undoubtedly provoke severe
counter-measures; lastly, the restrictions which Henry had imposed on those bishops he had allowed to attend the council
illustrated his continuing concern at the recent pattern of
papal intervention in his dominions.

All these points appear to have been discussed when king and
pope met between Gisors and Chaumont, on the border of Normandy
and the Vexin, on 23 November 1119.[2] On the political issues
Calixtus appears to have accepted the king's defence of his
conduct towards Duke Robert, and the king's readiness for a
peace with France removed most further difficulties. The problem

---

[1]Below, pp. 735, 738-9.
[2]The meeting took place in a church equidistant from Gisors and Chaumont-
en-Vexin, perhaps that of Trie-Château (ar. Beauvais). OV, ed. Chibnall,
vi.282-90, Malmesbury in WMGR ii.482, §406, WMGP, p. 265, Hugh the Chanter,
pp. 76-81 (*Hist. York*, ii.168-72), Eadmer, pp. 258-9.

of Thurstan was more intractable; on hearing the news of his consecration the king had sworn never to allow him to return to England unless he made a profession, and had begun the process of taking the archbishopric into his hands, while the pope had already granted Thurstan his pallium, though this may not have been known to the king.[1] The pope pressed the archbishop's claims, but the king refused to act without the advice of a council in England and stood by his oath. Though Henry also raised the matter of the customs of his kingdom it seems unlikely that any large measure of agreement was reached. If then the meeting was generally described as friendly, serious differences remained.

This was soon shown when Cono of Palestrina was appointed as legate for France, England, and Normandy at the beginning of December, for it was Cono's action in 1115 in Normandy which had so alarmed Henry earlier.[2] In February 1120 Bishop William of Exeter came to the pope at Valence with the object of securing a profession from Thurstan and a legatine commission for Archbishop Ralph, though these were conceivably alternatives; his failure can be tested against the uncompromising letters issued on Thurstan's behalf at the beginning of March, immediately before he left the Curia. The archbishop of Canterbury was suspended from office, and Christ Church placed under an interdict, if Thurstan was not restored to York within a month; a letter to the king, containing similar provisions with the further threat of an interdict on both provinces, was entrusted to the archbishop of Tours and the bishop of Beauvais, but was delivered by intermediaries soon after Easter (18 April), together with letters from Cono. Under such pressure the king and legate agreed to a meeting, probably at Vernon, on 30 May.[3]

---

[1] Hugh the Chanter, pp. 74-5, 78-9, 81 (*Hist. York,* ii.166-7, 170-2), Eadmer, pp. 257-8.
[2] Above, p. 710; Hugh the Chanter, pp. 83, 89 (*Hist. York,* ii.174, 181), Schieffer, *Die päpstlichen Legaten in Frankreich,* pp. 207-12. At what point Thurstan was offered, and refused, an English legation before March 1120 is not clear.
[3] Hugh the Chanter, pp. 85-94, 101-4 (*Hist. York,* ii.177-86, 192-4), which include JL 6773, 6774, 6767, 6831. JL 6774 and Hugh, pp. 101-2, are paraphrased in Symeon, ii.258, 262. More summarily see WMGP, p. 266.

After some discussion the king agreed to restore Thurstan to
the archbishopric provided that his return was delayed for some
time. His services to the king in the following months further
assisted his cause; he played an active part in securing the
peace between Henry and Louis VI which culminated that summer
in the homage William, Henry's heir, did to Louis for Normandy;
he interceded successfully with Cono on behalf of the Norman
bishops whom he had summoned to his legatine council at Beauvais
on 18 October 1120, and threatened with excommunication for
their failure to attend. After a further interview with the
legate at Gisors about the beginning of November Henry returned
to England[1] and at a council, probably that held at London at
Epiphany, persuaded Archbishop Ralph of the impossibility of
further resistance, even had the disaster of the White Ship left
the will to attempt it. On 31 January 1121 Thurstan sailed for
England; he came to the royal court at Windsor where the king
was celebrating his marriage feast, and was solemnly received
at York on 20 February.[2]

125

c.JUNE 1121. LEGATION OF PETER PIERLEONI, CARDINAL PRIEST OF SANTA MARIA IN TRASTEVERE

See Tillmann, pp. 26-7, Brett, *English Church*, p. 41.

Peter Pierleoni, a member of a family which had been outstanding in the papal service for almost a century, and himself the
future anti-pope Anacletus II,[3] arrived in Northern France

---

[1]Hugh the Chanter, pp. 94-9 (*Hist. York*, ii.186-90); for the council at
Beauvais see particularly Clarius of Sens in *Bibliothèque historique de
l'Yonne*, ii.535; for the homage of prince William see Symeon, ii.258 and
Suger, *Vie de Louis VI le Gros*, p. 112.

[2]Hugh the Chanter, pp. 99-101 (*Hist. York*, ii.190-1), Eadmer, pp. 291-2.
Reg. ii, nos. 1241, 1243, illustrate the composition of the meeting.

[3]The abundant literature on Peter is summarized in Hüls, pp. 189-91, 225,
amongst which see particularly P. Fedele, *Archivio della R. Società Romana
di Storia Patria*, xxvii (1904), 399-440. His influence at the curia at this
time is emphasized by L. Pellegrini, *Contributi dell'Istituto di Storia
Medioevale*, ii (1972), 525-6.

before May 1121 as legate for France and England; his commission is said to have extended to Ireland, Scotland, and the
outer isles.[1] In France he often acted in concert with cardinal
Gregory, his later rival as Innocent II. Eadmer claims that this
legation was one of a number sent out by Calixtus after the
capture of the anti-pope Burdinus at the end of April, though
Peter at least must have left Italy before then.[2] Abbots and
other messengers crossed the channel to announce his impending
arrival, and the king sent his nephew John of Bayeux and Bishop
Bernard of St. Davids to escort him to England. Their instructions were to entertain the legate only from the royal demesne,
allowing him to levy no procurations. He came to the royal
court as the king was engaged in his expedition against North
Wales, probably in June, and it was these preoccupations, as
well as the customs of the kingdom, which Henry advanced as
reasons for not summoning the council without which the legate
could not pursue his plans.[3] Two documents appear to show him
at London, confirming the privileges of the monks of Westminster
and granting them an indulgence, but the texts present some
marked peculiarities, if they are not wholly fabricated.[4] On his
return the legate spent three days at Canterbury, where he was
shown texts of the primacy forgeries, and sailed from Dover
before mid-September.[5]

In Anglo-Norman sources even before the schism of 1130 Peter
was not well regarded, and his mission was chiefly remembered
for the lavish gifts which he received from the king and many
churches; if it had any specific purpose no source records

---

[1]Schieffer, *Die päpstlichen Legaten in Frankreich*, p. 214; Peter's earliest
dated appearance as legate is at Oudenburg on 1 May 1121 (*Chronicon monasterii Aldenburgensis*, pp. 45-50); Eadmer, p. 295.

[2]Eadmer, p. 294.

[3]Eadmer, pp. 295-7; the king held his court at Westminster at Whitsun (29
May) before the Welsh expedition (*ASC*, ed. Plummer, i.250, ed. Clark, p. 41,
trans. Whitelock *et al.*, p. 187).

[4]*PUE* i, nos. 12, 13. In form these are quite unlike the relatively numerous documents issued in Peter's name in 1121 and 1123-5; besides those texts
cited by Schieffer, above, n. 1, compare also *Papsturkunden in Frankreich*,
Neue Folge iv (ed. Ramackers), nos. 15, 16, vii (ed. Lohrmann), no. 29.

[5]Eadmer, pp. 296-7, *J. Wig.*, p. 16 (*Flor. Wig.* ii.76). These events are
placed by Eadmer before the arrival in England of Gregory as bishop-elect of
Dublin. He was made deacon at Salisbury in the fourth week of September.

it.[1] After the Lateran council in April 1123, Peter returned to France as legate; late in 1123 he was in Normandy, but there is no evidence that he ever returned to England.[2]

126

c. FEBRUARY 1123. LEGATION OF HENRY, ABBOT OF SAINT-JEAN D'ANGÉLY

> See Tillmann, p. 27; Henry's career is described in full by C. Clark, '"This ecclesiastical adventurer": Henry of Saint-Jean d'Angély', *EHR* lxxxiv (1969), 548-60.

Abbot Henry had been sent by Calixtus II to escort Archbishop Ralph to the Curia in 1119, though without success.[3] Early in 1123 he was in England to collect Peter's Pence, and it seems likely that he attended the royal council at Gloucester on 2 February at which the new archbishop was elected to Canterbury, for he is said to have protested to the king at its outcome.[4] Nothing else seems to be known of his activities on this visit, though he was to be appointed abbot of Peterborough in 1127.

127

FEBRUARY 1123. ELECTION OF WILLIAM OF CORBEIL AS ARCHBISHOP OF CANTERBURY

> For the circumstances see D. Bethell, *EHR* lxxxiv (1969), 674-81 and Nicholl, *Thurstan,* pp. 84-91. The chief sources are *ASC*, ed. Plummer, i.251-2, ed. Clark, pp. 42-4, tr. Whitelock *et al.*, pp. 188-9; Symeon, ii.267-73; *J. Wig.*, p. 17 (*Flor. Wig.* ii.77-8); Hugh the Chanter, pp. 108-

---

[1] Eadmer, p. 296, Malmesbury in WMGP, p. 128; compare the very hostile accounts of Peter in OV, ed. Chibnall, vi.266-8 and *MGH Libelli de Lite,* iii.93-6 (by Arnulf of Lisieux).

[2] See e.g. JL 7056 (*Italia Pontificia* ed. P. Kehr, vi.324-5). For Peter's second legation see Schieffer, pp. 214-18 and the references in p. 724 n. 4 above.

[3] Hugh the Chanter, p. 63 (*Hist. York,* ii.156).

[4] *ASC*, ed. Plummer, i.252, ed. Clark, p. 43, tr. Whitelock *et al.*, p. 189.

  19 (*Hist. York*, ii.198-208); OV (ed. Chibnall), vi.318-
20; Gervase, ii.379-80.

Archbishop Ralph died at Canterbury on 20 October 1122, while
the king was in the North. After celebrating Christmas at Dunstable the king moved westwards, having sent out writs summoning
a council at Gloucester for 2 February. Its composition is
variously described, but the presence of a number of laymen, the
archbishop of York, the bishop of Durham, and the heads of
several northern houses as well as the higher clergy of the province of Canterbury is well attested. Some time before the council met, the secular bishops, notably Robert of Lincoln and Roger
of Salisbury, were seeking to secure the election of an archbishop who was not a monk; the death of Bishop Robert on 10
January did not weaken their determination.[1]

  Accordingly, when the council opened, the bishops urged their
case, though they were fiercely resisted by the monks of Christ
Church for two days; eventually, however, the monks were forced
to accept a list of four candidates presented to them by the
bishops, from whom they chose William of Corbeil, a former
clerk of Flambard and canon of Dover, who had recently become
first prior of the bishop of London's house of Augustinian
canons at St. Osyth.[2] According to the Anglo-Saxon Chronicle
the choice was contested not only by the monks but by the lay
magnates, who were overborne by the bishop of Salisbury, while
Hugh the Chanter suggests that the new archbishop was unknown to
the king. Archbishop Thurstan offered to consecrate him according to the ancient custom, but Canterbury's partisans refused.
Accordingly he was consecrated at Canterbury on 16 February by
a number of his suffragans; he returned to the king's court at
Woodstock about 11 March, and from there the two archbishops
left for Rome, accompanied by a substantial embassy of eccle-

---

[1] Hunt., pp. 244-5.
[2] For St. Osyth see two studies by D. Bethell, 'The Lives of St. Osyth of
Essex and St. Osyth of Aylesbury', *Analecta Bollandiana*, lxxxviii (1970),
75-127, esp. 90-4, and 'Richard of Belmeis and the Foundation of St. Osyth's',
Transactions of the Essex Archaeological Soc., 3rd Ser., ii (1970), 299-
328.

siastics.[1] They travelled separately, and when Archbishop William arrived at the Curia he met formidable opposition; Hugh the Chanter and the Durham *Historia Regum* are in general agreement that the charges made against his election were that it was made in the king's court, and not by the clergy of Canterbury, further that he had not been consecrated by the proper person, and that a secular clerk had been promoted to preside over monks.[2] The king's request, letters from the emperor on his behalf, and the intercession of the archbishop of York eventually secured William's confirmation as archbishop, and in a bull dated 21 May 1123 Calixtus recorded this and the grant of the pallium. It may perhaps have been of importance that the form of William's election conformed closely to the procedure laid down in the Concordat of Worms, reached the previous autumn.[3]

The presence of both archbishops and the bishop of Glasgow at Rome afforded an opportunity for pursuing two other controversies, that of the subjection of Glasgow to York, and that of the primacy. When Canterbury's forged privileges were produced Thurstan objected that he had set out to attend the Lateran council, not for litigation, though he had some copies of documents in the case. Though the Canterbury bulls were derided, judgement was postponed; according to the Durham chronicle the case was to be referred to a legatine council to be held in England. The last bull in favour of a member of the embassy is dated 25 May, and they probably returned to Normandy very soon after that.[4]

---

[1] According to *UGQ*, p. 5, William left England on 13 Mar. The composition of the embassy is most fully described in *ASC*.

[2] The Durham historian was particularly well informed about events at Rome in 1123, perhaps through the monk Robert, who secured *PUE* ii, no. 5 on the monks' behalf.

[3] Leyser in *TRHS* 5th Ser., x (1960), 79-83.

[4] *PUE* iii, nos. 7, 8; the king crossed to Normandy, where the ambassadors found him on their return, on 11 June (Symeon, ii.273, interpreted, with some hesitation, in the light of *ASC*, ed. Plummer, i.253, ed. Clark, p. 44).

128
18-27 MARCH 1123. FIRST LATERAN COUNCIL

For the council in general see JL i, pp. 809-11, Hefele—
Leclercq, v (1), 630-44, Foreville, *Latran*, pp. 50-69,
U. Robert, *Histoire du pape Calixte II*, pp. 162-77. The
canons (Mansi, xxi.281 ff.) are best edited in *Conciliorum
oecumenicorum decreta*, ed. J. Alberigo *et al.*, pp. 190-4,
used here.

The Lateran council, reckoned in the Latin West as the ninth
ecumenical council, met in the third week in Lent, 1123, as the
crowning event of Calixtus' programme of reconciliation. The
only surviving summons is addressed to Archbishop Baudri of
Dol, and is dated 25 June 1122; it calls him with the suffragans and abbots of his province to a council to be held at Rome
on 18 March 1123. Similar letters appear to have been addressed
to the archbishops of Canterbury and York for the same time,
though these were not delivered before the end of October.[1] In
fact no English delegation attended the council, since the king
delayed his bishops until after the consecration of Archbishop
William, and they probably did not arrive in Rome until May
1123. To excuse their absence Henry sent a clerk and two Norman bishops.[2]

The number of prelates who attended is uncertain, for contemporary estimates varied from less than two hundred to almost
a thousand. The well-informed historian at Durham agrees with
Abbot Suger, who was present, in speaking of three hundred
bishops taking part.[3] The text of the canons is also difficult
to establish, as there is still no edition based on a study of

---

[1]U. Robert, *Bullaire du pape Calixte II*, ii, no. 304 (JL 6977); according to Hugh the Chanter, p. 108 (*Hist. York*, ii.198) the letters arrived
between the death of Archbishop Ralph on 20 October 1122 and the beginning
of Advent (3 December).

[2]Hugh the Chanter, p. 110 (*Hist. York*, ii.200); it is possible that the
monk Robert of Durham was also there (see Leyser in *TRHS* 5th Ser., x (1960),
80-2). *PUE* ii, no. 5 for Durham and JL 7071 for Glastonbury are both dated
15 May, and at least six more bulls for English beneficiaries were issued
in the next ten days.

[3]Symeon, ii.269; Suger, *Vie de Louis le Gros*, p. 214.

the abundant manuscript tradition. The *textus receptus* of Mansi
(the β version of *Conciliorum oecumenicorum decreta*) is clearly
of little authority. While there is more general agreement on
canons 1-17 of the α tradition, the manuscripts even here diverge widely in detail.[1]

The canons show few departures from the recent pattern of
papal legislation, but the return of the papacy to Rome and
defeat of the anti-pope are reflected in a provision denouncing
the ordinations of Burdinus, and in others protecting pilgrims
and certain Italian and specifically Roman ecclesiastical interests. The pope's concern for the maintenance of the Truce of God
and for the progress of the crusade in Spain and the Holy Land
also finds a mention. More strikingly, c. 16, which exists in
several versions, denounces the public ministrations of abbots and
monks with unusual vigour; among the omissions are any explicit
mention of either investiture or the mechanics of election.[2]

There are five English manuscripts of the canons. The first
is found in the single surviving complete copy of the Durham
Historia Regum,[3] which is also found in all essentials in another
Durham book:

Cambridge, Peterhouse ms. 74, fos. 119^V-120, at the end of
    a copy of Lanfranc's abbreviation of Pseudo-Isidore.

The Canterbury version is found in two other copies:

Cambridge, Corpus Christi Coll. ms. 19, fos. 333^V-334, added
    at the end of Ivo's *Decretum*, but wrongly ascribed to
    the Council of Rheims in a rubric.

---

[1]The β sequence is found at the end of Book IV of the Collection in Thir-
teen Books and some copies of Anselm of Lucca's *Collectio Canonum*. For the
manuscripts see now S. Kuttner, *Bulletin of Medieval Canon Law*, NS, i (1971),
10 and n. For the α text see also Cl. Leonardi, *Bullettino dell'Istituto
storico Italiano per il medio evo e Archivio Muratoriano*, lxxv (1963), 57-
70.

[2]The terms of the Worms concordat were attacked with great bitterness
during the council according to *Gerhohi praepositi Reichersbergensis opera
inedita*, i.83; c. 3 prohibits the consecration of any but canonically elected
bishops, without specifying the proper forms of election.

[3]Symeon, ii.269-72, Cambridge, Corpus Christi Coll. ms. 139, fo. 127^{r-v}.

Durham Cathedral Lib. ms. B. IV. 18, fo. 97, added at the
   end of another copy of Lanfranc's collection, with extracts from St. Gregory and materials on the Canterbury
   primacy.

The only copy from a secular community is found in:

Hereford Cathedral Lib. ms. O. ii. 7, fos. i^V-ii^V, added on
   the flyleaves of a canonical ms. described above (p. 696).

The Canterbury and Durham versions contain a number of the
α canons; the Hereford text alone includes c. 16 and part of
c. 18 in forms related to those found in the β sequence.[1]
   It does not appear that the Lateran decrees exercised any
great direct influence in England, but much of their substance
became widely known through the legatine council of 1125, which
was attended by most of the higher clergy and recorded in a
much larger number of manuscripts.

129

1124-1125. LEGATION OF JOHN OF CREMA, CARDINAL PRIEST OF ST.
   CHRYSOGONUS

On this legation see Tillmann, pp. 27-30, Schieffer, *Die
   päpstlichen Legaten in Frankreich*, pp. 225-6, Brett,
   English Church, pp. 42-7. For John's career see particularly Zoeppfel, *Die Papstwahlen*, pp. 310-13, Schmale,
   Studien zum Schisma, pp. 34-8, Zenker, pp. 59-62, Hüls,
   pp. 176-8.

In 1123 Calixtus II had promised to send a legate to England to
resolve the primacy issue; at the same time the dispute between
the archbishop of York and the Scottish bishops was becoming

---

[1]The relation of the English copies to the other versions is discussed
in a paper to be printed in the *Proceedings of the Sixth International
Congress of Medieval Canon Law* (1980).

more acute, notably with the appointment of Prior Robert of
Scone to the see of St. Andrews early in 1124. In the mind of
King Henry, however, these matters were probably quite overshadowed by the importance of securing a divorce between his
nephew, William Clito, and the daughter of the count of Anjou,
doubly dangerous during the Norman revolt of 1123/4. The case
had probably first been discussed before the legates Peter and
Gregory at their synod at Chartres on 12 March 1124, which was
attended by at least some of the Norman clergy.[1] By the beginning of June, however, Calixtus had sent John of Crema, a
cardinal who stood among the closest of the pope's advisers, as
a special legate, and it was his judgement in favour of the
divorce which the pope confirmed in letters dated 26 August.[2]
No commission for John survives in Calixtus' name, and in the
event the legate was detained by the king in Normandy until
after the pope's death on 13 December. As soon as the news
reached Normandy Archbishop William renewed his application for
a legate to resolve the primacy dispute in England, while at
about the same time the king summoned representatives of all
the vacant churches of England to Normandy, and appointed a
number of new prelates.[3] In Lent the legate crossed the Channel,
accompanied by both archbishops and by Simon and Seffrid,
bishops-elect of Worcester and Chichester, in time to sing the
Easter High Mass in Canterbury Cathedral on 29 March.[4] He stayed
in the South long enough to attend the consecration of Bishop
Seffrid on 12 April, before setting out on a visitation which,
according to the Anglo-Saxon Chronicle, took him to every
bishopric and abbey of the kingdom.[5] Meanwhile the new pope,

---

[1]Schieffer, *Die päpstlichen Legaten in Frankreich*, pp. 215-16.
[2]Robert, *Bullaire du pape Calixte II*, ii, no. 507 (JL 7165); for the date
of the legate's arrival in Normandy see *Lanfranci Opera*, ed. Giles, i.333.
The circumstances of the divorce have been discussed most recently by S.B.
Hicks, 'The Anglo-Papal Bargain of 1125: the Legatine Mission of John of
Crema', *Albion*, viii (1976), 301-10.
[3]Hugh the Chanter, p. 120 (*Hist. York*, ii.209); *Chron. Battle*, pp. 132-4;
Reg. ii, nos. 1424-7 are all most probably to be attributed to early 1125.
[4]*ASC*, ed. Plummer, i.255, ed. Clark, p. 47, trans. Whitelock *et al.*, p.
192; Gervase, ii.381-2.
[5]*ASC* loc. cit.; *J. Wig.*, pp. 18-19 (*Flor. Wig.* ii.79); 'Historia Sele-
beiensis' in *The Coucher Book of Selby*, i. (27); Brett, *English Church*,
pp. 42-3.

Honorius II, issued a number of bulls on 12/13 April empowering
John to act as legate for England and Scotland and probably
another to Thurstan commanding him to attend the legate in his
dealings with the Scottish bishops; this was no doubt among the
points discussed at John's meeting with King David at Roxburgh
before he returned south for the legatine council in September.[1]

Shortly after the council the legate, preceded by the two
archbishops, the bishops of Lincoln and Glasgow and the abbots
of St. Albans and Sherborne, crossed the Channel to Normandy.
Here the king and legate agreed on a compromise over the issue
of the primacy, upon which the two archbishops were ordered
either to agree or to abandon their litigation. They then proceeded separately to Rome, arriving about Christmas.[2]

John's legation was subsequently cited by Gilbert Foliot as
a model of judicious reform, though he is unlikely to be a
first-hand witness. In the Annals of Winchester and Henry of
Huntingdon he appears very differently. Both stories are in
essence the same: the legate who displayed such hostility to a
married clergy was himself found in the most compromising of
circumstances, and left the country in confusion. In detail they
are irreconcilable, but their substance is lent considerable
support by a story in the Anacletian version of the *Liber Pontificalis* that John of Crema was deposed for some time under
Honorius, and by the charges of incontinence levelled against
him during the schism after 1130.[3] However, whatever their
truth, John's legation was the first since 1070 where a direct
emissary of the pope was able to exercise widespread authority
in England.

---

[1]Symeon, ii.276-8 (JL 7201, 7203-4); *PUE* ii.101.
[2]Hugh the Chanter, pp. 122-4 (*Hist. York*, ii.210-2); Nicholl, *Thurstan*,
pp. 95-6; Bethell in *JEH* xix (1968), 156.
[3]*GFL*, no. 170, pp. 240-1; Hunt., p. 246; *Ann. Mon.* ii.47-8; *Liber Pontificalis prout extat in codice manuscripto Dertusensi*, pp. 80, 208.

130

8 SEPTEMBER 1125. LEGATINE COUNCIL AT WESTMINSTER

> For this council see Brooke, *English Church and the Papacy*, pp. 102, 169-70, Nicholl, *Thurstan*, pp. 93-5, Brett, *English Church*, pp. 43-5, Foreville, *Latran*, pp. 69-70.

The commission of Honorius to John of Crema had particularly empowered him to celebrate solemn synods, and the crowning achievement of his mission was the council he held in September.[1] The only surviving summons (no. I) is in the name of Archbishop William of Canterbury, and calls Urban of Llandaff with the archdeacons, abbots, and priors of his diocese to a council to be held at London on 8 September; presumably this was the common form which may be compared with that of the two legates in 1070.[2]

The deliberations of the council lasted three or four days; the king remained in Normandy throughout the legation, but the attendance of a number of the laity as well as of many of the lower clergy is recorded by the Anglo-Saxon Chronicle (no. II) and the thirteenth century Annals of Margam (no. III), here apparently following a good lost source, as well as the preface to the canons (no. IV) preserved in the chronicles of Durham and Worcester.[3] The council made a considerable impression on contemporaries, as is attested by its appearance in a number of annals usually indifferent to such events.[4]

It is also reflected in the large number of apparently independent manuscripts containing the canons of the council. The Durham tradition is represented by:

---

[1]Symeon, ii.277 (JL 7201).

[2]No. IV gives 9 Sept.; nos. I and II, Hunt., p. 245, Hugh the Chanter, p. 121 (*Hist. York*, ii.210), Ann. Winchcombe (ed. Darlington), p. 125, all give 8 Sept. No. IV, while clearly placing the council at Westminster Abbey, treats London and Westminster as interchangeable; although only no. III and Gervase, ii.381 among the other sources give Westminster we follow the traditional ascription. For 1070 see above, p. 568.

[3]For the apparent sources of the Annals of Margam see above, p. 668.

[4]*Ann. Mon.* ii.47, Ann. Chichester in *UGQ*, p. 94, *The Chronicle of Holyrood*, p. 116: 'Magna fames et magnum concilium' (following a southern source).

Cambridge, Corpus Christi Coll. ms. 139, fo. 129^{r-v} (= A),
printed in Symeon, ii.278-81. A copy made in the late
15th cent. BL Add. 34193, fos. 202^{v}-3 is almost certainly
drawn from a similar source but lacks some of the idio-
syncracies of A. Generally only those variant readings
found in both are recorded in the apparatus.

This version has an elaborate dating clause, in which it is
unique, followed by a prologue found also in the Worcester
Chronicle, here represented by

Oxford, Corpus Christi Coll. ms. 157, pp. 375-7 (= B).
Apparently an autograph copy, this is followed in all
essentials by the other manuscripts of the text and the
other later compilations dependent on it.[1] The 14th-cent.
canonical compilations from Worcester in London, Lambeth
Palace ms. 171, fo. 7^{v} and Oxford, Bodl. ms. Rawlinson
C. 428, fo. 111^{r-v} have the same version apparently from
the same source. The text of B was printed in *Flor. Wig.*
ii.81-3 and *J. Wig.*, pp. 20-2.

Independent copies of the canons without the prologue are also
found in these twelfth-century manuscripts.

Aberystwyth, NLW 17110E (the Book of Llandaff), cols. 58-61
(= L). This has an inaccurate rubric added later,[2] but
otherwise presents a good text directly associated with
one of the participants; it is best edited by Evans in
Book of Llandaff, pp. 49-51, see also p. 347.
Hereford Cathedral Library ms. O. ii. 7, fo. 151^{r-v} (= H), a
corrupt text added on the end leaves of a copy of the
Collection in XVII Books, between the councils of 1108
and 1127. Its more extreme errors are not noted.
Hereford Cathedral Library ms. P. i. 3, fo. 101^{r-v} (= P), a
better text added at the end of a miscellaneous collection
of documents on English church government (fully described

---

[1]See above, pp. 506, 569, 696-7.   [2]Brett, *English Church*, p. 52 n.

by Holtzmann in *Neues Archiv*, 1 (1933), 284-6).

London, Lambeth Palace 351, fo. 93^{r-v} (= C), added at the
end of an abstract of Lanfranc's collection possibly
associated with Canterbury.

Oxford, St. John's Coll. ms. 125, fos. 89^{v}-90 (= O), at the
end of a composite text of Ivo's *Pannormia* and Burchard's
Decretum, of unknown origin, after the Councils of Westminster (1138) and London (1143), below pp. 795, 771.[1]

There was another text of the canons, probably also with a date
and prologue, in the copy of the Collection in IV Books which
was destroyed in Warsaw in 1944.[2]

The manuscript tradition therefore derives from at least the
five cathedral archives of Canterbury, Durham, Hereford, Llandaff, and Worcester, and the close agreement of their texts in
all essentials seems to show the circulation of a quasi-official
version of the canons. The text below is based on B, a good
text as early as any other, except where there is a consensus
against it; select variants from the other manuscripts are noted.
The canons were printed in Sp. ii.33-4, W. i.408-9, Labbe, x.914-
18, Mansi, xxi.330-3.

The chief source for this legislation is the First Lateran
Council, celebrated two years earlier. Of the seventeen canons
in the received text Westminster incorporates the substance of
seven; seven of the rest bore largely on events outside England,
where provision against a false coinage was scarcely necessary
in 1125.[3] Only the forms for electing bishops and the subordination of monks to their bishops do not find the mention one
might expect. The phrasing of some of the canons and the appearance of c. 5 may well owe something to the earlier councils of
Rheims and Toulouse in 1119, both of which the legate had
attended. Equally, however, as the Anglo-Saxon chronicler remarked, there are a number of provisions which hark back to
Anselm's council of 1102, the last English enactments on general
issues. One may suppose that the English clergy had as much as

---

[1]Z.N. Brooke, *English Church and the Papacy*, pp. 237-8.
[2]Above, p. 720 n. 1.
[3]*ASC*, ed. Plummer, i.255, ed. Clark, p. 46, tr. Whitelock *et al.*, p. 191,
Hunt., p. 246, *J. Wig.*, p. 18 (*Flor. Wig.* ii.79); compare C. of Lateran I
(1123) c. 13.

the legate to do with the final form the canons were to take.

I. *Summons to the council*

Aberystwyth, NLW 17110E, col. 58. Printed *Book of Llan-daff*, p. 49, Sp. ii.33, W. i.408, Labbe, x.914, Mansi, xxi.329.

Summonitio Willelmi Cantuariensis archiepiscopi.

Willelmus Cantuariensis archiepiscopus Urbano Landavensi episcopo salutem. Litteris istis tibi notum facere volumus quod Iohannes ęcclesię Romanę presbiter cardinalis atque legatus legis ordinatione nostraque coniventia concilium celebrare disposuit Lundonię in nativitate beatę semper virginis Marię. Propterea precipimus ut in prefato termino in eodem loco nobis occurras cum archidiaconibus et abbatibus et prioribus tuę dyocesios, ad definiendum super negotiis ęcclesiasticis et ad informandum seu corrigendum quę informanda vel docenda seu corrigenda docuerit sententia convocationis nostrę.

II. *Anglo-Saxon Chronicle 1125 E*

Bodl. ms. Laud. Misc. 636, fo. 84^{r-v}. Facsimile ed. White-lock in *Early English Manuscripts in Facsimile*, iv.167-8; printed in *ASC*, ed. Thorpe, i.376-7, ed. Plummer, i.255, ed. Clark, pp. 46-7. Trans. Thorpe, ii.221-2, Whitelock *et al.*, pp. 191-2 (used here).

On þes ilces gæres sende se papa of Rome to ðise lande an cardinal, Iohan of Creme wæs gehaten. He [fo. 84^v] com first to þone king on Normandi, 7 se king hine underfeng mid micel wurðscipe, beteahte hine siððon þone ærcebiscop W. of Cantwara-byrig; 7 he hine ledde to Cant-warabyrig 7 he wæs þær under-fangen mid micel wurðscipe 7

In the course of this same year the pope of Rome sent to this country a cardinal called John of Crema. He came first to the king in Normandy, and the king received him with great honour, and then com-mended him to William, arch-bishop of Canterbury; and he conducted him to Canterbury and he was there received with

mid micel processionem, 7 he
sang ðone hehmesse on Eastren-
dæi æt Cristes wefod, 7 siððon
he ferde ofer eall Englalande
to ealle þa biscoprices 7 ab-
botrices þa wæron on þis lande
7 ofer eall he wæs underfangen
mid wurðscipe 7 ealle hine
iæfen micele gife 7 mære. 7
siððon he heolde his concilie
on Lundene fulle þreo dagas on
Nativitas Sanctę Marię, on September, mid ærcebiscopes 7 mid
leodbiscopes 7 abbotes 7 læred
7 lawed, and bead þær þa ilce
lagas þa Anselm ærcebiscop
hæfde æror beboden, 7 feala ma
þeah hit litel forstode, 7
þeonen he for ofer sæ sone
æfter Sancte Michaeles messe,
7 swa to Rome.

great honour and with a great
procession, and he sang High
Mass on Easter Day at Christ's
altar, and then he went over
all England to all the bishoprics and abbacies that there
were in the country and he was
received with honour every-
where, and they all gave him
great and splendid gifts. And
then he held his council at
London for a full three days
at the Nativity of St. Mary,
in September, with archbishops
and diocesan bishops and
abbots and clerics and laity,
and promulgated there the same
laws that Archbishop Anselm
had previously promulgated, and
many more, though it was of
little avail. And from there
he went overseas soon after
Michaelmas, and so to Rome.

III. *Annals of Margam s.a. 1125*

> Cambridge, Trinity Coll. ms. O. 2. 4. (1108), p. 9.
> Printed by T. Gale in *Historiae Anglicanae Scriptores
> Quinque* (Oxford, 1687), p. 5 and *Ann. Mon.* i.11.

Hoc in tempore Iohannes cognomine Cremensis, presbiter quidam
cardinalis de Roma missus, venit primum ad regem Henricum in
Normannia, et ab eo permissus omnem perlustravit Angliam. [a]Ad
ultimum vero concilium maximum cogens apud Westmonasterium
omnium episcoporum, abbatum, priorum necnon et clericorum,
canonicorum, scholasticorum eciam et laicorum potencium, in

-----

[a]*The passage* Ad ultimum ... effectis *is not in Dublin, Trinity Coll. ms.
507 (E. 4. 23), which contains the greater part of these annals.*

excelso trono quatuor dies presedit, ipsis eciam archiepiscopis sibi subpedaneis effectis.[1]

IV. *Canons of the council*

A

Anno ab incarnatione Domini MCXXVI,[a] pontificatus autem domni
papę Honorii secundi anno primo, regnante piissimo et glorioso
Henrico Anglorum rege, Willelmi magni filio, anno vero regni
ipsius XXV,

AB

Celebrata est synodus Lundonie in ęcclesia beati[b] apostolorum
principis apud Westmonasterium mense Septembrio nona die eiusdem mensis, id est v idus Septembris,[c] ubi [p. 376] post multarum discussionem causarum promulgata sunt hęc capitula et ab
omnibus confirmata, numero xvii. Pręfuit autem huic[d] synodo
Iohannes de Crema, sanctę[e] et apostolicę ecclesię de titulo
sancti Grisogoni presbiter cardinalis et[f] domni papę Honorii
in Angliam legatus, cum Willelmo Cantuuariensi et Turstino
Eboracensi[g] arciepiscopis et cum episcopis diversarum provinciarum numero xx et abbatibus circiter xl, et cum innumera
cleri et populi multitudine. Sunt autem hęc capitula.[h]

[1][i] Sanctorum patrum vestigiis inherentes, quenquam in ęcclesia per pecuniam ordinari auctoritate apostolica prohibemus.[2]

[2] Interdicimus etiam ut pro chrismate, pro oleo, pro baptismate, pro penitentia, pro visitatione infirmorum seu unctione,
pro communione corporis Christi, pro sepultura, nullum omnino
pretium exigatur.[3]

---

[a]*The* I *over an erasure;* MCXXV BL *Add ms. 34193.*   [b]Petri *add* A.   [c]id
est ... Sept. *om.* A.   [d]illi A.   [e]Romane *add* A.   [f]predicti *add* A.
[g]A, *but not Add. ms. 34193, reverses the order of the archbishops.*   [h]Sunt
... capitula *om.* A.   [i]Primum capitulum B, *whose numbering we follow.*

---

[1]The passage has points of contact with no. II and with Gervase, ii.381.
[2]CC. of Westminster (1102), c. 1, Toulouse (1119), c. 1, Lateran I (1123),
c. 1.
[3]CC. of Rheims (1119), c. 4, Rome (1099), c. 12, Toulouse (1119), c. 9.

[3] Statuimus preterea et apostolica auctoritate decernimus ut
in consecrationibus episcoporum vel abbatum benedictionibus seu
in dedicationibus ęcclesiarum non cappa, non tapete, non manutergium, non bacinia[a] et nihil omnino per violentiam nisi
sponte oblatum fuerit penitus exigatur.[1]

[4] Nullus abbas, nullus prior, nullus omnino monachus vel
clericus, ęcclesiam sive decimam seu quęlibet beneficia ęcclesiastica de dono[b] laici sine[c] proprii episcopi auctoritate et
assensu suscipiat. Quod si presumptum fuerit, irrita erit
donatio huiuscemodi, et ipse canonicę ultioni subiacebit.[d][2]

[5] Sancimus[e] pręterea ne quis ęcclesiam sibi sive[f] prebendam
paterna vendicet hereditate aut successorem[g] sibi in aliquo
ęcclesiastico constituat beneficio. Quod si presumptum fuerit,
nullas vires habere permittimus, dicentes cum psalmista, 'Deus
meus, pone illos ut rotam', qui[h] dixerunt, 'Hereditate possideamus sanctuarium Dei'.[i][3]

[6] Adicientes quoque statuimus ut clerici qui ęcclesias seu
beneficia habent ęcclesiarum, et ordinari quo liberius vivant
subterfugiunt, cum ab episcopis invitati fuerint si ad ordines
promoveri contempserint, ęcclesiis simul et beneficiis earum
priventur.[4]

[7] Nullus in decanum, nullus in priorem nisi presbiter, nullus
in archidiaconum nisi diaconus promoveatur.[5]

---

[a]bacinia LCPO; bachinia H; baccinia A; baccilia B.   [b]vel manu *add* A.
[c]nisi P.   [d]subiacebit ABLCP; subiaceat OH.   [e]Sancimus BCP; Sanctimus A;
Statuimus OH; Sanximus L.   [f]sibi sive: seu O.   [g]successori B; successore P.   [h]qui: et sicut B.   [i]pone ... Dei: etc. O; C *adds* nobis *after*
possideamus.

[1] C. of Rome (1099), c. 18, Poitiers (1100), c. 13 (both reading 'bacinos').
Compare Eadmer, p. 198.
[2] CC. of Winchester (1072), c. 5, Westminster (1102), c. 22, Rheims (1119),
c. 2, Lateran I (1123), cc. 8 (18).
[3] Ps. 82, 14, 13, CC. of Westminster (1102), c. 8, Toulouse (1119), c. 8,
Rheims (1119), c. 4.
[4] Compare *EA* 255, ll. 24-8.
[5] CC. of Westminster (1102), c. 4, Toulouse (1119), c. 2, Lateran I (1123),
c. 6.

[8] Nullus in presbiterum, nullus in diaconum nisi ad certum titulum ordinetur. Qui vero absolute fuerit ordinatus sumpta careat dignitate.[1]

[9] Nullus abbas, nullus omnino clericus vel laicus quenquam per episcopum[a] in ęcclesia ordinatum absque proprii episcopi iudicio presumat eicere. Qui autem secus facere presumpserit, excommunicationi subiaceat.[b][2]

[10] Nullus episcoporum alterius[c] parrochianum ordinare aut[d] iudicare presumat.[e] Unusquisque enim suo[f] domino stat aut cadit, nec tenetur aliquis[g] sententia non a[h] suo iudice prolata.[3]

[11] Nemo excommunicatum alterius presumat in communionem[i] suscipere. Quod qui[j] scienter fecerit, et ipse communione careat christiana.[4]

[12] Precipimus etiam ne uni personę in ęcclesia archidiaconatus aut diversi[k] tribuantur honores.[5]

[13] Presbiteris, diaconibus, subdiaconibus, canonicis uxorum, concubinarum et omnium omnino[l] feminarum contubernia auctoritate apostolica inhibemus preter matrem aut[m] sororem vel[n] amitam, sive illas mulieres quę omni[o] careant suspitione. Qui huius decreti[p] violator extiterit confessus vel convictus, ruinam proprii ordinis patiatur.[6]

---

[a]ecclesiam B.   [b]subiacebit BH.   [c]presumat *add* B.   [d]*om.* A.   [e]*om.* B.
[f]sub P.   [g]*om.* O.   [h]non a AB; a non COH; ante LP.   [i]communione BH.
[j]si B; *om.* H.   [k]in ecclesia ... diversi ALCPOH; duo archidiaconatus vel
diversi ordinis B.   [l]omnino omnium B.   [m]*om.* B.   [n]*om.* B.   [o]omni BCOH;
omnino ALP.   [p]decreti huius AC.

[1]C. of Chalcedon, c. 6 (Hinschius, pp. 285-6), C. of Piacenza (1095),
c. 15 (in *Decretum*, Dist. LXX), and see above, p. 675 n. 3.
[2]Compare C. of Lateran I (1123), c. 4.
[3]*Epistola Calixti Secunda*, c. 12, *Decreta Dionysii*, c. 3, *Decreta Iulii*,
c. 12 in Hinschius, pp. 138-9, 196, 468.
[4]Burchard, xi.36-9, C. of Lateran I (1123), c. 2.
[5]CC. of Poitiers (1078), c. 2, Clermont (1095), cc. 10, 12 in Somerville,
Councils of Urban II, i.76-7.
[6]CC. of Westminster (1102), cc. 5, 6, London (1108), passim, Rheims
(1119), c. 5, Lateran I (1123), c. 7.

[14] Usuram[a] et turpe lucrum clericis omnimodis[b] prohibemus. Qui vero super crimine tali confessus fuerit aut convictus, a gradu proprio deiciatur.[1]

[15] Sortilogos, ariolos et au[p. 377]guria quęque sectantes, eisque consentientes, excommunicari precipimus, perpetuaque notamus[c] infamia.[2]

[16] Inter consanguineos seu affinitate propinquos[d] usque ad septimam[e] generationem matrimonia contrahi prohibemus. Si qui vero taliter coniuncti fuerint, separentur.[3]

[17] Interdicimus etiam ut viri proprias uxores de consanguinitate impetentes, et testes quos adducunt, non suscipiantur, sed prisca patrum in omnibus[f] servetur auctoritas.[g][4]

B

Placet vobis? Placet. Placet vobis? Placet. Placet vobis? Placet.

P

Responderunt episcopi, Placet.

131

25 JANUARY 1126. LEGATINE COMMISSION FOR WILLIAM, ARCHBISHOP OF CANTERBURY

> For this grant see Tillmann, pp. 30-3, Dueball, *Die Suprematstreit,* pp. 99-100, Nicholl, *Thurstan,* pp. 96-7, Bethell in *JEH* xix (1968), 156-7, Brett, *English Church,* p. 47.

---

[a]Usura B.   [b]omnino LO.   [c]dampnamus A.   [d]coniunctos B.   [e]*om.* B, *with a lacuna.*   [f]in omnibus *om.* B.   [g]*All but* BP *end.*

---

[1]Hinschius, pp. 314, 323, C. of Rheims (1049), c. 17 in the ed. by Blumenthal in *Deutsches Archiv* xxxii (1976), 34.
[2]C. of London (1075), c. 8.
[3]CC. of Westminster (1102), c. 25; compare C. of Lateran I (1123), c. 9.
[4]C. of Rouen (1074), c. 10; compare *Decretum,* C. 35 q. 6.

The ambassadors who accompanied the legate John to Rome in the
winter of 1125/6 were charged not only with securing an agreed
compromise over the issue of the primacy, but also with obtaining a legatine commission for Archbishop William. Such a proposal had been advanced on behalf of Archbishop Ralph in 1120,
but according to Hugh the Chanter the king was now doubly
interested. Not merely would it offer Canterbury some recom-
pense for a partial surrender over the primacy, it would also
help to avoid a repetition of the mission of Cardinal John.[1]
Apparently on the advice of Archbishop Thurstan, Honorius agreed
to the plan, and commissioned William as his legate for the
correction of abuses and celebration of councils in a bull of 25
January.[2]

The evident threat to the position of Thurstan which this
represented was met in part by a letter the pope wrote to the
king at about the same time, in which he urged that the archbishop should suffer no grievance or injury.[3]

*Bull of Honorius II conferring a legation on William, archbishop
of Canterbury*

> BL mss. Cotton Claudius E. v, fo. 255[r-v] (= A), Cleopatra
> E. i, fos. 31[v]-32 (= B); also in the 15th-cent. mss. Can-
> terbury D & C Register A, fo. 11 (from B) and London, Lam-
> beth Palace 482, fo. 85. Printed from B in W. i.409,
> calendared JL 7284.

Honorius episcopus, servus servorum Dei, dilectis fratribus et
filiis episcopis, abbatibus, baronibus et ceteris clericis et
laicis[a] per Angliam et Scotiam constitutis, salutem et

---

[a]et laicis *om.* B.

[1]Hugh the Chanter, pp. 87, 123 (*Hist. York*, ii.178, 212).

[2]Ibid., pp. 123-6 (*Hist. York*, ii.212-4); no ms. gives the year of the
bull, but it must fall between the date of John's legation and the council
of 1127. The conjectural 1127 of W. i.409 and JL 7284 conflicts with the
clear testimony of the Chanter, *J. Wig.*, p. 22 and *Chron. Angliae Petriburgense*, p. 82. Further, the day is given in the surviving text, and between
1 January and 14 February 1126 eleven other bulls were issued for English
beneficiaries, while none survive for the similar period in 1127 (Brett,
English Church, pp. 242-3, Bethell, *JEH* xix.156n.).

[3]Hugh the Chanter, p. 128 (*Hist. York*, ii.216).

apostolicam benedictionem.

Sponsa Christi, sacrosancta ęcclesia in firmamento apostolicę fidei radicata, tanquam devota mater [fo. 255^v] et propicia, consuevit mitibus et humilibus filiis vitę pabula ministrare, tam iis qui longe positi sunt quam iis qui prope. Propinqui siquidem per exhibitam sibi nostrę personę praesentiam, longinqui vero per legatorum nostrorum ministerium visitantur. Quoniam igitur vos tanquam unicos et speciales beati Petri filios[1] fore cognoscimus, karissimo fratri nostro Guillelmo Cantuariensi archiepiscopo in Anglia et Scotia vices nostras[a] commisimus. Quatenus constitutus illic a nobis apostolicę sedis legatus, caritatis vestrę fretus auxilio, ad honorem Dei et sanctę Romanę ęcclesię et animarum vestrarum salutem, corrigenda corrigere et firmanda valeat, operante Domino, confirmare. Quapropter universitati vestrę mandando praecipimus ut ei, sicut legato nostro, humiliter obędire et, cum ab eo invitati pro ęcclesiarum statu et christianę religionis incremento fueritis, ad eius vocationem unanimiter convenire et synodales cum eo studeatis celebrare conventus.

Datę Laterani viii kl' Februarii.

132

13-16 MAY 1127. LEGATINE COUNCIL AT WESTMINSTER

Archbishop William held his first legatine council, and the only one whose acts have survived, immediately after the royal council at London. It lasted for three days, with a recess for Sunday, 15 May, and was attended by a great number of the clergy and laity.[2] Archbishop Thurstan refused to attend after the

---

[a] vices nostras *om.* B.

---

[1] The same phrase was to be used of Hugh of Reading in 1128 and 1131, for which see below, pp. 750, 755.
[2] Hunt., p. 247. A number of royal charters were probably issued at about this time: *Reg.* ii, nos. 1477-84 and *Misc. D. M. Stenton,* p. 32 n. *Reg.* ii, no. 1484 may refer to events at either the royal or the ecclesiastical council.

quarrel over his rights at the Christmas court of 1126,[1] and Ranulf of Durham fell ill on the way, being represented by proctors. The proceedings were noisy and overcrowded. Bishop Urban of Llandaff attempted to pursue his claims against the bishops of St. Davids and Hereford over disputed diocesan frontiers, but subsequently told the pope that he could obtain no judgement in so ill-regulated an assembly; accordingly he appealed to Rome.[2] Apart from the narrative in the Worcester chronicle and texts dependent upon it,[3] the council is only mentioned by Hugh the Chanter for the quarrel of the archbishops, and by Henry of Huntingdon; this contrasts with the widespread notice of the council of 1125.[4]

The canons are introduced by the narrative printed below (no. I) in the manuscripts of John of Worcester, here represented by:

A   Oxford, Corpus Christi Coll. ms. 157, pp. 377-9. The 14th-cent. Worcester mss., Lambeth Palace 171, fos. 7^V-8 and Oxford, Bodl. Rawlinson C. 428, fos. 110-1 include the same narrative and conclusion, and are apparently dependent upon John.

The canons only (no. II) are found in three independent manuscripts:

C   Cambridge, Corpus Christi Coll. ms. 19, fo. 334^V, at the end of a small collection of canonical material added to an early 12th-cent. copy of Ivo's *Decretum* from Christ Church, Canterbury.
H   Hereford Cathedral Lib. ms. O. ii. 7, fos. 151^V-2, after the canons of 1125 (q.v.).

---

[1]Hugh the Chanter, pp. 129-31 (*Hist. York*, ii.217-9).
[2]*Book of Llandaff*, pp. 34-8 (JL 7305-8), 52.
[3]Which here include Gervase, ii.382.
[4]It is however possible that the slight reference in *Chron. Angliae Petriburgense*, p. 83: 'Willelmus Cantuariensis archiepiscopus, apostolicae sedis legatus, Concilium Londoniae celebrat, plura ibi proponens capitula', derives from some earlier and independent source.

R London, BL ms. Royal 10. A. viii, fos. 148^V-149, an early
addition to a copy of Ivo's *Pannormia* and sermons made
*c.*1200; the book has been severely damaged by fire.

H and R are preceded by the same rubric and apparently derive
from a common source. C is independent, and is followed by a
copy of the king's writ confirming the council's acts (no. III),
a part of which is quoted by the Worcester chronicle. The text
below is based on C, with select variants from A, H, and R. The
canons were printed from a Worcester version in Sp. ii.35-6,
Labbe, x.920-2, W. i.410-1, Mansi, xxi.355-8.

Canons 1 and 4-7 represent an elaboration of the principles
set out in 1125, though it is noticeable that c. 5 follows the
wording of the Lateran council of 1123 more closely than that
of Westminster. The provisions against clerical marriage also
show points of contact with Anselm's council of 1108. More
generally, as in 1125, there are a number of canons which follow the pattern of earlier English legislation rather than that
of other contemporary papal and legatine councils.

I. *Chronicon ex chronicis of Worcester s.a. 1127*

Oxford, Corpus Christi Coll. ms. 157, pp. 377-9. Printed
in *Flor. Wig.* ii.85-8 and *J. Wig.*, pp. 23-5.

Willelmus Dorubernensis archiepiscopus congregavit generale
concilium omnium episcoporum et abbatum et quarunque religiosarum personarum totius Anglię apud monasterium sancti Petri in
occidentali parte Lundonie situm. [p. 378] Cui concilio presedit
ipse sicut archiepiscopus Cantuuariensis et legatus apostolicę
sedis, considentibus secum Willelmo episcopo Wintoniensi, Rogerio
Særesberiensi, Willelmo Execestrensi, Herveo Eliensi, Alexandro
Lincoliensi, Eoverardo Norðuuicensi, Seifredo Cicestrensi,
Ricardo Herefordensi, Godefrido Bathoniensi, Iohanne Hrofensi,
Bernardo de Sancto David Walensi, Urbano Glamorgatensi seu Landavensi, David Pangornensi. Ricardus Lundoniensis et Robertus

Cestrensis[a] iam obierant,[1] nec aliquis in sedem illorum eousque successerat. Turstanus autem Eboracensis archiepiscopus directis nuntiis ac litteris rationabili causa ostendit se conventui ipso adesse non potuisse. Rannulfus vero Dunholmensis episcopus eo tendens infirmitate correptus est, nec iter ceptum perficere potuit, sicut prior ęcclesię et clerici quos illuc direxerat sub testimonio veritatis attestati sunt. Wigornensis autem episcopus Symon ad parentes suos trans mare iverat, et nondum reversus erat.[2] Confluxerant quoque illuc magnę multitudines clericorum, laicorum tam divitum quam mediocrum, et factus est conventus grandis et inestimabilis. Sedit autem tribus diebus, id est tertio idus Maii et die sequenti, tercioque post hunc qui fuit xvii kl' Iunii.[3] Acta sunt ibi de negotiis secularibus nonnulla; quędam quidem determinata, quedam dilata, quędam vero propter nimium ęstuantis turbę tumultum ab audientia iudicantium profligata. Quę autem communi episcoporum consensu in ipso concilio decreta sunt et statuta sicut illic publice recitata sunt et suscepta in hoc opere placuit annotare. Sunt igitur hęc:

   (*Then follow the canons, no. II below*)

... p. 379 ... Rex igitur cum inter hęc Lundonie moraretur, auditis concilii gestis, assensum prebuit, auctoritate regia et potestate concessit et confirmavit statuta concilii a Willelmo Cantuuariensi archiepiscopo et sanctę Romanę ęcclesię legato apud Westmonasterium celebrati.

II. *Canons of the council*

Statuta concilii a Will' Cantuariensi archiepiscopo et sancte Romane ęcclesię legato apud Westmon' celebrati anno incarnationis Domini nostri Iesu Christi MCXXVII, regni vero Henrici

---

[a]*Lambeth 171, Bodl. Rawlinson C. 428 and several copies of the Worcester chronicle here read* Coventrensis.

---

[1]On 16 Jan. 1127 and 22 Aug. 1126.
[2]Simon was a Lotharingian, who had been chancellor to Queen Adeliza (*J. Wig.*, p. 18); a Llanthony cartulary (PRO C115 A 9, fo. 114) contains a charter of Bishop Simon which refers to a similar visit after 1131. Compare also R.W. Eyton, 'The Staffordshire Chartulary', pp. 214-5.
[3]15 May, when the council did not sit, was the first Sunday after the Ascension.

gloriosi regis Anglorum anno xxvii.[a]

[1] Ecclesias et ecclesiastica beneficia, prebendas[b] seu quoslibet ecclesiasticos honores vendi vel emi auctoritate beati
Petri apostolorum principis et nostra omnino prohibemus. Qui
vero hoc preceptum violasse convictus fuerit, clericus quidem
etiamsi[c] canonicus regularis sit[d] vel monachus ab ordine
proprio[e] deponatur; laicus vero exlex et excommunicatus habeatur et eiusdem ecclesię vel beneficii potestate privetur.[1]

[2] Ordinari quemquam per pecuniam in ecclesia Dei vel promoveri auctoritate sedis apostolicę et nostra[f] modis omnibus
interdicimus.[2]

[3] Exactiones certas pecuniarum pro recipiendis canonicis,
monachis et[g] sanctimonialibus condemnamus.[3]

[4] Nullus in decanum nisi presbiter, nullus in archidiaconum[h]
nisi diaconus constituatur. Quod si quis ad hos honores infra
predictos ordines iam designatus est, moneatur ab episcopo ad
ordines accedere. Quod si iuxta monitionem[i] episcopi ordinari
refugerit, eadem[j] ad quam designatus fuerat[k] careat dignitate.[4]

[5] Presbiteris, diaconibus, subdiaconibus et omnibus canonicis
contubernia mulierum[l] penitus[m] interdicimus. Quod si concubinis

[a]*This is the preface of* C; Concilium a Willelmo Cantuariensi archiepiscopo sancteque sedis Romane legato atque ab universis (omnibus R) Anglie
episcopis, assensu videlicet gloriosi regis Henrici omniumque baronum suorum
in Ascensione Domini apud Lundoniam celebratum HR; *om.* A.   [b]*om.* A.
[c]etsi R.   [d]sit regularis C.   [e]*om.* A.   [f]et nostra *om.* A.   [g]can., mon.
HR; mon., can. et C; can., modo et A.   [h]archidiaconatum A.   [i]admoni-
tionem C.   [j]ea R.   [k]est HR.   [l]illicitarum *add* A.   [m]*om.* HR.

[1]CC. of Westminster (1102), c. 15, Rheims (1119), c. 1; compare C. of
Lateran I (1123), c. 8.
[2]CC. of Lateran I (1123), c. 1, Westminster (1125), c. 1.
[3]CC. of Melfi (1089), c. 7, Rome (1099), c. 17; compare J. H. Lynch,
Simoniacal entry into religious life, p. 98.
[4]CC. of Westminster (1102), c. 4, Lateran I (1123), c. 6, Westminster
(1125), c. 7.

(quod absit) vel forte[a] coniugibus adheserint, ęcclesiastico
priventur ordine,[b] honore simul[c] et beneficio. Presbiteros vero
parrochiales (si qui tales fuerint) extra chorum eicimus et
infames esse decernimus. Archidiaconis vero et ministris quibus
hoc incumbit, auctoritate Dei et nostra precipimus ut omni
studio et sollicitudine procurent ab ęcclesia Dei hanc perniciem omnino[d] eradicare. Quod si qui in hoc neglegentes vel
(quod[e] absit) consentientes inventi fuerint, primo et secundo
ab episcopis digne corripiantur,[f] tercio vero[g] canonice severius
corrigantur.[h][1]

[6] Concubinę vero presbiterorum et canonicorum, nisi ibi legitime nupserint, extra parochiam expellantur. Quod si postea
culpabiles inventę fuerint, in cuiuscunque territorio inventę
fuerint,[i] a ministris ęcclesię capiantur. Et sub excommunicatione precipimus ne ab aliqua potestate maiore vel minore[j]
detineantur, sed libere eisdem ministris ęcclesię[k] tradantur
et ęcclesiasticę disciplinę vel servituti episcopali iudicio[l]
mancipentur.[2]

[7] Ut nullus archidiaconus in diversis episcopatibus diversos
archidiaconatus teneat sub anathemate prohibemus; immo ei cui
prius assignatus est tantum adhereat.[3]

[8] Episcopi presbiteros, abbates, monachos, priores subditos
firmas[m] tenere inhibeant.[n][4]

[9] Decimas sicut Dei summi dominicas ex integro reddi precipimus.[5]

---

[a]*om.* A.   [b]*om.* HR.   [c]simul honore R.   [d]*om.* R.   [e]in hoc ... vel
quod *repeated* A.   [f]corrigantur A.   [g]*om.* HR.   [h]corripiantur A.
[i]invente fuerint CHR; sint A.   [j]min. vel mai. A.   [k]ecclesie ministris
HR.   [l]servitio C.   [m]firmam A.   [n]prohibemus R.

---

[1]CC. of London (1108), cc. 1, 2, 4, 6, Rheims (1119), c. 5, Lateran I
(1123), c. 7, Westminster (1125), c. 13.
[2]C. of London (1108), cc. 2, 8, Brett, *English Church*, p. 149.
[3]C. of Westminster (1125), c. 12, Brett, *English Church*, pp. 210-11.
[4]C. of Westminster (1102), cc. 3, 9, 21.
[5]CC. of Winchester (1070), c. 14, Windsor (1070), c. 10.

[10] Ut nulla persona ęcclesias vel decimas seu quęlibet[a] ęcclesiastica beneficia det vel accipiat sine consensu et auctoritate
episcopi canonica auctoritate vetamus.[1]

[11] Nulla abbatissa, nulla[b] sanctimonialis carioribus utatur
indumentis quam agninis vel cattinis nigris.[c2]

III. *Royal writ confirming the acts of the council*

> Cambridge, Corpus Christi Coll. ms. 19, fo. 334[v]. Printed
> in Rymer (1816), i.8 and *EHR* lxxii (1957), 690, n. 5.
> Calendared as *Reg.* ii, no. 1476.

Henricus rex Anglię archiepiscopis, episcopis, abbatibus,
comitibus et baronibus Anglię et fidelibus sanctę ęcclesię
salutem.

Sciatis quod auctoritate regia et potestate concedo et confirmo statuta concilii a Willelmo Cantuariensi archiepiscopo et
sanctę Romanę ęcclesię legato apud Westmonasterium celebrati,
et interdicta interdico. Si quis vero horum decretorum violator
vel contemptor extiterit, si ęcclesiasticę disciplinę humiliter
non satisfecerit, noverit se regia potestate graviter cohercen-
dum, quia divinę dispositioni resistere praesumpsit.[3]

Teste Rogerio episcopo Salesberię et Gaufrido cancellario et
Rannulfo comite Cestrię apud Lundoniam.

133

1128-1130. ABBOT HUGH OF READING AS PAPAL EMISSARY OVER PETER'S
PENCE

The sole source for these events is the collection of

---

[a]alia *add* A.   [b]vel A.   [c]*om.* AR.

[1]CC. of Winchester (1072), c. 5, Lateran I (1123), c. 4, and compare
'c. 18', Westminster (1125), c. 4, Brett, *English Church*, pp. 141-4.
[2]Compare C. of Westminster (1138), c. 15.
[3]The substance, though not the wording, recalls the Conqueror's writ
printed above, no. 94.

letters printed from Edinburgh UL ms. 104 in *PUE* iii, nos.
15-23, 25, on which see Brett, *English Church*, pp. 48,
168-9.

At the end of April 1128, the pope summoned Hugh, first abbot
of the royal abbey of Reading, to Rome by 18 November. His
monks, the king and Hugh himself all opposed the summons, particularly since the abbot's kinsman, Matthew of Albano, was
said to be expected to visit England in the near future (although
there is no evidence that he ever came).[1] In October the pope
repeated his summons, whether Matthew came to England or not. By
May 1129 Hugh was at Rome, and prepared for a long stay. It is
possible that Honorius originally intended to retain him perma-
nently as a member of the Curia, but by 16 June he had decided
to send him back to England as 'sub proprio iure atque dominio
nostro ... specialem beati Petri et sancte Romane ecclesie clericum'. Among his duties was to be arranging the better payment of
Peter's Pence, over which the pope had become seriously disturbed.
In the autumn[2] Hugh wrote to Honorius, describing his negotiations with the king, which had produced agreement on the size
both of the arrears and of the sum at which it should be fixed
in future, though the second figure is now uncertain. No other
special functions of Hugh as a papal representative are recorded
before his promotion to Rouen in 1130 and the events of the
schism after Honorius' death.[3]

134

30 SEPTEMBER-4 OCTOBER 1129. LEGATINE COUNCIL AT LONDON

Soon after the king returned from a two-year stay in Normandy

---

[1]Hugh's family connections and his part in these events are discussed by
T. Waldman, 'Hugh "of Amiens", Archbishop of Rouen 1130-64', pp. 3-7,
15-18. Matthew of Albano celebrated the Council of Rouen in October 1128,
but did not leave France for Rome until after 29 October 1129 (Schieffer,
Die päpstlichen Legaten in Frankreich, pp. 229-33, Hüls, pp. 96-8).

[2]The date for payment of arrears was set for Martinmas (11 November),
which seems not to have passed when Hugh wrote; the king did not return to
England from Normandy until 15 July 1129 (Symeon, ii.283).

[3]Below, pp. 754-7.

Archbishop William summoned a solemn council to London.[1] Though
four bishoprics were vacant, according to the Anglo-Saxon
Chronicle (no. I) there was an unusually comprehensive summons
of the regular clergy, and the council lasted the five days
from Monday to Friday, longer than any other of the reign. While
Huntingdon (no. II) gives 1 August, the date of the nomination
of Henry of Blois to the bishopric of Winchester appears to
confirm the date given by the Chronicle.[2]

For all the solemnity of its convocation, the council made
a poor impression on those contemporaries who noticed it at all,
and no direct record of any legislation it may have promulgated
has survived. It was chiefly remembered for its ineffective
measures against married clergy. The enforcement of these decrees, stern enough in their conception, was entrusted to the
king, who used them merely as a pretext for extortion, much as
he had done in Anselm's day.[3]

According to a Gloucester copy of the Worcester *Chronicon*
written *c.*1200, which is followed by the slightly later Annals
of Tewkesbury, the council also authorized the celebration of
the feast of the Conception of the Virgin:

> ... in concilio apud Lundoniam congregato in presentia
> eiusdem regis Henrici, ex auctoritate apostolica confirmata
> est festivitas conceptionis sancte Dei genitricis Marie.[4]

Encouraged by Eadmer earlier, quite widely celebrated, and

---

[1]Symeon, ii.283, *J. Wig.*, p. 29. Though the sources agree that the council met at London, comparison with the evidence for 1125 above suggests
that it may well have sat at Westminster.
[2]The short notice in the Annals of Margam (*Ann. Mon.* i.12) is apparently
independent of nos. I and II though close to both: '... fitque concilium
totius Angliæ apud Lundoniæ ad festum Sancti Michaelis; in quo tamen nihil
omnino nisi de uxoribus presbyterorum decernitur. Sed post quinque dies
nepos regis, Henricus nomine, ex abbate Glastoniæ, rege iubente, episcopus
efficitur Wintoniæ'. *J. Wig.*, p. 29, gives the date as October, and Symeon,
ii.283 says that the nomination was made in a solemn assembly at Winchester,
so it should perhaps be placed on 11 October (following Ann. Winchcombe,
s.a.), not on the conventional 4 Oct.
[3]Above, pp. 695, 698.
[4]Dublin, Trinity Coll. ms. E. 6. 4(503), fo. 119^v, printed in *J. Wig.*,
p. 29 n. 5; though the manuscript itself cannot safely be attributed to
Gloucester the general character of the interpolations in the later section
shows a close association with that house; compare *Ann. Mon.* i.45, Ann.
Winchcombe, s.a., *Cart. Gloucester*, i.15.

championed by Hugh of Reading, Bishop Gilbert of London, Anselm of Bury, and Osbert of Clare among others, the feast had been opposed by a party of court clergy led by Roger of Salisbury, Bernard of St. Davids, and the dean of St. Pauls in 1128. It seems likely that this dispute, and the claim that the feast had been prohibited in an unspecified council, gave rise to the decision of 1129.[1]

I. *Anglo-Saxon Chronicle 1129 E*

> Bodl. ms. Laud. Misc. 636, fo. 87. Facsimile ed. Whitelock in *Early English Manuscripts in Facsimile,* iv.173; printed in *ASC*, ed. Thorpe, i.379, ed. Plummer, i.259-60, ed. Clark, p. 51. Trans. Thorpe, ii.226, Whitelock *et al.*, p. 195 (used here).

Ða sone be þes kynges ræd 7 be his leue, sende se ærcebiscop Willelm of Cantwarbyrig ofer eall Englaland 7 bead biscopes 7 abbotes 7 ærcedæcnes 7 ealle þa priores, muneces 7 canonias þa wæron on ealle þa cellas on Englaland, 7 æfter ealle þa þet Cristendome hæfdon to begemen 7 to locen, 7 þet hi scolden ealle cumen to Lundene at Michaeles messe 7 þær scolden sprecon of ealle Godes rihtes. Þa hi ðider comen þa, began þet mot on Monendæig 7 heold on an to ðe Fridæig. Þa hit eall com forð, þa weorð hit eall of earcedæcnes wifes 7 of preostes wifes, þet hi

Then soon by the advice and permission of the king, Archbishop William of Canterbury sent over all England and ordered bishops and abbots and archdeacons and all the priors, monks, and canons that there were in all the cells in England, and all those that had to care for and look after Christianity, all to come to London at Michaelmas and there to discuss all God's dues. When they arrived there, the meeting began on Monday and continued right on to the Friday. When it all came out, it turned out to be all about archdeacons' wives and priests' wives, that

---

[1]*Letters of Osbert of Clare*, ed. E.W. Williamson (London, 1929), pp. 11-16, 65-8. Of the extensive modern literature see particularly E. Bishop, *Liturgica Historica* (Oxford, 1918), pp. 238-59, Southern, *St. Anselm*, pp. 290-6 with the references in E.J. Kealey, *Roger of Salisbury*, pp. 137-42 and Barlow (1979), p. 195.

scolden hi forlæten be Sanctes
Andreas messe [30 Nov.], 7 se
þe þet ne wolden done, forgede
his circe 7 his hus 7 his ham,
7 nefra ma nan clepunge þær to
na hafde mare. Þis bebæd se
ærcebiscop Willelm of Cantwara-
byrig 7 ealle þa leodbiscopes
ða þa^a wæron on Englalande, 7
se kyng hem geaf ealle leue
ham to farene, 7 swa hi ferdon
ham, 7 ne forstod noht ealle
þa bodlaces, - ealle heoldon
here wifes be þes kynges leue
swa swa hi ear didon.

they were to give them up by
St. Andrew's Day, and anyone
who would not do so, should
forgo his church and his house
and his home, and nevermore
have a claim to them. This was
ordered by William of Canterbury, the archbishop, and all
the diocesan bishops that were
in England, and the king gave
them all permission to go home,
and so they went home, and all
the orders availed nothing -
they all kept their wives by
permission of the king as they
had done before.

II. *Henry of Huntingdon, Historia Anglorum s.a. 1129*

> Printed in Hunt., pp. 250-1; the earlier editions are
> listed there on pp. ix-x. Here printed from Cambridge,
> Corpus Christi Coll. ms. 280, fo. 135^{r-v} (= A), BL Arun-
> del ms. 48, fo. 116^{r-v} (= B) and BL Add. ms. 24061, fos.
> 50^v-51 (= C).

Tenuit [rex] igitur concilium maximum ad kalendas Augusti apud
Lundoniam, de uxoribus sacerdotum prohibendis. Intererant
siquidem illi concilio Willelmus Cantuariensis archiepiscopus,
Turstanus Eboracensis archiepiscopus, Alexander Lincoliensis
episcopus, Rogerus Salesbiriensis,^b Gillebertus Lundoniensis,^b
Iohannes Roucestrensis, Siffridus Sudsexcensis, Godefridus
Bathensis,^c Simon Wigornensis, Everardus^d Nordwicensis, Bernardus
Sancti Davidis, Herveus primus Heliensis episcopus. Nam Win-
toniensis et Dunelmensis et Cestren[fo. 135^v]sis^e et Hereforden-

---

^a wa *ms.*   ^b episcopus *add* B.   ^c God. Bath. *om.* C.   ^d Eward AC.   ^e episcopus *add* A.

sis obierant.[1] Hi columpne regni erant et radii sanctitatis hoc
tempore. Verum rex decepit[a] eos simplicitate Willelmi archiepiscopi. Concesserunt namque regi iusticiam de uxoribus sacerdotum, et inprovidi habiti sunt, quod postea patuit cum res
summo dedecore terminata est. Accepit enim rex pecuniam infini-
tam de presbiteris et redemit eos. Tunc, sed frustra, conces-
sionis sue penituit episcopos cum pateret in oculis omnium
gentium deceptio prelatorum et depressio subiectorum.

135

THE SCHISM OF 1130 AND THE COUNCIL OF RHEIMS IN 1131

See in general H. Klewitz, *Reformpapsttum und Kardinalkolleg*, pp. 209-59, P.F. Palumbo, *Lo scisma del MCXXX*,
esp. pp. 393-4, H. Bloch, *Traditio*, viii (1952), 159-264,
F.-J. Schmale, *Studien zum Schisma des Jahres 1130*, esp.
pp. 220 ff., and M. da Bergamo, *Contributi dell' Istituto
di storia medioevale*, i (1968), 265-302. For the council
see Hefele—Leclercq, v.694-9 and R. Somerville, in *Bull.
of Medieval Canon Law*, NS v (1975), 122-30, citing
earlier literature.

On the night of 13/14 February 1130 Honorius II died, and two
successors were elected; a party directed by the chancellor,
Cardinal Aimeric, chose Gregory of St. Angelo, who took the name
of Innocent II, while a rather larger body, chiefly of the older
cardinals, chose Peter Pierleone, the legate to England of 1121,
as Anacletus II. Uncertainty over the procedure for an election
and bitter personal divisions within the body of the reforming
cardinals made the resolution of this schism more complex than
ever before.

Before the middle of June Anacletus had secured virtually

---

[a]deinceps B.

---

[1]The other absentees were William of Exeter, already blind, and Urban of
Llandaff, at the height of his quarrel with Bernard of St. Davids. David of
Bangor was rarely in England.

complete control in Rome, and Innocent was compelled to flee
to Pisa, and thence, early in September, to France. The abbot
of Cluny recognized him at once; at a meeting of the clergy of
northern France at Étampes Louis VI and his bishops accepted
him too, and Abbot Suger was sent to Cluny with a formal embassy
to this effect at the end of October. At the Council of Clermont (18 November) messengers from Lothar and the German clergy
announced the outcome of a similar meeting at Würzburg, and
Innocent had secured the support of the French and German kings,
as well as that of the most influential of the religious, headed
by Cluny, Cîteaux under the potent impulsion of St. Bernard,
and Prémontré.

King Henry meanwhile still held aloof. Agents of Urban of
Llandaff had been in Rome as the schism broke out; they seem to
have accepted Innocent at once, for his first bulls as pope were
issued on Llandaff's behalf on 25 February, two days after his
consecration.[1] On 3 March Innocent wrote to Abbot Hugh of Reading, who had been named a 'specialis beati Petri filius' the
previous year, announcing his election and urging Hugh to continue the active collection of Peter's Pence. By 28 March the
pope had heard of Hugh's promotion to Rouen, which he hastened
to confirm.[2] In August agents of Bishop Urban were at Genoa
with the pope again, while Bernard of St. Davids may also have
been there, perhaps as the king's agent.[3] All this while Henry
ordered his clergy to take no action until a choice was made;
it seems clear that the propaganda of both parties was current
in England.[4] In the autumn the king crossed to Normandy, where

---

[1]JL 7405-6 (Book of Llandaff, pp. 55-6); such precipitate action has its
parallel in the bull issued by Anacletus on 24 February at the request of
Archbishop Adalbero of Hamburg/Bremen (JL 8372, Palumbo, Lo scisma, p. 650).
[2]PUE iii, nos. 22, 25, 26; above, no. 133.
[3]JL 7421-2 (Book of Llandaff, pp. 56-7); the letter from Cardinal John
(probably of Crema) on p. 58 is here associated with this second Llandaff
mission, though it may belong with the bulls of February. The letter from a
Cardinal Gregory associated with it is yet more problematic.
[4]Henry II cited his grandfather's conduct in 1130 as a precedent for his
suspension of litigation at the curia at the outbreak of the schism of 1159
(below, p. 838). Innocent's circular letter on his election (JL 7407) is
only known in England from the archives of Urban and Hugh of Rouen (Book of
Llandaff, p. 54, PUE iii.97); Anacletan propaganda is represented by the
letter of Peter of Porto in Historia Novella, ed. Potter, pp. 7-9, WMGR

Gerard of Angoulême was active on behalf of Anacletus, while Hugh of Rouen was probably Innocent's chief advocate.[1]

At the beginning of January Louis VI met Innocent at Fleury and escorted him north to Orléans. Thence the pope moved to Chartres. Henry left Normandy, accompanied by the Norman bishops, and came to meet him there on 13 January, falling at his feet and making lavish gifts to the cardinals. Henceforward Henry's dominions accepted Innocent apparently without reservation; from 17 January 1131 onwards bulls for England and Normandy followed in rapid succession.[2]

The climax of these negotiations occurred on 9/10 May, when there was a great gathering of churchmen at Rouen; the pope arrived surrounded by a large body of cardinals, the archbishop of Tarragona, the bishop of Chartres and the abbots of Cluny,

---

ii.532-3, §454) and a letter from the anti-pope of 25 Feb. 1131 generally addressed (P. Baumgarten, 'Ein Brief des Gegenpapstes Anaclet (II.)', *Neues Archiv* xxii (1896), 576, Palumbo, *Lo scisma*, p. 671). Both texts are found in rather later 12th-cent. mss., BL Royal 5. A. xiii, from Worcester, and Oxford, Corpus Christi Coll. 137. See also *J. Wig.*, pp. 29 n., 44.

[1]On Gerard's efforts see particularly Arnulf of Lisieux, *Invectiva*, in *MGH Libelli de Lite*, iii.102-3 and H. Claude in *Mélanges St. Bernard*, pp. 80-4. Various explanations of Henry's final decision were given by contemporaries. According to *Chronique de Morigny*, p. 53 he acted in imitation of Louis VI, and Suger, *Vie de Louis VI le Gros*, p. 260 seems to agree. OV vi.418-20 offers independent confirmation of the partisan claim of the *Vita Petri Venerabilis* (*PL* clxxxix.20) that he was chiefly moved by the adherence of Cluny. This has some force in view of Henry's extensive patronage of Cluny at the time, for which see C.N.L. Brooke in *Il monachesimo nella riforma ecclesiastica* (Milan, 1971), pp. 137-40, D. Lohrmann in *Pierre Abélard: Pierre le Vénérable*, 191-203, and *Letters of Peter the Venerable*, ed. Constable, i.190-1, ii.259. The *Vita Prima S. Bernardi*, Book ii, by Ernald, however, describes Bernard's mission to the king in Normandy and success in winning him to Innocent's cause 'ab episcopis Angliae penitus dissuasum' (*MGH Scriptores*, xxvi.101, *PL* clxxxv.271), a passage to be received with caution. For the part of Hugh of Rouen see above, p. 750, *Letters of Peter the Venerable*, i.24-5 (no. 17), ii.105-7, JL 7487 (*Papsturkunden in Frankreich*, Neue Folge ii, no. 11), OV v.442, *Chronique de Morigny*, p. 60 and the discussion in Waldman, 'Hugh "of Amiens", Archbishop of Rouen 1130-64', pp. 24-7.

[2]OV vi.418-20, *Vita Prima S. Bernardi* in *MGH Scriptores*, xxvi.101, *PL* clxxxv.271, *Innocentii II Vita a Bosone conscripta* in *Pontificum Romanorum ... Vitae*, ii.175, JL 7449 (*PL* clxxix.76), *Historia Novella*, ed. Potter, pp. 9-10 (WMGR ii.533-4 §454), *Reg.* ii, no. 1687, JL 7440 (*Book of Llandaff*, pp. 63-5), *Papsturkunden in Frankreich*, Neue Folge ii, nos. 8, 9, JL 7441 (*PL* clxxix.72-4). For the likelihood of the presence of the abbot of Cluny see *Letters of Peter the Venerable*, ii.138, 259.

Clairvaux, and St. Denis. Hugh of Rouen, the bishops of Lisieux
and Séez and the prior of Carlisle were among Henry's clergy.
By then Innocent's success north of the Alps was largely secure,
and at Rouen he issued the first surviving summons to a council
to be held at Rheims on 18 October 1131.[1]

Henry returned to England before the council, where his chief
representative was Archbishop Hugh of Rouen. Suger mentions the
presence of bishops from England, but only Bernard of St. Davids
and representatives of Urban of Llandaff are known to have been
there, in the interests of their own sees. The acts of the council are not found in known manuscripts of English provenance.[2]

136
24 APRIL 1132. COUNCIL AT LONDON

The case raised by Urban of Llandaff against his neighbours at
Hereford and St. Davids at the papal curia had been pursued
almost without intermission since the legatine council of 1127.
However, whether deliberately or not, the litigants had never
appeared together in Rome, and the resources of Llandaff were
being exhausted by constant embassies.[3] On 12 August 1131 Innocent summoned Urban and Bernard of St. Davids to the council
of Rheims in October, but Urban's representatives excused him
on grounds of ill health. Accordingly on 21 November the pope
ordered him to appear before the three archbishops of Canterbury, York, and Rouen on the second Sunday after Easter, 1132,

---

[1]*Historia Novella*, ed. Potter, p. 10, Torigny (ed. Howlett), p. 119,
William of Jumièges, *Gesta Normannorum Ducum*, ed. Marx, pp. 308-9 (an interpolation by Torigni), JL 7472-6 (*PL* clxxix.93-7), *PUE* i, no. 15, *Reg.* ii,
no. 1691 (*Facsimiles of English Royal Writs to 1100*, n. to pl. **xx**). This
meeting may well have been the occasion for renewing the legation of Archbishop William of Canterbury, apparently referred to this year in *Historia
Novella*, ed. Potter, p. 11 (WMGR ii.535 §456); he had certainly received it
before 7 March 1132 (JL 7549, *Book of Llandaff*, p. 65). See further C.R.
Cheney, *Revue de Droit Canonique*, xxviii (1978), 89.

[2]Suger, *Vie de Louis VI le Gros*, p. 268, OV vi.422, *Chronique de Morigny*,
pp. 57-61.

[3]The fullest modern account of the chronology of the dispute and calendar
of the documents is that in Conway Davies, i.147-90, ii.621-33; see now also
W. Davies, '*Liber Landavensis*: its construction and credibility', *EHR* lxxxviii
(1973), 335-51.

to receive a delegated judgement (no. I).[1] This order was repeated in a second bull of 13 February 1132, apparently in
response to a protest by Urban, for here the final decision was
expressly reserved to the pope.[2]

No record of the judgement survives, and the bare mention by
Huntingdon (no. II) gives no indication of the outcome. However
the record of further meetings the next year and Urban's death
on a last appeal make it clear that there was no effective and
decisive judgement.[3] At the time of the Council of Rheims the
bishop of Hereford had only just been consecrated, but it is
quite likely that he too appeared at London to resist Urban's
claim on his diocese. It may well be that a charter of Archbishop William recording a judgement which confirmed Hereford
in possession of disputed territory in the Golden Valley by
virtue of a commission from Pope Innocent refers to events at
London at this time.[4]

Another charter of Archbishop William (no. III) shows that
the council concerned itself with matters other than the affairs
of Llandaff, for it records the surrender of the church of
Calke to the canons there by Abbot William of Chester,[5] though
this surrender is not said explicitly to be the consequence of
a conciliar judgement. Private transactions of this kind are not
recorded for the earlier councils of the reign.

It seems likely that a royal council was held at this time,
for the king's charter granting his college at Dover to Archbishop William speaks of the gift as first made at Northampton
in 1131 'sed apud Westmonasterium confirmata communi celebrato
concilio', and the witness list includes the three archbishops

---

[1]*Book of Llandaff*, pp. 56 (and 61-2), 58-9 (and 62-3), 59, 60 (and 64-5),
65-6 (JL 7406, 7474, 7477-8, 7484).
[2]Ibid., pp. 62, 65 (JL 7542, 7549).
[3]Hunt., p. 253, P. Baumgarten, *EHR* ix (1894), 531-2.
[4]The charter is best edited by M. Cheney in *EHR* lvi (1941), 179 n.; the
judgement was delivered 'communi nostro et fratrum nostrorum episcoporum
iudicio' which certainly suggests an ecclesiastical council. No other similar occasion is known between Robert's consecration in 1131 and King Henry's
death.
[5]The house at Calke (later moved to Repton) was founded before 1120 (*Misc.
D. M. Stenton*, p. 32 n. which refers to the benefactions of Earl Richard,
who died in the White Ship); Abbot William held office 1121-40.

with nine other English bishops. It may have been during this
that a grant was made to Kenilworth in the presence of Bishop
Roger of Chester and his household 'in domo Sauhali halbergerii
quando concilium celebratum fuit apud Lundon' iii kal Maii'
[29 April]. Whether these two councils may usefully be distinguished must remain uncertain.[1]

I. *Letter of Innocent II to Urban of Llandaff, 21 November 1131*

    Aberystwyth, NLW ms. 17110 E, coll. 75-76. Printed *Book
    of Llandaff*, pp. 66-7. Calendared in JL 7511, Conway
    Davies, ii.631-2.

Innocentius episcopus, servus servorum Dei, venerabili fratri.
U. Landavensi episcopo salutem et apostolicam benedictionem.

    Ut lis et controversia que inter te et fratrem nostrum B.
episcopum sancti David de parrochialibus terminis agitatur
finem acciperet, et utraque ęcclesia de cętero conquiesceret,
festivitatem beati Luce quo ad nostram venires presentiam,
eidem episcopo de sua quęrimonia responsurus, tibi terminum
constituimus. Predictus [col. 76] autem frater noster B. episcopus, clericorum et laicorum caterva stipatus, eodem termino
nostro se conspectui optulit, agere preparatus. Verumtamen
corporali egritudine detentum non posse venire tres sacramen-
tales qui a tua parte fuerant delegati tactis sacrosanctis
ewangeliis firmaverunt. Nos igitur, utriusque ęcclesię inopie
et laboribus providentes, negotium hoc venerabilibus fratribus
nostris G. Cantuariensi, T. Eboracensi et Hugoni Rotomagensi
archiepiscopis in regno Anglie pertractandum commisimus. Placet
autem nobis ut, si fieri potest, inter te et prefatum B.
episcopum per eorum consilium et deliberationem pax et concordia reformetur. Precipiendo ergo tibi mandamus ut, omni occasione seposita et absque apellatione, proxima Dominica quę
legitur 'Ego sum pastor bonus', cum litteris et privilegio
predecessoris nostri felicis memorie pape Honorii[2] et aliis

---

[1] *Mon.* iv.538 (*Reg.* ii, no. 1736), R.W. Eyton, 'The Staffordshire Chartulary', p. 206.
[2] *Book of Llandaff*, pp. 30-3 (JL 7304); compare pp. 34-48, esp. 41-5
(JL 7369).

instrumentis ac superstitibus testibus quos ante ipsius presentia[m] produxisti, eisdem te fratribus representes. Quatenus ipsi et tuas et predicti fratris[a] nostri B. episcopi rationes audire et plenius intelligere et quod preceperint nobis valeant intimare. Quod si subterfugeris et te presentare et agere contempseris, cavendum est ne dampnum de absentia tua sustineas, illumque possessorem et te petitorem constituamus.

Dat' Trecis xi kl' Decembris.[1]

II. *Henry of Huntingdon, Historia Anglorum, s.a. 1132, 1133*

> Printed Hunt., p. 253. The text below is based on Cambridge, Corpus Christi Coll. ms. 280, fo. 136[r-v] (= A), collated with BL ms. Arundel 48, fo. 117 (= B) and BL ms. Add. 24061, fo. 51 (= C).

Post Pascha fuit magnum placitum apud Lundoniam, ubi de pluribus quidem et maxime de[b] discordia episcopi sancti Davidis et episcopi Clamorgensis de finibus parrochiarum suarum tractatum est ...

Anno xxxiii ... ad[c] capud ieiunii [8 Feb.] fuit conventus apud[d] Lun[fo. 136[v]]doniam super episcopos sancti Davidis et Clamorgensis, et pro discordia archiepiscopi et Lincoliensis episcopi. Ad Pascha [26 Mar.] fuit rex apud Oxeneford in nova aula,[e] ad Rogationes [30 Apr.-3 May] fuit iterum conventus apud Winceastre super rebus predictis.

III. *Charter of Archbishop William of Canterbury, 1132 x 1136*

> BL Add. Charter 7214. Printed I.H. Jeayes, *Descriptive catalogue of Derbyshire Charters* (London, 1906), pp. 66-7 and C.R. Cheney, *English Bishops' Chanceries 1100-1250* (Manchester, 1950), p. 150 with facs. as pl. 1. Original 141 mm x 115 mm, sealed on a tongue on the left, with

[a]fratribus *ms.* [b]*om.* B. [c]apud A. [d]ad B. [e]et *add* B.

[1]For other English bulls issued at Troyes at this time see *PUE* i, no. 16, ii, no. 14.

wrapping tie at foot; two horizontal folds and one verti-
cal. Fragmentary elliptical seal in reddish-brown wax.
The seal has stained parts of the centre to the point of
illegibility.

Willelmus Dei gratia Cantuar' archiepiscopus et sedis apostolice
legatus Rogero eadem gratia Cestrensi episcopo et Rannulfo
comiti[1] et omnibus sancte Dei ecclesie fidelibus per Angliam
salutem et Dei benedictionem.

Notum omnium devotioni sit quoniam Willelmus abbas Cestrensis in presentia nostra [et arc]hiepiscoporum Eboracensis et
Rotomagensis et aliorum episcoporum [qui co]ncilio Lundonie
interfuerunt, quod celebravimus in dominica quando cantatur
'Ego sum pastor bonus' tempore Henrici regis,[2] canonicis de
Calc reddidit ecclesiam suam de Calc et quietam clamavit, et
omnia sua que per illum vel per suos illis ablata fuerunt reddere vel restaurare de suo promisit, et quod etiam cartam comitis de eadem re quam habuerant quamque per ipsum perdiderant
restitueret. Unde volo et firmiter precipio ut eadem ecclesia
amodo ad opus predictorum canonicorum ad serviendum Deo libera
et quieta permaneat. Rogo etiam vos omnes ut pro amore Dei[a] et
nostro eandem ecclesiam consilio vestro et auxilio muniatis.
Val'.

Endorsed in a 12th-cent. hand De restitutione de Kalc facta
coram W. archiepiscopo Roberto priori L[undonie].[3]

---

[a] *interlined.*

---

[1] Roger, bishop of Chester 1129-48, and Ranulf, earl of Chester 1129(?)-
1153.
[2] This suggests, without proving, that the king was dead, and that the
charter was issued between 1 December 1135 and 21 November 1136.
[3] If the endorsement is to be believed, this is much the earliest occurrence of Prior Robert, who was still in office in 1154 (*Heads*, p. 182).

137

DECEMBER 1135-APRIL 1136. ROYAL CHARTERS OF LIBERTIES

Following the precedent of Henry I (above, p. 652), Stephen
tried to strengthen an insecure succession by issuing charters
of liberties: the first, brief and very generally worded,
accompanied his coronation oath, and so may be dated c.22 December 1135;[1] the second, much ampler, has a dating clause which
attaches it to the Easter court at Oxford early in April 1136.[2]
Although there are various more general clauses, it is primarily
a charter of liberties for the Church, and this is emphasized
at the outset by the references to the archbishop of Canterbury
(on whose adherence Stephen's 'election' and coronation had
depended), and the pope, whose confirmation he claims to have
had.

The first charter survives in the bifolium BL ms. Harl. 458,
fo. 3[V], 13th cent. (French translation, fo. 4[V]) (H); and in ms.
Cotton Claudius D. ii, fo. 71[V] (68[V]), written in the Guildhall,
City of London, early in the 14th century (C);[3] printed *Statutes
of the Realm*, i, Charters of Liberties, p. 4; W. Stubbs, *Select
Charters* (9th edn., 1913), p. 142; *Regesta*, iii, no. 270. We
print from H, noting variants of C. C may just possibly be a
copy of a different original, but it seems more likely that it
has been touched up by a scribe used to later formulas.

Of the second charter three originals survive: Salisbury,
Dean and Chapter C. 2 (s; scribe unidentified);[4] Exeter, D.& C.

---

[1] On the date of Stephen's coronation, see note to *Regesta*, iii, no. 270.
[2] Round, *Geoffrey de Mandeville*, pp. 18-23, 262-6, discusses the massive
witness list and related lists; ms. h dates it 'in communi concilio'.
[3] Originally part of a book now divided between London, Guildhall, Cor-
poration RO, Liber Custumarum, fos. 1-84, 86-102, 173-186, BL ms. Cotton
Claud. D. ii, fos. 1-24, 30-40, 42-115, 124-135, 266-277, and Oxford, Oriel
Coll. ms. 46, fos. 109-211. See N.R. Ker, 'Liber Custumarum, and other
manuscripts formerly at the Guildhall', *Guildhall Miscellany*, i (1952-9),
37-45, cited there as ms. D; also Ker, *Medieval Manuscripts in British
Libraries*, i.20-2; C.N.L. Brooke, G. Keir, and S. Reynolds, 'Henry I's
charter for the City of London', *Journ. of the Society of Archivists*, iv
(1973), 558 ff., esp. p. 573.
[4] Our text below is based on s, with significant variants of the other
originals; but see note 1, p. 765. On the distribution of the charter see
R.L. Poole, *Studies in Chronology and History* (ed. A.L. Poole, Oxford,
1934), pp. 309-13; corrected by C.R. Cheney, *Bull. J. Rylands Lib.* xxxviii
(1955-6), 337-8.

2529 (e; scribe unidentified); Oxford, Bodl. ms. Rawl. Q. a. 1,
fo. 26, from Hereford, in a scrap book of Hearne's (h: scriptor
xiii; see T.A.M. Bishop, *Scriptores Regis*, Oxford, 1961, no.
595; cf. nos. 739, 241 for s and e). All are in facsimile in
Regesta, iv, plates III-V; text in *Regesta*, iii, no. 271, which
we reproduce, collated with the originals, and revised to conform with our conventions. Copies in William of Malmesbury,
Historia Novella, c. 464, ed. Potter, pp. 18-20; Richard of
Hexham, pp. 148-50; York Minster Lib., Magnum Reg. Album, pt.
iii, fos. 73^V, pt. iv, fo. 72; Canterbury, D.& C. Reg. E, fo.
40; Reg. I, fo. 72^V.

Printed: *Regesta*, iii, no. 271; also W. i.412-13; Sp.
ii.38; *Statutes of the Realm*, Charters of Liberties, p. 3
(with facs. of e); Newburgh, ed. Hearne, iii.711-13
(from h); C. Bémont, *Chartes des libertés anglaises
(1100-1305)* (Paris, 1892), pp. 8-10; Stubbs, *Sel. Charters*, pp. 142-4; William of Malmesbury, *ut supra* (and
ed. Stubbs, RS ii.541-2); *Early Yorks. Charters*, i (ed.
W. Farrer), no. 133. On the date of the charters, see
J.H. Round, *Geoffrey de Mandeville* (London, 1892), pp.
22-3; *Regesta*, iii, nos. 270-1 nn. For comment, see H.A.
Cronne, *The Reign of Stephen* (London, 1970), pp. 125 ff.,
Barlow (1979), pp. 91, 304.

I. *King Stephen's first, or coronation, charter of liberties*

Stephanus[a] rex Angl(orum) iustic(iis), vicecomitibus, baronibus
et omnibus ministris et fidelibus suis Francis et Anglicis,
salutem. Sciatis me concessisse et presenti carta mea confirmasse omnibus baronibus et hominibus meis de Anglia omnes
libertates et bonas leges quas Henricus rex Angl(orum)[b] eis
dedit et concessit. Et omnes bonas leges et bonas consuetudines
eis concedo quas habuerunt tempore Edwardi regis.[c] Quare volo
et[d] precipio quod habeant et teneant illas omnes[e] bonas leges
et libertates de me et heredibus meis, ipsi et heredes sui,

---

[a]C *adds* Dei gratia.   [b]C *adds* avunculus meus.   [c]regis Edwardi C.
[d]C *adds* firmiter.   [e]omnes illas C.

libere et quiete et plenarie. Et prohibeo ne quis eis super
hiis molestiam vel impedimentum vel diminutionem faciat super
forisfacturam meam. Teste Willelmo Mart(el). Apud Lond(oniam).

II. *King Stephen's 'Oxford' charter of liberties for the Church*

Ego Stephanus Dei gratia assensu cleri et populi in regem Anglię[a] electus et a Willelmo Cantuar(iensi) archiepiscopo et
sanctę Romanę ecclesię legato consecratus, et ab Innocentio
sanctę Romanę sedis pontifice postmodum[b] confirmatus, respectu
et amore Dei sanctam ęcclesiam liberam esse concedo[1] et debitam
reverentiam illi confirmo. Nichil me in ęcclesia vel rebus
ęcclesiasticis simoniace acturum vel permissurum[c] promitto.
Ęcclesiasticarum personarum et omnium clericorum et rerum eorum
iusticiam et potestatem et distributionem bonorum[d] ęcclesiasti-
corum in manu episcoporum ęssę perhibeo et confirmo. Dignitates
ęcclesiarum privilegiis earum confirmatas et consuetudines
earum antiquo tenore habitas inviolate manere statuo et concedo.

Omnes ęcclesiarum possessiones et tenuras quas die illa
habuerunt qua Willelmus[e] rex Angl(orum) avus meus[f] fuit vivus
et mortuus sine omni calumpniantium reclamatione eis liberas et
absolutas esse concedo.

Si quid vero de habitis vel possessis ante mortem eiusdem
regis quibus modo careat ęcclesia deinceps repetierit indulgen-
tię et dispensationi meę vel restituendum vel discutiendum
reservo.

Quecumque vero post mortem ipsius regis liberalitate regum,[g]
largitione principum, oblatione vel[h] comparatione vel qualibet
transmutatione fidelium eis collata sunt confirmo.

Pacem et iusticiam me in omnibus facturum et pro posse meo
conservaturum eis promitto.

Forestas quas W(illelmus) rex[i] avus meus et W(illelmus)[i]

---

[a]Anglie s; Anglorum eh.   [b]*om.* e.   [c]eh *add* esse.   [d]honorum h.
[e]W. e.   [f]rex ... meus s; rex avus meus e; avus meus rex h.   [g]e *adds* vel.
[h]*om.* b.   [i]W. rex ... W. s; Will' rex ... Will's b; W. ... W. h.

---

[1]Cf. Henry I's charter, above, p. 654, c. 1.

secundus[a] avunculus meus instituerunt et tenuerunt,[b] illas[c]
michi reservo. Cęteras[d] omnes quas rex Henricus[e] superaddidit,
ęcclesiis et regno quietas reddo et concedo.

Si quis autem[f] episcopus vel abbas vel alia ęcclesiastica
persona ante mortem suam rationabiliter sua[g] distribuerit vel
distribuenda statuerit, firmum manere concedo. Si vero morte
preoccupatus fuerit, pro salute animę eius ęcclesię consilio
eadem fiat distributio.

Dum vero sedes propriis pastoribus vacuę fuerint,[h1] ipsę et
omnes earum possessiones[i] in manu et custodia clericorum vel
proborum hominum eiusdem ęcclesię committantur[j] donec pastor
canonice substituatur.

Omnes exactiones et iniusticias et meschenningas sive per
vicecom(ites) vel per[k] alios quoslibet male inductas funditus
exstirpo. Bonas leges et antiquas et iustas consuetudines in
murdris et placitis et aliis causis observabo et observari
precipio et constituo.

Hęc vero omnia concedo et confirmo salva regia et iusta dignitate mea, testibus W(illelmo) Cant(uariensi)[1] archiepiscopo,
et Hugone archiepiscopo Roth(omagensi), et H(enrico) episcopo
Winton(iensi), et Rogero episcopo Sar(esberiensi), et Alexandro
episcopo Linc(olniensi), et Nigello episcopo Eliensi,[m] et
Ebr(ardo) episcopo Norwich(ensi), et Sim(one) episcopo Wirec(es-
trensi), et Bern(ardo) episcopo sancti David, et Aud(oeno)
episcopo Ebroic(ensi), et Ricardo episcopo Abrinc(ensi), et
Roberto episcopo Heref(ordensi), et Ioh(anne) episcopo Rovec(es-
trensi), et Adel(oldo)[n] episcopo Carl(eolensi), et Rogero

---

[a]om. e. [b]habuerunt e. [c]om. eh. [d]h adds vero. [e]rex Henr's s;
rex H. e; Henr' rex h. [f]om. eh. [g]om. h. [h]h adds et. [i]ipse ...
poss. sh; ipsas et earum poss. omnes e. [j]committam e. [k]om. h.
[l]Minor differences of abbreviation of names (and in a very few cases of
order of witnesses) are not noted; all Christian names save the second W. de
Albini are extended in one or other original. For full details see facsimiles in Regesta, iv, plates III-V. [m]h om. the bishop of Ely.
[n]Athelulf' e; A. h.

[1]Cf. ibid. On the interpretation of this clause see M.E. Howell, Regalian
Right in Medieval England (London, 1962), pp. 29-30, who supposes that
Stephen in principle surrendered regalian right by this clause; but it is
not clear that he is making more than a concession on the manner in which a
vacant see was administered: see below, p. 868 (Const. of Clarendon, c. 12).

cancellario, et Henrico nepote regis.,[a] et R(oberto) comite
Gloec(estrie), et Willelmo comite Warenn', et Rannulfo comite
Cestr(ie), et R(ogero) comite Warwich', et Roberto de Ver, et
Milone Gloec(estrie), et R(oberto) de Oilli, et B(rientio)
filio comitis constabulariis, et W(illelmo) Martel, et Hugone
Big(ot), et Umfrido de Boh(un), et Simone de Belloc(ampo) dapi-
feris, et W(illelmo) de Albini, et Eudone Martel pincernis, et
Roberto de Ferr(ariis), et W(illelmo) Pevr(ello),[b] et S(imone)
de Silvanecta,[c] et W(illelmo) de Albini, et Pag(ano) filio
Iohannis, et H(amone) de sancto Claro, et Ilb(erto) de Laci.
Apud Oxenef(ordiam). Anno ab incarnatione Domini M^{mo}C^{mo} XXX^{mo}
VI^{to}, scilicet regni mei primo.[d]

138

1138-9. LEGATION OF ALBERIC, CARDINAL BISHOP OF OSTIA

> The best modern account of the legation is in Tillmann,
> pp. 38-41, based on Richard of Hexham, pp. 169 ff.; John
> of Hexham, pp. 297 ff.; *J. Wig.*, pp. 48 f. (see also
> sources cited, below, pp. 768-72; D. Nicholl, *Thurstan,*
> pp. 229-32).[1]

In the summer of 1138 the eminent French Cluniac, Alberic,
recently consecrated cardinal bishop of Ostia (3 April) came
to England as legate for England and Scotland; his function was
to celebrate the end of the schism, following the death of the
anti-pope Anacletus II on 25 January 1138; to visit the Scottish and English kings and their churches; to make peace between
the two kingdoms - the battle of the Standard was fought on 22
August while Alberic was in England; to settle the troubled
churches of the border; and to preside over a council of the

---

[a]h *adds* R(ogero) de Fisc(anno).   [b]e *adds* de Notingeh'.   [c]Saintliz e;
sancto Licio h.   [d]sed ... primo se; in communi concilio h.

---

[1]On Alberic, monk of Cluny, abbot of Vézelay 1131-8, cardinal bishop of
Ostia 1138-48, see R. Manselli in *Archivio della Società Romana di Storia
Patria,* lxxviii (1955), 23-68; Zenker, pp. 15-20.

English church and the election of a new archbishop of Canterbury. The election of Archbishop Theobald and the council of
Westminster (December 1138) are dealt with below, pp. 768-79.
Since Alberic's meeting with the Scots clergy and nobles was
intended to settle the church on both sides of the border and
restore Bishop Adelold to Carlisle, it seems relevant to include
John of Hexham's narrative of these events.

*John of Hexham's narrative of Alberic of Ostia's legation in
1138*

> From Cambridge, Corpus Christ Coll. ms. 139, fo. 139 (C),
> collated with Paris, BN ms. nouv. acqu. lat. 692, fos.
> 47^v-8 (Pb; select variants only);[1] ed. T. Arnold, in
> Symeon, ii.297-9.

Directus est autem ab eodem papa legatus Anglię et Scottię
Albericus Hostiensis episcopus, natione Gallicus, professione
monachus Cluniacensis et in eodem cenobio supprioris officio ad
disponendas regulares observationes prelatus monachis cunctis,
excellentia virtutis et plenitudine eruditionis instructus.
Veniens vero in Angliam adiunxit sibi socios sui laboris Rod-
bertum episcopus Herefordensem et Ricardum primum abbatem de
Fontibus.[2] Profectusque ad regem Scotię reverenter receptus
est a fratribus Hagustaldensis [ecclesie]^a et Aldufus episcopus cum eo. Ante triduum autem adventus eius ad locum illum,
Eadgarus filius Cospatrici comitis cum satelliciis suis eruperat
e castris regis Scottię predam agens de quadam villa territorii
Hagustaldensis. Irruerunt etiam in quandam villam fratrum
Hagustald(ensium),^{b} interfectisque tribus hominibus fratrum et
capta preda eiusdem vici, priorem Hagustaldensem, quem contigit

---

^{a}*Ins. in later hand* C; *om.* Pb. ^{b}Hagustaldensis fratrum (*marked for
transposition*) C; fr. Hagustald' Pb; *perhaps* ecclesie *is missing, as Arnold
suggested.*

---

[1] On this ms. (12th-13th cent., probably from Scotland) see J.M. Todd and
H.S. Offler in *Scottish Hist. Rev.* xlvii (1968), 151-9.
[2] Robert de Béthune, bishop of Hereford (1131-48), and Richard I, abbot of
Fountains (1132-9), who died at Rome on 30 April 1139 (*Heads,* p. 132).

eadem nocte ibi adesse, contumeliis et ludibrio dehonestaverunt.
Super iniuria hac satis compatienti animo legatus regem expostu-
lavit apud Karlel, et ad correctionem violentię huius[a] animos
regios adduxit. Per triduum vero cum episcopis et principibus
regni Scottię, qui ei ex regio precepto ibi occurrerant, quę
corrigenda erant correxit, et quę statuenda erant statuit.
Aldulfum episcopum in gratiam eiusdem regis et in sedem suam
de Karlel recipi impetravit. Iohannem Glascuensem episcopum,
qui omisso episcopali officio apud Tironas monachatui se con-
tradiderat, ex apostolica auctoritate revocavit. Scottos quoque
et Pictos in hoc sibi acquiescentes habuit, ut infra festum
sancti Martini omnem captivitatem ad Karlel reducerent et
libertati donarent, nullusque eorum ecclesias violare, femineo
sexui vel pueris vel senibus cedem inferre ulterius presumeret.
Ipsius etiam regis genibus provolutus ab hostilitate eum usque
ad festum sancti Martini cessare compulit. His ibi ita dispositis in die sollempni sancti Michaelis ad Hagustaldensem ecclesiam reversus, in Suthangliam profectus est. Siquidem Northym-
bria universa inculta et in solitudinem redacta fuit. Quotquot
enim supererant, vel ad asilum monasteriorum confugerant, vel
per solitudines delituerant; potentes intra oppida se conclu-
serant.

Igitur ex auctoritate apostolici precepti ad festum sancti[a]
Nicholai apud Lundonias in Uuestmonasterio [C, fo. 140[v]] convenerunt ad eundem legatum Albericum episcopi, abbates et primores regni, anno pontificatus Innocentii papę ix et regni
Stephani regis tercio ...

(*A brief account of the council follows: see pp. 769-70.*)

139

DECEMBER 1138. LEGATINE COUNCIL OF WESTMINSTER

In the letter of invitation to this council, the papal legate
indicates that the main session will be on Sunday, 11 December
1138, and that its business will be to take part in the

---

[a]*Ins. in later hand* C.

consecration of the bishop of Exeter, the election of a new
archbishop of Canterbury, and other ecclesiastical and papal
affairs; those summoned are asked to arrive on the Thursday or
the Friday, i.e. 8 or 9 December.[1] In the event the *acta* of the
council are dated 13 December, apparently the day when the
canons were promulgated; the bishop of Exeter was consecrated
on the following Sunday (18 December), and Theobald, abbot of
Bec, was elected archbishop on 24 December, and consecrated on
8 January 1139.[2] What most directly concerns us now was the
issuing of its disciplinary canons, on 13 December. These canons
fall into three groups. The first nine are for the most part a
reissue of the main definitions of Westminster (1125), not
greatly altered, but with rather more elaborate sanctions, notably (in the case of clerks irregularly ordained by another
bishop) the reservation to the Holy See of the relaxation from
the penalty. The same reservation was made in a canon aimed to
protect ecclesiastics against assault. This canon was repeated
in the council of 1143 and is the most important of the second
group (canons X-XIII), which introduce a new emphasis on the
defence against violence of every kind, from violence against
clerks to the activity of clerks who act as knights, and seem
to echo the first signs of the disorder which was shortly to
become the anarchy. The remainder of the canons are assorted
disciplinary measures of greater or less importance.

   Brief mentions of the council also occur in John of Worcester (p. 53, incorporating phrases from the *acta*),[3] Henry of
Huntingdon (p. 265),[4] John of Hexham (Symeon, ii.299, derived

---

[1]Richard of Hexham's narrative (followed by John of Hexham, in Symeon,
ii.299) gives 6 Dec. as the opening date. The *acta* of the council (incorporated in John of Worcester, Richard of Hexham and Gervase of Canterbury)
seem to give 13 Dec. as the day when the canons were promulgated. The Ann.
Winchcombe say that Theobald was elected archbishop in the council on 10
Dec. (s.a. 1139, ed. R.R. Darlington, p. 128) - but see n. 2. Henry of
Huntingdon dates the council, quite vaguely, to Advent (p. 265). On this
council, see Voss, p. 21, Barlow (1979), pp. 93-4.
   [2]Cf. Saltman, *Theobald,* pp. 12 f.; for the date, also Le Neve, ii.4.
   [3]Cf. also Gervase, ii.384; but this is only an abbreviated version of
Gervase, i.109.
   [4]Followed, with slight additions, by Torigny, p. 135; also mentions in
Diceto, i.252; Newburgh, ed. Howlett, i.34-5; Roger of Wendover, ed. H.O.
Coxe, ii.225; Paris, *Chron. Maj.* ii.169-70; Ann. Wenlock, Cambridge, Corpus

from Richard of Hexham) and the *Life of Christina of Markyate,*
pp. 162-3. *The Memorials of the Abbey of Fountains*[1] have an
account of how the abbot of Fountains went with other abbots to
meet the legate (presumably on this occasion), and subsequently
accompanied him to the papal curia.

John of Worcester assigns to the council the consecration of
the bishop of Exeter (see p. 772 n. 1), the blessing of the
abbot of Westminster, and the degradation of the abbots of
Battle, Crowland, and Shrewsbury (cf. below). There is an
account of the resignation of Warner abbot of Battle 'ante
Natale Domini', without reference to the council, in the Chronicle
of Battle abbey.[2]

This council is stated to have been the occasion of a forged
charter of King Stephen to Westminster Abbey, composed in the
mid-twelfth century.[3] The dating clause was evidently based on
the *acta* of the council. But the lengthy witness list is, with
one or two possible exceptions, consistent with a date at the
close of 1138 or the beginning of 1139, and may well incorporate
a sound tradition of the higher clergy present, though not perhaps a complete list (see p. 774 n. g.). It included the following ecclesiastics: Archbishop Theobald (either he is an addition
to the list, or it was not drawn up until after his election),
Henry bishop of Winchester, Roger bishop of Salisbury, Alexander bishop of Lincoln, Nigel bishop of Ely, Geoffrey bishop of
Durham, Robert bishop (? of Hereford), Robert bishop (? of Bath),
Everard bishop (of Norwich), Robert bishop (? of Exeter, though
only consecrated on 18 December), Simon bishop (of Worcester),
Bernard bishop (of St. Davids), Adelold bishop (of Carlisle),

Christi Coll. 111, fo. 9; Ann. Wigmore, Manchester, John Rylands Lib. Lat.
215, fo. 2; possibly also by the Continuatio Roffensis, ed. Liebermann, in
UGQ, p. 48. Other mentions occur in Ann. Winchcombe (see above, p. 769 n. 1)
and Worcester (*Ann. Mon.* iv.378), and the *Chron. Angliae Petriburgense* (ed.
J.A. Giles, London, 1845, p. 90; s.a. 1138 it gives the arrest of the bishop
of Lincoln; s.a. 1139 the deposition of the abbot of Crowland by the legate
Alberic).

[1] Ed. J.R. Walbran *et al.*, i (Surtees Soc., 1863 for 1862), pp. 70-2.
[2] Ed. Searle, pp. 140-1. For the legate Alberic and the council cf. Tillmann, pp. 38 f.; above, pp. 766-8.
[3] *Reg.* iii, no. 928 - see note, and on the context of the forgery, P. Chaplais in *Misc. D.M. Stenton*, pp. 89-110, esp. p. 97. Cf. below, p. 774 n. g.

Seffrid Pelochin bishop (of Chichester), Roger bishop (unidenti-
fiable), Geoffrey abbot of St. Albans, Ingulf abbot of Abingdon, 'Walter' abbot of 'Evesham' (the abbot of Evesham at this
time was Reginald Foliot; but it seems most likely that Evesham
is a mistake for Eynsham, whose abbot was called Walter), Robert
abbot of Thorney, Walter abbot of Ramsey, Martin abbot of Peterborough, Roger abbot of Tewkesbury, Edward abbot of Reading,
Gilbert abbot of Colchester.

The *acta* of the council are derived from three types of
manuscript:

(*a*) C. *Richard of Hexham,* who gives the *acta* embedded in a
       narrative: Cambridge, Corpus Christi College, ms. 139
       fos. 43^V-44^V, from Sallay or Sawley, perhaps origi-
       nally from Fountains; on this ms. see P. Hunter Blair
       in *Celt and Saxon* (ed. N.K. Chadwick) (Cambridge,
       1963), pp. 63-118; D. Baker in *Studies in Church History,*
       xi (1975), 83-123.

(*b*) G. Gervase of Canterbury (below, p. 973 n. 3) who
       includes the letter of summons (I):
       Ga - BL ms. Cotton Vespasian B. xix, fos. 38^V-40 (13th-
       cent., from Canterbury).
       Gc - Cambridge, University Library ms. Ff. 1. 29, fos.
       19^V-20, 27^V-28^V (see Stubbs' note ad loc.); 14th-cent.
       On these mss., see Stubbs, ibid., pp. l-lv.

(*c*) Texts of *acta* without Richard of Hexham's narrative.
       E. Cambridge, Emmanuel College, ms. 38 (from Pershore
       Abbey), fos. 78^V-79, in a 12th-cent. copy of Isidore on
       the Pentateuch.
       J. Oxford, St. John's College, ms. 125, fos. 87-8 (with
       heading 'Concilium London' sub rege Stephano'; followed
       by Councils of London, 1143 and Westminster, 1125, in a
       12th-cent. copy of Ivo's *Pannormia* (see Z.N. Brooke,
       English Church and the Papacy, pp. 237-8).

The variants between the texts are considerable, and - save
that there is a measure of agreement between E and G - they
seem to be independent of one another. The present text is that
of C, with errors corrected from the other mss.; the variants
of J alone are consistently noted. The text of G is somewhat

inferior, and E is an abbreviated and careless text: only
selected variants (and especially readings in which they agree)
have been noted.

> *Printed texts:* W. i.413-16, from Sp. The *acta* were first
> printed by Twysden, coll. 326-9 (Richard of Hexham) and
> 1346-8 (Gervase); subsequently in Sp. ii.39-44 (from
> Richard of Hexham, Matt. Paris, etc.); Labbe, x.992-8;
> Mansi, xxi.507-20; Richard of Hexham, ed. R. Howlett,
> *Chrons. Stephen etc.*, iii.172-6; and Gervase, i.105-9.

I. *Letter of summons by the papal legate, Alberic of Ostia, to
the prior and monks of Christ Church Canterbury etc.*

From Ga, fos. 38^v-39; Gc, fos. 19^v-20; ed. Stubbs, Gervase, i.106.

Albericus Dei gratia Hostiensis episcopus, apostolice sedis
legatus, dilectis in Christo fratribus Ieremie priori totique
conventui, H(elewiso) archidiacono, clero, nobilibus, populo
Cantuarie salutem et benedictionem.

Susceptum apostolice legationis officium nos constringit, et
cor nostrum instanti sollicitudinis pulsat aculeo, ut ecclesiis
regimine destitutis idoneum pastoris solatium providere studea-
mus. Veruntamen Cantuariensis ecclesie diuturna desolatio nos
vehementius angit, quippe que et diadema regni habet, et omnibus ecclesiis Anglie, ordinata pastore, futura est exemplum
ruine vel resurrectionis. Proinde caritati vestre his apicibus
nostris insinuamus, quod episcopos et abbates omnes ceterasque
religiosas huius regni personas, apostolica auctoritate convo-
cavimus ad colloquium quod Lundonie habere disposuimus apud
Westmonasterium Dominica Adventus Domini qua[a] cantabitur
'Gaudete in Domino', quatinus ibi Deo volente Exoniensem electum consecremus,[1] et de ordinatione ecclesie Cantuariensis,[b]

---

[a]que Ga.   [b]Cantuarie ecclesie Gc.

[1] *J. Wig.*, loc. cit., gives Sunday, xvi Kal. Jan. as the day when the
bishop of Exeter was consecrated. 17 Dec. 1138 was a Saturday, and as consecrations were apparently always performed on Sundays, the date here fore-
cast seems more likely to be correct.

de ceteris etiam ecclesiasticis atque apostolicis negotiis
divino pre[Ga, fo. 39]eunte auxilio tractemus. Eapropter vobis
precipimus, ut prima dominica Adventus Domini litteras istas
coram universo clero et populo Cantuariensi exponi faciatis, et
invocata Sancti Spiritus gratia, premissisque orationibus, indicto ieiunio et elemosinis, talem vobis preficiendam providea-
tis personam cui sacrorum canonum auctoritas in nullo valeat
obviare, cui etiam comprovinciales episcopi pariter debeant
assentire, et cui dominus vester[a] rex nec possit nec debeat
assensum suum iuste denegare. Quocirca dilectioni vestre mandamus et apostolica auctoritate precipimus, ut tot et tales
personas illuc generalitatis vice vobiscum adducatis, que omnium
vestrum voce loquantur et cunctorum in se preferant assensum.
Certi autem estote quia iuste postulationi vestre in quantum
poterimus secundum Deum consilio et auxilio non deerimus. Precipimus etiam ut quinta aut sexta feria ante predictum terminum
Lundoniam veniatis, quatinus de hoc et de ceteris negotiis
aliquantulum vobiscum deliberare valeamus. Valete.[b]

II. *Narrative of Richard of Hexham*

[c]Supranominatus vero legatus [sc. Albricus], ut predictum est,
per episcopatus ac monasteria ad curiam regis Anglie reversus,
quendam alium legatum nomine [Petrum][d] qui nuperrime a domno
papa Innocentio venerat, ibidem repperit. Igitur Turstinum
Eboracensem archiepiscopum et omnes episcopos atque abbates
ac priores canonicorum per totam Angliam summoneri fecerunt,
ut ad festum sancti Nicholaii [*sic*] in civitate Lundonia ad
generale concilium convenirent. Quibus prefinito tempore ac loco
cum S(tephano) rege Anglie congregatis, de ecclesiasticis causis
cum illis ambo legati tractare ceperunt; Albricus tamen priorem
locum optinuit. Fuit autem concilium huiusmodi.[c]

---

[a]noster GaGc.   [b]*Followed in Gervase (pp. 107-9) by* Idus Decembris (anno
Domini MC xxxviii Gc) celebrata est sinodus ... (*abbreviated from the* acta
*of the council) and the canons. After the canons is an account of the elec-
tion of Archbishop Theobald and the jealousy of the bishop of Winchester.*
[c-c]*In* C *only*; JE *start* Anno ...; J *has title* Concil' London' sub rege Stephano.   [d]*om.* C; *the name is supplied by* J. Wig. (*p. 53*). *Possibly to be
identified with Peter of Pisa, but there are several other possibilities*
(*Brixius, pp. 45-6*).

[Acta of the council]

Anno ab incarnatione domini M C XXX VIII pontificatus autem[a] domni pape Innocentii secundi[a] anno ix, regnante piissimo et illustrissimo[b] S(tephano) rege Anglorum, Henrici magni regis nepote, anno vero regni ipsius tercio,[c] celebrata est synodus Lundonie in ecclesia sancti[d] Petri apostolorum principis apud Westmonasterium mense Decembris,[d] tertia decima die eiusdem[e] mensis: ubi post multarum discussionem causarum, promulgata sunt hec capitula et ab omnibus confirmata, numero xvii. Prefuit autem illi synodo Albricus Hostiensis episcopus et predicti domni pape Innocentii[f] in Angliam et Scottiam legatus, cum episcopis diversarum provinciarum xvii[g] et abbatibus circiter xxx et cum innumera cleri ac[h] populi multitudine. [i](Vacabat autem tunc temporis Cantuariensis ecclesia et infirmabatur Turstinus Eboracensis archiepiscopus: Willelmum tamen ecclesie sancti Petri Eboracensis decanum cum quibusdam clericis suis illuc direxit.)[i] Sunt autem hec capitula.

Capitulum I.[j][1] Sanctorum patrum canonica instituta sequentes auctoritate apostolica interdicimus ut pro crismate, [C, fo. 45] pro oleo, pro baptismate, pro penitentia, pro[k] visitatione infirmorum seu desponsatione mulierum seu[l] unctione, pro communione corporis Christi, pro sepultura, nullum omnino pretium exigatur: quod[m] qui presumpserit, excommunicationi subiaceat.

II. Sancimus[n] etiam ut ultra octo dies corpus Christi non

---

[a]*om. JE.* [b]*piissimo et illustrissimo C; nobilissimo JE; J continues Stephano Anglorum rege.* [c]*anno ... tercio C; tertio vero (om. E) anno regni ipsius JE.* [d]*beati ... Decembri J, J. Wig.* [e]*om. J, J. Wig.* [f]*om. J.* [g]*xvii E; numero xvii JG; xviii C, J. Wig. (the difference may consist in counting or not counting the bishop of Exeter, consecrated 18 December, but even so it is doubtful if there were more than 16 English and Welsh bishops at this time before the consecration of Archbishop Theobald).* [h]*ac C; et JG; E om. the whole passage et cum innumera ... hec capitula.* [i]-[i]*In C only (almost the same words in John of Hexham, p. 299).* [j]*Numbers given as in J (EG also have numbers); om. C.* [k]*seu pro EG; G om. visitatione infirmorum seu and ins. pro visitatione infirmorum after mulierum.* [l]*seu CJ; pro E; seu pro G.* [m]*quod CJ; et EG.* [n]*Sancimus C; Statuimus JEG.*

---

[1]Cf. C. of Westminster (1125), c. 2; cf. Brett, *English Church,* pp. 164-6.

reservetur, neque ad infirmos, nisi per sacerdotem aut per diaconem[a] aut (necessitate instante) per quemlibet[b] cum summa reverentia deferatur.

III.[1] Item apostolica auctoritate sancimus ut in consecrationibus episcoporum vel abbatum benedictionibus non cappa, non indumentum ecclesiasticum, neque quicquam ab episcopo vel a ministris eius exigatur; et[c] in dedicationibus quoque ecclesiarum non tapete, non manutergium, non bacinia, nichilque omnino preter procurationem[d] sacris canonibus institutam[e] requiratur.

IV. Si quis episcopus in diocesi sua per alium episcopum ecclesiam consecrari fecerit, apostolica auctoritate prohibemus, ne quid inde ultra procurationem[d] eiusdem episcopi exigat.

V.[2] Nullus omnino de manu laici ęcclesiam seu quecunque[f] ecclesiastica beneficia accipiat. Cum autem investituram per episcopum aliquis acceperit, precipimus ut super ewangelium iuret se nichil propter hoc per se vel per aliquam[g] aliam personam dedisse alicui vel promisisse; si autem[h] presumptum fuerit, [i]irrita huiusmodi donatio erit, et tam dator quam acceptor ultioni canonice[j] subiaceat.[i]

VI.[3] Sancimus preterea ne quis ecclesiam, seu quelibet beneficia ecclesiastica[k] paterna sibi vendicet hereditate aut successorem sibi in ecclesiastico constituat beneficio.[l] Quod si

---

[a]diaconem CGa; diaconum JGc; diaconos E.   [b]aut (necessitate ... quemlibet C; vel per (*om.* EG) quemlibet clericum instante necessitate (*om.* E) JEG.   [c]*om.* JEG.   [d]procurationem CJ; corredium G; corr' E.   [e]institutam CJ; institutum G; instituta E.   [f]quecunque C; queque JE; quelibet G (*as 1125, 1127*).   [g]aliquam *ins. in margin* C; *om.* JEG.   [h]si autem C; Quod si J (*as 1125*); Et si EG.   [i-i]irrita ... subiaceat CJ; irritum fore decernimus EG (*also omitting the whole of c. VI save these three words*).   [j]erit huiuscemodi donatio ... canonice ultioni J.   [k]beneficia ecclesiastica C; ęcclesiastica beneficia J.   [l]*om.* J.

---

[1]Cf. ibid., c. 3.
[2]Cf. ibid., c. 4 and C. of Westminster (1127), c. 10.
[3]Cf. C. of Westminster (1125), c. 5. The quotation is from Psalm 82, 14, 13.

presumptum fuerit, irritum fore decernimus, cum psalmista dicentes[a] 'Deus meus, pone illos ut rotam qui dixerunt: hereditate possideamus sanctuarium Dei'.

VII.[1] Clericos a non suis episcopis absque litteris proprii
episcopi ordinatos a susceptorum officiis ordinum[b] inhibemus,
solique Romano pontifici eorundem plenaria restitutio reservetur nisi religionis habitum susceperint.

VIII.[2] Sanctorum patrum vestigiis inherentes, presbiteros,
diaconos,[c] subdiaconos uxoratos aut concubinarios ecclesiasticis
officiis et beneficiis privamus, ac ne quis eorum missam audire
presumat, apostolica auctoritate prohibemus.

IX.[3] Feneratores[d] clericos et turpia lucra sectantes et pup-
blica secularium negotia[e] procurantes ab officio et beneficio
ecclesiastico[f] nichilominus removendos esse censemus.

X.[4] Si quis clericum aut monachum vel sanctimonialem vel[g]
quamlibet ecclesiasticam personam occiderit, incarceraverit vel
nefarias ei manus[h] intulerit, nisi tercio summonitus satisfecerit, anatemate feriatur. Neque quisquam ei preter Romanum
pontificem nisi mortis urgente periculo[i] modum penitentie

---

[a] cum psalm. dic. C; dic. cum psalm. J (*as 1125*).   [b] officiis ordinum C;
ord. offic. JEG.   [c] J *adds* vel.   [d] Venatores G.   [e] officia J.   [f] et beneficio ecclesiastico CGa; ecclesiastico et beneficio J; et ecclesiastico beneficio EGc.   [g] seu EG.   [h] ei manus CJ; eis manus G; manus eis E.   [i] *om.*
nisi ... periculo J.

---

[1] Cf. CC. of Winchester (1070), c. 3; London (1075), c. 4; Westminster
(1125), c. 10.
[2] Cf. CC. of Westminster (1127), c. 5; London (1102), c. 6.
[3] Cf. C. of Westminster (1125), c. 14.
[4] Cf. C. of Rheims (1131), c. 13; C. of Pisa (1134), c. 12 (Mansi, xxi.461,
490). The Pisa canon has the words: '... (si) quis ... in clericum vel
monachum violentas manus iniecerit, anathemati subiaceat: et nullus episcoporum illum absolvere presumat, nisi mortis urgente periculo, donec apostolico conspectui presententur'. Cf. also C. of London (1143), c. 2 and n.
The privilege is cited by John of Salisbury (*Policraticus*, v. 5, ed. C.C.J.
Webb, i.297), probably after the decree of 1139, but with a possible remi-
niscence ('nisi per Romanum pontificem') of this canon.

finalis iniungat.[a] Si autem[b] inpenitens mortuus fuerit, corpus eius inhumatum remaneat.[c]

XI.[d1] Si quis res ecclesiarum[e] mobiles vel[f] inmobiles violenter usurpare presumpserit, nisi post canonicam vocationem[g] emendaverit, eum excommunicari precipimus.

XII.[d2] Apostolica auctoritate prohibemus ne quis absque licentia[h] episcopi sui in possessione sua[i] ecclesiam vel oratorium constituat.[j]

XIII.[3] His subiungimus quoque[k] auctoritatem Nicholai pape dicentis: 'Cum discreti sint milites Christi a militibus seculi, non convenit militem ecclesie seculo militare, per quod ad effusionem sanguinis necesse sit[l] pervenire. Denique sicut turpe[m] est laicum missas facere sacramenta corporis et sanguinis Christi conficere, ita ridiculum et inconveniens est clericum arma sustollere et ad bella procedere, cum Paulus apostolus[n] dicat 'Nemo militans Deo implicat, etc.'[o]

XIIII.[4] Item[p] adicimus hoc decretum Innocentii pape dicentis Victrico Rotomagensi [C, fo. 45[v]] archiepiscopo:[q] 'Monachi diu morati in monasteriis,[r] si postea ad clericatum[s] pervenerint,

---

[a]iniungat finalis J.   [b]Si autem C; Etsi J; Si EG.   [c]maneat EG.
[d]J *transposes cc. XI and XII, and for c. XII reads* Apostolica auctoritate prohibemus ne quis sine licentia sui episcopi ecclesiam aut oratorium cónstruat.   [e]res ecclesiarum EG; ecclesiarum res C *marked for transposition*; ecclesiarum res J.   [f]aut J.   [g]vocationem canonicam J.   [h]precepto JEG.
[i]sua C; *om.* E; propria G.   [j]construat G (*as* J: *see* n. d).   [k]subiungimus quoque C; subiunximus EG; adnecti placuit J.   [l]sit necesse J.   [m]aut pernitiosum *add.* EG; et perniciosum *add.* J.   [n]egregius J; egregius predicator G.   [o]implicat *om.* J; *for* etc. EG *read* se secularibus negotiis.
[p]om. EG.   [q]om. Victrico ... archiepiscopo JEG.   [r]in monasteriis conversati J; in monasteriis morati EG.   [s]clericatus honorem JEG.

---

[1]Cf. C. of Windsor (1070), c. 11; C. of Lateran I (1123), c. 20 (Alberigo, pp. 190-4).
[2]Cf. C. of Lateran I (1123), cc. 7, 18 (Alberigo, pp. 190-4).
[3]From a letter of Pope Nicholas I of ?861, JE 2688. The immediate source of the canon is not clear: of the collections known in England at this time, it occurs in Ivo's *Decretum*, vi.120; *PL* clxi.474. The quotation at the close is from II Tim. 2, 4: 'Nemo militans Deo implicat se negotiis saecularibus'.
[4]Innocent I's letter is JK 286. The fathers of the council may have known it from Pseudo-Isidore (Hinschius, p. 529), or Ivo's *Tripartita*. It was later included in *Decretum*, C. 16 q. 1 c. 3.

non debent aliquatenus a priore[a] proposito deviare.' Sicut in
monasteriis positi fuerunt,[b] ita et[c] in clericatus ordine degere
debent; et quod diu servaverunt, id[c] in altiori gradu positi
amittere non debent.

XV.[1] Prohibemus etiam apostolica auctoritate[d] sanctimoniales
variis seu grisiis, sabellinis, marterinis, hereminis, beverinis pellibus[e] et anulis aureis uti, sive torturam capillorum
et compositionem capillorum facere.[f] Huius[g] decreti que inventa
fuerit violatrix, anathemati subiaceat.

XVI.[2] De omnibus primiciis rectas decimas dari,[h] apostolica
auctoritate precipimus. Quas qui reddere noluerit, anathematis
in eum sententia proferatur.

XVII.[13] Sancimus preterea ut si magistri scolarum aliis scolas
suas legendas pro precio locaverint, ecclesiastice vindicte
subiaceant.

   [*Conclusion of Richard of Hexham's narrative.*]

In hoc autem concilio tractatum est de archiepiscopo ad Cantuariensem ecclesiam eligendo, que ut supradictum est tunc
proprio pastore carebat. Tandem vero post proximam Epiphaniam
hec causa finem habuit, cum Beccensis cenobii abbas nomine
Teobaldus electus prefate ecclesie archipresul a supradicto

---

[a]a priore C; priori JEG.   [b]fuerint J.   [c]*om.* JEG.   [d]auctoritate
apostolica JG.   [e]sabellinis ... pellibus: herminiis, sabelinis, beverinis,
marterinis pellibus J; EG *place* hereminis (E vel hereminiis) *after* pellibus.   [f]*om.* sive ... facere JEG.   [g]Cuius EG.   [h]dare EG.   [1]*For this
canon* JEG *read* Magistri scolarum si aliis scolas suas (*om.* Gc) regendas
commiserint, prohibemus ne quicquam propter hoc (E propter hoc ne quicquam;
G ne propter hoc quicquam) ab eis exigant. Quod si fecerint, ecclesiastice
vindicte subiaceant (J *adds* Hoc placet). JEG *end here.*

---

[1]Cf. C. of Westminster (1127), c. 11. The furs listed are vair (*variis*),
gris - probably miniver - (*grisiis*), sable (*sabellinis*), marten (*marterinis*), ermine (*hereminis*), and beaver (*beverinis*). This is important early
evidence for the use of these furs in England. See C. Brooke and G. Keir,
London 800-1216 (London, 1975), pp. 259-61; E.M. Veale, *The English Fur
Trade in the later Middle Ages* (Oxford, 1966).
   [2]Cf. C. of Westminster (1127), c. 9.
   [3]Barlow (1979), pp. 225-6.

Alberico consecratus est.

In eodem autem concilio depositus est abbas de Cruland, et prior ecclesie sancti Albani martyris nomine Godefridus[a] in loco eius restitutus; et abbatie que est iuxta Hastingas que dicitur ad Bellum, abbas nomine Adam ellectus est;[1] quos utrosque predictus Albericus benedixit. Invitavit quoque omnes episcopos et abbates plurimos Anglie ad generale concilium quod domnus papa Innocentius ad medium Quadragesime Rome celebraturus erat.[2] Dum autem hec agerentur de pace reformanda inter duos reges sepissime ac diligentissime cum pluribus, et maxime cum regina Anglie tractavit.

140

APRIL 1139. SECOND LATERAN COUNCIL

For the council in general see Alberigo, pp. 195-6 (bibliog.), 197-203 (text); Mansi, xxi.523-46; Hefele—Leclercq, v.i.721-46; Foreville, *Latran*, pp. 73-95, 180-94; supplemented by Richard of Hexham, pp. 176-7; *The Life of Christina of Markyate*, pp. 162-7; Torigny, p. 65; R.L. Poole, 'The English bishops at the Lateran Council of 1139', *EHR* xxxviii (1923), 61-3; Saltman, *Theobald*, pp. 14-15; C.R. Cheney, *Medieval Texts and Studies* (Oxford, 1973), pp. 204-5; Barlow (1979), p. 112.

The Life of Christina, pp. 162-3, describes a discussion at the Council of Westminster of December 1138 as to who should compose the English delegation. In the event, it consisted of Theobald, newly consecrated archbishop of Canterbury, four bishops - identified by Richard of Hexham as Rochester, Worcester, Coventry and Exeter - four abbots,[3] and Henry archdeacon

---

[a]C *adds* et alter, *cancelled*.

[1]The new abbot of Battle was Walter de Lucy, elected, according to the *Chron. Battle*, pp. 140-3 (ed. Brewer, p. 65), on 8 Jan. 1139; cf. *Heads*, pp. 29, 42 (for Crowland).   [2]i.e. the second Lateran Council of 1139.

[3]*The Life of Christina of Markyate*, pp. 162 ff., describes how Geoffrey abbot of St. Albans was chosen, but in the end, by Christina's persuasion, was prevented from going.

of Huntingdon. En route, while staying at Bec, Henry was made
aware of the newly finished *Historia Regum Britanniae* of
Geoffrey of Monmouth, and this led him to refer to the visit
in one of his letters;[1] yet in his own *Historia* he made no
reference to the Lateran Council. Theobald took the occasion
to receive his pallium from the pope.[2]

On 1 March, shortly before the council, Henry of Blois,
bishop of Winchester, was appointed papal legate for England,
apparently in compensation for his failure to secure the archbishopric of Canterbury. He held it until 1143.[3] The council
met early in April for about one week. Theobald was back in
England by August.[4]

The canons promulgated in the Council were almost immediately
incorporated in Gratian's *Decretum*; thus they were by the mid
and late twelfth century well known in England.[5] Yet apart from
the texts in copies of Gratian, there is no ms. of English
provenance known to contain them.[6]

The Council was in large measure designed to celebrate the
end of the papal schism of 1130. From the English point of
view, however, the most important event was the discussion of
the rival claims of King Stephen and the Empress Matilda to the
English throne. The debate was described by Gilbert Foliot in
GFL, no. 26 (written in 1143-4), and by John of Salisbury in
HP (ed. Chibnall, pp. 83 ff.; ed. Poole, pp. 85 ff.). There
are discussions of it by R.L. Poole in his edition, pp. 107 ff.;

---

[1]In Torigny, pp. 65-6; cf. C. Brooke, in *Studies in the Early British
Church*, ed. N.K. Chadwick (Cambridge, 1958), p. 231, and n. But see also OV.
vi.380-1 n.   [2]Saltman, *Theobald*, pp. 14-15.
[3]See below, pp. 781-810; Tillmann, pp. 41-50; Böhmer, *Kirche und Staat*,
pp. 340 ff.; L. Voss, *Heinrich von Blois*, pp. 22 ff., 38, 41-53.
[4]Foreville, *Latran*, p. 78: the opening date of II Lateran is variously
given as 3, 4, or 8 April by the sources, but it was apparently concluded
by the 9th or 10th. See below, p. 783.
[5]On the reception of Gratian in England, see John of Salisbury, *Letters*,
i, p. xx and n. (where John's legal learning is unduly depreciated). John's
letters show that Gratian was known in England at latest by the late 1150s;
in all probability copies were circulating by *c*.1150.
[6]Bodl. Lat. misc. d. 74, fos. 96ᵛ-97ᵛ (cf. Cheney, *Medieval Texts and
Studies*, p. 205 n.), contains a partial copy of them in a 12th-cent. ms. of
Ivo's *Pannormia*, but the book is probably of French provenance, though in
later centuries perhaps in the library of the Franciscans at Chester (Ker,
p. 50). The text of the canons breaks off early in c. 28, where the leaf
ends; c. 6 omits all after *careant*. Canon 15 of the Council is referred to
in *PUE* iii, nos. 313, 317.

in *GF*, chap. vii; and by G. Constable in Peter the Venerable,
Letters, ii.252-5.

Professor Constable points out that it is possible (as was
thought before Poole wrote his discussion of the problem) that
John's account refers to a debate before the pope in 1136: it
is almost certain that Stephen had submitted his claim to the
pope in that year.[1] 'While accepting this as a possibility',
write Morey and Brooke (*GF*, p. 105 n.), 'we feel that it is
probable that John's and Gilbert's account refer to the same
occasion ...' The similarities and differences are discussed
both by Constable and in *GF*. In any event it is agreed that the
case was debated in the Lateran Council, that the Empress's
case was presented by Ulger, bishop of Angers; if John's version refers to the same occasion, Stephen's advocates were
Arnulf, archdeacon of Sées (later bishop of Lisieux), and
Lupellus, clerk to William, archbishop of Canterbury.

141

29 AUGUST-1 SEPTEMBER 1139. LEGATINE COUNCIL OF WINCHESTER

The following accounts of this council and the councils
of Winchester and Westminster of 1141 are found in William of Malmesbury, *Historia Novella,* cc. 470-8, 492-6,
501-2, ed. K.R. Potter, pp. 28-34, 52-6, 62-4; ed. Stubbs,
ii.550-5; cf. Sp. ii.44 and W. i.419 (from Mat. Paris).

The background to this council was essentially political. In
the summer of 1139 King Stephen moved against Roger, bishop of
Salisbury, and his family; on *c.*24 June he had him arrested in
Oxford. Henry of Blois, the king's brother, bishop of Winchester and papal legate (see p. 780), summoned the king to a
legatine council at Winchester, which was described at length
by William of Malmesbury (below).[2] The *Gesta Stephani* (pp. 80-1)

---

[1] Constable, loc. cit., citing *Life of Christina,* pp. 162-3.
[2] For the context, see M.I. Megaw, 'The ecclesiastical policy of Stephen,
1135-9: a reinterpretation', in *Essays in British and Irish History in
Honour of J.E. Todd,* ed. H.A. Cronne, T.W. Moody, and D.B. Quinn (London,
1949), pp. 24-45; H.A. Cronne, *The Reign of Stephen,* pp. 38-9, 129 ff.;

speaks of a council at which it was 'firme statutum' that
bishops' castles should be handed over to the king; and at
which the king subsequently did penance for his assault on the
bishop of Salisbury and his episcopal nephews of Lincoln and
Ely. But it seems clear that Stephen was not present at the
legate's council, and there seems to be some confusion here;
as also in John of Hexham's mention of it, which seems to con-
fuse it with the council of 1143 (see p. 794). The council of
Winchester was also referred to by Huntingdon (p. 265) and Ann.
Waverley, *Ann. Mon.* ii.227.[1] The annals describe it as a legatine council held in August in which legate and archbishop
begged the king to restore the castles he had taken from the
bishops. The affair was soon overshadowed by the arrival of the
Empress Matilda, who landed in England about the end of September.

We reproduce the text of K.R. Potter's edition of the *Historia Novella,* based on collation by R.A.B. Mynors of all the
mss. We have reproduced his apparatus (with minor corrections).
The basis is ms. Ce[1], BL Royal 13. D. ii (12th cent., from
Margam), which represents the author's final revision, occasionally checked by Ce[2] (BL Addit. 38129, early 15th cent.);
the variants represent classes of mss. identified by Stubbs and
Mynors as A and B, which we call a and b.

Of a the mss. are: Bodl. ms. Laud. Misc. 548 (12th cent.);
Oxford, All Souls Coll. ms. 35 (13th cent., from St. Martin,
Louvain); Cambridge, Trinity Coll. ms. R. 7. 10 (748) (12th
cent.).

Of b the mss. are: BL Royal ms. 13. B. xix (14th-15th cent.);
Bodleian, Bodl. 712 (2619) (14th cent., written for Robert
Wyvill, bishop of Salisbury); Cambridge, Trinity Coll. R. 7. 1.
(739) (13th cent., probably used by Savile); BL Royal 13. D. v
(13th cent.).[2]

R.H.C. Davis, *King Stephen,* pp. 34-5; *Gesta Stephani,* pp. 80 ff. For this council, see
also Voss, p. 34, Barlow (1979), p. 130; Kealey, *Roger of Salisbury,* pp. 190-8.

[1]Subsequently by Paris, *Ch. Maj.,* ii.171; etc.
[2]Shown by Stubbs and Mynors to be a b ms., and used by Matthew Paris
(Mynors in Potter's edn., pp. xl-xli; R. Vaughan, 'The handwriting of Matthew Paris', *Trans. Cambridge Bibliographical Soc.,* i (1949-53), 376-94,
esp. p. 391).

William of Malmesbury, Historia Novella s.a. 1139

... [470] Hoc regis factum in diversas sententias solvit ora
multorum. Quidam dicebant iure castellis alienatos episcopos
videri, que preter scita canonum edificassent: illos evangelis-
tas pacis esse debere, non architectos domorum que auctoribus
maleficii forent refugium.[a] Hec amplioribus rationibus et
sermonibus agebat Hugo archiepiscopus Rothomagi,[1] quantum illa
facundia poterat maximus regis propugnator. Alii contra,
quorum partibus assistebat Henricus Wintoniensis episcopus,
sedis apostolice in Anglia legatus, frater regis Stephani, ut
ante dixi; quem nec fraterna necessitudo, nec periculi metus,
a vero tunc[b] exorbitare cogebat. Sic porro dicebat: si episcopi
tramitem iusticie in aliquo transgrederentur, non esse regis,
set canonum iudicium; sine publico et ecclesiastico concilio
illos nulla possessione privari debuisse: regem id non[c] recti-
tudinis zelo, set commodi sui compendio fecisse; qui castella
non ecclesiis, ex quarum sumptibus et in quarum terris con-
structa erant, reddiderit, set laicis eisdemque parum religiosis
contradiderit. Ista vir ille tum privatim, tum etiam publice
coram rege affirmans, eiusdemque aures de liberatione et restitutione pontificum appellans, omnem consumpsit operam, in
nullo auditus: quapropter, vigorem canonum[d] experiendum ratus,
concilio, quod quarto kalendas Septembris celebraturus erat
Wintonie, fratrem incunctanter adesse precepit.

[Potter, p. 29] [471] De concilio habito pro captione
                          episcoporum.
Dicto die omnes fere episcopi Anglie, cum Thetdbaldo archiepiscopo Cantuarie qui Willelmo successerat, venerunt Wintoniam.
Archiepiscopus Eboracensis Turstinus pro[e] valitudine qua grava-
batur, vix enim animi viribus corpus regebat, ceteri vero pro
guerra, litteris absentiam [Ce[1], fo. 115] suam excusarunt.[f]

---

[a]maleficii *after* refugium ab.   [b]tunc *om*. ab.   [c]b *adds* ex.   [d]canoni-
cum Ce1.   [e]pro: qui pro a.   [f]excusabant a.

---

[1]Hugh of Amiens, previously abbot of Reading, archbishop of Rouen 1130-
64 (*Heads*, p. 63; above, p. 750 and n.; the subject of an Oxford D.Phil.
thesis by T. Waldman, 1970).

Lectum est primo in concilio decretum Innocentii pape, quo iam
a kalendis Martii, si bene commemini,[a] partes sollicitudinis
sue idem apostolicus domino episcopo Wintoniensi iure[b] legationis in Anglia iniunxerat. Exceptum id summo favore, quod,
diuturnitate temporis temperantiam suam ostendens episcopus,
non se prerupta legatum promulgasset iactantia. Processit
deinceps in concilio sermo eiusdem, latialiter ad litteratos
habitus, de indignitate[c] captionis episcoporum: quorum Sales-
beriensis in camera curie, Lindocoliensis in diversorio suo
intercepti essent; Eliensis exemplum simile veritus, veloci
profugio ad Divisas se calamitati exemisset. Scelus miserabile,[d]
regem ab incentoribus ita fuisse seductum, ut hominibus suis,
presertim episcopis, in curie sue pace manus inici iussisset.
Adiecta esset regio dedecori celestis iniuria, ut, sub obtentu
culpe pontificum, ecclesie possessionibus suis spoliarentur.
Sibi regis contra Dei legem[e] excessum tanto dolori esse, ut
mallet se multo dispendio et corporis et rerum suarum affici,
quam episcopalem celsitudinem tanta indignitate deici. Quin
etiam regem de emendatione peccati multociens commonitum;
postremo[f] [Potter, p. 30] concilii vocationem non abnuisse.
Proinde archiepiscopus et ceteri consulerent in medium quid
opus esset facto: se ad executionem concilii nec pro regis, qui
sibi frater erat, amicitia,[g] nec pro dampno possessionum, nec
etiam pro capitis periculo, defuturum.

[472] Dum[h] hec ille sensim per amplificationem exponit, rex,
cause sue non diffisus, comites in concilium misit, querens cur
vocatus esset. Responsum est a legato ex compendio: non debere
illum, qui se Christi fidei subiectum meminisset, indignari si
a ministris Christi ad satisfactionem vocatus esset, tanti
reatus[i] conscius quantum nostra secula nusquam vidissent. Gentilium quippe seculorum opus esset episcopos incarcerare et possessionibus suis exuere. Dicerent ergo fratri, quod, si consilio suo placidum commodare dignaretur assensum, tale illi
Deo auctore largiretur, cui nec ecclesia Romana, nec curia

---

[a]memini a.   [b]iura b.   [c]indignatione ab.   [d]mirabile Ce[1].   [e]legem
Dei ab.   [f]ab add tunc.   [g]amicitia after regis ab.   [h]cum ab.
[i]reati a.

regis Francie, nec ipse comes Thetbaldus frater amborum, sapiens profecto vir et religiosus, ex ratione contraire posset, set quod favorabiliter complecti deberent. Consulte vero in presentiarum rex faceret, si vel rationem facti sui redderet, vel canonicum iudicium subiret. Ex debito etiam oportere ut ecclesie faveret, cuius sinu exceptus, non manu militum, in regnum promotus fuisset. Cum^a dicto comites egressi nec multo post cum^b responso reversi sunt. Comitabatur eos Albericus quidam de Ver, homo causarum varietatibus exercitatus. Is responsum regis retulit, et [Potter, p. 31] quantum potuit causam antistitis^c Rogerii, episcopus enim Alexander aberat,^{d} quem manutenuit,^{e} gravavit; modeste tamen, sine ulla verborum^f contumelia: quamvis quidam comitum, astantes^g iuxta, crebro loquelam eius interrumperent, probra in episcopum iacientes.

[473] Hec ergo fuit summa dictorum Alberici: multis iniuriis Rogerium episcopum affecisse regem Stephanum: rarissime ad curiam venisse, quin homines sui, de eius potentia presumentes, seditiones movissent.^{h} Qui cum sepe^i alias, tum nuper apud Oxenefordum fecissent impetum in homines et in ipsum nepotem comitis Alani; in homines etiam Hervei de Liuns, qui esset tante nobilitatis, tanti supercilii, ut nunquam regi Henrico petenti animum indulserit in Angliam venire. In iniuriam ergo regis Stephani redundare, pro cuius amore venerit, quod ei^j tanta vis illata sit. Episcopum Lindocoliensem, ex veteri odio in Alanum, seditionis per^k homines suos auctorem fuisse. Episcopum Salesberiensem inimicis regis clam favere, dissimulata interim pro tempore versutia: id regem ex multis indubitanter comperisse; eoque potissimum, quod Rogerium de Mortemer, cum militibus regiis quos ducebat,^{l} in summo de Bristowiensibus metu, nec una nocte idem episcopus Malmesberie manere dimisisset. Omnibus esse in ore, quod, statim ut imperatrix venisset, ille ad eam cum nepotibus et castellis se^m conferret. Rogerius itaque captus sit non ut episcopus, set ut regis serviens, qui et

---

^{a}cum] sic cum ab. ^{b}proviso ab. ^{c}antistis Ce^1. ^{d}abierat ab.
^{e}quem manutenuit *om.* ab. ^{f}verba a. ^{g}stantes ab. ^{h}monuissent Ce^1.
^{i}sepe *om.* Ce^1. ^{j}ea Ce^{1}Ce^2. ^{k}super b. ^{l}ductitabat ab. ^{m}se *after* ille ab.

procurationes eius administraret et solidatas acciperet. Castella [Ce¹, fo. 115ᵛ] non per violentiam rex eripuerit, set
episcopi [Potter, p. 32] ambo gratanter reddiderint, ut calumpniam de tumultu quem in curia concitaverant evaderent. Aliquan-
tum pecuniarum[a] rex in castellis invenerit, que ipsius legitime
essent; quia eas[b] tempore regis Henrici, avunculi et anteces-
soris sui, ex fisci regii redditibus Rogerius episcopus[c] colle-
gisset. Eis tamen, sicut et castellis, idem presul pro timore
commissorum in regem libens cesserit; inde non deesse testes
regi. Ipsum proinde velle ut pacta inter se et episcopos rata
permanerent.

[474] Reclamatum est ab episcopo Rogerio contra sermones
Alberici, quod nunquam regis Stephani minister fuisset, nec
ipsius solidatas[d] accepisset: mine quinetiam ab animoso viro,
et qui malis erubesceret frangi, prolate,[e] si iustitiam de
rebus sibi ablatis in illo concilio non invenisset,[f] eam in
audientia maioris curie querendam.[g] Leniter legatus, ut cetera:
omnia que dicuntur contra episcopos prius in concilio ecclesiastico et accusari et an vera essent decuisset inquiri, quam in
indempnes contra canonum decreta sententiam proferri. Rex
itaque faciat, quod etiam in forensibus iudiciis legitimum est
fieri, ut revestiat episcopos de rebus suis: alioquin iure
gentium dissaisiti[h] non placitabunt.

[475] Dictis in hunc modum utrobique multis, causa petitu regis
in posterum diem dilata,[i] nec minus in crastino[j] ad adventum
archiepiscopi Rothomagensis posttridie prolongata. Is ubi venit,
omnium suspensis [Potter, p. 33] animis quidnam afferret, dixit
se concedere ut episcopi castella[k] haberent si se iure habere
debere per canones probare possent; quod quia non possent,
extreme improbitatis esse contra canones niti velle. 'Et esto,'
inquit, 'iustum sit ut habeant: certe, quia suspectum est
tempus, secundum morem aliarum gentium, optimates omnes claves

---

[d] [a]aliquantulum pecunie a.   [b]a *qdds* in.   [c]episcopus Rogerius ab.
[d]soliditates a.   [e]prolati a.   [f]inveniret ab.   [g]querenda Ce¹.
[h]dissaisati ab.   [i]prolata a.   [j]crastinum Ce¹Ce².   [k]castella episcopi b.

munitionum suarum debent voluntati regis contradere, qui pro
omnium pace debet militare. Ita omnis controversia episcoporum
infirmabitur:[a] aut enim secundum canonum scita iniustum est ut
habeant castella; aut, si hoc ex[b] indulgentia principali tolera-
tur, ut tradant claves necessitati temporis debent cedere.'

[476] His predictus subiecit[c] causidicus Albericus: significa-
tum esse regi quod murmurarent[d] inter se pontifices, pararentque
aliquos ex suis contra eum Romam mittere. 'Et hoc,' ait, 'lau-
dat vobis rex, ne quisquam vestrum presumat facere; quia, si
quis contra voluntatem suam et regni dignitatem ab Anglia
quoquam iret,[e] difficilis ei fortassis reditus foret. Ipse
quinetiam quia se gravari videt, ultro ad Romam appellat uos.'[f]

[477] Hec postquam rex partim quasi laudando, partim minando
mandasset, intellectum est quo tenderet. Quapropter ita
discessum est, ut nec ipse censuram canonum pati vellet, nec
episcopi in[g] eum [Potter, p. 34] exerere[h] consultum ducerent:
duplici ex causa, seu quia principem excommunicare sine apostolica conscientia temerarium esset; seu quoniam audirent, quidam
etiam viderent, gladios circa se nudari. Non enim iam ludicra
erant verba, set de vita et sanguine pene certabatur.[1] Non
omiserunt tamen legatus et archiepiscopus quin tenorem officii
sui prosequerentur: suppliciter enim pedibus regis in cubiculo
affusi, oraverunt ut misereretur ecclesie, misereretur anime et
fame sue, nec pateretur fieri discidium inter regnum et sacer-
dotium. Ille dignanter assurgens, quamvis a se facti eorum
amoliretur invidiam, malorum tamen preventus consiliis, nullam
bonarum[i] promissionum exhibuit efficaciam.

---

[a]infirmabatur ab.   [b]pro ab.   [c]predictus subiecit Çe[1]; addidit predictus ab.   [d]minitarent a; minarentur b.   [e]ierit a.   [f]vos *after* ultro ab.
[g]om. ab.   [h]exercere b.   [i]bonorum a.

---

[1]Cf. Virgil, *Aeneid,* xii.764-5.

142

7-10 APRIL 1141. LEGATINE COUNCIL OF WINCHESTER

The only contemporary account of any importance is that
of an eye-witness, William of Malmesbury, given below.[1]

On 2 February 1141 Stephen was captured at the battle of Lincoln, and the bishop of Winchester, as papal legate, attempted
to lead the English Church to support the coronation of the
empress. He proceeded to summon 'a legatine council of the
English Church, which in the best Hildebrandine manner would
proclaim that Stephen had been cast down by the judgement of
God, elect Matilda as Lady, and proceed to London to consecrate
her as queen in Westminster Abbey'.[2] According to the *Historia
Novella* all the bishops came, and the legate consulted bishops,
abbots, and archdeacons separately. William of Malmesbury
favoured the empress, but had no special brief for the bishop
of Winchester, and although the council decreed in her favour,
he emphasizes the bishop's failure. The representatives of the
citizens of London, who claimed a special role in king- or
queen-making,[3] demanded the king's release, and a strong plea
was made on behalf of Stephen's queen to the same effect. Thus
the council failed to establish the empress's position; and
her subsequent visit to London and Westminster, after a brief
initial success, proved a fiasco. She and the legate were compelled to flee before the coronation could be accomplished. In
the confused fighting in and around Winchester which followed,
the empress's half-brother and chief supporter, Robert earl of

---

[1]There is a brief mention in the annals of Plympton (*UGQ*, p. 28), 'post
peractum Pascha', of a council at Winchester at which both Archbishop
Theobald and Henry, bishop of Winchester and legate, were present, 'communi
assensu et fidei sacramento confirmantes imperatrici regni successionem'.
Ralph Niger, *Chronica*, ed. R. Anstruther (Caxton Soc. 1851), p. 185, briefly
summarizes William of Malmesbury's narrative. For the date, see below:
Monday—Thursday after the octave of Easter, 1141.

[2]R.H.C. Davis, *King Stephen* (London, 1967), p. 57; for the background,
see ibid., pp. 52 ff.; for the council, pp. 57-8; for what follows, pp. 58-
65.

[3]For London's role, ibid.; for the history of the claim, M. McKisack in
Studies in Medieval History presented to F.M. Powicke (Oxford, 1948), pp.
76-89; cf. C. Brooke and G. Keir, *London 800-1216* (London, 1975), pp. 36-9.
On the issues between Stephen and Matilda, see above pp. 780-1; *GF*, chap. 7.

Gloucester, was captured; eventually, early in November, the
earl and the king were exchanged. At another legatine council
at Westminster on 7 December, the English Church returned to
its allegiance to Stephen and the legate attempted to undo, and
excuse, his previous démarches (below, pp. 792-4).[1]

William of Malmesbury, Historia Novella s.a. 1141

> Ed. Potter, pp. 52-6; ed. Stubbs, ii.574-7; also printed
> W. i.420-1; Sp. ii.45-6. For mss. see p. 782 (Ce^2 has a
> long hiatus after the second sentence.)

[492] [Ce^1, fo. 119] Quomodo solempni concilio imperatricem in
dominam Anglie confirmaverint.

Feria secunda post octavas Pasche, concilium archiepiscopi
Cantuarie Thedbaldi et omnium episcoporum Anglie multorumque
abbatum, legato presidente, Wintonie ingenti apparatu inceptum.
Si qui defuerunt legatis et litteris causas cur non venissent
dederunt. Cuius concilii actioni quia interfui, integram rerum
veritatem posteris non negabo; egregie quippe memini. Ipsa die,
post recitata scripta excusatoria quibus absentiam suam quidam
tutati sunt, sevocavit in partem legatus episcopos, habuitque
cum eis archanum consilii sui; post^a mox abbates, postremo
archidiaconi convocati. Ex concilio nichil processit in publicum; volutabatur tamen per omnium mentes et ora quid foret
agendum.

[493] Quomodo legatus debitam et legitimam successionem imperatricis in regnum commendaverit.

Feria tercia hoc fere sensu legati cucurrit oratio: digna-
tione pape se vices eius in Anglia tenere; ideoque per eius
auctoritatem clerum Anglie ad hoc concilium congregatum, ut de
pace patrie, que grandi periculo naufragabatur, consuleretur in
medium. Tempore regis Henrici^b avunculi sui singulare domicilium

---

^{a}*om.* ab. ^{b}H. Ce^1; Henrici *ceteri.*

---

[1]Davis, *King Stephen,* esp. pp. 65-6.

pacis in Anglia fuisse; ita ut per vivacitatem, animositatem,
industriam eiusdem precellentissimi viri non solum indigene,
cuiuscumque potentie vel dignitatis essent nichil turbare
auderent, set etiam eius exemplo finitimi quicumque reges et
principes in otium et[a] ipsi concederent, et subiectos vel
[Potter, p. 53] invitarent vel compellerent.[b] Qui videlicet
rex, nonnullis ante obitum annis, filie sue quondam imperatrici,
que sola sibi proles ex desponsata quondam coniuge supererat,
omne regnum Anglie, simul et ducatum Normannie, iurari ab omnibus episcopis simulque baronibus fecerit, si successore masculo
ex illa, quam ex Lotharingia duxerat, uxore careret. 'Et invi-
dit,' inquit,[a] 'atrox fortuna precellentissimo avunculo meo, ut
sine masculo herede in Normannia decederet. Itaque quia longum
videbatur dominam expectare, que moras ad veniendum in Angliam
nectebat, in Normannia quippe residebat, provisum est paci
patrie, et regnare permissus frater meus. Enimvero, quamvis ego
vadem me apposuerim inter eum et Deum[c] quod sanctam ecclesiam
honoraret et exaltaret, et bonas leges manuteneret, malas vero
abrogaret; piget meminisse, pudet narrare, qualem se [Ce[1], fo.
119[v]] in regno exhibuerit: quomodo in presumptores nulla
iustitia exercita,[d] quomodo pax omnis statim ipso pene anno
abolita; episcopi capti, et ad redditionem possessionum suarum
coacti; abbatie vendite, ecclesie thesauris depilate; consilia
pravorum audita, bonorum vel suspensa vel omnino contempta.
Scitis quotiens eum tum per me tum per episcopos convenerim,
concilio presertim anno predicto[e] ad hoc indicto, et nichil
nisi odium adquisierim. Nec illud quemquam, qui recte[f] pensare
velit, latet, debere me[g] fratrem meum mortalem diligere, set
causam[h] patris immortalis multo pluris facere. Itaque quia Deus
iudicium suum de fratre meo exercuit, ut eum, me nesciente, in
potestatem potentium [Potter, p. 54] incidere permitteret; ne
regnum vacillet, si regnante careat, omnes vos pro iure legationis mee huc convenire invitavi. Ventilata est hesterno die
causa secreto coram maiori parte cleri Anglie, ad cuius ius[i]

---

[a] *om.* b.   [b] impellerent ab.   [c] Deum et eum b.   [d] exercitata ab.
[e] preterito ab.   [f] rectum Ce[1].   [g] *om.* A.   [h] causa a.   [i] Ce[1] *om.* ius; *add.*
in margin examen.

potissimum spectat principem eligere, simulque ordinare. Invocata itaque primo, ut par est, in auxilium divinitate, filiam
pacifici regis, gloriosi regis, divitis regis, boni regis, et
nostro tempore incomparabilis, in Anglie Normannieque dominam
eligimus, et ei fidem et manutenementum promittimus.'

[494] Quomodo Londonienses in concilio.

Cumque omnes presentes vel modeste acclamassent sententie, vel
silentes non contradixissent, subiecit legatus:[a] 'Londonienses,
qui sunt quasi optimates pro magnitudine civitatis in Anglia,
nunciis nostris convenimus, et conductum ut tuto veniant misi-
mus. Eos quia confido non ultra hunc diem moraturos, bona
venia usque cras sustineamus.'

[495] Feria quarta venerunt Londonienses, et, in concilium
introducti, causam suam eatenus egerunt ut dicerent, missos se
a communione quam vocant Londoniarum, non certamina set preces
offerre,[b] ut dominus suus rex de captione liberaretur. Hoc
omnes barones, qui in eorum communionem iamdudum recepti fuerant,
summopere flagitare a domino legato et ab archiepiscopo, simulque
ab[c] omni clero qui presens erat. Responsum est eis a legato
ubertim et splendide; et, quo minus fieret quod rogabant, eadem
oratio que pridie habita. [Potter, p. 55] Adiectum quinetiam,[d]
non decere ut Londonienses, qui precipui habebantur in Anglia
sicut proceres, illorum partes foverent[e] qui dominum suum in
bello reliquerant, quorum consilio idem sanctam ecclesiam
exhonoraverat, qui postremo non ob aliud ipsis Londoniensibus
favere videbantur nisi ut eos pecuniis emungerent.

[496] De clerico regine.

Interea surrexit quidam, cuius nomen, si bene memini, Christianus, regine ut audivi clericus, porrexitque cartam legato; qua
ille sub silentio lecta, voce quantum potuit exaltata dixit non
esse legitimam, nec que[f] deberet in tanto, presertimque sul-
limium et religiosarum personarum, conventu recitari. Preter

---

[a] *om.* ab.   [b] afferre ab.   [c] *om.* ab.   [d] etiam a.   [e] faverent b.
[f] nec que ab; neque Ce[1].

cetera enim que reprehensibilia et notabilia erant scripta,
testem appositum qui preterito anno, in eodem quo tunc sede-
bant capitulo,[1] venerabiles episcopos maxima verborum affecerit[a]
contumelia. Ita illo tricante, clericus legationi sue non
defuit, set preclara fiducia litteras legit in audientia, quarum
hec erat summa: rogabat regina obnixe omnem clerum congregatum,
et nuncupatim[b] episcopum Wintonie fratrem domini sui, ut eundem
dominum regno restituerent,[c] quem iniqui viri, qui etiam homines
sui essent, in vincula coniecissent. Huic suggestioni retulit
legatus verba in eandem sententiam qua et Londoniensibus. Illi,
communicato consilio, dixerunt se decretum concilii convicaneis
suis relaturos, et favorem suum quantum possent prestituros.
Feria quinta solutum est concilium, excommunicatis ante multis
qui regiarum erant partium; nominatim Willelmo Martello, qui
quondam pincerna [Potter, p. 56] regis [Ce[1], fo. 120] Henrici,
tunc dapifer Stephani. Iste immaniter exulceraverat legati
animum, multis rebus eius interceptis et surreptis.

143

7 DECEMBER 1141. LEGATINE COUNCIL OF WESTMINSTER

For the circumstances and literature, see above, pp. 788-9.

William of Malmesbury, Historia Novella s.a. 1141

Ed. Potter, pp. 62-4, ed. Stubbs, ii.583-5; also printed
W. i.421; Sp. ii.46-7.

[501] De concilio quo legatus temptavit lenire causam recep-
           tionis imperatricis in dominam.
Interea legatus, immodici animi pontifex, qui quod semel

---

[a] effecerit a.   [b] nuncupatum b.   [c] restitueret Ce[1].

---

[1] This presumably means that the council was held in the chapter-house
of the cathedral priory; and may refer back to another council there in
1140 - but more probably the reference is to the Council of Winchester of
Aug.-Sept. 1139. But 'capitulum' may be used in the sense of 'meeting' of
bishops.

proposuisset non ineffectum relinquere vellet, concilium pro
iure legationis sue apud Westmonasterium die octavarum sancti
Andree coegit. Eius concilii actionem non ita exacta fide pro-
nuntio ut superioris, quia non interfui. Auditum est lectas in
eo litteras domini apostolici, quibus modeste legatum argueret
quod liberare fratrem suum dissimulasset; delicti tamen superioris gratiam facere; et magnopere cohortari, ut quocumque modo,
vel ecclesiastico vel seculari, posset, ad germani liberationem
accingeretur. Regem ipsum in concilium introisse, et apud sanctum conventum querimoniam deposuisse, quod homines sui et eum
ceperint, et afflictione contumeliarum paulo minus extinxerint,
qui iusticiam eis nunquam negasset. Ipsum legatum magnis elo-
quentie viribus factorum suorum invidiam temptasse alleviare:
quod scilicet imperatricem non voluntate sed necessitate
[Potter, p. 63] recepisset, quippe cum recenti adhuc fratris
sui clade, omnibus comitibus vel fugatis, vel eventum rei
suspecta mente prestolantibus, ipsa cum suis muros Wintonie
circumsonasset; ipsam quecumque pepigerat ad ecclesiarum ius
pertinentia obstinate fregisse. Quin etiam certis auctoribus ad
se delatum eam et suos non solum dignitati sue, sed et vite,
struxisse insidias: ceterum, Deum pro sua clementia secus quam
ipsa sperasset vertisse negotia, ut et ipse perniciem vitaret,
et fratrem suum vinculis eximeret. Itaque iubere se de parte
Dei et apostolici, ut regem, voluntate populi et assensu sedis
apostolice inunctum, quantis possent viribus enixe iuvarent;
turbatores vero[a] pacis, qui comitisse Andegavensi faverent ad
excommunicationem vocandos, preter eam que Andegavorum domina
esset.

[Ce[1], fo. 121[v]] [502] Quomodo quidam fautor imperatricis locu-
                 tus fuerit pro imperatrice.
Hec eius verba non dico quod omnes[b] gratis animis exceperint,
certe nullus expugnavit; omnes clerici[c] vel metu vel reverentia
frenarunt ora. Unus fuit laicus, imperatricis nuncius, qui palam
legato interdixit, ne per fidem quam ei pactus fuerat quicquam

---

[a] *om.* a.   [b] ab *add* clerici.   [c] *om.* ab.

in illo concilio statueret quod eius honori adversum foret:
fidem ab eo[a] imperatrici factam,[b] ne fratrem suum ullo auxilio
iuvaret,[c] nisi forte viginti[d] milites nec plures mitteret. Quod
in Angliam ipsa venisset, frequentibus epistolis eius factum:
quod regem cepisset, quod in captione[e] [Potter, p. 64] tenuis-
set, ipso potissimum conivente actum. Dixit[f] hec et alia
pleraque magna verborum austeritate, nichil omnino legato
blanditus: nec vero ullo sermonum pondere ille moveri potuit ut
iram proderet, semel incepti, ut prius dixi, sui non segnis
insecutor.[g] Fuit ergo[h] hic annus, cuius tragedias compendio
digessi, fatalis et pene perniciosus Anglie; in quo cum aliquo
modo sibi ad libertatem respirandum putasset, rursus in erump-
nam recidit, et, nisi Dei misericordia mature occurrat, diu
herebit.

144

c.14 MARCH 1143 (?). LEGATINE COUNCIL OF LONDON

The chroniclers of the period offer two alternative occasions
for the group of canons printed below. John of Hexham ascribes
two canons to the council of 1139 in which Henry of Blois disputed with the king on the affair of Roger of Salisbury and
his episcopal nephews: the canons are those which our council
has in common with 1138, and his account has verbal links with
both versions.[1] Henry of Huntingdon and some satellites ascribe

---

[a]ab *add* hanc.   [b]factam imperatrici a.   [c]adiuvaret b.   [d]ei xx a;
xx ei b.   [e]captionem a.   [f]ab *add* nuntius.   [g]executor ab.   [h]b *om.*
ergo.

---

[1]Printed in Symeon (we quote the text as in Cambridge, Corpus Christi
Coll. ms. 139, fo. 141), ii.301: '... ecclesiastica severitas potenter ul-
ciscitur in eos *qui* vel in lesionem *clericorum manus nepharie iniciunt,* vel
res ęcclesię diripiunt, sive excommunicationi subiacent vel in ea obeunt
...' (words in italics are in C. of Westminster (1138), cc. 10-11; 'qui ...
clericorum manus iniciunt ... res ecclesie diripiunt', are in C. of London
(1143), cc. 1-2). It is not, of course, impossible that the canons in question were also promulgated in 1139. John of Hexham elsewhere (p. 313) mentions a council at London in mid-Lent at which William dean of York (soon
to be bishop of Durham) was present.

the same two canons to London and the mid Lent of 1143.[1] Two
later chroniclers have confused the issue: William of Newburgh
by introducing verbal links with 1138 into the narrative, Roger
of Wendover by inserting into Henry of Huntingdon's account a
rustic privilege vouched for by no earlier document.[2] All three
texts are printed below.

In Oxford, St. John's Coll. ms. 125, the canons occur in a
group of three councils: first London 1138; next these canons,
headed 'aliud concilium apud Lond(oniam)'; and thirdly, Westminster 1125. These canons were printed by Wilkins from this
ms. under the year 1138. They are also to be found, without
heading, in four other English mss.; and in a completely different order in two French mss. of Anglo-Norman provenance, the
thirteenth-century decretal collections *Sangermanensis* and
Abrincensis, under the title 'Concilium Remense celebratum sub
Eugenio papa'.[3] In this disguise they were at one time accepted

---

[1]Huntingdon, p. 276, from which Torigny (pp. 145-6), Hoveden (i.206),
Newburgh (ed. R. Howlett, *Chrons. Stephen, etc.* i.43 - quoted below) and
Roger of Wendover (ed. H.O. Coxe, ii, London, 1841, pp. 232-3 - also quoted
below; cf. Paris, *Chron. Maj.* ii.175) derive their accounts, although Newburgh and Wendover have other information to add to Henry of Huntingdon. To
this list could probably be added the annals of Waverley (*Ann. Mon.* ii.229),
which adds to a short mention seemingly based on Torigny a reference to those
who 'res ecclesiasticas et cemiteria fregebant', which is reminiscent of the
phrase 'qui ecclesiam cimiteriumque violaverit' in Wendover, but not derived
from Huntingdon or Torigny (nor, verbally, from the canons of the council;
but cf. c. 1). For a possible reference in the *Liber Eliensis*, see p. 806.
   There is also a brief account, apparently of the same council, in Gervase (ed. Stubbs, i.122) sub *anno* 1142: 'coacto apud Londonias concilio,
presidente Henrico Wintoniensi episcopo et apostolice sedis legato cum
venerabili Theobaldo Cantuariensi archiepiscopo, considentibus episcopis
Anglie et abbatibus plurimis, in talium actores, preceptores, executores,
sed et in castellorum fundatores, monachorum vel clericorum spoliatores
ceterosque malefactores sententia excommunicationis publice ac solempniter
prolata est ...'.
   To this council too may perhaps be attributed the reference in the
preface to Alfred of Beverley's annals: 'In diebus silencii nostri, quando
non poteramus reddere Deo que Dei erant ... quod propter praesentem excommunicatorum multitudinem secundum Londoniensis concilii decretum a divinis
cessabamus, ... expulsis ad regis edictum de sedibus suis ecclesiae nostrae
columpnis, diu graviterque vexatus sum ...'(*Aluredi Beverlacensis annales,*
ed. T. Hearne, Oxford, 1716, pp. 1-2; cf. A. Gransden, *Historical Writing
in England* c.*550 to* c.*1307*, London, 1974, p. 212).
   [2]On this see J.S.P. Tatlock, *The Legendary History of Britain* (Berkeley
and Los Angeles, 1950), p. 282 and n. Compare C. of Rouen (1096), c. 2 in
OV v. 20-1.
   [3]For these collections, see C.N.L. Brooke, in *Traditio*, xiii (1957),
471-3. The title in *Abrincensis* runs 'Remense concilium'.

as genuine canons of the council of Rheims of 1148; and in
these mss. they are indeed placed end to end with the genuine
canons of Rheims (they form cc. 1-14 in Sang., and the genuine
canons cc. 15-32), but the break between the two is clearly
perceptible, and there is no doubt that they are identical with
the canons in St. John's 125.

The English provenance of all the mss. indicates that the
canons came from an English council; the age of the mss. precludes a date much after the middle of the twelfth century;
and the form and subject matter of the canons suggests the circumstances of the anarchy of Stephen's reign - in particular the
emphasis on physical violence and the details for the administration of anathemas. Two of the canons repeat the prescriptions
of the 1138 council; and the form of two canons and the words
of another establish a link with that of 1151.[1] They can be
dated *c*.1138-53 with considerable confidence (and see p. 800
n. 2).

It cannot be decided with any certainty whether these canons
belong to August-September 1139, to March 1143, or to another
council unrecorded. The most rational conclusion is to associate
them with the contemporary notice in Henry of Huntingdon - both
ms. J and Henry ascribe their councils to London[2] - and thus
place this stern effort to curb the anarchy by *force majeure* to
the last year of Henry of Blois's legateship and to a period
considerably later than the tentative anathemas of 1138.[3] And
this has been the conclusion adopted by a succession of scholars,
led by Heinrich Böhmer.[4]

There is a clear reference to c. 1 in a charter of Henry of
Blois as bishop and legate (i.e. 1139-43), printed in Voss,
p. 148: 'Audistis ... quoniam in concilio Sathane tradiderimus

---

[1]Cf. cc. 11-12 and the notes to C. of London (1151). The council here
attributed to 1143 is quoted in 1151 in such a way as to suggest that they
are related more closely to one another than either to C. of Westminster
(1138).
[2]John of Hexham ascribes his council to Winchester - correctly, for the
date given.
[3]Cf. above, p. 769.
[4]*Kirche und Staat*, p. 346, n. 5; Tillmann, p. 44, n. 171; Voss, pp. 34-
6, 47, who suggests the possibility that there was another council in June;
Barlow (1979), p. 131.

eos omnes qui possessiones ecclesiasticas et eorum bona diri-
piendo invadunt'; on this ground he calls on the justiciar and
citizens of London to restore to the canons of St. Martin-le-
Grand property near Cripplegate which had been taken from them.

It was in this council that William Cumin, chancellor of
the Scottish king, who had attempted to force himself on the
bishopric of Durham, was excommunicated and deprived of all his
benefices, including the archdeaconry of Worcester.[1] It is
likely that the story of his intrusion was somewhat embroidered,
since in later years he was pardoned, received patronage from
Archbishop Theobald and King Henry II, and was restored to his
archdeaconry. It is possible that the legatine council mentioned in one of Theobald's charters referred to this occasion:
he bears witness to the settlement of a case between Bermondsey
priory and the collegiate church of St. Martin-le-Grand, London.[2]

Thus the manuscripts fall into two classes:

1. A. Aberdeen, UL ms. 161, fos. 94-8, a theological and legal
      miscellany, 12th cent.

   C. Cambridge, Corpus Christi Coll. ms. 130, fo. 123^{r-v}, Lan-
      franc's Collection, 12th cent.

   B. Oxford, Balliol Coll. ms. 218, fos. 69^v-70^v, Julian of
      Toledo, Prognosticon, 12th cent.[3]

   Jo. Oxford, St. John's Coll. ms. 96, fo. 149^{r-v}, *Vitae sanc-
      torum,* from Pershore abbey, 12th cent.

   J. Oxford, St. John's Coll. ms. 125, fos. 88-9, see pp. 735, 771.

All these mss. are of the mid or late twelfth century, and
in quality there is little to choose between them: certainly
none is a copy of any other. We have followed the consensus of
mss. where the reading is doubtful, and J where this criterion

---

[1] See *GFL*, nos. 33-4 and pp. 539-40; Le Neve, ii.30, 105; John of Hexham
in Symeon, ii.309, 312-14; *PUE* ii, nos. 29-31; Lawrence of Durham, *Dialogi*
(ed. J. Raine, Surtees Soc. lxx, 1880), pp. 7-8.

[2] Saltman, *Theobald,* no. 169, pp. 391-2 (cf. Voss, p. 148). Saltman referred this to Imar's council in 1145, but it seems more likely that it
occurred in one of Henry of Blois's councils, and that Theobald bore witness
since Henry was an interested party, as dean of St. Martin-le-Grand.

[3] The text of B is incomplete: it ends with c. 14 at the foot of fo. 70^v,
at the end of a quire. On the ms., see R.A.B. Mynors, *Catalogue of the mss.
of Balliol College, Oxford* (Oxford, 1963), p. 215.

seems inadequate; the spelling is normally also that of J. The
minor variants of B, which are legion, have been ignored.

2. Sang. Paris, BN ms. lat. 12459: *olim* Saint-Germain-des-Prés,
   Lat. 381, the decretal collection known as the *Collectio
   Sangermanensis*.
   Abr. Avranches, Bibl. de ville, ms. 149, *olim* Mont-Saint-
   Michel, 249, the similar decretal collection known as the
   Collectio Abrincensis I.

These mss. are both of the early 13th century, and have been
fully described and analysed by H. Singer, 'Neue Beiträge über
die Dekretalensammlungen vor und nach Bernhard von Pavia',
Sitzungsberichte der Kais. Akademie der Wiss. in Wien, Phil.-
Hist. Klasse, clxxi (1913), 68-404 (the relevant passages are
pp. 125 ff., 356 ff.). Their readings are of less authority
than the mss. of class 1, but select readings are noted, and
where the two agree, they are given the siglum α.

   Printed texts. W. i.417-18 (from J: see above), 421-2
   (from Hoveden and Matt. Paris); Sp. i.47 (from Hoveden);
   Mansi, xxi.515-18, 603-4 (from W.).

I. *Henry of Huntingdon, Historia Anglorum s.a. 1143*

   From Huntingdon, ed. Arnold (RS), p. 276, collated with
   BL Arundel ms. 48, fo. 171*a*; Royal 13. B. vi, fo. 151;
   Cambridge Univ. Lib. Gg. 2.21, fo. 90^v (no significant
   variants).

Octavo anno rex Stephanus interfuit concilio Lundonie in media
Quadragesima. Quod, quia nullus honor vel clericis vel ecclesie
Dei a raptoribus deferebatur, et eque capiebantur et redimebantur clerici ut laici, tenuit Wintoniensis episcopus, urbis
Romane legatus, concilium apud Londoniam clericis pro tempore
necessarium. In quo sanccitum est ne aliquis qui clerico violenter manus ingesserit ab alio possit absolvi quam ab ipso
papa et in presentia ipsius; unde clericis aliquantulum sereni-
tatis vix illuxit.

II. *William of Newburgh, Historia rerum Anglicarum*

> From BL mss. Stowe 62, fo. 12^V;^{a} Cotton Vesp. B. vi, fo.
> 118; Newburgh, ed. Howlett (RS), i.43.^{1}

[Rex] *concilio* quod sequenti *anno Lundoniis* ab Henrico *Wintoniensi episcopo*, apostolice sedis *legato*, pro quiete et prero-
gativa ordinis *cleric*alis celebratum est, benigne *interfuit*,
et favoris regii suffragium non negavit. Nam quia tunc in Anglia
malis increscentibus parum sacris deferebatur ordinibus,
eratque fere in omnibus sicut populus sic sacerdos,^{2} *in* eodem
concilio statutum *est* ut quicumque in *cleric*um vel in monachum
violenter manus^b iniceret, excommunicatus sollempniter denun-
tiaretur et ad Romanum pontificem *absolv*endus mitteretur.

III. *Roger of Wendover, Chronica s.a. 1142 (sic)*

> From Bodl. ms. Douce 207 (21781), fo. 114^V; BL Cotton
> ms. Otho B. v, fo. 2^V (defective owing to the fire of
> 1731). Ed. H.O. Coxe, ii.232-3; Paris, *Ch. Maj.* ii.175.

Willelmus [*sic*] *Wintoniensis episcopus* et sedis apostolice
legatus in media Quadragesima *apud Londonias concilium, rege*
presente et episcopis, celebravit. *Nullus* enim *honor vel* reverentia *ferebatur Dei ecclesie vel* eius ordinatis a predonibus
sceleratis, sed *eque clerici et laici capiebantur, redimebantur*
et in vinculis tenebantur. *Sanccitum est* ergo ibi et generaliter
constitutum, *ne aliquis qui* ecclesiam cymiteriumque violaverit,
vel in *cleric*um aut virum religiosum *manus* iniecerit *violenta*s,
ab alio quam ipso papa possit absolvi. Statutum est etiam ut
aratra in campis cum ipsis agricolis talem pacem habeant in
agris qualem haberent si in cimiterio extitissent. Excommunicaverunt autem omnes qui contra hoc decretum venirent candelis

---

^{a}*The text is based on this ms.* ^{b}violenter manus BL *Stowe 62;* manus
violenter *Cotton Vesp. B. vi.*

---

^{1}The words in italics are those which Newburgh and Wendover have in common with Henry of Huntingdon.
^{2}Cf. Isa. 24, 2; Hosea 4, 9.

accensis, et sic miluorum rapacitas *aliquantulum* conquievit.

IV. *Canons probably to be ascribed to this council*

[1][a1] Sanctorum patrum vestigiis inherentes novis morbis nova remedia procuramus. Statuimus igitur ut si quis possessiones ecclesiasticas invaserit, diripuerit vel depopulatus fuerit uel quoquo modo[b] distraxerit, anathema sit.

[2][2] Si quis clerico vel aliis ęcclesiasticis personis manum iniecerit vel in carcerem vel in vincula miserit vel redemerit, anathema sit, nec solutionem mereatur nisi mortis articulo instante priusquam a domno papa solvatur. Locus vero in quo clericus vel[c] alia ecclesiastica persona tenta fuerit, vel vinculis mancipata, et omnia circumiacentia castella et rura, civitates etiam vicine quę capientis vel tenentis fuerint, a divino officio cessent et cum lugente lugeant.[3]

[3] Prohibemus etiam ne sacrum crisma vel oleum[d] contemptoribus vel excommunicatis tradatur.[4] Tradetur[e] autem cum hac observatione archidiaconis, ut et episcopi de ipsis securi sint,[f] et

---

[a]*The order in Sang. and Abr. is 1, 10, 14, 15, 2, 4, 5, 11, 12, 9, 8, 7, 13, 16, 3, 6, and 17. Heading in J*, Aliud concilium apud Lond'.   [b]quomodo Jo.   [c]BC *add* aliqua.   [d]crisma vel oleum ABJoα; oleum vel crisma JC.   [e]Tradatur BJo.   [f]C *adds* quod.

---

[1]The opening words are identical with C. of Westminster (1125), c. 1 (cf. 1138, c. 8, etc.). For the subject matter, cf. C. of Windsor (1070), c. 11, C. of Westminster (1138), c. 11.

[2]Cf. C. of Westminster (1138), c. 10, C. of Lateran II (1139), c. 15 (Alberigo, p. 200; Mansi, xxi.530: 'ut si quis ... in clericum vel monachum violentas manus iniecerit, anathematis vinculo subiaceat; et nullus episcoporum illum presumat absolvere, nisi mortis urgente periculo, donec apostolico conspectui presentetur ...'). It is probable that this canon was the source used by the council of London, but it so closely follows the canon of 1131 (cf. C. of Westminster (1138) above, p. 776 n. 4) that the relation to Lateran II cannot be used as firm evidence for the date of the present council. The 1139 canon was a very celebrated one: it is cited, for instance in *PUE* iii, nos. 313, 317. On Rheims 1131 and II Lateran, see R. Somerville in *Bulletin of Med. Canon Law*, v (1975), 122-30.

[3]Cf. Ecclus. 7, 38; Rom. 12, 15.

[4]For chrism see Brett, *English Church*, pp. 164-6; D.C. Douglas in *Domesday Monachorum of Christ Church, Canterbury* (London, 1944), pp. 4-6, 77-9.

archidiaconi de presbiteris, quod ipsi prelatorum mandatis et
ęcclesiasticis preceptis per omnia sint parituri.[a]

[4][1] Clerici qui excommunicatorum consiliis et negociis commu-
nicant vel in domibus et[b] familia eorum versantur, quamlibet
nobiles fuerint, tam ordinis sui quam beneficiorum ęcclesiasti-
corum periculo[c] subiaceant, nisi a summo pontifice[d] veniam
mereantur.

[5] Prohibemus nichilominus ne divinum officium celebretur,
sed nec campana pulsetur in urbe vel in castro vel in rure, ubi
aliquis excommunicatorum presens fuerit.

[6] Statuimus etiam ut excommunicatorum corpora insepulta
maneant; qui vero ea infra cimiterium vel in lapide vel in
ligno extra in aqua vel in domibus clericorum posuerit, a
sacerdote eiusdem loci excommunicetur; nec nisi ab episcopo[e]
eiusdem [J, fo. 88ᵛ] provincie solvatur, unius anni penitentia
corrigendus.

[7] Si quis[f] episcoporum vel sacerdotum aliquem vinculo anathematis innodaverit[g] et ille metu mortis vel imminentis periculi
vel animo fraudandi satisfactionem infra certum terminum promiserit, et ob hoc solutionem meruerit, nisi infra promissum[h]
terminum solvat quod promisit, morte preventus maneat insepul-
tus si vero sine termino hoc ipsum promiserit et infra tres
menses non solverit, simili pena teneatur.

[8][2] Decernimus ut sacerdotes qui divina officia celebrare in-
[h]ibiti nichilominus celebraverunt[i] et ob hoc anathemate vincti
sunt, degradentur et bonis ecclesiasticis priventur, nisi a[j]

---

[a]parituri sint BAbr.   [b]vel in Bα.   [c]pericula Jo.   [d]pontifici A.
[e]C *adds* illius.   [f]C *adds* vero.   [g]enodaverit JC.   [h]*om.* J; intra terminum promisum α.   [i]celebraverint C.   [j]C *adds* summo.

[1]Cf. C. of Westminster (1125), c. 11 and n.; C. of Lateran II (1139),
c. 3 (Mansi, xxi.526-7); Alberigo, p. 197.
[2]Cf. *Decretum*, c. 11 q. 3 cc. 5-6.

domno papa veniam consequantur. Qui vero eandem sententiam nondum passi sunt, nisi infra xl dies resipuerint, eadem pena
plectantur.

[9] Prohibemus omnibus presbiteris ne capellariam potentum
suscipiant vel in curiis eorum administrent nisi per manum
episcopi eiusdem[a] diocesis; ad hoc ingrediantur sacramento
astricti quod episcopalibus mandatis atque preceptis[b] per omnia
obedient et excommunicatos ad divina officia non admittent.[c]
Qui vero contra fecerint ab ordine pariter et beneficiis ęcclesiasticis[d] cadant.

[10] Clerici qui ab alienis ecclesiis dominorum vel parentum
suorum violentia[e] vel aliquo modo sine auctoritate episcopi
eiusdem loci reditus perceperint, pariter ipsi[f] et fautores sui
tamdiu anathemati subiaceant, donec ecclesias et omnia quę inde
perceperint, in integrum spoliatis restituant. Sacerdotes vero
qui interim per ipsos in eisdem ęcclesiis administraverint,
memorata pena feriantur et insuper degradentur.

[11][1] Qui sciens communicaverit excommunicato tanquam ex nomine
excommunicatus habeatur. Si vero rex communicaverit, in quemcumque locum venerit, presente excommunicato, nec divinum officium celebretur nec campana pulsetur. Quod si capellani curie
vel sacerdotes[g] loci celebrare presumpserint, ilico ab episcopo
eiusdem[h] loci excommunicentur et ab ordine cadentes ęcclesiasticis beneficiis careant.

[12] Qui[i] ob rapinam vel invasionem rerum [J, fo. 89] ęcclesiasticarum anathematis gladio percussus ad satisfactionem venerit,
nec dampnum resarcire poterit, antequam absolvi mereatur,

---

[a]ipsius Jo.   [b]*om.* J.   [c]admittant Jo.   [d]ab ordine ... ecclesiasticis CJ; pariter ab ordine et beneficiis ecclesiasticis AJo; pariter ordine
et ecclesiasticis beneficiis α; ab ordine et ęcclesiasticis bonis B.
[e]uiolentia ABα; *om.* CJoJ.   [f]episcopi (*sic*) Jo.   [g]C *adds* eiusdem.
[h]ipsius Jo.   [i]Bα *add* uero.

---

[1]Cf. C. of Westminster (1125), c. 11.

sacramento astringatur, se annuatim sicut tunc ei iniunctum
fuerit soluturum donec totum persolverit.

[13] Precipimus ut quotiens aliquis episcoporum alii confratri
et coepiscopo denuntiaverit se canonicam iusticiam in possessionem vel in[a] personam alicuius exercuisse, postulans ut et
ille coepiscopus eandem iusticiam denunciet aut faciat; ilico
sine dilatione obtemperet aut periculum ordinis incurrat.

[14] Prohibemus et modis omnibus interdicimus omnes exactiones
et indebitas castellorum operationes[1] fieri. Si quis de redemptione clericorum sciens aliquid perceperit vel obsides eorum
tenuerit vel ipsos, anathema sit.

[15][2] Prohibemus et modis omnibus interdicimus ne sacerdotes,
diaconi, subdiaconi exactores, vel prepositi laicorum existant.
Quod si existere presumpserint, anathematis gladio percellantur
et deinceps a beneficiis ęcclesiasticis cadant.

[16] Prohibemus omnibus modis[b] sacerdotibus capellanis ne divinum officium in munitionibus et[c] turribus celebrare presumant,
postquam in ęcclesia alia[d] eiusdem loci prohibitum fuerit; quod
si presumpserint, ab ordine pariter[e] et bonis ęcclesiasticis[f]
cadant.

[17] Precipimus ut ante proximum Pascha corpora nominatim excommunicatorum in cimiteriis sepulta inde exportentur; provide-
antque universi episcopi ut hoc sine fraude effectui mancipetur,
ne forte alia pro aliis exportentur. Deus unus est, in quo nisi
unum fuerint pastores ęcclesie nec poterunt[g] subditis iusticiam

---

[a]*om.* Jo.   [b]modis omnibus A.   [c]vel AJo.   [d]alia ecclesia AJo.
[e]pariter ab ordine Jo.   [f]ecclesiasticis bonis A; beneficiis Sang.; ecclesiasticis beneficiis Abr.   [g]poterint Jo.

---

[1]i.e., labour services due at the lord's castle, presumably in construction (cf. C. of London (1151), c. 1).
[2]Cf. C. of Westminster (1102), c. 9 (and C. of Westminster (1175), c. 10
and n.).

recte exhibere. Hinc est quod et nos episcopi adinvicem colligati sumus compromittentes quod iusticiam recte exhibebimus.
Sciat[a] itaque unusquisque quia quod quis dicit veritati debet,
et[b] quod promittit, fidei.

145

*c.*SEPTEMBER 1143. LEGATINE COUNCIL OF WINCHESTER; *c.*18-30
NOVEMBER 1143. LEGATINE COUNCIL OF LONDON

On these councils see Voss, pp. 47-8; Tillmann, p. 46.

The chronology of the last councils presided over by Henry of
Blois, bishop of Winchester, as papal legate, is far from clear.
The simplest solution is as follows. On 26 September 1143 the
legate consecrated his nephew, William FitzHerbert (St. William
of York) as archbishop of York, at Winchester after consider-
ing his credentials at a gathering which is very likely the same
council at which the issue was adumbrated of the rent of
50*s.* 7*d.* claimed by the archbishop of Canterbury from the abbot
of St. Augustine's, Canterbury - 'a mere bud on the forest tree
of the parent suit' of the abbey's exemption.[1] On the octave of
St. Martin, 18 November, at a council in London, the legate is
said to have summoned the bishops of Ely and Chester/Coventry
to Rome (below, p. 806); at the end of the month, about the
thirtieth (below, p. 809), also at a council in London, the
legate confirmed the decision of this suit made in the summer.
Thus we may have three councils, in September, and on 18 and
*c.*30 November; but in all probability the November meetings

---

[a]Sciant C.   [b]etiam C.

---

[1]On the York election and consecration, see D. Knowles, *Historian and
Character and other essays* (Cambridge, 1963), chap. 5; D. Baker in *Studi su
S. Bernardo di Chiaravalle* (Bibliotheca Cisterciensis, vi, Rome, 1975), pp.
115-80. On the St. Augustine's case, see esp. Saltman, *Theobald*, pp. 64-
75, esp. 67-8; D. Knowles in *Downside Review,* 1 (1932), 401-15; for its
later history E. John in *Bulletin of the John Rylands Library,* xxxix (1956-
7), 390-415 (the case is compared above with *Bleak House,* chap. i).

represent a single council. None of these dates is without difficulty, as will be seen if we look more closely at each in
turn.

1. The evidence for these councils mainly depends on the
chronicle of St. Augustine's abbey (see below), a late and
prejudiced source. It is best known in the form given to it by
William Thorne in the fourteenth century; a venerable tradition
ascribes the section running to 1220-1 to Thomas Sprot, and
there are good reasons for believing that the first part of the
chronicle originally concluded at this date. But there appears
to be no ms. older than the fourteenth century, and more analysis of the manuscript tradition is needed before the question
can be settled. The narrative of the suit is cast in the shape
of a statement by Henry of Blois himself, which also appears
separately in two fourteenth-century cartularies of the abbey;
and it incorporates within it an act of the bishop enshrining
the confirmation of *c*.30 November. In the narrative the bishop
is made to say that although he found no just base for the
archbishop's claim, none the less, acting with the bishop of
Hereford as papal judge-delegate, he compelled the monks to
pay. It looks as if the monks had at least tampered with the
instrument, or possibly taken advantage of the enmity between
Henry and Theobald in the later 1140s to obtain an *ex parte*
statement from the former. None the less, an authentic basis of
some kind seems certainly to lie behind the document as it now
exists. In particular, the list of bishops present at the first
meeting rings true. Durham and Carlisle are included - as could
only happen in legatine gatherings of both provinces - but not
York, who was evidently still to be consecrated; of the major
English bishops Ely alone is missing, which conforms with other
evidence to be considered below. Uhtred of Llandaff is given
the title 'Glamorgan', current in the early twelfth century,
forgotten later.[1] Furthermore, the decision recorded in the
documents seems itself to be authentic, and was confirmed in
papal bulls which have not been questioned.[2] In return for a

---

[1] Cf. Conway Davies, ii.613-25, esp. nos. L18, 20-4, 39, 57.
[2] *PUE* ii, no. 34 (17 Apr. 1144); JL 8581 (21 Apr. 1144).

prebend in St. Martin's, Dover, held by the monks, and two mills near Dover, the archbishop renounced his rent, and agreed to concede chrism, to dedicate their churches and to grant orders to the monks without further exaction.

The presence of the bishop of Durham in the list of bishops - he was consecrated on 20 June - and the confirmation in November have led to the dating of this council 20 June x November;[1] but it is extremely probable that it was the same occasion which saw the examination and consecration of the archbishop of York, and his absence from the list in any case makes a date later than September unlikely.

2. 18 November occurs only in the *Annals of Waverley:*[2] 'In oct(avis) sancti Martini sedit concilium apud Londoniam, ubi legatus summonuit episcopos Eliensem et Cestrensem Romam ire. Inde et ipse Romam ivit, mortuo iam papa Innocentio ....' The *Liber Eliensis* (p. 324, cf. p. 435) ascribes an appeal of Bishop Nigel to Rome in the presence of the legate to a council which has been identified as that of mid Lent 1143 (see p. 795). The other difficulty is that by 18 November the news of Pope Innocent II's death had reached England, and it would normally be presumed that Henry of Blois's legateship had lapsed. The precise state of law on this question in the 1140s is not entirely clear.[3] But it seems probable that the meeting or meetings of November were summoned to discuss what should be done in the

---

[1]*Handbook of British Chronology*, 2nd edn., ed. F.M. Powicke and E.B. Fryde (London, 1961), p. 549.

[2]*Ann. Mon.* ii.229, checked by BL ms. Cotton Vesp. A. xvi, fo. 83[V].

[3]In the late 12th cent. a local legate had to receive confirmation of his legation from a new pope (cf. Tillmann, pp. 34, 144); and we have no reason to doubt that this was already the assumption in the 1140s. But it could well be that he would use the title until he had been refused such confirmation. Celestine II lived too short a time, in all probability, to settle the matter; and John of Hexham specifically says that Henry failed to get confirmation from Lucius II (Symeon, ii.315-16). There is evidence that Archbishop Theobald was addressed as legate before confirmation by Pope Adrian IV, and later dropped the title for a time in 1159-60 (*GFL*, pp. 505-6). But an act of courtesy by a pope who knew he was going to confirm the legateship is quite understandable, and in 1159-60 the English church officially recognized no pope, so that the title could have been embarrassing. *De facto* Theobald was confirmed in his legateship by both Anastasius IV and Adrian IV, and probably also by Alexander III. On all this see pp. 820-1, and esp. C.R. Cheney, 'The deaths of Popes and the expiry of legations in twelfth-century England', *Revue de Droit Canonique*, xxviii (1978), 84-96.

aftermath of the pope's death, and the occasion may well have
been taken to sort out problems like that of the bishop of Ely
and cases like that of St. Augustine's. The legatine style in
the charter of c.30 November, if genuine, remains a difficulty,
though even this could be justified as a statement of a compromise made two months before. In any event it is hard to set
aside the evidence both of the Waverley annals and of the St.
Augustine's chronicle; and the appeal of the bishop of Ely to
Rome is likely to have been made[1] at the end of the year:
there are other grounds for believing that he was in England in
mid 1143, and he is known to have been in Rome in May 1144.[2]

Sufficient has now been said to justify the inclusion of the
bishop of Winchester's narrative of the councils of ? September and late November, even though a doubt remains as to its
authenticity in its present shape, and as to the precise date
of the councils here discussed.

The bishop of Winchester's narrative of the case between Theo-
  bald, archbishop of Canterbury, and the monks of St.
  Augustine's abbey on the customary payments by the monks to
  the archbishop

The narrative occurs in two cartularies of St. Augustine's, BL ms. Cotton Claudius D. x, fo. 20^{r-v} (Td);
PRO E164/27, fos. 12-13^{v} (Tp); also in the two 14th-cent.
mss. of the earlier version of the chronicle of St.
Augustine's (to 1220), ms. Cotton Tiberius A. ix, fos.
130^{v}-131 (Tt); Lambeth Palace Lib. ms. 419, fos. 132^{v}-133
(Tl); and in William Thorne's version of the chronicle,[3]

---

[1]Or repeated, if it was first made in March.   [2]*Liber Eliensis,* pp. 324-7, 435.
[3]William Thorne's chronicle runs to 1375; the two mss. cited above break
off in 1220. A superficial and highly selective comparison has shown that
for the passage here in question the mss. which run to 1220, though both
of the fourteenth century, represent an earlier form, revised and in part
rewritten by Thorne. This confirms the traditional view that Thorne used an
earlier chronicle (ascribed, on grounds no longer known, to Thomas Sprot),
of the early thirteenth century, which in its turn was evidently based on
contemporary notes and records. Beyond that it would be quite unsafe to go
in the present state of knowledge: see the helpful notes by E. John in
Bulletin of the John Rylands Lib., xxxix (1956-7), 390 n., and M.A.F. Borrie,
'The Thorne Chronicle', *British Museum Quarterly,* xxxi (1966-7), 87-90 (with
particular reference to BL Addit. 53710).

which was printed by Twysden, col. 1803-6; hence W. i.422-
3. Twysden based his text on a ms. which subsequently
passed into the Phillipps collection (8138) and is now BL
Addit. 53710 (pp. 49-50), and Cambridge, Corpus Christi
Coll. ms. 189, fos. 61(60)^V-62(61). The text is based on
a collation of Td, whose spelling is normally followed,
Tp, Tl, and Tt; select variants only are given; Thorne
made some revisions, and variants of his mss. are not
noted.

Incarnationis dominice anno[a] millesimo centesimo quadragesimo
tercio concilio adunato apud Wintoniam presidente Henrico
eiusdem civitatis episcopo et apostolice sedis legato, considentibus[b] archiepiscopo Tidbaldo Cantuariensi, cum confratribus
et coepiscopis Rodberto Lundon(ie), Gozelino Salesbir(ie),[c]
Alexandro Lincoln(ie), Seyfrido Cicestrie, Rodberto Herefordie,
Rodberto Batonie, Rogerio Cestrie, Willelmo Dunelmie, Ascelino
Rovecestrie, Simone Wigornie, Adelulfo Kardullie, Uhtredo
Clamorganie, una cum abbatibus et ceteris pluribus religiosis
ac secularibus, controversia magna de quinquaginta solidis et
septem denariis inter Thibaldum archiepiscopum Cantuarie et
monachos eiusdem et Hugonem abbatem sancti Augustini eiusdemque
monachos iam diucius habita, quinetiam in consistorio summi
pontificis Innocencii secundi sepius agitata, tandem eodem papa
iubente michi Henrico[d] in hac patria vices suas agenti et Rodberto Herefordie episcopo, ipso archiepiscopo cum suis, et
abbate cum suis eandem iussionem singulis litteris deferentibus,
quia de illa causa plenior noticia in Anglia haberi poterat,
commissa est terminanda. Congruo igitur tempore utraque parte
ad presignatum concilium evocata, cum didicissemus in privilegiis Romanorum pontificum monasterium beati Augustini ut ius
proprium sedis apostolice muniencium, nulliusque alterius dicioni
subditum, abbatem et monachos predicti loci neque subiectionem,
neque consuetudinem, neque redditum aliquem seu in magno sive in

---

[a]TdTp *place* anno *after* quadrag.   [b]considente Td.   [c]Tp *has adjectival
endings for some bishoprics,* Salesbiriensi ...; *the consensus of other mss.
for at least some subst. forms seems to make clear this was not intended
in the archetype; and even* Tp *reads* Cicestrie.   [d]TlTt *add* Wynton' episcopo.

minimo archiepiscopo et ecclesie sancte Trinitatis solvere
debere, licet supradictos quinquaginta solidos et septem denarios se iam diucius faterentur dedisse pro oleo et crismate nec
aliter illa habere potuisse; quod eciam, sicut antea in presencia domini pape Innocencii litteris eiusdem testantibus, ita
et in nostra se probaturos plurimis allegacionibus et testibus
offerebant, archiepiscopum vero nullam honestam causam de^a qua
eosdem denarios habuisset vel exigere posset comperissemus,
consultum duximus tam anxiam causam, tam gravem utriusque ecclesie laborem amicabili modificacione sedare, et matri ecclesie
nostre Cantuarie, cui nos episcopi professi sumus debitum
honorem, licet ecclesie beati Augustini videamur gravamini
reservare. Consuluimus utique et quodammodo coegimus abbatem et
monachos, ut darent archiepiscopo et ecclesie sancte Trinitatis
possessionem aliquam liberam sexaginta solidos valentem, quippe
ut potenti vicino et in multis pernecessario, utpote in
dacione olei et crismatis,[1] in dedicandis ecclesiis, in ordinibus faciendis, in iusticiis ceterisque negociis prout postulatus; ista videlicet condicione, ut illa possessione semel
accepta, sibi ab inde proprium haberet, et ecclesia sancti
Augustini a memoratorum denariorum solucione inperpetuum foret
libera, et secundum privilegia sua maneret in omnibus quieta.
Eodem vero anno quia Romam ituri eramus, convocatis iterum
fratribus circa festivitatem sancti Andree apud Londoniam
archiepiscopus cum monachis suis predictam convencionem dum
executam fuisse testaretur literasque nostras super prefata
censura ne quis hinc inde posset eam violare exigeret. Habito
fratrum consilio litteras huius terminacionis racionabili eius
peticioni sigillatas dedimus, abbati quoque et fratribus similiter fecimus. Quarum tenor iste est.

Henricus Dei gratia Winton(iensis) episcopus et apostolice
sedis legatus universis sancte Dei ecclesie fidelibus salutem.
Scire volumus universitatem vestram Hugoni abbati et monasterio
beati Augustini Cantuarie a Tidbaldo Cantuar(iensi) archiepis-

---

^{a}*om.* Td.

---

[1] See p. 800 n.4 and refs.

copo et ecclesia sancte Trinitatis de quinquaginta solidis et septem denariis controversiam motam et sepius in consistorio domini pape Innocencii secundi summi pontificis agitatam, et tandem eodem iubente amicabili composicione interveniente per nos hoc modo terminatam. Monasterium beati Augustini prefato archiepiscopo et ecclesie sancte Trinitatis duo molendina apud Dovram et viginti solidatas de prebenda quam monasterium beati Augustini habet in ecclesia sancti Martini de Dovra, hac condicione [Td, fo. 20^v] dedit, ut nec eidem archiepiscopo nec alicui successorum suorum per se sive per ministros suos ab eodem monasterio vel fratribus aliquid ulterius exigere liceat. Fuit autem controversia hec in presencia supradictorum episcoporum ceterorumque terminata.

Henry of Blois and Theobald duly went to Rome to argue before the pope as to the future administration of the English Church and of the province of Canterbury, and the monks of St. Augustine's also sent a delegation to seek confirmation of their privileges. Theobald raised a small question still outstanding: the customary payment by monks to archbishop of 'bread and drink and rams'; this had been commuted for a payment of three shillings, and it was arranged that it should be abolished in exchange for the grant by monks to archbishop of land worth three shillings per annum. This was confirmed by Pope Lucius II in a bull dated from the Lateran on 17 April 1144 (Thorne, col. 1805-6; *PUE* ii, no. 34 (= JL 8581); Saltman, *Theobald*, pp. 68-9).

146

1145. LEGATION OF IMAR, CARDINAL BISHOP OF TUSCULUM

This note is based on, and in part reproduces, A. Morey and C.N.L. Brooke, 'The Cerne Letters of Gilbert Foliot and the Legation of Imar of Tusculum', *EHR* lxiii (1948), 523-7, esp. pt. II, pp. 526-7. See also Tillmann, pp. 50-1.[1]

---

[1] Imar, like Alberic of Ostia, was an eminent Cluniac; he was a cardinal from 1142. In the schism of 1159 he became one of Victor IV's chief supporters and died at Cluny, which he kept for a while on Victor's side, in 1162 (Zenker, pp. 44-6 and references).

In May 1144 Pope Lucius II announced his intention of sending legates to this country in a letter to Bishop Bernard of St. Davids (JL 8607). Some time after 30 May two cardinals, Imar of Tusculum and Alberic of Ostia, were sent as legates to France where they remained as late as 19 November, but there is no record of any visit to England by the legates in that year. Early in 1145, Imar came to England alone, and an important object of his journey was to advance the issue of the promotion of William FitzHerbert to the see of York (see p. 804). It seems likely that St. Bernard and his associates, who opposed the granting of the pallium to the recently consecrated archbishop, delayed Imar's journey to England, and he may never have come as Lucius's legate; it is certain that he acted for Lucius's successor, Eugenius III: Lucius died on 15 February 1145, and Eugenius was elected on the same day. The most likely reconstruction is that Imar arrived in England in April or early May 1145, and left again some time after 10 June.

On 10 June Imar was in Winchester, where he heard two appeals of close concern to Gilbert Foliot, then abbot of Gloucester (*GFL*, nos. 40-3), those relating to the disputed succession to the abbacy of Cerne, and to the rights of Gloucester's dependency, Ewenny priory. It is possible that the meeting of 10 June was a council, but we have no evidence to confirm this, and a more likely candidate for a legatine council is his meeting with the bishops and abbots in London, which cannot be precisely dated.

The meeting of bishops and abbots is recorded in two documents describing the settlement of the suit between the bishop and monks of Rochester Cathedral, one by the legate Imar (printed below), the other by Archbishop Theobald: Theobald gives the place as London, adds Edward abbot of Reading, Walter abbot of Ramsey, Aimar prior of Lewes, and Clarembald prior of Bermondsey to the list of assessors, and adds certain details to the account of the case itself, none of substance. Theobald's charter is printed in Saltman, *Theobald,* pp. 450-1, no. 223; Imar's in *PUE* ii, no. 45, from Textus Roffensis (Rochester Cathedral

Library MS. A. 3. 5),[1] fos. 203^V-204 (mid-12th-cent. addition
to early 12th-cent. ms.; copies in BL Stowe ms. 940, fos. 106^V-
107; London, Society of Antiquaries, ms. 177, fo. 93: Thorpe's
collection), collated by BL ms. Cotton Domit. x., fos. 124
(125)-125(126), whence *Reg. Roffense,* p. 41.

GFL, no. 65, in which Gilbert Foliot, as abbot of Gloucester,
excuses himself from attending a meeting with the archbishop,
very likely refers to an unrecorded council in the period 1145-8.

Cardinal Imar's report on the case between the bishop and monks
of Rochester on the manors of Lambeth (Surrey), and Hadden-
ham (Bucks)

Imarus Dei gratia Tusculanus episcopus, apostolicę sedis legatus, omnibus matris ęcclesię filiis ad quos litterę istę pervenerint, salutem. Rei gestę memoria litteris provide committi-
tur, ne lites semel sopitę in futuro iterum instaurentur.
Proinde universitati vestrę per pręsentia scripta notum esse
volumus quod inter Ascelinum Rofensem episcopum et eiusdem loci
monachos, ęcclesię scilicet beati Andreę, super iure maneriorum
Lamhetham et Hendenham controversia huiusmodi orta est. Asserebant prędicti monachi memorata maneria sibi ad victum proprium
a rege Anglorum Willelmo iuniore et Lamfranco pię recordationis
Cantuariensi archiepiscopo et Gundulfo Rofensi episcopo concessa rationabiliter et donata et ad eiusdem rei evidentiorem
probationem eorumdem cartas et confirmationes et sequentium
regum Anglorum Henrici et Stephani et Anselmi Canturiensis
archiepiscopi in medium proferebant. Contra quę cum pręfatus
Ascelinus Rofensis episcopus nichil firmum, nichil validum
responderet nec se in pretaxatis maneriis ius habere probare
posset, assidentibus nobis venerabilibus fratribus Teobaldo
Cantuariensi [fo. 204] archiepiscopo, Rodberto Lundoniensi,
Henrico Wintoniensi, Alexandro Linco[l]niensi, Ebrardo Noruuicensi, Sifredo Cicestrensi episcopis, Gaufrido sancti Albani,
Gervasio Westmonasterii, Petro Scireburn(ensi) abbatibus et

---

[1]See facsimile edition, ed. P. Sawyer (Early English Manuscripts in
Facsimile, 2 vols., Copenhagen, 1957-62), ii. Saltman, *Theobald,* pp. 291-2,
attributes a charter of Theobald to Imar's council; but see above, p. 797.

magistro Hilario[1] et aliis quam pluribus religiosis personis ipsa maneria cum omnibus suis appenditiis, secundum quod carte donationis et confirmationis continebant, ipsis monachis adiudicavimus et ipsos possessores constituimus; ipso eorum episcopo promittente quod deinceps, sine vexatione et inquietatione, monachos bona et possessiones suas habere permitteret et pacem eis servaret, quod et ipsi firmiter observare precepimus; ad cuius rei argumentum ipsos monachos in osculo pacis recepit. Nos itaque predictorum fratrum iustis petitionibus facilem prebentes assensum tam sepedicta maneria quam alia omnia eorum bona et possessiones, quas in presentiarum iuste possident vel in futuro legitime habituri sunt, iura etiam, consuetudines, libertates rationabiliter indultas auctoritate officii quo fungimur ipsis confirmamus, et presentis scripti attestatione roboramus.

147

NOTE ON ARCHBISHOP THEOBALD'S PRIMACY, 1145-61

Between 1139 and 1143 Theobald was subject to the authority of Henry of Blois, bishop of Winchester, as papal legate. After 1143 the legateship was never again granted to Henry. 'But it was some years before the threat was lifted, and Henry and the bishop of St. Davids meanwhile were intriguing to be made archbishops in their own right. Theobald was abroad in 1143 and 1144, and the fruit of his visit to the pope was the confirmation of his "primacy", an event which called out a letter of effusive thanks from Gilbert Foliot to the papal chancellor, the English Cardinal Robert Pullen, and some verses of obscure rejoicing from Osbert of Clare. It soon appeared, however, that this was not the end of Theobald's difficulties. Primacy he had achieved, but primacy over whom? From now on he claimed to be primate of all England, and to be metropolitan over Wales. Yet the bishop of St. Davids continued to claim his independence, and Theobald had to argue with him in the pope's presence again

---

[1]Presumably the future bishop of Chichester.

in 1147. The claim died, for the time being, with Bishop Bernard early in 1148, but at the Council of Rheims it was made clear to Theobald that his primacy did not extend over York. In his later years he altered his formal title to "primate of the English", and the reflection of his disappointment can be seen in Becket's refusal to use the title "primate". But Theobald received consolation in 1150: Henry of Winchester's case was finally repudiated, and Theobald was made legate for the English church.'[1]

For the general setting, see Saltman, *Theobald,* pp. 19 ff.; for the chronology of Theobald's primacy and titles, *GFL*, pp. 505-6; Saltman, *Theobald*, pp. 190 ff.; *GF*, pp. 88 ff.; for Henry of Blois's bid to be archbishop, Voss, pp. 45 ff., 53 ff.; John of Salisbury, *HP*, ed. Chibnall, pp. 91 ff.; for the claims of St. Davids, Conway Davies, i.190-232; *GF*, pp. 151 ff.; M. Richter, *JEH* xxii (1971), 177-89; *Nat. Lib. of Wales Journ.* xv (1967-8), 197-214.

The grant of primacy of Theobald, dated 5 May 1145, is *PUE* ii, no. 43.

Once securely established in the saddle, Theobald strove to preserve a united province in a divided land; if he had been granted primacy over York, he would no doubt have aimed to preserve a united church in England as a whole. This involved the summoning of provincial councils from time to time, but we are very imperfectly informed as to their frequency. Only from one, that of 1151 (no. 150), have any canons survived; but it is evident from the *Letters* of John of Salisbury that it was Theobald's practice to consult his suffragans and other advisers on all matters of policy and on important lawsuits. The council of London referred to in Saltman, *Theobald,* no. 232, in which Gilbert earl of Pembroke (died Jan. 1148-9) made the archbishop confirm the grant of the church of Everton (Hunts.) to the monks of St. Neot's, may well have fallen in the period 1145-8, since the archbishop presumably presided.

The early letters of John of Salisbury largely consist of reports or consultations on legal cases for Theobald, and so

---

[1] *GF*, pp. 91-2, below, p. 820 .

contain references to several councils of the period. *Letters,* i, nos. 14-16, refer to a council or councils in 1156 (see pp. 829-35); nos. 124-5 to that of June-July 1160 (pp. 836 n., 838-40). Two other letters refer to councils which cannot be dated; but the period of John's service as Theobald's adviser in ecclesiastical cases, especially on those which involved appeals, seems to have been *c.*1154-61: to these years belong all but a handful of the first letter collection, and perhaps indeed all.[1]

I. *John of Salisbury, Letters, no. 70*

> *Letters,* i, no. 70 from Paris, BN ms. lat. 8625, fo. 11, Cambridge, UL ms. Ii. 2. 31, fo. 127.

Archbishop Theobald tells Richard de Belmeis, bishop of London (1152-62) that one Alice de Valognes has complained that the bishop was about to pronounce a judgement against her without due hearing. The archbishop instructs the bishop to give her due hearing, then consult his colleagues at a meeting of bishops in London shortly due, and proceed to judgement on their advice. The nature of the case and its outcome are unknown.

... Precipimus itaque ut ei audientiam debitam prebeatis, et tunc secundum Deum causa debitum finem sortiatur. Convenient Lond(oniam) nobiscum auctore Deo in brevi fratres nostri, ut de eorum consilio, si interim vestro officio exequendo diligentiam placuerit adhibere, causam hanc tutius poteritis[a] diffinire.

II. *John of Salisbury, Letters, no. 92*

> JS, *Letters,* i, no. 92, from Paris, BN ms. lat. 8625, fo. 15.

John of Salisbury had been presiding over a diocesan synod on

---

[a]poteritis *Paris ms.;* positis *Cambridge ms.;* possitis *J. Masson, edition of Paris, 1611, perhaps rightly.*

---

[1]For these dates, see JS, *Letters,* i; but see also ibid. ii, p. x n. 5.

the archbishop's behalf, and an issue arose as to whether certain clerks cited before him were not under the jurisdiction
of the bishop of Chichester.[1] John reserved the case for the
archbishop, who was absent through illness, and it appears that
this meant that it would be discussed in a provincial council,
shortly to meet. The letter is John's explanation to the bishop
of Chichester, and is an interesting illustration of the relation between a diocesan and a provincial synod. For that reason
we quote it in full. The archbishop was ill on and off from
1155, so it can be dated 1155 x 61 (cf. JS, *Letters*, i, pp.
xxxvii, 14, etc.); and it is possible that it refers to the
Council of London of 1160 (see p. 836).

Ex litteris quas michi vestra serenitas destinavit planum est
prudentiam vestram suggestione malignantium adversus innocen-
tiam meam fuisse circumventam. Siquidem illi quos vestros
parrochianos esse asseritis a domino archiepiscopo per decanos
et alios officiales suos sepe citati sunt, et cum in sua contumacia pertinaces semper invenirentur tandem denuntiatum est
eis sub interminatione anathematis ut copiam sui in sinodo
facerent. Illis itaque absentibus immo potius se contumaciter
absentantibus, presentes fuerunt officiales archidiaconi per
quos illi sepissime citati fuerant. Cum autem per eos et de
citationibus et de contumaci responsione absentantium consti-
tisset, rem ad consultationem domini archiepiscopi, licet
sinodus aliud suaderet, credidi referendam. Michi namque fere
tota sinodus reluctabatur et nonnulli detrahebant dicentes me
dissimulare iustitiam Cant(uariensis) ecclesie et domini archiepiscopi ob favorem vestrum qui, accepto tempore languoris

---

[1]See note to JS, *Letters*, i.141: there seems to be no doubt that this
was part of the boundary dispute between Chichester and Canterbury, although
the letter has no heading in the ms. The five or seven intervening parishes
might suggest that the issue was a Chichester enclave in the see of Canterbury rather than the Canterbury enclave in Chichester. But there seems little
doubt that the reference is to the Canterbury peculiar in the diocese of
Chichester, consisting of the deaneries of Pagham, Tarring, and Southmalling,
with the 'Pallant' in Chichester (*Acta of the Bishops of Chichester*, ed.
H. Mayr-Harting, pp. 54-5; I.J. Churchill, *Canterbury Administration*, London,
1933, i.75-8). For a possible reference to a meeting of bishops etc.,
*c.*1145-8, see p. 812.

eius, ex insperato in ipsum insurgere decrevistis et Cantuariensis ecclesie terminos ingredi et eam his que centum annis quiete
possedit mutilare. Stupebant autem omnes super tanti ausus perti-
nacia inpunita cum aut quinque aut septem interiacentes parro-
chie, ut aiunt, oculate fidei manifestent fundum de quo agitur
nullo modo ad Cicestrensem[a] ecclesiam pertinere. Erant quoque
presentes clerici qui sibi vim et atroces iniurias illatas
querebantur, et vicinis constabat omnibus quod eisdem parrochia-
nis sacerdotes nostri per totum annum omnia divina ministrant.
Hec et multo plura ad dominum archiepiscopum et pro parte mea
invito prolata sunt, adeoque undique conclamatum ut et ego de
dilatione nonnullam suspicionem contraherem. Precepit ergo ut
contumaces parrochianos suos vestros, sicut decanus et sinodus
suadebant,[b] anathemati subiugarent.[c] Ego vero die sequenti hoc
illi decano, ceteris audientibus, sicut iniunctum fuerat denun-
tiavi. Et hec est illa mea sententia quam ex ignorantia iuris
processisse vestra discretio deprehendit et reprehendit. Me
siquidem sermone et scientia fateor inperitum et qui non suffi-
cio tueri quicquid volueritis inpugnare. Nam ad hoc quis ido-
neus? Sed nescio an ex vestra prudentia istud processerit quod
illi qui semper nostre fuerunt iurisdictioni subiecti, concipi-
entes spiritum sapientie grandioris, vocationes illius cui etsi
non episcopali iure tamen metropolitico subiecti fuerunt dedig-
nati sunt facere copiam sui vel ad hoc ut fori prescriptione
uterentur. Scio enim hoc ex alto processisse consilio. Non tamen
hec allego ad excusationem mei si me esse in culpa pronuntia-
veritis, quia malo a vobis veniam postulare quam uti rationibus
iuris vel allegare mandatum domini et necessitatem obsequendi.
Ad reliqua seorsum respondebitur. Consulo tamen ut dominum meum
ante concilium videatis.

148

MARCH-APRIL 1148. PAPAL COUNCIL OF RHEIMS

        In general, see Mansi, xxi.711-36; Hefele-Leclercq, v,
        i.823-38; Foreville, *Latran*, pp. 101-6; N.M. Häring in

---

[a]Cistrensem *ms.*   [b]suadebat *ms.*   [c]subiugaret *ms.*

Scholastik, xl (1965), 55-90, and *Mediaeval Studies*,
xxviii (1966), 39-59; JS, *HP*, ed. Poole, pp. xxxi-lvii,
4-42, 93-6, ed. Chibnall, pp. xl-xli, 4-42. See also
Gervase, i.134.

In the course of 1147 Pope Eugenius III sent messengers to summon the council to meet at Rheims in March 1148.[1] This was not
well received by King Stephen, who in 1147-8 and fitfully in
the years which followed, was attempting to assert his control
over the English Church and to keep a check on journeys to and
from the papal Curia. It is recorded that he expelled the papal
legate who came to invite the English bishops to attend.[2] The
course of events is discussed in Saltman, *Theobald*, pp. 25 ff.;
GF, pp. 89 ff.

The outcome was that Stephen sent three bishops to Rheims,
Robert of Hereford, William of Norwich, and Hilary of Chichester; he attempted to prevent the archbishop of Canterbury and
the other bishops from going. 'The archbishop was even compelled
to stage a little comedy: he conducted a solemn consecration of
the bishops of Llandaff and Rochester at Canterbury, in the
king's presence, a few days before the council was due to open;
then he slipped away in "a fishing smack which he had hired and
hidden in a remote bay ... that would carry no more than a
dozen men", as John of Salisbury tells us, and so, as the pope
is alleged to have said, "swimming rather than sailing" he
reached the council.'[3]

The main session of the council opened on 21 March; the pope
left Rheims *c*.19 April. The *Historia Pontificalis* and the
letters of Gilbert Foliot[4] reveal some of the business concern-

---

[1] For what follows see Tillmann, p. 51.
[2] Ibid., citing *UGQ*, p. 81 (*Continuatio S. Augustini*).
[3] *GF*, p. 89; John of Salisbury, *HP*, ed. Chibnall, p. 7; Gervase, i.134.
The consecration took place on 14 March in the king's presence; the council
opened at Rheims on 21 March. Of the other bishops, Roger of Coventry was
on crusade; Jocelin of Salisbury may conceivably have been at Rheims (Saltman, *Theobald*, p. 26). The rest seem to have stayed away. Oxford, Corpus
Christi Coll. ms. 137 (12th cent. English miscellany), fos. 99^v-100, has the
'creed' and an attendance list, which includes Theobald, William of Norwich
and the archdeacons Walter and Geoffrey of York (i.e. York and Nottingham:
see C.T. Clay in *Yorks. Arch. Journal*, xxxvi (1944-7), 274-5, 283).
[4] *GFL*, nos. 74-8; cf. *GFL*, pp. 108 and ff.; *GF*, pp. 89 ff. JS, *HP*, ed.
Chibnall, pp. 6-8, describes Stephen's intervention and the archbishop's
arrival at Rheims; pp. 49, 78 ff. the aftermath in England.

ing England discussed at the council or while it was in session.
The pope suspended the English bishops who had stayed away, but
granted the archbishop of Canterbury full power to release all
of them except the bishop of Winchester who, as the king's
brother, was apparently suspected of complicity in Stephen's
activities. Theobald was also granted power to preside over the
election to the see of Lincoln. The bishop of Hereford died at
Rheims on 16 April. Gilbert Foliot was made vicar of the diocese, and subsequently 'elected' bishop, though whether by a
genuine election or by papal provision is not clear: in either
case the promotion was evidently due to an arrangement between
pope and archbishop.[1] The long-standing suit between Gloucester
abbey and the archbishop of York was postponed at the instance
of Bernard, abbot of Clairvaux, until the new archbishop, Henry
Murdac, abbot of Fountains and Bernard's disciple, could take
up residence in his see; Stephen was preventing his entry,
since he had supplanted the king's nephew, William FitzHerbert.[2]

Theobald returned to England, but was immediately sent into
exile by the king. Some months later he returned again under
the protection of Hugh Bigod, earl of Norfolk.[3] An uneasy truce
between king and archbishop followed until 1152, when Theobald
was in exile again for refusing to anoint and crown Stephen's
son Eustace; in 1153, after Eustace's death, Theobald and Henry
of Winchester joined in presiding over the reconciliation between Stephen and the future Henry II, which led to the Treaty
of Winchester of November 1153 and the succession of Henry II
at the end of 1154.

Henry of Blois, bishop of Winchester, had meanwhile reconciled himself to the pope, and submitted to the ignominy of
being neither papal legate nor an independent archbishop - as
he and the bishop of St. Davids had claimed they were entitled
to be in the 1140s. Henry of Blois was abroad once, or more

---

[1]See discussion in *GF*, pp. 96 ff.; *GFL*, no. 77. For the bishops released
from suspension, see Saltman, *Theobald*, p. 27.

[2]*GFL*, nos. 75, 128 and nn. Doubtless the resignation of Bernard, abbot
of Cerne, foreshadowed in *GFL*, no. 64, also took place at Rheims; he returned to Gloucester abbey where he had been a monk, and was later abbot
of Burton (*Heads*, pp. 31, 37).

[3]JS, *HP*, p. 49; Gervase, i.136.

probably twice, in 1148-9 and 1149-50, and was relieved of the
sentence of suspension passed against him at Rheims.[1]

Canons of the council appear in two English mss. of known
provenance: Durham Cathedral B. IV. 18, fos. 98^V-99^V (Lanfranc's collection abridged, written at Canterbury in the early
12th cent., later moved to Durham);[2] Lincoln Cathedral ms. 193,
fos. 206-207^V (12th cent. canonical ms., at Lincoln since the
12th cent.).[3] They are also in BL ms. Egerton 749, fos. 138^V-
140: 12th cent., *Pannormia* of Ivo of Chartres. They are also in
the interpolated version which incorporates the canons of the
Council of London of March 1143 in two Norman mss., the *Collec-
tiones Sangermanensis* and *Abrincensis* (Paris, BN ms. lat.
12459; Avranches, Bibl. de Ville, ms. 149; see pp. 795-6).

149

1150-1161. THE LEGATESHIP OF THEOBALD, ARCHBISHOP OF CANTER-
BURY

Between October 1149 and 20 March 1150, and probably in the
early months of 1150, Theobald was made papal legate for
England, and possibly for Scotland too; thus his jurisdiction
over York *de facto* was secured, while the jurisdiction of his
see *de iure* was set aside (see p. 814). See Saltman, *Theobald*,
pp. 30-1 and *passim*; Tillmann, p. 33; *GF*, p. 92 n. 1 (but see
Le Neve, ii.99 and n. 4); *GFL*, pp. 505-6.

The legation was granted by Pope Eugenius III, and confirmed
by his successors. There are grounds for thinking that Theobald
did not regard himself as legate after the papal schism of 1159
until the formal recognition of Alexander III *c*.July 1160
(Cheney, *Revue de Droit Canonique*, xxviii (1978), 91-2).

In 1150 and again in 1151-2, England was visited by John
Paparo, first as cardinal deacon of Sant'Adriano then as
cardinal priest of S. Lorenzo in Damaso, but only as a traveller

---

[1]JS, *HP*, pp. 78 ff.; the case for two visits is discussed by Dr. Chibnall,
ibid., pp. 91-4; for one visit in JS, *Letters*, i.253-4.

[2]Z.N. Brooke, *English Church and the Papacy*, pp. 81-2, 232.

[3]Ker, p. 117, cf. p. 115. There is a brief extract in BL ms. Add. 11440,
fos. 110^V-111.

on his way to and from Ireland, where the cardinal conducted an
important legation.[1]

150

*c.*18 MARCH 1151. LEGATINE COUNCIL OF LONDON

> See Saltman, *Theobald,* pp. 33 ff., 547-9; Barlow (1979),
> pp. 101, 131.

The only contemporary chronicler to notice the council was
Henry of Huntingdon,[2] who dates it mid Lent 1151: in that year
mid-Lent Sunday fell on 18 March. He also complains that it was
the occasion of three appeals to Rome. One of these appeals was
from the monks of Ely, against the clerk Henry who had usurped
some of their properties: this was but one stage in a long-
drawn-out dispute.[3] The chronicler also makes this the occasion
for his celebrated remark that appeals to Rome had not been the
custom in England before the legateship of Henry of Winchester;
but he tells us little that is concrete about the council's
activities. Nevertheless, it may be to him that we owe the
earlier of the two surviving texts of the canons of the council.

As in 1143, the canons of the council of 1151 were concerned

---

[1]See Tillmann, p. 52; J.A. Watt, *The Church and the Two Nations in Medieval Ireland* (Cambridge, 1970), pp. 28 ff., esp. 31, and nn. On his movements
in England, see note in *English Episcopal Acta,* i, *Lincoln,* ed. D. M. Smith,
p. 139.

[2]No. I. This was printed in Sp. ii.44 s.a. 1140/1; W. i.424 s.a. 1151.

[3]The *Liber Eliensis* (ed. Blake, p. 350) specifically says that the case
of the monks of Ely against the archdeacon of Ely was settled at a London
council held about this time, which may safely be identified with the present council; and it seems very likely that the other dispute (set in motion
at this stage by the same proctor, the monk Richard) was brought up on the
same occasion. The other case had been re-delegated to the archbishop and
the bishop of Chichester in December 1150; but when the delegates attempted
to settle the dispute, Richard appealed to the pope once again (*Liber Eliensis,* pp. 344-62, 405-7, *PUE* ii, nos. 64-5, 67, etc.). It is possible that a
case between the monks of Belvoir and Gilbert parson of Hallaton and Geoffrey de Normanville, was heard in this council. It was settled before the
archbishop at London in a council in the presence of Robert bishop of Lincoln and Hilary bishop of Chichester (Saltman, *Theobald,* nos. 14-15; *English
Episcopal Acta* i, ed. D.M. Smith, no. 78). As the archbishop was legate it cannot be earlier than 1150, and this council, or that of December 1152, or some
other unrecorded, are all possible occasions.

primarily with the temporary conditions - of confusion and
secular violence - produced by the anarchy. It also owed something to the 1143 council both verbally and in the substance
of one or two of its canons. But in the main the members of
the council were trying 'to seek out new remedies', as stated
in the preamble.

> P. Paris, BN ms. lat. 6042, formerly Colbert 3969, fo. 121.
> The council is added at the conclusion of a mid-12th-
> cent. ms. of Henry of Huntingdon's chronicle, a ms. end-
> ing in 1147, which belonged to the abbey of Mont-Saint-
> Michel, and is probably a copy of that which Henry himself
> gave to Robert of Torigny, later abbot of Mont-Saint-
> Michel.[1]

The other text is of the late twelfth or early thirteenth century, and comes in the decretal collection *Roffensis,* of the
'English' or 'Canterbury' group.[2]

> R. BL ms. Royal 10. C. iv, fo. 145[r-v].

The spelling of P is followed unless the contrary is stated.

> *Printed texts* (not in W or Sp - but see p. 821 n. 2).
> Mansi, xxi.749-52; Saltman, *Theobald,* pp. 547-9 (from a
> collation of P and R). First printed by Baluze (from P)
> in his *Miscellaneorum lib. septimus* (Paris, 1715), pp.
> 81-3; hence in Mansi's ed. of Baluze (ii, Lucca, 1761,
> p. 121) and Mansi's *Concilia.*

---

[1]The manuscript is described in Torigny, ed. L. Delisle (Rouen, 1872-3),
i, pp. lv-lxi. There is great confusion about the history and relationships
of the texts of Henry's work, and a final decision on the problems of the
Paris ms. must wait for the new edn. by Dr. D.E. Greenway (OMT).

[2]Cf. C. Duggan, *Twelfth-Century Decretal Collections* (London, 1963),
pp. 76-8, 173-87, esp. 177.

I. *Henry of Huntingdon, Historia Anglorum s.a. 1151*[1]

Tedbaldus Cantuariensis archiepiscopus, et apostolice sedis
legatus, tenuit concilium generale apud Lundonias in media
Quadragesima, ubi rex Stephanus et filius suus Eustachius et
Anglie proceres interfuerunt, totumque illud concilium novis
appellationibus infrenduit. In Anglia namque appellationes in
usu non erant donec eas Henricus Wintoniensis episcopus, dum
legatus esset, malo suo crudeliter intrusit; in eodem namque
concilio ad Romani pontificis audientiam ter appellatus est.

II. *Canons of the council*

[a]Anno dominice incarnationis MCLI, papatus domini Eugenii pape
tertii incipiente septimo, Anglorum rege Stephano regnante anno
sexto decimo, presidente Tebbaldo Cantuariensi archiepiscopo,
tocius Britannie primate et sedis apostolice legato, anno tertio decimo, celebratum est Londonie concilium mense Martio in
quo statuta hec fuerunt que subterannexa sunt.[a]

[1] Multorum experimenta morborum novas nos cogunt medicinas
querere[2] ut tribulationibus que invenerunt nos nimis[3] possimus
remediis salubribus obviare. Sancimus igitur ut ecclesie et
possessiones [R fo. 145[v]] ecclesiastice ab operationibus et
exactionibus quas vulgo tenserias sive tallagias vocant omnino
libere permaneant,[b] nec super his eas aliqui de cetero inquie-
tare[c] presumant.[4] Qui vero contra hoc decretum venire tempta-
verint, divino in terris eorum cessante officio tandem donec

[a-a]*So* P; *om.* R (R *also om. numbers of chapters*).   [b]perananeant P.
[c]inquietatie P.

---

[1]Ed. T. Arnold (RS), p. 282, collated with mss. Cambridge, Corpus Christi Coll. 280, fo. 199, UL Ii. 2.3, fo. 203[v]; London, BL Royal 13. B. vi,
fo. 153[v]; Oxford, Bodl. Bodley 521 (2182), fo. 104[v] (variants insignificant).
An abbreviated version of Henry's account is in Gervase (i.147; cf. also
ii.388) and a verbatim copy in 'Walter of Coventry' (Coventry, ed. Stubbs,
i.176). There is a passing mention in the 14th-cent. *Chron. Angliae Petriburgense,* ed. J.A. Giles (London, 1845), p. 94 (s.a. 1150).
[2]Cf. C. of London (1143), c. 1.   [3]Cf. Ps. 45, 2 (46, 1).
[4]Cf. C. of London (1143), cc. 1, 14. On *tenserias* see J.H. Round, *Geoffrey de Mandeville* (London, 1892), pp. 215, 218 n., 414-16: he shows that

condigne satisfaciant, anathematis sententia percellantur. Sane
operationes regi debitas fieri non prohibemus, regio tamen
precedente mandato.[1]

Capitulum ii. Quia vero ecclesie per Angliam constitute occasione placitorum corone regis pertinentium attenuantur supra-
modum[a] et destruuntur, nolumus eas sicut hactenus super eisdem
placitis baronibus respondere. Ideoque precipimus quatinus[b]
huius nostre institutionis[c] transgressoribus et terris eorum
episcopi in quorum parrochiis fuerint iusticiam satagant ecclesiasticam exercere. Qua in re si episcopi neglegentes extiterint,
ab eisdem damna ecclesiis illata[d] requirantur.

Capitulum iii.[2] Preterea statuimus ut qui pro invasione seu
pro[e] rapina rei ecclesiastice anathematis vinculo innodantur,
absolvi nullatenus mereantur donec ablata integre restituant
vel ecclesie que damnum passa est sufficienter caveant quod
universum debitum infra tempus quadrimenstre persolvant.
Verumtamen si de rebus mobilibus eorum qui dampna inferunt
eadem resarciri non poterunt,[f] supportandos eos esse putamus
ut fideiussoriam prestantes cautionem vel ea deficiente iuratoriam ad annue prestationis solutionem secundum suas facultates
episcopi taxatione teneantur. Si quis autem eos aliter absolvere
presumpserit, eadem damna[g] resarcire compellatur.

Capitulum iv. Illud quoque adicientes dicernimus[h] ne liceat de
cetero alicui ecclesiastice persone post invasoris seu raptoris

---

[a] *om.* R.   [b] R *adds* de.   [c] constitutionis R.   [d] ecclesiis illatas R;
ecclesie P.   [e] *om.* R.   [f] poterint R.   [g] *om.* R.   [h] dicernimus P; decernimus R.

---

it was in relatively common use at this time for forcible exactions, sometimes (perhaps commonly) forced payments in return for protection. *Tallagias*
is the first known use in English sources of a word which later became very
common for tallages or taxes. We are much indebted to Mr. R.E. Latham for
advice and help from material for the *Dict. of Medieval Latin from British
Sources*; see meanwhile his *Revised Med. Lat. Word-List*, pp. 475, 480.

[1] On the canon as a whole, see Saltman, *Theobald*, pp. 34-5.
[2] Cf. C. of London (1143), c. 12.

excommunicationem[a] de damno ecclesie illato ultra vicesimam
partem debiti aliquid remittere. Qui vero remiserit, si episcopus est, per sex menses, si alia ecclesiastica persona per
annum integrum ab officio[b] suspendatur.

Capitulum v. Sanctorum patrum[c] vestigia secuti[1] precipimus ut
hi qui anathematis sententia condemnantur, si per annum integrum in ea pertinaciter perseverent, infames et detestabiles[d]
habeantur, ut neque in testimoniis[e] neque in causis audiantur
et in principis sit potestate ipsos[f] exheredare.

Capitulum vi. Prava nimis et statutis canonum[g] contraria ino-
levit consuetudo ut in ecclesiis Anglie clerici passim et sine
delectu recipiantur.[2] Quod ne de cetero fiat modis omnibus
prohibemus.

Capitulum vii. Nichilominus etiam[h] presentis scripti auctoritate
statuendum esse censemus, ut quotiens sacerdotibus innotuerit
predam sive rapinam rerum ecclesiasticarum ad loca in quibus
degunt devenisse, divina[i] ibidem officia celebrare non presumant donec episcopi vel archidiaconi super hoc mandatum
suscipiant, vel ipsa rapina restituatur. Cessantibus autem
matricibus ecclesiis capelle que intra munitiones[j] constructe
sunt, non expectata cessandi iussione, ab administratione divi-
norum cessent. Sacerdotes vero qui huius sanctionis contemptores extiterint per annum integrum officio proprio careant;
quod si sepius in hac re neglegentes reperti fuerint, pro arbitrio episcopi sui maiori severitati[k] subiciantur.

Capitulum viii. Hoc quoque presentis sanctionis pagina firmandum

---

[a]excummucationem P.   [b]ab officio P; *om*. R.   [c]patrorum P.   [d]det. et
infames R.   [e]testimonio R.   [f]eos R.   [g]statutis canonum P; sanctorum
patrum statutis R.   [h]et R.   [i]divina R; diurna P.   [j]R *adds* earum.
[k]*om*. R.

---

[1]Cf. ibid., c. 1 and n.
[2]The wording is obscure; the canon is no doubt partly attacking clerks
wandering from diocese to diocese without licence (cf. C. of Westminster
(1175), c. 5 and Index s.v. 'Commendatory letters').

esse credimus[a] ne quis in civitate vel portu, neque in vico,
neque in castro, neque omnino[b] alicubi locorum, nova vectigalia
que vulgo pedagia dicuntur instituere vel instituentibus[c] consentire audeat.[1] Huius autem statuti[d] temeratores, quia rem
exemplo perniciosam inducunt, anathemati subiciendos non dubi-
tamus.

151

7 DECEMBER 1152. LEGATINE COUNCIL OF LONDON

This council seems only to be recorded in a letter of Gilbert
Foliot, bishop of Hereford, to Pope Eugenius III, reporting on
a case in which he was papal judge-delegate, which had been
heard at a meeting of the legate and his suffragans - i.e.
Archbishop Theobald and the bishops of the province of Canterbury - at London on 7 December; the context establishes the
date 1152.[2] The case was a long and complicated dispute between
the monks of Ely and a clerk called Henry, son of William the
Breton, archdeacon of Ely. Henry had a charter from Bishop Hervey
of Ely granting his father the manor of Stetchworth. The monks
claimed that it was a forgery; this issue was tried before the
archbishop and Hilary, bishop of Chichester, at mid Lent 1150,
and Henry was acquitted of forgery. On this basis the manor was
formally restored to Henry by Nigel, bishop of Ely. 'But the
issue of right was still not settled, and after various démarches
Canterbury and Chichester, again appointed delegates, heard the
case once more, including Henry's claim for damages since possession had not been restored ... The monks appealed, and Eugenius III delegated the case to Gilbert [Foliot], instructing him

---

  [a]credidimus R.   [b]*om.* R.   [c]instituentibus R; institutionibus P.
[d]instituti R.

---

  [1]In this context, *pedagia* echoes the phrase *exactio pedaticorum* in C.
of Lateran I (1123), c. 14, which refers to a tax on travellers. This is
the earliest known use of *pedagia* in a British source (ex inf. R.E. Latham
— cf. p. 823 n. 4; Latham, *Revised Medieval Latin Word-List*, p. 338).
  [2]See below, and *Liber Eliensis,* ed. E.O. Blake, pp. 405-7.

to settle first the question of damages, then, if the monks
wished ... to settle the question of right. [Gilbert Foliot,
Ep.] 295 describes the pleading before Gilbert, which took
place at Northampton on 18 November (1152) and was carried on
in London on 7 December, but suspended by Henry's appeal. Henry
failed to prosecute his appeal, and on 28 September 1153 Pope
Anastasius IV settled the case in favour of the monks ...'[1]

> All the documents in the case are laid out in *Liber Elien-*
> *sis,* ed. E.O. Blake, pp. 344-62 (lib. iii, cc. 96-114),
> and discussed, ibid. pp. 405-7, with full evidence for
> the dates of the various stages. See also *GFL*, nos. 295-
> 6 and nn.

Liber Eliensis — report by Gilbert Foliot, bishop of Hereford

> *Liber Eliensis,* iii, c. 108, pp. 355-8 = *GFL*, no. 295,
> *ad fin.*; also *PUE* ii, no. 74; based on Ely, EDC/1 (dep.
> in Cambridge UL), fos. 166^V-169; Trinity Coll. Cam-
> bridge O. 2.1, fos. 159^V-161; Bodl. ms. Laud Misc. 647,
> fos. 96-7; BL Cotton Titus A. i, fos. 44-46^V.

(After pleading at Northampton, 18 Nov. 1152.) Unde ne obscuri-
tatem veritas pateretur et iustitiam H(enrici), si qua erat,
sententia preceps obrueret, diem sibi octavas beati Andree
Lundonie, quo dompni legati et suffraganeorum suorum futurus
erat conventus, grave sustinentibus monachis constituimus. Ipso
vero die Lundonie sedentes adhibito nobis domino episcopo Lundoniensi nostri copiam fecimus et, quia Henricus eorum, quos
premiserat, neminem exhibebat, per dompnum Lundoniensem episcopum et per personas alias a domino legato, quid super
sepedicta restitutione fateretur, inquisivimus. Qui negotii
penes se gesti non immemor Henrico restitutionem quam dicebat
se nunquam fecisse respondit. Deficiente itaque circa hunc
articulum Henrico, monachos a sepedicta quinquaginta librarum
petitione absolvimus, quas post factam Henrico restitutionem

---

[1]*GFL*, p. 358 (note to no. 295).

sibi non fuisse ablatas H(enrici) dictis et ratione cognovimus.
Monachi[s] vero de petitione reliqui, centum scilicet librarum,[1]
sibi sententiam dici postulantibus, cum ad pronuntiandum quod
sentiebamus operam sapientum consilio preberemus, H(enricus)
non expectans sententiam, ad audientiam vestram diem kalendas
Augusti [1 Aug. 1153] nominans appellavit. Monachi vero se in
longum protrahi attendentes, audientiam vestram ad 'Quasimodo
geniti' [26 April, 1153] appellantes, iniuncte nobis imposuere ...[a]

152

c.DECEMBER 1154. ROYAL CHARTER OF LIBERTIES

The same mss. which contain Stephen's first charter also contain the only surviving text of a similarly brief, and quite
general, confirmation of liberties which may be presumed to have
been issued about the time of Henry II's coronation, 19 December 1154.[2] It survives in the fragmentary BL ms. Harl. 458,
fo. 3[v] (13th cent.: see p. 762; French translation on fo. 4[v])
(H): and in BL ms. Cotton Claudius D. ii, fo. 73[v] (C), whence
Sp. ii.51; W. i.426; *Statutes of the Realm*, i, Charters of
Liberties, p. 4; W. Stubbs, *Select Charters* (9th edn., 1913),
p. 158; etc. For comment, see Stubbs, pp. 157-8. We print the
text of H, with C's variants noted. See p. 762: C's text seems
to have been improved to conform with later tastes.

Henricus[b] rex Angl(orum),[c] dux Norm'[d] et Aquit' et comes Andeg'[d]
omnibus comitibus, baronibus, et fidelibus suis Francis et
Anglicis salutem. Sciatis me ad honorem Dei et sancte ecclesie

---

[a]*The rest of the sentence is missing in the mss.*   [b]C *adds* Dei gratia.
[c]Anglorum C.   [d]Normannie ... Andegavie C; H *om. first* et.

[1]See ibid., p. 361, n. 2.
[2]See Eyton, pp. 1-2. Henry landed on 8 December and held court at Winchester; then passed on to Westminster for the coronation on the 19th, and
spent Christmas at Bermondsey. He was back in London-Westminster in late
March (Eyton, pp. 6 ff.), but this charter reads like a preliminary announcement of his well-known intention to restore the status quo of his grandfather's time.

et pro comuni emendatione totius regni mei, concessisse,[a] red-
didisse et presenti·carta mea confirmasse Deo et sancte ecclesie et omnibus comitibus,[a] baronibus et[b] hominibus meis omnes
concessiones et donaciones et libertates et liberas consuetudines quas rex H(enricus)[c] avus meus eis dedit et concessit.
Similiter etiam omnes malas consuetudines quas ipse delevit et
remisit, ego remitto et deleri precipio et[d] concedo pro me et
heredibus meis. Quare volo et firmiter precipio quod sancta
ecclesia et omnes comites et barones et homines mei,[e] omnes
illas consuetudines et donationes et libertates et liberas consuetudines habeant et teneant, libere et quiete, bene et in
pace et integre, de me et heredibus meis, ipsi[f] et heredes
sui,[g] adeo integre[h] et quiete et plenarie in omnibus sicut rex
H(enricus)[i] avus meus eis dedit et concessit et carta sua confirmavit. Teste Ricardo de Lucy apud Westm(onasterium).

153

1156. COUNCIL OF LONDON

This council is known to us only from records of two or three
cases[1] which were discussed at it: the case between William de

---

[a] C *adds* et.   [b] C *adds* omnibus.   [c] Henricus C.   [d] C *om.* precipio et.
[e] omnes mei homines C.   [f] sibi C.   [g] heredibus suis C.   [h] libere C.
[i] Henricus C.

---

[1] It is possible that the case of Osbert, archdeacon of Richmond, accused
of poisoning William FitzHerbert, archbishop of York, in 1154, came before
this council: at some date in 1156 it was tried before a panel of bishops,
and Osbert was ordered to establish his innocence by compurgation. Instead
he appealed to the pope, and John of Salisbury, writing for Archbishop
Theobald, spoke of consideration of the case in the following terms: 'Cum
ergo, intervenientibus multis dilationibus, quaestio ex necessitate protracta esset, et actor, S(imphorianus) scilicet, secundum subtilitatem
legum et canonum accusationem non posset implere, inspectis sacris canonibus, de consilio venerabilium fratrum nostrorum Ric(ardi) Lond(oniensis),
Hi(larii) Cicestr(ensis), Iocel(ini) Sar(esberiensis), Rodb(erti) Exon(iensis) episcoporum et aliorum sapientum qui aderant, quia verbum istud per
totam insulam divulgabatur, iam dicto archidiacono purgationem indiximus
trium manu archidiaconorum, adhibitis secum aliis quattuor diaconis, diem
praestandae purgationis praefinientes ...'. But as the day approached the
archdeacon appealed to the pope (JS, *Letters*, i, no. 16; cf. ibid., Appendix III; *GFL*, no. 127).

Turba, bishop of Norwich, and Walkelin, archdeacon of Suffolk,
which is the theme of two of John of Salisbury's letters; and
the privileges of St. Albans abbey against the bishop of Lincoln, as appears from a brief reference in the long account of
the issue in Matthew Paris's *Gesta abbatum s. Albani.*

The first case is only known to us from John's letters to
the pope, the first in the name of Archbishop Theobald, the
second on his own account; in spite of the archdeacon's knavery,
entertainingly described by John, he remained in office for
about thirty years longer.[1]

The second case was a part of one of the numerous disputes
between a bishop and a great Benedictine abbey as to the extent
and nature of its exemption from episcopal control. St. Albans'
rights had a slight basis in earlier history, but they developed
essentially as a result of two circumstances: the close bond
between Abbot Paul (1077-93) and his uncle, Archbishop Lanfranc,
which established a special relationship with the archbishop;
and the devotion of Pope Adrian IV (1154-9) to the saint and
the abbey under whose shadow he had been born.[2] Such was
Adrian's devotion that he seems to have chosen his name as pope
in honour of Adrian I (772-95), of whom St. Albans tradition
asserted that he had 'canonized' the saint and given some
privileges to his abbey when visited by the founder, King Offa.
Of the twelve bulls granted by Adrian IV to Abbot Robert de
Gorron (1151-66), only two are mentioned in this passage, that
promulgating the cult of St. Alban, and that exempting the
abbey's *parochia* from the Pentecostal procession to Lincoln
cathedral.[3] These were but limbs of the main issue, begun by

---

[1] On Walkelin, see Le Neve, ii.67; JS, *Letters,* i.22 n. 'He had been a
clerk of Bishop Everard, and occurs as archdeacon from 1143 till 1185 x 6.'
On Bishop William de Turba (1146/7-1174), see Le Neve, ii.56; Knowles, *EC*,
pp. 31-3, etc.

[2] See J. Sayers, 'Papal privileges for St. Albans Abbey and its Dependen-
cies', *The Study of Med. Records,* ed. D.A. Bullough and R.L. Storey (Oxford,
1971), pp. 58 ff.; R.L. Poole, *Studies in Chronology and History* (Oxford,
1934), pp. 291 ff. Adrian's father appears to have been a tenant of the
abbey who became a monk there late in life. See note in JS, *Letters,* ii,
pp. 10-11 n.

[3] *PUE* iii, nos. 100 (and ff.), 118. On the bulls for St. Albans, see J.
Sayers, art. cit., pp. 58 ff., esp. 59-60 and 60 n. 1; and on the general
context, Knowles, *MO*, pp. 582, 587 ff., and in *Downside Review*, l (1932),

the grant of the bull *Incomprehensibilis* of 5 February 1156, and continued by *Religiosam vitam* of 14 May 1157, which provided the foundation for the abbey's exemption. The bishop did not surrender without an argument, but the dispute was finally settled before a gathering of king and clergy in March 1163.[1] The extract below establishes the date for the council: after the end of May but well before 28 October.[2]

I. *John of Salisbury, Letters, nos. 14, 15*

> JS, *Letters*, ed. W.J. Millor, H.E. Butler, and C.N.L. Brooke, i, nos. 14-15 (text established by Millor and R.A.B. Mynors from Paris, BN ms. lat. 8625, fos. 30, 35; for no. 14 collated with Cambridge, UL ms. Ii. 2. 31, fo. 121[v]: variants not noted).

(*Ep. 14: Archbishop Theobald to Pope Adrian IV*)
Caritatis fraterne compassio nos admonet pro venerabili fratre nostro Willelmo Norwic(ensi) episcopo vestre maiestati suppli-care, ut vexationibus, quas ei Walchelinus archidiaconus inces-santer continuat, finem debitum inponi precipiatis. Quod quam necesse sit, vestre sinceritati innotescere procuravimus iniqui-tatis odio et abominatione scandali[3] potius quam aliquo perso-narum intuitu. Factum est siquidem Lond(onie) nuper cum conven-tum celebraremus, exigentibus quibusdam necessitatibus. Iam dictus episcopus venerabilem fratrem nostrum Lond(oniensem) episcopum, cui videlicet et Wigorn(ensi) episcopo cognitionem accusationis, qua Walchel(inus) inpetitur, delegastis, misera-bili admodum supplicatione convenit, ut saltem ea die, que ei tunc tertia fuerat peremptoria constituta, post multas ei mul-torum bonorum virorum vexationes eius admitteret probationes,

---

213-18. There is a passing mention of the return of the abbot of St. Albans from the Curia in the spring of 1156 in the chronicle of Vézelay (iii.1563, *Monumenta Vizeliacensia*, ed. R.B.C. Huygens, Turnhout, 1976, p. 506). He was at Vézelay on 15 Apr.

[1]J. Sayers, art. cit., p. 64; *Reg. Lincoln*, i, no. 104 (8 Mar. 1163); *Gesta abbatum S. Albani*, i.150-7; cf. Eyton, pp. 59-60.
[2]Cf. R.L. Poole, *Studies*, pp. 271-2; JS, *Letters*, i.22 and n.
[3]Cf. Ps. 118, 163.

quod iam dicto archidiacono iuxta mandati vestri formam ablata restituisset vel iustitiam exhibuisset,[1] nisi in omnibus per ipsum Walchel(inum) stetisset. Produxitque in medium copiam virorum religiosorum, abbatum, archidiaconorum, priorum et clericorum, eorum testimonio quod allegaverat probaturus. Processerunt et alii quamplures illese opinionis viri, qui amore iustitie et ad confusionem iniquitatis dicebant se paratos esse probare, quod sepe dictum archidiaconum audierant offerentem episcopo remissionem omnium restitutionum quas reposcebat, et insuper de propria lx marcas argenti, ea conditione, ut ei absolutionem criminum suorum idem episcopus impetraret, et episcopum repudiasse, partim quia non poterat, partim ne videri posset tantorum criminum redemptionem recepisse. In quibus, cum universi tam clerici quam laici supra modum scandalizarentur, dissimulare non potuit nec voluit dominus Lond(oniensis) predictas probationes tunc tertio productas fuisse, sed Walchel(inum) nulla trium citationum peremptoriarum apparuisse, et adiecit, quod sine Wigorn(ensi) episcopo, cui condelegata erat cause congnitio et non apparebat die condicto, nichil discernere poterat vel debebat. Sit itaque vestre discretionis, pater, si placet, sepius dicti archidiaconi subterfugiis, in quibus confidit, obviare, et vexationibus tam diu afflicti episcopi pacis remedio subvenire.

(*Ep. 15: John of Salisbury to Pope Adrian IV*)
Inmoderatus amor tantam michi dedit audaciam ut sollicitare presumam pro meis et amicorum meorum necessitatibus, cum sim pulvis et cinis,[2] apostolicam maiestatem. Verum pro his fiducialius supplico quos vobis, pater amande, et sancte Rom(ane) ecclesie fideliores agnosco. Inter quos est venerabilis pater dominus.Norwic(ensis), qui sicut promptiori et pleniori devotione apostolatui vestro submittitur et in ecclesia Anglorum fructuosius famulatur, ita manifestis calumpniis sepius affligitur et indebitis vexationibus mandatorum vestrorum occasione prosternitur, sicut ex rescriptis episcoporum potestis percipere.

---

[1]Walkelin's plea was evidently the *exceptio spolii*.
[2]Gen. 18, 27.

Walchel(inus) archidiaconus comprehensus in operibus manuum suarum,[1] ut non modo mandatum vestrum sed iustitiam Dei evacuet, et sacrarum constitutionum laqueos et iudicum manus effugiat, religionem vestram circumvenire nititur sub pretextu non habite restitutionis, cum tamen per ipsum steterit, si quid ei deest, quominus eam habuerit. Taceo quod in redemptionem criminis multa promisit in contemptum sedis apostolice, ab ea reversus plura commisit. Ad iniuriam vestram venio: spurium quem ei revertenti a vobis focaria peperit, de sacratissimo nomine vestro appellari precepit Adrianum. Eandem reliquit pater gravidam, sed provida dispositione statutum est, ut si forte pepererit masculum, appellent Beneventum, quia illic peregrinatur pater, si feminam, dicatur Adriana. O verum Romani pontificis amicum! qui et in flagitiis ipsius habet memoriam, et de bonitate vestra, quam impune deludit, nequitie sue nomen imponit! Hic est, domine, hic est qui sanctum episcopum ea sola ratione persequitur, quia criminibus eius episcopus adversatur. Cum videatis iniquum, cuius crimina manifesta sunt precedentia ad iudicium, non ponetis cum eo malitie portionem,[2] licet ille vos, quantum in se est, infamie sue reddat participem. Cum enim, etsi non deiectus, a vobis redire debuerit vel correctus, facta sunt semper hominis illius novissima deteriora prioribus;[3] dicam, pater, dicam quod consona voce omnium fama concelebrat, 'qui hunc dimittit, iustitie inimicus est, et vitio consensus, iustitie, honestatis et continentie[a] profanator.' Wigorn(ensis) episcopus, cui commissa est causa eius, in executione mandati vestri piger est, et in proximo insulam egressurus. Placeat ergo vobis ei subrogare quemcumque volueritis in Anglia iustitie amatorem, ut causa episcopi quandoque debitum finem sortiatur.

---

[a] incontinentie *Paris ms.*

---

[1] Cf. Ps. 9, 17.
[2] Cf. Ps. 49 (50), 18-19; and for *crimina manifesta,* a generally accepted canonical principle, *Decretum* C. 2 q. 1 cc. 15-16, 21 and *dictum post* c. 20.
[3] Cf. Matt. 12, 45 (and Luc. 11, 26); II Pet. 2, 20; and cf. note to JS, *Letters,* i.25.

II. *Matthew Paris, Gesta Abbatum Sancti Albani*

> The text is from Matthew Paris's autograph, BL Cotton ms.
> Nero D. i, fo. 43; ed. W. Wats, pp. 72-3; also in H.T.
> Riley's edition of the *Gesta* (RS, 1867-9), i.129-31, from
> BL ms. Cotton Claud. E. iv, fo. 116^v. Paris's narrative
> was based on the work of Adam the Cellarer and the papal
> bulls; on it, see R. Vaughan, *Matthew Paris*, pp. 182-5.
> The extract starts immediately after the abbot's return
> from the papal Curia in May 1156.

Paucis itaque post hec evolutis diebus, congregantur apud
Lond(oniam) archiepiscopi, episcopi, abbates, multarumque ecclesiarum prelati cum comitibus et baronibus tocius regni, ut nego-
cia regni et ecclesie pertractarent, cum Theob(aldo) Cant(uariensi) archiepiscopo, apostolice sedis legato, eidem concilio
presidente. Episcopus vero Linc(olniensis) Robertus cognomento
de Querceto, id est de Chesnei, audiens Robertum abbatem cum
specialibus quibusdam et singularibus privilegiorum libertatibus a Roma redisse, noluit illuc venire, sed missis nunciis
suam allegavit impotenciam; timens ne in illo concilio privilegiis huius ecclesie ostensis et auditis, aut clericorum suorum
iram eis assensum prebendo incurreret, et sic libertati sue et
ecclesie sue derogaret, aut eis contradicendo domini pape
offensam subiret. Adest tamen Robertus abbas suis stipatis
amicis, qui quadam die episcopis congregatis litteras apostolicas porrexit, in quibus eisdem episcopis dominus papa precipie-
bat, quatinus festivitatem sancti Albani per singulas ecclesias
eorum devotissime celebrandam denunciarent. Hiis auditis, omnes
unanimiter apostolico precepto parere se velle cum summo honore
fatentur.

Hiis siquidem responsis abbas exhilaratus[a] alias litteras
domini pape de solempni processione clericorum et laicorum
Hertfordensis provincie, per singulos annos huic ecclesie ex-
hibendo, Lincolniensis clericis astantibus, perlegi fecit.

Quibus auditis indignati ipsum abbatem et capitulum suum ad

---

[a] exhileratus *ms. Nero D. i.*

audientiam apostolicam appellaverunt, prefigentes diem appellationi diem dominicam qua cantatur 'Gaudete in Domino' [16 Dec.,
1156], sumentes occasionem de hoc, quod dominus papa in eisdem
litteris interdicebat ne clerici vel laici inter Hertfordensem
provinciam constituti iteratam processionem ad Linc(olniensem)
civitatem facere a quolibet compellerentur.

   Robertus abbas domum revertitur, hec conventui nuncians.
Quo prosequi volente, venit Hugo Dunelm(ensis) episcopus,
utriusque ecclesie tunc fidelis amicus, partes suas interponens,
ut utraque ecclesia inter se amicabiliter componerent. Locus et
dies ab utraque ecclesia, fide interposita, constituitur, quo
res de reformacione pacis die apostolorum Simonis et Iude [28
Oct.] apud sanctum Neotum actitaretur. Adest episcopus
Linc(olniensis) R(obertus) cum Ricardo Lundon(iensi) et Gille-
berto Herefordensi (postea London(iensi))[a] cum copiosa clericorum multitudine. Adest et Robertus [abbas][b] cum suis. Illis
vero hac de re altercantibus, tandem dictis episcopis cum
episcopo Dun(elmensi) mediantibus, inter utramque ecclesiam
compositio formata est. Huius vero compositionis forma a
predicto episcopo G(illeberto) Herefordensi cognomento Folioth
dictata est; utriusque ecclesie sigillis concessa et confirmata est. Nam duobus ex fratribus nostris, cum medietate ciro-
graphi huius ecclesie sigillo sigillati Linc(olniensem) ecclesiam adeuntibus, medietatem alteram Linc(olniensis) ecclesie
sigillo signatam ab eis absque reclamacione vel more etiam
dispendio receperunt.

154

1159-60 AND JUNE-JULY 1160. THE PAPAL SCHISM AND THE COUNCIL
OF LONDON

On 7 September 1159 two elections took place in Rome; the two
popes-elect, Roland, formerly papal chancellor, and Octavian,
took the titles of Alexander III and Victor IV respectively.

---

[a]*interlin. ms.*   [b]*om. ms. Nero D. i; supplied in Claud. E. iv.*

The Emperor Frederick Barbarossa came swiftly to the support of
Victor, and in February 1160 at the Council of Pavia all those
who accepted Victor gathered and announced their decision:
Victor was recognized by most of the prelates of the Empire and
a number in north and central Italy. The kings of France and
England were pressed to follow suit, but they were at war, and
apparently took no decision till a peace treaty was made between them in May. 1160.[1] The first document printed below is
Henry II's writ of c.December 1159 intended to ensure that
neither pope was accepted in the province of Canterbury[2] until
he had himself come to a decision. In May 1160 King Louis VII
agreed to delay while Henry consulted the church of his kingdom.[3] The prelates of England were summoned to London in June
or early July[4] to formulate advice to the king as to which
pope he should recognize. The ensuing council is described by
Archbishop Theobald as the church of the English meeting at
the command of the king (no. II below). It was clearly more
than a provincial council, and though Theobald had held a legatine commission from Pope Adrian IV, and was to hold one again
from Alexander,[5] this could hardly be his authority for summoning

---

[1] These events are described in detail and the sources discussed by M.G.
Cheney, 'The recognition of Pope Alexander III ...', *EHR* lxxxiv (1969), 474-
97; the editors are much indebted to Mrs. Cheney for help in drafting this
section. Cf. also P. Classen, 'Das Konzil von Toulouse 1160: eine Fiktion',
Deutsches Archiv, xxix (1973), 220-3.

[2] Presumably similar writs were addressed to the other archbishops of
Henry's empire, or at least to the archbishop of York.

[3] Arnulf of Lisieux, *Letters,* ed. F. Barlow, no. 23; this and letters
24-5, 27-8, and the letters of John of Salisbury (below) and Gilbert Foliot
(no. 133) are the chief sources for the process by which the English Church
came to accept Alexander; Arnulf's *Letter* 28 is a formal statement of the
case for Alexander addressed to the English archbishops and bishops, evidently intended for the council of London, which Arnulf tells us in no. 27
he could not attend in person. For the dating of these letters, see Cheney,
loc. cit.; Barlow, locc. citt. and nn.

[4] F. Barlow in *EHR* li (1936), 264-8; cf. JS, *Letters,* i.263 n. The preparations for the council are described ibid. pp. 214-15 (no. 124). On the
Council of London see T.A. Reuter, 'The Papal Schism, the Empire and the
West, 1159-1169' (Oxford D.Phil. thesis, 1975), pp. 230-1. Reuter suggests
that the documents in BL ms. Cotton Otho C. xiv, fos. 90 ff. are 'traces of
the dossier of documents which lay before the council of London when it met
in June 1160 to consider the schism'. On these events see also L. Grill,
'Das Wirken des Abtes Aelred von Rievaulx für Papst Alexander III. bei
König Heinrich II. von England', *Cîteaux,* xviii (1967), 370-84.

[5] Cf. *GFL*, p. 506; C.R. Cheney, *Revue de Droit Canonique,* xxviii (1978),
90-2.

a council when he was not in a position formally to recognize
a pope whose legate he might be. The meeting at London was
followed by a meeting of Norman magnates, lay and clerical,
with the king at Neufmarché, and then towards the end of July
by a meeting of the kings of France and England at Beauvais,
at which they formally accepted the validity of Alexander's
election and received his legates. King Henry announced his
decision to Pope Alexander in a letter dated at Rouen, presumably on his return from Beauvais (no. III below). King Louis
seems to have been determined to act with King Henry, presumably in order to prevent the division of his kingdom between
two obediences; the decision of the Council of London was
therefore of much more than local importance.

The king's right to make the decision between the rival
popes on behalf of his subjects was asserted in the writ
addressed to Archbishop Theobald (no. I) and explicitly accepted
by Theobald,[1] as it had been by Anselm (Southern, *St. Anselm*,
p. 154). The Council of London therefore issued no public
announcement and did not even commit its decision to writing.
Messengers carried to the king a letter from the archbishop
which made it clear that only one course of action would be
acceptable, but neither the king nor the church was publicly
or finally committed until the declaration at Beauvais.

I. *Christmas 1159.*[2] *Writ of King Henry II on the papal schism*

Neither pope is to be recognized until the king has decided
between them.

> From Bodl. ms. Rawlinson Q. f. 8 (27836), fo. 11 (no. 6a),
> 12th cent. Printed by Saltman in *Theobald,* p. 543 and in
> *BIHR* xxii (1949), 154-5. For the ms., which was at Ely
> in the 14th cent., see Saltman in *BIHR* and A. Duggan,
> 'Manuscript Transmission of Letter Collections relating
> to the Becket Dispute' (London Ph.D., 1971), pp. 68-82,
> 442-56, A. Duggan (1980), pp. 38-46, 233-5).

---

[1] JS, *Letters,* i.190-2.
[2] Cf. Eyton, p. 49: Henry spent Christmas 1159 at Falaise, and in any event
a date a few months after the double election of Sept. 1159 is indicated.

Henricus rex Angl(orum) et dux Norm(annorum) et Aquit(anorum)
et comes Andegav(orum) Theobaldo Cantuar(iensi) archiepiscopo,
episcopis, abbatibus et toti clero sibi subiecto, salutem.
Sicut ad vestram potest pervenisse noticiam, cardi[fo. 11ᵛ]nales
sancte Romane ecclesie post obitum Adriani pape felicis memorie
inter se divisi duos, Roll(andum) scilicet cancellarium, et
Octovianum in summum pontificem elegerunt. Et quia similis
scissura fidei contraria tempore avi mei H(enrici) regis in
apostolica sede accidisse dinoscitur, et ipse sicut catholicus
princeps et sapiens neutri electo sine sano et salubri consilio
assensum prebere festinavit, mando vobis et precipio quatinus
neutriᵃ de supradictis electis assenciatis vel obediatis neque
occasione huius negotii sive appellacionis Angliam exeatis,
donec ex maturo sicut decet consilio divina disponente gratia
quid michi et vobis super hac re agendum sit certius intelliga-
mus et vobis notificemus. Erit igitur discretionis vestre et
studium ita iurisdictionem vestram moderare in iusticia omnibus
exhibenda sive conservanda ut nullus de vobis iuste conqueri
debeat neque detrimentum paciatur, ex hoc quod sibi non liceat
ad sedem apostolicam appellare. T(estibus) Phill(ippo) Baio-
c(ensi) et Rotroc(o) Ebroic(ensi) episcopis, apud Phalesiam.

II. *Archbishop Theobald's letter to King Henry II*

> JS, *Letters,* i, no. 125, from Paris, BN ms. lat. 8625,
> fo. 14; Cambridge UL ms. Ii. 2.31, fo. 123ᵛ.

In eo maxime viget et proficit gloria principis Christiani si
pium Deo a quo omnis principatus est impendit famulatum; eique
pacis, exultationis et glorie perpetuatur hereditas, qui procel-
las componit ecclesie laborantis et fideli et felici procurat
obsequio ut exultans sponsa cupitis sponsi queat emplexibus
inherere.[1] In se vero provocat omnipotentem manum altissimi qui
naufragium Christi pleno miserationis affectu non excipit, qui

---

ᵃnautri ms.

---

[1]Cf. Prov. 7, 18; Cant., *passim.*

ecclesie collisiones aut operatur aut negligit et abutens potestate concessa consensu fovet malitiam quam non reprimit aut
extinguit. Collisio siquidem populorum indubitata regnorum sub-
versio est et fomes scismatis est predampnati a Domino et iam
iam labentis indicium principatus. Speramus autem in patre
misericordiarum, auctore consolationum[1] quod thronus vester
benedictione perpetua solidabitur et quod filii vestri et filii
filiorum solium regni quod ab eo accepistis et salubri administratione disponitis feliciter hereditabunt, cum in subditis
vestris tantam ipso propitio invenerimus concordie[a] unitatem
ut fidem eorum in petra ecclesie solidatam esse fidelissimis
et manifestissimis constet indiciis. Cum enim ex mandato vestro
Anglorum convenisset ecclesia, proposita est in auribus sapientum questio super qua fidei vestre sinceritas, ut oportuit,[b]
optimates regni vestri dignata est consultare. Lecta sunt hinc
inde plurima quibus pars alterutra suam sententiam tueri
poterat vel errorem. Deinde in medium prolata est norma fidei,
regula gerendorum que in patrum sanctionibus invenitur,[2] ut sic
innotesceret universis utrius cause facies ei commodius posset
aptari; adeoque, propitiante patre misericordiarum,[3] processum
est ut ex assertionibus partium veritas eluceret cum et testes
ab insperato procedentes apud nos causam veritatis instruxerint
et nefanda scismatici opera preconante fama[4] publicarentur.
Itaque secundum ea que proposita sunt, non quidem iudicatum est
quia nec licuit, non statutum aliquid in preiudicium regie
maiestatis quia nec debuit, sed quod licuit, quod debuit, quod
iussio maiestatis vestre[c] exegit, consilium, Deo teste et iudice,
formatum est quod fidelis prudentia subditorum vero principi
dictare debuerat non rogata; illud quoque ut prima sicut iustum
est vobis gratia debeatur, et operis gloria consummati, prout
precepistis sine omni publicatione in libris conscientie

---

[a] concordie *Camb. ms.; om. Paris.*   [b] oportui *Paris.*   [c] vestre serenita-
tis *Camb. ms.*

---

[1] Cf. II Cor. 1, 3.
[2] See *Decretum,* D. 23 c. 1 (election decree of 1059) and D. 79, *passim.*
[3] See n. 1 above.
[4] Cf. Martianus Capella, *De nuptiis,* i.17 (63).

signari[1] fecimus, quos vobis a latoribus presentium magistro
Barth(olomeo) archidiacono et Willelmo de Ver capellano vestro[a]
iussimus aperiri.[2] Nam predictus archidiaconus scrutiniis et
deliberationibus interfuit universis et vota singulorum et
omnium exploravit nobiscum. Et que accipietis ab eo de nostro
pectore processisse non dubitetis. Eos vobis commendamus rogan-
tes attentius ut personas eorum, si placet, commendatas habeatis et nostras que in manibus eorum sunt petitiones benigne[b]
admittatis.

III. *Letter of Henry II announcing to Pope Alexander III his*
  recognition

> From Vienna, Österreichische Nationalbibliothek, ms.
> 629 (= cvp 629), fo. 51 (no. 68),[3] where it is copied
> from a transcript sent with a covering letter from the
> pope to Eberhard, archbishop of Salzburg (dated 20 Jan.
> 1161); printed from this ms. in S. Tengnagel, *Vetera*
> *Monumenta* (Ingolstadt, 1612), p. 411 (no. 58), and from
> Tengnagel in *HF* xv.762; hence also *PL* cc. 1383; Delisle,
> *Recueil*, i.248-9, no. 139.

Karissimo domino et patri suo A(lexandro) Dei gratia summo
pontifici, H(enricus) rex Anglie [*sic*] et dux Normannie et
Aquitanie et comes And(egavie), salutem et debitam in Christo
subiectionem. Novit satis vestra discretio quam fideles sancte
Romane ęcclesię antecessores nostri semper extiterunt, qui in
simili casu non nunquam probaverunt, cum in sancta ecclesia
peccatis exigentibus exorto scismate, katholicam secuti sunt
unitatem. Hanc ergo patrum meorum approbans et sequens

---

[a]nostro *Masson, fort. recte; Camb. om.* cap. vestro.   [b]benignus *Camb.*

---

[1]Cf. Apoc. 22, 10.
[2]'Bartholomew, later bishop of Exeter, and William de Vere, brother of
the first earl of Oxford, clerk of Archbishop Theobald, later a canon regular of St. Osyth, clerk and justice to Henry II, and bishop of Hereford,
1186-98' (JS, *Letters*, i.217 n.; cf. *Complete Peerage*, revised ed., x, Appendix J, pp. 114-15).
[3]The Admont letter collection, on which see G. Hödl in *Deutsches Archiv*,
xxv (1969), 347-470, esp. pp. 454-7; also ib. xxvi (1970), 150-99, esp. p.
196; cf. M.G. Cheney in *EHR* lxxxiv (1969), 482 n. 3.

devotionem, quia vestram electionem veritate credo subnixam,
vos in patrem et dominum, vos in summum pontificem et katholi-
cum, cum universis tam clero quam populo mee potestati a Deo
commissis in vestris legatis recepi sollempnitate debita et
veneratione. Vos igitur clementissime rogo, et cum omni humilitate obsecro, ut me in proprium et spiritalem filium recipiatis,
et in meis peticionibus me si vobis placet exaudiatis. Latorem
presentium fratrem R., in cuius ore mea negotia posui, plenius
vobis exprimenda, benigne suscipiatis, et his que ex parte mea
vobis dixerit assensum et effectum adhibeatis. Ego ad vestram
voluntatem sum paratus, et me et mea vobis expono, arbitrio
vestro penitus exponenda. Teste cancellario, apud Rotho(magum).

155

EARLY 1161. COUNCIL OF CANTERBURY

This council is only recorded in Gilbert Foliot's *Letter* 134,
in which he describes the election of Adam, prior of Bermondsey, as abbot of Evesham, in an ecclesiastical council at
Canterbury. It was evidently held at Canterbury owing to the
final illness of the archbishop, who died on 18 April 1161.
Gilbert was writing to the prior and convent of La Charité-sur-
Loire, the mother house of Bermondsey, to ask them to release
Adam; the election had already had the approval of the archbishop and the king. The *Ann. Bermondsey* (p. 441) date the
election 16 April;[1] but it is possible this refers to the completion of the process after the prior of La Charité had given
his consent.

Gilbert Foliot, Letters, no. 134

> *GFL*, no. 134 (ed. J.A. Giles, no. 254), from Bodl. ms.
> e Mus. 249 (27835), fos. 180[V]-181.

-----

[1]For the date, see *GFL*, pp. 178, 533; *Heads*, pp. 47, 115. Adam was a
monk of La Charité, prior of Bermondsey 1157-61 and abbot of Evesham 1161-
89, when he died. The date 16 Apr. depends on the *Ann. Bermondsey*, of evil
fame, but evidently based in the main on well-recorded annals for this
period (see *Heads*, pp. 6, 114); the year 1161 is confirmed by Evesham annals.

G(ilebertus) Dei gratia [Herefordensis]^a episcopus venerabili
fratri et amico priori Karitatis et toti conventui, salutem et
sincere dilectionis affectum.

Quanta fratres in Christo dilectissimi karitatis plenitudine
vos et vestram domum amplectamur, nec verba explicant nec operis
argumenta declarant. Si quid tamen vestrum est apud nos a nostra
id solicitudine non reputamus alienum - leta vestra lete suscipimus. Si quid quod absit secus accidit, non id vobis tantum
incumbit quod et nos non aliena mentis afflictione pariter
sustinemus. Vestre si quid vel eorum in quibus vos promoveri
certum est promotionis oportunitas, si quando nobis occurrit,
non eam negligere, non eam nos otiose preterire permittit illa
proculdubio qua vobis astringimur devotio karitatis. Unde cum
conventu fratrum et coepiscoporum nostrorum [fo. 181] necnon et
aliorum religiosorum virorum qui ad expedienda negotia ecclesiastica Cantuarie convenerant de electione abbatis Eveshamie
tractaretur, nostro quidem consilio licet alii quamplures
aliorsum tenderent ad hoc tandem omnium inclinata est voluntas,
ut specialem filium ecclesie vestre priorem Bermundesheye illi
quorum erat electio eligerent, alii vero quorum in hoc expecta-
batur assensus unanimiter assentirent. De quo licet morum
merita et honesta eius apud nos conversatio sancte et laudabiliter enuntiarent, in hoc non parum gavisi sumus nobis tam favorabiliter fuisse aplausum, quod de vestre scola discipline
prodeuntem tanti nominis discipulum^b pastoralis magisterio cul-
minis dignum diceremus. Iam vota nostra concurrunt: quod nos
probamus domnus noster rex Anglie approbat, domnus Cantuariensis
idem sua auctoritate confirmat. Iam ad vos omnium nostrum spectat intentio, ut supremam manum adhibeatis - huius enim operis
consummatio a vestra dependet sententia. Inde est quod dilecte
nobis fraternitati vestre pro desolata iamdiu ecclesia Eve-
shamis que suum expetit et expectat electum preces affectuose
porrigimus quatinus sue electioni vestrum prebentes assensum
quem sibi elegit pastorem concedatis et quod ad honorem Dei et
sancte utilitatem ecclesie pia devotione inchoavimus benigno
favore mancipetis effectui. Valete.

---

^aLondonien' *ms.* *(see* GFL, *p. 178 n. 3).*   ^bdiscipulii *ms.*

156

MAY 1162. COUNCIL AT WESTMINSTER FOR THE ELECTION OF THOMAS BECKET AS ARCHBISHOP OF CANTERBURY

The fullest account is still that in L.B. Radford, *Thomas of London before his consecration* (Cambridge, 1894), chap. viii.

Archbishop Theobald died 18 April 1161;[1] on 23 May 1162 the monks of Christ Church, Canterbury, agreed to the election of Thomas Becket, archdeacon of Canterbury and royal chancellor, as his successor, and a few days later a delegation from the chapter elected him in the presence of young Henry, the king's eldest surviving son, and of the bishops and other notables of the kingdom, in the monks' refectory in Westminster Abbey.[2] The formal procedure was identical with that followed for the election of Ralph and Theobald: election by the monks of Canterbury, or their representatives, followed by confirmation by the bishops and other magnates, of a candidate whom the king and most of the bishops had clearly already approved. The ground had evidently been carefully prepared, though all opposition had not been cleared out of the way; but in 1162, as in 1138, there was no sign of the conflict between chapter and bishops which had occurred in 1114 and 1123, and was a feature of all elections to Canterbury in the late twelfth century.

The only thing certain about Becket's appointment is that it came on royal initiative: Henry II wished to have his friend and chancellor as archbishop.[3] The reasons for the long delay and the attitude of many of those concerned are not so clear. William of Canterbury seems to say that the king did not make up his mind

---

[1] Le Neve, ii.4.

[2] Le Neve, ii.4 (by a slip giving the election as in the king's presence); cf. Radford, pp. 205 ff.; *MB* ii.366; iv.14-16 (Lives of Becket by Grim and Roger of Pontigny, *al.* the 'First Anonymous'), etc.; Diceto, i.306-7; Gervase, i.169-70. (We accept as probable the attribution of the first Anon. to Roger of Pontigny, doubted by Robertson, the editor of *MB*.)

[3] So e.g. the Lives by William of Canterbury, John of Salisbury, Grim, William FitzStephen, Herbert of Bosham, etc.: *MB* i.6-7; ii.305, 365-6; iii.35, 180-1; etc.

until some time after Theobald's death, Herbert of Bosham that
he kept his wishes secret for a while; Edward Grim and Roger of
Pontigny imply that some effort was needed to win the monks of
Canterbury to the election.[1] Since the tradition was for a monk,
or at least a regular, to be elected, one can readily under-
stand why there were doubts and also why the biographers writing
at or near Canterbury after the martyrdom hesitated to admit as
much. In any event it was not until the spring of 1162 that the
matter was settled: Henry told Becket of his plan; Thomas
resisted; Cardinal Henry of Pisa, one of the papal legates in
France at this period, urged him to accept,[2] and Becket gave
way. The king sent him to England to attend to other business
and with him sent the justiciar, Richard de Lucy, to see to the
election. Richard took three bishops, Exeter, Chichester, and
Rochester,[3] to Canterbury to discuss Becket's election with
them; and there on 23 May he was nominated. Later in the month
the meeting at Westminster was held in the young Prince Henry's
presence and his election formally made and confirmed.[4] On 2
June he was ordained priest by the bishop of Rochester, who
after some argument had allowed the claims of Henry of Blois
bishop of Winchester - precentor of the province acting for the
dean, the bishop of London, who had died on 4 May[5] - to consecrate Thomas; this ceremony the bishop of Winchester performed,
with numerous assistants, on 3 June.[6] Soon after, a party

---

[1] MB i.6; iii.180; ii.366; iv.16. The monks' opposition is also referred
to in the *Thómas Saga*, ed. E. Magnússon (RS, 1875-83), i.72-83, esp. 72-3,
perhaps based on the lost life by Robert of Cricklade (see E. Walberg, *La
tradition hagiographique de S. Thomas Becket* (Paris, 1929), pp. 24-33).

[2] So William of Canterbury, John of Salisbury, and Roger of Pontigny, *MB*
i.8; ii.305-6; iv.18; for another account of Becket's resistance, see Bosham,
MB iii.180 ff. Very different is the account in Gilbert Foliot's *Multiplicem*, *GFL*, no. 170, pp. 230-2, implying that Becket grasped at the archbishopric. On Henry of Pisa, see Tillmann, p. 53; Brixius, pp. 54-5, 108; Zenker,
pp. 96-101, esp. 101. A former Cistercian, he signed as cardinal from 1151
to 1166.

[3] Three bishops and Richard de Lucy, Grim *MB* ii.366; Guernes de Pont-
Saint-Maxence, 431-4, names the bishops and adds the abbot of Battle, Walter
de Lucy, Richard's brother; Roger of Pontigny gives only two bishops and
names Exeter and Chichester (*MB* iv.14, 16). John of Salisbury was also
present at the election (*Letters*, ii, no. 175).

[4] See p. 843 n. 2.   [5] Le Neve, i.2.

[6] Le Neve, ii.4; Diceto, i.307; Gervase, i.169-71; on the argument as to
who should consecrate him, see Bosham, *MB* iii.188.

consisting of Adam abbot of Evesham, John of Salisbury, and another clerk fetched the pallium on his behalf from the pope at Montpellier, and Becket received it on 10 August.[1]

Apart from Becket's own opposition and some resistance from the monks, the one discordant note in these proceedings which was recorded at the time was the opposition of Gilbert Foliot, then bishop of Hereford, soon to be translated to London. The gossip of the time was that Foliot wished to be archbishop himself; this he formally denied, and, however that may be, he did not carry his opposition at the time to the point of preventing a unanimous election.[2]

157

MAY 1163. PAPAL COUNCIL OF TOURS

What follows is based on R. Somerville, *Pope Alexander III and the Council of Tours (1163)* (Berkeley, Los Angeles, London, 1977). This includes a full treatment of the English evidence and involvement which makes only a brief summary necessary here; the attendance list is also edited and annotated by T. Reuter in *Annuarium Historiae Conciliorum*, viii (1976), 116-25. See also Foreville, *Latran*, pp. 118-20; Mansi, xxi.1167-88 (canons on coll. 1175-84); Hefele-Leclercq, V. ii.963-77.

At Montpellier in May 1162[3] and Tours in 1163 Alexander III held

---

[1] Le Neve, ii.4; C.C.J. Webb, *John of Salisbury* (London, 1932), pp. 104-5; Gervase, i.172; Diceto, i.307; Guernes, ed. Walberg, 596 ff.; William of Canterbury, FitzStephen, *MB* i.9; iii.36.

[2] See *GF*, pp. 149-51 and *GFL*, nos. 170, 220, for his denial. In no. 170, p. 231, however, Gilbert Foliot admits his opposition and claims that he suffered severely for it. It is also mentioned by William of Canterbury and Grim (who call him by anachronism bishop of London), FitzStephen, Roger of Pontigny (*MB* i.9; ii.367; iii.36; iv.17; etc.). In *GFL* no. 170, pp. 230-1, Gilbert gave a very foreshortened and partisan account of the election of Becket.

[3] It seems that no English bishops were present; Henry's dominions were represented by the bishops of Évreux and Bayeux (Somerville, p. 7). We are very grateful to Professor Somerville for lending us a copy of his book before publication; and also to Dr. T. Reuter for his help in this section: see now Reuter, art. cit.

councils whose prime purpose was evidently to assert his standing against the anti-pope. At Tours he was on the territory of
both his main supporters, Henry II of England and Louis VII of
France. Partly for this reason, the canons of Tours were quite
often copied in English mss., although neither the council nor
its canons were of comparable importance to those of the Third
Lateran of 1179.

Late in 1162 Alexander III sent the subdeacon Theoduinus to
invite the English prelates to the council; Henry II permitted
them to attend on condition that no new custom would be brought
into the kingdom, nor its dignity in any way reduced by any
action of the council.[1] The council opened on 19 May 1163. A
remarkable attendance list survives, and shows that both the
archbishops of Canterbury and York were present, with the bishops
of London, Ely, Salisbury, Norwich, Chichester, Rochester, Exeter
Coventry, Llandaff, and St. Asaph and the elect of Worcester; and
from the northern province, Durham. In addition, the bishop of
St. Davids was probably present.[2] Winchester, Lincoln, and Bath
were excused on the ground of illness.[3] The Scottish bishop of
Dunkeld was also present, but seated (it seems) well away from
the archbishop of York to avoid awkward questions about jurisdiction. The Norman verse chronicler Étienne de Rouen in his
Draco normannicus suggests that the issue of Canterbury and
York was a point of major discussion;[4] this is doubtless exaggerated, but evidently there was a wrangle about seating and

---

[1]Somerville, pp. 8 ff., 82; JL 10834 = *MB Epp.* 21; Diceto, i.310; cf.
Tillmann, pp. 54-5; Cheney, *BL*, p. 92, citing Rymer, *Foedera,* I, i (1816), 44.
[2]Somerville, pp. 27-9; Reuter, art. cit., pp. 122-5; from BL ms. Cotton
Vitell. A. xvii, fo. 16ᵛ. Although known to W. Holtzmann and Z.N. Brooke, the
list was first thoroughly investigated, and edited, by Professor Somerville
and Dr. Reuter. For St. Davids, see Reuter, p. 120 n. 27; Somerville, pp. 24-
5, 89; Giraldus, *Opera,* iii.155. On English participation see Herbert of
Bosham, *MB* iii.254-5; for abbots, below, and p. 847 n. 1. Doubtless there
were more abbots and priors present, perhaps including some of those who
received privileges at this time (see Somerville, pp. 29-31).
[3]*Diceto,* i.310.
[4]*Draco normannicus* in *Chrons. Stephen etc.*, ii.742-52. For Canterbury and
York see also the brief note in the 12th-cent. list of papal councils in an
English ms., BL Cotton Faust. A. viii, fo. 84ᵛ; 'in ea synodo Thomas Cantuar'
archiepiscopus sedit ad dexteram, Rogerus Eborac' ad sinistram' - but the
author may have taken this from an English council. There is also a passing
reference in the annals of Horsham, Cambridge, Trinity Coll. R. 14. 9, fo. 9ᵛ.

a complaint from the archbishop of York; to this the pope returned the diplomatic answer that Tours cathedral was not so
designed as to allow for an organized arrangement of the participants. In a similar way Matthew Paris tells us that the abbots
of St. Albans and Bury were prevented from effectively disputing
their precedence.[1] Perhaps some diplomatic confusion was arranged by a papal Curia in no position to take a strong line
with the participants. There was evidently a discussion of the
question whether Gilbert Foliot should renew his profession on
translation from Hereford to London;[2] an attempt to secure the
canonisation of Anselm of Canterbury was referred to a meeting
of English bishops.[3] The archbishop of Canterbury and, it would
seem, a number of other participants, used the occasion to win
confirmation of privileges from the pope.[4]

The theologian John of Cornwall, who has left us an account
of the Christological debate which was inspired by discussion
at Tours, was presumably of English origin. His later career was
in the service of Walter of Coutances, also Cornish by origin,
archbishop of Rouen.[5] But it is far from clear that he was himself present at Tours.

The canons occur among English mss. in Newburgh and in canon
law mss., mostly decretal collections; they were frequently
either adjacent to or intermingled with canons of the Council of
Westminster of 1175.[6]

---

[1] *Gesta abbatum S. Albani*, ed. H.T. Riley, i (RS, 1867), pp. 177-8.
[2] Somerville, pp. 59, 99; cf. *GF*, p. 148 and n. 2.
[3] *MB Epp.* 25; R.W. Southern, *St. Anselm and his Biographer*, pp. 339-40;
below, p. 850.
[4] Somerville, p. 58; Bosham, *MB* iii.255. For a list of privileges granted
at or soon after the council, see Somerville, pp. 30-1.
[5] John of Cornwall, *Eulogium*, ed. N.M. Häring, in *Mediaeval Studies*, xiii
(1951), 253-300, esp. 257; Somerville, pp. 60-1. On John's career see Le
Neve, ii.106; and in general, E. Rathbone, in *Recherches de théologie anc.
et méd.*, xvii (1950), 46-60.
[6] See p. 974; Brooke in *Traditio*, xiii (1957), 471-80 (the table on p.
480 was corrected by S. Kuttner in *Traditio*, xvii (1961), 536-7). Sets of
canons occur in Newburgh, i.136-7 and these collections: *Belverensis*, Bodl.
ms. e Mus. 249, fos. 121-2; *1 Dunelmensis*, Durham Cathedral ms. C. III.1,
fo. 14^{r-v}; *Fontanensis*, Bodl. ms. Laud Misc. 527, fos. 43^{v}-44; *Bridlington-
ensis*, ms. Bodl. 357, fos. 132-133^{v}; *Claudiana*, BL ms. Cotton Claud. A. iv,
fo. 195^{r-v}; Durham Cathedral ms. B. IV. 17, fos. 172^{v}-173; and stray canons
occur elsewhere. There are also some Tours canons in the Collections *Tanner,
Sangermanensis* and *Abrincensis I* (see pp. 795-6, 798).

158

1 OCTOBER 1163.[1] ROYAL COUNCIL OF WESTMINSTER

Already in 1162 Henry II began to have doubts about Becket's
actions, and after the king's return to England at the turn of
the year occasions of friction began to multiply. Different
points are emphasized by different biographers and chroniclers;
but it is clear that personal misunderstanding was mingled with
disputes between Becket and royal tenants-in-chief,[2] with
sheriffs and other royal officials,[3] and with royal exaspera-
tion on some notorious cases of criminous clerks (as Henry
thought) inadequately punished;[4] also that an obscure phase in
the old primacy controversy between Becket and Roger of Pont
l'Évêque, archbishop of York, aggravated a difficult situation.
According to the anonymous author of the *Summa causae inter
regem et Thomam,*[5] the royal Council at Westminster which opened
on 1 October (see below) was summoned solely to establish the
archbishop of Canterbury as primate of all England; doubtless
this is a partisan statement from the Canterbury side, and very
likely an oversimplification. In any case the king took the
opportunity to make a formal protest against the activities of
archdeacons in church courts, and the activity of felonous
clerks.[6] He urged Becket to state formally his acceptance of a
royal statement of customs which the archbishop refused to do,
according to Roger of Pontigny,[7] except *salvo ordine suo*; and

---

[1]This was evidently the opening date, and is only specified in the *Summa
causae, MB* iv.201. Henry II's attitude to his relations with the Church in
1162 may be gauged by the reissue of the canons of Lillebonne of 1080 in a
Norman council in 1162: these included a close scrutiny of episcopal jurisdiction (M. Brett in *JEH* xxvi (1975), 307; P. Chaplais in *Journ. Soc. of
Archivists,* iv (1970-3), 627-32).

[2]For his disputes with the earl of Clare (Hertford) and William of Eynsford, see FitzStephen (*MB* iii.43) and Diceto, i.311-12. Cf. Bosham (*MB*
iii.251); Gervase, i.174.

[3]On payments to sheriffs, see Grim and Pontigny, *MB* ii.373-4; iv.23-4.

[4]See below, pp. 857-62; the *cause celèbre* was that of Philip de Broi,
canon of Bedford (see p. 860 n.; *MB* ii.374-5; iii.45; iv.24-5).

[5]An early account from the archbishop's point of view, but preserved in
Gilbert Foliot's archives (see *GFL*, pp. xxxix, 1 (n. 7), lii, 3), printed
in *MB* iv.201 ff. On the primacy dispute in the 1160s, see esp. A. Heslin
(Mrs. Duggan), in *Studies in Church History*, ii (1965), 165-78.

[6]So especially *Summa causae, MB* iv.201-2.

[7]*MB* iv.26-7; cf. ibid. pp. 202-4 (*Summa causae*).

the account in the 'Anonymous of Lambeth', printed below, makes
this the first occasion on which Becket raised his celebrated
defence against trial of clerical offenders in secular as well
as ecclesiastical courts, 'Non iudicabit Deus bis in idipsum'.
No conclusion was reached at Westminster, nor at a meeting of
king and archbishop at Northampton soon after,[1] and the next
few weeks were filled with diplomatic activity. It is probably
true, as Roger of Pontigny asserts, that the king made various
efforts to detach the bishops from the archbishop, but the
earliest surviving account of Clarendon (see p. 853), in Gilbert
Foliot's letter *Multiplicem*,[2] seems conclusive that these efforts
were not wholly successful. An embassy was sent to the pope,
and from the pope and cardinals came letters recommending moderate and flexible behaviour to the archbishop - or so Roger of
Pontigny asserts,[3] for they do not survive; he tells us that
they were brought by Philip, the energetic Cistercian abbot of
l'Aumône, who came with the new bishop of Hereford, Robert of
Melun, and the count of Vendôme, to enforce this attitude on
him. With them he went to Oxford or Woodstock,[4] where Becket
and the king had an inconclusive discussion, and Henry determined to summon the Council of Clarendon.[5]

It is a curious fact that, although this council was apparently held at the opening of October, and ended, if Herbert of
Bosham's account is correct, in the king's rapid departure on
the second day, on Sunday 13 October the king and the archbishop
presided over the translation of the relics of St. Edward the
Confessor in Westminster Abbey, in the presence of fourteen
bishops, five abbots (including Laurence of Westminster), and
a number of secular notables.[6] It would be natural to think that

---

[1]Pontigny, *MB* iv.27; for the following events he remains the fullest witness. His account of Henry's intrigues with the bishops is ibid. iv.30.

[2]*GFL*, no. 170, pp. 233-4.

[3]*MB* iv.31. On Philip, abbot of l'Aumône, see Tillmann, pp. 53-5; Knowles,
EC, pp. 59-60; JS, *Letters*, i.262 n.

[4]See *GFL*, p. 233 n. 1: Gilbert Foliot (ibid.) and Bosham (*MB* iii.277)
place it in Oxford, Guernes (910), Grim and Pontigny (*MB* ii.373; iv.32) in
Woodstock. They are only 8 miles apart.

[5]Pontigny, *MB* iv.33.

[6]The evidence for this, and a full discussion of the problem of the date,
are laid out by F. Barlow in *Edward the Confessor* (London, 1970), pp. 325-7
(cf. pp. 282-4). The translation is mentioned by Herbert of Bosham (*MB*

the council and the translation were connected, and it is possible that our only authority, the *Summa causae*, has misdated
the council: that it really began on or soon after 13 October.
But it is also possible that the translation had been planned
as the dénouement to the council, and that, in fact, king and
archbishop met again on the thirteenth for the event. Of
Becket's biographers, only Herbert of Bosham mentions the translation, and he not in the context of this council.[1] This makes
it seem slightly more probable that the translation was not
intimately linked to the two[2] days of meetings described by the
biographers.

It is possible, though far from certain, that a provincial
council was held about this time to consider and complete the
process for the canonization of St. Anselm.[3]

The best account of the council of Westminster is given
below, from the early though anonymous Life of Becket known as
the 'Anonymous of Lambeth', only known from Lambeth Palace
Library ms. 135, fos. 6^v-7; from this it was printed by J.A.
Giles, *Vita S. Thomae*, ii (London-Oxford, 1846), pp. 88-9, and
by Robertson in *MB* iv.95-7.

---

iii.261), but clearly not in its precise chronological setting. This is given
by Richard of Cirencester, *Speculum Historiale*, ed. J.E.B. Mayor (RS, 1863-
9), ii.326-7, who dates it Sunday, 13 Oct. 1163: a late source, but the
dating clause is exceptionally convincing, as Barlow points out, since 13
Oct. was a Sunday in 1163, and was also the date remembered in later times
for the translation of St. Edward; the list of those present, including the
bishop of Lisieux, adds conviction; and there is some confirmation in
Coventry, i.185; cf. Paris, *Ch. Maj.* ii.221. While the bishops were in London, three of them were involved in a usurious bond of William Cade's, evidently for a loan made to expedite the business of the Michaelmas audit at
the Exchequer (H. Jenkinson in *Essays in History presented to R.L. Poole*,
Oxford, 1927, pp. 196 ff., 208).

[1]*MB* iii.261.
[2]Herbert's account seems to make clear that he thought the council effectively lasted one day, and the king left early on the next (*MB* iii.266-75,
esp. 274-5); and he was present (p. 272: 'audivimus ... Hic est discipulus
qui ... audivit et scripsit hec'). But he was writing more than twenty years
later and is not always reliable in chronology (see below, p. 895 n. 3).
[3]See R.W. Southern, *St. Anselm and his Biographer* (Cambridge, 1963), pp.
339-40: from Tours on 9 June the pope had remitted the matter to a provincial
council, and there are some indications that this may have acted, but no
direct evidence (*MB Epp.*, 23; above, p. 847).

The Anonymous of Lambeth

Non multo post autem episcoporum, abbatum et procerum cetum
Londonie colligi contigit, ob negotia regia, pacisque regni
firmamentum. Inter ceteras vero que proposite sunt illic queri-
monias, accusati sunt archidiaconi super subditos non prela-
cionis tenere modestiam sed exercere tirannidem, calumniis
fatigare laicos et indebitis exactionibus clericos. De cleri
quoque numero producti sunt quidam variis flagiciorum crimi-
nationibus impetiti. Tales enim precipue dicebantur regni turbare pacem, novisque facinorum inmanitatibus debachare,
securitate per ordinis privilegium evadendi. Correctionem igitur horum rex instanter ab episcopis flagitabat. Amplius autem
institit, ut in clericos publicorum criminum reos de ipsorum
consilio sibi liceret, quod avitis diebus factum sua curia
recolebat; tales enim deprehensos et convictos aut confessos,
mox degradari, sicque penis publicis, sicut et laicos subdi
tunc usurpatum est. Hoc idem sibi licere cum instantius rex
postularet per episcopos decerni, substiterunt quidem ipsi diutius caventes admittere, quod legi divine videbatur obviare.
Dicit enim Naum propheta: 'Non iudicabit Deus bis in id ipsum'.[1]
Contra Deum itaque bis iudicandos censuisse videri poterant, si
post degradationem in convictis penam mortis aut mutilationis
infligi consensissent. Cavit hoc prudentissimus et [ms., fo. 7]
rectissimus iudicum rex Salomon. Cum enim Abyathar sacerdos
reus mortis appareret sicut et Ioab, quia contra Salomonem
declinassent post Adoniam fratrem eius ut rex fieret, non tamen
sicut Ioab sic et Abyathar Salomon morte punivit, sed a sacer-
docio tantum amovit dicens: 'Vade in Anathot, agrum tuum: es
quidem vir mortis, sed hodie te non interficiam, quia portasti
archam Domini coram patre meo David.'[2] Talibus itaque cum
archiepiscopo moti pontifices, ad regis arbitrium legem ponere
dubitarunt, presertim ne trahi posset in preiudicium et calumniam innocentium, ut vel ad purgationem urgerentur vel nocen-
tium sorti subderentur. Hinc itaque contencionis exordium, hinc
enim arbitratus rex archiepiscopum cum episcopis in insidiis

---

[1] See above, and below, p. 857 and n. 4.
[2] III Reg. 2, 26.

sibi sedere, regiarumque dignitatibus consuetudinum velle contraire, primum ira non parum excanduit, et deinde promissionem
de servandis illis extorquere prosiliit. Illi vero, tractatu
seorsum diutius habito, volentes regis iram sedare, cautam
putaverunt procurasse responsionem, dum ordine suo salvo peti-
cionem fieri concesserunt. Additionem autem, quam providerant
ad cautelam, pars regis interpretata est ad captionem, et super
ea detrahenda diutius certatum est, sed episcopis unanimiter
subsistentibus tunc optentum non est. Unde soluto conventu terri-
biliter efferatus rex et minax abscedens, exinde pontificalium
concussionibus rerum officiales suos gravius insistere iussit. ...

159

*c.*25-30 JANUARY 1164. ROYAL COUNCIL OF CLARENDON

I. *The council*

The failure of the Council of Westminster and the subsequent
negotiations evidently led Henry II to try to force the archbishop to accept a written statement of essential customs in
the areas of dispute. To this end a very carefully drafted set
of constitutions was prepared - by Richard de Lucy and Jocelin
de Bailleul, according to Becket's own account, by John of Oxford, if an early Canterbury ms. is to be believed.[1] William of
Canterbury and Bosham, indeed, speak as if the Constitutions
were drawn up during the council, but they are so carefully
composed that we may be sure they were in draft at least before the council met, and version II below perhaps represents
such a draft of the early clauses.

Gervase gives the date of the council as 13 January, St.
Hilary's day; but Diceto's date, 25 January, is more probable,

---

[1] For authorship, see *MB Epp.* 195-6; BL ms. Cotton Claud. B. ii, fo. 26
(below, p. 877 n. a) - the secular magnates must have had the help of some
of the abler clerks. Bosham ascribes them to Henry's counsellors (below,
pp. 885-6) and describes the tripartite chirograph which was the final
form of the Constitutions: one part was given to the archbishop of Canterbury, one to York, the third kept in the royal archives. For the next
sentence see *MB* i.18; iii.279 (= below, pp. 885-6).

since the Constitutions themselves are dated 30 January:[1] evidently they were passed after some days of discussion, but
there is no indication in the sources of proceedings as long as
at Northampton in October. Indeed, the sources are not helpful
on the details of the council and its discussions. The earliest,
Gilbert Foliot, tells us in his letter *Multiplicem*[2] that all the
bishops - and he names ten, all the bishops of the province
save Norwich who can have been present[3] - stood firm for three
days against the king's demand for an 'absoluta promissio' to
observe the royal customs. Then, Gilbert tells us, 'terga dedit
dux militie'; to his colleagues' stupefaction, after a brief
exit, Thomas returned and announced that it was God's will that
he should perjure himself. Several of the biographers, on the
other hand, assert that it was Thomas who held firm, and William of Canterbury, Edward Grim, Guernes and Roger of Pontigny
name the bishops of Salisbury and Norwich, fearful for royal
disfavour, among those who, with the lay lords, led by the
earls of Cornwall and Leicester, urged submission.[4] It is

---

[1] Below, p. 883; Gervase, i.176; Diceto, i.312 (and p. 313 on the Constitutions). The document is dated the 4th day before Candlemas, 2 Feb.; that
is, presumably, equivalent to the 3rd before the kalends of February, i.e.
30 Jan., but 29 Jan. may be intended. For indications of chronology in
Herbert of Bosham, see below p. 886 and n. 2. On Clarendon see also Hoveden,
i.221-2.

[2] *GFL*, no. 170, pp. 233-4.

[3] With minor differences, in the same order as in the Constitutions (pp.
877-8): this is roughly in order of seating (i.e. with London and Winchester
first, then in order of seniority of consecration), save that Gilbert puts
himself last. But both lists give Lincoln (1148) and Chichester (1147) before Salisbury (1142), and it may be that Gilbert had before him, or in his
mind, a copy of the Constitutions. The bishop of Norwich is in the list in
the Constitutions, but omitted from *Multiplicem,* perhaps by accident - but
see below.

[4] William of Canterbury, Grim, Roger of Pontigny (*MB* i.16-17; ii.381-2;
iv.34-5); and Guernes, 938-9; they add accounts of appeals to Thomas by two
leading Templars (cf. *Records of the Templars,* ed. B.A. Lees, London, 1935,
no. 18). Roger of Pontigny describes the bishop of Norwich as a young man
related to the king, evidently confusing him with the bishop of Worcester,
Henry's first cousin. Bosham (*MB* iii.279; below, p. 885) gives the bishops
as Winchester and Salisbury (Winchester was indeed an old enemy of Henry
II's, and Bosham's confusion, if such it was, is understandable). On the
identification of the bishops, see Knowles, *EC*, p. 62 n. For Becket's lonely
stand, see FitzStephen, Anonymous of Lambeth, *MB* iii.48-9; iv.99 ff.; cf.
also John of Salisbury, *MB* ii.311. Grim's account confirms Foliot's to this
extent, that the general submission of the bishops followed that of the archbishop.

significant, perhaps, that Norwich is the only omission from
Gilbert Foliot's list of the bishops who held out. Doubtless the
bishops were readier to resist the king than the biographers
imply; doubtless too, they were less united than Gilbert asserts.[1]

It may well be that Becket had assumed, from his conversa-
tions with the abbot of L'Aumône, that a mere verbal submission
would be sufficient; and also the king may have assumed that
Becket would take the lead in giving way.[2] It seems clear that
Becket felt himself in a position of acute difficulty, and both
at Clarendon and at Northampton in October was under almost un-
bearable strain. His loneliness is stressed by FitzStephen, who
tells us that two of the archbishop's leading clerks had been
frightened away from his service about this time.[3] The dénouement may well have been as described by Roger of Pontigny: the
archbishop agreed to keep the customs of the kingdom in good
faith; and the king then called on the bishops to give their
assent likewise. The bishop of Salisbury alone hesitated, but
at the archbishop's bidding assented too, 'and had a reprimand
from Henry for his pains'.[4] Only then did the king have the
text produced;[5] and this precipitated a new crisis, which was
averted by a verbal acceptance of the chirograph, to which the
archbishop did not set his seal: 'adquievit ad tempus assensu
et in verbo veritatis stipulatione archiepiscopus, et ille
Eboracensis, et episcopi omnes, statuta illa firmaverunt servanda regi legitime, sine dolo malo, et in bona fide'.[6]

---

[1] The fullest modern account of the council is in Knowles, *EC*, pp. 60-5;
cf. Knowles, *TB*, pp. 87 ff. An aerial photograph of Henry's palace at Clarendon (near Salisbury), by Professor J.K.S. St. Joseph, is reproduced in
Knowles, *TB*, facing p. 90; cf. R.A. Brown and H.M. Colvin in *The History of
the King's Works*, ed. H.M. Colvin, ii (London, 1963), 910-18.

[2] So Knowles, *EC*, pp. 60-1, based on Guernes, 887-910, esp. 900, and
Roger of Pontigny, *MB* iv.31-2.

[3] *MB* iii.46, on Robert Foliot, archdeacon of Oxford and later bishop of
Hereford, and Jordan, archdeacon of Chichester (on this passage see M.G.
Cheney in *Church and Government in the Middle Ages*, Cambridge, 1976, p.
153). FitzStephen also describes how Henry II sent John of Canterbury to be
bishop of Poitiers and John of Salisbury into exile, allegedly to separate
them from Becket.

[4] Knowles, *EC*, p. 64.   [5] See above and p. 852 n. 1.

[6] FitzStephen, *MB* iii.48-9. Mrs. M.G. Cheney has shown that the phrase in
FitzStephen's text (*MB* iii.48, at n. 9) that suggests that the bishops sealed
the chirograph occurs only in one ms. (art. cit. p. 149). As has often been
observed, this is contradicted by all the other evidence, including

The immediate sequel to the Council was a letter from the king supported (willy-nilly) by the archbishop, to the pope, asking for confirmation (see p. 894). The pope refused; and the best texts of the Constitutions which survive carry with them glosses indicating which the pope approved and which he specifically rejected (see below). They were discussed again late in 1164 in the papal Čuria, and in Becket's presence, and it is probable that these glosses related to the pope's statement on this second occasion rather than to his immediate reaction (see p. 895).[1] Meanwhile Becket had repented, and twice tried to cross the Channel with a view to humbling himself before the pope in person: he failed to escape the country, but the pope duly absolved him for his failure to resist the king at Clarendon. The submission had failed.

II. *The Constitutions (introduction and commentary)*

The Constitutions described how a 'recordatio et recognitio cuiusdam partis consuetudinum et libertatum et dignitatum

---

FitzStephen's own (*MB* iii.66; cf. esp. Bosham, ibid., p. 288; Foreville, pp. 123-4 n.; Knowles, *EC*, pp. 64-5 n.). In *MB Epp.* 60 the bishop of Poitiers, writing in June 1164, asserts that Becket gave no absolute guarantee, nor written support, to the Constitutions.

[1] The pope's first reaction to Henry II's request for confirmation was a refusal, which may not have been based on detailed study of the constitutions; when they were discussed in Becket's presence in November they were read out in full, and this is the most likely occasion for the individual reactions noted in the glosses. Becket repeated the condemnation at Vézelay in 1166 (*MB Epp.* 194-6, 198); though curiously, discrepancies between the summary in his condemnation and the full text suggest that he had no text with him at Vézelay (see pp. 875-6). There is no evidence of a written condemnation of individual constitutions by the pope, but he himself referred to his condemnation much later in *MB Epp.* 401, and there can be no doubt that he was reckoned to have condemned the offending clauses quite unambiguously: on this, John of Salisbury in particular was quite clear (see *MB Epp.* 194 = JS, *Letters,* ii, no. 168; also ib. nos. 229-30, 288); and the papal condemnation is described in general terms by several of the biographers: William of Canterbury, Grim, Herbert of Bosham, Roger of Pontigny (*MB* i.46; ii.404; iii.341 ff.; iv.62-4; Guernes, 2547 ff.). The pope condemned nos. 1, 3-5, 7-10, 12, 15, and tolerated 2, 6 (but see note *ad loc.*), 11, 13-14, 16. The most consistently attacked were 1, 3, 4, 7, 8, 15. Grim says that Becket immediately condemned these (*MB* ii.380); Bosham (below) quotes 1, 3, 4, 7, 8, 12 at length; Anon. Lambeth quotes 8, 4, 7, 3, 15 (*MB* iv.102) as repugnant. At Vézelay Thomas specifically cited the same cc. as in Grim.

antecessorum suorum' was made in the king's presence; and they
are specified as the customs of King Henry 'avi sui et aliorum';
later the document says that 'quedam pars' of the customs and
dignities recognized 'presenti scripto continetur', and finally
introduces the chapters with the words 'Incipiunt consuetudines
quas avitas vocant'. *Avita,* ancestral - but more particularly,
grandfatherly:[1] can the description be justified? Let us look
at each in turn.[2]

1, *on advowsons,* condemned by the pope. This simply states
that cases on advowson are for the king's court alone. But the
facts of life were more complex, as we might in any case deduce
from the presence of this chapter. 'The Crown never withdrew
this claim; and the papacy never abandoned the contrary assertion ...'[3] There is some evidence of co-operation between the
courts in the time of Henry I;[4] in the time of Stephen and the
early years of Henry II the Church courts had jurisdiction in
most of the cases known.[5] But John of Salisbury, *Letters,* i,
no. 102, presupposes that both courts had a say: the proctors
of the earl of Cornwall (see above, p. 853) asserted that a
church had been occupied 'contra consuetudinem totius ecclesiae
et regni Anglorum, contra constitutionem regis et antiquam
omnium procerum dignitatem'. In Henry II's later years the

---

[1]Cf. *Dict. of Medieval Latin from British Sources,* fasc. i, ed. R.E.
Latham (London, 1975), p. 171.

[2]This commentary owes much to notes generously provided by Professor C.R.
Cheney; although for its form we are alone responsible. Cheney, *BL* (*From
Becket to Langton,* Manchester, 1956), surveys the aftermath, 1170-1213 -
see esp. chap. iv. This apart, the most useful commentaries on the Constitutions are by Herbert of Bosham printed below, and in Foreville, chap. iii.
See also Z.N. Brooke, *English Church and the Papacy* (Cambridge, 1931),
pp. 201-8, and many books and arts. cited below.

[3]Cheney, *BL,* p. 109, a crucial passage, immediately citing a letter of
Alexander III to Henry II which entered the *Decretals* (*Extra* 2, 1, 3): see
BL, p. 109 n., for other references. According to Bosham (below) Becket also
objected on the ground that this drew clerks to secular tribunals. For a
definition of the nature of a benefice, see G. Olsen in *Studia Gratiana,*
xi (1967), 433-46, esp. 441. On the practice in Normandy, J.W. Baldwin in
French Hist. Studies, vi (1969-70), 1-30, esp. 15-17.

[4]Cf. H.G. Richardson and G.O. Sayles, *Governance of Mediaeval England*
(Edinburgh, 1963), pp. 315-16, citing *Cart. Ramsey,* i.138-9 (temp. Henry I)
and F.M. Stenton in *EHR* xxxii (1917), 47 f. (1156 x 9).

[5]See Cheney, *BL,* p. 7; Saltman, *Theobald,* pp. 163-4. See esp. JS,
Letters, i, nos. 2, 78 (in the church courts, though a royal command was
involved), 80, 85, 102.

king's court seems to have handled most of the cases, though
the Church courts did not lose their jurisdiction altogether;
no doubt it was evident to secular and ecclesiastical lawyers
alike that advowsons had a spiritual and a material element.[1]
C. 1 greatly oversimplifies the custom of Henry I's reign, but
expresses fairly enough the aspiration of the royal courts
under Henry II. It looks forward, rather than back.

2, that *grants of churches* 'de feudo regis' be not made
without royal assent; this was tolerated by the pope (but see
note *ad loc.*) and doubtless reflected the normal practice of
Henry I's reign. But in so far as it hinted at royal control
over grants of churches in general, it also looked forward,
even to the Statute of Mortmain. Version II (probably a draft)
has a slightly different version, evidently corrupt; it is not
clear that 'in elemosinam' meant anything different from 'in
perpetuum'.

3, *on criminous clerks*, condemned by the pope. Where c. 1,
on advowsons, is simple and clear, this, the central and most
famous clause of the Constitutions, is complex and ambiguous.
The early summaries make two points plain in its interpretation.
Becket specifically condemned at Vézelay in 1166 the proposition 'quod clerici vel viri religiosi trahantur ad iudicia
secularia':[2] its prime aim - and the first objection to it -
was that it would draw into the royal court clerks accused of
crime: 'Ut clericus accusatus de furto, vel rapina, vel huiusmodi, primo veniat in curiam regis'.[3] Secondly, it involved a
double judgement, in the ecclesiastical and secular courts, to
which Thomas objected, quoting the famous text: 'Non iudicabit
Deus bis in idipsum'.[4]

---

[1]Cheney, *BL*, pp. 7, 108-17; J.W. Gray in *EHR* lxvii (1952), 481-509.
[2]*MB Epp.* 196 (*MB* v.390). Cf. Anon. of Lambeth, *MB* iv.102: 'Quod clerici
veniant ad vocationem regis et iustitie sue pro qualibet causa.'
[3]FitzStephen, *MB* iii.47.
[4]A Latin rendering of the Septuagint version of Nahum, 1, 9, familiar to
theologians, as Dr. Beryl Smalley has shown, from the *Glossa Ordinaria* and
commentaries deriving from St. Jerome's; but also to be found in canon law
texts. See *CCSL* 76A (1970), pp. 534-5; B. Smalley, *Becket Conflict and the
Schools* (Oxford, 1973), pp. 125 ff.; eadem, in *Atti del II Congresso inter-
nazionale della Soc. Italiana di Storia del Diritto* (Florence, 1971), pp.
749-55; cf. Z.N. Brooke, op. cit., p. 205 n.; *Decretum*, C. 13 q. 2 c. 30.

The constitution, however, says nothing of a second punishment: the final clause only stipulates that the Church cannot
protect the degraded clerk 'de cetero',[1] which, literally taken,
does not determine whether there shall be a second judgement
and a second punishment in the same case. It is evident that the
final wording reflects debate and an attempt to compromise: to
define only what the king and his supporters felt they must insist on; and modern commentaries on the clause and its background, most notably that of Dr. Charles Duggan,[2] have established that the clause presupposes learned argument as well as
considerations of practice, on both sides.

The practice of Henry I's time seems quite obscure. Before
that date there had occurred the celebrated cases of Odo,
bishop of Bayeux, and William of Saint-Carilef, bishop of Durham, of the 1080s; and in both cases it was claimed that the
king had condemned and arrested the bishop, not as bishop, but
as a secular official: 'non clericum nec antistitem ... sed
comitem meum ... non antistitem sed tirannum', as Orderic makes
William I excuse his treatment of the bishop of Bayeux; and in

---

On criminous or felonous clerks, see esp. C. Duggan in *BIHR* xxxv (1962),
1-28, with additional theological evidence in Smalley, locc. cit.; from the
rich earlier literature the following retain their value: F.W. Maitland in
EHR vii (1892), 224-34 (= *Collected Papers*, ii (Cambridge, 1911), 232-50);
Maitland, *Roman Canon Law in the Church of England* (London, 1898), pp. 132-
47; R. Génestal, *Le Privilegium Fori en France* ... (2 vols., Paris, 1921-4),
esp. ii.95-114; G. Le Bras, *L'immunité réelle* (Paris, 1920); H.W.R. Lillie,
'St. Thomas of Canterbury's opposition to Henry II', *Clergy Review*, viii
(1934), 261-83; Foreville, pp. 125-31, 137-57. On the wider legal context,
A. Dumas in *Dict. de Droit Canonique*, vi (1954), 235-83, esp. 255 ff. On
the context in English legal practice L.C. Gabel, *Benefit of Clergy in England in the Later Middle Ages* (Northampton, Mass., 1928-29), esp. pp. 18-
29; C.R. Cheney, 'The punishment of felonous clerks', *EHR* li (1936), 215-36;
Councils, ii.1436-7, Index s.v. *Privilegium Fori*; A.L. Poole in *Hist. Essays
in Honour of J. Tait*, ed. J.G. Edwards *et al.* (Manchester, 1933), pp. 239-46.
Cf. also W. Ullmann in *Studia Gratiana*, xiii (1967), 455-89. On practice in
Normandy, Génestal, ii.106 ff.; J.W. Baldwin in *French Hist. Studies*, vi
(1969-70), 24-7. 'Non iudicabit ...' is indicated as the basis of Becket's
argument by Bosham, below, p. 887, and quoted by William of Canterbury, Grim,
Anon. Lambeth, and the *Summa causae* (*MB* i.28; ii.388; iv.96, 202).

[1] In the context this can only mean 'further, henceforth'. No. V (p. 884),
probably a late draft, has this last clause as a separate item; but it hardly
makes sense on its own and this may well be due to a copyist misunderstanding a marginal addition in his exemplar.

[2] Art. cit., esp. pp. 3 ff., 15 ff., 25 ff.

the *De iniusta vexatione Willelmi episcopi* Lanfranc is made to
apply the same distinction both to William and to Odo.[1] The
Leges Henrici primi presuppose that accusations against the
clergy are for the bishops' courts to handle; the second charter of Stephen of 1136 confirms this (see p. 764) - but by
implication suggests that this was not the consistent practice
of Henry I's reign. Shortly before Stephen's death, Osbert
archdeacon of Richmond was accused of poisoning William Fitz-
Herbert, archbishop of York; the accusation, Archbishop Theobald told the pope in 1156,[2] was made in a royàl council, and
the king claimed jurisdiction 'propter atrocitatem criminis et
quia eo presente initiata erat'. After Henry II's accession it
was taken from the king's court, 'cum summa difficultate in manu
valida, cum indignatione regis et omnium procerum, iam dictam
causam ad examen ecclesiasticum revocavimus'. Becket himself
spoke in 1163 of exemption 'speciali privilegio' as the existing custom, but it is not entirely clear what he meant.[3] The
little that we know suggests that there had been compromise and
sometimes co-operation in handling major cases, and that claims
to jurisdiction from both sides were not surprising in the mid
twelfth century. But our information is defective, for the
cases cited were *causes célèbres*, and the real issue was how
to handle lesser folk and more ordinary crimes. There is no
doubt that much of the argument in 1163 turned on this. Fitz-
Stephen in his summary of the growing argument cites a canon of
Bedford who spoke contemptuously of a royal justice in his cups,
an obscure clerk in Worcestershire who killed his lover's father,

---

[1]OV, ed. Chibnall, iv.42, 100 (cf. note *ad loc.*); *De iniusta vexatione*,
in Symeon, i.170-95, esp. 184. (We do not accept the view of H.S. Offler in
EHR lxvi (1951), 321-41, that the tract is of the second quarter of the 12th
cent.: cf. M. Gibson, *Lanfranc of Bec* (Oxford, 1978), pp. 220-1; above, p.635
n.2).But if it were it would illustrate the view of the case taken in the
generation before Clarendon.) For what follows see the succinct summary in
Warren, pp. 461 ff.
[2]JS, *Letters*, i, no. 16; on this case, see ibid. pp. 261-2; D. Knowles,
Historian and Character and other essays (Cambridge, 1963), pp. 92-7;
A. Morey in *Cambridge Hist. Journ.*, x.352-3 (1952).
[3]*MB Epp.* 29, to the pope: this is stated in the context of a general
defence of clerical immunity; it may refer to Stephen's charter, or to existing custom; or to a divine privilege supported by canon law. For another case
of a bishop (Gilbert Foliot himself) trying to wrest jurisdiction from a lay
court in the years before Clarendon, see *GFL*, no. 117 (1148 x 63).

and another clerk who stole a silver chalice from the church
of St. Mary-le-Bow in London.[1] In all these cases, he tells us,
the king claimed jurisdiction and the archbishop refused it. In
the immediate situation the king appeared as the aggressor; but
no doubt he thought he was fighting against recent innovations
by the church courts, and for equal justice on all offenders.
Behind the argument lay a deep issue of prejudice, all the
pent-up feelings between clergy and laity - the clergy tradi-
tionally anxious to avoid secular courts, since their unction
separated them from lay jurisdiction and they feared that lay
courts would deal unfairly with them; the laity on the other
hand regarding clerical privilege as unfair and unjust in itself, and in practice used as a screen for all manner of mis-
demeanour. And behind the prejudices lay a complex legal history.
The one thing wholly clear is that Clarendon c. 3 did not
describe an existing process, nor, so far as we can tell, the
procedure of any previous age. It was essentially an attempt to
resolve a sophisticated and complex legal argument.

Herbert of Bosham, describing the state of the case at Westminster in October 1163, and speaking as a theologian, asserts
that the king 'quorumdam fretus consilio utriusque iuris se
habere peritiam ostentantium' demanded that criminous clerks be
handed over to the *curia*, i.e. the royal court, citing both
human and divine, that is canon, law in support and especially
in canone "tradatur curiae"'.[2] However contemptuous Herbert
may have been, there can be little doubt that Henry's advisers
included men of legal learning. From the royal side the Constitution seems to incorporate four ideas: that royal courts should
have jurisdiction, which was Henry's original and general claim;
that what was done in ecclesiastical courts should be subject to
surveillance by officials of the royal court; that in so far as

---

[1] *MB* iii.45-6. The case of Philip de Broi, canon of Bedford, is referred
to by many sources (esp. *MB* i.12; iii.45, 265; iv.24-5), and it seems that
the royal justice had attempted to reopen the case after an acquittal in
the bishop's court. Newburgh, i.140, reports a rumour that more than a
hundred murders had been committed by clerks since 1154.

[2] *MB* iii.266-7. The reference is doubtless to *Decretum*, C. 11 q. 1 cc. 18,
31, passages from Pseudo-Isidore quoted by C. Duggan, art. cit., p. 6; their
meaning and origin are discussed ibid. pp. 6-7, 9 ff.

there was a powerful counterclaim by the church, this should be
met by accepting the possibility that both secular and church
courts had jurisdiction over aspects of such cases; and that
convicted clerks should be handed over to the royal courts for
punishment. (If the constitution says nothing of punishment,
this may well have been a slight attempt to meet Becket's objections; but it was not a concession of substance.) Of these,
the first two essentially reflect Henry II's basic attitude.
The third may well owe something to memories of Bishops Odo and
William of Saint-Calais. There can be little doubt that the
fourth was derived from Roman Law, from the use of *Novella* 123;
the doctrine of this Novel, that someone accused of crime in
the bishop's court should be degraded and handed over to a
secular judge for punishment, was cited and discussed by canonists contemporary with Becket.[1] This reveals that the matter was
the subject of serious debate among legal experts; the texts in
Gratian were in themselves not free from ambiguity; and it had
usually been taken for granted that the ecclesiastical courts
could hand over obdurate offenders to the secular courts when
they wished - a doctrine which was to have a large future in
the trial of heretics.

On Becket's side, both the intervention of the lay courts
and the secular punishment were objectionable: the first offended
the *privilegium fori*, which defended clerks from secular tribunals, the second *privilegium canonis*, which defended them from
violence.[2] Above all, his famous objection to the double punishment,[3] later adopted by Pope Alexander III himself, was supported
by a body of contemporary canonical opinion and had been referred
to by John of Salisbury in his *Policraticus,* dedicated to Becket
himself as chancellor.[4]

---

[1]Rufinus (*c.*1157 x 9) and Stephen of Tournai (*c.*1160): see Duggan, art.
cit., pp. 25-7, for the use of this and Novel 83; and for the canonists,
ibid. pp. 19 ff.

[2]Cf. Génestal, *Le Privilegium Fori* (p. 858 n. 1); index to *Councils* ii, s.v.
Privilegium Fori, Priv. Canonis. For Peter the Chanter's views see J.W. Baldwin, *Masters, Princes and Merchants* (Princeton, 1970), i.145-6, ii.101-2.

[3]See pp. 857-8 n. 4.

[4]C. Duggan, art. cit. pp. 15-18; he cites John of Salisbury, *Policraticus,*
viii.18 (ed. C.C.J. Webb, Oxford, 1909, ii.364) on pp. 17-18 and p. 17 n. 5.
Cf. also St. Bernard, *Ep.* 126 (*Opera*, ed. J. Leclercq *et al.*, vii.318;
PL clxxxii.279), citing Nahum against a double judgement.

As for criminous clerks, the *privilegium fori* survived, and
*c.*1168-9 we find Gilbert Foliot himself in the act of tactfully
but firmly demanding that the royal justices hand over two
clerks to the church courts.[1]

4, on the need for 'archiepiscopis, episcopis et personis
regni' to have *royal licence to leave the kingdom,* condemned by
the pope. This clause could be construed as a crucial support
to c. 8 in checking appeals, and the papal condemnation is
understandable; the pope objected to any control by royal power
on the clergy's movements (see p. 865). None the less, it was
undoubtedly the custom, and remained the practice, for the king
to expect to be asked permission when ecclesiastics went abroad.
The issue had arisen with the Lateran Councils of 1123[2] and
1139, with the Councils of Rheims in 1148 and Tours in 1163;[3]
and in the last case the pope promised the king that his permission for the English bishops to attend was not a precedent,
which might create a custom or diminish the king's dignity.[4]

Persone could mean either all rectors of benefices or only
dignitaries. The phrase reads more naturally here, and even
more so in c. 11, if it means dignitaries, or at least promi-
nent clerics, and seems to have been so interpreted;[5] Herbert
of Bosham (below, p. 888) seems to interpret the phrase as
'magnates of the realm', contrasting *personarum regni* with
privatorum.[6]

----

[1]*GFL*, no. 197. See below for modification in 1176. See also the important
passage in Cheney, *BL*, pp. 107-8, citing esp. Diceto, i.402-3, 410, etc.;
Peter of Blois, *Ep.* 73 (*MB Epp.* 794). Cheney points out that Becket's successor argued for co-operation and justice; and that in later generations
the felonous clerk was in the Church's hands, but his chattels went to the
sheriff.

[2]Hugh the Chanter (ed. Johnson), p. 108.

[3]Above, pp. 779, 818, 846. For other cases, cf. Henry of Blois' with-
drawal in 1155 (Torigny, p. 186: 'absque licentia regis et quasi latenter').
On this clause, cf. Foreville, p. 153.

[4]*MB Epp.* 21; Cheney, *BL*, p. 92.

[5]The material for the *Dict. of Med. Lat. from British Sources,* kindly
made available to us by Mr. R.E. Latham, shows examples of both usages, and
that both were common. The rendering 'magnate' for *persona regni* in Latham,
Revised Med. Latin Word-List, p. 345, is based on this and c. 11, but in
neither case is an interpretation which could include secular magnates at
all likely.

[6]Cf. his use of the phrase at *MB* iii.393.

5, on the techniques for enforcement used by the spiritual
courts, forbidding exaction of a *vadium ad remanens* or an oath
from excommunicates for future good behaviour; condemned by
the pope. This clause attempted to restrict the exactions from
an excommunicate to *vadium et plegium standi iudicio ecclesie*;
i.e. it condemned the oath to bind the excommunicate for the
future. It accepted excommunication as a means for spiritual
courts unprovided with police to enforce attendance.[1]

6, against accusation of laymen *ex officio* in spiritual
courts, tolerated by the pope.[2] In a full recent commentary on
this clause, Professor R.C. Van Caenegem has shown not only
how it reflects Henry II's indignation against archdeacons and
rural deans who made accusations, unsupported by broadly-based
testimony, but also runs parallel to Henry's schemes for reform
in the royal courts.[3] It repeated in substance a decree made
c.1154-8, and reissued for Normandy in 1159;[4] and we know of
the earlier English decree from FitzStephen's vivid account of
Henry and his advisers' angry handling of a rural dean in the
diocese of York, which he uses to illustrate one of the principal bones of contention even before Becket's promotion.[5]

This clause lays down that there must be adequate and suitable witnesses - though the archdeacon shall not lose what is
due to him - and offers the help of the sheriff in summoning a
jury of twelve *legales homines de visneto* to establish the truth
in a case. Professor Van Caenegem shows in detail how this constitution of 1164 led to the definition of the jury of present-
ment in the years which followed, especially in the Assize of
Clarendon in 1166.[6] But the clause did little to mend the

---

[1]Cf. Pollock and Maitland, i.478; F. Makower, *Const. Hist. and Constitution of the Church of England* (London, 1895), pp. 242-3, 468 n. 3; Foreville,
pp. 126 n. 1, 140; below, c. 10.
[2]But see p. 880 n. a, which may reflect uncertainty as to the pope's attitude.
[3]*Church and Government in the Middle Ages: Essays presented to C.R.
Cheney* ... (Cambridge, 1976), pp. 64-70 and 71 ff.
[4]Van Caenegem, pp. 68-70, citing FitzStephen, *MB* iii.43-5; Torigny,
p. 327. Cf. C.H. Haskins, *Norman Institutions* (Cambridge, Mass., 1918),
pp. 329-33.
[5]*MB* iii.43-5, which can be dated 1158.
[6]Van Caenegem, pp. 71 ff.; cf. Pollock and Maitland, i.151-2; on canonical methods of accusation, ibid. ii.656-8; and for later use of *ex officio*
procedure, below, ii.262 n. 4.

reputation of deans and archdeacons, who remained butts for the
satirists and for Henry II's sharp enquiries - see below, p.
940 .

7, against *the excommunication of tenants-in-chief,* and
royal officials, condemned by the pope. FitzStephen notes this
among the original issues which were coming to a head in 1163:
Becket excommunicated William of Eynsford for ill-treating
Canterbury protégés; the king objected violently and Becket
absolved William.[1] The *Gesta abbatum* of St. Albans cites a
case in 1159 when judges-delegate hesitated to excommunicate a
tenant-in-chief and the abbot had to go to the gates of Toulouse
to seek help from the king. It is possible, however, that the
authors of the *Gesta* really had this constitution in mind when
they spoke of a royal edict.[2] Thus it was and remained customary
for the king to claim that only with his leave could his tenants
and officers be excommunicated:[3] and in the 1190s Archbishop
Hubert Walter presided over a court which upheld a complaint
from William de Stuteville, baron and sheriff, that he had been
excommunicated - but in this case the offending prelate was the
archbishop of York. Becket, meanwhile, had regarded the constitution as a serious breach of the clerical power to bind and
loose, and when he excommunicated a whole posse of royal officials in 1166, he chose the great abbey of Vézelay on a major
festival to make his breach of this constitution as public as
possible.[4] In 1165-6 Gilbert Foliot attempted in two *causes*
célèbres, the affair of the canons of Pentney and of the marriage of the first earl of Oxford, to avoid obeying papal instructions, which might have led to a breach of the constitution,
without open disobedience to the pope. In the former case, in
the end, he and the bishop of Norwich obeyed the pope and in

---

[1]*MB* iii.43; cf. Diceto, i.311-12 and the commentary of H. Mayr-Harting
in *EHR* lxxviii.221. FitzStephen places Henry's angry retort at Windsor,
evidently in 1163, but perhaps more probably in March than *c.*August as
Eyton proposed (Eyton, pp. 61, 64).
[2]*Gesta abbatum S. Albani* (RS), i.163; cf. H. Mayr-Harting, loc. cit.
[3]Cf. the case cited in Cheney, *BL,* p. 98; and, for what follows, Cheney,
Hubert Walter, p. 98. For 13th-cent. cases and difficulties, below, ii.283
n. 1.
[4]See below, pp. 888-9, for Bosham's account of Becket's attitude; and,
for Vézelay, see Esp. *MB Epp.* 194-8.

1169 were denounced by the king for their pains (below, p. 937).;
in the latter, it was not until 1172 that his threat to execute
a final papal mandate induced the earl to consummate his marriage.[1]

8, on *appeals,* condemned by the pope. The essential objection, as in c. 4, is to the principle that the king can decide·
on issues of such importance to the church. After c. 3 this was
perhaps the most important constitution, as it was evidently
one of the most ineffective. It forbids appeals to proceed from
any ecclesiastical court - archdeacon's or bishop's - via the
archbishop's court to the pope without royal consent.[2] Herbert
of Bosham observed how the king and his supporters found themselves in the necessity of making appeals to the pope, and the
constant posture of appeal of Gilbert Foliot and other English
bishops must have brought this constitution into derision.[3]

In practice appeals had been growing steadily in the previous
thirty years, and the early letters of John of Salisbury show
that numerous appeals were going to Rome in Henry II's early
years on cases often quite trivial. The king and his officials
do not seem to have taken strong action to check this, although
as with c. 7 the St. Albans chroniclers claimed that he had
made his prohibition before 1164.[4] In some of the episcopal
appeals against Becket it is not clear that a royal licence was
sought or obtained, but the Anstey case seems to confirm that
this was normal.[5] The case law suggests that a reasonable degree

---

[1]*GFL,* nos. 159-64; cf. *GF,* pp. 184-5.

[2]We do not accept the interpretation of H.G. Richardson and G.O. Sayles,
Governance of Mediaeval England (Edinburgh, 1963), pp. 306-9, who argue that
it applied only to cases commencing in an archdeacon's court. It is hard to
imagine the point of such a clause, and this is evidently contrary to contemporary interpretation: cf. e.g. Bosham, *MB* iii.283 (= below, p. 889), 393.

[3]Ibid., and see *GF,* pp. 162 ff., and esp. 162 and reference.

[4]*Gesta abbatum S. Albani* (RS), i.178. For the background, see JS, *Letters,*
i, esp. nos. 2, 68, 84, for good examples of quite humble litigants appealing.

[5]See *GF,* pp. 184-5 n., for evidence that in at least one case the bishops
appealed without royal licence; but it seems fairly evident that this was a
special case and not the normal procedure, which is represented by *GFL,* no.
203 (not 204 as in *GF,* p. 185 n., line 10). In the case of Richard of Anstey,
we know that he obtained at least one royal licence, even though the archbishop's official report gives no indication of this (JS, *Letters,* i, no.
131; for the licence, see his diary of expenses, ed. P.M. Barnes, in *Misc.*
D.M. Stenton, p. 19; for the case, see also Barnes, pp. 1-24; Cheney, *BL,*

of co-operation was quite usual; and the evidence of the *causes
célèbres* in which the king felt himself personally involved
suggests that there was normally no serious objection to the
king being present at a meeting of the court held by papal
judges-delegate.[1] The king continued to insist that he have a
reasonable check on litigants whom he suspected of disloyal
purposes, and discussion of c. 4 has shown that it remained
customary for men of standing to apply for royal licence to go
overseas. In a formal sense, this was the issue on which the king
most obviously gave way after Becket's murder. Whether he would
or could have seriously impeded the flow of appeals is far from
clear; at least he renounced any overt attempt to do so.[2]

9, on *frankalmoign tenure,* condemned by the pope. This clause
established the assize *Utrum,* and was doubtless condemned because it envisaged a process by which the king's court decided
whether the case was one of frankalmoign or not, before it
could come to the church court. In practice it seems quite
readily to have been accepted as a normal procedure, although
occasionally cases went to the church courts in Henry's later
years. E.G. Kimball showed that this issue had at one time been
argued in the lay courts; that there was some evidence of a
change in Stephen's time which this clause was doubtless intended
to check or reverse; and that there may have been a Norman precedent for the assize.[3] Before long the assize ceased to be a

---

pp. 54-8, esp. 55; Saltman, *Theobald,* pp. 154-6, who points out that silence
on the royal licence in John of Salisbury's *Letters* is not evidence against
the practice).

[1] H. Mayr-Harting in *JEH* xvi (1965), 41-2.
[2] For the history of appeals and its relation to the issue see esp. Cheney,
BL, pp. 47-86; M.G. Cheney in *EHR* lvi (1941), 177-97; C. Duggan, *Twelfth
Century Decretal Collections* (London, 1963), pp. 1 ff. and *passim*; A. Morey,
Bartholomew of Exeter (Cambridge, 1937), chap. iv; for older views, F.W.
Maitland, *Roman Canon Law in the Church of England* (London, 1898), pp.
122-31; Z.N. Brooke in *Cambridge Hist. Journ.* ii, no. 3 (1928), 213-28; Z.N.
Brooke, *English Church and the Papacy from the Conquest to the Reign of John*
(Cambridge, 1931), pp. 211-14.
[3] *EHR* xlvii (1932), 1-11; cf. *Royal Writs in England from the Conquest to
Glanvill,* ed. R.C. Van Caenegem (Selden Soc., 1959), pp. 86-7, 325 ff.;
Pollock and Maitland, i.246-50; Cheney, *BL,* p. 107 and n. 3 for a case in
the Church courts in 1175. Cf. also G.D.G. Hall's note on *Glanvill* (NMT,
1965), x, 12, pp. 126, 191. There is a short but valuable paper on the
assize by S.E. Thorne in *Columbia Law Review,* xxxiii (1933), 428-36; see esp.
pp. 428-9, where he adduced evidence in favour of earlier secular control.

preliminary enquiry as here envisaged and became a full propri-
etary action.

10, offering the aid of a royal official in bringing a contumacious layman who refused to attend or make satisfaction to
a church court, condemned by the pope. Doubtless the pope condemned it because it forbade excommunication before the royal
official had tried to bring the offender to justice. It permitted him to be put 'sub interdicto', which may possibly in
this context have meant a minor form of excommunication or
simply a threat to excommunicate before the royal official had
been asked to bring the man to court.[1] The clause was of little
importance, and ignored by Herbert of Bosham.

11, that *ecclesiastical dignitaries* who hold in chief *are* as
it were *barons* and act as such, joining in judgements of the
king's court, short of judgements involving mutilation or
death; this the pope tolerated. This clause expressed the familiar view of Lanfranc, that a bishop was both bishop and baron
(above, p. 859). The sting in the clause was its relevance to
the case of John the Marshal against Becket (below, pp. 894-
8), which Becket had regarded as raising the issue of clerical immunity and in which the bishops found themselves invited
to judge their ecclesiastical superior.[2] But the clause itself
essentially established a point of legal procedure. For *persone
regni*, see c. 4.

12, on the procedure *in vacancies and for elections in archbishoprics, bishoprics, and monastic houses* under royal patronage, condemned by the pope. This is one of the most lucid of
the constitutions; apart from the words 'salvo ordine suo' at
the end, it represented in unequivocal terms Henry II's interpretation of existing practice; and it can reasonably be said
that the clause both describes the custom of Henry I's reign and
the procedures of Henry II's, from which in general he was never

---

Like Miss Kimball, he suggested some change in Stephen's reign. See now also
A.W. Douglas, 'Frankalmoin and jurisdictional immunity: Maitland revisited',
Speculum, liii (1978), 26-48.

[1] The precise meaning is not clear.
[2] Cf. *MB Epp.* 74, 223 (*MB* v.139, 494: in the latter case Thomas sees himself as Christ before Pilate, Matt. 27, 11).

compelled to withdraw.

It deals first with regalian right in vacancies. There is
doubt how much Stephen had surrendered in his second charter
(pp. 764-5), but it is evident that in practice Stephen tried to
exercise the right to draw revenues in a vacancy, and Henry II
evidently 'exercised regalian right from the beginning of his
reign'.[1] Becket as chancellor apparently received the revenues
of three vacant bishoprics.[2] As archbishop he resisted what
the churches commonly regarded as a burden and abuse, and in
the long run Henry was made to promise not to keep bishoprics
and abbeys vacant for more than a year, save 'urgente necessitate ...' (below, p. 996). 'No doubt it was "urgente necessitate"', comments Dr. Howell, 'that the king was obliged to keep
the wealthy see of York vacant for the last eight years of his
reign ...'[3]

The canonical process of election to bishoprics was by the
cathedral chapter, and freely; abbots were elected under the
Rule of St. Benedict by their communities, but in cases in
which a free election was held in the community it was quite
common for a bishop and a group of local monastic superiors to
be present, especially in cases of difficulty.[4] The procedure

---

[1]M.E. Howell, *Regalian Right in Medieval England* (London, 1962), p. 32;
cf. pp. 32 ff. for a full commentary on this clause so far as it related to
regalian right. Cf. Foreville, p. 369; and for the European context, esp.
in Germany, R.L. Benson, *The Bishop-Elect* (Princeton, 1968), pt. ii;
J. Gaudemet in *Dict. de Droit Canonique,* vii (Paris, 1965), pp. 493-532, esp.
501-5; P. Classen, in *Vorträge und Forschungen,* xvii (Sigmaringen, 1973),
451-3.

[2]JS, *Letters,* i, no. 128 (p. 223, cf. p. 266 and n.); cf. Howell, pp. 32-3.

[3]Howell, p. 34.

[4]See *Decretum,* D. 61-3, etc.; J. Gaudemet in *Le istituzioni ecclesias-
tiche della 'Societas Christiana' dei secoli XI-XII* (Milan, 1974), pp. 476-
89; R.L. Benson, *The Bishop-Elect* (esp. p. 23 and refs.): a study mostly of
status and office, not of the process of election, but with much useful
material and bibliography, esp. pp. 39-40, 230-1 on election in the royal
palace or chapel. For abbatial elections, *Regula S. Benedicti,* c. 64; *Decretum,* C. 18 q. 2 and *dictum post* c. 8. There is little evidence for the precise procedure of episcopal elections in the late 1150s and early 1160s,
although there are abundant indications of royal and achiepiscopal influence:
see esp. JS, *Letters,* i, nos. 128-9, 133. On episcopal elections under
Stephen and in the early years of Henry II, see Saltman, *Theobald,* pp. 90-
132. On monastic elections, Knowles, *MO,* chap. xxiii, esp. pp. 397-8 (Henry
I), 398 (Stephen), 399 (Henry II). For a case of monastic election with
bishops and abbots present, JS, *Letters,* i, no. 109 (evidently the result
of a dispute); for other recent elections, *GFL,* nos. 134-7. Adrian IV had
denounced lay interference in elections in JL 10139 of 1156.

laid down in this constitution, however, had doubtless been followed for some elections both to bishoprics and abbeys in Henry
I's reign, had certainly been followed for the elections of
Theobald and Thomas himself as archbishops (pp. 769, 843-5) -
though in the latter case the king was represented by the Justiciar Richard de Lucy - and could reasonably be regarded as normal and customary. Some chapters had from time to time tried
to stage, or succeeded in staging, a real election outside the
royal chapel; this had probably been not uncommon under Stephen;
and there is little evidence for monastic elections in the royal
chapel in Henry's early years. But the practice described in
this constitution appears to have been normal for episcopal
elections thereafter. For later episcopal elections, see below,
pp. 956-65.[1] The full procedure, including homage, continued
the compromise of 1106-7, which had been intended by the pope
as a temporary concession (above, p. 690). For the view of
Becket and his *eruditi*, as reported by Bosham, see pp. 889-91.

13, on the provision of mutual help between the king and
ecclesiastical courts in cases in which justice has been forc-
ibly withheld, of *deforcement*;[2] tolerated by the pope. This is
a clause of little importance, but illustrates the clarification
of procedures which is a part of the Constitutions.

14, that chattels of persons under *sanctuary* are not pro-
tected; tolerated by the pope. Again, perhaps a clarification,
or possibly reflecting a difficult case; but not a major issue.

15, that cases of *debt*, with or without an oath, should be
handled by the royal courts, condemned by the pope. The doctrine
of the church courts was that they had jurisdiction in cases of
oaths and perjury. A bull of 1151 shows us a Norman case in
which the church courts tried to enforce a debt under oath; and
an early letter of John of Salisbury describes a case between
tenants-in-chief which one of them took on appeal to the papal

---

[1]Also Foreville, pp. 368-88; H. Mayr-Harting in *JEH* xvi (1965), 50-2;
Cheney, *BL*, p. 20.

[2]This word came to be common in the technical legal sense of 'deforce',
but in this context, as Mr. R.E. Latham has pointed out to us, it seems to
have the general sense of 'force'. The meaning of 'iustificare' at the end
of c. 13 is not clear; possibly the king expected prelates to excommunicate
those who were contumacious in the king's court.

curia.[1] *Extra* 3, 22.3, shows us Pope Lucius III (writing 1181
x 4) asking the help of the archbishop of Canterbury in pursuit
of a debt incurred by Peter of Blois at the time of the Third
Lateran Council in 1179. The royal courts accepted that the
church courts had jurisdiction over oaths, but issued prohibitions against the use of this jurisdiction to settle 'pleas
concerning the debts ... of laymen', as the author of *Glanvill*
says, on the basis of a royal assize, which presumably means
this constitution.[2] In practice the royal courts allowed jurisdiction when the debts related to wills or marriages.

16, against the ordination of villeins' sons without their
lords' leave, tolerated by the pope. This may have been included
as a reaction to specific scandals: it was not a point at issue.[3]

Conclusion. 'In the Constitutions of Clarendon [Henry II]
gave what is on the whole an accurate description of the customary practice in his grandfather's reign, erring, if anything,
on the side of moderation ... On the other hand ... Henry II
committed a fatal blunder in publishing the Constitutions, which
was a novelty.'[4] Thus Z.N. Brooke in 1931. More recent studies
have suggested some modifications. That Henry reckoned the
constitutions 'on the whole' to be those of his grandfather, no
one doubts; and very broadly the claim was justified. In several
cases we can see the practice of Stephen's reign being deliberately turned back even before 1164.[5] But in the crucial c. 3
(criminous clerks) he and his counsellors were seeking for a
new solution, and in c. 8 (appeals) facing a problem which Henry
I had hardly faced; and in many clauses one is made to see his
legal advisers looking the present squarely in the face - trying

---

[1]JL 9458 (10 March 1151); JS, *Letters,* i, no. 71, probably c.1154-8 (cf.
Le Neve, i, 5, 9 for the dates of the dean and archdeacon mentioned).

[2]*Glanvill,* ed. Hall, x, 12, p. 126; and see the editor's comments, pp.
191-2. See also Pollock and Maitland, ii.197-203; the jurisdiction of the
church courts over clerical debts only slowly died out (ibid. ii.199; cf.
i.447 n.; below, ii.1417, Index s.v. debt).

[3]Early canon law, as represented by a decretal of Gelasius in Gratian's
Decretum, D. 54 c. 12, concurred with the Roman Civil Law in refusing ordination to an unfree man unless he had his lord's permission. The word 'rusticorum' was evidently meant to refer, as it usually did, to unfree tenants.

[4]*English Church and the Papacy,* pp. 205-6.

[5]See esp. cc. 1, 8, 12. Cc. 4, 7, 11, 12 represent good examples of the
revival or reassertion of the known custom of Henry I's time.

to provide solutions to the actual problems of the developing
royal courts of the late twelfth century. Of this cc. 6 and 9
provide illustrations. Several of the minor clauses, furthermore, probably helped to establish legal procedures by the act
of publication. We have seen that c. 15 was treated as an
assize by the author of *Glanvill*, although 'this silliness' as
G.D.G. Hall called it was hardly an ornament to the English
law; but c. 9 seems also to have established itself, and Dr.
Howell argued that the publication of c. 12 played an important
part in underpinning Henry II's practices. Henry was suffi-
ciently pleased with the Constitutions to imitate them in 1166
and 1176 in the assizes of Clarendon and Northampton, and sup-
plement them in 1169 (p. 926). Yet they also drew sharp attention to the points on which Henry was attempting new law, or
practices palpably contrary to the canons, and so drew from the
pope who had the strongest motive of any pope of the century
to favour the English king, however informally, a clear condemnation.

III. *Texts*

The following have been included: the text of the Constitutions;
an abbreviated version which comes from a good and early ms. and
may represent a draft made late in the composition of the Constitutions; and the narrative of Herbert of Bosham. Although cast in
the form of a narrative and giving valuable details, it is essentially a commentary on the major points in the Constitutions; and
it is for this that it is included here, as the most substantial
contemporary discussion.

Numerous copies survive of the Constitutions, but all seem to
derive from the Canterbury text of the 'chirograph'; and the
large majority go back to the excellent Canterbury text incorporated in Alan of Tewkesbury's collection of the Becket correspondence made *c.*1176.[1] Since texts of the supplementary

---

[1] On Alan's collection, see esp. A.J. Duggan, 'The Manuscript Transmission
of Letter Collections relating to the Becket Dispute and their use as contemporary Sources' (Univ. of London Ph.D., 1971), pp. 123-85 (A. Duggan (1971));
revised in *Thomas Becket: a Textual History of his Letters* (A. Duggan (1980));
see also JS, *Letters*, ii, xlix-lii, lviii-lxiii (based on Dr. Duggan's work,

constitutions of 1169 almost invariably occur with or close to
texts of the Constitutions of Clarendon, references for 1169
are given here as well as for 1164: the first folios refer to
1164, the second to 1169.

Of Alan of Tewkesbury's collection three good copies survive.

Ab. BL ms. Cotton Claudius B. ii, fos. 26-27^V, 27^V-28: probably the fair copy of Alan's first recension, written at
Canterbury *c*.1176.[1]

Ac. Cambridge, Corpus Christi College 295, fos. 11-12,
12^{r-v}: early 13th cent., a good copy of Alan's third
recension, probably made at Canterbury.[2]

Ag. Oxford, Bodleian Library, Bodl. 937 (3088), fos. 1-2^V,
4^{r-v} (and see p. 873 n. 4): early 13th cent.; part of a
small group of documents which are attached to a large
collection of copies taken from Alan, second recension, in
order to make more complete a copy of the 'Lambeth' version
of the Becket correspondence.[3]

Later copies of Alan's collection are: Cambridge, Trinity
Hall ms. 24, fos. 124-125^V, 126, a mid-13th-cent. copy of the
second recension collated with other texts (bk. i only survives); BL ms. Arundel 219, fos. 15^V-18^V, 19^{r-v}, a 14th-cent.
abbreviated copy of Ac (bks. i-iii); Vatican ms. Lat. 1220,
fos. 68^V-69^V, 69^V-70, a 14th-cent. copy of Alan's second

---

owing much also to Sir Roger Mynors's study of the text of letters of John of
Salisbury in these mss., which has confirmed the use we make of them). Dr. Duggan shows that the *marginalia* of Ab, the earliest and most important of these
mss., range in date from 1176 to *c*.1190, but she also shows that the earliest
seems to have been written in 1176 (A. Duggan (1980), p. 122), and it therefore seems likely that part at least of the text of Ab was written in that
year. In any event Alan's main editorial task presumably fell shortly after
John of Salisbury's departure to be bishop of Chartres in the summer of 1176.
Cf. JS, *Letters*, ii, pp. lxi-lxiii; but see A. Duggan (1980), pp. 87 ff., 168,
indicating a date 1174 x 6 for Alan's work.

[1]For the date, see above; for descriptions of the ms. A. Duggan (1980),
pp. 100-23; JS, *Letters*, ii, pp. li-lii.
[2]A. Duggan, pp. 134-7; JS, *Letters*, ii, p. 1.
[3]A. Duggan, pp. 131-4; JS, *Letters*, ii, p. lii.

recension (and see below);[1] Cambridge, Trinity College ms.
O. 5. 40, unfoliated, a 17th-cent. transcript made for Thomas
Gale, based on Ac collated with Ab.

A Canterbury text independent of these is preserved in William of Canterbury's Life of Becket:

Aw. Winchester College, ms. 4, pp. 15-18, 42-4 (= *MB* i.18-23,
53-5), a 13th-cent. copy of the Life written 1172 x 4.[2]
From this Life was derived the text of 1164 in Gervase,
i.178-80 (mss. Ga, fos. 67-8; Gc, fos. 50^V-51^V; for
1169, see p. 930). A version also based on William of
Canterbury was copied in the early 13th cent. Glasgow
Reg. Vetus, now at Blairs College, Aberdeen.[3]

Other texts are in:

1. The *Summa cause inter regem et Thomam,* an early compilation, probably from Becket's circle, or in some sense of
Canterbury origin, though surviving in mss. derived from the
archives of Gilbert Foliot, bishop of London:[4] Oxford, Bodl. ms.
b   E Mus. 249 (27835), fos. 68^V-70 (Fb) (*c.*1180) and Bodl. ms.

---

[1]A. Duggan (1980), pp. 124-9; an important ms., since it is the fullest witness to Alan's second recension, as Dr. Duggan has shown. But for the text of the Constitutions it is late and unreliable, and its witness is in any case confused by including a text of the *Causa exilii* (see below).

[2]For the date of the Life, see E. Walberg, *La tradition hagiographique de S. Thomas Becket* (Paris, 1929), p. 116. Aw is the only known ms. of the Life (apart from the extracts in the Glasgow register), and was presented to Winchester College by the founder. William's *Miracula* also occur in a ms. at Montpellier, which, however, lacks the life (*MB* iv, pp. xxiv-xxvi, 442 ff.; cf. JS, *Letters,* ii. p. lv).

[3]On this ms., see G.R.C. Davis, *Medieval Cartularies of Great Britain* (London, 1958), p. 133, no. 1150, with note of 17th-cent. transcript in Brechin Castle; no. 1151 is a 15th-cent. copy of no. 1150 now in the Scottish Rec. Office in Edinburgh (Hist. Room R.2/3) = *Reg. Glasgow,* ii.593-5.

[4]The document describes the events, especially the councils, of 1163-4, from the point of view of Becket, laying emphasis at the end on the plight of his clerks and supporters; at the outset it states that the Council of Westminster was summoned to demonstrate the primacy of Canterbury. An origin in Becket's circle seems clearly indicated; and this is consistent with the text of the Constitutions, which shows only minor divergences from Ab and its colleagues, often in common with Ag. On the mss. see Duggan, chap. 4; *GFL*, pp. xxxv-liv, 2-11, 14-16; and on Sd, M. Cheney in *Church and Government in the Middle Ages: Essays pres. to C.R. Cheney* (Cambridge, 1976), pp. 147 ff.

Sd   Douce 287 (21861), fos. 44-45^V (Sd) (*c.*1200) (in both cases 1164 only; for their texts of 1169, see p. 929).

H   2. Substantial extracts in Herbert of Bosham's Life (H), below, pp. 885-9, and a complete text (from p. 878 n.h) at the end of the compilation consisting of the Life, *Liber Melorum,* homily and Constitutions, ms. Arras 375 (649), fos. 65^V-66^V (see p. 885), from Saint-Vaast, Arras, under rubric 'Causa exilii et martyrii b. ... Thome martyris et pontificis Cantuariensis'.

3. Roger of Crowland's *Quadrilogus,* i.l b, in Paris, BN ms. Lat. 5372, fos. 17^{r-v}, 17^V-18 (both 1164 and 1169); Bodl. ms. e Mus. 133 (3512), fos. 31-32^V (1164 only).[1]

4. Numerous mss. of a small collection of documents called the 'Causa exilii', commonly attached to Elias of Evesham's *Quadrilogus*, but sometimes separately, and invariably followed by 1169 (13th-15th cents. unless otherwise noted). Cambridge, Corpus Christi Coll. ms. 59, fos. 257^V-258; Trinity Coll. ms. B. 1. 23, fos. 167-169, 169^{r-v}; O. 5. 39 (17th-cent. transcript), unfoliated; UL ms. Ee. 2. 29, fos. 217, 216^V (15th-cent. extract, 1169 only); Ff. 4. 46, fos. (2), fragment of 1164 (the rest is missing), 138, conclusion of 1169; Durham Cathedral Lib. ms. B. IV. 44, pp. 109-11, 111-12; Durham UL ms. Cosin V. iii. 12, fos. 40^V-41^V, 41^V-42; London, BL mss. Arundel 15, fos. 68-70, 70^{r-v}; Arundel 52, fos. 39^V-40, 40^V; Cotton Faust B. viii, fos. 115-116^V, 116^V-117; Cotton Vesp. B. xiv, fos. 90^V-92, 92^{r-v}; Vitell. C. xii, fos. 225-226^V, 226^V-227; Harl. 2, fos. 71^V-73, 73^{r-v}; Harl. 4242, fos. 61-63, 63; Royal 13 C. vi, fos. 128-129, 129; Stowe 52, fos. 66^V-67^V, 67^V-68; Oxford, Corpus Christi Coll. 38, fos. 86-87^V, 87^V; University Coll. ms. 69, pp. 86-90, 90-2; Paris, BN ms. lat. 5616, fos. 96^V-98^V, 98^V-99^V; Rome, Bibl. Vallicelliana B. 60, fos. 68-69^V, 69^V-70 (there is also an undated fragment of 1164, cc. 13-17, on fo. 73): Vatican ms. Lat. 1220, fos. 37-38, 38 (in *Causa exilii*: for the ms. see above).

---

[1] On Roger of Crowland and these mss. see A. Duggan (1980), pp. 205 ff., 278-84; also A. Duggan in *Thomas Becket, Actes du Colloque International de Sédières,* ed. R. Foreville (Paris, 1975), pp. 5-7.

5. Texts closely connected with 4 or otherwise probably of
Canterbury origin: BL ms. Addit. 11506, fos. 10-11, 11^{V},
*c.*1200, with the Lives by John of Salisbury and Alan of Tewkesbury;[1] Lambeth Palace Lib. ms. 1212, fos. 168^{V}-169, 169^{r-v},
13th-14th cent. Canterbury register. There is a stray text of
cc. 2-15 in Paris, BN ms. lat. 14663, fo. 193^{V} (15th cent., from
Saint-Victor, Paris).

6. Wendover, *Flores Hist.*, ed. H.G. Hewlett (RS, 1886-9),
i.26-30 (1164; for 1169 see pp. 929-30); the chief mss. are BL
Cotton Otho B. v, Part ii, fos. 20-1, and Bodl. Douce 207
(21781), fos. 121^{V}-122; hence Paris, *Ch. Maj.*, ii.223-5.

7. *Summaries and extracts.* Apart from the abbreviated version on pp. 883-5, and Herbert of Bosham's extracts, pp. 886-9,
the most interesting are: the brief summary in the 'Anonymous of
Lambeth' (see above, p. 850), *MB* iv.102; a similar summary in
John of Salisbury's and Becket's accounts of the archbishop's
condemnation of them at Vézelay in 1166 (JS, *Letters*, ii, no.
168; *MB Epp.*, 194-6, 198); and a French summary in Guernes,
2391-2546. It is a curious fact that the summaries of the clauses as
condemned at Vézelay suggest that Becket had no copy of the Constitutions with him. In clause 1, the summary speaks of cases on
churches and tithes, not advowsons; in clause 4 he inserts a
specific reference to travelling at the pope's summons; clause
15 is made a general prohibition of episcopal coercion in cases
of perjury and breach of faith; and the order of the clauses
is 7, 15, 3, 1, 8, 4. It could perhaps be argued that Becket
possessed no copy in his years of exile; and it is noticeable
that there is no full copy in the mss. representing the earlier
versions of his letter collections, before that of Alan of
Tewkesbury. Yet it hardly seems credible that he had no access
to the Constitutions, and it is much more likely that he kept
possession of the Canterbury copy of the chirograph, on which
all these texts are evidently based. What seems much more possible, though still surprising, is that the condemnation of the

---

[1] On this ms. see A. Duggan (1980), p. 95; JS, *Letters*, ii, pp. xlviii-xlix.
The lives and documents are followed (after a change of hand and quire) by
the later letters of John of Salisbury.

individual constitutions at Vézelay was unpremeditated,[1] and
that he had left his copy behind.

Printed editions. The Constitutions were first printed
in the 1495 *Quadrilogus* (*Vita et processus S. Thome
Cantuariensis*, Paris, 1495, fos. (g v^v)-(g vi^v) - 1169
is on (g vi^v)-(g vii) (reprinted in Salamanca in 1526);
from Vat. Lat. 1220 (Alan's second recension), via the
17th-cent. transcript in Vat. Lat. 6027, by F. Christianus
Lupus [Wolf], *Epistolae et Vita divi Thomae* (2 vols.,
Brussels, 1682), *Vita,* pp. 163-9 (in *Causa exilii*), and
Epistolae, i.25-6 (abbreviated); and frequently elsewhere,
including Sp. ii.63-5, W. i.435-6; most accessibly by
Robertson in *MB* i.18-23 (William of Canterbury) and *MB
Epp.* 45;[2] W. Stubbs, *Select Charters*, 9th edn., ed. H.W.C.
Davis (Oxford, 1913), pp. 163-7.

This edition. The only texts which we have any reason
to suppose independent of Alan of Tewkesbury are Aw, H,
Fb, and Sd, all evidently derived from the basic Canterbury text which he used. Our aim must therefore be to
reconstruct this text, and for this Ab is the natural and
necessary base, checked by Ac and Ag, with a little help
from Fb, Sd, H, and Aw, which are, however, inferior witnesses. In view of the great interest of the Constitutions,
we have included most of the variants of Ac, Ag, Fb, and
Sd (where the two latter agree), a fair number from Aw,

---

[1] Herbert of Bosham tells us that he did not discuss the censures in advance with his clerks, and this may possibly indicate that Becket himself
was undecided as to the form of the censures until the last moment (*MB*
iii.387, 391-2). In a letter written at the time, John of Salisbury says
that Thomas refrained from excommunicating the king because he was told
that Henry was seriously ill (*MB Epp.* 194 = JS, *Letters,* ii, no. 168), and
this seems to make it certain that some change of mind occurred.

[2] As usual, Robertson's apparatus was of little use, and he quoted variants
from Bodl. 509, which contains no copy of the document (presumably by confusion with Bodl. 937, Ag). Between our text and his there will be found a
number of minor differences, but none of great substance. The most significant are the ambiguity about the papal attitude to c. 6 (see p. 880 n. a),
and *tractetur* for *terminetur* at the end of c. 7 (p. 880 n. k). The only
divergence of more than a word or of word order among the mss. is at the end
of c. 9; but the omission of a clause in some mss. seems due only to a scribal slip.

and a few from H. In principle, variants of later mss.
might be of interest, showing differences in the later
understanding of the Constitutions. We have found, however, only a host of minor divergences of no historical
interest: for the interpretation and use of the Constitutions, the summaries and epitomes (see above) are more
valuable.

IV. *The Constitutions of Clarendon*

Rescriptum illarum consuetudinum quas avitas vocant: quando et
coram quibus facta est earum recognitio.[a]

Anno ab incarnatione domini millesimo centesimo sexagesimo
quarto, papatus Alexandri anno vi,[b] illustrissimi regis Anglorum
Henrici secundi anno x,[c] in presentia eiusdem regis, facta est
recordatio et recognitio cuiusdam partis consuetudinum et libertatum et dignitatum antecessorum suorum, videlicet regis Henrici
avi sui et aliorum, que observari et teneri deberent[d] in regno.
Et propter dissensiones et discordias que emerserant inter
clerum et iusticias domini regis et barones regni de consuetudinibus et dignitatibus regni, facta est ista recordatio vel
recognitio[e] coram archiepiscopis,[f] episcopis et clero, et comitibus et baronibus et proceribus regni. Et easdem consuetudines
recognitas per archiepiscopos et[g] episcopos et[g] comites et[g]
barones, et per nobiliores et antiquiores regni, Thomas Cantuariensis[h] archiepiscopus et Rogerius Eboracensis archiepiscopus et Gillebertus Londoniensis episcopus et[g] Henricus
Wintoniensis episcopus et Nigellus Eliensis episcopus et Willelmus Norwicensis episcopus et Robertus Lincolnensis episcopus et

---

[a]earum recognitio Ab; recognitio Ac; *no rubric in* Ag; FbSd *have rubric but*
om. rescriptum ... recognitio; Aw *om. the whole preamble, and starts in c. 1.*
Ab[1] *has at foot of fo. 26:* Hec ex mandato regis digessit Iohannes Oxeneford'
potius utens phrasi sordida quam stilo militari si Latino utendum fuerat. Sed
iniquas leges stilus ineptus decet.   [b]quarto Ab; vi Ab[1]; iiiio Ac; vi
AgFbSd (*correctly* vi).   [c]decimo Ab; xi Ab[1]; xo Ac; xi AgFbSd (*correctly* x)
(Ag *has* in presentia domini regis).   [d]debent Ab (?) *before corr.*, Ac;
deberent Ab[1]Ag.   [e]ista recognitio Ab (*before corr.*), Ac; ista recordatio
vel recognitio Ab[1]; hec recordatio vel recognitio AgFbSd (*but* Fb *reads* vel
recordatio).   [f]Ab *adds* et.   [g]et *om.* AgFbSd (Ag *reads* et barones).
[h]FbSd *add* sancte memorie; *om.* Cant. Ag.

Hylarius Cicestrensis episcopus et Iocelinus Saresberiensis
episcopus et Ricardus Cestrensis episcopus[a] et Bartholomeus
Exoniensis episcopus et Robertus Herefordensis episcopus et
David Menevensis episcopus et Rogerius Wigornensis episcopus
electus[b] concesserunt, et in verbo veritatis viva voce firmi-
ter promiserunt, tenendas et observandas domino regi et heredi-
bus suis, bona fide et absque malo ingenio, presentibus istis:
Roberto comite Leghecestrie, Reginaldo comite Cornubie, Conano
comite Britannie, Iohanne comite de Augo, Rogerio comite de
Clara, comite Gaufrido de Mandevilla, Hugone comite Cestrie,
Willelmo comite de Arundel, comite Patricio, Willelmo comite de
Ferrariis, Ricardo de Luci, Reginaldo de sancto Walerico,
Rogerio Bigod, Reginaldo de Warenn', Richerio de Aquila, Willel-
mo de Braosia, Ricardo de Camvilla, Nigello de Mobrai, Simone de
Bellocampo, Hunfrido de Boum, Matheo de Herefordia,[c] Waltero de
Meduana, Manassero Biseth dapifero, Willelmo Maleth, Willelmo
de Curci, Roberto de Dunestanevilla, Iocelino de Baillolio,
Willelmo de Lanvalis, Willelmo de Caisneto, Gaufrido de Ver,
[Ab, fo. 26^v] Willelmo de Hastinges, Hugone de Moravilla, Alano
de Nevilla,[d] Simone filio Petri, Willelmo Maudut camerario,
Ioanne Maudut, Iohanne mariscallo, Petro de Mara,[e] et multis
aliis proceribus et nobilibus regni, tam clericis quam laicis.

Consuetudinum vero et dignitatum regni recognitarum quedam
pars[f] presenti scripto continetur. Cuius partis capitula hec
sunt.

Incipiunt consuetudines quas avitas vocant.[g]

Prima. *Hoc dampnavit sancta Romana ecclesia sub papa Alexandro
tertio.*[h]

---

[a] et Ricardus ... episcopus Ag *puts after* Wigornensis episcopus.   [b] episcopus electus Ab[1]Ac; electus AbFbSd; episcopus et ... Ag (*see n. a*).
[c] Herofordia Ab (*in list above* AcAg *read* Gaufrido comite, Ac Willelmo de
Ferrariis, *om.* comite).   [d] Alano de Nevilla AbAc; *om.* AgFbSd: *see n. e*.
[e] AgFbSd *add* Alano de Novavilla.   [f] Ag *adds* in.   [g] Incipiunt ... vocant Ab;
He sunt consuetudines quas Henricus secundus rex Anglie petiit sibi confirmari a sancto Thomas Cant' archiepiscopo Ac; *om.* AgFbSd.   [h] AbAc *have the
numbers in rubric* (Prima, ij[a], iij[a], iiij[a], Quinta, Sexta, vij[a], ..., Decima,
..., xvij[a] Ab), *the papal condemnation or toleration in the margin (some
letters in* Ac *cut away*) (primum hoc capitulum dampnavit Rom' ecclesia sub
papa Alex' tercio Ac); AgAwFbSd *om. throughout (for* Aw *see n. a, p. 877).* H
starts here with Primum ...

De advocatione et presentatione ecclesiarum,[a] si controversia emerserit inter laicos, vel inter clericos et laicos,[b] vel inter clericos, in curia domini regis tractetur et terminetur.

ii. *Hoc toleravit.*

Ecclesie de feudo domini regis non possunt in perpetuum dari absque assensu et concessione ipsius.

iii. *Hoc dampnavit.*

Clerici retati et accusati de quacunque re, summoniti a iusticia regis, venient[c] in curiam ipsius, responsuri ibidem de hoc unde videbitur curie regis quod sit ibi[d] respondendum, et in curia ecclesiastica unde videbitur quod ibidem sit respondendum; ita quod iusticia regis[e] mittet in curiam sancte ecclesie ad videndum qua ratione res ibi tractabitur. Et si clericus convictus vel confessus fuerit, non debet de cetero eum[f] ecclesia tueri.

iv. *Hoc dampnavit.*

Archiepiscopis, episcopis et personis regni non licet exire de[g] regno absque licentia domini[h] regis; et si exierint, si domino regi placuerit, assecurabunt quod nec in eundo nec in moram faciendo, nec in redeundo, perquirent malum vel[i] dampnum domino regi vel regno.

Quinta. *Hoc dampnavit.*

Excommunicati non debent dare vadium ad remanens, nec prestare iuramentum, sed tantum vadium et plegium standi iudicio ecclesie ut absolvantur.

---

[a]Aw *starts with* si, *om.* De ... ecclesiarum, *under heading* Consuetudines avite regis.   [b]inter cler. et laic. AbAcFbSd; inter laic. et cler. AgAw (Sd *om.* vel inter clericos).   [c]veniant Ag.   [d]ibi sit Ag.   [e]reg. iust. Ag.   [f]de cetero eum AbAgAw; eum de cetero AcFbSd.   [g]de AbAc; a AgFbSd.   [h]Ag *om.* domini.   [i]vel AbAc; sive AgFbSd.

vi. *Hoc toleravit.*[a]

Laici non debent accusari nisi per certos et legales accusatores et testes in presentia episcopi, ita quod archidiaconus non perdat ius suum nec quicquam quod inde habere debeat. Et si tales fuerint qui culpantur, quod non velit vel non audeat aliquis eos accusare,[b] vicecomes requisitus ab episcopo, faciat[c] iurare duodecim legales homines de visneto seu[d] de villa coram episcopo, quod inde[e] veritatem secundum conscientiam suam manifestabunt.

vii. *Hoc dampnavit.*

Nullus qui de rege teneat in capite, nec[f] aliquis dominicorum ministrorum eius excommunicetur nec terre alicuius eorum[g] sub interdicto ponantur, nisi prius dominus rex si in terra fuerit conveniatur, vel iusticia eius si fuerit extra regnum,[h] ut rectum de ipso[i] faciat, et ita ut quod pertinebit ad curiam regiam[j] ibidem terminetur, et de eo quod spectabit ad ecclesiasticam curiam ad eandem mittatur ut ibidem tractetur.[k]

viii. *Hoc dampnavit.*

De appellationibus, si emerserint, ab archidiacono debent procedere ad episcopum, et[l] ab episcopo ad archiepiscopum; et si archiepiscopus defuerit in iusticia exhibenda, ad dominum regem perveniendum est[m] postremo, ut precepto ipsius in curia archiepiscopi controversia terminetur, ita quod non debet ulterius procedere absque assensu domini regis.

ix. *Hoc dampnavit.*

Si calumpnia emerserit inter clericum et laicum, vel inter

---

[a]toleravit AcH; dampnavit Ab *marg.* vel alio l(ibro) toleravit Ab[1] *(i.e. in the revised version(s) of Alan of Tewkesbury's collection the reading was* toleravit, *which therefore seems slightly the preferable reading; but it may be due to a scribal slip, and incorrect; and see above,* p. 863 n. 2). [b]accusare eos AgFbSd.   [c]faciat AcAgFbSd; faciet Ab.   [d]seu AbAc; sive AgFbSd.   [e]*om.* FbSd.   [f]vel Ac.   [g]illorum AcAw.   [h]extra regnum fuerit AcAw.   [i]ipso AbAc; eo AgFbSd.   [j]regiam curiam Ag.   [k]tractetur AbAc *(over erasure)* AgFbAw; terminetur SdH *and most printed edns.*   [l]et *om.* AgFbSdAw.   [m]perveniendum est FbSdAb; proveniend' est Ag; est perveniendum AcAw.

laicum et clericum, de ullo tenemento quod clericus ad elemosinam velit attrahere, laicus vero ad laicum feudum, recognitione
duodecim legalium [Ab, fo. 27] hominum per capitalis iusticie
regis considerationem terminabitur, utrum tenementum sit perti-
nens ad elemosinam sive ad feudum laicum,[a] coram ipsa iusticia
regis. Et si recognitum fuerit ad elemosinam pertinere, placitum erit in curia ecclesiastica. Si vero ad laicum feudum,
nisi ambo tenementum de eodem episcopo vel barone advocaverint,
erit placitum in curia regia.[b] Sed si uterque advocaverit de
feudo illo eundem episcopum vel baronem, erit placitum in curia
ipsius, ita quod propter factam recognitionem seisinam non
amittat, qui prius saisitus fuerat, donec per placitum disra-
tionatum sit.[c]

Decima. *Hoc dampnavit.*

Qui de civitate, vel castello, vel burgo, vel dominico
manerio domini[d] regis fuerit, si ab archidiacono vel[e] episcopo[f]
super aliquo delicto citatus fuerit, unde debeat eisdem respondere, et ad citationes eorum satisfacere noluerit,[g] bene
licet eum sub interdicto ponere, sed non debet excommunicari,
priusquam capitalis minister domini[h] regis ville illius[i] conveniatur, ut iusticiet eum ad satisfactionem venire. Et si
minister regis inde defecerit ipse erit in misericordia domini[j]
regis, et exinde poterit episcopus ipsum accusatum ecclesiastica
iusticia cohercere.

xi. *Hoc toleravit.*

Archiepiscopi, episcopi et universe persone regni que[k] de
rege tenent in capite habent[l] possessiones suas de domino rege
sicut baroniam, et inde respondent[m] iusticiis et ministris regis
et secuntur[n] et faciunt[o] omnes rectitudines et consuetudines

---

[a]laic. feud. Ag.   [b]regis Ag.   [c]sit AbAc; fuerit AgH; FbSdAw *om.* donec
... sit (*presumably due to homoeoteleuton in a ms. reading* fuerit; Sd *reads*
saisitus fuerit).   [d]*om.* Ac.   [e]Ag *adds* ab.   [f]Ac *adds* et.   [g]noluerit
satisfacere AcAw.   [h]*om.* AgFbSdAw.   [i]vel loci *interlineated in* Ag.
[j]domini AbAcAw; *om.* AgFbSd.   [k]qui AcH.   [l]habeant Aw.   [m]respondeant
AgFbSdAw.   [n]sequantur Ag (*and* Aw *after corr.; Gervase reads* sequuntur:
see p. 873).   [o]faciunt AbAc; faciant AgFbSd (*and* Aw *after corr.*).

regias; et sicut barones ceteri[a] debent interesse iudiciis
curie domini[b] regis cum baronibus, usque[c] perveniatur in iudicio ad diminutionem membrorum vel ad mortem.

xii. *Hoc dampnavit.*

Cum[d] vacaverit archiepiscopatus vel episcopatus vel abbatia
vel prioratus de[e] dominio regis, debet esse in manu ipsius et
inde percipiet omnes redditus et exitus sicut dominicos. Et cum
ventum fuerit ad consulendum ecclesie, debet dominus rex mandare potiores personas ecclesie et in capella ipsius domini[f]
regis[g] debet fieri electio, assensu domini[h] regis et consilio
personarum regni, quas ad hoc faciendum vocaverit. Et ibidem
faciet electus homagium et fidelitatem domino[i] regi, sicut ligio
domino, de vita sua et de menbris et de honore suo[j] terreno,
salvo ordine suo, priusquam sit consecratus.[k]

xiii. *Hoc toleravit.*

Si quisquam de proceribus regni defortiaverit[l] archiepiscopo
vel episcopo vel archidiacono de se vel de suis[m] iusticiam
exhibere, dominus rex debet eos iusticiare.[n] Et si forte aliquis
diffortiaret domino regi rectitudinem suam, archiepiscopi et
episcopi[o] et archidiaconi debent eum iustificare,[p] ut domino
regi satisfaciat.

xiv. *Hoc toleravit.*

Catalla eorum qui sunt in forisfacto regis non detineat
ecclesia vel cimiterium contra iusticiam regis, quia ipsius
regis sunt,[q] sive in ecclesiis, sive extra fuerint inventa.

---

[a]ceteri barones Ag.   [b]domini AbAc; *om.* AgFbSdAw.   [c]AgFbSd *add* quo.
[d]Cum AbAcSdAw; Dum AgFb.   [e]in Ag.   [f]*om.* AgFbSdAw.   [g]*om.* Aw; ipsius
regis Ag.   [h]domini AbAcAw; ipsius Ag; *om.* FbSd.   [i]*om.* AgFbSd.   [j]*om.* Ag.
[k](sit *expunct.* then) consec. sit Ac.   [l]defortiaverit AbAw; diffortiaverit
AcAgFbSd.   [m]vel de suis AbAcAw; suisve AgFbSd.   [n]eos iusticiare AbAc;
iusticiare AgHAw; iustificare FbSd.   [o]H *ends here, at the end of a folio,
with the rest completed in a 17th-cent. hand.*   [p]iustificare AbFb; iusticiare AcAgSdAw.   [q]regis sunt AbAcAw; sunt regis AgFbSd.

xv. *Hoc dampnavit.*

Placita de debitis que fide interposita debentur vel absque interpositione fidei sint in iusticia[a] regis.

xvi. *Hoc toleravit.*

Filii rusticorum non debent ordinari absque assensu domini de cuius terra nati esse dinoscuntur.[b]

xvii. Facta est autem predictarum consuetudinum et dignitatum regiarum recordatio[c] a prefatis archiepiscopis et[d] episcopis et[d] comitibus et[d] baronibus et nobilioribus et antiquioribus regni apud Clarendo[Ab, fo. 27[v]]nam, quarta die ante purificationem sancte Marie perpetue Virginis,[e] domino Henrico filio regis cum patre suo domino rege[f] ibidem presente.[g]

Sunt autem et alie multe et magne consuetudines et dignitates sancte matris ecclesie, et domini regis, et baronum regni, que in hoc scripto non continentur, que salve sint sancte ecclesie, et domino regi et heredibus suis, et baronibus regni, et in perpetuum inviolabiliter observentur.[h]

V. *The Constitutions: abbreviated version*

The following version of cc. 1-7 occurs only in a single 12th-cent. ms. of Becket's correspondence, Bodl. ms. Rawlinson Q. f. 8 (27836), in Ely Cathedral Library in the 14th cent. It may be an abbreviated version of a full text, or a summary noted by the clerks who composed this Becket collection; it has been plausibly suggested[1] that it is the fragmentary copy of a draft version, made fairly late in the process of composition.

---

[a]curia Ag.   [b]Aw *ends here.*   [c]reg. recordatio AcAgFbSd; recordatio reg. Ab.   [d]et AbAc; *om.* AgFbSd.   [e]perpetue Virginis AbAc; *om.* AgFbSd. [f]Ag *om.* domino rege.   [g]FbSd *end here.*   [h]Sunt autem ... observentur AbAc; Has predictas consuetudines quia T. Cant. archiepiscopus scripto et sigillo suo confirmare noluit, exulavit. Quas tamen quia verbotenus confirmaverat, statim penitens se ipsum a missarum celebratione suspendit ... Ag; Ab *adds (marg.)* Expliciunt constitutiones quas Henricus rex Anglie peciit sibi confirmari a beato Thoma martire.

---

[1]By A. Saltman, *BIHR* xxii (1949), 156-7.

From Bodl. ms. Rawlinson Q. f. 8 (27836), fos. 11^V-12;
ed. A. Saltman in *BIHR* xxii (1949), 155-6, with commentary pp. 156-7; cf. A. Duggan, 'The Manuscript Transmission of Letter Collections relating to the Becket Dispute'
(p. 871 n. 1), pp. 71-2, A. Duggan (1980), pp. 39-40.

[1] De presentationibus ecclesiarum placitum inter laicos sive
inter clericos, sive inter clericos et laicos, in curia regis
terminetur.

[2] Elemosine (*sic for* Ecclesie) de feudo regis non possunt
dari in elemosinam in perpetuum, nisi per licentiam regis.

[3] Clerici qui calumpniati fuerint et rettati de quacumque
re, summoniti per iusticiam regis veniant in curiam regis
responsuri ibi[a] de hoc quod ipsi curie videbitur ibi respondendum, et inde ad curiam sancte ecclesie ibi ad respondendum vel
faciendum quod iustum fuerit; et iusticia regis mittat in
curiam ecclesie ad videndum quo iure res tractetur.

[fo. 12] [4] Episcopis sive aliis personis non licet exire a
regno Anglie nisi per licentiam regis.

[3b] Clericum convictum[b] et confessum non debet ecclesia tueri.

[5] Excommunicati non debent dare pro absolutione sua pignus,
nisi vadium et plegium standi iudicio ecclesie, nec prestare[c]
iuramentum.

[6] Laici non accusentur nisi per legitimos accusatores et
legales testes et in presentia ipsius episcopi causa tractetur,
salvo tamen iure archidiaconi.

[7] Barones regis vel servientes vel aliqui qui in capite de
rege teneant non excommunicentur, donec domino regi prius

---

[a]ubi *ms.*   [b]convuctum *ms.*   [c]prare *ms.*

ostendatur, et in curia regis quod ad iusticiam regis pertinet
et in curia ecclesiastica sit quod ibi pertinet.

VI. *Herbert of Bosham on the Council of Clarendon*

> From Arras, Bibl. de Ville ms. 375 (649), fos. 37^V-41^V
> (early 13th cent., from Saint-Vaast, Arras);[1] printed in
> *MB* iii.278-89.

Verum rex regni et sacerdotii pacem ut videbatur zelans, sed
et sibi et archipresuli suo minus in hoc previdens, nec ullum
deprehendens in hoc malitie fucum, mox apud [fo. 38] quandam
nobilem et preclaram regis propriam mansionem, que ex re nomen
habet Clarendune,[2] regnum convocat universum, presules regni
et proceres. Et infra dies paucos conveniunt universi, ubi in
omnium conspectu et primus ante omnes archipresul in pretacta
forma se obligat, quod videlicet regias consuetudines foret
observaturus bona fide, verbo illo suppresso, scilicet salvo
ordine; et quasi iuratoriam adiciens cautionem hoc se facturum
in verbo veritatis confirmavit. Et id ipsum et in eadem forma
sigillatim universi pontifices. Cum vero multorum et magnorum
suasionibus et consiliis, quicquid prius apud prefatum illud
castellum, videlicet Oxeneford spopondisset, vix inductus
fuisset ad obligationem hanc, hec tamen ut induceretur potissima
causa fuit, caritas videlicet fraterna et compatiens, quibusdam
enim fratrum suorum coepiscoporum fraterne compatiebatur, illis
metuens magis quam sibi, gloriose videlicet memorie generoso
viro Henrico tunc Vuintoniensi et Iocelino tunc Salesberiensi
episcopis: quibus nisi fieret sic, tum ex antiquo odio, tum
quia in presenti propter ecclesie negotium habebantur suspecti,
aut captio aut quod deterius imminere videbatur.[3] Et quidem
archipresulis et pontificum ad regias et ut nominabantur avitas
consuetudines observandas in genere obligatio talis. Et incontinenti facta obligatione in forma hac, per quosdam regni

---

[1] We omit the rubric (before 'Et ut' p. 886) 'De consuetudinibus exactus'.
[2] For the site of the palace at Clarendon, see Knowles, *TB*, p. 87 and
plate facing p. 90; R.A. Brown and H.M. Colvin in *History of the King's
Works*, ii (London, 1963), pp. 910-18.
[3] See above, p. 853 and n. 4.

proceres, qui has nosse debuerant, facta est regiarum consuetudinum recognitio,[1] et sicut publice ita et expressim recensen-
tur. Verum cum plereque iam fuissent expresse et multo plures
ut videbatur forent exprimende adhuc, archipresul interlocutus
est se nec esse de antiquioribus regni, ut pristinas regum
consuetudines sciret, nec in archipresulatu diu fuisse, unde et
dicebat se nescire de his; et preterea quod inclinata esset iam
dies, tantum negotium differendum in crastinum. Placuit sermo
et in sua se receperunt hospitia, in crastino[2] revertentes in
idipsum. Et que pridie intermisse fuerant consuetudines regie
recognite sunt et expresse et in scriptum cyrographi[3] modo
confectum redacte, et regiarum consuetudinum nomine censite.
Quarum tamen multe, ut perhibebant multi, nequaquam regie, sed
ut iam dicere cepimus odio archipresulis ad ancillandam ecclesiam evomitum emulationis et invidie virus: [fo. 38[V]] ipso
etiam rege ignorante quod inimici homines sic inter ipsum et
archipresulem suum hac astutia dissensionis zizania seminare
intenderent.[4] Nec enim rex qui adhuc iuvenis, sicut nec archipresul suus novus, pristinas regni consuetudines nisi ex
aliorum relatu cognoscebat.

Et ut illarum consuetudinum seu libertatum vel dignitatum,
quas regias vocabant et que tunc [sunt] nobis proposite, inter-
seramus hic aliquas. Prima, ut decreti funesti cyrographi
propriis utar verbis, fuit hec.

[1] De advocatione et presentatione ecclesiarum si controversia
emerserit inter laicos, vel inter laicos et clericos, vel inter
clericos, in curia domini regis tractetur et terminetur.

Sic mox in primis respondit archipresul evidentissime clericos ad secularia iudicia pertrahi, et ecclesiasticam iurisdictionem in secularem converti. Advocatio quippe ecclesiarum iuri

---

[1]See p. 852; the last clause, of course, echoes the words of the document.
[2]Herbert seems to indicate that the proceedings lasted two days; in fact
the council probably lasted five or six (see pp. 852-3); and it may be that
Herbert represents fairly enough the proceedings of the last two days, and
that we are now at the 29 or 30 January 1164; or he may have misremembered.
[3]See p. 852 n. 1.
[4]Cf. Matt. 13, 25.

spirituali, quo is qui vulgo ecclesie persona dicitur curam
spiritualem et regimen animarum adipiscitur, accedit et inni-
titur, unde cuius est de iure principali cognoscere, et de
accessorio, cum unum de altero pendeat et sibi invicem innexa
sint et adnexa. Alioquin si istud quod perniciosa quorundam
adinventione ius advocationis nominatur, merum seculare ius et
her[ed]itarium est: vendatur, ematur, et etiam aliorum instar
secularium in monomachiam deducatur. Duppliciter igitur argue-
bat archipresul funestum adinventum hoc, tum quia clericos
trahebant ante iudicem non suum, tum quia id unum controversia
non de cognitione secularis, sed potius iudicis ecclesiastici
est.

Huic vero funesto aliud, non tamen continuo sed tercium in
cyrographo, decretum subiungebatur prophanius, cuius sunt hec
verba et talis sanctio.

[3] Clerici retati vel accusati de quacunque re, summoniti a
iusticia regis venient in curiam ipsius responsuri ibidem de
hoc unde videbitur curie regis quod sit ibi respondendum, et in
curia ecclesiastica unde videbitur quod ibi sit respondendum:
ita quod iusticia regis mittet in curiam sancte ecclesie ad
videndum qua ratione res ibi tractabitur. Et si clericus convictus vel confessus fuerit, non debet de cetero eum ecclesia
tueri.

Hac ut nominabant consuetudine sic in scriptum redacta,
advertit mox archipresul et certius magis intellexit quam ex
priori propinari sibi serpentine emulationis virus; et mox
testatus est totius funesti cyrographi ipsa [fo. 39] verba
sicut insipide elegantie, sic plena malicie et plane libertatis
cleri subversionem: adiciens: 'Ecce' inquit 'quia iuxta funestum
canonem hunc clerici tam in criminali quam in civili causa ad
seculare iudicium pertrahuntur. Et denuo iudicatur Christus
ante Pilatum presidem. Et quod adhuc penalis servitutis accedit
cumulo, contra Domini in propheta mandatum clerici bis iudica-
buntur in idipsum et duplex eorum consurget tribulatio.[1] Quod
si sic omnium sceleratorum excedet adhuc deterior clericorum

---

[1]See p. 857; Nahum 1, 9 (Vulgate).

conditio. Huic vero subsequens erat funesti cyrographi decretum alterum.

[4] Archiepiscopis, episcopis et personis regni non licet exire
de regno absque licentia domini regis. Et si exierint, si regi
placuerit assecurabunt quod nec in eundo nec in moram faciendo,
querent malum vel damnum regi vel regno.

Archipresul vero obiecit huic quod huius promulgationis
edicto cessarent ad loca sancta peregrinationes et vota et
etiam evacuaretur obedientia, et quod maxime personis regni
regnum preclarum carcer fieret, et sic deterior personarum
regni conditio quam privatorum. Quid enim si aliqua personarum
peregre proficisci se voverit, aliave forte iusta causa et
honesta traxerit ad transmarina? Quid si forte sicuti interdum
solet inter viros apostolicos et Anglorum reges simultas oborta,
ad concilium aliasve ecclesie necessitates expediendas vocat
hic, inhibet ille. Nonne oportet obedire magis huic quam illi?
Christi vicario quam regi terreno? Oportet quidem: quanto magis
Deo quam homini. Verum personis ecclesiasticis regibus obligatis
sic et votum et obedientia secundum obligationis huius formam
de regum penderet arbitrio: verum ut archipresul interloquendo
subiecit. Decens quidem est et congruit sic ut quevis personarum
regni, si ob causam exire regnum disposuerit, a rege prius
licentiata recedat: sed iuratoria cautione se obligare ad hoc,
ne absque licentia exeat, sicut irreligiosum et indecens.

His vero consequens erat adhuc cyrographi decretum septimum.

[7] Nullus qui de rege teneat in capite, vel aliquis dominicorum
ministrorum eius excommunicetur, nec terre alicuius eorum sub
interdicto ponantur, nisi prius rex, si in terra fuerit, conveniatur, vel iusticia eius, si extra regnum fuerit, ut rectum
de ipso faciatur. Et ita ut quod pertinebit ad curiam regiam
ibidem terminetur et de eo quod spectabit ad curiam ecclesiasticam ad eandem mittatur ut ibi tractetur.

[fo. 39ᵛ] Hoc cyrographi decreto perhibebat archipresul plane
exauctorari ecclesiam, et sacerdotes in presenti Domini Sabaoth,
velut selecti quidam aliorum duces et principes, militie sue

privari cingulo, qui a summo omnium principe et qui omnium
principum aufert spiritum,[1] acceperunt gladium et liberam habent
ligandi et solvendi potestatem super reges ipsos et principes.
Iuxta quod rex ipse et propheta: Ad alligandos, inquit, reges
eorum in compedibus et nobiles eorum in manicis ferreis.[2]
Exauctorarentur, inquam, Christiane militie duces sacerdotes
sic, quorum est discernere inter sanctum et prophanum, inter
pollutum et mundum, et ad quorum qui leprosus fuerit separatur
arbitrium.[3]

Huic vero mox subsequens cyrographi decretum octavum.

[8] De appellationibus, si emerserint, ab archidiacono debent
procedere ad episcopum, et ab ipso ad archiepiscopum. Et si
archiepiscopus defecerit in iusticia exhibenda, postremo ad
regem est perveniendum ut precepto ipsius in curia archiepiscopi
controversia terminetur, ita quod non debet ulterius procedere
absque assensu regis.

Huic in prima facie cervice erecta archipresul se opposuit
proclamans, huic promulgato sic, ipsos archipresules, si con-
senserint, manifeste periurii reos, qui in susceptione pallii
inter cetera de appellationibus deferendis Romano pontifici
expressim iuraverunt: adiciens etiam dire et funeste tolli hoc[a]
omnium refugium oppressorum, quibus tanquam ad matrem omnium
Romanam ecclesiam libere recurrere perhibetur.

Post hoc inter pleraque alia supponitur cyrographi decretum
duodecimum.

[12] Cum vacaverit archiepiscopatus vel episcopatus vel abbatia
vel prioratus de dominio regis, debet esse in manu eius, et inde
percipiet omnes redditus et exitus sicut dominicos.

Huic mox respondit archipresul breviter, res pauperum fisco
minime applicandas, et hoc forte, sicut contra clementiam et
magnificentiam regiam, que etiam tanquam aliene divitie

---

[a]hic *ms.*

---

[1]Cf. Ps. 75, 13 (76, 12).   [2]Ps. 149, 8.
[3]Cf. Levit, 10, 10; 13-14, *passim.*

nequaquam sunt redemptio anime principis,[1] quod etsi illorum
qui precesserunt nos temporibus aliquando sic, minime tamen
tanquam sacrilegium hereditarium hoc trahendum ad consequen-
tiam. Sed ecclesie semper clamandum, semper obviandum, et
quatenus potest resistendum; et si sustineatur quod corrigi non
potest, tamen consentiendum nunquam.

Sequitur vero in eodem irregulari canone. Et cum ventum
fuerit ad consulendum ecclesie, debet dominus rex mandare
potiores personas ecclesie, et in capella regis fiet electio.

Et quidem [fo. 40] archipresul, tanquam validus canonice
electionis patronus, prehabito cum eruditis suis consilio,
sicut in aliis et in hoc, mox respondit, sicut canonem novum et
novam ex ipso electionis formam introductam, apostolicarum sanc-
tionum priscis iam et usitatis institutis sicut penitus diver-
sam et adversam; nec licere sibi absque viri apostolici, seu
potius totius universalis ecclesie auctoritate, novitati tam
singulari et singularitati tam nove, presertim super tantis
personis ecclesiasticis constituendis in insulana credita sibi
ecclesia, novam auctoritatem prestare, vel assensum, etiam etsi ecclesie plurimum expediret sic. Hoc enim esset iam velut
particulare quoddam scisma in ecclesia facere ex suo sensu et
suo spiritu, a generalibus et iam usitatis sanctorum patrum
sanctionibus sic recedere: addens quod hec electionis forma
nova in Anglia, velut quedam in corde maris scintilla, mox per
universum ecclesiarum orbem incendium grande de facili ex se
posset producere. Nam si ad votum suum et nutum hanc electionis
formam adinvenit in regno suo rex Anglorum, quidni similiter
facturi in regnis suis audientes hoc et reges ceteri? Addens
etiam quod novus canon hic plane canonice electionis libertati
et honori plurimum derogaret: cum nisi urgentissima ratio
interveniat, eo in loco eligendus sit antistes, ad quem consecrandus est, non quidem in presentia principis etsi de principali
coniventia et assensu. Quis enim principis presentiam non paveat?
Quis non exhorrescat? Quis nominabit libere, nisi quem desidera-
verit aut[a] quem postulaverit princeps? Quod sancti patres

---

[a] ad *corr.* *to* aut *ms.*

---

[1] Cf. Prov. 13, 8.

religiose et sapienter providentes statuerunt, ut nec in curia
nec in aula seu camera, nec etiam in principum capella seu ora-
torio pontificum aut fieret aut confirmaretur electio.

Adiciebat etiam decere minime ut ecclesiastici principes,
persone tam celebres, tam magnifice, quibus tot populorum regimen, tot animarum cura et tot ecclesiarum sollicitudo credita
est, in talibus et talium presertim locis que quorumlibet
laicorum seu etiam regum deputata sunt obsequiis aut eligantur
aut confirmentur electi. Et obiectis sibi mox respondit, quia
etsi in hoc Anglorum regno ab aliquorum regum retro temporibus
sit factum sic, magis hoc tirannice usurpatum quam constitutum
legittime. Adiecit tandem de variis electionum figuris, de
quibus per utriusque testamenti paginam ecclesiastice nos
hystorie [fo. 40^V] edocent, ex quibus in ecclesia primitiva
catholicos seculi principes ecclesiasticis electionibus et
negotiis non nunquam interfuisse manifestum, verum secundum
profectum fidei et varias circa ecclesiam rerum vicissitudines
varia sanctorum patrum super electionum figuris dispensatio
invenitur. In quibus aliter statutum reperitur inter ecclesie
nascentis primordia, aliter vero nunc, quando iuxta prophete
vaticinium posita est in superbiam seculorum; unde et ab hac
electionis forma, quam nunc universalis ecclesia suscepit,
approbat et observat absque ecclesie auctoritate recedere tutum
minime. Et quidem archipresulis responsum ad hec sic.

Ex istis itaque constitutis funestis que iam expressimus,
odio archipresulis ad ecclesiastice libertatis oppressionem ab
ecclesie inimicis fabricatis, sic quisque mox videre potest
quam manifesta, quam iusta archipresulis nostri primo exilii et
demum martyrii causa fuerit. Quod alicuius martyrum causa iustior
fuerit aut apertior, ego nec audivi nec legi: qui potest doceat,
cum tamen et de illis pleraque alia restent adhuc funesto illi
decreti cyrographo inserta forme et sanctionis consimilis.

Verum non est meum, non est mee mensure, non parvitatis mee,
ad regias seu ecclesiasticas consuetudines dignitatesve aut
libertates se extendere. Nichil parvitati mee et dignitatibus
illis, nec mee mensure est vel scientie probare illas vel
improbare: ipsorum potius regum et pontificum consideratio hec.

Solum quod audivi, quod vidi, hic testor.[1] Unum scio quia hec
que iam expressimus et alia nonnulla similia his, numero ni
fallor quasi decreta capitulatim distincta sedecim, prefato
inserta cyrographo, plena iam erant inter regem et archipresulem dissensionis materia. Et hoc decreti cyrographum, ab ipso
originali mutuatum, favente Domino, in historici huius voluminis
fine integre postponemus[2] ut cunctis martyris huius historie
lectoribus liquido pateat, etiam preter ea que iam posita, quam
clara, quam aperta, quam perspicua primo exilii et postea martyrii fuerit archipresulis causa. Domino quidem omnium iudice
mirabiliter quidem, sed equissime disponente, ut cuius fuerant
odio introducte et quibus semetipsum accusans videbatur quodam
modo consensisse, per eundem ipsum postea in proprio ipsius
cruore sint abolite, delens sic hoc, quod adversum nos erat
decreti per cyrographum, quod erat contrarium nobis; palam etiam
triumphans principatus et potesta[fo. 41]tes in semet ipso.
Nam ut de aliis nunc preteream, ipsius regis advertentis se et
corde toto et corpore ad archipresulem suum in fine reversi,
huic de quo nunc agitur presenti decreti cyrographo renuntia-
vit, renuit et vim eius omnem et auctoritatem explosit: quod
plane liber, quem Melorum inscripsi quem historie huic subiunxi,
edocet.[a] Quod si michi obieceris multa de iniquis statutis illis
per regnum observari adhuc, breviter respondeo et certissime regem
ipsis, ut diximus, renuntiasse et Christi sponsam ecclesiam in sanguine
martyris Christi triumphali evicisse. Si rex penitens et renuntians perseveraverit, Deus novit, Deus velit, rex ipse viderit.
Et si, ut michi obicis, funesti illius cyrographi consuetudines
alique vim habent, et tanquam de stirpe noxia de nocivis ampu-
tatis nonnulla quasi spuria vitulamina male excrescant, adhuc
sperandum quod ad archipresulum martyris successorum instantiam,

---

[a]*In margin of ms.:* In libro melorum (see p. 874) ii°, melorum [? ...]
notula. Consuetudines *(the ref. seems to be to Liber Melorum, ii.9, in*
Herberti de Boseham Opera, *ed. J.A. Giles, ii, London-Oxford, 1846,*
pp. 39-40).

[1]Cf. I Joh. 1, 1 ff. (but a common refrain in Herbert, as in many other
medieval biographies).
[2]See p. 874. The 'volume' contained the Life, the *Liber Melorum,* his
homily on the martyr's feast and the Constitutions (se *MB* iii.158-9).

per regum clementiam, cum crebro et devote martyris et martyrii
cause extiterint memores, inperfectum supplebitur, et plene a
facie olei computrescet servitutis ecclesiastice iugum.¹ Aut si
non, habebunt altissimo disponente sic martyris successores
archipresules his diebus carnis sue exercende probandeque virtutis materiam. Sed quasi preoccupantes, necdum est de his que
nunc hic tangimus locus; revertamur ad hoc quod in presenti
agitur, iam propositam plenam et ni fallor solum ex his que
pretetigimus, preter alia que hic preterimus, totius ecclesie
iudicio iustissimam dissensionis causam et materiam. Quam
totius ecclesie primas vir apostolicus sua que omni preest auctoritate iustificavit confirmans, sicut sequentia declarabunt.
Revertamur inquam ad plenam iam dissensionis causam. Iam enim
plana, iam ampla dissensionis materia, post modicum exilii, et
postmodum martyrii causa ...²

[fo. 41ᵛ] ... Scripto vero expressas, ut iam diximus, consuetudines continente ad cyrographi formam confecto et propalato,
postulat rex ab archipresule et coepiscopis ut ad cautionem
maiorem et firmitatem, sigilla sua appendentes apponant.³ Verum
archipresul etsi vehementer motus et contristatus, dissimulat
tamen, regem exacerbare tunc nolens. Et caute quidem non de
plano negat, sed differendum dicebat adhuc. Et si paratos ad
faciendum, adiciebat tamen propter negotii magnitudinem decere
dilationem vel modicam, cum iuxta sapientem absque consilio
nichil faciendum sit grave,⁴ et exinde post deliberationem aliquantulam, ipsum et episcopos alias super hoc decentius
requirendos. Scriptum tamen dictas consuetudines continens
recipit, premeditate quidem et provide ut causam videlicet suam
secum scriptam haberet. Alteram vero scripti partem suscepit
Eboracensis archiepiscopus: rex vero ipse terciam, in regum
archivis reponendam. Et sic a curia recessimus versus civitatem
Wintoniam proficiscentes.

---

¹Cf. Isa. 10, 27.
²At this point we omit a rhetorical apostrophe.
³See pp. 852 n. 1, 854 n. 6.   ⁴Cf. Eccles. 32, 34.

160

6-13 OCTOBER 1164. ROYAL COUNCIL OF NORTHAMPTON

After Clarendon Henry II sent Geoffrey Ridel (now archdeacon of
Canterbury) and John of Oxford to the pope to seek confirmation for the Constitutions - though it is doubtful if the pope
saw or commented on a full text at this time. They also asked
that the archbishop of York be made legate for the whole kingdom. This was refused, though York was appointed legate for
Scotland later in the year,[1] and meanwhile some kind of legateship is said to have been conferred on the king himself. Soon
after, reports reached the pope that Becket was undergoing a
course of penance and had suspended himself from his priestly
functions, and on 1 April Alexander III sent him a bull of
absolution.[2] Further efforts to reconcile king and archbishop
made no headway, and Thomas tried twice to escape and visit the
pope in person.

It is reported that John of Oxford, on his knees before the
pope, had sworn that unless the pope acted as Henry wished,
Becket's life would be in peril.[3] However that may be, as the
year advanced the king prepared for a further onslaught. He
chose two cases in which he reckoned that the jurisdiction of
the royal court could be most plausibly and effectively used
for the archbishop's undoing, and summoned him to the royal
court in September to answer the first case against him. This
was a complaint by John the Marshal that he had not received
justice in the archbishop's baronial court in a land plea. The
archbishop, for his part, claimed that John's oath to this
effect was made on a troper not on the gospels, as if to avoid
a charge of perjury; but the fact was that the archbishop failed

---

[1]Tillmann, p. 56 and n. 20. For the king as legate see JS, *Letters*, ii,
no. 275; C.R. Cheney, *Pope Innocent III and England* (Stuttgart, 1976),
pp. 38 n., 56.

[2]*MB Epp.* 50 (prob. 27 Feb.), 52 (1 Apr.): the difference in date suggests
that the royal embassy arrived some weeks before reports of Thomas's penances.
Cf. William of Canterbury, Grim, FitzStephen, Bosham, Roger of Pontigny, the
Anon. of Lambeth, *MB* i.24-5; ii.389-90; iii.49, 292 ff.; iv.37-40, 103-4;
Knowles, *EC*, pp. 65-6.

[3]Roger of Pontigny, *MB* iv.38.

to answer the summons to the royal court.[1] A further summons
was made to a solemn royal council at Northampton in October,
and there Thomas was made to answer John's complaint; and also
made to answer a series of demands for repayment or accounts
of money handled by him as chancellor.[2] The council opened,
according to the most probable chronology,[3] on Tuesday, 6 October, and continued through a week of stormy and dramatic meetings, to its climax on Tuesday 13 October, when the archbishop
fled. The story has never been better told than by William
FitzStephen, who was present and seems to have based his narrative on detailed notes made at the time or soon after.[4] Variant
versions of major incidents are referred to in the notes.

On 13 October Thomas escaped from Northampton by night, and
on 2 November he crossed to Flanders, passing on to the papal
court at Sens, where the Constitutions of Clarendon were read
out and the papal condemnation confirmed (see pp. 855, 914);
and at the end of the year Thomas was settled in the Cistercian
abbey of Pontigny.

From the Vita Sancti Thome of William FitzStephen

The following is based on collation of all the mss., but minor
variants of individual mss. have not been noted; we have based

---

[1]See Knowles, *EC*, pp. 69-70 n., dismissing the statement of William of
Canterbury and Grim, that Becket was ill in September (*MB* i.30, ii.390; see
on the other side esp. FitzStephen, *MB* iii.52 (below, p. 899) and *GFL*, no.
170, p. 235). For the case of John the Marshal see also Roger of Pontigny,
MB iv.40-1, 43.

[2]Details in Knowles, *EC*, pp. 69-70, based on FitzStephen (below, pp. 897-901);
also Roger of Pontigny, *MB* iv.40 ff.

[3]See Knowles, *EC*, pp. 163-6, showing that the dates given by FitzStephen
are consistent and probably correct. Diceto gives 13 Oct. and Gervase *c*.12
Oct. (3rd day before St. Calixtus) for opening of the council; Bosham starts
it on Thursday, the 6th before St. Calixtus (14th) and ends it on the following Tuesday - his calendar for 1164 may have been awry (see next note),
but the main sessions ran from a Thursday to a Tuesday (Diceto, i.313;
Gervase, i.182; *MB* iii.296-301). Bosham wrote in the 1180s; on FitzStephen
see also below.

[4]Cf. Knowles, *EC*, p. 163. It is improbable that so consistent a pattern
of dates, with weekdays correct for 1164, could have been produced without
notes made at the time. At *MB* iii.70 he gives the date of Thomas's escape
from England as 2 November; this is confirmed by Bosham, *MB* iii.324-5, who
makes it, however, a Tuesday. (All Souls Day, 2 Nov., was a Monday in
1164.)

our text on Sd and Sl, which probably alone represent the original, full text of the *Life*.[1] Sd already incorporates some early
changes, but has to be our base ms., since a lacuna in Sl
deprives us of its text of the greater part of this extract. Sh,
Sa, and Sj represent a revised and abbreviated version, although
Sh has kept some of the passages omitted in Sa and Sj. Where we
have only the witness of Sd, Sj, and Sh it is often difficult
to be sure with minor differences whether they are due to slips
in Sd or revision in Sj and Sh.

Sd. Oxford, Bodl. ms. Douce 287 (21861), fos. 11-16, late
   12th cent. (or early 13th) from Lessness abbey (also
   used on pp. 874, 929).

Sl. BL ms. Lansdowne 398, fos. 25-26^v; 15th cent.

Sh. Hereford Cathedral ms. O. iv. 14, fos. 204-208, 14th
   cent., in Hereford Cathedral Library since 15th cent.
   and possibly from Worcester.

Sa. London, Lambeth Palace Lib. ms. 138, fo. 212^{r-v} (fragment only), early 13th cent.

Sj. BL ms. Cotton Julius A. xi, fos. 126-132^v, late 12th or
   early 13th cent., at one time in the Franciscan library
   at Hereford. There is a 17th-cent. transcript in Cambridge, Trinity Coll. ms. O. 5. 45 (1326).

The *Life* was first printed in J. Sparke, *Historiae Angli-
canae scriptores varii* (London, 1723), variously bound
as ii, part i or part ii; subsequently ed. J.A. Giles,
Vita S. Thome, i (London-Oxford, 1846), pp. 213-38; hence
by Migne in *PL* cxc.103-92; also in *MB* iii.49-70.

William FitzStephen's narrative

[38] Unde[a] rex postmodum aliud generale edicit[b] concilium,

---

[a]Unde SdSl; *om.* SjSaSh.   [b]generale edicit Sl[1]SjSa; gen. edidit Sd;
gen. Sh; ed. gen. Sl (*before corr.*).

---

[1]See the important paper of M.G. Cheney in *Church and Government in the
Middle Ages: Essays presented to C.R. Cheney* (Cambridge, 1976), pp. 139-56;
on ms. Sd see above, pp. 873-4; on FitzStephen see also C.N.L. Brooke and G.
Keir, *London 800-1216* (London, 1975), pp. 112-21, and p. 88 n., where there
is some account of the mss. containing the description of London without the
rest of the Life; these are ignored here.

locum designans apud Norhamtun(am) octava sancti Michaelis feria
tertia. Concilii dicta dies[a] aderat; ipsa die venimus Norhamtonam. Regem ea die non vidit archiepiscopus, quia rex circa
rivos aquarum et fluenta in avibus celi ludens veniendo Norham-
ton(am) sero intravit. Crastino mane dicta missa et horis, archiepiscopus ad curiam venit ad castrum regis. In cameram primam[1]
intromissus, sedit regem expectans, qui tunc missam audiebat;
cui venienti venerabiliter assurgens vultum exhibuit constan-
tem, placidum, ad osculi consuetam Anglis gratiam offerendam
verecundum, recipiendam paratum, si rex preoccuparet.[b] Ad oscu-
lum receptus non est.

[39] Primam sumpsit archiepiscopus loquendi materiam de Willelmo de Curci, qui unum hospitiorum suorum occupaverat, pete-
batque a rege ut illud sibi vacuari preciperet; precepit.
Secundus sermo eius fuit quod ad vocationem ipsius pro verbo
quod ei moverat Iohannes Marescallus venerat. Siquidem Iohannes
petebat ab archiepiscopo terram unam, membrum quoddam ville
archiepiscopalis Pageham. Et aliquot diebus pro causa illa sibi
designatis cum brevi regis in curiam archiepiscopi venerat, ubi
cum non proficeret, nullo siquidem iure munitus quod tunc lex
erat, probavit tandem defectum curie archiepiscopi, sed super

---

[a] *om.* SjSa.   [b] preoccupasset Sd.

---

[1] Northampton castle was replaced by a railway station in the 19th cent.;
for a reconstruction of the rooms here described, see Knowles, *EC*, pp. 169-
70; cf. *King's Works*, ii (1963), 750-3 (R.A. Brown and H.M. Colvin). The
prima camera was evidently an outer room, perhaps communicating with the
chapel. The hall and (inner) chamber which figure below were in the main
residential block to the south-west of the bailey. C. 39 describes the
events of Wednesday 7 Oct. In the notes that follow no attempt is made to
compare the authorities in detail; for this see Knowles, *EC*, pp. 66-89.
After FitzStephen's the fullest narrative is that of Herbert of Bosham (*MB*
iii.296-322), whose chronology, however, is evidently confused (see above);
there are also narratives of some fullness by William of Canterbury, Alan
of Tewkesbury, Edward Grim, Roger of Pontigny, and Guernes (*MB* i.30-41;
ii.326-35, 390-9; iv.41-54; Guernes, 1383-2055); there are also accounts in
Gervase, i.182-9 (based on William of Canterbury, Alan of Tewkesbury and
Herbert of Bosham) and Diceto, i.313-14; etc. The narratives present many
minor differences, especially for 13 Oct., mostly of little significance.

librum troporum extractum desub pallio suo,[1] causantibus iusticiariis curie archiepiscopi quod neque librum ad hoc neque
talem attulisse deberet. Reversusque ad regem literas citationis
archiepiscopi in curia regis ei responsuri emeruerat, presti-
tuta[a] liti die Exaltationis sancte Crucis. Ad diem autem illam
archiepiscopus non venerat, sed miserat regi milites quatuor
cum litteris suis et vicecomitis Cantie, pariter attestantis
iniuriam Iohannis et inperfectum probacionis eius. Sed quid?
Indigne ferens rex quod ab eo citatus archiepiscopus in propria
persona non venerat, hoc si vellet allegaturus, male tractavit
nuntios ipsius molestus eis in ira et minis; tamquam qui contra
regis citationem in curiam eius excusationem falsam, nullam et
inutilem[b] attulerant; et tandem datis vadibus vix eos[c] relaxavit. Et [Sd, fo. 11[v]] aliam diem ex instantia Iohannis (primam
scilicet concilii diem), pro eadem causa prefixit,[d] litteris
suis ad vicecomitem Cancie de archiepiscopo citando[e] emissis.
Nec[f] tunc enim,[g] nec diu ante, ei scribere voluerat, quia eum
salutare nolebat. Nec aliam per literas sibi directas sollen-
nem et primam, ut antiqui moris erat, habuerat archiepiscopus
ad concilium[h] citationem. Dixit inquam archiepiscopus se ex
mandato regis pro causa Iohannis venisse; ad quod rex ait
Iohannem esse in eius servitio Lond(onie), venturum autem in
proximo, et tunc de eorum causa cognosceret. Erat siquidem
Iohannes ille cum thesaurariis et ceteris fiscalis pecunie et
publici eris receptoribus Lond(onie), ad quadrangulam tabulam
que dicitur calculis bicoloribus, vulgo Scaccarium; potius
autem est regis tabula nummis albicoloribus ubi etiam placita
corone regis tractantur. Ea[i] die inter regem et archiepiscopum
nil amplius actum est, sed dixit rex ei ut ad hospitium iret,
in crastino ad causam suam reverteretur. Rediit.

---

[a]prestita Sd.   [b]Sd *adds* excusationem (nimis inutilem Sl).   [c]vix eos
SjSaSh; eos vix Sl; eos Sd.   [d]prefixerat Sd.   [e]archiep. citando SlSjSs
Sh; citatione ipsius Sd.   [f]non Sd.   [g]*om*. Sd.   [h]Sd *om*. ad concilium.
[i]Ea Sd; Eo Sl; Ea prima SaSjSh.

---

[1]See p. 894 : he is alleged to have sworn on a troper, the most modest of
liturgical books (a collection of musical adornments or additions to mass
and offices, or later, a book of sequences) rather than on a gospel book.
Cf. *GFL*, no. 170, p. 235 and n.; Roger of Pontigny, *MB* iv.41.

[40] Secunda die,[1] considentibus episcopis, comitibus,[a] baronibus Anglie omnibus, Normannie pluribus, preter Rophensem episcopum qui nondum venerat, et quendam alium,[b] archiepiscopus
lese maiestatis corone regie arguitur, quia scilicet, ut supra
narratum est, a rege citatus pro causa Iohannis, neque venisset
neque idonee se excusasset. Archiepiscopi depulsio nullum locum
habuit, allegata[c] Iohannis supradicta iniuria et iurisdictione
huius causa sua[d] propria et curie sue integritate. Rex exigit
iudicium. Archiepiscopi ratio nulla est approbata.[e] Visum est
omnibus ex reverentia regie maiestatis et ex astrictione ligii
homanagii quod domino regi archiepiscopus fecerat,[f] et ex fidelitate et observantia terreni eius honoris, quam ei iuraverat,
quod parum esset defensus vel excusatus; quia citatus a rege
neque venerat neque corporis infirmitatem vel necessariam que
differri non posset ecclesiastici officii[g] administrationem
per nuntios allegaverat; condempnandumque eum dixerunt in penam
pecuniariam omnium bonorum suorum mobilium ad misericordiam
regis. De proferendo iudicio distantia fuit inter episcopos et
barones, utrisque alteris illud inponentibus, utrisque se excu-
santibus. Aiunt barones: 'Vos episcopi pronuntiare debetis
sententiam; ad nos non pertinet:[h] nos laici sumus, vos persone
ecclesiastice sicut[i] ille, consacerdotes eius, coepiscopi eius.'
Ad hec aliquis episcoporum, 'Immo vestri potius est hoc officii,
non nostri; non enim est hoc iudicium ecclesiasticum, sed seculare. Non sedemus hic episcopi, sed barones. Nos barones et vos
barones pares hic sumus. Ordinis autem[j] nostri rationi frustra
innitimini, quia si in nobis ordinationem attenditis, et in
ipso similiter attendere debetis. Eo autem ipso quod episcopi
sumus, non possumus archiepiscopum et[k] dominum nostrum iudicare.'
Sed quid? Rex hac audita[l] de pronuntiando controversia motus

---

[a]comitibus SdSa; comitibus et SlSjSh.   [b]preter ... alium SdSlSh; Roffensis
episcopus et quidam alius nondum venerat SjSa.   [c]allegata SdSl; allegata
tamen SjSaSh.   [d]om. SjSaSh.   [e]Sa ends here.   [f]archiep. fecerat SdSl; fec.
arch. SjSh.   [g]eccl. off. SdSl; offic. eccl. SjSh.   [h]Sd adds hoc.   [i]Sd
adds et.   [j]om. Sd.   [k]Sl breaks off here, resuming after the end of our
extract. Henceforth Sd, collated with plausible variants of Sj and Sh (revised edn., see p. 896), whose readings are preferred when Sd seems probably
at fault.   [l]hac audita SjSh; aud. hac Sd.

---

[1]Thursday, 8 Oct. Knowles, *EC*, pp. 67 ff.

est; et controversari super hoc desitumest. Dominus Winton(iensis) inpositus dicere, tandem et invitus pronuntiavit. Archiepiscopus autem, quia sententie vel recordationi curie regis Anglie non licet contradicere, sustinuit consilio episcoporum; adacta ad mitigandum et honorandum regem sollenni in manum ipsius missione, quasi concessione iudicii, ut moris est ibi; et omnibus episcopis datis vadibus preter Gilebertum illum Lundoniensem qui rogatus pro eo spondere noluit, que eius[a] singularitas notam fecit.

[41] [Sd, fo. 12] Post eadem die conventus est archiepiscopus de trecentis libris perceptis de castellaria Eye et Berchamsted'. Archiepiscopus litis declinatione premissa, ut qui ad hoc citatus non fuit, ait ut non in lite se hanc pecuniam et multo plurem misisse ad reparationem palatii Lond(onie) et castrorum predictorum, ut cernere erat. Rex noluit esse auctor eius quod hoc[b] per eum factum esset. Exigit iudicium. Archiepiscopus gratia regis reddere adquiescens pecuniam hanc, quoniam omnino nolebat ut quantalibet pecunia esset irarum inter eos[c] causa, semotim laicos fideiussores, comitem Gloecestrie et Willelmum de Eisnesford' et tertium quendam, homines suos, interposuit. Sub hoc fine die illa discedunt.

[42] Die tertia certi condictione[d][1] convenitur archiepiscopus per internuntios de quingentis marcis ex causa fideiussionis regis in exercitu Tolose pro eo[e] erga quendam Iudeum ibidem.[f]

---

[a] eum Sd (eius ... notam Sj; eum ... notam Sd; eius ... notum Sh).
[b] om. Sd.   [c] irarum inter eos SjSh; inter eos ir. Sd.   [d] conditione *mss.*
[e] fideiussionis regis pro eo Sh; fid. regis in ex. Tolose Sd; commodati in ex. Tolose et aliis quingentis marcis ex causa fid. regis pro eo Sj.
[f] ibidem SjSh; ibi Sd.

---

[1] Friday, 9 Oct. 'certi condictione' is clearly the right reading, as was pointed out in *MB* iv, p. xxvii. 'certi condictio' was a term in Roman Law for an action based on a civil law obligation claiming that a *certum* (a fixed sum, *certa pecunia,* or some other fixed item, *certa res*) was owed by the defendant (cf. W.W. Buckland, *Textbook of Roman Law*, 3rd edn., ed. P. Stein, Cambridge, 1963, p. 683). Presumably it here means that the action was for a known sum of money. Bosham (*MB* iii.298) confirms that the claim was for 500 marks, not 1000 as the revision in Sj, printed in Robertson's text, suggests.

Item convenitur actione tutele de omnibus perceptis ab archiepiscopatu vacante, seu aliis episcopatibus et abbatiis tempore
cancellarie[a] eius vacantibus; iubeturque super hiis omnibus
regi rationem exponere. Respondit archiepiscopus se non ad hoc
venisse paratum vel citatum. Super hoc si conveniri deberet
loco et tempore, domino suo regi quod iuris esset faceret.
Exegit rex ab eo super hoc cautionem fideiussoriam. Dixit ille
se oportere super hoc habere consilium suffraganeorum et clericorum suorum. Rex sustinuit. Ille discessit, et ex illa die
amplius ad hospitium eius non venerunt eum videre barones vel
alii milites, intellecto regis animo.

[43] Quarta die[1] ad hospitium domini archiepiscopi venerunt
omnes persone ecclesiastice.[b] Cum episcopis semotim, cum abbatibus semotim, super huiusmodi tractatum habuit, consilium
captavit. Consilio domini Wintoniensis[c] ordinatoris eius, qui
ei ad hoc auxilium validum promisit, temptatum est si regem
pecunia posset[d] delinire, et optulit ei duo millia marcarum.
Rex noluit. Fuerunt aliqui de clero qui dicerent archiepiscopo,
quod pro debito officii suscepti ecclesiam Dei tueretur, personam suam et dignitatem attenderet, regem honorificaret in
omnibus, salva Dei et ecclesiastici honoris reverentia; nichil
adversi esse quod timere deberet, cum ei nullum crimen, nulla
turpitudo inponeretur. Cantuariensi ecclesie redditus fuerat
liber a cancellaria et omni regis seculari querela; cum quelibet etiam abbatia vacans monachum alienum, abbatem sibi electum
recipere nolit, nisi immunem ab omni obedientia abbatis eius
sibi dimissum. Aliis secreto regis aure et mente inclinatiori-
bus, longe alia mens erat dicentibus, 'Dominus rex ei in ira
molestus est. Ex certis signis animum regis interpretamur hunc

---

[a]cancellarii Sd.   [b]pers. eccl. Sd; eccl. pers. ille SjSh.   [c]dom.
Winton. Sd; nobilis Henrici Winton. episcopi SjSh (*evidently revision*).
[d]posset Sd; possent SjSh.

---

[1]Saturday, 10 Oct. Presumably Alan's remarkable debate among the bishops
(*MB* ii.326-8) was based on the meeting here described, as in Knowles, *EC*,
pp. 72-3. But it is essentially a dramatic device to indicate, in a very
interesting way, a range of different attitudes among the bishops (cf. *GF*,
pp. 280-1).

esse quod dominus archiepiscopus super omnibus et super reddendo archiepiscopatu omnino misericordie regis se supponat.'
Inter quos et Hylarius Cicestrensis in partem regis inclina-
tior[a] ait ei, 'Utinam posses esse non archiepiscopus et remanere Thomas.' Hic etiam alias dixit de eo, 'Omnis plantatio
quam non plantavit pater celestis eradicabitur';[1] quasi diceret
quia electionem eius regis declarata voluntas precessit. De
quo archiepiscopus postea in exilio suo alicui dixit: 'Et hic
inter fratres locum optinuit Iude proditoris.' Postmodumque,
ante revocationem et pacem archiepiscopi, quasi a Deo percussus
expiravit.[2] Iste Cicestrensis prosecutus pro se et aliis quibusdam complicibus suis sit, 'Ex convictu et familiaritate cancellarie regem melius nostis quam nos. Indubitatum est vobis [Sd,
fo. 12[v]] contendendo an cedendo melius vincatur. In cancellaria
ei, et in pace et in gwerra, probe et laudabiliter officiosus,
non sine invidia tamen, laudem invenistis; qui vobis tunc in-
viderunt nunc regem accendunt adversus vos. Quis de tanto
ratiocinio, de tam incerta pecunia, posset spondere pro vobis?
Dicitur regem dixisse quod non amplius in Anglia simul eritis,
ille rex vos archiepiscopus. Ad misericordiam eius relinquere
omnia tutius est, ne forte, quod absit, vos tamquam cancellarium
et rationalem suum pro pecunia sua conventum, tanquam reum
repetundarum et fideiussoribus carentem retineat vel manum in
vos mittat; unde ecclesia Anglie dolorem et regni facies contrahat ruborem.' Dicebat aliquis: 'Absit ut sic sibi et corporis
sui saluti consulat, et Cantuariensem ecclesiam[b] que eum sibi
elegit inhonoret. Nullus hoc suorum fecit antecessorum; et
tamen persecutiones in diebus illis passi sunt. Preterea beneficium archiepiscopale, villas et huiusmodi, in manu domini
regis forte posset, salvo iure ecclesie, refutare ad tempus;
suum officium vero nequaquam.' Ita in varias consulti distra-
hebantur[c] sententias, alius sic, alius[d] non sic.

---

[a]inclinatior SjSh; inclinatus Sd.   [b]Sd *places* ecclesiam *after* inhonoret.
[c]detrahebantur Sd.   [d]alius Sd; alius vero SjSh.

---

[1]Matt. 15, 13.
[2]Bishop Hilary died *c.*13 July 1169 (on him *GFL*, p. 532 and references,
esp. to H. Mayr-Harting in *EHR* lxxviii (1963), 209-24).

[44] Quinta dies,[1] que et Dominica erat, tota consiliis dedita est; vix reficiendi hora respirare licebat. Archiepiscopus ab hospitio non recessit.[a]

[45] Sexta die,[2] languor repente (ut fit) ortus eum moratus est quo minus ad curiam iret. Siquidem renes eius frigore et dolore contremuerunt; oportuitque cervicalia calefacere et vicissim apponere. Quo audito, rex misit omnes comites suos, barones plurimos, responsum captati consilii querens ab eo et proponens, velletne de reddenda ratione receptorum tempore cancellarie de vacantibus ecclesiis fideiussoriam prestare cautionem, et super hoc curie sue stare iudicio. Respondit per episcopos archiepiscopus, quod si liceret ei pro corporis adversa valitudine, in crastino ad curiam veniret, facturus quod deberet.

[46] In crastino[3] mane ad quoddam altare sancti Stephani prothomartyris celebravit missam 'Etenim sederunt principes.'[b] Illius misse cantationem statim insidiantes ei regis delatores ei nuntiant, maligne interpretantes quod pro se quasi altero Stephano prothomartyre contra regem et suos iniquos eum persequentes, archiepiscopus illam missam celebraret.

[47] Post ad curiam vadit. Obiter precedenti eum ait Alexandro crucis sue baiulo, 'Melius egissem si in nostris instrumentis

---

[a]recessit Sd; dicessit SjSh.   [b]principes Sd; om. SjSh.

---

[1]Sunday, 11 Oct. Knowles, *EC*, pp. 73-4, suggests that the discussions recorded under Saturday continued throughout the Sunday.

[2]Monday, 12 Oct. On the illness, which evidently began on the Sunday night (Bosham and Pontigny, *MB* iii.300, iv.44; cf. Grim, ii.392), see Knowles, *EC*, pp. 167-8. Guernes, 1508 ff., seems to place it earlier, but has probably confused the order of events; Grim, loc. cit., has somewhat telescoped them.

[3]'The scenes of the following day, Tuesday, 13th October, are among the most celebrated in English domestic history' (Knowles, *EC*, p. 76). All the main narratives describe the events of the day at length, and they are disentangled in Knowles, *EC*, pp. 76-89 (on the mass introit, p. 77 and n.). On the archbishop of York and his cross, see A. Heslin, art. cit., p. 848 n. 5; on the appeals, p. 914. On the request (p. 913) for permission for Thomas to depart, see *EC*, p. 88 n.: Grim says that it was for permission to go to Canterbury, Bosham to leave the country; FitzStephen just to depart, which seems the most likely (cf. *MB* ii.334; iii.312).

venissem.' Proposuerat enim quod nudis pedibus incedens et
revestitus et crucem baiulans ad regem intraret, ei pro pace
ecclesie supplicaturus. Sed ab hoc proposito eum clerici sui
averterunt, neque quod crucem tollere vellet putaverunt. Intra-
turus in aulam castri, cum equo descendisset, crucem quam
previam baiulaverat Alexander Walensis in manibus[a] accepit.
Aderat ibi ad hostium aule episcopus predictus[b] Lond(oniensis),
cui Hugo de Nunant quidam archidiaconus Luxoviensis, qui cum
archiepiscopo venerat et de domo eius erat,[c] 'Domine presul
Lund(oniensis), ut quid sustines quod crucem ipse baiulat?'
Episcopus, 'Bone homo, semper fuit stultus, et semper erit.'
Omnes ei[d] ingresso viam cedebant. In cameram se recepit; loco
solito sedit; episcopi iuxta eum, Lond(oniensis) propius. Qui
aderant obstupuere omnes, et in eum oculi omnium intendebant.
[Sd, fo. 13] Episcopus Lond(oniensis) suadebat ut crucem uni
clericorum suorum traderet; paratum eum dicebat quasi vellet
totum regnum turbare. 'Crucem' ait Lond(oniensis) 'in manibus
tenetis; si modo rex gladium suum accipiat, en bene ornatum
regem, bene ornatum archiepiscopum'. Archiepiscopus: 'Si fieri
posset, meum' inquit 'esset semper eam in manibus propriis
ferre; nunc autem scio quid faciam, equidem ut pacem Dei con-
servem persone mee et Anglorum ecclesie. Dicis ut libet; tu si
hic ego sis, aliter sentias. Si autem dominus rex, ut dicis,
modo gladium acciperet, hoc utique signum pacis non esset.'
Forte memor erat archiepiscopus in quam arto res fuerat apud
Clarendonam, quando erumpentibus lacrimis nuntii regis ad eum
venerunt.

[48] Vocati ad regem omnes episcopi multam ibi introrsus moram
faciunt, et cum eis Rogerus ille[e] archiepiscopus Eboraci, qui
ultimus ad curiam veniebat, ut conspectior haberetur,[f] et de
consilio illo regis esse non videretur; qui et suam e regione
anticrucem sibi preferri faciebat, quasi 'pila minantia pilis'.[1]

---

[a]manibus SjSh; manus Sd.   [b]Sd *adds* Gileb'.   [c]Sd *adds* ait.   [d]ei Sd;
enim archiepiscopo SjSh.   [e]*om.* Sd.   [f]haberetur Sd; ingrederetur SjSh.

---

[1]Lucan, *Phars.* i.7.

Prohibitus etiam a domino papa, litteris sibi emissis, ne in provincia Cantuariensi crucem antesignatius[1] eius ferret; sed accepta prohibitione, de falsa domini Cantuariensis suggestione appellationem interposuerat, qua se tutum gerebat.[a] Interim in silentio clam[b] ait archiepiscopo suus in divina pagina magister Herbertus,[2] 'Domine, si forte miserint manus impias in vos, in promptu habeatis excommunicationis in eos ferre sententiam; ut tamen spiritus salvus fiat in die Domini.' Cui Willelmus filius Stephani, qui[c] ad pedes archiepiscopi assidebat, aliquantulum clare dixit ut audiret archiepiscopus: 'Absit hoc ab eo; non ita fecerunt sancti apostoli et martires Dei, cum caperentur et raperentur sublimes; potius, si hoc contigerit, oret pro eis et ignoscat, et in sua patientia animam suam possideat. Si enim eum pro causa iusticie et libertatis ecclesiastice pati contigerit, prestante Deo,[d] anima eius erit in requie, memoria in benedictione. Si sententiam in eos proferret, videretur omnibus quod ex ira et inpatientia hoc quod posset in ultionem sui fecisset. Et proculdubio contra decreta ageret; ut scribit beatus Gregorius Ianuario archiepiscopo: "Nil te ostendis de celestibus cogitare sed terrenam te habere conversationem significas, dum pro vindicta proprie iniurie, quod sacris regulis prohibetur, maledictionem anathematis invexisti."'[3] Iohannes Planeta hec audiens lacrimas erumpentes laborabat retinere. Similiter et Radulfus de Dici, archidiaconus Londoniensis ecclesie,[e4] plurimum ea die ibi lacrimatus est. Archiepiscopus

---

[a]SjSh *insert:* Nec (Ne Sh) mirum si dolor et gemitus et (*om.* Sh) contricio cordis obsedissent archiepiscopum: nam audierat quod ea die vel per sententiam qualemcumque caperetur, vel si hoc evaderet facta contra eum pravorum coniuracione occideretur congressus, quasi rege nesciente; *om.*. Sd. [b]in sil. clam Sd; silentio SjSh.   [c]Sd *adds* ei.   [d]Domino SjSh.   [e]ecclesie Sd; postea decanus SjSh.

---

[1]Standard-bearer; probably a mistake for 'antesignatus' (see *Dict. of Med. Lat. from British Sources,* ed. R.E. Latham, i.94).

[2]Of Bosham; both he and FitzStephen were present (see below).

[3]*Decretum,* C. 23 qu. 4 c. 27 (ultimately from Gregory the Great, *Reg.* ii.47, ed. P. Ewald and L.M. Hartmann, *MGH Epp.* i (1891), 148-9). On John Planeta, one of Becket's clerks (FitzStephen, *MB* iii.131), see D.E. Luscombe, *School of Peter Abelard* (Cambridge, 1969), pp. 58-9 n.

[4]Diceto was archdeacon of Middlesex, 1152/3-80, dean of St. Paul's 1180-c.1200 (Stubbs, in Diceto, introd.; Le Neve, i.5-6 and refs., 15-16).

talia audiens conferebat in corde suo. Post modicum idem Wil-
elmus filius Stephani, volens loqui archiepiscopo et a quodam
marescallo regis qui cum virga sua astabat prohibitus, dicente
quod nullus ei loqueretur, post intervallum intendens in archiepiscopum erectione oculorum et motu labiorum signum fecit ei,
quod crucis sue exemplum et Crucifixi quam tenebat imaginem
respiceret, et quod in oratione esset. Archiepiscopus signum
illud bene intellexit, et fecit sic confortatus in Domino. Quod
post plures annos archiepiscopus in Galliis exul apud sanctum
Benedictum supra Ligerim[1] eidem Willelmo ad dominum papam eunti,
inter ceterarum angustiarum suarum recordationem memoravit ...

FitzStephen proceeds with an 'apostrophe to the king on
the clerical immunities' (Robertson), and on the nature of
martyrdom, here omitted: *MB* iii.59-61.

[50] [Sd, fo. 14] Deus bone, quam multi clericorum et militum
qui aderant veras et luculentas de contemptu mundi proferebant
sententias, cum solus ibi crucem tenens sedebat archiepiscopus,
et omnes suffraganei episcopi eius[a] et comites et barones ad
regem evocati[b] essent et elongati ab eo. Dicebat aliquis: 'O
seculum captiosum, cuius tamquam maris tranquilli, quamvis aliquando serena sit superficies, intus tamen tempestates habet
absconditas.' Alius aliquis: '"Omnium rerum vicissitudo est."[2]
Amor Domini feudum non est. O honores mundi, in quibus etiam
que sperantur timenda sunt.'

[51] Episcopi introrsus cum rege colloquentes inter cetera
dixerunt ei quod ipsa die cum venissent ad archiepiscopum, male
tractationis redarguti sunt ab eo, quod scilicet nuper eum in-
micius tractassent cum baronibus et severius iusto iudicassent,
et inaudito more; quoniam etsi pro una absentia quam supersisam
regis[c] dicunt, non tamen contumacia iudicari deberet, non

---

[a]ep. eius SjSh; eius ep. Sd.   [b]vocati Sd.   [c]om. SjSh.

---

[1]Saint-Benoît-sur-Loire or Fleury.
[2]Cf. Terence, *Eun.* 276.

deberent eum condempnasse ad misericordiam regis in penam pecuniariam omnium bonorum mobilium. Hoc enim modo destrui posset
Cant(uariensis) ecclesia, si rex inmisericors eum obdurare
vellet, et ipsis episcopis baronibusque[a] captiosum tale in tali
casu posset esse iudicium. Sed constitutum esse in singulis
comitatibus summam unam pecunie, condempnatis in penam pecuniariam ad misericordiam regis solvendam. In Londoniis siquidem centum solidi constituti sunt. In Cantia, que mari propius
admota piratas a littore Anglie habet arcere, que et primum
sibi ictum in bellis contra hostes alienigenas vendicat, quo
maius est ei onus, maior est ei data libertas; et ibi quadraginta solidi constituti sunt taliter condempnatis. Ipseque
domicilium et sedem suam habens in Cantia, saltem ad legem
Cantie iudicari et taxari deberet. Dicebant etiam episcopi quod
adhuc ipsa die, infra decem dies date sententie, eos ad dominum
papam appellaverat; et ne de cetero eum iudicarent pro seculari
querela, que de tempore ante archiepiscopium[b] ei moveretur,
auctoritate domini pape prohibuerat.

[52] Motus rex misit ei comites suos et barones plurimos
querere ab eo si huius appellationis et prohibitionis se gereret
auctorem; maxime cum homo eius ligius esset, tenereturque ei et
communi sacramento et speciali apud Clarend(onam) stipulatione
in verbo veritatis quod legales[c] suas dignitates, in bona fide,
sine dolo malo, et legittime conservaret. Inter quas hec una
est, ut episcopi eius omnibus assint iudiciis preterquam iudicio
sanguinis.[1] Querere etiam ab eo si vellet cavere datis vadibus
de ratiocinio cancellarie reddendo, et super hoc curie eius
stare iudicio. Ad quod ille, respecta Crucifixi imagine, animum
et vultum firmans, et residens, ut suam archiepiscopi conservaret
dignitatem, luculentam et equalem ut nec in uno verbo subsis-
teret orationem habuit huiusmodi.

---

[a]baronibus Sd.   [b]archiepiscopium Sd; archiepiscopum Sj; archiepiscopatum Sh.   [c]legales SjSh; regales (*? over erasure*) Sd.

---

[1]See pp. 881-2, Const. of Clarendon, c. 11.

[53] 'Viri fratres, domini regis comites et barones, ego equidem domino nostro regi ligio, homanagio, fidelitate et sacramento astrictus sum, sed sacramentum maxime sacerdotale comites habet iustitiam et equitatem. Honori et fidelitati domini regis teneor, tam devota quam debita subiectione, propter Deum obsequium in omnibus prestare, salva Dei obedientia et dignitate ecclesiastica, et persone mee honore archiepiscopali, litem declinans, ut qui neque ad exponendum ratiocinium,[a] neque ad causam aliquam preter quam ad causam Iohannis [Sd, fo. 14^v] vocationem habui, neque alii in causa responsioni faciende vel iudicio audiendo teneor hic obnoxius. Fateor et recolo me plurimas administrationes et dignitates a domino rege suscepisse, in quibus ei fideliter deservivi, citra vel[b] ultra mare; et etiam redditibus meis propriis omnibus in servitio eius expensis, quod gaudeo, eris plurimi debitorem me creditoribus obligavi. Cum autem ex permissione divina et domini regis gratia archiepiscopus electus consecrari deberem, ante consecrationem a rege immunis dimissus sum et ecclesie Cant(uariensis) redditus liber, quietus et solutus ab omni regis querela seculari, licet modo in ira hoc[c] diffiteatur; quod probe plurimi vestrum noverunt omnesque ecclesiastice huius regni persone. Vosque huius veritatis conscios oro, obsecro et obtestor ut domino regi hec suggeratis, contra quem testes nominare, sicut[d] est licitum, non est tutum, nec modo opus est quia non litigo. Post consecrationem disposui honorem et onus susceptum[e] opere excolere, et ecclesie Dei aliquatenus prodesse, cui conspiciebar preesse. Qua in re si non datur prodire, si nequeo facere, reflante adversitate, non domino regi, non alii cuiquam, sed principaliter peccatis meis id[f] imputo. Potens est Deus augere gratiam cui et cum voluerit.

[54] 'De reddendo ratiocinio fideiussores dare non possum. Omnes episcopos et opitulares amicos meos iam hic obligavi, neque ad hoc cogi debeo, quia michi hoc adiudicatum non est.

---

[a] rocinium Sd.   [b] vel Sd; et SjSh.   [c] in ira hoc Sd; hoc in ira SjSh.
[d] sicut Sd; si Sh; etiamsi Sj.   [e] Sj *adds* opera et.   [f] *om.* Sd, *leaving space.*

Neque in causa sum ratiocinii, quia ad causam illam non vocatus fui, neque aliquam habui ad causam citationem preterquam ad causam cum Iohanne Marescallo. Quod autem de prohibitione facta hodie episcopis seu appellatione michi instatis, recognosco equidem me coepiscopis meis dixisse quod pro una absentia, non tamen contumacia, severius iusto me condemnaverunt, et preter morem et exemplum longe retro vetustatis. Unde et eos appellavi, prohibens ne de seculari querela temporis ante susceptum archiepiscopium me iterum hac pendente appellatione iudicent; et adhuc appello; et tam personam meam quam Cantuariensem ecclesiam sub Dei et domini pape colloco protectione.'

[55] Finierat: proceres alii[a] cum silentio ad regem revertebantur, verba eius pensiculantes et examinantes. Alii dicebant: 'Ecce prohibitionis ex ore eius audivimus blasphemiam.'[1] Aliqui baronum et stipatorum lateris regii, obtorto collo incedentes, et obliquis oculis respicientes eum, loquebantur inter se aliquantulum clare et ut ipse audiret: 'Rex Willelmus, qui subegit Angliam, novit clericos suos domare. Ipsum fratrem suum Odonem Baiocensem episcopum rebellem sibi cepit.[2] Stigandum Cant(uariensem) archiepiscopum[b] nigranti iniectum puteo perpetuo carcere dampnavit. Pater etiam domini nostri regis Gosfridus comes Andegavie, qui et Normanniam in manu forti sibi subdidit, Arnulfum[c] Sagiensem electum et plures clericorum eius fecit evirari, et eunuchatorum ante se in pelvi afferri membra; quia citra assensum eius electioni Sagiensis.ecclesie de se facte assensum prebuit, et se electum gerebat.'

[56] Rex responso archiepiscopi accepto, instat episcopis, precipiens et obtestans per homanagium et fidelitatem sibi

---

[a] alii Sd; illi Sh; *om.* Sj.   [b] arch. Cant. Sd.   [c] *om.* Sj.

---

[1] Cf. Matt. 26, 65; Marc. 14, 64.
[2] See pp. 858-9. For the legends of Stigand's last years, see E.A. Freeman, *Hist. of the Norman Conquest,* iv (Oxford, 1871), pp. 333-4. The elect of Sées maltreated by Count Geoffrey and his men was called Gerard (see F. Barlow, in *Letters of Arnulf of Lisieux* (Camden 3rd ser. lxi, 1939), p. xxxiv); FitzStephen confuses him with the bishop of Lisieux, who was active in the case.

debitam et iuratam, ut simul cum baronibus de archiepiscopo
sibi dictent sententiam. Illi se excusare ceperunt per interpositam archiepiscopi prohibitionem. Rex non adquievit,
asserens quod non teneat hec eius simplex prohibitio contra
hoc quod Clarend(one) factum et iuratum fuerat. [Sd, fo. 15]
E contra regi ingerunt episcopi, quod apponere, et in quo super
eos manum aggravare, possit archiepiscopus, si ab eis prohibitioni et appellationi paritum non fuerit; et pro bono regis et
regni, velle et debere prohibitioni facte[a] adquiescere. Tandem
rege suaso, episcopi captato consilio suo ad archiepiscopum
intrant. Flebat Robertus Lincolniensis episcopus et quidam alii
lacrimas vix continebant. Tunc prefatus Cicestr(ensis) sic orsus
est: 'Domine archipresul, salva gratia vestra, habemus quod de
vobis plurimum queramur. Plurimum nos episcopos vestros offendis-
tis; in angiportu magno nos inclusistis, quasi inter malleum[b]
et incudem nos misistis, hac prohibitione vestra; cui si non
paruerimus inobedientie, si paruerimus constitutionis et offense
regie, vinculis illaqueamur. Nuper enim apud Clarend(onam)
vobiscum congregati a domino rege conventi fuimus de observandis
regalibus suis dignitatibus, et ne forte hesitare possemus, ipsas de quibus loquebatur consuetudines suas regales scriptas
nobis ostendit. Tandem illis spopondimus assensum, promisimus
observantiam; vos primo loco nos suffraganei vestri postmodum
ex vestro precepto. Ad hec cum super hoc exigeret a nobis dominus rex cautionem iuratoriam, et per sigillorum nostrorum
inpressionem, diximus sufficere sibi debere pro sacramento sacerdotali quod dicebamus ei in verbo veritatis regales suas illas
dignitates nos observaturos, in bona fide sine dolo[c] malo,[1] et
legittime. Dominus rex persuasus adquievit. Quo contra nunc nos
venire compellitis, interdicendo ne ei quod de nobis exigit
adesse possimus iudicio. Ab hoc gravamine, et ne quid ad lesionem
nostram addatis, dominum papam apellamus, et hac vice prohibitioni vestre obedientiam prestamus.'

---

[a]et appellationi ... facte SdSj; facte vol'it Sh (*omission by homoeoteleuton*, prohibitioni ... prohibitioni).   [b]*om.* Sd.   [c]Sh *adds* et ingenio.

---

[1]See p. 854.

[57] Archiepiscopus: 'Quod dicitis, audio, et Deo propitio
apellationis prosecutioni adero. Clarend(one) autem nichil con-
cessum est a me, vel a vobis per me, nisi salvo honore ecclesiastico. Ut enim vos ipsi dicitis, has tres ibi retinuimus
determinationes, "in bona fide, sine dolo malo, et legittime",
per quas salve sunt ecclesiis[a] dignitates quas e iure pontifi-
cio habemus. Quod enim contra fidem ecclesie debitam et contra
leges Dei est, non potest in bona fide et legittime observari;
item, non est[b] regis dignitas, ubi ecclesiastica quam obser-
vandam[c] iuravit perit libertas. Ad hec, easdem quas dicitis
dignitates regales scriptas, dominus rex summo pontifici con-
firmandas transmisit; et reportate sunt, ab eo potius improbate
quam approbate. Exemplum nobis dedit et[d] doctrinam, ut et nos
ita faciamus, parati cum ecclesia Romana recipere que recipit,
respuere que respuit. Preterea si lapsi sumus Clarendon(e) -
caro enim est infirma - spiritum resumere debemus et in virtute
Spiritus Sancti contra hostem antiquum eniti; qui utrumque
procurat, ut et qui stat cadat et qui cecidit non resurgat. Si
sub stipulatione in verbo veritatis ibi concessimus vel iura-
vimus[e] iniusta, nostis quia illicita iurantes nullo iure obligantur.'

[58] Redeunt ad regem episcopi et eius pace a iudicando excu-
sati, a baronibus summoti seorsum sedent; nec minus a comitibus
et baronibus suum exigit rex de archiepiscopo iudicium. Evocan-
tur quidam vicecomites et secunde dignitatis barones antiqui
dierum ut addantur eis, et assint iudicio. Post aliquantam
moram ad archiepiscopum redeunt proceres. Comes Legrecestrie
Robertus, qui maturitate etatis et morum aliis preminebat,[f]
quibusdam aliorum imponens ut pronuntiarent [Sd, fo. 15[v]]
renitentibus cepit negotium Clarend(one) habitum articulatim
commemorare, ut superius fecerat archiepiscopo minus hylaris
Hylarius Cicestrensis episcopus, quasi inde manifesta erat regie
maiestatis lesio, et promissionis in verbo veritatis ibi facte
transgressio: dicebatque archiepiscopo quod suum audiret

---

[a]Sj *adds* nostris.   [b]Sj *adds* Christiani.   [c]conservandam Sd.   [d]in Sd.
[e]roboravimus Sj.   [f]Robertus ... preminebat *om.* Sj.

iudicium. Sed non plura passus, ait archiepiscopus: 'Quid est
quod facere vultis? Venistis me iudicare? Non debetis. Iudicium
est sententia lata post controversiam. Ego hodie nichil dixi ut
in causa. Ad nullam causam huc vocatus fui preter quam ad
causam Iohannis, qui mecum non est expertus. Ad hec me iudicare
non potestis. Ego qualiscumque pater vester sum, vos autem
proceres palatii, laice potestatis[a] seculares persone. Iudica-
tionem vestram non audiam.' Recedunt proceres. Post intervallum
surgens archiepiscopus et crucem suam[b] baiulans, hostium petebat,
quod tota die districtissime observatum[c] quasi ultro apertum est
ei. Aliquis maliloquus prosequens eum periurum regis exire dixit;
aliquis tanquam proditorem eum recedere, et domini sui regis
iudicium asportare. Ille in aula hominibus plena[d] ad fascem
lignorum non visum sibi offendit, sed non cecidit. Ad hostium
ubi equi sui erant venit; suum ascendens, magistrum Herbertum,
qui equum proprium propter pressuram nimiam tam cito habere non
poterat, secum ad hospitium transvexit, ad monasterium sancti
Andree. O quantum sustinuit in illa die in spiritu martirium!
- sed felicior rediit a conspectu concilii, qui dignus habitus
est ibi pro nomine Iesu contumeliam pati.[e]

[59] Facta oratione ante altare, crucem postea secus aram beate
Marie deposuit. Sedit, et domestici eius circa eum; tunc ait
ei[f] Willelmus filius Stephani: 'Ista equidem, ista fuit amara
dies.' Cui ille: 'Ultima erit amarior.' Et post modicum suos
hortatus ait, 'Quisque vestrum in silentio et in pace sua se
habeat, amarum verbum de ore vestro non exeat. Nulli maledico
quicquam respondeatis; sinite eos convitiari. Superioris persone est hoc pati; inferioris, hoc facere. Ut illi suarum linguarum ita nos nostrarum aurium domini simus. Non michi male-
dicitur, sed ei qui[g] quod mali dicitur in se recognoscit.'

[60] Rex audito[h] quod eum aulici turpiloquio prosequerentur,
rogatus a Robert de Milidono Hereford(iensi) episcopo[i] vel forte

---

[a]potestatis SdSh; potestates Sj.   [b]om. Sd.   [c]observatum *mss.*; obsera-
tum Sj[1] *Robertson.*   [d]plena SdSh; om. Sj.   [e]Sj *places* o quantum ... pati
after asportare *above.*   [f]om. Sd.   [g]qui Sd; om. SjSh.   [h]Sj *adds* ipsius
archiepiscopi discessu et; *and om.* ips. arch. discessum *below.*   [i]ep. Heref. Sd.

ab aliquo edoctus ipsius archiepiscopi discessum, dum adhuc
non perrexisset, misit precipiens ut post eum voce preconia per
vicos clamaretur, ne quis eum turpiloquio vel convitio lederet;
ne quis omnino ei vel alicui suorum in aliquo molestus esset
articulo. Archiepiscopus illo sero inter suos ut solebat come-
dit. Post cenam milites eius omnes qui aderant, reddito ei
homanagio suo et impetrata licentia, cum lacrimis ab eo dis-
cesserunt. Postea tres episcopos, Walterum Rophensem, capellanum suum, et duos quos ordinaverat, Robertum Hereford(ensem),
Rogerum Wigorn(ensem), misit regi archiepiscopus, querere ab eo
licentiam et conductum prestari sibi in crastino recessuro.
Regem illi invenerunt hilarem, sed distulit in crastinum mane
eis respondere. Responso nuntiorum accepto archiepiscopus moram
illam responsi reg(is)[a] aliquid sibi afferre periculi veritus
est.[b]

[61] Nox erat,[1] hora ad complendum dicta. Dixit sociis archiepiscopus se velle in ecclesia vigilare. Una quidem preteri-
tarum noctium in vigiliis et orationibus pernoctaverat in
ecclesia cum clericis suis, facta afflictione, positisque genibus ad invocationem uniuscuiusque sancti vel sancte in letania
sua nominate. Aiunt ei quidam de clericis suis: 'Volumus et nos
vobiscum in ecclesia vigilare.' Ille 'Ne utique; nolo vos [Sd,
fo. 16] vexari.' In noctis intempeste silentio tertius recessit,
nullo clericorum, nullo militum suorum comitatus. Quod cum in
crastino rex et omne concilium cognovissent, captato quid factu
opus esset consilio, omnes possessiones Cant(uariensis) ecclesie
archiepiscopo in pace remanere dimisit, nullo eius officialium
amoto, quia in appellatione hinc inde erant. Et[c] qui causas
istas prosequerentur ad dominum papam misit incontinenti post
eum ad calces eius archiepiscopum Eborac(ensem) et episcopos
quatuor, Gilebertum Lond(oniensem), Hylarium Cicestr(ensem),

---

[a]regis Sj; regii Sh; reg' Sd.   [b]Sh *adds* et maxime quia postea duo
magni ... (*from John of Salisbury's Vita S. Thome, c. 18* = MB *ii.313, lines
4-11, ending* iuramentis).   [c]Et SdSh; Dominus autem rex Sj.

---

[1]Cf. Ioan. 13, 30.

Bartholomeum Exon(iensem), Rogerum Wigorniensem et comites duos
et barones duos et clericos domesticos domus sue tres. Reliquum
diei et concilii insumitur in tractando de copiis pedestribus
in Gwaliam rebellem et regem Resum federifragum ducendis; scribi-
turque a singulis personis tam ecclesiasticis quam secularibus
in regis rogantis auxilium promissa bellatorum peditum multitudo. Solvitur concilium ...

161

1164-70. THE EXILE OF THOMAS BECKET, PAPAL LEGATIONS AND EMBAS-
SIES, AND MEETINGS OF BISHOPS

On 13 October 1164 the Council of Northampton came to its
climax and abrupt conclusion; the archbishop and the bishops
appealed to the pope against each other.[1] The king immediately arranged for an embassy consisting of the archbishop of
York and the bishops of London and Chichester to wait on the
count of Flanders, the French king, and, most important, to
visit the pope at Sens, to explain Henry's conduct, to accuse
Becket of treachery and to ask for judgement on him. The embassy failed: the pope temporized, Louis VII gave Becket asylum,
first at Pontigny, then (1166-70) at Sens, and the bishops hesitated to follow up their appeal.[2] The years of Becket's exile
were punctuated by a series of appeals and legations, all perhaps serious in intent; but the appeals became in due course a
continuous and formal process designed to prevent the archbishop from proceeding to extreme measures, whereas the legations presented a series of experiments in procrastination or
reconciliation.

Appeals. The appeal of 13 October 1164 was never carried
through. It 'may well have been quashed by the pope at Sens:

---

[1]See above, pp. 909-10, and *GF*, p. 162 and n. 1. For the wider history of
ecclesiastical diplomacy in this period, see T.A. Reuter, 'The Papal Schism,
the Empire and the West, 1159-1169' (Oxford D.Phil. Thesis, 1975).

[2]Knowles, *EC*, pp. 92 ff.; Guernes de Pont-Saint-Maxence, *Vie de S.
Thomas*, 2246 ff.; Roger of Pontigny, *MB* iv.60-1; on the meeting at Sens,
see esp. Alan of Tewkesbury in *MB* ii.336-41.

There is no special record of its burial'.[1] In 1165-6 Gilbert
Foliot, bishop of London, was harassed by mandates from archbishop and pope to hand over churches which had been seque-
strated from Thomas's clerks; Gilbert 'asked the king to
release him from this dangerous burden (GFL, no. 168), and par-
ried the mandates by a second appeal'.[2] In June 1166 Becket,
now papal legate for England save the diocese of York, prepared
to excommunicate the king; in the event, after receiving a
report that Henry was seriously ill, he excommunicated a number
of his advisers on Whit Sunday, 12 June, at Vézelay, but spared
the king himself. Numerous leading men 'in England not already
singled out reckoned the sword hung over them. Gilbert was able
for once to rally substantial support for a series of appeals,
of which the appeal of the bishops was the most formal and
formidable. This was apparently the first appeal *ad cautelam,*
an anticipatory appeal, that is, against a sentence which had
not been pronounced, but might fall on them at any moment.'
This was made by the English bishops on 24 June and confirmed
on 6 July; but it was transformed by the pope into a 'general
investigation of the case by papal legates' (see below). On 29
November 1167 Gilbert Foliot and the bishop of Salisbury, possibly aided by the bishop of Winchester - who later became a
staunch supporter of Becket - renewed their appeal against all
Becket's actions past and future.[3] This seems to have staved
off the excommunication with which Becket threatened Foliot at
the turn of 1167 and 1168,[4] and in April 1168 the pope released
the bishops from their appeal. Early in 1169 there were rumours
that Becket was once again preparing to use the weapon of excommunication. 'At the beginning of Lent Gilbert issued once
again an appeal *ad cautelam*. The archbishop treated it as
invalid and excommunicated him on Palm Sunday [13 April]. After
some hesitation ... Gilbert decided to behave as one excommunicate. He submitted to the pope, but his submission was accom-

---

[1]*GF,* p. 162.
[2]*GF,* p. 162; for the quotations which follow, ibid., pp. 162-3.
[3]*GF,* pp. 162 ff. (we quote from pp. 162-3); *GFL,* pp. 218-19 and nos.
181-2; *EC,* pp. 95 ff.
[4]JS, *Letters,* ii, pp. xxxvii-xxxviii and nos. 227, 236-8, 240, 244.

panied by a full defence of his appeals, a defence which was
repeated at greater length in the literary debate between Canterbury and London devised by Gilbert or one of his supporters
about the same time.'[1] Gilbert was absolved on 5 April 1170;
but the coronation of the young King Henry in June led the pope
to restore the ban in September.[2] This was forwarded by Thomas
at the end of November, along with similar letters excommunicating the bishop of Salisbury and suspending the archbishop of
York. This step was crucial in the events which led to the
tragic dénouement of 29 December; no more appeals were made,
and after the murder, in the course of 1171-2, the three chief
episcopal offenders in the affair of the coronation were by
slow and careful process absolved and released.[3]

Legations. On 24 April 1166 the pope issued his bull appoint-
ing Thomas legate for England save the bishopric of York; soon
after he confirmed Thomas's primacy, but in such terms as were
not acceptable to Thomas, since York was still not subjected to
him.[4] The events of the summer made it clear to the pope that
some further check on Thomas's actions, and some more effective
diplomatic action, were needed. Late in 1166 embassies went to
Rome from the king, the bishops, and the archbishop. The result
of these, and especially of the diplomatic skill and energy of
John of Oxford, dean of Salisbury, the leader of the king's
party, was that Alexander appointed two cardinals, William of
Pavia, cardinal priest of St. Peter ad Vincula, and Otto, cardinal deacon of St. Nicholas in Carcere Tulliano, as legates, the
former well known to take a friendly view of Henry II, the latter
a supporter of Thomas.[5] The sending of the commission was announced in December 1166, but it was evidently intended that
their progress should be slow, perhaps to allow for the political situation in Italy - the pope had to face invasion by the

---

[1]*GF*, p. 163; *GFL*, pp. 270-1, cf. no. 212 and *MB* iv.213-43.
[2]*GFL*, pp. 282-3.
[3]*GFL*, pp. 288-9; JS, *Letters*, ii, p. xliv and nos. 306-7.
[4]*MB Epp.* 172-3 (legation) and 170 (primacy); *GFL*, pp. 218-19; cf. *GF*,
p. 154 n.
[5]For what follows, see JS, *Letters*, ii, pp. xxxii-xxxvi, and nos. 212-15,
222-3, 225, 227-35, etc.; *MB Epp.* 283, 286-8; Tillmann, pp. 56-68; Foreville,
pp. 182 ff.; on the cardinals, Zenker, pp. 118-23, 171-4.

Emperor Frederick Barbarossa - to clear. Nor were the legates given powers to settle the dispute in the event of an impasse. They left Rome in March 1167, and arrived in Normandy eventually in October. On 18 November, between Gisors and Trie, they tried to bring king and archbishop together; but Thomas faced them with the Constitutions of Clarendon and reiterated that he could 'only promise observance with the proviso "saving the honour of God, the liberty of the Church, fair treatment for himself and restitution of the confiscated lands of Canterbury"'.[1] A meeting with Henry II and some of the English bishops took place at Argentan on 27-9 November. Nothing was achieved, although the cardinals lingered till July 1168 before returning to the papal Curia.

Meanwhile, in May 1168, Alexander III had made preparations for a different kind of diplomatic gesture. Henry II had several friends among the French Grandimontines and Carthusians, and the pope attempted to exploit the influence of these retired ascetics over the king. He wrote to Simon of Mont-Dieu, the Carthusian, and Bernard de Corilo (de la Coudre), a Grandimontine, to approach and warn the king; another Carthusian, Engelbert of Val Saint-Pierre, was added to their number, and the three holy men succeeded in bringing Thomas and Henry together at Montmirail on 6 January 1169. Thomas knelt before the king, but the customary verbal battle ensued; Thomas agreed to keep the customs only 'saving his order'; the conference broke up, and Louis VII, who was at hand to help, became (not for the first time) restive in his support of Thomas.[2] Another meeting was attempted on 7 February, and John of Canterbury, bishop of Poitiers, tried to arrange a conference between king, archbishop and a group of Grandimontines. This the archbishop rejected: he had neither the resources nor the patience left for another such meeting.

---

[1] Knowles, *TB*, p. 119; Tillmann, p. 60 and n. 35; *MB Epp.* 331; JS, *Letters*, ii, nos. 230-1. On Argentan, see *MB Epp.* 339. For what follows, see *MB Epp.* 424, cf. 423, 451; JS, *Letters*, ii, pp. xxxiv, xli, and no. 286; Tillmann, pp. 62-4; Foreville, pp. 189 ff. On Henry II and the Grandimontines, see E.M. Hallam (-Smith) in *Journal of Medieval History*, i (1975), 165-86.

[2] Knowles, *TB*, p. 120; *MB* iii.424-5. For the meeting of 7 Feb., Tillmann, p. 64.

On 28 February the pope appointed yet another legation, this time of curial officials not of the standing of cardinal: Gratian and Master Vivian.[1] Gratian, a nephew of Eugenius III, was the most steadfast of all the legates in Thomas's support, and Vivian, archdeacon of Orvieto, was persistent in his efforts for peace. Again, nothing was achieved. Fruitless meetings were held in Normandy in August-September, and Gratian presently returned to the Curia; Vivian stayed on in France, and on 18 November arranged a further meeting of Thomas, Henry, and Louis at Montmartre. The meetings in September failed because the king insisted on a clause 'saving my dignities', the archbishop 'saving the liberty of the Church', and Henry refused the kiss of peace; the meeting at Montmartre, however, ostensibly failed only because of the king's refusal of the kiss of peace.[2] Meanwhile the pace of diplomatic action was hastening: the decrees of 1169 were already promulgated (see pp. 926-39); on 19 January 1170 the pope commissioned Rotrou, archbishop of Rouen, and Bernard, bishop of Nevers, to restore Thomas or threaten Henry with an interdict on his continental dominions.[3] They were not given the opportunity to complete their mission, for presently Henry went into England and presided at the coronation of his son; but after the events of Whitsun, he seems to have reckoned that the interdict could be held off no longer. At Fréteval on 22 July peace was patched up, and at the turn of November and December the archbishop returned to Canterbury.[4]

Meetings of bishops. Apart from the Council of Oxford of c.January 1166 (p. 920) only three formal meetings of bishops are recorded in this period, although there were doubtless others, apart from the informal parleys of which we have some record. About 24 June 1166 and again on 6 July - this time at Northampton - the English bishops met to make their appeal against the Vézelay censures and the archbishop's future

---

[1]*MB Epp.* 476, cf. 492, 560; Tillmann, pp. 64-7; Foreville, pp. 196-9; JS, *Letters*, ii, pp. xxxiv f., xli f., and nos. 289, 291.
[2]*MB Epp.* 582-3, 605-7, 610; *MB* iii.446 ff.
[3]*MB Epp.* 623; Tillmann, pp. 67-8; Foreville, pp. 199-201.
[4]See esp. JS, *Letters*, ii, nos. 302-4, and pp. xliii f.; also Knowles, *TB*, pp. 131 ff.; Foreville, pp. 308-17.

actions.[1] It is not known how many were present, but presumably
a fair gathering must have been needed to account for the con-
fident presumption of *GFL*, nos. 166-7, in which the bishops of
the province of Canterbury and 'persone per eorundem dioceses
locis pluribus (*or* variis) constitute' inform pope and archbishop of their appeal. After the return of John of Oxford,
c.February 1167, he himself summoned a meeting of English
bishops to hear the pope's decisions and the king's instructions. 'Was he to be exalted' wrote John of Salisbury to the
pope of John of Oxford, 'by such mighty privileges that on his
return to England he could by your authority summon the bishops
and the clergy of England and instruct them not to obey the
archbishop of Canterbury, nor go to him when summoned; and that
men lawfully excommunicate, without making satisfaction or
giving any security at all, still persisting in their sacrilege,
should be absolved?'[2] When 'John arrived', he said in another
letter, 'the pontiffs and Pharisees of our day gathered in
council, and took counsel therein how they might destroy the
anointed of the Lord, absolve men excommunicated yet impenitent,
abolish God's law and the canons, and commit and uphold the
crime of disobedience without fear of judgement'.[3] Although
this need not be taken as a literal transcript of the agenda,
we need not doubt that the meeting took place, nor that several
of the bishops were present at the meeting of Henry II and the
legates at Argentan in November 1167 and Montmirail in January

---

[1]See above, p. 915 ; *MB Epp.* 209, pp. 421-2: on p. 422 the meeting at
Northampton is referred to as future: 'Concilium quoddam habituri sunt in
octavis Apostolorum episcopi et omnes abbates apud Norhamtonam' (Nicholas
guestmaster of Rouen to the archbishop). In JS, *Letters*, ii, no. 198 (1166-7)
John speaks as if no meeting of bishops to discuss the Church's peace had
recently taken place.

[2]JS, *Letters*, ii, no. 213: 'Nunquid tantis erat privilegiis extollendus,
ut in introitu suo vestra auctoritate convocatis episcopis et clero Angliae
mandaret ne Cantuar(iensi) archiepiscopo obedirent vel ad ipsum vocati
accederent, et ut iure excommunicati sine satisfactione et cautione omni
absolverentur in sacrilegiis perseverantes?' Cf. ibid., no. 219.

[3]JS, *Letters*, ii, no. 234 (to Cardinal Albert, later Pope Gregory VIII):
'Collegerunt item pontifices et nostri temporis Pharisaei in adventu Iohannis ... concilium, et in eo consilium inierunt quomodo perderent christum
Domini, excommunicatos inpoenitentes absolverent, evacuarent divinae legis
et canonum sanctiones, et sine crimine committerent et tuerentur inobedien-
tiae crimen.'

1169.[1] But these were exceptional gatherings for political and
diplomatic action; no other serious meeting of the bishops is
recorded until after the murder of Thomas Becket on 29 December
1170.

162

1166, *c*.JANUARY. COUNCIL OF OXFORD; 1166, JANUARY x MARCH.
ASSIZE OF CLARENDON

The Council of Oxford was summoned by Henry II to deal with one
of the rare outbreaks in England of the Cathar heresy. 'The
English Church had hitherto been remarkably free from this problem. The heresies of the early eleventh century, so far as the
evidence goes, touched it not at all; nor did the Petrobrusian
and other movements of the early twelfth. In the second half of
the twelfth century, when the Cathar churches were flourishing
and multiplying in many parts of the continent and establishing
a regular hierarchy of heretical bishops in France and Italy,
only one invasion of heretics into England is known. About 1160
a small group of Flemish [or German] Cathars landed in the
country. In due course the bishops became anxious about them;
Roger of Worcester consulted Gilbert [Foliot of London]; a
council was held under the direction of the king, and the
Cathars were whipped and expelled by the lay power after condemnation by the Church, early in 1166. Between the Council of
Oxford in 1166 and the days of Wyclif outbreaks of heresy were
very infrequent in England, and very small affairs compared with
the successes of the Cathars and the Waldensians on the continent.'[2]

The fullest account is that of William of Newburgh, quoted
below: he gathers into a single narrative their arrival *c*.1160
and expulsion in 1166, and so appears to telescope all the
events before the Council of Tours of 1163; but there is no

---

[1]*MB Epp.* 339, 451-2; JS, *Letters*, ii, no. 288.
[2]*GF*, pp. 241-2; cf. *GFL*, nos. 157-8 and nn. See also W.L. Wakefield and
A.P. Evans, *Heresies of the High Middle Ages* (New York, London, 1969),
pp. 245-7.

doubt that his account refers to the council of 1166. *Ann. Tewkesbury, Ann. Mon.,* i.49,[1] and Diceto (i.318) both date it 1166, the letter to early 1166, and it seems likely that it followed the court of Christmas 1165, which was probably held at Oxford.[2] The king went overseas in March.

Of these heretics Walter Map (in his otherwise very confused account of the Cathars, *c.*1181) said: 'In Anglia nondum venerunt nisi sedecim, qui precepto regis Henrici secundi adusti et virgis cesi disparuerunt.'[3] Writing at about the time of the council, St. Ailred of Rievaulx wrote in his *De anima* of them: 'Audivi plures ex eis teneri in vinculis, coactumque a rege concilium, ut cum sapientibus quid de talibus agendum sit deliberaret. Nam et nuptiis detrahunt et sacramentum altaris exsufflant, carnis negant resurrectionem et baptismatis virtutem evacuant.'[4]

Gilbert Foliot's letters were probably written about the end of 1165. The bishop of Worcester had consulted him as to their treatment. After citing precedents from St. Augustine for treatment both lenient and severe, Gilbert advised that they be placed in solitary confinement and treated with moderate severity - including lashes - until a gathering of clergy (in the second letter, of bishops) can determine what is to be done.[5]

---

[1] Whence *Ann. Worcester, Ann. Mon.,* iv.381.
[2] Cf. Eyton, pp. 88 ff.
[3] *De nugis curialium,* i.30, ed. M.R. James, p. 58.
[4] *De anima,* i.59-60; ed. A. Hoste and C.H. Talbot, *Opera Omnia,* i (Turnhout, 1971), pp. 703-4; also ed. C.H. Talbot (London, 1952), p. 91; quoted by F.M. Powicke in Walter Daniel, *Life of Ailred,* pp. ci-cii, with useful notes on the heretics and the council. See also A. Borst, *Die Katharer* (Stuttgart, 1953), p. 94 and n.; Pollock and Maitland, ii.547 f.; H. Maisonneuve, *Etudes sur les origines de l'Inquisition* (2nd ed., Paris, 1960), pp. 114-15.
[5] The two letters appear essentially to duplicate one another, and it is unlikely that both were sent (see *GF*, p. 27). In both he suggests confinement until the council can decide; in no. 157 he also recommends moderate flogging, in no. 158 confinement only, and adduces the arguments from Augustine; in both he suggests that they be visited by the bishops' clerks who can dispute with them.
The doctrines noted by Ailred and William of Newburgh were characteristic of the dualist Cathars, although the nature and extent of their condemnation of marriage has been much disputed. It is clear that they cannot have regarded marriage, which led to the creation of evil matter (as they saw it) and the imprisonment within it of more spirits, as a sacrament.

Two chapters in the *Assize of Clarendon* related to ecclesiastical affairs and are printed below; the second (c. 21)
also deals with the heretics condemned at Oxford, and this has
been used to date the Assize to the early months of 1166. Henry
II went abroad in March. There has been some dispute in recent
years whether the surviving texts of the *Assize* precisely represent a text produced or promulgated in 1166. If we accept their
essential authenticity, it makes little difference if some
clauses were later altered, since it is unlikely that cc. 20-1
were affected.

On the *Assize,* see J.C. Holt, 'The Assizes of Henry II:
the Texts', in *The Study of Medieval Records: Essays in
Honour of Kathleen Major* (Oxford, 1971), pp. 85-106,
answering the condemnation of H.G. Richardson and G.O.
Sayles in *The Governance of Mediaeval England* (Edinburgh,
1963), pp. 198-203, 438-9, and *Law and Legislation from
Æthelberht to Magna Carta* (Edinburgh, 1966), pp. 88-131;
Warren, pp. 281-2, suggests a compromise, allowing for
revision after 1166; R.C. Van Caenegem in *Church and
Government in the Middle Ages : Essays presented to C.R.
Cheney* (Cambridge, 1976), pp. 42-4, 73-4, accepts Holt's
argument and puts the chief elements in the Assize in
their legal and historical context, with full references
to earlier literature. On the date, see *Gesta Henrici II,*
ii, pp. lix-lxiv; Eyton, pp. 88-92, esp. 89 and n.

I. *William of Newburgh, Historia Rerum Anglicarum*

From BL mss. Stowe 62, fos. 38-9 (S); Cotton Vesp. B. vi,
fo. 130[r-v] (V).[1] Printed in *Chrons. Stephen etc.*, ed. R.
Howlett, RS, i.131-4; also in Sp. ii.59-60; W. i.438-9.
This passage is translated, with commentary, in Wakefield
and Evans (above, n. 2 p. 920), pp. 245-7.

---

[1]The earliest two mss.: Stowe 62 is contemporary with the author, 12/13th
cent., and comes from Newburgh priory, his own house; Vesp. B. vi is of
the early 13th cent., from Oseney abbey (select variants only).

De hereticis Angliam ingressis et quomodo exterminati sunt.

Hisdem diebus erronei quidam venerunt in Angliam, ex eorum ut creditur genere quos vulgo Publicanos vocant. Hii nimirum olim ex Gasconia incerto auctore habentes originem, regionibus plurimis virus sue perfidie infuderunt. Quippe in latissimis Gallie, Hispanie, Ytalie, Germanieque provinciis tam multi hac peste infecti esse dicuntur, ut secundum prophetam[1] multiplicati esse super numerum videantur. Denique cum a presulibus ecclesiarum et principibus provinciarum in eos remissius agitur, egrediuntur de caveis suis vulpes nequissime, et pretenta specie pietatis, seducendo simplices, vineam Domini Sabaoth tanto gravius quanto liberius demoliuntur. Cum autem adversus eos igne Dei fidelium zelus succenditur, in suis foveis dilitescunt, minusque sunt noxii; sed tamen occultum spargendo virus nocere non desinunt. Homines rusticani et idiote atque ideo ad rationem hebetes peste vero illa semel hausta ita imbuti, ut ad omnem rigeant disciplinam, unde rarissime contingit eorum aliquem, cum e suis latebris proditi extrahuntur, ad pietatem converti. Sane ab hac et ab[a] aliis pestibus hereticis immunis semper extitit Anglia, cum in aliis mundi partibus tot pululaverint hereses. Et quidem hec insula cum propter incolentes Britones Britannia diceretur, Pelagium in oriente heresiarcham futurum ex se misit, eiusque in se processu temporis errorem admisit: ad cuius peremptionem Gallicane ecclesie pia provisio semel et iterum beatissimum direxit Germanum. At ubi hanc insulam expulsis Britonibus natio possedit Anglorum, ut non iam Britannia sed Anglia diceretur, nullius umquam ex ea pestis heretice virus ebullivit: sed nec in eam aliunde usque ad tempora regis Henrici secundi, tanquam propagandum et dilatandum introivit. Tunc quoque Deo propicio pesti, que iam irrepserat ita est obviatum, ut de cetero hanc insulam ingredi vereretur. Erant autem quam viri quam femine paulo amplius quam triginta, qui dissimulato errore quasi pacifice huc ingressi sunt, propagande pestis gratia, [S, fo. 38^V] duce quodam Gerardo in quem omnes tanquam preceptorem ac principem respiciebant. Nam solus erat

---

[a] *om.* V.

---

[1] Cf. Ps. 39, 6.

aliquantulum litteratus; ceteri vero sine litteris et idiote
homines plane impoliti et rustici, nationis et lingue Teutonice.
Aliquandiu in Anglia commorantes, unam tantum mulierculam
venenatis circumventam susurriis, et quibusdam ut dicitur
fascinatam prestigiis suo cetui aggregarunt. Non enim diu
latere potuerunt, sed quibusdam curiose indagantibus quod pere-
grine essent secte deprehensi, comprehensi, tentique sunt in
custodia publica. Rex vero nolens eos indiscussos vel dimittere
vel punire, episcopale precepit Oxonie concilium congregari.[a]
Ubi dum sollempniter de religione convenirentur, eo qui litteratus videbatur suscipiente causam omnium et loquente pro omnibus,
Christianos se esse et doctrinam apostolicam venerari responderunt. Interrogati per ordinem de sacre fidei articulis, de
substancia quidem superni medici recta; de eius vero remediis,
quibus humane infirmitati mederi dignatur, id est divinis
sacramentis perversa dixerunt: sacrum baptisma, eucharistiam,
coniugium detestantes, atque unitati catholice quam hec divine
imbuunt subsidia, ausu nefario derogantes. Cunque sumptis de
scriptura sacra divinis urgerentur testimoniis, se quidem ut
instituti erant credere, de fide vero sua disputare nolle responderunt. Moniti ut penitentiam agerent, et corpori ecclesie
unirentur, omnem consilii salubritatem spreverunt. Minas quoque
pie pretentas ut vel metu resipiscerent deriserunt, verbo illo
dominico abutentes: 'Beati qui persecutionem patiuntur propter
iusticiam, quoniam ipsorum est regnum celorum.'[1] Tunc episcopi,
ne virus hereticum latius serperet precaventes, eosdem publice
pronunciatos hereticos corporali discipline subdendos catholico
principi tradiderunt. Qui precepit heretice infamie caracterem
frontibus eorum inuri et spectante populo virgis cohercitos
urbe expelli, districte prohibens ne quis eos vel hospicio
recipere, vel aliquo solatio confovere presumeret. Dicta sentencia ad penam iustissimam ducebantur gaudentes, non lentis
passibus preeunte magistro eorum et canente, 'Beati eritis cum
vos oderint homines.'[2] In tantum deceptis a se mentibus seduc-

---

[a] congraegari S.

---

[1] Matt. 5, 10.   [2] Luc. 6, 22.

torius abutebatur spiritus. Illa quidem muliercula quam in
Anglia seduxerant metu supplicii discedens ab eis, errorem con-
fessa reconciliacionem meruit. Porro detestandum illud collegium cauteriatis frontibus iuste severitati subiacuit: eo qui
primatum gerebat in eis [S, fo. 39] ob insigne magisterii
inustionis gemine, id est in fronte et circa mentum, dedecus
sustinente. Scissisque cingulo tenus vestibus publice cesi, et
flagris resonantibus urbe eiecti, algoris intolerancia - hiems
quippe erat - nemine vel exiguum misericordie impendente misere
interierunt. Huius severitatis pius rigor non solum a peste
illa que iam irrepserat Anglie regnum purgavit, verum etiam ne
ulterius irreperet, incusso hereticis terrore precavit.

II. *The Assize of Clarendon*

> From Oxford, Bodl. ms. Rawlinson C. 641, fo. 20 (C) (12th-
> cent. legal collection); BL ms. Royal 14. C. ii, fo.
> 276^{r-v} (Hr) (Roger of Hoveden's *Chronica*); ed. Stubbs,
> *Hoveden,* ii, pp. cv (from C), 248; *Gesta Henrici II*, ii,
> p. liv (from Hr); Stubbs, *Select Charters* (edn. of 1913),
> pp. 170-3 (from C). Cf. Holt (above, p. 922), pp. 86 ff.

... [20] Prohibet etiam dominus rex ne monachi vel canonici vel
aliqua domus religionum[a] recipiant aliquem de populo minuto[b]
in monacum vel canonicum vel fratrem, donec sciatur de quali
testimonio ipse fuerit, nisi ipse fuerit infirmus[c] ad mortem.

[21] Prohibet etiam dominus rex quod ullus[d] in tota Anglia
receptet in terra sua[e] vel soca sua vel domo sub se aliquem
de secta illorum renegatorum qui excommunicati et signati
fuerunt[f] apud Oxeneford'. Et si quis eos receperit ipse erit[g]
in misericordia domini regis, et domus in qua illi fuerint
portetur[h] extra villam et comburatur. Et hoc iurabit unusquisque
vicecomes quod hoc tenebit, et hoc iurare faciet omnes ministros

---

[a]religionis Hr.   [b]de minuto populo Hr.   [c]inf. fuerit Hr.   [d]Prohi-
bet ... ullus C; Prohibet dominus rex ne aliquis Hr.   [e]terram suam Hr.
[f]excomm. ... fuerunt C; fuerint excommunicati et signati Hr.   [g]ipse erit
C; sit Hr.   [h]asportetur Hr.

suos, et dapiferos baronum[a] et omnes milites et francostenentes
de comitatibus ...

1166. LEVY FOR THE DEFENCE OF THE HOLY LAND. See p. 1022.

163

c.OCTOBER x NOVEMBER 1169. ROYAL CONSTITUTIONS CONCERNING THE
    CHURCH

> See M.D. Knowles, Anne J. Duggan, and C.N.L. Brooke,
> 'Henry II's Supplement to the Constitutions of Clarendon',
> *EHR* lxxxvii (1972), 757-71, with an edition of the texts,
> on which ours is based, on pp. 763-71. This article
> established the authenticity of the 'constitutions' against
> a recent expression of dissent,[1] and fixed their date.

'At the meeting between king and archbishop at Bures [Normandy]
on 1 September [1169], in the presence of the papal legates
Gratian and Vivian [see p. 918], Henry was clearly apprehensive
that an interdict on his realm might be proclaimed.'[2] In October
or November the archbishop 'prepared letters ... declaring an
interdict' on England from 2 February 1170, unless there was
peace by that date. It seems clear that these constitutions,
and the oaths which accompanied them, were Henry's answer to
the threat. Writing soon after 18 November 1169, Becket told his
representatives in the Roman Curia that Henry had sent Geoffrey
Ridel to London to exact oaths to observe the constitutions, and
with Richard archdeacon of Poitiers and other officials to

---

[a]et ... baronum C; et barones Hr.

---

[1]In H.G. Richardson and G.O. Sayles, *The Governance of Mediaeval England*
(Edinburgh, 1963), p. 308 and n.; see also their *Law and Legislation from
Æthelberht to Magna Carta* (Edinburgh, 1966), p. 93; cf. Knowles, Duggan
and Brooke, p. 758 n. 1 - also for *MB Epp.* 598, 'the garbled account sent by
a friend to Becket, which reads, however, much more like the fruit of contemporary rumour and panic than a later forgery'.
[2]For this and what follows, art. cit., p. 760.

summon the bishops to London to take oaths that no messenger or letters should be received from pope or archbishop, nor interdict obeyed, nor any of the king's faithful subjects excommunicated.[1] The version in Alan of Tewkesbury's collection (no. 1 below) says that they were made ('constituit') by the king in Normandy, and sent to Richard de Lucy, Geoffrey Ridel, archdeacon (of Canterbury) and Richard (of Ilchester) archdeacon of Poitiers, to be sworn and observed against Pope Alexander and Archbishop Thomas; and that they were carried by Wimer (later sheriff of Norfolk and Suffolk, 1170-87) and Walter of Grimsby, sheriff of Lincoln (1170-5). A rubric and gloss in ms. Ab give the date 1169 (p. 937 n. a). William of Canterbury quotes the decrees in his Life of Becket (1172 x 4) and says that an oath renouncing Alexander III was imposed on children of twelve 'and on all others, including the monks of Canterbury';[2] there may be exaggeration here, but William FitzStephen confirms that an attempt was made to extract the oath from laymen of twelve or fifteen years and more.[3] The date of these efforts is clarified by the version in Gervase of Canterbury 'where the day of St. Denis (9 Oct.) is given as the opening date when letters sent became actionable, and St. Martin's day (11 Nov.) as the time when those previously arrested should be brought to trial.[4]

There is some difference, at least of emphasis, in the accounts of the effects of the king's command on the bishops. William FitzStephen says that the archbishop of York refused to take the oath or allow his subjects to do so.[5] Foliot, it would seem probable, was abroad on, or about to set out on, his journey to seek absolution from excommunication.[6] The other bishops, according to FitzStephen, allowed their subjects to take the oath, but he does not say that they them-

---

[1]*MB Epp.* 610, dated art. cit., p. 759 n. 2. For a comparison of the oaths with those taken at Würzburg in 1165, see W. Ullmann in *Historisches Jahrbuch*, xciii (1973), 265-300, at p. 297 and n. 97a.
[2]*MB* i.53-5.   [3]*MB* iii.102.
[4]Art. cit., p. 759; Gervase, no. 3 below. What follows is from art. cit., pp. 760-1.
[5]*MB* iii.102.
[6]See discussion in art. cit., p. 760 n. 7.

selves swore, and John of Salisbury, corroborated by Becket, asserts that Henry of Winchester did not, and Thomas also excepts from the charge of swearing the bishops of Norwich and Chester ...[1] The attempt to corral the bishops at London failed entirely according to Thomas, and Clarembald, the intruded abbot of St. Augustine's, Canterbury, was the only prelate to swear. Nevertheless, many of the clergy and laity took the oath, unwillingly, and the archbishop, when he heard of the whole situation, wrote a letter of general absolution from the oath.[2]

The differences between the three surviving versions may be explained by the hypothesis that they represent texts sent to different recipients: that in Alan's collection seems designed for the royal justices, although even this may be somewhat abbreviated;[3] that preserved in Foliot's archives softens the clause attacking Foliot himself and may well be a version intended for his eyes; that in Gervase, which emphasizes the duties of sheriffs and has a clause unique to it dealing with laymen coming or going overseas, is very likely that intended for the sheriff of Kent. Most of the clauses are self-explanatory in their context, or simply confirm Constitutions of Clarendon (Alan, cc. 2, 3). The most curious is Alan, c. 10, ordering prosecution of the bishops of London and Norwich for contravening Constitutions of Clarendon, c. 7, by laying an interdict on the lands of the earl of Norfolk and excommunicating him. The case was by now somewhat stale: the earl had been fighting the canons of the small house of Pentney since 1164-5, and was still under the ban in March 1170.[4] No doubt this 'constitution' was meant primarily or solely as a warning to prelates less inclined to resist the archbishop than Gilbert Foliot, but it sets an edge on a harsh list of injunctions; the Pentney case is also a symbol of the whole dispute in miniature, showing us the church

---

[1] *MB Epp.* 593 (= JS, *Letters,* ii, no. 296), 650, 610 (esp. p. 176).
[2] Art. cit., pp. 760-1.
[3] See discussion in art. cit., p. 762.
[4] See art. cit., pp. 762-3; *GFL,* nos. 159-61; *MB Epp.* 644 (p. 250) and cf. *MB Epp.* 728.

courts, and the pope in person, defending obscure folk against
the mighty, but also, be it said, canons against a layman.

Texts. 1. The mss. of the version in *Alan of Tewkesbury's* collection of the Becket correspondence, and other Canterbury
sources, are the same used in the Constitutions of Clarendon,
and are listed on pp. 872-3. Our text is based primarily on
Ab, with collations of Ac and Ag, and some use of Aw (William
of Canterbury). Ag has also a text of 2 (see below).

   2. The text which derives primarily from the archives of
Gilbert Foliot, bishop of London, was edited by A.J. Duggan in
'The Manuscript Transmission of Letter Collections relating to
the Becket Dispute' (Univ. of London Ph.D., 1971), Appendix B,
pp. 415-17, and thence in art. cit. It is based on:

   Fb. Oxford, Bodleian, Bodl. ms. e Mus. 249 (27835), fo. 89,
      letter collection from Gilbert Foliot's archives, *c.*1180
      (see p. 873).
   Sd. Bodl. ms. Douce 287 (21861), fo. 87^V, misc. collection
      of Becket materials, also largely deriving from Foliot
      archives, *c.*1200 (see pp. 874, 896).
   Ag, fo. 3^{r-v}.
   Hr. Hoveden, i.231-2, collated with BL Royal 14. C. ii, fos. 101^V-102.
   Q. Roger of Crowland, *Quadrilogus,* Paris, BN ms. Lat. 5372,
      fo. 94^V.
   W. Roger of Wendover, *Flores Historiarum,* ed. H.G. Hewlett
      (RS), i.36, collated with BL ms. Cotton Otho B. v, fo. 22^V
      (mutilated in the fire of 1731) and Bodl. ms. Douce 207
      (21781), fo. 122^V.

On Hoveden's sources, see A. Duggan (1971), pp. 313-34, where
it is shown that his main source for letters etc. was a manuscript from the Foliot tradition, similar, though not identical,
to manuscripts Fb and Sd. But his text of 1169, version 2, contains readings from a manuscript of version 1, and we have only
incorporated his variants where they have some support from
other manuscripts. Similarly, Wendover (A. Duggan (1971), pp. 335-44)
evidently altered his text, or used a corrupt copy, so that its

relation to other surviving manuscripts cannot now be ascertained; its private readings have been ignored. Roger of Crowland incorporated a part of *MB Epp.* 598 into his text: this illustrates the fact that he was compiling from a rich diversity of earlier sources. Only select readings are noted; for a full collation, see Duggan, loc. cit.

3. From Gervase, ms. Ga, fos. 83-4, collated with Gc, fos. 63^V-64^V; ed. Stubbs, i.214-16 (see pp. 771, 928, 973 n. 3).

1. *Alan of Tewkesbury's Text*	2. *The Foliot Text*	3. *Gervase of Canterbury's Text*
		(Some clauses have been transposed to make comparison possible.)

Hee sunt^a constitutiones quas constituit rex Henricus in Normannia, et mandavit iusticiis suis Ricardo de Luci et duobus archidiaconis, Galfrido Ridel^b et Ricardo^c Pictavensi, et omnibus principibus et populis Anglie, iuranda et	He sunt constitutiones quas rex Henricus decrevit observari et fecit edicto publico promulgari contra ecclesiam proscripto sancto Thoma.^{a} Hec sunt capitula que rex mandavit iusticiis observanda per Walterium de Grimesbi et Wine-	Ille vero alia et enormia querens diverticula, novas pravitates in Angliam misit, mandans et districte precipiens ut omnes senes cum iunioribus eas custodirent, et ut omnes earum observationem compellerentur iurare. [Ga, fo. 83^V] Harum^a

1. *Alan of Tewkesbury's text* (Ab, with significant variants of Ac, Ag and Aw). ^{a}Ab *adds* etiam; Aw *om. the whole paragraph.* ^{b}Ag *adds* archidiacono Cantuariensi. ^{c}Ag *adds* archidiacono.	2. *The Foliot Text* (Fb, collated with SdAg, omitting minor errors: select variants only from HrQW). ^{a}He ... Thoma Ag; Edicta que rex Anglie metu interdicti promulgari fecit diebus illis Q; Item iusticiariis suis significavit per literas sub hac forma W; *om.* FbSdHr.	3. *Gervase of Canterbury's text* (Ga, collated with Gc, whose minor variants are not noted.) ^{a}Gc *adds* autem.

servanda contra
papam Alexandrum
et beatum[a] Thomam
Cantuariensem ar-
chiepiscopum. Harum
latores fuerunt
Wimerus presbiter
et postea[a] vice-
comes, et Gwalterus
de Grimesbi.[a]

merum capellanum.[a]

traditionum ista
est forma.

Capitulum i. Si[b]
quis inventus fue-
rit ferens litteras[c]
domini pape vel
aliquod mandatum
archiepiscopi Can-
tuariensis[d] con-
tinens interdictum
Christianitatis in
Angliam capiatur,

[1] Si quis inven-
tus fuerit ferens
litteras domini
pape vel mandatum,[b]
aut Cantuariensis,[c]
continens in se[d]
interdictum Christ-
ianitatis in An-
gliam,[e] capiatur et
retineatur[f] donec

[1] Si quis a fest-
ivitate sancti Dio-
nisii inventus
fuerit in Angliam
ferens litteras
domini pape vel
Tome archiepiscopi
Cantuariensis vel
aliquod mandatum[a]
ex parte eorum de

---

[a]Ag om. beatum and pos-
tea and adds at end
clericus et vicecomes
Lincolie.   [b]Aw starts
here, with rubric Nove
constitutiones regis.
[c]lit. fer. Ag.   [d]Cant.
arch. Aw.

---

[a]Hec ... capellanum
FbSdAg (Ag reads per
Winemerum); ... Henri-
cus rex ... faciens
grave edictum et exe-
crabile contra Alexan-
drum papam et Thomam
Cantuariensem archiepi-
scopum, cuius capitula
hec sunt Hr; Idem rex
iusticiariis suis con-
tra beatum Thomam archi-
episcopum W Douce ms.,
not in Otho; om. Q.
[b]Ag ins. aliquod.
[c]AgHr ins. archiepiscopi.
[d]in se SdAgQ; om. FbHrW.
[e]Angliam AgFbSdQ; Anglia
HrW(?).   [f]Both Hr and
Q continue here as in
version 1, and Q incor-
porates some phrases
from MB Epp. 598.

---

[a]Gc adds eorum.

et de eo sine dilatione iusticia fiat sicut de traditore regis et regni.

rex vel iustic(ie)[a] voluntatem suam de eo preceperit.

interdicto, capiatur et statim fiat de eo iusticia sicut de traditore domini regis et regni sui. Verumtamen illi qui capti sunt cum mandato vel litteris huiusmodi ante festum sancti Martini custodiantur usque ad eundem terminum et postea fiat de eis iusticia sicut preceptum est.

ii. Preterea[a] nullus clericus vel monachus vel conversus vel alicuius convers[fo. 28]ionis[b] permittatur transfretare vel redire in Angliam, nisi de transitu suo habeat litteras iusticie, et de reditu suo litteras domini regis. Si

[2] Nullus[b] clericus vel canonicus vel monachus vel conversus vel alicuius religionis transfretare permittatur [vel redire in Angliam][c] nisi de transfretatione sua habeat litteras iustic(ie)[d] vel de reditu litteras domini regis. Si quis

[7] Nullus clericus vel canonicus vel mo[fo. 84]nacus, vel cuiuscumque religionis Dei fuerit, permittatur transfretare nisi habeat litteras de passagio suo. [6] Si clericus vel canonicus vel monacus vel conversus, ceu cuiuscumque

---

[a]*om.* Aw.   [b]conversationis Ac.

[a]vel iustic(ie): iusticie Ag.   [b]Item nullus HrW (*om.* vel canonicus Hr).   [c]vel ... Angliam HrQ, *marg. ins. in* Ag; *om.* FbSdW.   [d]iustic' FbSd; iusticiarii W; iusticie Q; iusticie et Ag (*not* vel); iusticiarum Hr (*for* vel AgHr *read* et; AgQ *add* suo *after* reditu).

quis aliter inven-
tus fuerit agens,
capiatur et incar-
ceretur.

aliter inventus
fuerit,[a] capiatur
et retineatur.[b]

religionis fuerit,
de ultra mare
venerit, exquira-
tur et si nil huius-
modi cum illo inven-
tum fuerit, nisi
habeat litteras
domini regis de
passagio suo, non
procedat ulterius,
sed quam citius
poterit revertatur;
et si aliquod huius-
modi super eum in-
ventum fuerit, capia-
tur et incarceretur.
[Cf. c. 5, p. 934.]

iii. Ne aliquis
appellet ad papam
vel ad archiepisco-
pum.
iv. Ne aliquod
placitum teneatur
de mandatis pape
vel archiepiscopi,
vel aliquod manda-
tum illorum[a] in
Anglia ab ullo
homine recipiatur.[b]
Si quis inventus

[4] [N]ullus appel-
let ad dominum
papam neque ad
Cantuariensem,[c]
neque aliquod placi-
tum ex eorum mandato
teneatur neque ali-
quod mandatum eorum
in Anglia[d] recipia-
tur. Et si quis
tenuerit vel recep-
erit vel tracta-
verit, capiatur et

[4] Nulla fiat apel-
latio ad dominum
papam neque ad
Thomam Cant(uarien-
sem) archiepiscopum,
nec aliquod placi-
tum eorum mandato
teneatur. Et si
quis a festo sancti
Dionisii inventus
fuerit hoc faciens,
capiatur et reti-
neatur et omnia

---

[a]eorum Aw.   [b]accipia-
tur Ag.

[a]AgQ *ins.* agens.   [b]Ag
has et ret. *over erasure
and adds* vel incarcere-
tur; et inc. *in* Q.
[c]Cantuariensem FbAg
(Cant') SdQ; Cant. ar-
chiepiscopum Hr; Thomam
arch. W.   [d]Angliam Fb.

fuerit aliter[a]
agens, capiatur et
incarceretur.

retineatur. [3][a]
Nullus ferat manda-
tum aliquod domini[b]
pape vel Cantuarien-
sis, et si inventus
fuerit qui tulerit
capiatur et reti-
neatur.

catalla eius et
possessiones capi-
antur in manu
domini regis, sive
episcopus fuerit
sive abbas vel
monachus aut cano-
nicus[a] aut clericus
vel[b] cuiuscumque
ordinis fuerit.

[5] Si quis laicus
venerit de ultra
mare, ubicumque
aplicuerit intente
exquiratur utrum
portet aliquid quod
sit contra honorem
domini regis. Et si
quid tale super eum
inventum fuerit,
capiatur et incar-
ceretur. Et similiter
fiat de laicis qui
veniunt ad mare
transfretare.

v. Generaliter quo-
que interdictum est
quod nullus ferat
aliquod mandatum
clerici vel laici
domino pape vel
archiepiscopo. Si

---

[a]al. inv. fuerit Aw.

[a]W *om.* c. 3 (Nullus ...
Nullus).   [b]domino
FbQ.

[a]aut canonicus Gc; *om.*
Ga.   [b]*om.* Gc.

talis inventus
fuerit, capiatur et
incarceretur.

vi. Si episcopi vel
clerici vel abbates
vel laici senten-
ciam interdicti
tenere voluerint,
sine dilatione de
terra eiciantur et
tota eorum cognatio,
ita quod de catal-
lis suis nichil
secum ferant.

[5] Si episcopi vel
abbates vel clerici
vel laici senten-
tiam interdicti
tenuerint, sine
dilatione a terra
eiciantur et tota
eorum cognatio, ita
quod nichil de
catallis suis secum
deferant;[a] et
catalla eorum et
possessiones in
manu domini regis
seisiantur.

[2] Si episcopi vel
abbates, cuiuscum-
que ordinis sint,
vel quicumque
clerici vel laici
sententiam inter-
dicti tenuerint,
statim eiciantur a
terra et tota cog-
natio eorum, et
tali modo ut nil
ferant de catallis
suis secum, sed
omnia catalla eorum
et omnes posses-
siones sue in manu
domini regis seisian-
tur.

vii. Ut catalla
omnium pape vel
archiepiscopo
faventium, et omnes
possessiones eorum
et omnium eis per-
tinentium, cuius-
cumque gradus vel
ordinis vel sexus
vel conditionis
sint, capiantur et
in dominica manu

[a] ferant AgQW.

domini regis con-
fiscentur.

viii. Ut omnes
clerici qui reddi-
tus habent in Anglia
sint summoniti per
omnes comitatus, ut
infra tres menses
veniant in Angliam
ad redditus suos,
sicut diligunt
redditus suos; et
si[a] non venerint ad
terminum statutum,
redditus in manu
regis capiantur.

[6] Omnes clerici
qui redditus habent
in Anglia sint sum-
moniti per omnes
comitatus ut infra
tres[a] menses sint
in Anglia[b] ad red-
ditus suos, sicut
eos diligunt, et
amodo in Angliam
redire; et si ad
terminum prefixum
non venerint, red-
ditus eorum in manu
domini regis seisi-
antur.

[3] Omnes clerici
qui habent redditus
in Anglia et sunt
extra Angliam, sum-
moneantur per omnes
comitatus et pro-
vincias quod infra
festum sancti
Hylarii redeant in
Angliam, et si non
venerint ad termi-
num illum, omnes
redditus eorum capi-
antur in manus
domini regis et ipsi
sint sine spe rever-
tendi. Et vice-
comites faciant hoc
scire archiepisco-
pis, episcopis de
provinciis suis.

ix. Ut denarii
beati Petri non red-
dantur ulterius
apostolico, sed
diligenter colli-
gantur et serventur
in thesauro regis,
et expendantur ad

[8] Denarii beati[c]
Petri colligantur,
et serventur quous-
que dominus rex
voluntatem suam inde
preceperit.

---

[a]sicut ... et si AbAcAw;
et Ag.

[a]quattuor Fb.   [b]sint
in Angl(ia) FbSdW; in
Anglia Hr; veniant in
Angliam AgQ.   [c]sancti
AgQ.

eius preceptum.

| x. Londoniensis et Norwicensis episcopi sint in misericordia regis et summoneantur per vicecomites et bedellos, ut sint contra iusticias regis ad rectum faciendum regi et iusticiis eius de eo quod contra statuta de Clarendune interdixerunt ex mandato pape terram comitis Hugonis, et excommunicationem quam dominus papa in ipsum fecerat per suas parrochias divulgaverunt sine licentia iusticiarum regis.[a] | [7] Episcopi[a] Lund(oniensis) et Norwic(ensis) summoneantur quod sint coram iustic(iis) domini[b] regis ad rectum faciendum quod contra statuta regni interdixerunt terram Hugonis comitis, et in ipsum sententiam anathematis tulerunt. |

---

[a]Ab *has final rubric:* Expliciunt constitutiones in Norm' a rege Henrico constitutas post transitum beati Thome anno dominice incarnationis millesimo centesimo sexagesimo nono; *in margin at foot of fo. 28:* Expliciunt constitutiones a rege H. in Normannia constitute quas idem rex decrevit observari et fecit edicto publico promulgari adversus ecclesiam proscripto sancto Thoma. Anno dominice incarnationis mclxix.

[a]Episcopus (epc') FbAg SdQ; Item H (episcopi *after* Nor.); Episcopi W. [b]*om.* AgHrQW (W *has* nostris *for* d. regis).

[8] Si quis Walensis
clericus vel laicus
applicuerit, nisi
habeat litteras
domini regis de pas-
sagio suo, capiatur
et custodiatur, et
omnes Walenses qui
sunt in scolis in
Anglia eiciantur.
[9] Omnes vero
vicecomites tocius
Anglie faciant
omnes milites et
libere tenentes et
omnes illos qui
quindecim annos
habent, de comita-
tibus suis, iurare
in pleno comitatu
et per omnes civi-
tates et burgos
quod hec mandata
super vitam et mem-
bra sua servabunt,
et missis servien-
tibus suis per omnes
villatas Anglie,
faciant iurare
omnes illos qui ad
comitatus non fuer-
unt quod hec mandata
cum ceteris tene-
bunt.

(*Gervase's post-
script*) Coacti sunt
itaque omnes per

universam Angliam
a sene decrepito
usque puerum Thome
archiepiscopi et
pape Alexandri obe-
dientiam abiurare.
Episcopi tandem in
unum coacti, et
auctoritate sua
sacramentum vulgi
corroborare rogati,
tam turpiter, tam
imprudenter contra
Deum cervicem eri-
gere, saltem veri-
cundia coacti con-
sentire noluerunt.

164

1170. THE INQUEST OF SHERIFFS

One clause in the Inquest of Sheriffs related to the practice
of the ecclesiastical courts and of clerical officials:[1] it is
reproduced below both in the well-known version intended for
the use of the justices (I), and in the lesser known version
which evidently represents the questions to be put to the witnesses (II). The former has been printed by Stubbs in Gervase,
i.217-19 and *Select Charters* (9th edn., ed. H.W.C. Davis), pp.
175-8, from the mss. of Gervase (see pp. 771, 973 n. 3). It is
omitted in Bodl. ms. e Mus. 222 (3592) fo. 155^{r-v} and Bodl. ms.
Rawl. C. 641, fos. 20-1. The latter text is in *GFL*, pp. 523-4,
from Bodl. mss. e Mus. 249, fo. 89^{r-v}, Douce 287, fos. 87^{v}-88.[2]

---

[1] c. 4 (c. 11 in second version) deals with the custody of archbishoprics,
bishoprics, and abbeys, but only as part of the administration of vacant
fiefs and escheats.

[2] It was first printed by J.A. Giles in *Vita S. Thomae*, ii (London-
Oxford, 1846), pp. 262-3.

The most recent commentary is by J.C. Holt, in *The Study
of Medieval Records,* ed. D.A. Bullough and R.L. Storey
(Oxford, 1971), pp. 86 ff., esp. p. 93 and n.; see also
J.H. Round, *Commune of London* (Westminster, 1899), pp.
125-36; *Red Book of the Exchequer,* ed. H. Hall (RS,
1896), i, pp. cclxvii-cclxxxiv; V.H. Galbraith in *EHR*
lxix (1954), 289-302.

I. ... Et similiter inquiratur per omnes episcopatus quid et
quantum et qua de causa archidiaconi vel decani iniuste et sine
iudicio ceperint, et hoc totum scribatur. (c. 12; c. 11 in
Gervase).

II. ... Dicetis quid et quantum archidiaconi vel decani ceperint iniuste et sine iudicio.

165
1171-2. THE RECONCILIATION OF THE BISHOPS

In September 1170 the pope had learned the details of the
coronation of the young king Henry in June, and he sent letters
excommunicating the bishops of London and Salisbury, and suspending the archbishop of York.[1] Becket's action in forwarding
these letters helped to precipitate his murder; and the murder
in turn checked for a time any move to absolve or restore his
episcopal colleagues. The archbishop of York was suspected of
stirring Henry's anger;[2] but it is hard to penetrate the veil
of prejudice which surrounded York at this time. John of Salisbury's collection of letters contains a strange and violent
onslaught on Archbishop Roger sent in protest by a group of
Canterbury clerks against rumours that he was to be restored,
and it may have been written by John himself.[3] In the same

---

[1] *MB Epp.* 699-700. For what follows, see Foreville, pp. 331-3; *GFL*, pp.
282-3, 289.
[2] Guernes 5126-33 directly accuses Roger, and FitzStephen has perhaps a
hint of a similar suspicion (*MB* iii.127-8); both FitzStephen and Bosham
indicate that it was the three bishops who stirred Henry's anger.
[3] *JS, Letters,* ii, no. 307 and cf. ibid., p.xliv; Roger's letter is ibid.,
no. 306.

collection is a curious account by Roger of his efforts to
exculpate himself. The pope commissioned the archbishop of
Rouen and the bishop of Amiens, who acted in the event through
substitutes, to hear his pleas and if possible raise his suspension. This they performed, and Roger's letter describing his
release is dated 13 December (1171).[1] At the foot of the leaf
which contains this letter in ms. Ab, BL Cotton Claudius B. ii,
fo. 349^V, is a note of the *capitula purgationis* extracted from
Roger on this occasion (printed *MB Epp.* vii.502). This we print
below: the first three of the four points exactly follow
(though with verbal differences) the pope's instruction (*MB
Epp.* 763); the fourth is an addition.

The bishops of London and Salisbury had already been absolved.
On 24 April 1171, after a reasonable delay, the pope commissioned the archbishop of Bourges and the bishop of Nevers to
arrange their absolution, and early in August, at Chaumont near
Gisors, the bishops of Nevers and Beauvais and the abbot of
Pontigny performed the ceremony.[2] Gilbert Foliot remained suspended until early 1172: on 28 February 1172 the archbishop of
Rouen and the bishop of Amiens were appointed to take his purgation and restore him, and this they accomplished at Aumâle on
1 May 1172.[3] By then the papal legates had arrived to treat with
the king himself.

*The capitula purgationis of Roger of Pont l'Évêque, archbishop
of York*

From BL ms. Cotton Claudius B. ii, fo. 349^V; printed in
MB Epp. vii.502 (also ed. J.A. Giles, *Vita S. Thomae,* ii
(London-Oxford, 1846), pp. 268-9).

---

[1]Monday, the feast of St. Lucy, immediately following *Gaudete* Sunday,
the 3rd in Advent, which fits for 1171. The papal instructions of 23 Oct.
1171 are *MB Epp.* 763-4 and in 765 Roger thanks the pope (see note to JS,
Letters, ii, no. 306). Canterbury Cathedral was reopened and purged shortly
before Christmas (Diceto, i.349; Gervase, i.229, 236; *MB* iv.169).
[2]Diceto, i.347; *GFL*, p. 289; *MB Epp.* 753; JL 11889; Foreville, p. 332.
[3]Diceto, i.351; *GFL*, p. 289; *MB Epp.* 767; JL 12143; Foreville, p. 333.

Hec sunt capitula purgationis quam prestitit Eboracensis quarta manu iuratorum quorum unus fuit magister Vacarius.[1]

Quod ipse consuetudines avitas super quibus vertebatur controversia inter regem et dominum Cantuariensem nec scripto nec iuramento firmaverat.

Quod ipse nec opere nec sermone nec per se nec per interpositam personam scienter aliquid machinatus est, quod dominum Cantuariensem in mortem traheret.

Quod litteras domini pape in Angliam destinatas de inhibitione coronationis filii regis nec recepit nec vidit, nec aliquid fieri fecit, qua minus eas videret vel reciperet.

Quod ipse in coronatione filii regis debitum iuramentum integre recepit, nec aliquid omisit quod in coronatione regis Anglie prestari solet.

166

1172. THE SETTLEMENT AND 'COMPROMISE' OF AVRANCHES

> For the events and details, see esp. Foreville, pp. 329–67; for the context and significance, M.G. Cheney, 'The Compromise of Avranches of 1172 and the spread of Canon Law in England', *EHR* lvi (1941), 177–97;[2] for the legation of Albert and Theoduinus, Tillmann, pp. 68–72.

There was talk in Rome in 1171 of sending Cardinal Otto once again; but in the event it was Theoduinus, cardinal priest of San Vitale, who accompanied Cardinal Albert, cardinal priest of San Lorenzo, the future Pope Gregory VIII; they were sent as legates to the territories of Henry II to make a settlement

---

[1] On Vacarius and his service to the archbishop of York, see R.W. Southern in *Medieval Learning and Literature: Essays pres. to R.W. Hunt* (Oxford, 1976), pp. 257–86, esp. 259–60, 283 ff. The papal instructions to Rouen and Amiens specified that there should be four compurgators, two dignitaries of his church and Masters Vacarius and Anger, if available, or two suitable substitutes (*MB Epp.* 763, p. 500, cited Southern, p. 283).

[2] And see above, pp. 855–71, esp. p. 866 n. 2; for a general view of the aftermath, Cheney, *BL*, and below, p. 951 n. 2. On Avranches, see also *Liber Pontificalis* (see p. 945 n. 6); Mansi, xxii.135–40.

after the murder of Thomas Becket.[1] They left the Curia in the
autumn of 1171, and by early December were in Henry's territories. Their task was to come to an understanding which would
permit the lifting of the interdict laid after the murder on
Henry's continental lands by the archbishop of Sens, and the
ban on Henry *ab ingressu ecclesie*.[2] Henry was far away in Ireland, and is said not to have heard of their coming for some
months. Then he settled the affairs of the island for the time
and sailed in mid April; by mid May he was in Normandy and
Maine, where he met the legates at Gorron on 16 May and again
in conference at the abbey of Savigny on the seventeenth. Henry
made a show of resistance to the legates' demands; but by the
nineteenth agreement had been reached, on Sunday 21 May the king
swore a solemn oath at Avranches and made a number of under-
takings; and his son, the young King Henry, swore too.[3] At Caen
on 30 May the king's reconciliation[4] was made public in the
presence of a wider gathering, including the archbishop of
Tours and a number of bishops.[5] The legates spent the summer in
Normandy: the restoration of the excommunicated bishops and the
suspended archbishop of York (p. 941) had already taken place; the
reconciliation of most of the supporters of Becket followed;[6] and
they negotiated peace between Henry II and Louis VII of France.
In September they concluded their main task. On 2 September the
pope confirmed the settlement (see below, no. III): on 27

---

[1]Albert had been cardinal deacon of Sant'Adriano since 1155-6, from 1158
cardinal priest of San Lorenzo in Lucina; in 1187 (Oct.-Dec.) he was Pope
Gregory VIII; Theoduinus was cardinal by 1166, later bishop of Porto (see JS,
Letters, ii, no. 234 n. 1 and refs.; G. Kleemann, *Papst Gregor VIII* (Bonn,
1912); P. Kehr in *Misc. F. Ehrle*, ii = Studi e Testi 38 (Rome, 1924), pp.
248-75; Brixius, pp. 57-8, 66, 126-7; Zenker, pp. 125-9). On their legation
see Tillmann, pp. 68 ff.; Foreville, pp. 335 ff.

[2]Foreville, pp. 334-5 and 335 n. 1.

[3]For the dates of the meetings at Gorron, Savigny and Avranches see *MB
Epp*. 771, 774 (= I below); in the latter Robertson's marginal date of 28
May is incorrect, since *Vocem iocunditatis* is the introit for the 5th Sunday after Easter = 21 May in 1172. For Henry's crossing, and for other
evidence, see Foreville, pp. 335 ff.

[4]Not from full excommunication; he had been excluded *ab ingressu ecclesie*: cf. Foreville, p. 335 and n. 5.

[5]*MB Epp*. 771, 774-5: in all these the meeting at Caen is in the future;
but see also Torigny, pp. 253 f.; *Liber Pontificalis* (see p. 945 n. 6).

[6]For all this and what follows, Foreville, pp. 340-1, 336-7, who notes
the papal bull for Herbert (of Bosham) and his colleagues, *MB Epp*. 778 of
24 June (1172).

September the legates presided at another meeting at Avranches when Henry repeated his oath and confirmed the agreement; on the 28th they held a legatine council of the clergy of Normandy and the neighbouring territories.[1] Their final task was to ensure that the process for filling the English vacancies, and for finding a successor to Thomas above all, was under way; but this is another story - see below, pp. 956-65. In or about April 1173 they received instructions to spread the news of Becket's canonization, solemnized by the pope on 21 February, announced in bulls of 10-12 March. Then they departed, their work apparently done - although the flight of the young king to Louis VII in March 1173 foreshadowed the dispute over the episcopal elections and the great rebellion which were to follow.[2]

The form of the oath and settlement at Avranches is described in the following documents.[3]

1. (= I below; *MB Epp.* 774). The legates' report addressed to William aux Blanchesmains, archbishop of Sens, himself papal legate for the French kingdom, a strong supporter of Becket and one of the most prestigious figures in the French hierarchy. It was written between 21 and 30 May 1172, since it speaks of the meeting at Caen as still in the future.

2. A closely similar report by the legates to Gilbert archbishop of Ravenna. *MB Epp.* 775, which Dr. Anne Duggan has shown

---

[1]See esp. *Gesta Henrici II* , i.32-4 (and Hoveden, ii.39-40; Mansi, xxii. 139-40; Foreville, pp. 336-7). The *Gesta* (i.33) describes it as a gathering 'cum archiepiscopis (*sic*), episcopis et clero Normanniae', but later describes a dispute between the archbishop of Tours and the bishop of Dol; presumably all Henry's more northerly possessions - Normandy, Touraine, Anjou, Maine, and Brittany - were represented. Tillmann, pp. 70-1 n. 115, thought the date 27 Sept. for Henry's oath a mistake. But the discovery of no. III below gives a plausible explanation of the double (or treble) process, as Foreville showed in detail (pp. 341 ff.; but cf. Warren, pp. 531-2 n.).

[2]Tillmann, p. 71; Eyton, p. 171; on the rebellion, see esp. Warren, pp. 117 ff. The papal bulls on the canonization are *MB Epp.* 783-5; JL 12199, 12201, 12203-4.

[3]For mss. and editions of texts printed below, see notes at head of I-III. On a spurious 'revocatio' of Henry II entered in a 15th-cent. ms., see F.W. Maitland, *Collected Papers*, iii (Cambridge, 1911), pp. 115-18. An interesting, incomplete pamphlet on the murder, the compromise, and the election of the new archbishop in BL ms. Lansdowne 398 is printed in *MB* iv.158-85; see esp. pp. 170-4.

derives from Hoveden.[1]

3. The legates' letter to Henry II confirming the terms of
the settlement. This speaks of Whitsun as imminent, so was
evidently written between 21 May and 4 June 1172. *MB Epp.* 772,
from Alan of Tewkesbury's collection, Hoveden, and Herbert of
Bosham's collection.[2]

4. The anonymous report, evidently, from the precision of
its dates,[3] a contemporary record, and probably written like
1 and 2 before the gathering at Caen; following the cardinals'
letters closely in form and substance, but with certain remarkable and significant differences (see below). Special stress is
laid on the king's repentance and the final sentence is notably
friendly to Henry; yet the terms of settlement are clearly
biased in a manner which suggests that the report was written
by or for a disciple or disciples of Becket. *MB Epp.* 771, from
Alan of Tewkesbury's collection.[4]

5. (= II below) The king's report, addressed to the bishop
of Exeter, JS, *Letters,* ii, no. 309.[5]

6. The king's oath, at Caen, as reported in the *Vita Alexandri III* in the *Liber Pontificalis.*[6]

7. (= III below) The fragment of the papal bull confirming

---

[1]A. Duggan (1971), p. 334 n. 1, shows that the only known source is Hoveden (ii.37-9, in Stubbs's edition) from which a 17th-cent. transcript in Cambridge, Trinity Coll. ms. O. 5.44 (unfoliated), *Gilberti [Foliot] ... Epistolae,* ed. J.A. Giles, ii (London-Oxford, 1846), no. 388, Mansi, xxii.138-
9, *HF* xvi.486, and the *MB* text all evidently derive. Sp. ii.99-101 reproduced Hoveden (= ii.35-40); but this was not reprinted by Wilkins.

[2]For mss. see A. Duggan (1971), pp. 334 n. 2, 390, 393-4, 438, 563. Hoveden, ii.36-7; Diceto, i.351-2. Herbert of Bosham's letter collection is Cambridge, Corpus Christi Coll. ms. 123. This text is no. 43, fo. 59^{r-v}, but
incomplete. No. 3 is in Alan's second recension, v.89 = 1st, v.95, BL ms.
Cotton Claud B. ii, fo. 350^V = 3rd, v.90, Cambridge, Corpus Christi Coll.
ms. 295, fo. 205^V. It is also in Bodl. ms. Laud Misc. 666, fos. 189^V-190^V
(cf. A. Duggan (1971), p. 438).

[3]See above, p. 943 n. 3 - it is the source for the dates 16-19 May and
confirms 21 and 28 May.

[4]See A. Duggan (1971), p. 563; Alan 2nd recension, v.88 = 1st, v.94, BL
ms. Cotton Claud. B. ii, fo. 350 = 3rd, v.89, Corpus Christi Coll. ms. 295,
fo. 205; also in Bodl. ms. Laud Misc. 666, fos. 187^V-189^V (cf. A. Duggan
(1971), p. 438).

[5]See notes to letter.

[6]*Liber Pontificalis,* ed. L. Duchesne (Paris, 1886-92), ii.425-6; for the
interpolated version see below, p. 950; Foreville, pp. 342 ff.; *Pont.
Romanorum Vitae,* ed. J.M. Watterich (Leipzig, 1862), ii.419-20; *PL,* cc. 38;
Duchesne, ii.426 n. 1.

the terms, dated 2 September (1172).

There are also accounts of the settlement in the chroniclers, but all these seem to rely for the terms on one or other, or more, of the documents. Thus the *Gesta*, i.31-3, gives a full version of the agreement, based on nos. 1-3, in fact presumably on the sources quoted at length in Hoveden, ii.36-9 (see nn. 1, 2 p. 945).[1] Diceto, i.351-2, is based on no. 3. Gervase, i.238-9 is based on the *Gesta*. Bosham in *MB* iii.543-4, cites 1 or 2.

Let us consider the elements in the settlement as they are laid out in the documents.

Henry II, of his own free will, purged himself of responsibility for the murder, swearing that he had neither ordered nor wished it ('nec precepit nec voluit', no. I below), and grieved *vehementer* when he heard of it. In the cardinals' letter to the king (no. 3) they assert that Henry had been anxious on the ground that the murder was committed 'occasione motus et turbationis quam viderunt in vobis ad illud facinus processisse'; and this is spelt out in the anonymous report, no. 4 which makes the king say 'se intelligere quod causa esset mortis archiepiscopi, et quidquid factum est propter eum factum est' - a version which we may regard as somewhat loaded, as is the same report on the theme of the constitutions (see below). Evidently the king confessed to a measure of responsibility, but denied on oath any murderous intention. The anonymous report adds two details, first the famous phrase that when he heard of the murder, 'plus inde doluit quam letatus est', and thereafter the observation (perhaps equally ambiguous) that he had not grieved so much for the death of either of his parents. In the *Liber Pontificalis,* however, he is made to swear that he grieved as much as if his own son had been killed.

Henry went on to make six promises. 1. Not to withdraw his obedience from Pope Alexander so long as the pope treated him as a catholic and Christian king; a promise particularly made by the younger Henry as well. This is omitted by the anonymous report and by the king (in no. II); but the legates are explicit in all their letters, including the one to the king, and

---

[1] The version in the *Gesta Henrici II* is perhaps closest to no. 2, above; this is virtually identical with no. 1, but of these, Roger of Howden, author of the *Gesta*, certainly knew 2 and does not seem to have known 1.

the same point is vouched for by the pope and in Henry's oath
in the *Liber Pontificalis*. It is a curious discrepancy.

2. To provide enough money to support 200 knights for the
defence of the Holy Land for a year: this is the same in all
versions, save that the anonymous values each knight at 300
aurei, while the king leaves the valuation to the Templars (the
anonymous also says 'secundum dispositionem templariorum');
the cardinals specify that the year starts 'ab instanti festo
Pentecostes'; and the whole clause is lost from the papal bull.

3. To take the cross at Christmas (1172) and set out on
crusade next summer (1173) unless the pope or his successor
allows him to stay. This is omitted by the king in no. II,
though included in the oath ('usque ad triennium', no. 6), but
clear in all the letters of the cardinals; the final phrases
survive in the papal letter to show that it was there. Both
cardinals and pope have a sentence allowing postponement if
Henry went to Spain against the Saracens 'pro urgenti necessitate'. The anonymous has a promise to go to Spain instead of
the clause promising to take the cross. The king's silence on
all this is probably significant. In spite of Gilbert Foliot's
assurance that Henry was longing to go on crusade in the 1160s,[1]
he successfully evaded any such call. Gerald of Wales, not
always a reliable witness on Henry II, alleges that his crusading vow was commuted in 1176 into a promise to found three
monasteries.[2] It is indeed the case that Henry's refoundations
of Amesbury and Waltham were set on foot in 1176-7, and the
foundation also of Witham followed in the late 1170s; and it is
probable that he negotiated on some of his plans with the cardinal legate in 1176, since both the two former foundations required papal approval, and Henry was doubtless keen to get all
the credit for his pious works that he could.[3] But the rest of

---

[1]*GFL*, no. 170, p. 241 (1166); cf. ibid. n. 3 and *GF*, p. 173 n. 1. On the
crusading initiatives of this period, see R.C. Smail in *TRHS* 5th ser. xix
(1969), 1-20, esp. 14.   [2]*Opera,* viii.170; below, p. 950.
[3]See Warren, p. 538 n. 1; Giraldus, *Opera,* viii.169-72; for Henry II's
patronage, see below, esp. p. 950 n. 1. For the foundations, D. Knowles and
R.N. Hadcock, *Medieval Religious Houses, England and Wales* (edn. of London,
1971), pp. 104-5, 135, 178; cf. esp. *Magna Vita S. Hugonis,* bk. ii, ed. D.L.
Douie and H. Farmer, i (NMT, 1961), pp. 46 ff.; cf. ibid. pp. xxiv ff. For
a suggestion that the idea of founding Witham was conceived in or before
1173, see Foreville, p. 343, n. 3; but cf. Farmer in *Magna Vita,* i, p. xxv
n. 1.

the story must remain doubtful. It is curious that the anonymous report does not include any promise to take the cross; but
we must believe that the cardinals supposed the king to have
made such an undertaking.

4. To renounce all customs against the churches of his kingdom introduced in his time, *tempore suo: tempore meo,* said the
king, 'quas quidem aut paucas aut nullas estimo'. There are
minor variations in the clauses - the pope says 'contra ecclesiam terre tue', and the pope and the cardinals agree (in no.
I it is almost a postscript to the letter) that he freed his
dignitaries or bishops from observing them; but the one major
divergence is in the anonymous report, which says that Henry
renounced 'prava statuta de Clarenduna et omnes malas consuetudines que in diebus suis in ecclesias Dei inducte sunt'. Evil
customs from before his time 'temperabit'. Herbert of Bosham,
perhaps inspired by the anonymous report (no. 4), speaks as if
Henry made a general renunciation of evil customs (*MB* iii.546).
These versions can only be reconciled by special pleading -
either by taking it that all that was evil in Clarendon was
introduced in Henry II's time, or that 'prava statuta' in the
anonymous report is governed by 'in diebus suis', i.e. that
reference is made only to those constitutions which were novel.
Neither interpretation is probable, and clearly the king thought
he had escaped without a total condemnation of Clarendon. We
are evidently in the presence of a diplomatic formula which
solved no particular issue: a reader studying the commentary
on Clarendon above may judge for himself how easy it was to
determine which customs were new and which old. The cardinals
were determined to be specific on appeals, and made of them a
separate clause. The narrower interpretation of the condemnation of the customs derives some support, furthermore, from the
remarkable letter written in the young king's name in his appeal
against the episcopal elections of 1173 (see below, pp. 958-9n.).[1]

---

[1] Paris, BN ms. lat. 14876, fos. 116-21 (12th-cent. copy), printed in *HF*
xvi.643-8. For further details see pp. 958-9 n. Here and below we assume that
the young king's letter is authentic, though tendentious. For what it is
worth, the pamphlet in Lansd. ms. 398 (see n. 3 p. 944) refers to a general
obliteration of Clarendon 'ad unguem' (*MB* iv.173-4).

The young king was present at Avranches and made to swear with
the old; but in the letter he says nothing of the settlement or
compromise, much of the evil customs which the martyr's blood
was shed to destroy. Specifically he claims that he himself
wished to abrogate Clarendon chapters 3, 7, 8, and 12, and he
makes clear that he does not think these were new customs, but
old and evil, which he wishes to abolish. The letter is most
elaborate on c. 12, since the occasion of it was the episcopal
and archiepiscopal elections, but it is very specific on the
others; and on c. 3 it promises an order that clerks shall not
be summoned 'ad seculares ... iudices, et ne manifesta exhibeant vel subeant iudicia' citing trial by battle and the
ordeals of water and iron. There is no suggestion in the letter
that the young king reckoned himself bound to this renunciation
by his promises at Avranches,[1] nor that he is renouncing customs
devised in his father's time. No doubt the letter was a bid for
papal support and made the most of his concessions; but for what
it is worth it lends some support to the evidence that the
settlement of 1172 involved no general rejection of the Constitutions.

5. To allow appeals to go freely to the pope, save that the
king might demand 'securitatem' from suspect persons; thus the
cardinals, and in no. II the king says in essence the same,
claiming that suspect appellants 'iurent quod in itinere illo
nec malum meum nec dedecus regni mei perquirent'; the oath in
no. 6 omits the qualification. This specific renunciation was
omitted from the anonymous report, though evidently implied in
the general renunciation of Clarendon which it contains.

6. To restore to the church of Canterbury her possessions in
full as they had been a year before the archbishop went into
exile; and to restore to favour and possessions all his supporters who had suffered in his cause. On these two points all
the versions seem to agree (but see p. 954 n. a).

Finally, the young king joined his father, swore to support

---

[1] Though he was so bound, needless to say, on freedom of appeals. Clerks
were specifically exempted from trial by battle in the supplementary concordat of 1176 (p. 996); this underlines that the young king was dealing,
in part at least, with real issues.

Alexander and repudiate the same customs (so the documents cited above on pp. 944-6 as 1, 2, 7; cf. a vaguer statement in 3, 4).

There are two further concessions which have sometimes been associated with this settlement. In the course of the 1170s Henry undertook three religious foundations or refoundations, and it has often been said that they were part of his penance for Becket's death. There is no evidence, however, to connect them with the settlement of 1172, and only the word of Gerald of Wales that they replaced his vow to go on crusade (see nn. 2-3 p. 947). On the other hand he was always interested in the more ascetic orders and may well have conceived the idea of one or more Carthusian foundations in this period to balance his generosity to Grandmont.[1]

There is a passage in some versions of the. *Vita Alexandri III papae* in the *Liber pontificalis* which seems to indicate that the two kings were to hold their kingdom from the pope - 'recipiemus et tenebimus' - they are made to say. This has been most thoroughly investigated by Professor Foreville, and we accept her conclusion that the words are an interpolation into the clause describing the royal oath of loyalty to Alexander, possibly made by hindsight in the light of John's submission of the kingdom to Innocent III; they are not in the earliest known ms. of the *Vita*.[2]

---

[1] The whole question of Henry II's foundations has been placed on a new footing by E. Hallam(-Smith), 'Henry II as a founder of monasteries', *JEH* xxviii (1977), 113-32; and for his wider activities as a patron, cf. her Univ. of London Ph.D. thesis, 'Aspects of the monastic patronage of the English and French Royal houses, *c.*1130-1272' (1976). Only one other writer relates three foundations (in this case not specified) to a penance, Ralph Niger (*Chronicles,* ed. R. Anstruther, London, 1851, p. 168, cited *JEH* xxviii.113 n.); Dr. Hallam-Smith shows that Henry's interests were far wider than had been supposed, and that an Augustinian house in Dublin and three Norman hospitals founded by him were actually dedicated to Thomas. Beyond that one can only say that the great majority of his foundations occurred in the 1170s and early 1180s, and that they may in part have been inspired by 'shock ... contrition' or 'an attempt ... to regain the favour and the support of the Church ...' (Hallam-Smith, art. cit., p. 132). On the Carthusians cf. esp. Knowles, *MO*, pp. 380-1.

[2] Foreville, pp. 342-56; she also quotes and studies the letter in Henry's name in Peter of Blois's letter collection (ibid., p. 349 n. 3 = *PL* cc. 1389(-90)), which seems to support the idea of feudal subjection and claims to have been written during the great rebellion (or some major rebellion by his sons). Her case against its authenticity as evidence of such an act of

No. I below tells of other promises made by the king, not to be written down;[1] but it is probable that this corresponds to the clause in the anonymous report (*MB Epp.* 771) which says 'Iniunxerunt ei etiam secretius ieiunia et eleemosynas, et alia quedam que ad communem audientiam non pervenerunt' - and it is unlikely that there were secret clauses of public significance.

All in all the king conceded little: apart from his renunciation of the attempt to check appeals, his concessions to the liberty of the church, as he himself said of the evil customs introduced in his own day, were 'aut paucas aut nullas'. But the public demonstration, three times repeated, of his reconciliation, shows that pope and cardinals set much store by what they had achieved: the full reconciliation of one of the most powerful kings in western Christendom to the Alexandrine cause and party, and his help towards the crusade.[2]

The choice of documents to be included here posed a peculiar problem, since all contribute something to our knowledge of the settlement; but some selection seemed unavoidable, and we have chosen what appeared to give as succinctly as possible one account from each of the three parties most concerned, the cardinals, the king, and the pope.

I. *The report of the Cardinals Albert and Theoduinus addressed to the archbishop of Sens*

From BL mss. Cotton Vitellius C. xii, fos. 279[v]-280 (Vi, 15th cent.) and Vespasian E. x, fos. 259 (258)-260 (259)

---

submission is very strong; yet the letter presents baffling problems, since it is apparently an integral part of Peter's first letter-collection of *c.*1184. See C.R. Cheney, *Pope Innocent III and England* (Stuttgart, 1976), p. 333 n. 33, and references. The whole question needs further investigation, but it seems most improbable that any such submission took place in 1172 and remains likely that the interpolation in the *Vita Alex. III* is related to the event of 1213 and its aftermath.

[1]But strangely the cardinals' letter to the archbishop of Ravenna (*MB Epp.* 775) speaks of other promises written 'in absolutionis eius charta'; this may, however, refer only to the repetition of the other promises by the young king (see also below, p. 953 n. c).
[2]On the aftermath see esp. H. Mayr-Harting in *JEH* xvi (1965), 39-53; Foreville, chaps. iii-iv; C. Duggan, *Twelfth-Century Decretal Collections*; Cheney, *BL*.

(Ve); Hereford Cathedral Lib. ms. O. iv. 14, fos. 223^v-
224^v (Sh) (both 14th cent.). Printed *MB Epp.* 774; also
in *Gilberti [Foliot]* ... *Epistolae*, ed. J.A. Giles, ii,
no. 387. On the mss. see A. Duggan, 'Manuscript transmission of Letter Collections relating to the Becket
dispute' (London Ph.D. thesis, 1971), p. 334 n. 1;
A. Duggan (1980), p. 179 and nn. In Vi and Ve it is in
a group of letters following Edward Grim's Life of Becket;
in Sh, a Becket miscellany, it follows FitzStephen's Life.
Vi is the least faulty text and provides the base and
spelling, with variants of Ve and Sh when they agree
against Vi or have something to contribute.

Venerabili fratri et in Christi visceribus amplectendo semper
amico, Willelmo Dei gratia Senonensi episcopo, apostolice sedis
legato, Albertus dignacione divina tituli sancti Laurentii in
Lucina et Theodinus tituli sancti Vitalis presbiteri cardinales,
apostolice sedis legati, quod promisit Deus diligentibus se.

   Quoniam exspectare vos credimus ut de statu nostro et iniuncti
nobis promotione negotii aliquid audiatis, idcirco qualiter
nobiscum et per ministerium mediocritatis nostre Deus egerit
hiis diebus, fraternitati^a vestre presenti scripto duximus in-
dicandum.^{b} Noveritis ergo quod postquam illustris Anglorum rex^c
venisse nos in regnum suum in veritate cognovit, totius obsta-
culo tarditatis amoto, de Hibernia in Angliam incumbentibus
sibi negociis pretermissis, de Anglia vero in Normannie partes
accessit, atque incontinenti plures ad nos nuntios et honora-
biles destinavit, inquirens a nobis^d quo loco potius convenire
cum eo et loqui vellemus. Placuit tandem ad Saviniense monasterium pro colloquio habendo concurrere, ubi religiosorum
virorum^e possemus orationibus adiuvari. Convenimus illuc, convenerunt et multe persone utriusque ordinis de regno ipsius, et
tractavimus di[Vi, fo. 280]ligentia qua potuimus quod ad salutem ipsius et iniunctam nobis obedientiam pertinebat. Cum autem

---

^{a}nostre ... fraternitati *om.* Ve. ^{b}intimandum Sh. ^{c}Anglorum rex ViVe;
rex Anglie Sh. ^{d}Ve *adds* in. ^{e}*om.* Ve.

non possemus in omnibus convenire,[1] recessit ipse a nobis velut
in Angliam profecturus et nos exspectavimus sequenti die ad
Abrincas civitatem ituri. Postera autem die venerunt ad nos
episcopus Lexoviensis et duo archidiaconi, et concesso quod
petebamus ad predictam processimus civitatem, ad quam Dominica
qua cantatur Vocem iucunditatis [21 May 1172] convenit cum
personis plurimis et ipse nobiscum, et cum tanta humilitate
quod fuerat condictum implevit ut illius exstitisse opus sine
dubitatione credatur qui respicit terram et facit eam tremere,
qui tangit montes et fumigant.[a][2] Sane quam timoratum Deo, quam
obedientem ecclesie se curaverit exhibere, non est opus presenti abreviatione referre. Satis enim ipsius opera manifestant
et manifestabunt adhuc plenius, sicut spes uber data est in
futurum.

Primum itaque, super mortem sancte memorie Thome quondam
Cantuariensis archiepiscopi, non de nostra exactione sed de
propria voluntate, tactis sacrosanctis evangeliis suam conscientiam expurgavit, iurans videlicet quod nec precepit nec voluit,
et quando audivit doluit vehementer. Quia vero quod factum
fuerat ex sua occasione factum esse timebat, de satisfactione
prestanda tale prestitit iuramentum. Primo quidem iuravit quod
a domino nostro papa Alexandro et eius catholicis[b] successoribus non recedet, quamdiu eum sicut catholicum regem et Christianum habuerint, et hoc ipsum fecit iurare filium suum maiorem
in charta absolutionis pro morte beati Thome.[c] Iuravit etiam
quod usque ad annum tantam pecuniam dabit templariis unde ad
defensionem terre Ierosolimitane ducenti milites valeant reti-
neri. Ab instanti vero Nativitate Domini usque ad triennium
crucem accipiet, sequenti estate Ierosolimam profecturus, nisi
per dominum papam steterit vel eius catholicos successores. Si
vero interim pro urgenti necessitate contra Sarracenos in His-
paniam iverit, quantum temporis in illo itinere consumpserit,

---

[a]facit ... fumigant ViSh; facit etc. Ve.   [b]catholicis Ve; catholice
ViSh.   [c]in charta ... Thome Sh (*also MB Epp. 775*); *om.* ViVe.

---

[1]The king's letter, no. II below, also stresses that it was a closely
argued negotiation.
[2]Ps. 103 (104), 32.

tantumden predictum spatium prolongare poterit. Abiuravit etiam
omnes consuetudines que contra ecclesias regni sui suo tempore
introducte videntur. Appellationes ecclesiasticarum causarum
ad dominum papam libere sinet fieri et tractari per eum causas
et suo fine concludi. Si quis tamen ei suspectus fuerit, securitatem ei faciet quod dampnum eius et regni sui non querat.
Possessiones Cantuariensis ecclesie si que sint ablate resti-
tuet, sicut habuit primo anno quando archiepiscopus[a] de terra
exiret. Id ipsum faciet et de personis que causa ipsius exisse
videntur; quibus etiam gratiam suam et bonam reddidit voluntatem, et hoc[b] quidem sub iuramento. Promisit autem et alia de
libera voluntate[c] gerenda que non oportet scripture serie deno-
tare. Hec autem scripsimus, ut agnoscatis eum obedientem ecclesie atque ad[d] divinum obsequium multo amplius quam adhuc fuerit
animatum. Noveritis ad hec[e] filium eius de predictis consuetudinibus dimittendis pariter cum eo iurasse. Sane quod ibi factum est, iterato adhuc, ne dubitationis locus alicui remaneret,
apud Cadomum in maiori frequentia personarum publice[f] statuit
se facturum. Relaxavit preterea episcopos de promissione quam
ei fecerant de consuetudinibus observandis, et promisit quod
non exiget in futuro. .

II. *King Henry II's report of the agreement, addressed to
    Bartholomew, bishop of Exeter*

> JS, *Letters,* ii, no. 309 = *MB Epp.* 773, based on Paris,
> BN ms. lat. 8562, fos. 88[v]-89.

... Hec enim sunt que me ad eorum instantiam observaturum
promisi: quod scilicet ab instanti festo Pentecostes usque in
annum tantam pecuniam dabo, unde ad arbitrium fratrum Templi
ducenti milites ad defensionem terre Ierosolimitane per annum
valeant teneri; et quod licebit appellationes fieri ad dominum
papam libere, ita tamen ut si quos suspectos habuerim, antequam
de regno exeant, iurent quod in itinere illo nec malum meum nec

---

[a]primo ... quando archiep. ViVe; uno anno antequam Sh.   [b]hoc Ve; *om.*
ViSh.   [c]voluntate voluntate Vi.   [d]ad ShVe; in Vi.   [e]ad hec Vi; adhuc
VeSh.   [f]*om.* Sh.

dedecus regni mei perquirent; et quod consuetudines que tempore
meo contra ecclesias terre mee inducte sunt dimittam, quas
quidem aut paucas aut nullas estimo; et quod possessiones
Cant(uariensis) ecclesie, si que ablate sunt plene restituam,
sicut habuit uno anno antequam archiepiscopus de Anglia egre-
deretur. Clericis preterea et laicis utriusque sexus pacem meam
et possessiones suas restituam, qui occasione prenominati archiepiscopi destituti fuerunt. Et hoc michi ex parte domini pape
in remissionem omnium peccatorum observandum iniunxerunt ...

III. *The acceptance and confirmation of the agreement by Pope*
   Alexander III, dated 2 September (1172)

> All that survives is in the late 16th-cent. transcript
> made for Robert Beale from the original then belonging
> to Henry Bourchier of the Inner Temple, BL ms. Add. 32100,
> fo. 251^{r-v}; ed. C. Johnson in *EHR* lii (1937), 466-7; *PUE*
> iii, no. 189 (for *ae* in the ms. we read *e*).

... nos aut catholicos nostros successores remanseris,[a] du-
cente Domino profecturus. Ceterum si contra Sarracenos in His-
paniam pro urgenti necessitate te contigerit proficisci, quantum
temporis fuerit ex quo arripueris iter elapsum, tantundem prescriptum spatium Ierosolymitane profectionis poteris prolongare.
Appellationes autem ad sedem apostolicam factas nec impedies
nec impediri permittes, quin libere fiant in ecclesiasticis
causis ad Romanam ecclesiam bona fide, absque fraude et malo
ingenio, et per Romanum pontificem tractentur et suum consequantur effectum: ita tamen ut[b] si qui tibi suspecti fuerint,
securitatem faciant quod malum tuum vel regni non querent.
Preterea consuetudines que contra ecclesiam terre tue tempore
tuo sunt introducte penitus dimittes, et personas ecclesiasticas regni tui ab earum observantia absolvisti. Possessiones
Cantuariensis ecclesie, si que ablate sunt, ita plene restitues,
sicut habuit uno anno antequam archiepiscopus de Anglia egre-
deretur. Porro clericis et laicis utriusque sexus pacem et

---

[a] remanserit ms. *For the run of this sentence cf. no. I.*   [b] *Or* aut ms.

gratiam tuam restitues et possessiones suas reddes, qui occasione sunt prenominati episcopi destituti. Que omnia te adim-
plere firmiter et servare iuramento prestito promisisti. Iuravit etiam primogenitus tuus qui est coronatus in regem de novis
consuetudinibus dimittendis. Pariter quoque ex fervore devotionis et fidei et abundantia sincere affectionis et reverentie,
quam ad Romanam ecclesiam et nos ipsos habetis, ambo iurastis
quod a devotione nostra et catholicorum [ms. fo. 251^v] successorum nostrorum quamdiu vos habuerimus sicut antecessores nostri
vestros antecessores habuerunt, et catholicos reges, minime
recedetis. Ut autem tam magnifica et insignis devotio in memoria
semper Romane ecclesie firmius habeatur et nullo unquam possit
tempore aliqua oblivione deleri, que predicta sunt rata et
firma habemus, et sigilli nostri munimine duximus roboranda,
et ea vobis in remissionem iniungimus peccatorum ut ad salutem
vobis proficiant sempiternam. Dat' Tusculan' 4 Non' Septembr.^{a}

167

LATE APRIL *and* JUNE 1173. COUNCILS OF LONDON

These two councils met for the election of the archbishop of
Canterbury, and to fill the other vacant sees, six in number.

The election to Canterbury was a contentious issue, for it
was in the 1170s and 1180s that the long-standing disagreement
between the monks of Canterbury Cathedral priory and the bishops
of the province as to which body formed the chapter who elected
the archbishop came to a head (see above, pp. 707-8, 726-7, 843,
and below, nos. 172, 178). As in 1162, the king was in France,
watching the event with close attention, but in the year following the Compromise of Avranches, he was naturally careful to
give some impression that the election was free. This did not
extend to all the elections, as is shown by the number of royal

---

^{a}Date ... ms. *The copyist adds* 'Anno 1174. In bulla plumbea filis sericis
rubeis' *and a representation of obverse and reverse of the bulla; with a note
that Robert Beale had seen and had the copy made, 14 Nov. 1551, and that the
original* 'is extant with Mr. Henry Bourchier of the Temple, gent.'. *All this
and the endorsement are ed. in full in EHR, loc. cit.*

clerks chosen (see p. 958). Negotiations started late in 1172.
The story has been worked out in detail in Foreville, pp. 373
ff.; by H. Mayr-Harting[1] and the editors of *GFL*, pp. 291 ff.,
esp. 292-3. The latter write as follows:

> Serious discussions began in February [1173]; and at a
> council held in London at the end of April [or early May]
> candidates were elected to all the bishoprics (except per-
> haps Bath, for which this seems to have taken place some-
> what earlier).[2] There was the customary dispute over the
> election to Canterbury between the bishops of the province
> and the monks of Canterbury.[3] The dispute was finally
> settled by the election of Richard, prior of Dover, on 3
> June.[4] In [*GFL*] no. 220 Gilbert describes an attempt
> to elect to Canterbury and the difficulties which arose.
> The discussions must have been spread over several months
> from the suggestion of the bishop of Bayeux late in 1172,
> through the election of the abbot of Bec in February and
> his withdrawal early in April, to the attempt to elect the
> abbot of Cerisy,[5] evidently at the council in late April;
> and the letter was written some time later ..., but before
> the final election on 3 June.

The letter opens with a sharp reference to his detraction
by the monks of Canterbury. But it closes with a suggestion

---

[1]*JEH* xvi (1965), 39-53. The early part of the story is most fully described in *MB* iv.176 ff. (pamphlet from BL Lansd. 398: see p. 944 n. 3),
beginning with meetings at Windsor in Sept.-Oct. 1172.

[2]*MB Epp.* 790 (cf. 791). For the elections, see Gervase, Diceto, below;
Ann. Winchester, *Ann. Mon.* i.61, which dates the election to Winchester to
1 May; Gervase dates the council *c.* end of April; *GFL*, p. 292 n. 3; Le Neve,
ii.45, 85, iii.2.

[3]Gervase, below; *GFL*, no. 220, shows that the dispute began somewhat
earlier than Gervase indicates. Bishop and monks had agreed to the election
of the abbot of Bec, but he had declined and been released on 5 April (Gervase, i.241-2). Foliot's letter shows that the crucial issue was already
who should announce the election (see below, pp. 961, 1017 ff., 1038; H. Mayr-
Harting, art. cit., pp. 50-2).

[4]See *GFL*, p. 292 n. 6; we prefer Gervase to the Canterbury annals in
UGQ, p. 6, which gives 15 June.

[5]The bishop of Bayeux was Henry de Beaumont, formerly dean of Salisbury
(bishop 1164-1205: see *GFL*, p. 530, corrected by JS, *Letters*, ii, p. xxv
n.); the abbot of Bec was Roger de Bailleul, 1149-79, the abbot of Cerisy,
Martin, *c.*1167-1185/90 (*GFL*, p. 292 n. 1).

that Henry go at least half-way to meeting the monks' wishes.
This is accompanied by a hint that Henry turn back ('revocetis') from his Norman candidates to an Englishman, or at
least someone living in England. One is inclined to suspect
that Gilbert had already come to an understanding with Odo
prior of Canterbury, and had his eye on a candidate; and
Gervase (below, p. 962) tells us that in the comparatively
brief interval between the fruitless council in late April
[-May] and the election of Richard, prior of Dover, early
in June, Richard himself and another monk went to ascertain
the king's wishes. The king refused to disclose his views,
but sent them secretly; Odo was allowed at least the show of
a free election, and Richard was elected. It seems likely
that all this was an elaborate face-saving device: the election was free, but Henry was allowed to state his wishes.[1]
... It is ... clear that the king had his way in the choice
of several of the bishops, as can be seen from the following
list of the elect. [Robert Foliot had been among the circle
of Becket's *eruditi*, his clerks, but had not shared his
exile.]

   Canterbury: Richard, prior of Dover; *Bath:* Reginald Fitz-
Jocelin, royal clerk and archdeacon of Wiltshire [?]; *Chichester:*
John of Greenford, dean of Chichester; *Ely:* Geoffrey Ridel,
royal clerk and archdeacon of Canterbury; *Hereford:* Robert
Foliot, archdeacon of Oxford; *Lincoln:* Geoffrey, son of
Henry II and archdeacon of Lincoln; *Winchester:* Richard of
Ilchester, royal clerk and archdeacon of Poitiers.

   The consecration of the archbishop-elect was fixed for
10 June, a week after his election, but it was prevented by
the intervention of the young king, Henry 'III', who took
exception to the elections - in particular because his consent had not been given (Gervase, as below).[2] The incident

---

[1] See Mayr-Harting, art. cit., p. 50.
[2] See also the long letter to the pope in the young king's name, preserved
in the fragmentary 13th-cent. group of letters attached to a 15th-cent. ms.
of St. Bernard's works from Saint-Victor, Paris, BN ms. lat. 14876, fos.
116-121; printed from Martène's transcript in *HF* xvi.643-8, and discussed
above, pp. 948-9. The authenticity of this long and tendentious attack on the

is described in [Foliot's *Letter*] no. 221, written shortly
after 10 June. The result was an appeal to the pope and the
postponement of the consecration of all the other bishops.
Between then and the settlement of the case in 1174 Gilbert
wrote to the pope on behalf of the elect of Ely (no. 225),
Hereford (no. 224), and Winchester (no. 223): he also wrote
to Cardinal William of Pavia in support of the bishop elect
of Winchester (no. 226). No. 222, for the elect of Bath,
refers to the legates' permission for an election, and does
not indicate any later difficulty, so it very likely belongs
to spring 1173. Similar letters on behalf of some of the
elect were sent by Arnulf of Lisieux, Bartholomew of Exeter,
John of Salisbury, and the prior and monks of Christ Church,
Canterbury.[1]

The dispute over the election of Richard to Canterbury
was settled by the pope early in 1174. His election was confirmed and he was consecrated by the pope in person at
Anagni on 7 April 1174; he was shortly afterwards given the
pallium and made ... legate.[2] Richard left Italy in May and
returned to England. On 23 June [at Saint-Jean de Maurienne]
he consecrated Reginald FitzJocelin to Bath; and on 6 October [at Canterbury] all the other bishops except Geoffrey
elect of Lincoln. Shortly after 6 October Gilbert wrote

'elections', coupled with a plea for true canonical freedom in preference
to ancestral customs - strange music from the mouth of any Angevin - is not
perhaps above suspicion; but it seems probable that it is a contemporary
broadside, and may well be the letter it purports to be, and reflect
manoeuvring of the young king's curia on the eve of the great rebellion of
1173-4. It is our sole source for the famous writ attributed to the old
king (fo. 117[v]); *HF* xvi.645: 'Henricus rex Anglorum, dux Normannorum et
Aquitanorum et comes Andegavensium (*sic*) fidelibus suis monachis Guintoni-
ensis ecclesie, salutem. Mando vobis ut liberam electionem habeatis, et
tamen nolo ut aliquem accipiatis nisi Ricardum clericum meum, Pictavensem
archidiaconum.' No doubt it represented Henry II's intention; we cannot
feel any confidence that the essential reference to Richard of Ilchester
occurred in a genuine writ. On the ms. see G. Laehr in *Festschrift A. Brack-
mann*, ed. L. Santifaller (Weimar, 1931), pp. 402-21, esp. pp. 403-4.

[1]Arnulf of Lisieux, *Letters*, ed. F. Barlow, nos. 92, 94-6, 98; JS, *Letters*, ii, nos. 311-21.
[2]For the province of Canterbury: Gervase, i.247; *Gesta Henrici II*, i.69-
70; Diceto, i.369-70.

no. 228 to Alexander III, pleading for the consecration of
Geoffrey, which did not take place.

He resigned Lincoln in 1182 and was archbishop of York from
1189 (consecrated 1191) till his death in 1212.

A curious sidelight is thrown on the period when Richard
was archbishop-elect by a passage in the Chronicle of Battle:
'... cum mox post electionem suam, consecratione sua non expectata, quedam publice statuenda decrevisset, dominus papa in
ipsius consecratione cuncta que a die electionis sue statuisse
visus est, in irritum redegit.'[1] But this more probably refers
to the handling of church property and conferment of benefices[2]
than to anything approaching legislation, and must be viewed
with reserve.

In the course of 1173 the papal subdeacon Nicholas paid a
visit, which is recorded by Diceto (i.378-9; cf. Tillmann,
p. 73); but this was to win support and money in the pope's
campaign against the anti-pope, and seems to have had no connection with the elections.

I. *Gilbert Foliot, Letters, no. 220*

> *GFL*, no. 220 to Henry II, defending himself for his part
> in the election; after describing the failure of the
> attempts to elect the bishop of Bayeux and the abbot of
> Bec, he goes on to the events of the council of late
> April 1173; Bodl. ms. e Mus. 249, fo. 190^V; *MB Epp.* 792;
> *Letters,* ed. Giles, no. 269.

Ad ultimum ad abbatem de Cereseio decursum est. Quod licet et
episcopis et omnibus terre vestre abbatibus omnibusque regni
vestri personis non solum grave videretur verum et indignis-
simum, ego tamen ne pax ecclesie turbaretur, nec quam desidera-
batis electio ulterius differretur - etsi cum multa ira et
indignatione omnium - tandem tamen optinui, ut si monachi

---

[1]Ed. E. Searle, p. 276; ed. J.S. Brewer, p. 144; below, p. 1009.
[2]As suggested in an interesting discussion of this passage by R.L. Benson, *The Bishop-elect* (Princeton, 1968), pp. 108-10.

Cantuar(ie) in electionis pronuntiatione episcopis regni vestri
vel modicam exhibere voluissent reverentiam,[1] in ipsum acqui-
escerent, et ne vester adversus eos turbaretur animus rem hoc
fine terminare permitterent. Verum hii sibi omnia usurpantes et
episcopos omnes a consilio et electione et electionis pronuntiatione severius excludentes, quod cum aliquantula modestia
agentes tunc optinere potuerunt, nimia utentes obstinacia
ulterius differri compulerunt. Qua in re si placet honori vestro
consulite, diligenter attendentes quid vobis magis expediat: an
monachis totum ascribere qui vobis nec hominio tenentur astricti
nec fidelitate, aut in eligenda maxima persona regni vestri
reverentiam aliquam episcopis attribuere, qui vobis aut hominio
aut fidelitate obligati honorem vestrum in Deo conservare duplici
necessitate tenentur obnoxii. Bonum est itaque si placet ut
rigorem monachorum quem tot[iens][a] de humilitate vestra conci-
piunt ea qua scitis mode[stia][a] et sapientia temperetis, et ad
aliquam si placet regni vestri personam ipsorum consilium
revocetis, et salvo iure utriusque partis in posterum de prima
voce in electione habenda (cum de eo agi fuerit oportunum) electionem ipsam per priorem et aliquem episcoporum simul aut alio
quocumque modo quod Deus vobis et consilio vestro revelaverit
pronuntiari faciatis, ut per sapientiam vestram pacificato
statu ecclesie, nebulam que ex dissensione hac regno vestro
adhuc impendet gratiam prestante Domino prorsus evacuetis.

II. *Gervase of Canterbury, Chronica, s.a. 1173*

> From BL ms. Cotton Vesp. B. xix, fos. 95-6 (Ga); Cam-
> bridge, UL ms. Ff. 1.29, fo. 73[r-v] (Gc) (see pp. 771, 973 n. 3):
> select variants only of Gc; ed. Stubbs, Gervase, i.243-5.

Dum hanc itaque diebus sacris Paschalibus molirentur explere
maliciam, convocati sunt episcopi et clerus Anglie ad Lon-
d(oniam) circa finem mensis Aprilis. Omis[Ga, fo. 95[v]]sa igitur

---

[a]*The margin of the ms. is cut away with the loss of a few letters.*

---

[1]See p. 957 n.3: here and in what follows Gilbert enunciates the problem
of who had the first voice in the election.

electione pastoris Cant(uariensis) ecclesie, electi sunt ad
libitum regis et curialium episcopi sex, videlicet Ricardus
Wintoniensis, Gaufridus Heliensis, R(obertus)[a] Herford(ensis),
R(eginaldus) Bathon(iensis), Lincolniensis, Cicestrensis. Novissime de electione Cant(uariensis) ecclesie conseritur sermo.
Sic erunt novissimi primi et primi novissimi, etcetera.[1] Prior
igitur Odo in medium vocatus, a prima petitione libere electionis non avellitur, sed obsecrat ut Cant(uariensis) electus
de sua id est de Cant(uarie) ecclesia sumatur. Consenserunt
utcumque episcopi, sed quia de regis beneplacito dubitabant,
decreverunt scriptis suis cum prioris nuntiis regium animum
pretemptare. Prior his libens annuit sed subito episcopi,
legationem hanc suspectam habentes, quod prius petierant
refutare ceperunt. Prior autem episcoporum mentes ad plenum
nosse desiderans, dixit abbatem de Cerasis virum esse commenda-
bilem, et regis non modica gratia pollere. Audientes episcopi
predictum abbatem utpote ignotum et alterius regni personam
refutaverunt, sed subito redeuntes ad cor,[2] consenserunt, con-
ditionem hanc interponentes, ut scilicet eorum esset electio et
episcopi Lond(oniensis) vox prima. Contradicente priore, insti-
terunt ut electio in scedula scriberetur, et sic ab utroque,
priore scilicet et episcopo London(iensi), in audientia legere-
tur; sed et hoc prior ut frivolum refutavit. Petierunt igitur
ut prior privatim inter eos electionem faceret, et episcopus
Londoniensis in audientia omnium eandem referret. Non consentiente priore, primum resumpserunt consilium, scilicet ut regis
assertio super electione facienda per fideles nuntios inquire-
retur. Missi sunt itaque ad regem in Norm(annia) monachi duo,
Ricardus[b] prior Dovorie et alius; qui regem satis gratiosum
repperientes, sed nullam sue voluntatis certitudinem reportantes,
ex precepto regis citissime in Angliam reversi sunt. Rex vero
per privatos nuntios Ricardo de Luci et avunculo suo comiti
Cornubie sue voluntatis revelavit archanum. Coacto igitur

---

[a]Ricardus Ga; R. Gc.   [b]Gc *om.* duo Ricardus.

---

[1]Cf. Matt. 19, 30; 20, 16; Marc. 10, 31; cf. Luc. 13, 30.
[2]Cf. Isa. 46, 8.

concilio apud Lond(oniam) in initio mensis Iunii, cum prior
Odo a petitione libere electionis minis vel blanditiis non
valeret avelli, etsi tarde tamen obtinuit quod petivit. Multis
itaque hinc inde sermonibus prolatis, tandem Ricardus prior
Dovorie Dominica octavarum Pentecostes[a] apud Westmonasterium
electus est. Sequenti die sabbati ab episcopis et electis Anglie,
clero et populo Cant(uariensis) ecclesie honorifice [Ga, fo. 96]
susceptus est, in crastino sicut dicebatur consecrandus. Sed cum
omnia tante consecrationi necessaria preparata fuissent, ecce
littere novi regis Henrici ex adversa parte in medium allate
sunt; quarum iste est textus:

'Henricus Dei gratia rex Anglie[b] et dux Norm' et comes
Andeg' regis Henrici filii caro et fideli suo Odoni[c] priori
Cant(uariensis) ecclesie et universo conventui, salutem et
dilectionem. Ex certa quorumdam relatione recepimus quod in
ecclesia vestra et etiam in provincialibus ecclesiis personas
quasdam minus congruas pater meus instituere attemptet. Et
quoniam absque assensu nostro id nequaquam fieri debet, qui
ratione regie unctionis regnum et totius regni curam suscepimus, super hoc Romanam sedem in multorum presentia apellavimus,
et appellationem factam venerabilibus patribus nostris et amicis
Alberto et Thedino cardinalibus, apostolice sedis legatis,
scripto et nuntio nostro denuntiavimus; qui sicut viri prudentes
apellationi detulerunt. Hanc etiam ipsam apellationem fidelibus
nostris Londoniensi, Exoniensi, et Wigorn(iensi) episcopis
scripto nostro denuntiavimus. Et quemadmodum appellavimus,
iterato sub testimonio vestro appellamus.'

Dubitantibus igitur episcopis et conferentibus quid facto
opus esset, cum quidam consecrationi consentirent, quidam apellationi deferrent, tandem assensu omnium consecratio illa
dilata est. Misit igitur Cant(uariensis) electus nuntios et
litteras tam suas quam omnium episcoporum et electorum Anglie
et conventus ecclesie Christi ad dominum papam, et ipse post
modicum in propria persona subsecutus est ...

---

[a]Gc *adds* iii nonas Iunii.   [b]*Sic* Ga *for* Anglorum; Angl' Gc (*but* Gc
reads Andegavie).   [c]Odoni Gc; O. Ga.

III. *Ralph de Diceto, Ymagines Historiarum, s.a. 1173*

From Lambeth Palace Lib. ms. 8 (Diceto's gift to St. Paul's),
fo. 83^{r-v} (Da) and BL ms. Cotton Claud. E. iii (also late
12th cent.), fo. 86^{v} (old 84^{v}) (Db); ed. Stubbs, i.368-9.

Da	Db
Littere regis patris, littere cardinalium, directe sunt in Angliam pridie nonas Iulii, plurimum exortantes ut de consilio Cantuariensis ecclesie communiter ageretur. Suffraganeis igitur super hoc conferentibus, Odo prior sancte Trinitatis et sanior pars conventus inauditum quiddam de novo ceperunt constanter asserere, quod et de suo collegio subrogandus esset antistes, et quod esset ab ipsis in publico nominandus. Et quia regis patris intererat plurimum diebus illis electionem concorditer celebrari, semotis duobus a multitudine [Da, fo. 83^{v}] monachorum, Odone scilicet priore Cantuariensi, Ricardo priore Dovorensi, cum eos monachi presentassent episcopis, ad sui prioris electionem unanimiter aspirantes, Gilebertus Lundoniensis episcopus consurgens in medium, cum prius ad laudem Odonis prioris plurima congesisset, de communi consilio coepiscoporum aliam declinavit in partem, dicens 'Nos Ricardum	II° nonas Iunii littere regis patris, littere cardinalium, directe sunt in Angliam plurimum exhortantes ut de consilio Cantuariensis ecclesie communiter ageretur. Suffraganeis igitur super hoc conferentibus, monachi Cantuarienses commune bonum sicut dicebatur impedire volentes, inauditum quiddam et intolerabile de novo ceperunt constanter asserere, quod et de suo collegio surrogandus esset antistes, licet hoc in ea sede nullis contigisset temporibus, et quod esset ab ipsis in publico nominandus. Semotis itaque duobus a multitudine monachorum, Odone scilicet priore Cant(uarie) et Ricardo priore Dourensis cenobii, cum eos monachi suffraganeis presentassent, ad sui prioris electionem obrepere molientes, Gilebertus Lund(oniensis) episcopus, consurgens in medium, de communi consilio fratrum ait, 'Nos Ricardum priorem eligimus', quem manibus comprehendens incepit alta voce 'Te Deum laudamus' multitudinem clericorum undique confluentium

priorem eligimus'; quem manibus comprehendens incepit alta
voce 'Te Deum laudamus'; multitudinem clericorum undique
confluentium eandem animavit
in vocem.

eandem animavit in vocem.
Monachi videntes suam inten-
tionem elusam accurrerunt
confusi.

Expletis ergo sollennibus que in applausu fiunt huiusmodi, Can-
tuar(iensis) electus, sicut omnes prius electi fidelitatem
regis iuraverant, sic et ipse iuravit salvo ordine suo; nulla
prorsus de regni consuetudinibus observandis habita mentione.
Hec acta sunt apud Westmonasterium, in capella sancte Katerine,
presente iusticiario regis et assensum prebente.

168

MAY 1175. COUNCIL OF WESTMINSTER

See especially C.R. Cheney in *EHR* l (1935), 385-8; M.G.
Cheney in *Studies in Church History*, xi (1975), 61-8;
C.N.L. Brooke in *Traditio*, xiii (1957), 471-80.

It is certain that this council took place in May 1175 (see
no. IV below), and possible that its formal sessions extended
from 11 May, the date of its opening given in the surviving
summons (no. I), to 18 May, the date given for the council in
no. IV; but 18 May may have been the only day of formal session,
in the presence of the two kings.[1]

The narrative of Roger of Hoveden's *Gesta Henrici II*, i.83-
91 (no. IV), seems to make it clear that it was a provincial
council of the province of Canterbury, held in the presence of
the two kings Henry.[2] It should not, however, be overlooked

---

[1]No. I invites the bishop of Salisbury to a council in London on the
Sunday 'Cantate Domino', i.e. the Fourth Sunday after Easter; in 1175 this
was 11 May and the coincidence of date makes it almost certain that the
letter refers to the present council. Diceto (no. III) gives 15 kal. *Iulii*,
evidently in error for *Iunii*. The third and fourth weeks after Easter were
one of the periods for provincial synods prescribed in *Decretum*, D. 18 c. 4.

[2]Cf. C.R. Cheney in *EHR* l (1935), 385-8; the absence of York and his
suffragans seems to make the point clear, even though York arranged for a

that the archbishop enjoyed the extra dignity of the legateship
over his province. The *Gesta* (no. IV) describes it as a council
of the archbishop of Canterbury and his suffragans - 'concilium
regionale' is Diceto's phrase (no. III) - and names all the
English bishops of the southern province save Geoffrey of Lincoln, elect but not consecrated;[1] the bishopric of Norwich was
vacant. Of the Welsh bishops, only St. Davids was present; St.
Asaph was an absentee, and the subject of a protest by his
clergy;[2] Bangor was vacant; Llandaff is not mentioned. The
Gesta also names three Benedictine and one Cistercian abbot;
this hardly seems likely to be a complete list. Gervase tells
us that the bishop of Worcester was absent through ill health,[3]
and that the bishops of London and Winchester sat on the
primate's right and left, as dean and precentor of the province,
with the rest of the bishops and abbots in order of consecration;[4] this is not, however, the order in which either the
bishops after Winchester or the abbots appear in the *Gesta*. The
Gesta makes the archbishop pronounce at least the prologue to
the canons; Gervase attributes the reading of the canons to his
chancellor Benedict,[5] who, he says, was made to utter the canons
after the archbishop's sermon. Since the sermon would normally
have opened the council, it may be that Gervase has confused

---

protest to be made on his behalf (see below), and was apparently in London
at the time (*York Minster Fasti*, ed. C.T. Clay, ii (1959), note to no. 105,
p. 145). Newburgh, i.203, specifically calls it 'provinciale concilium';
and the word 'provincialibus' or 'comprovincialibus' occurs on p.983.
Gervase, however, says 'convocato clero Anglie' as if it were a council of
both provinces (i.251).

[1] Geoffrey Plantagenet was bishop-elect of Lincoln 1173-82, later archbishop of York (el. 1189, consec. 1191; died 1212).

[2] See p. 992; Conway Davies, ii.437-43; *Heads*, p. 25. Godfrey was made to
resign both the bishopric and the abbacy of Abingdon in which he had enjoyed
a comfortable exile.

[3] Gervase, i.251; he adds nothing of substance except the points mentioned
here, and for the rest summarizes the *Gesta*. Roger of Worcester lived until
1179, and it seems likely that there is some confusion here, since his name
is among the bishops listed in the *Gesta*.

[4] See C. of London, 1075, c. 1.

[5] Giraldus supports Gervase in making Benedict read the canons: he tells
us that Benedict was discomposed by corrections suggested while he was reading by Bartholomew, bishop of Exeter. Giraldus refers to sermons by Bartholomew and Gilbert Foliot, immediately followed by Benedict's reading of the
canons (Giraldus, *Opera*, vii.58-60).

the events of the first and last day, and that it was the heads
for discussion, not the final canons, which Benedict announced.[1]
But it is also possible that 18 May was the only day of formal
session.

This is the one council of the period for which we possess,
as well as the published canons, a list of propositions for
consideration by the council. It was printed by Wilkins with
the date 1173; but it has been generally, though not univer-
sally, assigned to this council, since its rubric attributes it
to a council of Archbishop Richard, and twenty-two of its
thirty-seven items appear in the canons of 1175; the matter was
settled by Mrs. Cheney in her paper on the council.[2]

The letter of summons, no. I, instructed the bishop to whom
it was addressed to enquire into the abuses obtaining in his
diocese; no. II lists proposals for reforming the abuses
reported. Twenty-two of these are taken up in eighteen of the
nineteen canons of the council (no. IV: c. 11 is the one not
covered). The canons dealt with a number of important and not
so important matters of church discipline, especially clerical
incontinence and the problem of hereditary benefices (c. 1),
with the involvement of the clergy in secular life (cc. 2-4, 6,
10, 11), and with tithes (c. 13); listed approved Prefaces in
the mass (c. 15); made an important pronouncement on the public
nature of marriage (c. 18) and the place of consent in it
(c. 19);[3] and handled other topics. For all save three they
could provide a rubric which cited an accepted source in canon
law, a canon or group of canons, or a recent decretal; of the
three, one is given a biblical foundation (c. 6), one in Roman
Law (c. 14), and the third, which adds a prohibition of the
transfer of advowsons as part of dower to a well-worn denuncia-

---

[1]Cf. M.G. Cheney, art. cit. (above and following note), p. 62.

[2]*Studies in Church History*, xi (1975), 61-8, on which much of what follows is based.

[3]After a stern reiteration of the law that marriages of children must be
validated after they both reached the age of consent, exception is allowed
in urgent necessity, 'pro bono pacis' - doubtless a necessary concession
in the presence of Henry II, who habitually made marriage plans for his
children when they were very young (Brooke in *Proceedings of the Fifth
International Congress of Medieval Canon Law, Salamanca, 1976* (Vatican
City, 1980), p. 337 and n. 9).

tion of simoniac practices in the presentation to benefices,
slips in a unique reference to royal authority: 'tam regia quam
nostra freti auctoritate' (c. 9). The fathers of the council
accepted that their canons must be based on known canonical
authorities, and for the most part repeated securely accepted
principles; but they also took the first steps towards the more
elaborate legislation of the thirteenth century provincial
councils by adding an occasional provision to cover local circumstances.[1]

Of the fifteen propositions in no. II which were later
dropped, 'some may have been thought superfluous; was there
anything to be achieved by more local legislation against
usury? Some were, perhaps, thought impossible to enforce; could
legislation at Westminster stop the Welsh exchanging wives?
One proposition ran counter to Cistercian privileges about
tithe-paying; nothing could be done at the local level on such
a matter. A proposal that benefices should not be conferred on
persons without a tonsure was perhaps dropped because the council declared that archdeacons should tonsure clerks with too
much hair, with or without their consent.'[2]

But for seven or eight of the propositions which did not
become the basis for canons, evidence has been gathered to show
that the archbishop consulted the pope and in most cases received papal directives.[3] These cases are as follows:

---

[1]As is already true in the main with the canons of 1195 and 1200, below.
Cf. C.R. Cheney in *EHR* l (1935), 202-3. An elaborate study of the sources
of the canons was published by E. Seckel in the *Deutsche Zeitschrift für
Kirchenrecht*, 3. Folge, ix (1899-1900), 159-89, esp. 186-9. Seckel indicated
that the free treatment of the authorities cited amounted to falsification,
but this view has not commanded assent: the fathers of the council were
solely concerned to show on what authorities they had mainly relied. Seckel
also argued (esp. p. 176) that Gratian was the probable source (or the main
source) for all the early authorities. It would be surprising if it were not
so, and this has been confirmed by our investigations. In particular the
heading of c. 5 seems to presuppose a grouping of authorities as in Gratian,
not known in any other available source. (Cf. also W. Holtzmann in *Studia
Gratiana*, i (1953), 348-9.)

[2]M.G. Cheney, art. cit., pp. 62-3, citing II, cc. 11b, 21, 2, 7 (for
numeration see p. 979 n.); also IV, c. 4. On Cistercians, see below; and on
Cistercians and tithe, G. Constable, *Monastic Tithes* (Cambridge, 1964), esp.
pp. 190 ff. On usury see the qualification below, referring to II, c. 27.

[3]This is based on M.G. Cheney, art. cit., pp. 63-8, an important discussion greatly advancing our knowledge of this council and its relation to
papal decretals.

II, c. 1. For the enforcement of the need of episcopal institutions and against hereditary benefices. The archbishop excommunicated any who obtained churches without episcopal permission,[1] and wrote to the pope, who sent in answer JL 13817, addressed to archbishop and suffragans, confirming the excommunication and the need for episcopal approval of presentations, and also JL 13814,[2] giving the bishops authority to remove notorious offenders from their churches.

II, c. 2, part 2. That the Cistercians should not hold churches. Again, a papal letter was sent to the archbishop and his suffragans forbidding the Cistercians to hold churches and advowsons, and a general letter (JL 12412), issued certainly before October 1175, went to the Order in England.[3]

II, cc. 11a, 17 (formerly 12, 19). On the Jews, forbidding them to occupy church lands or take revenues from churches, and prohibiting fealty by Christians to Jews. On these two points the pope issued JL 13976, evidently to the archbishop and suffragans.[4]

II, c. 20 (22). To prevent appeals by men who had deserted their wives to live with other women. On this the pope issued JL 13823, addressed to the archbishop and suffragans.[5]

II, c. 26 (28). Prohibiting clerks from paying pensions from their churches to secure the succession. On this the pope issued JL 13816 dealing both with clerks who offered higher pensions in order to succeed, and with those who made similar arrangements with religious.[6]

II, c. 27 (29). When land was held in pledge, the profit

---

[1]Cf. M.G. Cheney, p. 64, and n. 7, citing *Collectio Wigorniensis*, ed. H.E. Lohmann, *Zeitschr. der Savigny-Stiftung für Rechtsgesch., Kan. Abt.* xxii (1933), 119, no. 4.50, and JL 13817.

[2]All the papal letters here cited are listed, with fuller references, in M.G. Cheney, p. 64, n. 8. For JL 13814 and 13817 see *Appendix Conc. Lateran.* (= Mansi, xxii.248-454), 28.14, 11.

[3]Ibid., 15.10.

[4]Ibid., 20.3. For the address see W. Holtzmann in *Festschrift Guido Kisch: Rechtshistorische Forschungen* (Stuttgart, 1955), p. 222 n. 5.

[5]*Appendix Conc. Lateran.*, 10.20.

[6]Ibid., 28.8. This deals with arrangements made by would-be parsons, not sitting incumbents, but it is part of the same problem; and cf. no. 29 (31) forbidding all expectatives, and the commentary in Cheney, *BL*, pp. 76-80.

should go towards repaying the principal. On this the pope
issued JL 13819, addressed either to archbishop and suffragans
or to the bishop of Exeter.[1] This was in effect a prohibition
of usury and so comprehended a part of c. 11b, forbidding
Christians to engage in usury.

II, c. 34 (36). That lepers shall not live among the healthy.
On this there is a papal letter, JL 13794, addressed to the
archbishop alone, or to the archbishop and suffragans, which
treats it as a matter of general custom that lepers live apart,
but is mainly concerned with lepers' marriages. 'Here the link
between proposition and decretal is less certain.'[2]

The proceedings and canons of the council are known from
four types of source.

1. *The chroniclers.*

Roger of Hoveden,[3] in both versions of his chronicle, Gervase
of Canterbury, and 'Walter of Coventry'.

Gesta Henrici II (by Roger of Hoveden), ed. Stubbs, i.83-91.

Ha. BL ms. Cotton Julius A. xi, fos. 64-7, 12th-13th cent.
    from Peterborough.

Hb. BL ms. Cotton Vitell. E. xvii, fos. 68-70^V, early 13th
    cent.; damaged in the fire of 1731, so that a few words
    are lost. There is a transcript by Humphrey Wanley in
    BL ms. Harl. 3666, fos. 38-42, by which the missing words
    can be checked.

Hoveden (Roger of Hoveden's revised version), ed. Stubbs,
    ii.72-8.

Hr. BL ms. Royal 14. C. ii, fos. 149^V-52, late 12th cent.[4]

---

[1]*Appendix* 16.3; see M.G. Cheney, p. 67.

[2]M.G. Cheney, p. 67; but see ibid., p. 68 esp. on the address. The link
remains likely and it is clear that in several cases the archbishop had
modified the original question.

[3]We assume that the *Gesta Henrici II* and Hoveden were both the work of
the chronicler Roger of Howden (or Hoveden), following D.M. Stenton in *EHR*
lxviii (1953), 574-82. On the use of texts in these chronicles, which still
raises a number of problems, see A. Duggan (1971), pp. 313-34; J.C. Holt,
art. cit. (p. 922). On the mss. see Stubbs's introductions.

[4]The only ms. of authority for Hoveden's chronicle to 1180. There is also
an abbreviated version in the excerpts from Hoveden in BL ms. Cotton Vitell.
A. xx fos. 155^V-156^V (late 13th cent.).

London, Inner Temple ms. 511.2, fo. 130^V, early 13th cent.[1]

Gervase (see pp. 771, 973 n. 3), ed. Stubbs, i.251-5 (cf.
    ii.398).

Ga (BL ms. Cotton Vesp. B. xix, 13th cent. from Canterbury),
    fos. 98-100^V.

Gc (Cambridge UL Ff. 1.29, 14th cent.), fos. 75^V-77^V.

'Walter of Coventry', ed. Stubbs, i.238-44.

Oxford, Magdalen Coll. ms. Lat. 36, fos. 54-6.

BL ms. Cotton Vitell. E. xiii, fos. 53-54^V.

Cambridge, Corpus Christi Coll. ms. 175, fos. 56^V-57^V (with
    the canons abbreviated).[2]

The original draft of the *Gesta* formed the source for all
these versions, and of this Ha is a faithful representative,
and Hb a useful check. We have noted Hb's variants where these
are of any significance (omitting minor errors), and we have
checked so far as possible in Wanley's transcript for words
missing in Hb (which are not very numerous) to see that nothing
significant is likely to have escaped us. Hr is an authoritative
ms. of the revision, but Hoveden or his scribes were not so
careful in copying the document in the revision, and its readings tell us almost nothing worth recording; the narrative is
simply an abbreviation of the *Gesta*.

To assess the value of Gervase's text is not so easy. It is
certain that he knew the *Gesta* and used it for his narrative
of the council; also that he had access to other information.[3]
His text is careless, and he omits c. 8;[4] most of his variants
are plainly errors, and none of his readings has any authority.
But his version of the liturgical c. 15 is so different that
one must suspect an alternative source here if nowhere else,

---

[1]An early 13th-cent. ms. from Rievaulx, not known to Stubbs. In physical
character it resembles Hr, and like Hr ends with an odd leaf of the annal
for 1181. But it shows many differences, some of which might repay study.
Its author has freely rewritten Hoveden's account of this council, and
removed the canons to the end of the book (fo. 130^V) where they follow
those of the Lateran Council of 1179; there they carry a rubric attributing
the council to 1179 or later. The text is derived from Hr or a twin and its
readings are of no value.

[2]The first two mss. represent the 'Intermediate Compilation', the third
Walter of Coventry. See Stubbs' edn., i, pp. x-xii, xxxix-xli.

[3]See above, p. 966; also Stubbs' marginal notes and use of small type to
indicate employment of the *Gesta* in this area of Gervase.

[4]Presumably by homoeoteleuton, since c. 8 begins 'Nullus' and c. 9 'Nulli'.

even allowing that a recital of familiar prefaces invited any
author or scribe, especially in a monastic *scriptorium*, to use
his memory. Furthermore, there are a small number of agreements
with independent texts, mostly in c. 15, and in two cases in
which Fb agrees with Ga against Ha, Ha and Gc are at one.[1]
Gervase is useless as an independent authority for the text,
but the version in Ga is of great interest, since it seems to
have provided the source of the texts in 3 below.

> 2. *Independent mss. of the preamble and canons.*

> Fb. Oxford, Bodl. e Mus. 249 (27835), fos. 132-133^V, in the
> decretal collection *Belverensis*, in a ms. of *c.*1180 mostly
> consisting of the letters and charters of Gilbert Foliot
> (bishop of London, 1163-87), probably written in his
> *scriptorium*, though later at Westminster abbey and Bel-
> voir priory.[2]

> L. Oxford, Bodl. ms. lat. th. d. 29, fos. 76-78, a late 12th-
> cent. copy of Lanfranc's Monastic Constitutions and theo-
> logical *sententiae* and extracts, once Dugdale's.[3]

> S. Oxford, St. John's Coll. ms. 115, fos. 148^V-149, *c.*1200,
> added at the end of a 12th-cent. patristic miscellany,
> after a small group of three crusading letters of the
> late 1180s, and John of Salisbury's Life of Becket.[4]

These three texts all start 'Ideo in ecclesia Dei ...'
(p. 983) and are without title. They have certain resemblances
among themselves, but e.g. L sometimes agrees with Ha against
Fb and S. L and S are relatively careless copies with a number
of variants which are evidently errors of their scribe or immediate exemplar.[5]

---

[1] None of these variants is of substance. Thus, in c. 6 (last sentence) Ga
and Fb read 'iudicium sanguinis' for 'sanguinis iudicium' (so Gc and Ha); and
in c. 9 'convictus vel confessus' for 'confessus vel convictus', on which Gc
and Ha agree (see n. ad loc.); but such minor points of word order may be of no
significance.
[2] See *GFL*, pp. xlii, 1, 2-11, esp. 8; but a slightly later date has been
suggested by R.W. Southern in *EHR* lxxxiii (1968), 785-7. The ms. is on any
showing late 12th-cent.   [3] See *Bodleian Lib. Record*, vi (1957-61) , 443.
[4] The letters are in the *Gesta,* ii.10-14, 62-3.
[5] There is a possible reference to a lost ms. in the late 14th-cent. catalogue of Dover priory, no. 211, ed. M.R. James, *Ancient Libraries of Canterbury and Dover* (Cambridge, 1903), p. 466: 'Statuta Ricardi archiepiscopi',
inc. 'Anno ab incarnacione'. No surviving copy opens like this, but it is possible that this is a garbled account of a ms. of the abbreviated version.

3. *Abbreviated texts.*[1]

14th century: London, Lambeth Palace ms. 171, fos. 9-10; Oxford, Bodl. ms. Rawlinson C. 428, fos. 111^V-113; both from Worcester Cathedral.

15th century: Antwerp, Museum Plantin-Moretus ms. 104, fos. 193^V-194^V; Cambridge, Corpus Christi Coll. ms. 84, fos. 192^V, 25^{r-v}, Peterhouse ms. 51, pt. ii, fos. 36^V-37; and 84, fos. 159^V-60; Trinity Coll. ms. O. 4. 14, fos. 118^V-119; Cambridge, UL ms. Gg. 6. 21, fos. 52-53, Addit. ms. 3575, fos. 314^V-316; Dublin, Trinity Coll. E. 2. 22 (526), pp. 155-6; Hereford Cathedral Lib. ms. P. vii. 7, fos. 122^V, 122*; Holkham Hall ms. 226, pp. 60-2; London, BL ms. Harl. 335, fo. 66^{r-v}; Lambeth Palace Lib. 538, fos. 147^V-149; Oxford, All Souls Coll. ms. 42, fos. 221^V-222^V, Balliol Coll. ms. 158, fos. 179^V-80, Exeter Coll. ms. 41, fos. 198^V-199.

In these texts the canons of 1175 are attached to a collection of councils: the 14th-cent. mss. contain earlier canons (see Index of mss.), followed by 1175 and later councils; the 15th-cent. mss. start with 1175; usually dated '1065'.[2] The 14th-cent. mss. omit cc. 8, 15, 16, 18; the 15th-cent. mss. omit these four and also cc. 10-11, 14. These texts have copious strange errors and misreadings of their own, and many minor variations, but taken as a group they agree in all essentials with Gervase, and in a number of minor variants with Ga against Gc.[3] By a slip the scribe of Ga dated the annal for 1175 to 1165, and the error was taken up by a scribe of the late 13th or early 14th cent., who has written at the foot of fo. 98^V,

---

[1] On these mss. see C.R. Cheney, *Medieval Texts and Studies,* pp. 166-7, with lists on pp. 166 n. 2, 167 n. 2; see also ibid. for one lost ms. (Cotton Otho A. xvi) and two mss. which may once have contained these canons (Bodl. Rawlinson C. 100 and Philadelphia Free Lib. Carson 4).

[2] All are dated 1065 except: Cambridge UL Add. 3575, undated (a contemporary hand has added the date 1165); Peterhouse 84, date lost; Dublin Trinity Coll. E. 2. 22 (526), 1365; Lambeth 538, 1066; Harl. 335, 1365. Wilkins cited Lambeth '17' (= Lambeth 171) and 'Eliensis' no. 235 (i.e. Bishop Moore's, now Cambridge UL Gg. 6. 21) in his apparatus.

[3] We have noted a few cases in which Ga and Gc have different readings and in which the consensus of the late mss. follows Ga, none in which the consensus agrees with Gc against Ga. Stubbs's ms. B of Gervase, Cambridge, Trinity Coll. ms. R. 4. 11 is ignored here, since it is an exact copy of Ga, possibly also from Canterbury; it is conceivably the source of the later texts, but lacks the note.

where the canons begin, 'Concilium apud Westm' tempore Ricardi archiepiscopi anno Domini $m^oc^olx \, v^o$'. This date is half way to 1065, and the note as a whole more than half way to what seems to have been the original title to the abbreviated versions: 'Concilium celebratum apud Westm' tempore Ricardi archiepiscopi anno Domini $m^olx \, v^o$'.[1] It seems probable that Ga is the source of all the later, abbreviated texts, and it comes from Canterbury, a not unlikely place for such collections to have been made. The readings of these late mss. have no original value; but the mss. are of interest since they show the value later put on the canons. Lyndwood made the canons respectable by attributing them to the thirteenth-century Archbishop Richard.[2] They were printed in at least one edition of the constitutions, that of Paris, 1504 (fo. 142^V).

4.*Individual canons in decretal collections*. We have seen that the earliest surviving text, in Fb, is in *Belverensis;* and it may well be that it was because it was copied without title in this and perhaps other, lost collections, that its canons were presently treated as canonical authorities in their own right. The canons carried about with them their individual rubrics, as in Fb, and so appeared to be independent canonical authorities. But in Fb they also followed the canons of the Council of Tours (see p. 847 n. 6) and canons of 1175 were sometimes regarded as additional canons of Tours. A full analysis has been given elsewhere.[3] This represented the state of knowledge in 1957; since new analyses and a full study of the decretal collections are in progress under the auspices of the Institute of Medieval Canon Law, it would be premature to provide revised lists now. We describe only the decretal which was used as a source in devising the canons, and a brief list of the collec-

---

[1] So the 14th-cent. mss.; the 15th commonly have 'incipit celebratum concilium ...' or 'Inc. conc. celeb. ...'; a few have 'Constitutiones celebrate ...' and Hereford P. vii.7 has only an explicit.

[2] Cheney, *Medieval Texts and Studies,* pp. 113, 166-7.

[3] See C.N.L. Brooke in *Traditio,* xiii (1957), 471-80, esp. 476-9; corrections by S. Kuttner in *Traditio,* xvii (1961), 536-7. For English decretal collections, C. Duggan, *Twelfth-Century Decretal Collections* (London, 1963). On the decretal-making process among those concerned in this council, see H. Mayr-Harting, in *Studies in Church History,* ii (1965), 186-96.

tions cited in the apparatus.[1]

C. 1 was based on a decretal, JL 12254, Alexander III to Roger bishop of Worcester, which occurs in *Belverensis* (Fb, fos. 122^V-123) and at least seventeen other collections, including *Extra* 1. 17. 3 (partially). The version in the council is entirely different, and readily distinguished; and we have noted it in seven collections. C. 12 purports to be based on a decretal, but all the known versions in the collections seem to derive from the council. The following collections are cited in the apparatus: *Abrincensis I* (c. 15: ed. Singer (above p. 798), p. 386); *Cheltenhamensis* (cc. 1 (2 versions), 6, 9, 10, 14: BL ms. Egerton 2819, fos. 92 (and 58), 42^V, 58^V, 92^V, 92^V); *Claudiana* (cc. 3, 4, 10: BL ms. Cotton Claud. A. iv, fos. 214, 214^{r-v}, 214); *Cottoniana* (cc. 10, 12: BL ms. Cotton Vitell. E. xiii, fo. 205 (both) - the ms. was severely damaged in the Cotton fire of 1731); *Fontanensis* (cc. 3, 6 (2 versions), 9, 10: Bodl. ms. Laud. Misc. 527, fos. 39, 39 (and 45^V), 44^V, 44^V); *Parisiensis I* (Prologue and cc. 1, 5: E. Friedberg, *Die Canonessammlungen zwischen Gratian und Bernhard von Pavia*, Leipzig, 1897, cc. 38b, 113-14, 7c; *Peterhusensis* (cc. 1, 12, 14: Cambridge, Peterhouse ms. 193, fos. 223^V, 223^V-224, 224); *Regalis* (cc. 10, 12, 14: BL Royal 15. B. iv, fo. 112 (all)); *Sangermanensis* (c. 15, ed. Singer (p. 798), pp. 311-12); *Tanner* (cc. 1, 9, 16: Bodl. ms. Tanner 8, pp. 594, 594, 641 - cf. W. Holtzmann in *Festschrift der Akad. Göttingen* (1951), pp. 83-145); *Wigorniensis* (c. 12: cf. H.E. Lohmann in *Zeitschrift der Savigny-Stift. für Rechtsgesch., Kan. Abt.* xxii (1933), 133, no. 7. 34).

This edition. We have printed IV from Ha, occasionally corrected by the consensus of Fb, S and L where it seems likely that Ha's reading is accidental or a slip; we have noted variants of Hb, but only occasionally of any of the *Gesta*'s derivatives; we have also noted variants of Fb, and of S and L where they could be significant, but rarely S's or L's private readings, which are numerous. We have included a few variants

---

[1]They represent only a preliminary selection, intended to illustrate the readings which may be found in texts of little authority, which are, however, independent of our chief sources.

from the decretal collections: as texts they are of little
authority, but they have some independent witness as they
derive from sister texts of Fb, not Fb itself.

Other mentions. Apart from the chronicles listed above, and
Diceto, whose account we print as no. III, there are brief
accounts or references in William of Newburgh, Gerald of Wales
(in the lives of the bishops of Lincoln), Robert of Torigny,
and the annals of Tewkesbury.[1] As no. V we print a letter from
the bishop of Salisbury ordering the monks of Reading to pay
tithes in accordance with the council 'recently celebrated at
Westminster' (see c. 13). It seems that the bishop of London
used the council as an occasion to ask for assistance for the
building fund of St. Paul's. A letter on behalf of the cathedral was issued by the bishop of Winchester about Ascension
Day in the year of Archbishop Richard's first Council at Westminster, i.e. *c.*22 May 1175; it refers to the interest in the
matter of the pope, the archbishop and the bishop of London;
and the bishop of London's letter on the same theme may also
have been issued on this occasion.[2] A letter of John of Salisbury refers to the discussion of the right of Herbert, archdeacon of Northampton, to his archdeaconry, first before the
bishop of Worcester, then in solemn council before the archbishop of Canterbury; and this seems likely to refer to the
present council. Soon after, Herbert was removed from Northampton, to be rewarded, it seems, with the archdeaconry of
Canterbury.[3] In the same year Gerald of Wales, acting on the
archbishop's behalf, deposed the archdeacon of Brecon, and on
his return to England was granted the archdeaconry himself,
and the deposition of his predecessor was confirmed; it is possible that this too took place at the council.[4] Finally, there

---

[1]See above, p. 966 nn.; Newburgh, i.203; Giraldus, *Opera*, vii.58-9; Torigny,
p. 269 (with a reference to the dispute between Canterbury and York); Ann.
Tewkesbury in *Ann. Mon.* i.51 (with specific mention of c. 15).
[2]W. Dugdale, *Hist. of St. Paul's Cathedral*, ed. H.E. Ellis (London, 1818),
p. 63; cf. R. Graham in *Journ. of the British Arch. Assoc.* 3rd ser., x
(1945-7), 73-6; *GFL*, no. 235.
[3]JS, *Letters*, ii, no. 324, and notes to the letter; cf. Le Neve, iii.30-1.
[4]Giraldus, *Opera*, i.27 (on Jordan, his predecessor, cf. JS, *Letters*,
i.134 n.), who refers to the involvement of the bishop of St. Davids; and
the bishop was at the council.

is what appears to be another reference to the council in a letter on a dispute about a church in the 'Register of Master David of London': David suggests to a clerical friend that they defer the matter until he comes to London at the archbishop of Canterbury's general summons.[1] But this may refer to some other occasion, and we cannot tell if business resulted.

We have seen that the canons of the council, owing to a misunderstanding, found a place in collections of papal decretals. Some of them were also repeated, no doubt more deliberately, in the Norman council of Rouen of 1190.[2]

I. *Summons to the council, early 1175*

Gilbert Foliot, bishop of London, evidently sends the summons as dean of the province of Canterbury: for the early history of the office see I.J. Churchill, *Canterbury Administration* (London, 1933), i.355 ff.; *GF*, pp. 227-9.

GFL, no. 234, from Bodl. ms. e Mus. 249 (27835), fos. 109^V-110 (Fb).

(Gilebertus) Dei gratia Lundoniensis episcopus venerabili fratri I(ocelino) Sar(esberiensi) eadem gratia episcopo, salutem que nunc est et quam speramus a Domino.

---

[1]Cf. Z.N. Brooke in *Essays in History pres. to R.L. Poole* (Oxford, 1927), pp. 227-45, esp. 230; it is letter 15, ms. Vatican Lat. 6024, fo. 142, ed. F. Liverani, *Spicilegium Liberianum*, i (Florence, 1863), p. 619. The letter concludes (ms. loc. cit.) 'Verbum illud de ecclesia vel capella de Dudinton', super quo iam eum [*sc.* latorem presentium] convenistis, in adventum vestrum Londonias ad generalem illam quam iam fecit dominus Cantuariensis vocationem differatis. Tunc enim, annuente domino Londoniensi, vobis occurram, et ad vestrum consilium et voluntatem exinde in verbo illo cedam vel contendam. Scitis enim et longe me melius quod sicut periculosum sua negligentia suo iuri cedere, sic et temerarium in alieni iuris invidiam litem improbam instituere.' The place-name Doddington or Dodington is common, and the chapel or church cannot be identified (no. 16 suggests the issue related to a pension from the church). Most of David's datable letters belong to the period *c.*1169-73, and none is later than 1179; the archbishop must be Richard and this is the only known council which fits the circumstances.
[2]Mansi, xxii.581-6: for Westminster c. 1, cf. Rouen, cc. 4, 6; for c. 3 (*ad fin.*), cf. c. 10; for c. 4, cf. c. 5; for c. 5, cf. c. 7; for c. 6, cf. c. 18; for c. 10, cf. cc. 9, 19; for c. 13, cf. c. 23; for c. 17, cf. c. 2. On this council see R. Foreville in *Church and Government in the Middle Ages* (ed. C.N.L. Brooke *et al.*, Cambridge, 1976), pp. 22-3, 38.

Quoniam in ecclesia regni huius vitia pullulant, et in vinea
Domini sarmenta succrescunt, consultioris falce iudicii succi-
denda visum est patri nostro Ricardo Cant(uariensi) Dei gratia
archiepiscopo totius Anglie primati et sedis apostolice legato,
secundum antiquam patrum consuetudinem, fratres et coepiscopos
suos et alios ecclesiarum prelatos [Fb, fo. 110] ad concilium
convocare ut que corrigenda fuerint, communicati censura consilii, vel omnino damnentur vel in melius Domino gratiam mini-
strante reformentur. Quia vero ad sollicitudinem nostram
pertinere dinoscitur fratres et coepiscopos nostros ad concilium
convocare, ab ipso ut id faciamus in mandatis accepimus. Inde
est quod fraternitati vestre ipsius auctoritate mandamus et in
vi obedientie iniungimus ut dominica qua cantatur 'Cantate
Domino canticum novum',[1] ob causam memoratam assessuri sibi
Lundonie sitis, et medio tempore cum omni cautela et diligentia
excessus quibus diocesis vestra laborat inquiratis, ut in medium
deducti correctioni subiaceant et censure. Ipsius etiam vobis
auctoritate iniungimus ut diocesis vestre abbatibus, archidiaconis, prioribus, et decanis locorum conventualium verbum hoc
notificetis, et eos ut designato loco et tempore in concilio
domino legato presentiam exhibeant ipsius auctoritate citetis.
Valete.

II. *Propositions for consideration by the council*

> From BL ms. Cotton Claud. A. iv (decretal coll. Claudiana,
> late 12th cent.), fos. 195[V]-196; printed from this ms. in
> W. i.474-5.

Concilium Ricardi Cant(uariensis) archiepiscopi.
[i] (N)ullus presumat intrare ecclesiam absque presentatione
advocati ecclesie, et impersonatione diocesiani episcopi, vel
officialis eius per ipsum.

ii Monachi albi non presumant amodo detinere decimas, quas
colunt in parrochiis ecclesiarum quas eedem habere solebant.

---

[1] Introit for 4th Sunday after Easter (see p. 965 n. 1).

Idem non presumant habere ecclesias contra statuta ordinis sui.

iii Clerici focarias non habeant. [c. 1]

iv Coniugati ecclesias non habeant seu ecclesiastica beneficia.
[c. 1]

v Filii non succedant patribus in ecclesiis. [c. 1]

vi Nullus det ecclesiam in dotalicium. [c. 9]

vii Nulli detur ecclesia qui clericale signum non habeat.

viii Excommunicationi subiaceant qui detinuerint decimas de
lana, de lino[a] et similibus. [c. 13]

ix Non pro communione vel crismate vel baptismate vel extrema
unctione[b] vel sepultura denarius vel aliquod pretium exigatur.
[c. 7]

x Clerici non eant ad tabernas vel potationes publicas. [c. 2]

xi Laici ecclesias ad firmam non habeant.

[xia] (12)[1] Iudei non recipiant fidelitatem a Christianis nec
Christiani faciant.

[xib] (13) Christiani non fenerentur.

xii (14) Ecclesie exhibeantur honorifice in libris et ornamentis et utensilibus necessariis.

xiii (15) Clerici comam non nutriant nec habeant vestes inordi-
natas. [c. 4]

---

[a]de lana de lino de lino ms.   [b]inunctione ms.

---

[1]Numbers in round brackets are those in Wilkins (roman numbers in W.).

xiiii (16) Amodo officium suum non exerceant qui in alienis episcopatibus furtive ordines susceperunt. [c. 5]

xv (17) Clerici publicis muneribus non fungantur nec causas sanguinis agant. [c. 3]

xvi (18) Non in ecclesiis vel locis consecratis iudicia sanguinis vel mortis exerceantur. [c. 6]

xvii (19) Iudei non presumant amodo evacuare parrochias ecclesiarum per occupationes suarum domorum vel terrarum.

xviii (20) Non occulta fiant matrimonia sed palam in facie ecclesie. [c. 18]

xix (21) Monachi firmas non teneant vel canonici claustrales curam parrochiarum agant. [c. 10]

xx (22) Uxorati relictis uxoribus aliis adherentes cum corripiuntur non appellent.

xxi (23) Walenses non vendant ecclesias vel dent in dotem vel consanguineis adhereant vel commutent uxores.[1]

xxii (24) Pro monachis, canonicis, monialibus in monasterio recipiendis nichil exigatur. [c. 8]

xxiii (25) Non dicantur prefaciones preter decem que statute sunt. [c. 15]

xxiiii (26) Non fiat intinctio corporis in sanguine Christi. [c. 16]

xxv (27) Vicarii perpetui qui personis ecclesiarum fideli sacramento obligantur se contra personam non erigant. [c. 12]

---

[1] Cf. Conway Davies, ii.451.

xxvi (28) Pensiones aliis non faciant clerici in ecclesiis occulte et sine assensu episcopi ut alii eisdem succedant.

xxvii (29) Terre non accipiantur amodo in pignus, quin fructus terre [ms., fo. 196] medio tempore percepti in sortem computentur.

xxviii (30) Laici non recipiant premia pro presentatione persone, nec episcopi pro personatione nec officiales sui. [c. 9]

xxix (31) Donationes ecclesiarum et presentationes personarum facte viventibus[a][1] irrite sint.

xxx (32) Non in vasis stagneis officia divina celebrentur. [c. 17]

xxxi (33) Victus in causa ei qui vicit expensas solvat. [c. 14]

xxxii (34) Ecclesia vel ambitus ecclesie hominem non tueatur qui ibidem hominem occiderit.

xxxiii (35) Non contrahatur matrimonium inter aliquos infra annos, nisi ex dispensatione inter principes vel magnos viros reconciliationis vel pacis causa. [c. 19]

xxxiiii (36) Leprosi inter sanos amodo non conversentur.

xxxv (37) Clerici vel monachi vel ecclesiis dediti non negocientur. [c. 10]

---

[a]*Perhaps for* personis viventibus *or something of the kind: see n. 1.*

---

[1]This must be a reference to expectatives, though as it stands evidently corrupt (cf. n. a above). See above, p. 969 n. 6, and Cheney, *BL*, p. 77.

III. *Ralph de Diceto, Ymagines Historiarum, s.a. 1175*

From mss. Da (Lambeth Palace Lib. 8), fo. 90^v; Db (BL Cotton Claudius E. iii), fo. 96^v; printed Diceto, ed. Stubbs, i.399.[1]

Habitum est concilium regionale Lundoniis apud Westmuster quinto decimo kalendas Iulii [*sic*] presidente Ricardo Cantuariensi archiepiscopo et apostolice sedis legato. Rogerus Eboracensis archiepiscopus concilio non interfuit, nec qui eius absentiam allegarent transmisit, cum iuxta priscam consuetudinem ad voca-tionem Cantuariensis ecclesie vel interesse debuerit vel iustam absentie causam per nuntios et per epistolam probabiliter allegare. Statuta concilii si bene revolveris perpauca reperies que tibi corpus canonum incorporare non possit.

By the phrase 'concilium regionale' is the following gloss:

Solius pape est concilium generale; Romane ecclesie et Constan-tinopolitane est concilium universale.

IV. *The narrative in the Gesta Henrici II of Roger of Hoveden and the canons of the council*

[s.a. 1175]^a Et reges ipsi[2] venerunt usque Barbefluctum ut transfretarent^b in Angliam; et ascensis navibus suis apud Barbefluctum, aplicuerunt in Angliam apud Portesmutam, septimo idus Maii feria sexta. Et venientes Lundonias invenerunt ibi Ricardum Cant(uariensem) archiepiscopum et suffraganeos suos, volentes ibidem concilium celebrare. Celebravit itaque predictus Cant(uariensis) archiepiscopus concilium apud Lundonias in Westmonasterio coram predictis regibus et assensu et voluntate

---

^{a}*The first paragraph as here printed is in the Gesta only (see n. 2).*
$_b$usque ... transfretarent Ha; apud ... transfretassent Hb.

---

[1]Hence Paris, *Ch. Maj.* ii.296; *Hist. Angl.* i.392.
[2]Henry II and his son, the young king Henry. This paragraph is consider-ably abbreviated in Hoveden; and abbreviated and revised in Gervase (see p. 966). On the bishops and abbots attending, see also p. 966.

ipsorum[a] die dominica[b] ante Ascensionem Domini, scilicet xv
kalendas Iunii. Huic autem concilio interfuerunt [Ha, fo. 64^v]
suffraganei predicti archiepiscopi[c] scilicet Walterius Rofensis
episcopus, Gillebertus Lundon(iensis) episcopus, Ricardus
Winton(iensis) episcopus, Ioscelinus Saresberiensis episcopus,[d]
Gaufridus Eliensis episcopus, Rogerus Uigorn(ensis) episcopus,
Reginaldus Bathon(iensis) episcopus, Rodbertus Herford(ensis)
episcopus, Bar(tolomeus) Exoniensis episcopus, Ricardus[e]
Cestrensis episcopus, Iohannes[e] Cicestrensis episcopus, episcopus de sancto David de Wallia,[f] abbas sancti Albani, abbas
sancti Aedmundi, abbas Rameseie,[g] abbas de Boxeleia. Et coram
prenominatis episcopis et abbatibus, Ricardus Cantuariensis
archiepiscopus in eminentiori loco[h] sedens hec verba in medio
proferens ait:

Ideo[i] in ecclesia Dei, secundum antiquam patrum consuetudinem concilia congregantur,[1] ut hii qui constituti sunt in
eminentiori cura pastorali vitam subditorum[j] de communi consilio regularibus institutis informent et enormitates que
pullulant incessanter consultiore censura compescant. Nos
itaque potius inherentes orthodoxorum patrum regulis quam aliquid de novo statuentes, quedam certa capitula[k] duximus in
medium promulganda que universis comprovincialibus[l] nostris
firmiter et inviolabiliter observanda iniungimus. Omnes enim[m]
sacrorum censemus canonum[n] transgressores qui statutis huius[o]
sacrosancte synodi[p] presumpserint contrahire.

[1] Ex decretali epistola Alexandri pape III ad Rogerum

---

[a]eorum Hb.   [b]Hb *adds* proxima.   [c]archipresulis Hb (*so also* Hr).
[d]Hb *places Salisbury before Winchester.*   [e]Ha *om.* Ricardus *and* Iohannes.
[f]Hb *adds* et.   [g]Aemundi, abbas Rameseie Ha; Aedmundi Hb.   [h]*om.* Hb.
[i]FbSL *start here.*   [j]in eminentiori ... subditorum HaHb; in eminentia pastorali vitam subditorum L; in eminentia pastorali vitam subiectorum FbS
and Paris. I (for references to decretal collections see p. 975).
[k]capitula FbSL *and Paris. I*; capitula dignum HaHb.   [l]provincialibus HaHb.
[m]autem L.   [n]cens. can. HaHb; canonum censemus FbS; L *places* cens. *before*
sacrorum.   [o]FbS *om.*   [p]concilii L.

---

[1]See *Decretum,* D. 18, *passim.*

Wigorn(ensem) episcopum.[a1]

Si quis sacerdos vel clericus in sacris ordinibus constitutus ecclesiam vel ecclesiasticum beneficium habens publice fornicariam habeat,[b] et semel,[c] secundo et tertio[d] commonitus fornicariam suam[e] non dimiserit, et a se prorsus non expulerit, sed potius in immunditia sua duxerit persistendum, omni officio et beneficio ecclesiastico spolietur. Si qui vero infra subdiaconatum[f] constituti matrimonia contraxerint, ab uxoribus suis nisi de[g] communi consensu ad religionem transire voluerint[h] et ibi in Dei servicio iugiter[i] permanere, nullatenus separentur, sed cum uxoribus suis[j] viventes ecclesiastica beneficia nullo modo percipiant.[k] Qui autem in subdiaconatu vel supra ad matrimonia convolaverint mulieres etiam invitas et renitentes[l] relinquant. Decernimus[m] etiam eiusdem epistole auctoritate ne filii sacerdotum in paternis ecclesiis amodo persone instituantur; nec eas qualibet occasione media non intercedente persona optineant. [II, cc. iii-v]

[2] [Ha, fo. 65] Ex concilio Cartag(inensi) III[n2]
Clerici in sacris ordinibus constituti edendi vel bibendi causa tabernas non ingrediantur nec publicis potacionibus intersint,[o] nisi peregrinationis necessitate compulsi. Si quis vero tale quid fecerit aut cesset aut deponatur. [II, c. x]

---

[a]ad Rogerum Wigorn' episcopum HaHb; *om.* FbSL.   [b]*om.* Hb.   [c]HbL *add* et.   [d]et tertio HaHb *and Regalis, Cheltenh., Peterhus., Tanner;* ac tercio L; tertioque FbS *and Paris. I.*   [e]*om.* Hb.   [f]subdiaconum HbS (*corr. to* subdiaconatum S[1]).   [g]*om.* L.   [h]velint Fb.   [i]vigilanter Ha.   [j]suis FbSL; *om.* HaHb.   [k]eccles. benefic. nullo modo percip. HaHb; eccles. benefic. nullatenus optineant *Tanner;* ecclesias vel (aut Fb) prebendas non habeant FbSL *Paris. I.*   [l]Fb *om.* et renitentes.   [m]Decernimus FbS *Paris. I;* L *places* Decernimus *after* auctoritate; Decrevimus HaHb.   [n]III HaHb; tercio FbS; *om.* L.   [o]intersint potationibus FbL.

---

[1]See p. 975 (and cf. C. of London, 1108; C. of Westminster, 1138, c. 8; for final paragraph, C. of Westminster, 1102, c. 8; C. of Westminster, 1125, c. 5; C. of Westminster, 1138, c. 6). For the topic, cf. J. Gaudemet in *Studia Gratiana,* xiii (1967), 339-69.
[2]Cf. *Decretum* D. 44 c. 4 (cf. C. of Westminster, 1102, c. 10).

[3] Ex concilio Toletano III[1]

Hiis qui in sacris ordinibus constituti sunt iudicium sanguinis agitare non licet. Unde prohibemus ne aut per se membrorum truncationes faciant aut inferendas iudicent. Quod si quis tale[a] fecerit concessi ordinis privetur officio[b] et loco. Inhibemus etiam[c] sub interminatione anathematis ne quis sacerdos officium habeat vicecomitis[d] aut prepositi secularis.[e] [II, c. xv]

[4] Ex concilio Agatensi[2]

Clerici qui comam nutriunt ab archidiacono etiam inviti tondeantur. Vestimentis etiam vel[f] calciamentis nisi que[g] honestatem et religionem deceant eis uti non liceat. Si quis autem contra hoc facere[h] presumpserit et commonitus[i] emendare noluerit excommunicationi subiaceat. [II, c. xiii]

[5] Ex diversis decretis Urbani, Innocentii et concilii Calcedon(ensis) et Cartag(inensis)[j][3]

Quia quidam clerici desperantes ab episcopis suis ordinari vel propter imperitiam vel vite incontinentiam vel nativitatis condicionem aut tituli defectum aut etatem minorem, extra provinciam suam[k] interdum etiam a transmarinis episcopis ordinantur

---

[a]si quis tale HaHb *Claudiana;* si quisquam (quis *Fontanensis*) tale quid FbS *Fontanensis;* si quid tale aliquid L.   [b]privetur officio HaHb; honore privetur FbSL *Fontanensis, Claudiana.*   [c]quoque FbS.   [d]officium habeat vicecomitis FbS *Claudiana Fontanensis* (vicecom'); habeat officium vicecomitis L; habeat vicecomitum Ha; habeat vicecomitatum Hb.   [e]HaHb *add* officium.   [f]etiam vel HaHb; vel L; etiam et FbS *Claudiana.*   [g]qui Ha. [h]facere HaHb L; agere FbS; venire *Claudiana.*   [i]communicatus S; commonitionibus L.   [j]Urbani ... Cartag' HaHb (Cartaginis Hb; Ha *reads* Innocentis); U. I. Calced' et Cartag' conciliorum S; Urbani, Innocentii, Cartaginensi (*sic*) et Calcedon' concilio L; *om.* Fb.   [k]vel vite incont. ... suam *om.* L.

---

[1]Cf. *Decretum,* C. 23 q. 8 c. 30, ex conc. Toletano *XI:* this does not include the final sentence below. Cf. also C. of London, 1075, c. 9.

[2]Cf. *Decretum,* D. 23 c. 22 (and cf. C. of Westminster, 1102, c. 24 and n.).

[3]Cf. *Decretum,* D. 70-2 *passim,* with specific reference to D. 70 c. 2 (Urban), D. 71 c. 2 (Innocent), D. 71 c. 4 (Chalcedon; cf. D. 70 c. 1; D. 71 c. 7), and D. 71 c. 6 (Carthage; cf. D. 72 c. 2). The order of the authorities seems to confirm that Gratian was the source used: see p. 968 n. 1. Cf. also C. of Winchester, 1070, c. 3; C. of London, 1075, c. 4; C. of Winchester, 1076, c. 2; C. of Westminster, 1125, c. 10; C. of Westminster, 1138, c. 7.

vel ordinatos se mentiuntur,[a] ignota sigilla episcopis suis
deferentes: statuimus talium[b] ordinationem irritam esse haben-
dam, sub interminatione anathematis inhibentes ne a quoquam ad
officii sui executionem suscipiantur. Episcopum quoque nostre
iurisdictionis qui talem sciens et prudens ordinaverit vel
susceperit, ab illius ordinis collatione ad quem eum ordinavit
vel suscepit[c] usque ad condignam satisfactionem se noverit esse
suspensum. [II, c. xiv]

[6][d] Cum ecclesia Dei secundum ewangelicum veritatem[1] domus
orationis esse debeat et non spelunca latronum et[e] sanguinis
forum; seculares causas[f] in quibus de sanguinis effusione vel
de pena corporali[g] agitur in ecclesiis vel in[h] cimiteriis
agitari sub interminatione anathematis prohibemus. Absurdum[i]
enim est et crudele[j] ibi sanguinis iudicium[k] exerceri ubi et
reis constituta est tutela refugii. [II, c. xvi]

[7] Ex concilio Triburiensi[2]

Dictum est solere in quibusdam locis pro perceptione crismatis nummos dari, similiter pro baptismo et communione. Hoc
simoniace heresis esse[l] detestata est sancta sinodus et anathe-
matizavit. Statuimus [Ha, fo. 65[v]] ergo ut de cetero nec pro
ordinatione nec pro crismate nec pro baptismo nec pro extrema
unctione nec pro sepultura nec pro communione nec pro dedica-
tione quicquam exigatur, sed gratis dona Christi gratuita dispensatione donentur. Si quis contra hoc[m] facere presumpserit
anathema sit. [II, c. ix]

---

[a]nunciuntur Hb.   [b]talem Hb.   [c]susceperit *Paris. I;* Fb *om.* ab illius
... suscepit.   [d]HaHb *have heading* item.   [e]et HaHb; aut FbSL *Fontanensis
(1, 2), Cheltenhamensis.*   [f]*om.* Fb.   [g]*om.* Hb.   [h]*om.* FbL *Fontan. (1),
Cheltenh.*   [i]absurde Ha.   [j]est et crudele HaHbL; et crudele est FbS
Fontan. (2), Cheltenh.; (est enim et crud. *Fontan. 1*).   [k]iudic. sanguinis
FbL *Fontan. (2), Cheltenh.*   [l]*om.* Hb.   [m]hec FbS.

---

[1]Cf. Matt. 21, 13; Marc. 11, 17; Luc. 19, 46.
[2]Cf. *Decretum,* C. 1 q. 1 c. 105. These forms of simony had been frequently condemned, e.g. at Tours in 1163 (Mansi, xxi.1178, c. 6); cf. C. of
Westminster, 1125, c. 2; C. of Westminster, 1138, c. 1; on chrism payments,
see Brett, *English Church,* pp. 164-6.

[8] Ex decreto[a] Urbani pape[1]

Nullus prelatus in recipiendo monacho vel canonico vel sancti-
moniali precium sumere vel exigere ab his[b] qui ad conversionem[c]
veniunt aliqua pacti occasione presumat. Si quis autem hoc
fecerit anathema sit. [II, c. xxii]

[9] Decretum novum[d][2]

Nulli liceat ecclesiam nomine dotalicii ad aliquem transferre
vel pro presentatione alicuius persone pecuniam vel aliquod
emolumentum pacto interveniente accipere.[e] Quod si quis fecerit
et inde in iure vel confessus vel convictus[f] fuerit, ipsum tam
regia quam nostra freti auctoritate patronatu[g] eiusdem ecclesie
in perpetuum privari statuimus. [II, cc. vi, xxviii]

[10] Ex decretis diversorum patrum[h][3]

Secundum instituta patrum nostrorum sub interminatione anathematis prohibemus ne monachi vel clerici[i] causa lucri negocientur; et ne monachi vel a clericis vel a[j] laicis firmas teneant,
neque laici ecclesiastica beneficia ad firmam[k] suscipiant. [II,
cc. xxxv, xix]

---

[a]decretis Fb (*Gervase omits c. 8 and numbers 9-19 as 8-18; see p. 971*).
[b]hiis Ha.   [c]conversionem FbSL; conversationem HaHb.   [d]Decretum novum
HaHb; *om.* FbSL.   [e]accipere FbSL *Fontanensis*; recipere HaHb; suscipere
before pacto *Cheltenh., Tanner.*   [f]vel conf. vel conv. (commotus Hb)
HaHbL; vel (*om.* Fb) conv. vel conf. FbS *Fontanensis, Cheltenhamensis,
Tanner.*   [g]patrocinio HaHb.   [h]Ex diversis decretis sanctorum patrum L.
[i]canonici L.   [j]vel a clericis vel a FbSL *Fontan., Regalis, Claudiana;*
a clericis vel a *Cottoniana, Cheltenh.;* a clericis vel HaHb.   [k]firmam
FbSL *Fontan., Regalis, Cotton., Cheltenh.;* firmas HaHb *Claudiana* (Hb *ends*
teneant vel suscipiant; L teneant).

---

[1]Cf. *Decretum,* C. 1 q. 2 c. 3; C. of Tours, c. 6 (see p. 986 n. 2); C. of
Westminster, 1127, c. 3 (with a slight verbal link). Cf. J.H. Lynch,
Simoniacal entry into religious life from 1000 to 1260 (Columbia, 1976),
pp. 153-5.
[2]See pp. 967-8; cf. M.G. Cheney in *EHR* lvi (1941), 194; for the wider issue,
cf. *Decretum,* C. 1 q. 3 cc. 2-8, 15; C. of Westminster, 1127, c. 1.
[3]Cf. *Decretum,* D. 88, esp. cc. 2, 9; C. 21 q. 3; C. 16 q. 7 c. 39; monks
were forbidden to hold farms in an undated decretal of Alexander III ('Rela-
tum est auribus' to the bishop of Norwich, ed. H.E. Lohmann in *Zeitschr. der
Savigny-Stiftung für Rechtsgeschichte, Kan. Abt.* xxii (1933), 98). Cf. C. of
Westminster, 1102, cc. 3, 21; C. of Westminster, 1127, c. 8.

[11] Ex concilio Meldensi[a][1]

Quicunque ex clero videntur esse arma non sumant nec armati
incedant, sed professionis[b] sue vocabulum religiosis[c] moribus
et religioso[d] habitu prebeant. Quod si qui contempserint tanquam sacrorum canonum contemptores et ecclesiastice auctoritatis prophanatores proprii gradus amissione multentur, quia non
possunt simul Deo et seculo militare.

[12] Ex decreto Alexandri pape III Norwic(ensi) episcopo misso[e][2]

Illud etiam de vicariis qui personis fide vel[f] sacramento
obligati sunt duximus statuendum quod si fidei[g] vel sacramenti
religione contempta personatum sibi falso assumentes contra
personas se erexerint, super hoc in iure vel[h] confessi vel convicti fuerint, de cetero in eodem episcopatu ad officii sui
executionem non admittantur.[i] [II, c. xxv]

[13] Ex concilio Rothomagensi[3]

Omnes decime terre sive de frugibus sive de fructibus[j] arborum
sive de aliis fructibus Domini sunt[k] et illi sanctificantur.
Sed quia multi modo inveniuntur[l] decimas dare nolentes, statuimus ut iuxta domini pape preceptum[m] admoneantur semel secundo
et tertio ut de grano, de vino [Ha, fo. 66] de fructibus arborum et de fetibus animalium et de lana, de agnis et de caseis,

---

[a]Fb *omits c. 11.*   [b]vocationis L.   [c]religionis Ha.   [d]religiosi Hb.
[e]Ex decreto Alexandri pape III (*om.* Hb) Norwic' episcopo misso HaHb; ex
cretali (*sic*) epistola Alexandri pape III ad Willelmum Norwicensem episcopum
missa S; Alexander papa ad W. Norw' episcopum Fb; *om.* L.   [f]et Ha *Cotton.,*
Peterhus. (sacramento: iuramento Ha; sacramentis Hb).   [g]fide HaHb.·   [h]super
... vel HaHb *Wigorniensis;* et super ... iure (*om.* vel) FbL *Regalis, Peterhus.;*
et super ... vel S.   [i]amittantur Ha; admittatur Hb *Regalis.*   [j]pomis FbSl
(*and Gratian*); fructibus HaHb.   [k]sive de aliis fruct. Domini sunt HaHbL; S
om. sunt; domini Fb (*om. the rest, as Gratian*).   [l]multi modo inven. HaHb;
modi inven. multi Fb; modo inven. multi S; multi inven. L.   [m]pape preceptum Ha; pape precepta Hb; nostri preceptum FbSL (*fort. recte*).

---

[1]Cf. *Decretum,* C. 23 q. 8 c. 6. Cf. C. of Windsor, 1070, c. 12; C. of
Westminster, 1138, c. 13.
[2]See p. 975.
[3]Cf. *Decretum,* C. 16 q. 7 c. 5, with some words from c. 4 (cf. the *Peni-*
tential of Bartholomew of Exeter, who was present in 1175, ed. A. Morey,
Bartholomew of Exeter (Cambridge, 1937), p. 257, citing cc. 5, 4 in that
order). Cf. C. of Winchester, 1070, c. 14; C. of Windsor, 1070, c. 10; C. of
Westminster, 1127, c. 9; C. of Westminster, 1138, c. 16.

et lino et canabe[a] et de reliquis que annuatim renovantur
decimas integre persolvant; quod si commoniti non emendaverint
anathemati se noverint subiacere. [II, c. viii]

[14][b1] Calumpniam et audaciam temere litigantium condempnando
in expensas[c] et alio multiplici remedio imperialis sanctio
compescit.[d] Quoniam igitur hoc[e] sacris institutis consonare
dinoscitur precipimus ut de cetero in causis pecuniariis[f] que
inter clericos agitabuntur victus victori in expensas condemp-
netur.[g] Qui autem solvendo non fuerit eum[h] arbitrio episcopi
sui puniendum relinquimus.[i] [II, c. xxxi]

[15] Ex decreto Pelagii pape[2]
Invenimus tantum decem prefationes[j] in sacro cathalogo recipi-
endas, id est:[k] unam in Albis Paschalibus, 'Et te quidem omni
tempore';[l] secundam in Die Ascensionis,[m] 'Qui post resurrectionem'; tertiam in Pentecosten,[n] 'Qui ascendens super omnes
celos';[o] quartam de Natale[p] Domini, 'Quia per incarnati verbi

---

[a]de vino ... lana et de agnis ... canabe Ha; de vino ... de agnis de
caseis de lino de canabe Hb; et vino de fructibus arborum de fetibus animalium de lana et lino et canabo et caseo Fb; de vino de fructibus arborum de
fetibus animalium de lana de lino de canabo de castaneis L; et vino et
fructibus arborum de fetibus animalium de lana et lino et canabo de caseis
(for de reliquis, de feno et de omnibus) S.   [b]Heading Item in Hb (and
Hoveden).   [c]in exp. condempn. Fb.   [d]compescat HaHb.   [e]igitur hoc HaHb;
ergo hoc L; ergo FbS; igitur Peterhus.   [f]peculiaribus Hb.   [g]in exp. cond.
FbSL Regalis, Cheltenh., Peterhus.; cond. in expensis HaHb.   [h]HaHb add in (non
solverit eum L).   [i]relinquimus FbSl; relinquo HaHb.   [j]tantum decem pref. HaHb;
dec. tantum pref. L; dec. pref. tantum FbS; Gratian has 1-9 as in our texts;
Gervase has 1-10 in the order 1-5, 9, 6, 7, 10, 8; Sangermanensis and
Abrincensis I 1-3, 6-8, 4, 5, 9, 10.   [k]reperiendas Ha; HaHb om. id est;
Fb om. recip.   [l]Et ... tempore HaHbS; Et te quidem in omni temp. L; Et te
Fb.   [m]secundam ... Ascensionis HaHb; aliam in die asc. Domini L; aliam
de ascensionis domini S; aliam de ascensione Fb.   [n]in Pent. HaHb; in die
Pent. L; die Pent' Fb; de Pentecostes S.   [o]Qui ... celos HaHbS; FbL om.
super omnes celos.   [p]quartam ... natale HaHb; quartam ... natali FbL;
quarta die Natal' S.

---

[1]Cf. Justinian, Inst. 4.16.1: '... et ut improbus litigator etiam damnum
et impensas litis inferre adversario suo cogatur.'
[2]Cf. Decretum, de consecratione, D. 1 c. 71 (nine prefaces); for the
tenth, D. 70, dictum post c. 2. This canon is referred to in the Ann. Tewkesbury (Ann. Mon. i.51), and quoted in The Customary of the Cathedral Priory
Church of Norwich, ed. J.B.L. Tolhurst (Henry Bradshaw Soc. 1948), pp. 201-2.

misterium';[a] quintam de Apparicione Domini, 'Quia cum unigeni-
tus tuus';[b] sextam de apostolis, 'Et te Domine suppliciter
exorare';[c] septimam de sancta[d] Trinitate, 'Qui cum unigenito
tuo';[e] octavam de cruce, 'Qui salutem humani generis';[f] nonam
de ieiunio quadragesimali tantummodo dicendam,[g] 'Qui corporali
ieiunio';[h] decimam de beata Virgine, 'Et te in veneracione beate
Marie'.[i] Huius igitur[j] decreti et domini pape Alexandri auctoritate districte precipimus[k] ne quis prefatis prefacionibus aliquam omnino[l] presumat adicere. [II, c. xxiii]

[16] Ex decreto[m] Iulii pape[1]
Prohibemus[n] ne quis quasi pro complemento communionis intingtam
alicui tradat eucharistiam.[o] Nam intingtum panem aliis Christum
prebuisse non legimus excepto illo tantum discipulo quem in-
tincta buccella magistri proditorem ostenderit,[p] non que sacramenti huius institutionem signaret. [II, c. xxiv]

[17] Ex concilio Remensi[2]
Precipimus[q] ne consecretur eucharistia nisi in calice [Ha, fo.
66[v]] aureo vel argenteo, et ne stagneum calicem aliquis episcopus amodo benedicat[r] interdicimus. [II, c. xxx]

---

[a]verbi misterium Ha; verbi HbL; *om.* FbS.   [b]tuus HaHb; FbSL *om.*   [c]Fb
om. supplic. orare (L *om.* Domine).   [d]*om.* FbL.   [e]Qui-tuo HaHbL; Qui cum
unig. et Spiritu Sancto S; Qui cum unig. Fb.   [f]humani generis Fb *om.*
[g]quadrages. tantummodo dicendam (dicebam Ha) HaHb; in quadragesima tantummodo (tantum L) dicendam FbSL.   [h]*om.* Fb.   [i]beate Marie Ha; *om.*.FbSL
(Hb *reads* ... de beata Maria, Et te ven. beate).   [j]ergo FbS; *om.* L.
[k]districte precipimus HaHb; districtius inhibemus FbL; districtius prohibemus S.   [l]prefatis ... omnino HaHb; memoratis ... omnino temere FbS;
pref. memoratis omnino aliquam temere L.   [m]decretis Fb; concilio Hb.
[n]Prohibemus FbSL *Tanner;* Inhibemus HaHb.   [o]tradat euch. (euk. Fb) FbLS
Tanner; euch. trad. HaHb.   [p]ostenderet SL.   [q]Precepimus Hb.   [r]aliquis
... benedicat HaHb; de cetero aliquis episcopus benedicat modis omnibus
FbS; episcopus al. ben. mod. omn. L.

---

[1]Cf. *Decretum, de consecratione,* D. 2 c. 7, pr. and §1.
[2]Cf. *Decretum, de consecratione,* D. 1 c. 45. Cf. C. of Winchester, 1070,
c. 16; JS, *Letters,* i.159.

[18] Ex decreto[a] Ormisde pape[1]

Nullus fidelis cuiuscunque[b] condicionis sit occulte nupcias faciat,[c] set benedictione accepta[d] a sacerdote publice nubat in Domino. Si quis ergo[e] sacerdos aliquos oculte coniunxisse inventus fuerit triennio ab officio suo[f] suspendatur. [II, c. xviii]

[19] Ex decreto[g] Nicholai pape[2]

Ubi non est consensus utriusque non est coniugium; ergo qui pueris dant puellas in cunabulis[h] nichil faciunt, nisi uterque puerorum postquam venerit[i] ad tempus discrecionis consentiat. Huius ergo[j] decreti auctoritate districtius inhibemus[k] ne de cetero aliqui quorum uterque vel alter ad etatem legibus[l] et canonibus determinatam non pervenit[m] coniungantur, nisi forte aliquando urgentissima interveniente necessitate[n] pro bono pacis coniunctio talis toleretur.[o] [II, c. xxxiii]

In hoc autem concilio clerici Rogeri Eboracensis archiepiscopi calumpniati fuerunt ius Eboracensis ecclesie de cruce portanda in diocesi Cantuariensis ecclesie. Preterea calumpniati sunt ibidem ex parte Eboracensis archiepiscopi episcopatum Lincolniensem et episcopatum Cestrensem et episcopatum Wigornensem et episcopatum Herefordensem de iure pertinere debere ad metropolitanam Eboracensium ecclesiam;[3] et super hoc predictum Cantuariensem archiepiscopum[p] appellaverunt ad Romani pontificis presentiam.[q] [Ha, fo. 67] Preterea appellaverunt ipsum

---

[a] decretis Ha.   [b] cuiusque HaHb (Hb *reads* condit, cuiusque).   [c] faciet Ha.   [d] accepta ben. Hb.   [e] vero Hb; quoque S.   [f] *om.* HaS.   [g] decretis Ha (decret' Fb).   [h] FbS *ins.* et e converso..   [i] venenerint Ha.   [j] *om.* FbSL.   [k] districtius prohibemus Fb; proh. districtius S; districtius L; inhibemus HaHbL (*but L has placed stray words* ergo districtius *after* coniugium *in the first clause, evidently misunderstanding a corrected exemplar*).   [l] HaHb *add* constitutam.   [m] pervenit HaHbFb; perveniet S; pervenerit L.   [n] urg. interv. nec. FbSL; urgente nec. interven. HaHb.   [o] FbSL *end here; henceforth* HaHb (*for Hoveden and Gervase see above, pp. 971-2*).   [p] Cant. arch. Hb (*and Hoveden*); arch. Cant. Ha.   [q] appellaverunt ... presentiam Ha; ad Romanum pontificem appellaverunt Hb.

---

[1] Cf. *Decretum,* C. 30 q. 5 c. 2; and on the attempt to enforce public ceremonies in the presence of a priest, J. Dauvillier, *Le mariage dans le droit classique de l'Église* (Paris, 1933), pp. 104-5; Brooke in *Proceedings of the Fifth International Congress of Medieval Canon Law* (Vatican City, 1980), pp. 335-42. Cf. C. of Westminster, 1102, c. 23.

[2] Cf. *Decretum,* C. 30 q. 2 c. 1; cf. above, p. 967 n. 3.

[3] For the earlier history of this claim, see p. 587.

Cant(uariensem) archiepiscopum ad Romanum pontificem super
iniuria et anathematis sententia quam intulit clericis Eboracensis archiepiscopi qui per eum ministraverunt[a] in ecclesia
sancti Osuualdi de Gloucestria, pro eo quod ad illum venire
nolebant ad ipsius summonitionem sicut clerici diocesis sue
fecerunt.

In ipso[b] concilio clerici ecclesie sancti Asafi[c] petierunt
a Cant(uariensi) archiepiscopo ut in vi obbediencie preciperet
Godefrido ecclesie sancti Asaf[c] episcopo ad sedem ecclesie sue
redire cui prefuit pontificali potentia,[d] vel ut predictus
archiepiscopus alium episcopum loco ipsius Godefridi insti-
tueret. Ipse[e] enim Godefridus episcopatum suum deseruit
paupertate et Valensium infestatione compulsus; veniensque in
Angliam a christianissimo rege Henrico benigne et honorifice
susceptus est. Et tradidit ei rex abbatiam Abbendonie vacantem
in custodia donec ad sedem propriam liberum haberet regressum.
Itaque prefatus Cant(uariensis) archiepiscopus in ipso concilio
ad instantiam prenominatorum clericorum et ammonitione Alexandri
summi pontificis, necnon et consilio venerabilium coepiscoporum
suorum, convenit iamdictum Godefridum ut in vi obbediencie ad
sedem propriam rediret vel curam pastoralem que sibi fuerat
commissa in manu ipsius libere et absolute resignaret. Ipse vero
Godefridus sperans quod abbacia de Abbendonia que tradita fuerat
ei ad custodiendum posset sibi[f] remanere, episcopatum suum nullo
cogente resignavit in manu Cant(uariensis) archiepiscopi et
tradidit ei anulum suum et baculum pastoralem; et ipse Cant(uariensis) privavit eum concessi ordinis dignitate et loco, et[g]
statuit loco ipsius et consecravit magistrum Adam ad episcopatum[h] sancti Asaf.

Et sic finito concilio dominus rex et cum eo rex filius suus[i]
arripuerunt iter suum in peregrinatione ad beatum Thomam Can-
t(uariensem) martirem ...

---

[a] ministrabant Hb.　　[b] Hb *adds* autem.　　[c] *om.* Hb (*left blank*).　　[d] presencia Hb.　　[e] ipsi Ha.　　[f] *om.* Hb.　　[g] privavit ... et Ha; archiepiscopus
Hb.　　[h] epm' Ha (*cf. Hoveden, ii.78:* rex dedit episcopatum sancti Asaf magistro
Ade Walensi, et abbatiam de Abbendune cuidam monacho (*see above p. 966 n. 2*)).
[i] eius Hb.

V. *Letter of the bishop of Salisbury citing c. 13*

> From Salisbury, D.& C. Muniments, Liber Evidentiarum C, no.
> 85 (13th-cent. copy); also in Salisbury Dioc. Recs. (now
> in Wilts. Record Office) Liber Evid. B, no. 56, and Registrum
> Rub., no. 56 (not collated); printed *Charters and Documents*
> *illustrating the history of* ... *Salisbury*, ed. W.R. Jones
> and W.D. Macray (RS, 1891), pp. 39-40.

[I]ocelinus Dei gratia Sar(esberiensis) episcopus dilectis
filiis abbati et conventui Rading(ensis) ecclesie salutem.

Mandatum domini Cant(uariensis) archiepiscopi suscepimus,
quatinus vos ad solutionem decimarum vestrarum ecclesie de
Bleberia[1] secundum constitutionem generalis concilii apud West-
m(onasterium) novissime celebrati[a] modis quibus possumus in-
ducamus, et si necesse fuerit districtius compellamus. Inde est
quod vobis per presentia scripta precipiendo mandamus quatinus
dictas decimas in garbis, in caseo, et lana et ceteris omnibus
sicut in prefato constitutum est concilio plenarie ecclesie de
Bleberia restituatis aut exinde presenciam vestram nobis apud
Sar(esberiam) die Lune proxima post festum beati Iacobi exibea-
tis,[2] sufficienter instructi docere qua ratione generalis concilii decretis obviare presumitis vel loco vestri sufficientem
responsalem transmittatis cum sigillo vestro et litteris
patentibus ratihabitionem[b] continentibus. Valete.

169

1175-6. THE LEGATION OF CARDINAL HUGO PIERLEONE AND THE LEGA-
TINE COUNCIL OF WESTMINSTER OF MARCH 1176

> The history of the legation is worked out in detail in
> Tillmann, pp. 73-7; Henry's concessions and their context
> are discussed in H. Mayr-Harting, 'Henry II and the

---

[a]celebraturi CB.   [b]ratihabitionem B; rati habitioni C.

---

[1]Blewbury (Berks.).   [2]Presumably 28 July 1175.

Papacy', *Journ. of Eccl. History*, xvi (1965), 39-53,
esp. pp. 48-9.

From October 1175 until July 1176 Hugo Pierleone, cardinal
deacon of Sant'Angelo, was papal legate *a latere* in England.
His chief function seems to have been to resolve problems remaining from the Compromise of Avranches of 1172, and Henry
recognized that he had granted the legate four concessions:
that no clerk was to be taken before a secular judge for any
criminal offences, save forest offences (cf. Const. Clarendon,
c. 3); that archbishoprics, bishoprics, and abbacies should
not be kept vacant for more than a year, save for urgent necessity; that clerks' murderers should be strictly dealt with by
the royal courts and suffer disinheritance as well as the normal penalties; and that clerks should not be compelled to trial
by battle (see p. 949 n.). In March 1176 he held a legatine council to settle the issues for which he had come, to resolve cases
etc. which had been brought to his notice, and to take stock of
the state of the English Church (see no. IV). The dispute for
precedence between the archbishops of Canterbury and York seems
to have caused some confusion, and Giraldus Cambrensis may be
right in claiming that the council failed of its main purposes
in consequence, or at least achieved less than had been hoped.
The extracts below describe the general context of the legation, give Henry's letter listing his concessions, Giraldus's
account of the presentation of the case for the metropolitan
status of St. Davids at the council; and documents which show
two law-suits, both concluded by groups of participants while
the council was in session.

I. *Roger of Hoveden, Gesta Regis Henrici II s.a. 1175*

    From BL ms. Cotton Julius A. xi, fos. 73^V-74 (Ha), and
    Vitell. E. xvii, fo. 75^{r-v} (Hb: defective; see p. 970);
    ed. Stubbs, i.104-5.

(1175) Et eodem anno paulo ante festum Omnium Sanctorum applicuit in Anglia quidam cardinalis nomine Hugozun, apostolice

sedis legatus, pro quo dominus rex Romam miserat; et invenit
dominum regem apud Wintoniam. Et dominus rex in obviam ei venit,
et rex filius suus cum eo, et eum cum debito honore et reverentia susceperunt. Et dominus rex per aliquot dies moram faciens
apud Wintoniam diutissime[a] tractavit de pace facienda inter
Rogerum Eboracensem archiepiscopum et Ricardum Cantuariensem
archiepiscopum, de capella sancti Oswaldi Gloucestrie[b] et de
cruce archiepiscopi Ebor(acensis) portanda. Et tandem per consilium regis inter predictos archiepiscopos in hunc modum convenit quod Cantuariensis archiepiscopus quietam clamavit
archiepiscopo Eboraci et liberam ab omni iurisdictione sua
capellam sancti Osuualdi Gloucestrie, sicut dominicam capellam
domini regis;[1] et absolvit clericos archiepiscopi Eboraci quos
vinculo excommunicationis innodaverat; et quod de cruce portanda, et de aliis controversiis que inter ecclesias suas
vertuntur, starent iudicio archiepiscopi Rothomagensis et
aliorum vicinorum episcoporum qui fuerint de regno Francie; et
quod sic pacem inter se haberent de predictis controversiis
usque ad primum festum sancti Michaelis sequens,[c] ita quod
neuter illorum alteri malum vel dampnum perquireret donec controversia illa determinata esset, et ad debitum finem perducta
per Rothomagensem [Ha, fo. 74] archiepiscopum et per vicinos
episcopos de regno Francie.

   Hiis itaque gestis, predictus cardinalis qui[d] in Angliam
per mandatum regis venerat, concessit et dedit domino regi
licentiam inplacitandi clericos regni sui de forestis suis et
de captione venationum. Ecce membrum Sathane! - ecce ipsius
Sathane conductus satelles! - qui tam subito factus de pastore
raptor, videns lupum venientem fugit. et dimisit oves sibi a
summo pontifice[e] commissas, pro quarum tutamine[f] missus erat a
Romana sede in Angliam.

---

[a]diutissime Hb; ductissime Ha.   [b]Gloucestrie Hb; Glucestr' Ha.
[c]usque ... sequens Ha; a primo festo sancti Michaelis sequente usque ad
finem v annorum subsequentium Hb (*cf. Hoveden, ii.86*); *but this relates to
a truce made in 1176 - see Stubbs's note* ad loc.   [d]qui Hb; que Ha.
[e]pontifice Ha; papa Hb.   [f]tutamine Ha; tutacione Hb.

---

[1]See J.H. Denton, *English Royal Free Chapels 1100-1300* (Manchester, 1970),
pp. 51-7, esp. 54-5.

II. *Ralph de Diceto, Ymagines Historiarum s.a. 1176*

From mss. Da, fos. 92^V-93, and Db, fo. 99^V (formerly 97^V);
ed. Stubbs, i.410 (cf. pp. 405-6) (for mss. see p. 964).

Hugo Petrileonis sue legationis in Angliam cancellato cursu v
nonas Iulii transfretavit; quid ei debeat Anglorum ecclesia
cupida libertatis, sequentis brevicule reserat continentia.

'Domino pape rex Anglorum. Propter reverentiam sancte
Romane ecclesie atque devotionem quam erga eam et paternitatem
ac dilectionem vestram et fratrum vestrorum habemus et semper
habuimus, licet plurimum resisterent et reclamarent regni
nostri maiores et magis discreti, ad instantiam viri discreti
et sapientis Hugonis Petrileonis, sancte Romane ecclesie cardinalis, apostolice sedis legati, amici et cognati[1] nostri, capitula que subscripta sunt in regno nostro tenenda concessimus.
Videlicet quod clericus de cetero non trahatur ante iudicem
secularem in persona sua de aliquo criminali, neque de aliquo
forisfacto, excepto forisfacto foreste mee, et excepto laico
feodo unde michi vel alii domino seculari laicum debetur servi-
cium. Concedo etiam quod archiepiscopatus,[a] episcopatus et
abbatie non teneantur in manu mea ultra annum, nisi urgente
necessitate et evidenti de causa que propter hoc non fuerit
inventa ut diutius teneantur. Concedo etiam quod interfectores
clericorum, qui eos scienter vel premeditati interfecerint,
convicti vel confessi coram iusticiario meo, presente episcopo
vel eius officiali, preter consuetam laicorum vindictam suam et
suorum de hereditate que eos contingit perpetuam sustineant
exheredationem. Concedo etiam quod clerici non cogantur facere
duellum.

III. *January X February 1176. Council of Northampton*

This was a royal council, famous for the promulgation of the
Assize of Northampton. After quoting the text of the Assize,

---

[a]Db *adds* et.

---

[1]It seems impossible to trace this relationship.

the *Gesta Henrici II* gives this account of ecclesiastical
business, part of which formed the background to the council
of Westminster of March 1176.

From the *Gesta Henrici* II, mss. (see p. 970) Ha, fos. 76^V-77;
Hb, fo. 77^{r-v} (some words missing); ed. Stubbs, i.111-12.

Ad predictum vero concilium quod celebratum fuit[a] apud North-
amptoniam venit Willelmus rex Scotie per mandatum domini regis,
et adduxit secum Ricardum episcopum sancti [Ha, fo. 77] Andree,
et Ioscelinum episcopum de Glascu et Ricardum episcopum de
Dunkeldan et Christianum episcopum de Galveia[b] et Andream
episcopum de Katenessa et[c] Simonem de Thouni episcopum[d] de
Murrevia,[1] et abbates et priores terre sue ad faciendam subiectionem ecclesie Angl(ie).

Tunc dominus rex exegit ab eis ut per fidem quam ei debebant[e]
et per sacramentum quod[f] illi fecerant eandem subiectionem
facerent ecclesie Anglie, qualem facere debebant[e] et solebant
tempore regum Anglie predecessorum suorum. Et illi responderunt
quod predecessores sui nunquam subiectionem aliquam fecerunt
ecclesie Anglie et quod nec ipsi ei aliquam facere deberent. Ad
hoc respondit Rogerus Eboracensis archiepiscopus quod episcopi
Scotie[g] subiectionem fecerant metropolitane ecclesie Eboraci
tempore predecessorum suorum et nominatim episcopus Glascuensis
et quidam alii episcopi Scotie;[h] et super hoc ostendit bullas
quas[i] inde pre manibus habuit.

Tunc magna orta est contentio inter Rogerum Eboracensem
archiepiscopum et Ricardum Cantuariensem archiepiscopum de
subiectione illa habenda. Dicebat enim Cantuar(iensis) archiepiscopus subiectionem illam deberi[j] fieri ecclesie Cantuarie,

---

[a]est Hb.   [b]Candida Casa Hb.   [c]*om*. Hb.   [d]ep. de Touni Hb.   [e]debeant
Hb.   [f]quam Ha.   [g]ep. Scotie Ha; ipsi de Glascu Hb.   [h]et nominatim
... Scotie *om*. Hb (*but see Stubbs's note*).   [i]quas Ha; et alia munimenta
necessaria que Hb.   [j]*om*. Hb.

---

[1]William I (the Lion), king of Scotland, 1165-1214; Richard, bishop of
St. Andrews, Jocelyn, bishop of Glasgow, Richard, bishop of Dunkeld, Chris-
tian, bishop of Galloway (Whithorn), Andrew, bishop of Caithness, Simon de
Tonei, bishop of Moray.

et Eboracensis archiepiscopus dicebat ecclesie sue. Et sic
finivit concilium illud. Et predicti episcopi Scotie accepta a
domino rege licencia recesserunt. Et exinde clam[a] miserunt
legatos suos ad Alexandrum summum pontificem postulantes ut
eos reciperet in manu sua et tutaret a subiectione illa quam
Anglicana ecclesia ab eis exigebat.

For the passage which follows, see below.

IV. *14-19 March 1176: Council of Westminster*

   From *Gesta Henrici II*, Ha, fos. 77-8 (75-6); Hb, fos.
   77^v-78,[1] ed. Stubbs, i.112-14.

Interim venit[b] ad curiam domini regis predictus Hugheszun [Ha,
fo. 77^v (75^v)] cardinalis ille, quem summus pontifex in Angliam
miserat; et per consilium domini regis submonuit omnes episcopos et abbates et priores tocius Anglie, quod essent in
media quadragesima apud Lundonias ad audiendum mandata et
precepta summi pontificis. Adveniente igitur media quadragesima
venerunt Lundonias dominus rex et rex filius suus[c] et predictus
cardinalis et Ricardus Cantuariensis archiepiscopus cum suffraganeis suis, et Rogerus Eboracensis archiepiscopus cum suffraganeis suis; et congregatis apud Westmonasterium in capella
monachorum infirmorum, predicto cardinale et predictis archiepiscopis cum suffraganeis suis, orta est dira lis et contencio
inter predictos archiepiscopos quis illorum[d] sederet a dextris
ipsius cardinalis. Volebat enim Ricardus Cantuariensis archiepiscopus a dextris ipsius sedere, et dicebat hoc de iure pertinere dignitati[e] ecclesie Cantuar(iensis).[f] Sed Rogerus
Eboracensis archiepiscopus contradicebat, asserens sedem illam
suam esse debere de antiquo iure ecclesie sue. Et dum ita

---

   [a]*om.* Hb.   [b]venit Hb, venit vel rediit (*interlin.*) Ha.   [c]suus Ha;
eius Hb.   [d]illorum Ha; eorum Hb.   [e]dignitati Ha; ad dignitatem Hb.
[f]Cantuarie Hb.

---

   [1]Select variants of Hb only (see p. 970). Cf. Hoveden, ii.92-3; Diceto,
i.405-6; Gervase, i.258-9; esp. ii.398; Ann. Winchcombe, ed. R.R. Darlington
in *Misc. D.M. Stenton*, p. 136.

contenderent irruerunt in Rogerum Eboracensium archiepiscopum
monachi et servientes, qui cum Cantuariensi archiepiscopo
venerunt, et arrepto illo pronum in terram proiecerunt et
pedibus suis conculcaverunt, et crebris ictibus ceciderunt eum,[a]
et cappam qua indutus fuerat fregerunt. Sed tandem semimortuus
vix e manibus eorum ereptus est. Quod cum predictus cardinalis
inspexisset doluit vehementer, et statim appellavit archiepiscopum Cantuariensem ad sedem apostolicam, inponens ei hoc fatum
fuisse per consilium eius[1] ad dedecus Romani pontificis et
ipsius. Et archiepiscopus Eboracensis qui, ut supradictum est,
verberatus fuerat, appellavit Cantuariensem archiepiscopum ad
[Ha, fo. 78 (76)] presentiam summi pontificis, imponens ei hanc
violentiam sibi factam fuisse a suis per consilium et voluntatem ipsius.[b] Similiter appellavit Galfridum Eliensem episcopum,
imponens ei quod violentas manus iniecerat in eum. Similiter
Cantuariensis archiepiscopus appellavit ipsum cardinalem ad
presenciam summi pontificis de suspecto gravamine.

Sicque finito concilio predictus cardinalis, convocatis
episcopis, abbatibus et prioribus et omni clericatu qui aderat,
coram illis renovavit predictam appellationem quam fecerat. Et
dato munere benedictionis permisit eos abscedere. Et Rogerus
Eboracensis archiepiscopus statim intravit[c] ad regem, et ostensis ei iniuriis que ei illata fuerant, commovit eum in iram et
odium adversus Cantuariensem archiepiscopum et Eliensem episcopum. Eadem vero die Cantuariensis archiepiscopus accessit ad
predictum cardinalem et spopondit ei pecuniam, et sedato eo,
uterque illorum remisit appellationem suam. Sed Eboracensis
archiepiscopus nullam cum eo inire voluit concordiam nisi in

---

[a]ciciderunt eum Ha; eum ciciderunt Hb.   [b]*The next two sentences are
reversed in Ha; it seems clear that Hb and Stubbs were right to give the
order in the text.*   [c]B *ins.* in ecclesia.

---

[1]For the strength of feeling against Archbishop Roger at Canterbury after
Becket's murder, see *MB Epp.* 777 = JS, *Letters*, ii, no. 307 (cf. ibid.,
p. xliv). Gervase (ii.398) transfers the blame for this attack from the
monks: 'sed advolantes ecclesiae Cantuariensis *suffraganei*, Rogerum a sede
deiciunt, caedunt et scindunt, et a concilio penitus eiciunt'; at i.258 he
says 'a quibusdam episcopis, clericis et laicis'. Diceto, i.405-6, says
that York especially blamed the bishop of Ely. See p. 1000 n.

presentia summi pontificis et per ipsum. Finito itaque concilio
recesserunt inde.

V. *Giraldus Cambrensis, De rebus a se gestis*

> From BL Cotton ms. Tiberius B. xiii,[1] fo. 163[V]; printed
> in Giraldus, *Opera,* RS, i.8; also in Wharton, *Anglia
> Sacra,* ii.475.

Qualiter canonici Menev(enses) tam regem quam legatum Hugui-
tionem super ecclesie sue dignitate convenerunt.

[C]um circiter clausum Pasche Hugutio cardinalis tituli
sancti Angeli fungens in Anglia legatione concilium generale
regni totius apud London(ias) convocasset, archidiaconi Mene-
ven(ses) et canonici discretiores ad protestandum pariter et
prosequendum si liceret ius dignitatis ecclesie sue scilicet
metropoliti cum coram cardinali Londonias advenerunt, episcopus
enim ipsorum quoniam in consecratione sua controversiam illam
abiuraverat contra sacramentum suum licet extortum venire
nolebat. Pretemptantes autem primo regis animum utrum inclinari
posset ad consensum pecuniamque non modicam, tam ipsi quam
consiliariis suis ad hoc offerentes cum plurimum circiter hec
laborassent, quia rex ille scilicet Henricus secundus morosus
erat in responsionibus, tandem responsum hoc acceperunt quod
numquam id tempore suo rex permitteret, nec capud Wallie dando
Walensibus archiepiscopum contra Angliam erigeret. Quo audito
fecerunt quod potuerunt: ius ecclesie sue et pristinam dignitatem coram legato, cuius tamen concilium per contentiones et
pugnas inter archiepiscopos duos, scilicet Cantuariensem Ricardum et Eboracensem Rogerum de prima sede et primacie dignitate
aborsu fecit, in puplica audientia sunt protestati.

---

[1]13th cent., containing Giraldus' *Speculum ecclesie* and *De rebus*. Giraldus
also has an account of the comments of Roger, bishop of Worcester, on the
archbishop of York's complaints (*Opera,* vii.62-4).

VI. *Notification by Roger, bishop of Worcester, as judge-*
delegate, of the conclusion of a dispute between the monks
of Saint-Évroult and the monks of Bermondsey[1]

From BL ms. Cotton Claud. A. viii, fos. 121^V-122 (16th-
cent. transcript); printed M.G. Cheney, *Roger bishop of*
Worcester, no. 58.

Universis sancte matris ecclesie filiis Rogerus Dei gratia
Wigornensis ecclesie vocatus episcopus, salutem. Manifeste improbitatis est a transactionibus [fo. 122] quibus equitas
patrocinatur recedere et per quietis inpatientiam contentiones
sopitas in nova litigia suscitare; unde omnium cognitioni
volumus innotescere controversiam que vertebatur inter dilectos
nostros abbatem et monachos sancti Ebrulfi et fratres de Bermundesey super ecclesia sancti Iohannis de Wideford absque spe
litis restaurande fine pacifico conquievisse. Cum enim dominus
Alexander papa tertius venerabili fratri nostro Roberto Herefordensi episcopo et nobis pariter causam que agebatur inter
prefatos fratres super prescripta ecclesia cognoscendam et
appellatione remota terminandam sub certa forma delegasset,
illustris comes Legrecestrie Robertus, quem ex maxima parte
causam contingebat, iamdictorum fratrum paci et tranquillit[at]i
studuit et ante litis ingressum omnem contentionis occasionem
liberali munificentia precidit. In mandato namque domini pape
continebatur insertum sibi ab abbate et fratribus sancti Ebrulfi
fuisse suggestum quod cum fratres de Bermundesey et Robertus
quondam comes Legrec' iunioris Roberti pater duas villas adinvicem commutassent etc.[2] Facta est hec concessio anno verbi

---

[1]On the same occasion Bishop Roger issued a general confirmation to the
monks of St.-Évroult of their *spiritualia* in the diocese of Worcester, at
the instance of Robert, earl of Leicester, 'anno verbi incarnati m. c. lxxv
Lond' tempore celebris congregationis archiepiscoporum, episcoporum, abbatum
et priorum Angl', regum patris et filii et magnatum regni Anglorum facte per
vocationem Hugonis Petrileonis sancti Angeli diaconi cardinalis, apostolice
sedis legati. Teste (*sic*) Roberto comite Leic', Roberto abbate Croilandie,
Iohanne de Salesb' thesaurario Exon' ecclesie, Simone archidiacono Wygorni-
ensi, Roberto capellano nostro et Roberto monacho, magistro Moyse et magistro
Silvestro, et aliis.' M.G. Cheney, *Roger*, no. 56, from Inspeximus of 1236 in
Arch. dép. Orne, H 925; abstract in Round, *Cal. Docts. France*, no. 650. For
Master Silvester see H. Mayr-Harting in *Studies in Church History*, ii (1965),
186-96.
[2]The centre of the document is missing.

incarnati 1175 (*sic*) Londini tempore celebris congregationis
archiepiscoporum, [episcoporum,] abbatum et personarum Anglie,
regum patris et filii et magnatum regni Anglorum facte per
vocationem Hugonis Petri Leonis sancti Angeli diaconi cardinalis, apostolice sedis legati. Testibus de concessione comitis
Roberto abbate de Croyland, Simone archidiacono Wigorn',
Roberto capellano nostro, magistro Moise, Ernaldo de Bosco,
Willelmo de Chiray, Willelmo de Diva, Willelmo de Wibetot,
Hugone de Campaines. Obligationi vero Roberti capellani comitis
interfuerunt in ecclesia sancti Bartholomei Ba(r)tholomeus
Exoniensis episcopus, et Iohannes de Salesburia thesaurarius
Exoniensis ecclesie et Simon archidiaconus Wigorn' et Robertus
capellanus et Robertus monachus, magister Silvester, feria quinta
post Dominicam qua cantatur Letare Ierusalem [18 Mar. 1176].
Fecit comes concessionem suam super prescripta ecclesia in domo
Roberti de Fuleham hospitis nostri. Robertus autem capellanus
se obligavit sexta feria post Dominicam predictam in ecclesia
sancti Bartholomei de Smethefeld in parte aquilonari.

VII. *The Chronicle of Battle Abbey*

Pleading in the case between Odo, abbot of Battle (1175-1200)[1]
and Godfrey de Lucy on the church of Wye (Kent).

> From BL ms. Cotton Domit. ii, fos. 124^V-130^V; ed. E.
> Searle, *Chronicle of Battle Abbey*, pp. 320-35; ed. J.S.
> Brewer, pp. 170-9. The loss of a quire in the ms. has
> deprived us of the conclusion of the case and of the
> chronicle.

Tunc temporis accidit quendam Hugonem Romane ecclesie diaconum
cardinalem a latere domini pape Alexandri missum legationis

---

[1]See above, pp. 963-4 (he had been prior of Christ Church, Canterbury,
in 1173-4; cf. *Heads*, pp. 34, 29); Godfrey, son of Richard de Lucy, was himself an eminent royal clerk and pluralist, later bishop of Winchester (*DNB;
GF*, pp. 279-80; Le Neve, i.47; ii.86-7; etc.). On this case see esp. Searle's
edn. and notes; E. Searle, 'Battle abbey and exemption: the forged charters',
EHR lxxxiii (1968), 449-80, esp. 454-9; S. Kuttner and E. Rathbone in *Traditio*, vii (1949-51), 281, and on Gerard Pucelle, pp. 296-303.

gratia venire in Angliam, qui convoca[fo. 125]tis archiepiscopis, episcopis, abbatibus et tocius regni clero, concilium
generale apud Westmonasterium concitavit, tum de negociis pro
quibus venerat tractaturus, tum de statu Anglicane ecclesie et
causis ecclesiasticis cogniturus. Abbate de Bello generali
edicto inter ceteros ad concilium vocato, scripsit ei predictus
legatus auctoritate apostolica speciale sibi dirigens mandatum
ut omni excusatione remota in presentia sua appareret, Godefrido de Luci super ecclesia de Wi responsurus et iuri pariturus.
Abbas suscepto hoc mandato, plurimum turbatus est animo, sciens
dominum regem predictam ecclesiam de Wi prefato Godefrido de
Luci, vacante ecclesia de Bello, absque omni exceptione dedisse
et confirmasse, ipsum quoque Godefridum ad presentationem
domini regis a Ricardo Cantuariensi electo fuisse susceptum,
et auctoritate qua electus potuit in ecclesia institutum, carta
nichilominus sibi a prefato electo super ipsius institutione
prestita, quam idem electus postmodum ab apostolica sede rediens
et a papa Alexandro consecratus, iam archiepiscopus, iam primas,
iam apostolice sedis legatus, omni qua fungebatur auctoritate
confirmaverat. Metuebat ergo cernens undique imminens periculum,
quoniam si adversus Godefridum litem iniret contra regie auctoritatis donationem et archiepiscopi institutionem ac utrorum-
que confirmationem, contraque dominum Ricardum de Luci sepedicti
Godefridi patrem, tocius Anglie post dominum regem iusticiam
capitalem irreverenter agere videretur. [fo. 125.ᵛ] Si vero
liti renuntians a causa deficeret, mox ecclesia de Wi Godefrido
absque ulla exceptione tota adiudicaretur, monasteriumque de
Bello annis singulis amissioni decem marcarum subiaceret. Recur-
rens igitur abbas ad nota et consueta devotionis et orationis
presidia, seseque fratrum commendans orationibus, dominum
regem adiit, quomodo in causam traheretur exposuit, prudenter
principis animum, cui se parti potius inclinaret, cupiens inda-
gare. Supplicabat regi ut se verbo simplici certum redderet, si
ecclesiam de Wi Godefrido de Luci concessisset necne, asserens
se nullatenus adversus ipsum Godefridum litem initurum, si sibi
de regis donatione posset certius innotescere. Rex donationem

per se factam sciens non esse canonicam,[1] cepit dissimulare
dicens, non se habere in memoria quod sepedictam ecclesiam
Godefrido concesserit vel confirmaverit. Abbas ab eo nichil
certum valens extorquere divertit ad archiepiscopum, sciscitans
ab eo si Godefridum ad presentationem domini regis in ecclesia
de Wi personam instituisset et institutionem auctoritate qua
fungebatur confirmasset. Archiepiscopo magna cum assertione
protestante se Godefridum non nisi ad portionem ecclesie, quam
Willelmus presbiter, de quo superius facta est mentio,[2] die qua
in fata concessit possederat, instituisse, nichilque super his
que archiepiscopum contingebant esse verendum, abbas quasi iam
secure litem ingressurus, iam de solo advocato cui causam suam
committeret defendendam cepit esse [fo. 126] sollicitus. Conveniens itaque quendam clericorum archiepiscopi, magistrum
scilicet Gerardum cognomento Puellam, virum quidem eruditissi-
mum et litteratissimum, postmodum vero Cestrensem episcopum,
causam suam sibi exposuit, rogans ut antique familiaritatis
gratia sub mutue vicissitudinis obtentu eam fovendam susciperet.
Clericus ille, audita et plenius cognita cause serie, respondit
causam illam dominum suum archiepiscopum contingere, nec se
partem aliquam posse tueri, quia domini sui actus velut minus
rationabiles videretur improbare. Illo sic excusante, abbas
magistrum Bartholomeum Exoniensem episcopum sibi olim familiarem[3]
expetiit, ut una cum clericis suis secum in causa sua staret.
Episcopus cognoscens quod adversus Godefridum de Luci esset
agendum, respondit eundem Godefridum Exoniensis ecclesie esse
canonicum, nec se causam alienam ad se non pertinentem contra
canonicum suum posse fovere. Pretendente episcopo huiusmodi
excusationem, declinavit abbas ad magistrum Iohannem Saresberi-

---

[1]This is an early example of the interpretation of regalian right to include the enjoyment of an abbey's patronage in a vacancy; it became an
established custom in the 13th cent. (cf. another case, relating to a cathedral chapter, in *Papal Decretals relating to the Diocese of Lincoln,* ed.
W. Holtzmann and E.W. Kemp, Lincoln Record Soc., 1954, pp. 28-9).

[2]*Chron.,* ed. Searle, p. 268; ed. Brewer, p. 140.

[3]Odo as monk of Christ Church, Canterbury, Bartholomew as clerk to Archbishop Theobald: cf. John of Salisbury, *Letters,* i, p. xxvii n., and pp.
222-3, etc.; A. Morey, *Bartholomew of Exeter,* chap. i. John of Salisbury,
also formerly Theobald's clerk, was by this time in the service or company
of Bartholomew (JS, *Letters,* ii, p. xlvi).

ensem, postmodum Carnotensem episcopum, eum de causa sua con-
sulens et auxilium postulans. Sed idem Iohannes se excusans,
'Canonicus' inquit 'sum Exoniensis ecclesie, nec Godefrido cum
eiusdem ecclesie socii et concanonici simus possum adversari'.
In hunc modum se excusabant omnes, quotquot habere credebat
amicos et familiares. Clerici domini regis et archiepiscopi
causam illam dominos suos dicebant contingere, nec se dominorum
suorum diffinitionibus posse contradicere. Episcoporum et
clericorum alii dicebant Godefridum esse cano[fo. 126^V]nicum
suum, alii concanonicum. Communis omnium et generalis erat
excusatio, se indignationem domini Ricardi de Luci patris sepedicti Godefridi nolle incurrere. Abbate in angustia posito
persuasit ei quidam ut cum quodam clerico legis perito, qui cum
legato de Italia venerat loqueretur, sicque cum eo ageret ut
cause sue susciperet advocationem, quia terrarum domini regis
nec indigena nec incola, nec beneficio seu quavis familiaritate
Cisalpinis obnoxius, non regem, non principem, non archiepiscopum, non episcopum, non quamlibet ecclesiasticam secularemve
regni personam in qualibet advocatione verebatur. Adquievit
abbas persuadenti, clericumque conveniens causam suam sibi exposuit, cuius advocationem clericus suscepit, ab abbate marcam
argenti recepturus. Iam securus abbas sese recepit hospitio,
litem ingressurus in crastino. Nocte superveniente cum iam hora
quietis instaret, affuerunt quidam a predicto clerico ad
abbatem transmissi, mandatum ipsius abbati viva voce exponentes,
quod scilicet causam super qua inter eos convenerat fovere non
poterat, quia domini regis et magnatum terre indignationi
subiacere nolebat. His auditis, nuntiisque qui venerant dimissis, iam omni spe consolationis succisa, anxiatus est in abbate
spiritus eius, sui quoque plurimum anxiabantur. Et quemadmodum
inter mestos solet frequenter accidere, qui cum mestitudinis
sue remedium non habeant, aliquid sepe loquuntur aut faciunt per
quod mestitudini sue amplius adiciunt, sic unus eorum qui cum
abbate erant [fo. 127] propinquus eius et ceteris familiarior
ad abbatem conversus dixit: 'Si michi domine ceterisque qui vos
contingunt propinquis, impensas sufficientes contulissetis,
quibus scolas frequentare possemus, in lege et decretis iampri-
dem exercitati, vobis in instanti et in aliis necessitatibus

possemus esse presidio. Nunc vero in scripturis bruti et
hebetes, a nobis ipsis consilium non habemus, nec ab aliis
prece vel pretio consequi valemus.' Ad hec abbas: 'Iam me'
inquit 'fere penitet quod studio legum animum non apposuerim'.
Omnibus qui aderant tum ex nature necessitate, tum ex nocturna
consuetudine quiescentibus, abbas parum aut nichil repausans
noctem totam aut noctis partem maiorem pervigil in oratione
transegit insomnem, se causamque suam Deo commendans, sanctoque
Martino ut sibi advocatus fieret humiliter supplicans. Celebratis in crastino divinis officiis, simpliciter cum suis ad locum
decisioni cause prefixum processit, parte adversa ex opposito
veniente cum advocatorum multitudine. Procurator et advocatus
principalis in causa partis adverse erat quidam magister Ivo
Cornubiensis,[1] qui procedens in medium litterasque patentes
Godefridi de Luci tunc in transmarinis scolas frequentantis in
publicum proferens, commissam sibi manifestavit cause procurationem et Godefridi ratihabitionem. Erat autem tunc ibi utpote
ad concilium vocati, cleri conventus maximus, non tamen presidente legato sed quibusdam suorum quibus cause commiserat
decisionem. Prefatus ergo magister Ivo sic exorsus ait. 'Satis
vobis domini iu[fo. 127^V]dices ex patenti testimonio litterarum
domini mei Godefridi de Luci credimus constare, ipsum utpote in
remotis extra hoc regnum partibus scolarum studia frequentantem
huic cause sue interesse non posse, michique causam eandem
procurandam commisisse. Cuius ego advocatione suscepta, non
minorem michi quam si dominus meus presens adesset postulo dari
audientiam, sed tanto diligentiorem quanto causam quam fovendam
suscepi constat esse iustiorem. Cum iam huic vite finem fecisset
vir venerabilis Walterus abbas de Bello,[2] domini mei Godefridi
patruus, totius monasterii dispositio in regie sullimitatis
devenit potestatem, adeo ut in domini regis fuerit arbitrio
monasterii ipsius regimen cui vellet committere, cum tamen in
voluntate non habuerit aliquem in eo nisi canonice electum
substitui. Nondum penes se deliberaverat maiestas regia cui

---

[1] Master Ivo later succeeded Godfrey de Lucy as archdeacon of Derby
(occurs e.g. *Reg. St. Osmund*, RS i.221, 243, 264, 267; in all these he seems
to witness as a member of Godfrey's household).
[2] Died 21 June 1171 (*Heads*, p. 29).

monasterialis prelationis conferret honorem, cum presbiterum
quendam Willelmum personam ecclesie de Wi contigit huic vite
renuntiare. Dominus rex ratione qua potuit de totius monasterii
corpore pro voluntate disponere, predictam ecclesiam de Wi in
fundo monasterii sitam domino meo Godefrido de Luci pietatis
et caritatis concessit intuitu et carta sua quam ad manum
habemus confirmavit, ut rex, ut fundi dominus, ut monasterii
illius preter cetera regni monasteria specialis patronus. Nec
quidem incongruum fuit domino regi de membris disponere, cui
totum corpus erat in potestate.' Et hec dicens, cartam domini
regis super donatione et confirmatione in [fo. 128] medium
protulit. Et adiciens 'Facta' inquit 'iure patronatus huiusmodi
donatione, vir venerabilis dominus Ricardus tunc Cantuariensis
electus, dominum meum Godefridum auctoritate qua potuit ad
presentationem domini regis suscipiens personam absque omni
exceptione instituit, datis sibi in testimonii munimentum institutionis sue litteris, sigillo quod tunc habere videbatur
apposito, licet nondum in plena potestate videretur constitutus.'
Proferensque in publicum litteras, 'En' inquit 'ipsius electi
testimonium. Sedem apostolicam postmodum adiens, ibique a domino
papa solenniter consecratus ac inde cum plena potestate archiepiscopi, primatis et legati denuo rediens, quod electus minus
antea facere poterat, iam confirmatus plena auctoritate insti-
tuendo et confirmando roboravit.' Et hec dicendo cartam archiepiscopi ipso etiam archiepiscopo presente in omnium oculis
ostendit, ita subinferens: 'Cum igitur' inquit 'huius ecclesie
de Wi non qualemcunque portionem sed ecclesiam totam cum omni
iuris sui integritate dominus meus Godefridus tam excellenti
auctoritate obtinuerit, dominus abbas et monachi de Bello ipsius
ecclesie medietatem contra regiam episcopalemque dignitatem
detinent occupatam. Ergo secundum plenam domini regis donationem
et domini archiepiscopi plenam institutionem plenam petimus
possessionem, ad maiorem parati probationem si forte iam edita
videatur minus sufficiens; abbati et monachis plena possessione
suscepta si quid questionis adversum nos habuerint responsuri,
et secundum iuris ordinem satisfa[fo. 128^V]cturi.'

Stupefactus ad hec abbas plurimum, stabat expers humani consilii, confisus tamen de divino, responsurus ad proposita. Cum

eos quos credebat amicos ut ad consilium suum venirent benigne
rogaret, omnes se modo quo predictum est excusaverunt, adeo ut
nec unus omnium qui aderant preter suos qui secum illo venerant
consilium sibi vel auxilium prestiturus procederet. Nemo enim
omnium timore domini regis et archiepiscopi et Ricardi de Luci
secum stare presumpsit, cognito quod eos causa contingeret.
Aderat illic inter ceteros magister Walerannus Baiocensis
archidiaconus, postmodum Roffensis episcopus,[1] qui tunc temporis
Cantuariensi archiepiscopo adherens, illic collateralis magistri
Gerardi Puelle residebat. Hic abbatem intuens in angustiis
positum, et divino ut creditur instinctu pietate motus, conversus ad magistrum Gerardum: 'Magister' inquit 'Gerarde, sic
omnes abbatem de Bello desolatum relinquemus? Dei odium incurrat
qui ei in hac necessitate deerit.' Surgensque et magistrum
Gerardum amica violentia manu iniecta post se trahens, 'Eamus'
inquit 'et abbatis assistentes consilio, ei in causa sua sub-
veniamus'. Venientibus ex insperato ambobus ad abbatis consilium,
abbas iam erat animequior et de causa sua securior. Non diu
protracto, sed maturato expeditoque consilio, redeunt pariter ad
iudicum consessum, ubi magister Gerardus agente magistro
Waleranno, immo Deo disponente procedens in spiritu fortitudinis,
non regem veritus, non archi[fo. 129]episcopum dominum suum, non
principes, non quoslibet eorum fautores, libera voce cepit in
hunc modum pro abbate allegare: 'Sicut ea' inquit 'que canonice
sunt inchoata, ut perfectionem obtineant sunt promovenda, sic
que contra iuris ordinem perperam sunt attemptata, in irritum
sunt revocanda aut in statum meliorem transformanda. Allegatum
est a parte adversa quod, monasterio Belli pastore orbato, totius
monasterii dispositio in manus domini regis devenerit, vacantem
interim ecclesiam de Wi in fundo monasterii sitam dominus rex
domino Godefrido de Luci contulerit, quodque eum regia auctoritate presentatum dominus noster Cantuariensis primum electus,
postmodum archiepiscopus ad eandem ecclesiam susceperit et
personam instituerit. Ad hec in primis salva pace domini regis
respondemus quod in rebus ecclesiasticis nichil iuris obtinet

---

[1]Clerk to Archbishop Richard, and bishop of Rochester 1182-4 (Le Neve,
ii.76).

potestas secularis. Licet ad tempus, in rebus monasterii pastore orbati visa fuerit maiestas regia pro potestate sibi iuris aliquid vendicasse, nichil tamen ad detrimentum monasterii abbatisve futuri de iure potuit vel debuit immutare, alienare, seu aliquatenus disponere, sed abbati futuro resignanda omnia in sua integritate conservare. Domini igitur regis super ecclesia de Wi in fundo monasterii sita nulla debuit esse donatio, quia vacantis cenobii non tam patronus quam custos, nullam in eo proprii iuris obtinuit possessionem, nec de iure alieno facere debuit donationem. Cum ergo palam sit quod sit irrita donatio, consequens omnino est ut etiam irrita debeat esse presentatio, [fo. 129^v] quia qui non potuit dare nec debuit presentare. Presentatus domino Cantuariensi electo per eum dicitur fuisse admissus, sed licet ratione precedentium minus canonica fuerit institutio, et ideo irrita, alia tamen consideratione nulla fuit nec esse potuit, quoniam electione archiepiscopi per summum pontificem nondum confirmata, electus admittendi vel instituendi non habuit potestatem.[1] Consecratus a domino papa archiepiscopus, et a sede apostolica in plenitudine potestatis reversus, quod minus antea fecerat dicitur solennius fecisse, et episcopali auctoritate confirmasse, sed nulla esse debuit vel potuit ipsius confirmatio, cum in ipsius consecratione sint omnia a summo pontifice cassata que ante consecrationem eius electionis tempore ab ipso fuerant instituta. Cum igitur electionis tempore facta fuerit presentatio et presentati institutio, dum omnia in consecratione revocantur in irritum, constat etiam quod quicquid circa presens negotium est attemptatum sub universitate concluditur, unde et in irritum proculdubio revocatur. Quia enim respectu apostolice auctoritatis modica aut nulla esse dinoscitur potestas episcopalis, que ab excellentiori dissolvuntur per inferioris ordinis gradum nequeunt accipere firmitatem. Totius itaque rei serie diligentius considerata, dum omnia in iuris ecclesiastici preiudicium perpetrata videntur, firmitatis sue non immerito robur amittunt, quoniam in ecclesiastice soliditatis radice non subsistunt. Plene institutionis postulat pars adversa be[fo. 130]neficium

---

[1]Cf. R.L. Benson, *The Bishop-elect* (Princeton, 1968), esp. pp. 167 ff.

cum potius beneficio portionis privari meruerit, quod in prefata ecclesia de Wi nullo rationis titulo dinoscitur possidere.
Spoliatum est iure suo vacans monasterium, nec tenentur iniuste
spoliati in iure suo respondere nisi primum restituti, unde et
dominus abbas de Bello pro monasterio suo agens iuris sui petit
restitutionem, postmodum paratus ad exhibendam iusticie pleni-
tudinem.' Cum in hunc modum magister Gerardus in omnium audientia perorasset, et allegationem suam legum ac decretorum que
hic inserere longum erat auctoritatibus comprobasset, iamque
pro allegatione partium ferenda esset sententia, delegati
iudices haud dubium quin adverse parti respectu potestatis
deferentes, sententiam sub dissimulatione reliquerunt et partibus ut componerent preceperunt. Abbas cui plus erat desiderio
pacis bonum quam lis atque contentio ex multarum consideratione
circumstantiarum decrevit compositionem non respuere, sciens
se iam nichil eorum que possederat amissurum, immo magis confisus se amplius adepturum. Formata est illic viris discretis
hinc inde intervenientibus huiusmodi compositio, ut scilicet
decimis de Bekewelle et Beawerdregge et Holeford ad sacristariam
monasterii de Bello ab antiquo assignatis in eadem assignatione
permanentibus, de cetero Godefridus de Luci totam ecclesiam de
Wi nomine vicarie perpetue sub pensione xv marcarum monasterio
annuatim solvenda possideret. Et quoniam ut predictum est Godefridus tunc temporis in transmarinis moram faciebat, in [fo.
130^V] reditu suo ad monasterium Belli in propria persona
accederet, instrumenta omnia que vel regis vel archiepiscopi
nomine super prefata ecclesia habere videbatur, monasterio
resignaret, munimentumque per quod compositio firmaretur a solo
monasterio reciperet. In hunc modum formata et hinc inde approbata compositione, abbas Deo et beato Martino gratias agens in
sua rediit, iam tanto hilarior quanto de causa sua securior ...

The chronicle describes the abbot's joyful return, and embarks
on Godfrey de Lucy's visit to fulfil his obligation under the
agreement; but breaks off before this is concluded owing to the
loss of a quire.

170

5-19 MARCH 1179. THIRD LATERAN COUNCIL

For the council in general see Mansi, xxii, esp. cols.
213-17, 239-40, 458-68 (attendance lists); Alberigo,
pp. 205-10 (bibliography etc.), 211-25 (canons); Foreville, *Latran*, pp. 134-58, 194-223 (and for composition,
pp. 387-90, cf. 140 and n. 123). On mss. of the canons,
see esp. U.-R. Blumenthal and M. Bertram in *Bulletin of
Medieval Canon Law* (forthcoming).[1]

Like the Second Lateran, the Third was summoned to celebrate
the end of a schism: the conclusion of the papal schism, peace
with the emperor, and the climax of the long pontificate of
Alexander III. Its canons included the election decree which
has formed the basis of papal electoral law ever since, and its
decrees reflected both the rapid growth of heresy and the wide
pastoral concerns of the pope and of many of the bishops. The
Second Lateran had been very shortly followed by the completion
and circulation of Gratian's *Decretum*. The epoch of Alexander
III saw unprecedented activity in the canon law courts, and
the first beginnings of decretal collections. Although the collections of this period are informal and unofficial, the council
gave a considerable stimulus to them; shortly before and shortly
after came the first attempts at systematic organization of
decretals, and the canons of the council itself occur frequently
in the collections of the 1180s and 1190s. Even apart from the
collections, the council and its canons were widely known and
extensively recorded - far more so than those of any previous
papal council - in the pages of English chronicles, and also of
one cartulary.

The summons was brought by the papal subdeacon Albert de
Summa in the summer of 1178;[2] the council was held in March

---

[1] See also the unpublished Inaugural-Dissertation of W. Herold, 'Die
Canones des 3 Lateran Konzils (1179)', Bonn, 1950-2.
[2] On the summons, see Tillmann, p. 78; cf. p. 79 n.; Foreville, *Latran*,
p. 133; cf. *Gesta Henrici II*, i.206, 209-10; Hoveden, ii.167, 171; Diceto,
i.429-30 (where the bishop of Winchester specifically has himself excused).

1179. The attendance lists show the following English and Welsh
bishops as present: Bath (Reginald FitzJocelin), Hereford
(Robert Foliot), Norwich (John of Oxford), Durham (Hugh du
Puiset), St. Asaph (Adam), and St. Davids (Peter de Leia).[1]
This may not be complete, but we have no clear evidence of the
presence of any other English bishop. Of the other clergy, Peter
of Blois, archdeacon of Bath, and Walter Map, were certainly
present.[2] Map tells us that he was at the council, and gives a
highly coloured account of how he made fun of Waldo, the founder
of the Waldensians. It was written by an eye-witness, probably
very soon after the council, since most of the *De nugis* was
composed or drafted c.1180-1; but its value is slight. 'No
doubt he was at the Lateran Council; very likely he was involved
in some discussion with the Waldensians; but this particular
account sits with others of heretics deliberately garbled, and
it is most unlikely that Waldo and his companions were treated
quite so shabbily as this.'[3] It has been suggested that Hugh de
Mareni, dean of St. Paul's, may have died on his return from the
council; but there is no positive evidence that he was there.[4]
Master Gerard Pucelle was exempted from clause 2, on schismatics,
in view of his visit to Cologne during the schism.[5]

English mss. containing canons of the council fall roughly
into two groups.

The *Gesta* gives a note of the Irish and Scottish bishops present; this is
repeated in Hoveden in similar words, with the addition of a statement on
the English bishops; explaining that there were only four present, and how
they excused the poor attendance: 'Episcopi autem Angliae constanter asseru-
erunt, quod ad generale concilium domini papae quattuor episcopi de Anglia
tantum Romam mittendi sunt' (Hoveden, ii.171). Cf. pp.779-80, 818, 846.

[1]Mansi, xxii.217, 467; the former list seems to include the archbishop
of Canterbury, but comparison of the lists suggests that 'Canterbury' is the
provincial heading. Although Gilbert Foliot of London (now an old man) was
apparently not present, he may have made a contribution to the election
decree by drawing the pope's attention to a Roman Law text suggesting the
principle of the two-thirds' majority, in a letter written in 1160 (*GFL*, no.
133, p. 176; cf. ibid. n. 4.
[2]For Peter, *Extra*, iii.22.3; for Walter Map, *De nugis curialium*, i.31,
ed. M.R. James (Oxford, 1914), pp. 60-2. Gerald of Wales tells us that some
canons of St. Davids were also present (see below).
[3]R.B. Brooke, *The Coming of the Friars* (London, 1975), p. 72; cf. pp.
151-2.
[4]*GF*, pp. 205-6 (for the date of Hugh's death see also Le Neve, i.5).
[5]Foreville, *Latran*, p. 143; *PL* cc. 1200; for the visit to Cologne see
JS, *Letters*, ii, pp. xxviii f., xxxi, xxxix.

1. *Decretal collections.*[1] These are mostly of the 1180s,
though some mss. have additions of the 1190s; but they all
represent collections first put together before 1190, mostly
before *c.*1185.

'English': *Cantuariensis*, BL ms. Royal 10. B. iv, fos. 62-5,
from Canterbury; *Roffensis*, BL ms. Royal 10. C. iv, fos. 137-
139^V, from Rochester; *Dunelmensis*, Durham Cathedral Lib. ms.
C. III. 1, fos. 11-12^V, from Durham. (*Regalis*, BL ms. Royal
15. B. iv, from Worcester, has two canons on fo. 108; cf. Duggan, p. 84).

'Bridlington': *Claudiana*, BL ms. Cotton Claud. A. iv, fos.
204^V-206^V (formerly 200^V-202^V).

'Worcester': *Claustroneoburgensis*, nos. 1-24;[2] *Cheltenhamen-*
sis, BL ms. Egerton 2819, fos. 11-16; *Cottoniana*, BL ms. Cotton
Vitell. E. xiii, fos. 204-10.

Appendix Concilii Lateranensis (*c.*1181 x 5), now generally
acknowledged to be of English origin;[3] the canons are an integral part of the *Appendix*, and survive in the following
English mss.: Cambridge, St. John's Coll. ms. F 11 (148), fos.
61^V-77^V; Lincoln Cathedral Lib. ms. 121, fos. 54-58^V.

They are also included in mss. of the Anglo-Norman school
probably of Norman origin, *Tanner, Sangermanensis,* and *Abrin-*
censis I;[4] but with the *Appendix* and *Collectio Tanner* one moves
into the world of cosmopolitan collections in which the canons
moved freely in the late twelfth century.

---

[1]The terminology used is as in C. Duggan, *Twelfth-Century Decretal Col-*
lections (London, 1963), to which we are much.indebted. The Institute of
Medieval Canon Law (Berkeley, California) has in hand the following major
works on this subject: *Studies in the Collections of 12th Century Decretals,*
ed. from the papers of Walther Holtzmann by C.R. and M.G. Cheney (Monumenta
Iuris Canonici, series B: Corpus Collectionum, iii, Vatican, 1979); *Decre-*
tales ineditae saec. XII, ed. from the papers of Walther Holtzmann by S.
Chodorow and C. Duggan (forthcoming); *Regesta decretalium saec. XII*, ed. as
above (forthcoming).

[2]Cf. F. Schönsteiner in *Jahrbuch des Stiftes Klosterneuburg*, ii (1909),
26-30.

[3]See esp. S. Kuttner in *Traditio*, vi (1948), 349 and nn.; S. Kuttner and
E. Rathbone in *Traditio*, vii (1949-51), 283-4; Duggan, p. 53, and in *Tradi-*
tio, xviii (1962), 459-68; *Studies in the Collections* (n. 1), pp. 116-34.

[4]See above, pp. 798, 975; W. Holtzmann, 'Die Dekretalensammlungen des 12.
Jahrhunderts: 1. Die Sammlung Tanner'; in *Festschrift zur Feier des*
200jährigen Bestehens der Akademie der Wissenschaften in Göttingen, Phil.-
Hist. Klasse (1951), pp. 83-145.

2. *Chronicles etc.* The canons (and brief accounts of the
Council) are in *Gesta Henrici II*, i.221-38; Hoveden, ii.172-89;
Newburgh, i.206-23; there are also extracts from cc. 14 and 9
in Diceto, i.430.[1] There are a few canons in Giraldus, *Opera*,
i.323-4; he also refers to the council at i.48; iii.50, 77,
109, 163, 168, and describes a protest by the canons of St.
Davids concerning the dignity of their church.[2] The canons are
in the cartulary of Rievaulx, BL ms. Cotton Julius D. i, fos.
7-18^V (formerly 3-14^V); *Cart. Rievaulx*, ed. J.C. Atkinson (Surtees Soc. 1889), pp. 362-76. They sit alone in Cambridge, Fitzwilliam Museum, ms. McClean 134, fos. 1-8^V, a 12th-cent. English
ms. of unknown provenance.[3]

171

1179. NOTE BY RALPH DE DICETO ON THE ECCLESIASTICAL COURTS

After describing the judicial and administrative arrangements
made by Henry II in 1179 (Diceto, i.434-5), Diceto comments on
the good harvest, and, as a further sign of divine blessing,
how matters were more considerately conducted in both civil and
ecclesiastical courts - and so he introduces the passage which
follows, which leads him into the problem of corruption in
church courts, and is a characteristic illustration of his
practical interest in the administration of canon law. In 1179
he was archdeacon of Middlesex.[4]

From Ralph de Diceto, *Ymagines historiarum*, mss. Da, fo.
99, and Db, fo. 106^V (see p. 964); ed. W. Stubbs, i.436-7.

---

[1]Whence Wendover and Matthew Paris (see Paris, *Ch. Maj.* ii.310-11). For
the Inner Temple ms. of Hoveden, see p. 971.

[2]Cf. Conway Davies, i.209, 288.

[3]See M.R. James, *A Descriptive Catalogue of the McClean Collection of
Manuscripts in the Fitzwilliam Museum* (Cambridge, 1912), pp. 281-2. The
canons now virtually comprise the whole ms.; James prints a note of the
former contents of the book in which they were once bound up, which seem
quite miscellaneous.

[4]Archdeacon 1152/3-1180/1, dean of St. Paul's 1180/1 to *c*.1200; Le Neve,
1066-1300, i.5-6, 15-16.

Rursus gratia celestis hoc anno terrenas potestates in eam erga subditos affectionem induxit, ut singulis querelas habentibus tam in foro civili quam ecclesiastico sancta consideratione prospectum esse non dubites. Eo namque decursum est ut in comitiis, sicut supra diximus, rege procurante presideant presules, et disceptationibus questionum forensium, que sanguinis penam non irrogant, audientiam suam accomodent. Rursus, ad consistorium archiepiscopi Cantuariensis, si veritas tibi comes fuerit, cum animi tranquillitate potes securus accedere pro merito cause calculum reportaturus. Ne sui siquidem assessores quos in dandis consiliis et litibus dirimendis habet assiduos, a via veritatis exorbitent, et in pecunie corruptelam partium studia litigantium universi negotii spem universam reponant, cur et quando terribiles in medium proponi scripturas civiliter introductum sit,[1] memoriter tenuerunt. Nam omnes communi sponsione devincti, tactis sacrosanctis evangeliis publice iuraverunt nemine deferente se conservaturos inposterum modis omnibus suas manus immunes a munere. Promisit illud idem archiepiscopus in verbo veritatis apud Pageham.[a]

172

21 OCTOBER 1184, 30 NOVEMBER-2 DECEMBER 1184. MEETINGS FOR THE ELECTION OF THE ARCHBISHOP OF CANTERBURY

As in 1173, the central issue was the dispute between monks and bishops as to who should elect; Gervase provides the only detailed narrative, but it is naturally coloured by the monks' point of view. Archbishop Richard had died on 16 February; the dispute was fought out between *c*.June and December; the monks had a preliminary meeting with the king on 4 August at Reading; they met again in late October. Finally, in December, came the postulation of Baldwin, bishop of Worcester, both by the bishops (2 December) and by the monks (16 December). The election

---

[a] Pageham Db.

---

[1] Cf. *Codex Justiniani*, 3.1.13.

was confirmed by Pope Lucius III at the request of the messengers of the king, the bishops, and the monks, by 15 March 1185. Baldwin was enthroned and received the pallium, brought by the papal notary Transmundus, on 19 May 1185. He probably received the temporalities about the same time.[1] The abortive meeting of 21 October 1184 (23 October according to Diceto) and the successful meetings of 30 November-2 December were gatherings of the English clergy, presumably of the province.

Gervase of Canterbury, Chronica, s.a. 1184

> From mss. Ga, fos. 125^V-128, Gc. fos. 98-100 (see pp. 771, 973 n.: select variants of Gc); ed. W. Stubbs, i. 313-20; also W. i. 488-9.

Rex autem Anglie misit nuntios et litteras ad conventum Cant(uariensis) ecclesie, precipiens ut cum priore suo plures ad eum mitterent monachos ad Winlesores. Quo cum venissent die ordinationis sancti Dunstani [21 Oct.] simul cum episcopis et clero Anglie, dixit ad monachos rex, 'Miseremini mei, domini mei et amici mei; vos enim estis fideles mei et amici, omnes fere nati de terra mea, unde michi magis tenemini. Rogo igitur vos per fidem quam michi debetis, loquimini cum episcopis meis, et inter vos [Ga, fo. 126 (127)] tale habetote consilium, quo Dei et sancte ecclesie honor conservetur, et regni status perseveret in pace, et ut honor debitus michi conservetur indempnis, quem predecessores mei in hac causa noscuntur habuisse.' Et plura in hunc modum. Cui cum prior breviter respondisset de benivolentia gratuita gratias agens, in eundem fere modum seorsum cum episcopis rex ipse absque mediatore locutus

---

[1]Le Neve, ii.5, citing Gervase, i.309-26 (see below); Diceto, ii.22-4, 36. See also JL 15387, 15388; *Ep. Cant.,* p. 4. Cf. H. Mayr-Harting in *JEH* xvi (1965), 51-2. For the process of translation see esp. Cheney, *Pope Innocent III and England,* pp. 71 ff. Diceto represents the bishops' viewpoint, Gervase the monks'; Diceto is briefer. He records a meeting of the monks in Reading on 4 Aug., and dates the next meeting 23 Oct.; in the dénouement, he states that the bishop of London, as dean of the Province, announced Baldwin's election (ii.22-4). On Transmundus, see Sheila J. Heathcote in *Analecta Cisterciensia,* xxi (1965), 35-109, 167-238, esp. 35-46.

est. Cum igitur episcopi et prior cum monachis convenissent
in unum de consilio regis tractaturi, dixerunt episcopi: 'Miramur admodum quod nos episcopos a consiliis vestris separatis,
cum simus ecclesie vestre professi et fidem debeamus ecclesie
Cant(uariensi) sicut et vos.' Et episcopus Bathon(ensis):[1]
'Non est' inquit 'aliquis princeps qui consilio nostro consi-
liari non valeat'. Pluraque in hunc modum proferebant. At
prior: 'Non' inquit 'separamus vos a consiliis nostris, cum
fidem omnimodam per professionem debitam ecclesie Cant(uariensi), ut dicitis, debeatis; sed sunt quedam consilia quibus
de iure interesse debetis: sunt et consilia que ad solum pertinent conventum, maxime in hac electione scilicet usque ad pub-
licam electionis pronunciationem. Rogamus igitur vos quatinus
in hac electione nobiscum stare velitis ut professi, ut fideles,
ut episcopi Cant(uariensis) ecclesie suffraganei, ut mater
vestra, scilicet Cantuariensis ecclesia etsi privata et privi-
legiata non valeat, canonica saltem gaudeat libertate.' Londoniensis autem ad hec indignans, nimia cecus senectute et
quasi lingua mutilata balbutiens, dixit: 'Fecistisne electionem?' Cui prior: 'Etsi aliquam fecimus nominationem nullam
tamen celebravimus electionem.' Lond(oniensis) ad hec: 'Nimium'
inquid 'processistis, qui sine nobis contra domini pape mandatum quempiam eligere presumpsistis.' Et prior: 'Nunquid super
hoc domini pape mandatum[a] habetis?' At illi: 'Utique habemus.'
Adlate sunt itaque vix tandem agente priore domini pape littere
precipientes quatinus infra xl dies episcopi Anglie, prior et
conventus Cantuariensis idoneam eligerent personam. Dixit autem
ille[b] Lond(oniensis): 'Audistisne quod dominus papa nos in
electione facienda vobis preposuit?' 'Fiat' inquit prior 'ut
vos in litteris suis dominus papa preposuerit, nos tamen penitus non exclusit, unde litterarum istarum petimus transcriptum
ut secundi, vos autem ut primo positi, bulla gaudeatis.' Cum
igitur super hoc rescripto tradendo, vel non tradendo, multa

---

[a] quempiam ... mandatum *om.* Gc (mandatum ... mandatum).   [b] ille Gc; *om.* Ga.

---

[1] No doubt the reference to the bishop of Bath, later the monks' candidate as Baldwin's successor, is significant (see below, p. 1036).

hinc inde prolata fuissent, ad hoc tandem perventum est ut
episcopi absque regis [Ga, fo. 126^v (127^v)] licentia litteras
illas transcribere non auderent. Si in tantillo episcopi matri
sue defecerunt, ut dicam nichilo, quid in summo facerent negotio in subsequentibus utique clarebit. Dum itaque de his et
huiusmodi cum monachis Cant(uariensibus) plura conferrent
episcopi, et rex interea aliis indulgeret negotiis, timens ne
si collocutione diutina consentirent ipse penitus ab electione
excluderetur, vel si dissentirent appellatione interposita
electio differretur, properavit episcopos a monachis segregare,
videlicet ut ipse, solus inter utrosque mediator existens,
omnium mentes ad libitum suum regeret, et utriusque partis simul
et electi, quasi ex sua liberalitate et studio gratiam obti-
neret. Evocati sunt itaque caute episcopi quasi cum rege seorsum essent locuturi, sed denuo non sunt reversi. Divisi itaque
ab alterutrum monachi scilicet et episcopi solius regis nutum
et nuntium expectabant. Nam solus discurrebat inter eos,^{a} nec
quicquam ex secretis quispiam scire poterat nisi quantum rex
proferre volebat. Nitebatur enim^b ut asserebat episcopos indu-
cere ad consentiendum persone quam prior et monachi nominaverant,
cui et ipse rex suum prebuerat assensum. Promiserat enim priori
et monachis in verbo regio cum iuramento post multa convitia
quod unum ex nominatis suis habituri essent archiepiscopum;
elaboratum est tandem ipso rege mediante ut eidem persone
utcunque episcopi consentirent. De persona igitur eligenda tandem utcumque sopita questione, de electione facienda et persona
nominanda mota est controversia. Dicebant enim episcopi quod
suum erat archiepiscopum Cant(uariensem) utpote suum metropoli-
tanum eligere, et quod episcopus Lond(oniensis) eiusdem scilicet
Cant(uariensis) ecclesie decanus personam debeat nominare. Retulit hec priori et monachis rex. At prior: 'Non' inquid 'fiet
istud. Ante prioratu Cant(uariensi) carebo, ante de ecclesia
exibo, ante in terra aliena exulabo. Non hec in diebus meis
Cant(uariensi) ecclesie inferetur contumelia, non persone mee
hec improperabitur infamia. Debet enim conventus Cant(uariensis)

---

^{a}inter eos disc. Gc. ^{b}quidam Gc.

de iure et antiqua consuetudine suum pastorem et pontificem
eligere, et qui prior est personam nominare. Iustumne est ut
episcopi absque conventu quemcunque voluerint Cantuaritis mit-
tant archiepiscopum? Nequaquam.' Audientes hec episcopi, indig-
nantes dixerunt: 'Non est ita, sed nostra est electio et
episcopi Londoniensis prima vox et nominatio.' Dum hec itaque
diutius usque in desperationem pacis [Ga, fo. 127 (128)] inter
eos rege mediante protenderetur altercatio, rex tandem mestus
ait ad priorem: 'Non potest, ut video, res ista hoc modo
procedere, quia non valeo vobis episcopos vel vos episcopis
concordare; medium aliquod^a videamus quo utriusque partis pax
et iusticia conservetur. Pax enim omnimodis amplectenda est,
cum ille valde sapiens fuerit qui dixit, fiat pax in diebus
nostris;[1] pro Deo pacem diligite, pacem querite et, quantum
potestis, paci consentite.' Innuit autem rex Randulfo de Glan-
villa prefecto Anglie, quem tunc forte secum duxerat, ut loqueretur, qui dixit: 'Perturbatio ista pessima est, et tam vobis quam
toti Anglicane ecclesie pernitiosa. Revertimini ad vos: non enim
potestis ita procedere quia nullo modo permittunt episcopi. Sed
animos vestros paulisper flectite, et ad mediam viam quam dominus repperit rex corda vestra inclinate. Indempnitati vestre
studet dominus meus rex; de iure vestro nichil peribit vel
parum, et forte facilius inclinabuntur episcopi ad consentiendum. Est autem hoc quod petit dominus rex ut concedatis, videlicet ut episcopus Londoniensis vel alius electionem dicat hoc
modo: "Nos episcopi et prior et conventus ecclesie Christi
Cant(uariensis) cum assensu domini regis eligimus istum"; vel
ut prior electionem pronuntiet et dicat, "Episcopi Anglie et
ego prior et conventus Cantuariensis cum assensu domini regis
eligimus istum." Quid enim nocebit si episcopos vestros in
electione nomine tenus preponatis?' Ad hec prior: 'Conferemus'
ait 'cum fratribus nostris et citissime responsum reportabo.'
Metuentes igitur et metientes monachi malitiam temporis, et
libertatem suam saltem palliatam habere cupientes, prebuerunt
assensum peticionibus regiis, sic tamen ut prior Cantuariensis
quod reliquum erat electionis exequeretur. Quo audito precepit

---

^{a}aliquid Gc.

---

[1]Cf. Ecclus. 50, 25.

rex ut hec pacis pactio scriberetur. Timentibus autem monachis
ne per hoc scriptum eis laqueus tenderetur invisus si episcopis
traderetur, dixit rex: 'Ne timeatis, non enim hac de causa
scriptum peto ut episcopis tribuatur, sed ne quid in re agenda
superfluum addatur vel necessarium subtrahatur.' Composito
autem scripto dato et accepto, rogavit episcopos rex ut si non
aliter vellent huic saltem forme pacis consentirent. Disputatum
est super hoc diutius, et tandem nec propter regis metum^a manifeste voluerunt contradicere, nec plane absque consensu coepiscoporum suorum qui ibi non aderant consentire. Cumque
videret rex eorum pertinatiam diemque protractum in vesperam,
distulit hoc negotium usque ad festum [Ga, fo. 127^v (128^v)]
sancti Andree, precipiens omnibus ut in predicta festivitate
omnes apud Lond(oniam) convenirent, sub certissima spe archiepiscopum de quo sermo habitus est suscipiendi. Iuravit quoque
priori et monachis rex quod numquam ab eis discederet, nec
quicquam conventionis inite aliquatenus mutaret, et quod episcopos ad consentiendum induceret; et quoniam^b priori et aliis
quibusdam verba dura et contumeliosa dixerat, cum osculo pacis
veniam petiit et omnes in pace dimisit. Igitur singuli ad
propria redierunt. Et denuo ad festum sancti Andree apud Lon-
d(oniam) convenerunt. Credens itaque prior promissionibus
regiis et sperans se iam iamque suum archiepiscopum suscepturum,
alacriter accessit, sed in ipso aditu omnia in contrarium
mutata conspexit. Nam a primo die in crastinum, de crastino in
diem tertium dilatum est negotium. Die vero tertia, quarto
scilicet nonas Decembris, cum monachi Cantuarienses una cum
priore suo resiederent colloquentes et mirantes admodum quorsum
ista dilatio tenderetur, misit ad eos rex Randulfum prefectum
Anglie aliosque spectabiles viros qui mentes monachorum tam a
spe apud Winlesores concepta quam a tota intentione sua tempta-
verunt deviare. Maxime tamen laboraverunt efficere ut monachi,
suo penitus omisso proposito, cum episcopis de faciendo tractarent negotio ac si nichil ante esset inchoatum. Quibus prior
in hunc modum respondit: 'Miramur admodum super his que nobis
affertis. Scitis enim quid convenit inter dominum nostrum regem

---

^{a}metum regis Gc. ^{b}quem Gc.

et nos, cum altera vice in presentia ipsius essemus. Unanimes enim fuimus de persona quam ei nominavimus, et cum ipse nobis suum prebuisset assensum de electione facienda sola remansit nominatio. Forma etiam eligendi scripto, ut scitis, commendata est. Sic a curia cum gratia domini regis recessimus, sic conventui nostro ea que facta sunt recitavimus, sic etiam nunc ad vocationem domini nostri regis[a] accessimus. Et quia nobis nova sunt et miranda que proponitis, nec eorum que diximus absque conventu nostro quicquam mutari poterit, domini regis presentiam optamus, ut cum illo presentialiter loquamur.' Relata sunt continuo regi que audita sunt. Ille vero nonnullis abbatibus secum assumptis et quasi de preteritis dissimulans dixit ad monachos: 'Ite domini mei, ite, et cum episcopis de pastore eligendo pacifice tractate, et quemcunque unanimi consensu [Ga, fo. 128 (129)] inter vos elegeritis, vel quodcumque feceritis, ratum michi erit et gratum meumque gratanter dabo assensum.' Cui cum prior respondisset ea que superius scripta sunt, que et nuntiis eius dixerat, ipse inter alia sic respondit:[b] 'Verum est: sic altera vice discessistis. Sed scitote quod a consilio regni mei nec volo recedere nec valeo, ne videar in regno meo scisma vel discordiam enutrire; sed pro Deo pacifice loquimini cum episcopis et abbatibus meis, et mementote quia vox populi vox domini.' Mira res! Nuper apud Windlesores festinavit quamtotius ab episcopis monachos separare, nunc e contrario nisus est tum per se tum per alios eos simul coadunare. Noverat enim mentes eorum et impetus, et quod in omnibus ecclesie necessitatibus maximis regis magis quam Dei favorem querebant. Fecerunt similiter et patres et predecessores eorum. Nam sancto Anselmo, tempore regis Willelmi, etiam obedientiam abnegaverunt; Theodbaldo archiepiscopo pro rege Stephano infesti fuerunt; sancto martiri Thome pro rege isto Henrico adversarii facti sunt; in electione Ricardi archiepiscopi supplantatores fuerunt; nunc etiam in electione ista aliquid sinistrum machinari conantur. Incurrerant enim quidam ex ipsis regis indignationem et odium, quam nunc quolibet modo mitigare curabant ...

---

[a] dom. regis n. Gc.   [b] respondit *after* ipse Gc.

In the end, after further negotiation, the prior named three candidates, the bishops Baldwin of Worcester as their nominee; and the argument was brought to a rapid conclusion by the sudden and unexpected formal celebration of the election of Baldwin by the bishops. After further exchanges Henry II went in person to Canterbury on 14 December; and on the 16th the monks duly elected Baldwin, in the king's presence, in the Chapter House at Westminster Abbey.[1]

By papal bulls of 17 and 18 December 1185 Baldwin was made legate for the province of Canterbury.[2]

1184-5. LEVY FOR THE DEFENCE OF THE HOLY LAND AND MEETING OF BISHOPS AND CLERGY: see below, no. 173

173

1166-90. LEVIES FOR THE DEFENCE OF THE HOLY LAND, AND THE SALADIN TITHE; AND MEETINGS OF BISHOPS (1184, 19 FEB. 1190)

See R.C. Smail, 'Latin Syria and the West, 1149-1187', *TRHS* 5th ser., xix (1969), 1-20, esp. 12-19; S.K. Mitchell, *Taxation in Medieval England* (New Haven, 1951), pp. 114-23; F.A. Cazel, 'The Tax of 1185 in aid of the Holy Land', *Speculum,* xxx (1955), 385-92.

In 1166, 1184-5, and 1188 plans were made to tax the faithful of Henry II's dominions to provide aid for the Holy Land. To the Crusading historian the first two are a part of the long and tortuous story of Henry II's many attempts to show interest in, and ultimate failure to join, a crusade.[3] To the historian

---

[1]See above, pp. 1015-16 and references; esp. Diceto, ii.23-4.

[2]JL 15520; *EHR* ix (1894), 536 ff.; dated Dec. 1185 but sent with the bulls of 12 Jan. 1186 announcing Pope Urban III's election (JL 15518-19; Hoveden, ii.305 f. See Tillmann, p. 34 n. 119; for Urban's bull on his election, see *GFL*, no. 269 and n.; *PUE* iii, no. 375 and n.).

[3]See Smail, p. 12; but substantial sums were somehow raised in the period 1185-7 (below, p. 1024 n. 1; Smail, p. 15). Mitchell, pp. 114 ff., seems to assume that some attempt was made to raise the taxes, but makes it clear that we have no evidence how successful they were.

of taxation they are of interest as the first experiments in taxing revenues and movable goods. The Saladin Tithe of 1188 was a much more substantial affair, and it was the prelude to the Third Crusade. The edict which led to the Saladin Tithe was issued in a royal council, but it was an ordinance issued by the king in a council which included prelates of his English and continental lands and barons of Anjou, Maine, and Touraine.

In 1165 Pope Alexander III, reacting to urgent appeals from the Latin kingdom, launched an appeal for a new crusade. It was alleged that Henry II was ready to set off in 1166;[1] but in the event the only outcome was a scheme for taxation on a new model in both the kingdom of France and England. There may have been a precedent in the tax levied by Louis VII before setting off on the Second Crusade in 1146.[2] There is evidence that the scheme in 1166 was for a tax of twopence in the pound on revenues and movables for the first year, followed by a penny in the pound for each of the four succeeding years, with certain exemptions, but in principle levied from all ranks of society able to pay.[3] There is a notice in the Pipe Roll which seems to indicate that substantial alms were carried to the east in 1166-7.[4] A similar tax was raised in the Latin Kingdom in 1183, and it seems that when the Patriarch of Jerusalem came to the west in 1184-5, Louis VII and Henry II planned a tax based on the levy of 1183.[5] This was to have been for three years: those with revenues of over £100 per annum paid £1 in £100 per annum; those with movables worth more than 100s., 5d. per 100s.; and so forth. How extensively this tax was levied is not known, although it seems certain that Henry sent

---

[1]*GFL*, no. 170, p. 241; see above, p. 947.

[2]Mitchell, p. 114 and refs.

[3]Mitchell, pp. 114-15, esp. nn. 3-6; Gervase, i.198-9; Torigny, pp. 226-7; Diceto, i.329.

[4]Smail, p. 12; *Pipe Roll 13 Henry II* (Pipe Roll Soc. xi, 1899), p. 194.

[5]Cazel, *Speculum*, xxx, 385-92 (establishing its date and authenticity); Mitchell, pp. 117-19; Smail, pp. 14-15; the ordinance for the French kingdom and Henry's French dominions (but with some reference also to England) was ed. W.E. Lunt, *EHR* xxxvii (1922), 235-42. Cazel, pp. 389, 391, argues that a letter of Archbishop Baldwin (Peter of Blois, *Ep.* 98, *PL* ccvii.306-8) refers to the collection of the tax in 1185 and shows that the ordinance of 1185 was also applied in England.

considerable sums to the Holy Land, and that this was not the
only occasion on which he did so.[1] In connection with this levy
a meeting of the English bishops and clergy was held in London.[2]

In July 1187 Saladin defeated the king of Jerusalem at the
battle of Hattin and made him prisoner; in October Jerusalem
fell. In November Duke Richard, the future Richard I, took the
cross, and on 21 January 1188 King Henry and King Philip II of
France followed his example.[3] A few days later Henry met the
magnates of his French dominions at Le Mans and promulgated the
tax, which was backed by a series of ordinances and also by a
group of privileges for crusaders authorized by the pope,
printed below. The king then crossed to England, and on 11
February 1188 in the royal Council of Geddington renewed the
ordinances for the tax, which was authorized for the English
kingdom.[4] Roger of Hoveden tells us that the king 'fecit recitari
omnia suprascripta capitula' at Geddington;[5] and Gervase lays out
cc. 5-12 below as edicts from the Council of Geddington. There
are sufficient variants in the texts to make tolerably clear
that Gervase had an independent source; but the difference in
standing between cc. 1-4 and 5-12, and the extent to which they
represent edicts of the two councils, is not entirely clear. The
reference to the pope in c. 5 might suggest that a group of
edicts are to follow which are not simply decisions of the
king's; but in fact the difference between the two sets is not
sustained. It seems best to print both as in the *Gesta* and
leave the question of their precise origin and status open.

The levy was in effect a tenth; and a levy of this kind on
such a scale was an alarming novelty, which provoked such a
reaction that the French king abandoned his attempt to collect

---

[1]Smail, pp. 14-15, esp. 15 n. 3 and refs; cf. above, p.1022; *Chronicles
and Memorials of the Reign of Richard I*, i, ed. W. Stubbs (RS, 1864), p. 26.
[2]*Gesta Henrici II*, i.311; cf. Hoveden, ii.383; W. i.488.
[3]Warren, p. 607; Smail, pp. 19-20 and refs.; *Chronicles and Memorials of
the Reign of Richard I*, i.14 ff., 32-3; *Gesta Henrici II*, ii.29-30. Cf.
Eyton,pp. 283-5. For the parallel French ordinance see Rigord, ed. H.F.
Delaborde (Paris, 1882-5), i.85-90.
[4]The ordinances printed below are placed by Roger of Hoveden in the *Gesta*
in the context of the council at Le Mans; the second set by Gervase (i.409-
10) in the Council of Geddington. Cf. Mitchell, p. 120.
[5]*Gesta*, ii.33; cf. Hoveden, ii.338.

it. In England the collection went forward, and the Pipe Roll
of 1 Richard I speaks of 25,000 marks going to the king; but
we cannot tell the full yield and the statements of the
chronicler Roger of Hoveden were evidently exaggerated.[1] On 6
July 1189 Henry II died at Chinon, and Richard ruled, and led
the Crusade, in his stead. One of the final preparations for
the crusade was in a meeting of bishops ('in conventu episcoporum') at Westminster on 19 February 1190, when Archbishop
Baldwin placed his see and church and its liberties under papal
protection before setting off for the east.[2]

We print below the text from *Gesta Henrici II*, with collations of the second set of ordinances from Gervase; there is a
full paraphrase or alternative version of both sets in Newburgh,
i.273-4.[3]

Ordinances relating to the Saladin tithe, from the Gesta Henrici
II, s.a. 1188

> From ms. Hb (p. 970), fos. 127-8, completed by Hh, BL ms.
> Harl. 3666, fos. 183-184 (*Gesta*);[4] ed. Stubbs, *Gesta,*
> ii.30-2; hence (cc. 1-4) Stubbs, *Charters* (edn. of 1913),
> pp. 188-9; collated with Hoveden, Hl (Bodl. ms. Laud
> Misc. 582, fos. 36-7) and, from c. 5, with Gervase, Ga,
> fos. 163-164, Gc. fo. 130^{r-v} (see pp. 771, 973 n.); ed.
> Stubbs, Hoveden, ii.355-7; Gervase, i.409-10. Variants
> of Ga or Gc alone are not noted.

---

[1]Mitchell, pp. 120-3; *Pipe Roll 1 Richard I* (ed. J. Hunter, Rec. Commission, 1844), p. 5. Roger of Hoveden in the *Gesta* tells us that Richard found
over £900,000 in gold and silver in his father's treasure (ii.76-7; but
perhaps for £90,000, since the equivalent is 100,000 marks in Hoveden,
iii.8; see Stubbs's note).

[2]Gervase, i.484; W. i.493 (from Paris, *Ch. Maj.* ii.357).

[3]Newburgh gives a version in this order: cc. 5, 1 (adding 'et de blado
futuri anni dabit similiter deciman'), 3, 7, 8; an additional clause giving
all who pay their tenth readily remission of 'medietatem pene sibi iniuncte';
then a part of c. 2 (but testified 'per septem legales homines'); cc. 10,
11, 12, 9 (the text has been checked by BL Stowe 62, fos. 88-9).

[4]Hb was burnt in the Cotton fire; following Stubbs we have completed its
text from Humphrey Wanley's very careful transcript in Harl. 3666, only
showing the details where there is any difficulty.

Henricus igitur rex Anglie, post crucis susceptionem, venit
usque Cenomannum,[a] et ibi ordinatum est ab eo in presencia
Ricardi filii eius comitis Pictavie et Willelmi Turonensis
archiepiscopi[1] et Balduuini Cantuariensis archiepiscopi et
Walteri Rothomagensis archiepiscopi, et in presentia Iohannis
Ebroycensis episcopi et Radulfi Andegavensis episcopi et
R(ainaldi) Cenomanensis et M(auricii) Namnetensis episcopi, et in
presentia [Hb, fo. 127^V] Hugonis de Nunaunt Cestrensis electi
et Elisiardi Sagiensis electi, et in presentia baronum Andegavie, Cenomannie, Turenorum, quod:

[1] Unusquisque decimam reddituum et mobilium suorum in elemosinam dabit[b] hoc anno, exceptis armis et equis et vestibus militum: exceptis similiter[c] equis et libris et vestibus et vestimentis et omnimoda capella clericorum et lapidibus preciosis
tam clericorum quam laicorum.

[2] Colligatur autem pecunia ista in singulis parochiis, presente presbytero parochie et archipresbytero et uno Templario
et uno Hospitalario et serviente domini regis et clerico regis,
serviente baronis et clerico eius et clerico episcopi; facta
prius excomunicatione ab archiepiscopis, episcopis, archipres-
byteris singulis in singulis parochiis super unumquemque, qui
decimam pretaxatam legitime non dederit, sub presencia et conscientia illorum qui debent, sicut dictum est, interesse.[d] Et
si aliquis iuxta conscientiam illorum minus dederit quam debuerit, eligentur de parochia quatuor vel sex viri legitimi qui
iurati dicant quantitatem illam quam ille debuisset dixisse,[e]
et tunc oportebit illum superaddere quod minus dedit.

---

[a]*Hoveden* (H1) *om. all that follows to* Turenorum *at the end of the paragraph, reading:* Cenomannum ubi consilio suorum ordinavit quod:.   [b]H1 *adds*
ad subventionem terre Ierosolomitane (*also* Newburgh).   [c]exceptis similiter
Hb; et exceptis H1 (*a note in* Hh *by* capella *below,* ? s. capellatura; *missing in* Hb).   [d]*In this sentence* H1 *puts* facta ... interesse (*om.* sicut
dictum est) *before* Colligatur ... episcopi.   [e]*? for* dedisse.

---

[1]Doubtless for Bartholomew, archbishop of Tours; the author of the *Gesta*
calls him William here and elsewhere (i.242; ii.209), perhaps by confusion
with the archbishop of Tyre.

[3] Clerici autem et milites qui crucem acceperunt[a] nichil de decima ista dabunt, sed de proprio suo et dominico, et quicquid homines illorum[b] debuerint ad opus illorum colligentur per supradictos et eis totum reddetur.

[4] Episcopi autem per literas suas in singulis parochiis episcopatuum suorum facient nunciari et[c] in die Natalis et sancti[d] Stephani et sancti Iohannis ut unusquisque decimam pretexatam infra Purificationem beate Virginis[e] penes se colligat,[f] sequenti die et deinceps, illis presentibus qui dicti sunt, ad locum quo vocatus fuerit, unusquisque[g] persolvat.

[5 (1)][1] Preterea statutum est a Romano pontifice[h] quod quicumque[i] clericus vel laicus crucem susceperit[j] ab omnibus peccatis[k] de quibus penituerit et confessus fuerit, auctoritate Dei et beatorum apostolorum suorum[l] Petri et Pauli[m] liberatus est et absolutus.

[6 (2)] Dispositum est autem[n] a regibus et[n] archiepiscopis et episcopis et aliis principibus terre[n] quod omnes illi tam clerici quam laici qui hoc iter non arripient decimas reddituum et mobilium[o] suorum huius[p] anni, et omnium catallorum suorum tam in auro quam in argento et omnibus aliis dabunt, exceptis vestibus et libris[q] et vestimentis clericorum et capellanorum[r] et lapidibus preciosis tam clericorum quam laicorum, et exceptis equis et armis et vestibus militum ad usum proprii corporis[s] pertinentibus.

[7 (3)] Dispositum est[t] etiam quod omnes clerici,[u] milites et

---

[a]acceperunt Hb; acceperint Hl.   [b]illorum Hh (*lost in* Hb); eorum Hl.
[c]*om*. Hl.   [d]Hb *ins*. et.   [e]Hl *adds* Marie.   [f]Hl *adds* et.   [g]Hl *adds* legitime.   [h]Romano pontifice Hb; domino papa Hl.   [i]GaGc *start here with* quicunque.   [j]acceperit GaGc.   [k]peccatis Hh; peccatis suis GaGc; *om*. Hl.
[l]suorum Hh; *om*. HlGaGc.   [m]GaGc *add* et summi pontificis.   [n]*om*. GaGc.
[o]et mobilium *om*. GaGc.   Punius GaGc.   [q]libris et vestibus GaGc.
[r]capella GaGc.   [s]ad us. prop. corp. HbHl; ad proprium corporis usum GaGc.
[t]Dispositum est HbHl; Notandum GaGc.   [u]GaGc *add* et.

---

[1]Cc. 5-12 are nos. I-VIII in Gervase, ed. Stubbs, i.409-10. There is no ms. authority for these numbers.

servientes qui hoc iter arripient decimas terrarum suarum et[a] hominum suorum habebunt,[b] et pro se nichil[c] dabunt.

[8 (4)] Burgenses vero et rustici[d] qui sine licencia[e] crucem acceperint nichilominus decimas dabunt.

[9 (5)] Dispositum[f] est etiam[g] quod nullus enormiter iuret, et quod nullus ludat ad aleas vel ad decios, et quod nullus post proximum Pascha utatur verio vel grisio vel sabelina vel escarleta,[h1] et quod omnes contenti sint duobus ferculis ex empto; et quod nullus aliquam mulierem secum ducat[i] in peregrinatione nisi aliquam forte[j] [Hb, fo. 128] lotricem peditem de qua nulla habeatur suspicio; et quod nullus habeat pannos decisos vel laceatos.[k]

[10 (6)] Dispositum[l] est etiam[m] quod quicumque[n] clericus vel[o] laicus redditus suos ante susceptionem crucis invadiaverit,[p] exitus huius anni[q] integre habeat, et transacto[r] anno creditor[s] rehabeat; ita quod fructus quos inde perceperit[t] in solutione debiti computentur,[u] et debitum post susceptionem crucis quamdiu debitor erit in peregrinatione non usuret.

[11 (7)] Statutum est etiam[v] quod omnes clerici et laici qui in hac peregrinatione proficiscentur possunt[w] licite invadiare[x] redditus suos, sive ecclesiasticos[y] sive alios, a Pascha cum[z] iter arripuerint usque ad tres annos, ita quod creditores quicquid de creditoribus[aa] contingat fructus omnes reddituum quos

---

[a]GaGc *add* decimas.   [b]habebunt HlGaGc; habeant Hb.   [c]nichil pro se Hl.   [d]vero et rustici *om.* GaGc.   [e]Hl *adds* dominorum suorum.   [f]Statutum GaGc.   [g]*om.* GaGc.   [h]scarlato GaGc.   [i]ducat secum al. fem. GaGc.   [j]forte aliquam HlGaGc.   [k]laceatos HlGaGc; lace[Hb; laceratos Hh.   [l]Dispositum HhHl(]situm Hb); Statutum GaGc.   [m]*om.* GaGc.   [n]GaGc *add* sive.   [o]sive GaGc.   [p]invadiaverat GaGc.   [q]GaGc *add* inde.   [r]transito Hl (*lost in* Hb).   [s]GaGc *add* redditus.   [t]preceperit Hl.   [u]computetur Hh (*lost in* Hb).   [v]*om.* GaGc.   [w]possint GaGc.   [x]GaGc *add* omnes.   [y]Hl *adds* sive laicos.   [z]cum HbHl; in quo GaGc.   [aa]debitoribus GaGc.

---

[1]For vair, gris, and sable, see C. of Westminster 1138, c. 15; *escarleta* refers to luxury cloths ('scarlet').

in vadio habebunt a predicto Pascha usque ad tres annos integre percipiant.

[12 (8)] Dispositum[a] est etiam quod quicumque in peregrinatione decesserit, pecuniam suam quam secum in peregrinatione attulerit ad sustentationem servientium suorum et ad auxilium terre Ierusalem[b] et ad sustentationem pauperum dividet, iuxta consilium discretorum virorum qui ad hoc constituentur.[c]

Hiis igitur preordinatis elegit viros ecclesiasticos et alios, quos constituit per terras suas transmarinas ad supradictas decimas sibi colligendas de omnibus tam clericis quam laicis qui crucem non acceperint.

174

1190 AND c.15-16 OCTOBER 1190. LEGATION OF WILLIAM DE LONGCHAMP, BISHOP OF ELY, AND LEGATINE COUNCIL AT WESTMINSTER

On 5 June 1190 Pope Clement III issued a bull announcing the appointment of the royal chancellor and regent William de Longchamp, bishop of Ely (1189-97), as legate for England, Wales, and the part of Ireland under English rule; the legation was renewed by Celestine III (1191), but not exercised after 1191-2 (see p.1042).[1] Most of his time was spent in political activity and conflict, ending in his exile; but he held one council (and, so far as our evidence goes, only one). According to Diceto, it was held on 15 October at Westminster, and the bishop of London (Richard FitzNeal) sat on the legate's right, Winchester (Godfrey de Lucy) on his left (no. I below). According to Gervase of Canterbury, the legate's summons was followed

---

[a]Statutum GaGc.   [b]Ierosolomitane H1GaGc.   [c]statuentur GaGc; *the paragraph which follows is in Hb (and Hh) only; H1 paraphrases, and GaGc proceed with the Council of Geddington, in which Baldwin archbishop of Canterbury preached, excommunicated those who embarked on war within seven years, and pursued his quarrel with his cathedral chapter.*

---

[1]Tillmann, pp. 85-7 (p. 86 for the council); cf. esp. JL 16505, 16765.

by a long discussion with the bishop of Rochester, who claimed
to be archbishop's chaplain and vicar of the diocese in Archbishop Baldwin's absence on crusade, and the prior of Christ
Church, on arrangements for the consecration of the bishop of
Worcester and seating at the council.[1] The bishop claimed the
seat on the legate's right; the legate cited the rival claim of
the bishop of London, then offered the seat to the prior, who
declined. As on other occasions, Diceto represents London,
Gervase Canterbury in these disputes. In the event, Gervase
does not tell us who took the coveted seat, but dates the council 16 October against Diceto's fifteenth.[2] In a passing reference, Giraldus dates it to a Tuesday, which supports the sixteenth.[3] No indication of the business discussed is given by
Diceto or Gervase or the Bury annals,[4] but both Jocelin of
Brakelond and Richard of Devizes seem to attribute to this
occasion attacks on the Black Monks (see nos. II, III), Jocelin
describing abortive decrees against them, Richard of Devizes
referring to it a decision to remove monks from Coventry Cathedral. In fact the legate was promulgating a papal bull against
the monks, who had not been able to defend their case. They were expelled at Christmas 1190, but the secular chapter was short-
lived; after many efforts the monks were restored in 1197-8.[5]

I. *Ralph de Diceto, Ymagines Historiarum s.a. 1190*

> From Da, fo. 119; Db, fo. 130^V (see p. 964); ed. Stubbs,
> ii.85.

Habitum est regionale concilium apud Westm(onasterium), presidente Willelmo Eliensi episcopo et apostolice sedis legato,
idibus Octobris. Ricardus Lund(oniensis) episcopus tertius iuxta
pristinam regni consuetudinem ad dexteram legati sedem optinuit:
Godefridus Winton(iensis) episcopus ad sinistram.

---

[1] Gervase, i.486-8.
[2] It is of course possible that the council lasted two days or more.
[3] Giraldus, *Opera,* iv.429-30.
[4] *UGQ*, p. 136: 'Willelmus Elyensis episcopus apostolice sedis legatus
concilium celebravit apud Westmonasterium.'
[5] On the Coventry case see Knowles, *MO*, pp. 322-4.

II. *The Chronicle of Jocelin of Brakelond*[1]

> From BL ms. Harl. 1005, fo. 141^v (135^v); ed. H.E. Butler
> (NMT, 1949), p. 54.

Cum cancellarius, episcopus scilicet Eliensis, legati fungeretur officio et concilium celebraret apud Lundon(iam), et quedam
decreta proposuisset contra nigros monacos, loquens de vaga-
cione eorum ad sanctum Thomam et ad sanctum Ædmundum peregrina-
cionis optentu, et contra abbates loquens, prefiniens eis certum
numerum equorum: respondit abbas Samson: 'Nos non recipimus
aliquod decretum contra regulam sancti Benedicti, que permittit
abbatibus liberam dispositionem habere de monachis suis. Ego
vero baroniam sancti Ædmundi servo et regnum eius; nec suffi-
ciunt michi tredecim equi, sicut quibusdam aliis abbatibus, nisi
plures habeam ad execucionem regie iustitie conservande.'

III. *The Chronica of Richard of Devizes*

> From Cambridge, Corpus Christi Coll. ms. 339, fo. 28;
> also in BL ms. Cotton Domitian xiii, fo. 74. Ed. J.
> Appleby, NMT, 1963, p. 13 (in context of events of 1190).

Willelmus apostolice sedis legatus concilium tenuit apud Westmonasterium, in quo, ne nil ageretur quod de se predicaretur
in posterum, omnem religionem de Coventrensi ecclesia eliminan-
dam et clericos prebendarios loco monachorum preiudicavit
substituendos.

175

7 APRIL 1191, 4 MAY 1191. MEETINGS AT WESTMINSTER AND CANTER-BURY FOR THE CONSECRATION OF THE BISHOP OF WORCESTER

Robert, son of William FitzRalph, archdeacon of Nottingham, was
elected bishop of Worcester on 1 July 1190, but his consecration

---

[1] This is in the context of later events (the capture of Richard I), but
no other legatine council is recorded in these years and the political circumstances of 1191-3 seem to make a later date impossible.

was delayed owing to the absence of the archbishop of Canterbury on the Third Crusade and a dispute as to who should consecrate him; in March 1191 news came that Archbishop Baldwin
had died before Acre on 19 or 20 November 1190.[1] The elect of
Worcester had by this date obtained a papal letter instructing
the legate, William de Longchamp, to perform the task if the
bishops of London and Rochester were unwilling. A meeting was
held at Westminster on Palm Sunday, 7 April, for the consecration, but was faced with an appeal from the monks of Canterbury
Cathedral priory against the consecration being performed anywhere but at Canterbury. The outcome was a meeting of bishops
at Canterbury on 5 May, when the bishop-elect was duly consecrated. On the following day, 6 May, the king's mandate for the
election of Archbishop Baldwin's successor reached Canterbury:
see below.

Gervase of Canterbury, Chronica, s.a. 1191

From mss. Ga, fos. 191^V (192^V)-192^V (193^V), and Gc, fos.
157^V-158 (select variants, ignoring word order: see
pp. 771, 973 n.); ed. Stubbs, i.490-3.

Applicuit interea Robertus electus Wigorniensis cancellario
legato domini pape deferens litteras ut eum in Westmonasterio
consecraret, si quidem Londoniensis et Roffensis episcopi de
facienda consecratione non consentirent. Appellaverat enim
uterque. Convenientibus igitur episcopis Anglie apud Westmona-
st(erium) Dominica Palmarum, vii scilicet idus Aprilis, ut in
consecratione Wigorn(iensis) apostolicum exequerentur mandatum,
venerunt et monachi tres Cantuarie missi a conventu, et eisdem
episcopis huiusmodi litteras porrexerunt.

    Reverendis in Christo dominis at fratribus W(illelmo) Dei
gratia Heliensi episcopo, apostolice sedis legato, domini regis
cancellario, ceterisque episcopis Cantuariensis ecclesie

----

[1]Gervase, i.488, 490; *Ep. Cant.*, pp. 329-30; Le Neve, ii.5. For the
rights of the bishop of Rochester, etc., see *Ep. Cant.*, pp. 325 ff.; for
the whole story see Stubbs, ibid., pp. lxxxiv ff.; on the bishop, Le Neve,
ii.100.

suffraganeis, Osbernus[a] prior et conventus ecclesie Christi
Cant(uarie) salutem ab auctore salutis. Noverit sanctitas vestra
nos ad sedem apostolicam appellasse, ne Wigorniensis electus
alias quam in ecclesia Cant(uariensi), sicut [Ga, fo. 192 (193)]
moris est, consecretur, et ne quis vestrum qui indempnitati
ecclesie Cant(uariensis) vinculo professionis providere tenemini, alias quam in eadem ecclesia eius consecrationi interesse
presumat. Valete.

Hec audientes episcopi qui convenerant una cum legato con-
ferebant in unum quid facto opus esset. Si enim in Westmonasterio,
ut dominus papa preceperat, non fieret[b] consecratio, legatus
apostolicum non exequeretur mandatum. Si vero ibidem fieret,
matri sue Cant(uariensi) ecclesie debitam obedientiam videren-
tur abnegare. Omnibus tandem placuit ut in mensem consecratio
differretur, apud Cant(uariam) facienda. Recognitum est ibidem
coram legato simul et episcopis Roffensem episcopum Cant(uariensis) ecclesie proprium ab antiquo fuisse capellanum, eumque
vacante Cant(uariensi) sede ad vocationem conventus debere Cantuariam[c] accedere, crisma conficere,[d] et cetera sacramentalia
ministrare, eumque in expensis procurare deberet qui archiepiscopatum custodiret. Vivente autem archiepiscopo, sed absente vel
egrotante, ad vocationem eiusdem simul et procurationem debet accedere. Hec michi qui hec scribo insinuavit idem G(ilebertus) Roffensis
episcopus, huic matricule, ut verbo suo utar, ad preces ipsius
inserenda. Venit igitur Cant(uariam) ad proximum Pascha a conventu vocatus idem episcopus, et in curia canonicorum sancti
Gregorii hospitatus est, ne videretur ignorantibus ad expensas
fuisse monachorum si in eorum curia haberet hospitium.

IIII nonas Maii convenerunt apud Cantuariam episcopi vi,
videlicet Heliensis qui et legatus et cancellarius, et God(efri-
dus) Wintoniensis episcopus, Reg(inaldus) Bathoniensis, Sein-
f(ridus) Cicestrensis,[e] Gil(ebertus) Roff(ensis) et ille Hugo
Cestrensis. Hi cum in ecclesia Cant(uariensi) convenissent in
unum, accersito electo Wigornensi, ceperunt eiusdem examinationem facere contra modum et formam ecclesie Cant(uariensis).

---

[a] O. Ga.   [b] fiat Gc.   [c] *om.* Ga.   [d] confiscere Ga.   [e] Gc *adds* episcopus.

Quod audiens prior Osbernus[a] una cum cantore et quibusdam fratribus accessit, rogans legatum ut secundum consuetudinem Cant(uariensis) ecclesie examinationem illam faceret et consecrationem. Respondit legatus quod sic non[b] deberet fieri, ad exemplum domini pape, qui sic facere consuevit. Cui prior, 'Dominus', inquit, 'papa quod sibi placuerit faciat; nos autem consuetudines huius ecclesie petimus observari. Si quandoque aliter vel alibi factum est, violentia fuit vel discreta dispensatio.' Hec audientes episcopi una cum legato surgentes, quod inceperant dimiserunt, indutique vestibus sacris interfuerunt de more processioni monachorum. Cum igitur ante [Ga, fo. 192^v (193^v)] magnum altare de more considerent episcopi, exsurgens Gil(ebertus) Roffensis episcopus dixit ad legatum:

'Nostis pater venerande quod dominus Baldewinus[c] Cant(uariensis) archiepiscopus peregre proficiscens vices suas in Anglia conservandas nobis commisit, unde nobis videtur quod omnia sacramentalia que in ecclesia Cant(uariensi) facienda sunt per manus nostras, sicut per proprium ecclesie capellanum, fieri debeant. Electio autem huius fratris nostri Wigornensis electi aliter quam debuit facta est; sed postea per vos in confirmatione aliquantulam accepit meliorationem. Allegat Londoniensis de iure decanatus sui, sed nichil ad nos. Nullam enim ei subiectionem debeo, in re nulla obedio, nec alteri, nisi soli domino meo Cant(uariensi) archiepiscopo: hunc igitur electum nostrum, ordinatum nostrum, a vobis tanquam legato consecrandum, salvo iure nostro, presentamus.' Legatus ad hec: 'Et nos illum per gratiam Dei sacrandum suscipimus, non de iure Heliensis episcopi, sed de auctoritate apostolice sedis legati. Consecrabimus eum auctoritate qua fungimur, salvo iure vestro, salvo[d] iure Lond(oniensis) episcopi.' Sacratus est itaque iiii nonas Maii[1] Robertus Wigorn(ensis) episcopus ad altare Christi, data professione de canonica subiectione quam debet archiepiscopo et Cantuariensi ecclesie. Die crastina venit in capitulum monachorum dominus legatus una cum novo Wigorn(ensi) episcopo et clericis tribus ... (*bearing the king's letters: see p. 1035, no. 177*).

---

[a]O. Ga.   [b]*om.* Gc (*fort. recte*).   [c]B. Ga.   [d]etiam *ins.* Gc.

---

[1]For 5 May (a Sunday) see Le Neve, ii.100.

176

1191, AFTER 29 SEPTEMBER. SYNOD AT YORK

This was an episode in the conflict of Geoffrey Plantagenet, archbishop of York (1191-1212) and Hugh du Puiset,
bishop of Durham (1153-95); on which see M. Lovatt, 'The
Career and Administration of Archbishop Geoffrey of York
(? 1151-1212)' (Cambridge Ph.D. thesis, 1974-5), pp. 41-7;
Hoveden, iii.168-9, 172; G.V. Scammell, *Hugh du Puiset,
Bishop of Durham* (Cambridge, 1956), pp. 178-81.

In the spring of 1191 Celestine III revoked Clement III's instruction against Hugh renewing his profession to Geoffrey. Hugh
appealed against this decision, but Geoffrey meanwhile had summoned him to make profession at a synod at York, some time after
Michaelmas. This Hugh refused to do on the ground that he had
already made profession to Archbishop Roger; Geoffrey excommunicated him but in due course the pope refused to accept the excommunication as valid. The dispute died slowly away after
various attempts at mediation and a decision by judges delegate against Hugh; a reconciliation was patched up in October
1192, without any full agreement.

It may be presumed that the synod to which Hugh was summoned
in 1191 was (at least in intention) a provincial synod.

177

22 OCTOBER 1191, NOVEMBER-DECEMBER 1191. MEETINGS FOR THE CANTERBURY ELECTION

The king's letters of 25 January 1191 from Messina which arrived
at Canterbury on 5 May 1191 recommended William, archbishop of
Monreale, for election to the archbishopric. In the event, the
king's suggestion was overlooked, possibly because the electors
already had news of the death of Archbishop William.[1] Monks and

---

[1] The royal letters are in *Ep. Cant.*, pp. 329-30 (see also Gervase, i.493-
4 for that to the monks). The archbishop of Monreale had met Richard I at
Messina in October 1190; he died at the siege of Acre (*Gesta Henrici II*,
ii.96, 128, 147; Hoveden, iii.22, 87).

bishops gathered for the customary discussion and disagreement
on 22 October, at London;[1] in the light of their dispute with
Archbishop Baldwin over his plan to erect a great collegiate
church in Lambeth, this election was particularly crucial to
the monks. The day fixed for the second meeting was 2 December,
at Canterbury. On 27 November the monks anticipated this col-
loquy, and elected Reginald, bishop of Bath; but on 26 December
he died, and the election was postponed for another eighteen
months.[2]

Ralph de Diceto, Ymagines Historiarum, s.a. 1191

From mss. Da, fo. 123[r-v], and Db, fo. 135[v] (133[v]: see
p. 964); ed. Stubbs, ii.102-3; also in W. i.494-5, from
Diceto, ed. Twysden.

... ximo kalendas Novembris. Ipsa die tractatum est de consilio
Cantuariensis ecclesie sicut rex Ricardus mandaverat. Convenerunt episcopi, convenerunt et monachi. Post longos tractatus
negotium tandem dilationem accepit.

Celestino pape suffraganei Cantuariensis ecclesie debitam
subiectionem.

Cum ad nostram pervenisset noticiam Baldewinum patrem nostrum
Cantuariensem archiepiscopum apud Acon viam universe carnis
ingressum, verentes ne monachi sancte Trinitatis in archiepiscopo substituendo sibi quippiam vendicare presumerent, de
communi consilio venerabilem fratrem nostrum Ric(ardum) Lun-
d(oniensem) episcopum, ad quem electi nominatio de iure dinoscitur pertinere, premisimus apud Cantuariam. Iunctus est ei comes
in itinere quidam regis iusticiarius. Igitur in ecclesia Cantuariensi [Da, fo. 123[v]] presentibus monachis et audientibus
Romane sedis audientiam appellavit, inhibens ex parte summi

---

[1] As is made clear both in the bishops' letter, below, and in the summons
to the prior and community sent in the king's name on 10 Oct., which also
confirms the date of 22 Oct. given by Diceto (*Ep. Cant.*, p. 348; for 2 Dec.,
see also *Ep. Cant.*, p. 349).
[2] Le Neve, ii.5. The delay was partly due to the king's absence and subsequent imprisonment, and to the political confusion in England (see *Ep. Cant.*,
p. xc).

pontificis ne quid in electione facienda presumerent attemptare citra conscientiam episcoporum et etiam citra regis assensum. Postmodum autem, ut nobis archipresulem eligeremus, ad vocationem domini Lundon(iensis), qui decanatum optinet inter suffraganeos, convenimus Lundoniis, convenerunt et monachi; dilationem accepit electio quibusdam dissensionibus ad invicem emergentibus. Dominus itaque Lund(oniensis), tocius Anglicane vicem gerens ecclesie, rursus Romane sedis audientiam appellavit, R(eginaldo) episcopo Bathon(ensi) cum reliquis episcopis contra monachos appellante. Paucis diebus elapsis constituimus accedere Cantuariam, ut sub presentia tam cleri quam populi, tam episcoporum quam monachorum, archiepiscopum eligeremus, diem ad hoc faciendum constituentes iiii^{to} nonas Decembris. Interim^a autem comes Moritonii domini regis frater, et dominus Rothom(agensis), Bathon(ensis), Rofensis, Hereford(ensis), Menevensis, Conventrensis episcopi, cum pluribus regni magnatibus pro quibusdam magnis regni negotiis transitum fecerunt usque Cantuariam. Cumque super negociis ipsis in palatio Cant(uariensis) archiepiscopi residentes tractarent, ingressi sunt coram eis G(aufridus) dictus prior et quidam monachorum, et manus inicientes in Bathon(ensem), et eum electum suum nominantes de medio residentium sustulerunt. Quos memorati presules et regni proceres e vestigio subsecuti, denuo vestram appellaverunt presentiam v^{to} kalendas Decembris.

178

29-30 MAY 1193. COUNCIL AT LONDON FOR THE ELECTION OF ARCH-
BISHOP HUBERT WALTER

For the context, see C.R. Cheney, *Hubert Walter,* esp. pp. 44 ff.

On 30 May the bishops met in what may be reckoned a provincial council, summoned by the bishop of London, to consider the election of the archbishop, following a royal mandate, and

---

^{a}interim Db; iterum Da.

instructions given personally to Queen Eleanor and William de
Ste-Mère-Église.[1] Diceto tells us that the bishop summoned
many heads of religious houses, and the justiciar also summoned
the monks of Canterbury. In the event, the bishops discovered
that the monks had already elected Hubert (the king's nominee)
on the previous day, 29 May; in spite of this they proceeded
also to elect him, or rather to postulate his election from the
pope, since he was already bishop of Salisbury. The translation
was duly confirmed by Celestine III and Hubert was enthroned
at Canterbury, when he received the pallium brought by the
nuncio Episcopellus on 7 November.[2] The two chief narratives
are printed below. Diceto represents the bishops, and Gervase
the monks (see pp. 956, 1015-16).

I. *Ralph de Diceto, Ymagines Historiarum, s.a. 1193*

From mss. Da, fo. 124^v, Db, fo. 137^{r-v} (see p. 964);
ed. Stubbs, ii.108-9.

... (quoting the royal letter) Commonitoriis igitur huiuscemodi
lectis in medium, ad vocationem domini Lundon(iensis) plures
convenerunt episcopi;[a] quidam sue causam absentie satis proba-
bilem vel per litteras vel per nuntios allegarunt. Convenerunt
ad vocationem eius plures locorum conventualium principales
persone. Dies dominica prefinita fuit electioni, scilicet tercio
kalendas Iunii. Mater itaque domini regis, Alienor regina,
Walterus quoque Rothomagensis archiepiscopus capitalis Anglie
iusticiarius, at alii regni magnates, ad regni pacem integre
conservandam omnem studuerunt impendere sollicitudinem,

---

[a] episcopi conv. Db.

---

[1] *Ep. Cant.*, pp. 364-5; Gervase, i.517-18. *Ep. Cant.*, p. 366 (no. ccccv)
is an instruction from Richard I not to elect Hubert, dated 10 July; this
had been preceded by a letter to Queen Eleanor of 8 June confirming her
instruction to see to Hubert's election, and telling her to ignore any letter he might send to the contrary, owing to the circumstances of his imprisonment (ibid., no. cccciii, pp. 364-5; cf. Stubbs in *Ep. Cant.*, pp. xc-
xci; Cheney, *Hubert Walter*, pp. 45-6).
[2] Cheney, *Hubert Walter*, p. 48; Gervase, i.521-3. Cf. Le Neve, ii.5, who
notes that Diceto, ii.111-12, gives the date 5 Nov.

quodam palliate^a pacis umbraculo suum velare propositum inten-
dentes, ut sub quadam qualiquali concordia partium studia di-
versissima iungerentur, quorum semper fuerant corda disiuncta.
De iusticiariorum dispositione Gaufridus prior Cantuariensis
et monachi, qui cum eo Lundoniam venerant, Cantuariam adierunt,
ubi Thomas gloriosus prothomartyr Cantuariensium sanguine
proprio tinctam sibi purpuram conquisivit. Et ut in terris
grande sibi nomen facerent, die sabbati predictam precedentis
dominicam prevenerunt episcopos, Hubertum quondam decanum
Eboracensem, quem aliquo spiritu revelante prenoverant ab episcopis eligendum, suum nominantes electum.

Viri quidam, medie manus homines, in capitulo Cantuarie presi-
dentes tanquam iusticiarii, nominationi facte prebuerunt assensum. Monachi prevenerunt episcopos, sabbatizantes non sabbato
mentis sed temporis. De quo dicit Moyses filiis Israel, 'Erit
vobis hodie sabbatum requietionis, et affligetis animas vestras.'[1] De quodam alio longe dissimili sabbato loquitur alibi
propheta dicens, 'Dabit dominus Deus sabbatum pro sabbato',[2]
scilicet pro pace temporali pacem eternam. Monachi cum exulta-
tione magna recedentes a capitulo, magnam intraverunt ecclesiam,
laudes debitas sicut sibi videbatur Domino decantantes, 'Te
Deum' scilicet 'laudamus.' Ab eorum mentibus excidisse non
debuit, quod cum aliquis in abbatem electus est sua collocandus
in sede, mediocri voce psalmus excurritur quinquagesimus, commissorum pristinam perpetrationem revocans ad memoriam, non
alicuius glorie temporalis titillationem importans. Monachi
prevenerunt episcopos, sed non in benedictionibus dulcedinis;[3]
nec enim in tanto monachorum collegio repertus est aliquis, qui
post suorum expletionem votorum populis ad propria reversuris
in fine sollempnem de iure posset dare benedictionem. Hubertus
a monachis Cantuariensibus prenominatus in sabbato renuntiet
diabolo per penitentiam, ne sub eius iugo retineatur. Die

---

^apatliate Da.

---

[1] Levit. 23, 31-2.
[2] Not traced (but cf. Levit. 23, 3; Ezek. 20, 12).
[3] Cf. Ps. 20 (21), 4 (3).

dominica, die constituta, die sanctificata, Hubertus Saresbiri-
ensis episcopus ab episcopis electus est in archiepiscopum.
Electionem factam Lundoniensis episcopus in publico recitavit
apud Westmonasterium in sede regia loco celebri, loco faciendis
electionibus archiepiscoporum a multis temporibus consecrato.
Walterus Rothomag(ensis) archiepiscopus capitalis Anglie iusticiarius dedit assensum, et auctoritate regia factam confirmavit
electionem. Igitur Lundon(iensis) episcopus, iuxta suorum
dignitatem predecessorum, et Deo laudes persolvendas exsolvit,
et benedictionem omnibus qui convenerant gratanter exhibuit ...

II. *Gervase of Canterbury, Chronica, s.a. 1193*

From mss. Ga, fo. 202^v-203, Gc, fo. 167^{r-v} (see pp. 771,
973 n.); ed. Stubbs, i.518-19.

... (quoting the royal letter) Regina vero et[a] Rotomagensis,
cum videretur[b] domini regis urgens esse mandatum, alios quoque
iusticiarios per Angliam dispersos, eo quod his diebus multis
et innumeris perturbaretur incommodis, nec valerent ulterius
tam utile tamque necessarium protelare negotium, viros [Ga,
fo. 203] industrios cum eis qui a rege venerant[c] cum litteris
commonitoriis Cant(uariam) miserunt ad conventum, monentes ut
in die dominica, iiii scilicet kalendas Iunii, Lund(oniam)
venirent, archiepiscopum per Dei gratiam electuri. Videntes
igitur monachi cum assensu regio sibi etiam nunc a Deo datam
eligendi libertatem, cum non viderent aliquem[d] in Anglia Huberto
prestantiorem, invocata sancte Trinitatis gratia, eum sabbato
mirantibus nuntiis et fere desperatis elegerunt. Prior itaque
G(aufridus) crastino Londoniam avolans prefatum electum suis
extraxit latebris, eumque[e] in contione episcoporum qui ad electionem faciendam convenerant Rothomagensi et regine regalibus
instituendum presentavit. Stupens ad hec R(icardus)[f] Londoniensis episcopus, qui sibi sollennitatem electionis reservatam puta-
bat, sed iam desperans, ne nil ageretur, priori et monachis
dixit: 'Bene fecistis qui nobis nostrum[g] adduxistis electum.'

[a]*om.* Ga.   [b]viderent Gc.   [c]venerunt Ga.   [d]aliquam Ga.   [e]cumque Ga.
[f]*om.* Ga.   [g]Ga *adds* R.

Cui prior: 'De vestro', inquid, 'electo, quid feceritis, vel
si quem elegistis, nos penitus ignoramus. Quod autem nostra de
iure debeat esse electio res in propatulo est cum regie curie
nostrum presentamus electum.' Factum est autem. Directi sunt
illico nuntii ipsius electi, et nuntii conventus, cum nuntiis[a]
regis ad curiam Romanam, pro pallio petendo et plenitudine
potestatis. Qui benigne a domino papa suscepti sunt.

Facte sunt interea exactiones durissime per totam Angliam
pro redemptione regis, ut omnes et singuli, tam ecclesiastice
quam seculares persone, quartam partem reddituum suorum solvere
cogerentur. Deinde calices ecclesiarum et ampulle, cruces et
candelabra, textus et turibula aurea vel argentea, capse etiam
sanctorum excoriate sunt et conflate, regiis assignate[b] ministris. Afflicta est precipue his diebus misera Cant(uariensis)
ecclesia, que tunsionibus et pressuris variis extenuata in
nichilum pene redacta est. Convocati sunt iterum et iterum apud
Lund(oniam) tam ecclesiastice quam seculares persone, ut sub-
tilius requirerent[c] si quid esset residuum ad solvendum. Cum
igitur apud Westmonasterium, absente Cant(uariensi) electo, considerent in unum et secum quererent, intravit quispiam crucem
baiulans, quem archiepiscopus Eboracensis stupentibus cunctis
a tergo subsequens presumsione stolida turbavit universos ...

179

10 FEBRUARY 1194. APPEAL TO THE POPE AGAINST COUNT JOHN AND WILLIAM DE LONGCHAMP

At the turn of 1193 and 1194 the intrigues of Count (later King)
John with the French king and against Richard I led Hubert
Walter, now justiciar as well as archbishop, to take firm
action. At a council of the realm held on 10 February 1194 John
was declared disseised of all his holdings in England. Roger of
Howden (Hoveden), who tells us this, goes on to describe a

---

[a] ipsius ... nuntiis Gc; conventus nunc nuntii Ga.   [b] excoriate ...
conflate ... assignate Ga *post corr.;* excoriata ... conflata ... assignata
Gc, Ga *ante corr.*   [c] exquirerent Gc.

meeting of the clergy in the infirmary chapel of Westminster abbey on the same day, to declare John excommunicate and to appeal to the pope against the legation of William de Long-champ, bishop of Ely (iii.236-7). For the setting, see Cheney, *Hubert Walter*, pp. 91 ff.

Roger of Hoveden, Chronica, s.a. 1194

> From Bodl. ms. Laud Misc. 582 (1582), fo. 133^{r-v} (Hb), and BL ms. Cotton Claud. B. vii, fo. 160^{r-v} (variants not noted); ed. Stubbs, iii.237.

Eodem die Hubertus Cant(uariensis) archiepiscopus et Hugo Lin-coln(iensis) et Ricardus Lundon(iensis) et Gilbertus Rofensis et Godefridus Wint(oniensis) et Wigorn(ensis) et Hereford(en-sis) episcopi, et Henricus Exoniensis electus, et abbates et clerici multi Cant(uariensis) diocesis, convenerunt in capella monachorum infirmorum apud Westmonasterium, et sententiam anathematis tulerunt in comitem Iohannem, et in omnes fautores eius et consiliarios, qui pacem et regnum regis Angl(ie) tur-baverunt vel turbarent, nisi relicta hostilitate ad satisfac-tionem venirent. Deinde appellaverunt ad presentiam domini pape contra Willelmum Eliensem episcopum, ne ipse de cetero fungeretur in Anglia legacionis officio; et appellationem suam sigillis suis confirmaverunt, et miserunt illam domino regi, deinde summo pontifici confirmandam. [Hb, fo. 133^v] Facta est autem hec appellatio quarto idus Februarii, feria quinta.

180

14-15 JUNE 1195. LEGATINE COUNCIL AT ST. PETER'S, YORK

This council was convened by Hubert Walter, archbishop of Can-terbury, during a visitation of the northern province soon after his appointment as papal legate by Pope Celestine III.[1] It was the only occasion on which an archbishop of Canterbury

---

[1] See Tillmann, pp. 34-6 and Cheney, *Hubert Walter*, pp. 119-22.

has held a legatine council at York. That it passed off without
overt opposition was probably due to the absence of Hubert's
rival, Archbishop Geoffrey of York. Whether attendance at the
council was limited to the diocese of York or extended to the
dioceses of Carlisle and Durham and Whithorn is not known. The
sees of Carlisle and Durham were both vacant. The proceedings
of the legation, and of the council in particular, are described
by two contemporary northern writers, William of Newburgh (no.
I) and Roger of Hoveden (no. II), the latter of whom copied the
canons of the council into his chronicle. With these canons we
meet a class of conciliar legislation which differs from that
of Westminster, 1175, setting a new model for some English
Church law (especially the diocesan statutes) of the next hundred years. In the main the canons of 1195 do not restate
general accepted principles of canon law, but provide new, detailed regulations on matters of clerical discipline, jurisdiction, and the like, not already set down with adequate precision.
Nevertheless, several of the canons of 1195 bear resemblance to
the canons of 1175; their intention seems in part to be the
codifying and underlining of regulations in the earlier council.

The canons are found in two main texts of Hoveden's chronicle
and in one other manuscript:

Hb. Bodl. ms. Laud Misc. 582 (Hoveden), fos. 153-154. Writ-
    ten in 1201 or soon after. The main text used by Stubbs
    in his edition of Hoveden, iii.294-7 (cf. ibid. i, pp.
    lxxviii-lxxx).
Hc. BL ms. Arundel 150 (Hoveden), fo. 114^{r-v}. Written in
    1201 or soon after. Stubbs considered that the Hc text
    of the chronicle was copied from Hb, but that the scribe
    referred occasionally to the authorities quoted by Hove-
    den. This gives Hc some colour of independent value.
L. Lambeth Palace Lib. ms. 145, fo. 138^{v}. Written c.1200,
    in isolation, on the front flyleaf of a Chrysostom from
    Crowland Abbey. There is no title to the canons. This
    text differs principally from Hb and Hc in omitting the
    last sentence, saving the authority and dignity of the
    Roman see, and in including a clause on pensions in

c. 12 which is not in Hb or Hc. Occasionally it offers
better readings than these manuscripts, but it has
numerous careless mistakes.

Printed by Henry Savile (1596), fos. 429^V-430^V in his
edition of Hoveden from Hb or a derivative, perhaps with
corrections from another manuscript (cf. Stubbs, ii, pp.
xiv-xix); whence Sp. ii.121-2 and W. i.501-3. Printed
from Hb and Hc by Stubbs, Hoveden, iii.294-7, who notes
the absence of the canons from other manuscripts of the
chronicle. Printed here from Hb, collated with L; selected
readings of Hc and S (= Savile) are noted where they depart from Hb.

I. *William of Newburgh, Historia Rerum Anglicarum, s.a. 1195*

Printed from BL ms. Stowe 62 fo. 139^{r-v}, with collation
of other manuscripts by R. Howlett, *Chrons. Stephen etc.*,
ii.442.

Defuncto igitur Dunelmensi episcopo, atque Eboracensi archiepiscopo ad placandam regis iram, que adversus eum vehementer
excanduerat, in transmarinis partibus constituto, Hubertus Cantuariensis archiepiscopus, et vices non tantum regias in regni
moderatione verum etiam apostolicas in ecclesiastica ordinatione
per totam habens Angliam, ostentaturus gloriam utriusque potestatis, Eboracam metropolim adiit, prelatos totius provincie
uti sollempniter sibi occurrerent atque assisterent, [fo. 139^V]
premissa auctoritate imperavit. Suppresso pro tempore primatis
nomine, ipsam ecclesiam metropolitanam nomine legati apostolice
sedis pompatice ingressus, potestatem in ea magnam exercuit; et
nullo obsistente vel reclamante, eo quod omnes vel terrore
eius perstricti vel metropolitano proprio minus essent devoti,
concilium magnifice celebravit. Quibus actis, et seculari quoque
pro tempore ibidem iurisdictione expleta, proprie se provincie
reddidit.

II. *Gervase of Canterbury, Chronica, s.a. 1195*

From Ga, fo. 205^V; Gc, fo. 170^V; ed. Stubbs, i.529 (minor variants of Gc not noted).

Eodem anno mense Iunio Hubertus Cantuariensis archiepiscopus, apostolice sedis legatus effectus, occidentales visitavit ecclesias, et apud Eboracum tam a monachis quam a clericis et laicis honorifice susceptus est. Deposuit autem certis[a] ex causis accusatum abbatem sancte Marie Eboraci et per Dunelmum[b] rediens misit abbates tres ut vice sua in diocesi Eboracensi alias circumquaque positas visitarent ecclesias. Festinabat enim redire Lundoniam ad expedienda regni negotia que hinc inde eum ex mandato regio distrahebant.[c]

III. *Roger of Hoveden, Chronica, s.a. 1195*

From Hb, fos. 152^V-154. Printed from Hb and Hc (see above) in *Chronica*, ed. Stubbs, iii.293-4, 297-8.

Harum igitur auctoritate literarum[1] predictus Cantuariensis archiepiscopus apostolice sedis legatus misit Eboracum Petrum priorem de Bineham[d] in Nortfolc[e] et magistrum Gervasium[2] cum literis domini pape et suis ad canonicos Eboraci et ad officiales Eboracensis archiepiscopi, mandans eis se illuc ex auctoritate legacionis sue in proximo venturum ad emendandum ea que essent emendanda et ad statuenda que secundum Deum fuerint statuenda. Et precepit eis ut ipsi convocato clero exhiberent ei tamquam apostolice sedis legato reverenciam debitam et honorem, adiungens se iam sentenciam excommunicacionis dedisse in omnes qui in hac parte mandato domini pape contradicerent, et super hoc misit literas suas patentes Simoni

---

[a]ceteris Ga.   [b]duelmum GaGc.   [c]distraebant Ga.   [d]Bynham Hc.
[e]Norfolc Hc.

---

[1]For the text of the pope's letters of commission (JL 17202, 17203, of 18 Mar. 1195) see *Ep. Cant.*, pp. 368-70; Diceto, ii.125-7; Hoveden, iii.290-3.
[2]Perhaps Master Gervase of Howbridge, later canon, chancellor, and dean-elect of St. Paul's, London.

Eboraci decano ut si quos ipse inveniret huic domini pape mandato rebelles denunciaret excommunicatos. Unde factum est quod
tam canonici quam officiales archiepiscopi Eboracensis responderunt nunciis legati quod eum reciperent tamquam apostolice
sedis legatum set non tamquam archiepiscopum Cantuariensem nec
tamquam primatem.

De adventu Huberti Cantuariensis archiepiscopi apostolice
sedis legati ad Eboracum.

Venit igitur legatus ille Eboracum die dominica, festo sancti
Barnabe apostoli,[1] et cum sollempni processione susceptus est
a clero et introductus in ecclesiam sedis chathedralis. Sequenti
die lune fecit ipse teneri assisas de omnibus placitis corone
regis, et de nova dissaisina, et de morte antecessorum, per
ministros suos.[2] Ipse vero et officiales sui tenuerunt placita
christianitatis. In sequenti die, feria tercia, perrexit legatus ille ad abbaciam sancte Marie Eboraci et ibi receptus est
ab eiusdem ecclesie monachis cum sollempni processione. Deinde
intravit capitulum monachorum et conquerentibus monachis quod
Robertus abbas eorum propter debilitatem et corporis sui egri-
tudinem domui sue prodesse non potuit, deposuit eum a cura
pastorali et ab administracione domus reclamantem et ad summum
pontificem appellantem.[a][3] In sequentibus autem duobus[b] diebus,
silicet feria iiii[a] et feria v[a],[c] congregatis in ecclesia sancti
Petri Eboraci Simone eiusdem ecclesie[d] decano et Hamone precen-
tore et Willelmo Testard et Gaufrido de Muschamp de Nothingham
et de Clivelande[e] archidiaconis et Iohanne cancellario et Roberto
preposito Beverlaci cum quibusdam eiusdem ecclesie canonicis[f]
et fere omnibus abbatibus et prioribus [fo. 153] et officiali-
bus et decanis et personis ecclesiarum Eboracensis[g] diocesis,

---

[a]et ab ... appellantem Hb; qui appellavit ad dominum papam Hc.   [b]om.
duobus Hc.   [c]om. silicet ... v[a] Hc.   [d]om. Simone eiusdem ecclesie Hc.
[e]om. Hamone ... Clivelande Hc.   [f]Iohanne ... canonicis Hb; canonicis eiusdem Hc.   [g]personis ec. Eb. Hb; rectoribus eiusdem Hc.

---

[1]11 June 1195.
[2]Traces of this session may appear in 'nova placita et nove conventiones
per Tomam de Husseburn' et magistrum Rogerum' in Yorkshire, *Chancellor's
Roll 8 Richard I*, ed. D.M. Stenton (Pipe Roll Soc., n.s. vii), pp. 171-3.
[3]Abbot Robert's appeal failed and he was succeeded in March 1197 by
Robert de Longchamp.

ipse legatus in eminenciori loco cathedratus sedit et concilium celeberimum celebravit,[a] in quo hec decreta subscripta[b] statuit servanda. (*No. IV follows.*)

In[c] concilio autem illo magister Petrus de Dinan exigebat sibi fieri plenariam saisinam de archidiaconatu de Westrihing quem Gaufridus Eboracensis archiepiscopus ei dederat, mandans capitulo Eboraci per literas suas ut eum reciperent et in stallum mitterent. Cui Simon decanus et capitulum Eboracense responderunt quod archiepiscopus non potuit archidiaconatum illum alicui dare, quia ultra terminum statutum in concilio Latranensi dare distulit, in quo concilio Alexander papa tercius constituit quod cum prebendas, ecclesias, seu quelibet officia in aliqua ecclesia vacare contigerit, non diu maneant in suspenso set infra vi menses personis que digne administrare valeant conferantur. Si autem episcopus ubi ad eum spectaverit conferre distulerit, per capitulum ordinetur. Quod si ad capitulum electio pertinuerit, et infra prescriptum terminum hoc non fecerit, episcopus secundum Deum cum religiosorum virorum consilio exequatur, aut si omnes forte neglexerint, metropolitanus de ipsis[d] secundum Deum absque illorum contradictione disponat.[1] Huius ergo dispositionis auctoritate et privilegii sui munimine a Celestino papa tercio ecclesie Eboracensi indulto[2] asserebant prefatus decanus et capitulum Eboracense quod ad illos spectat donacio predicti archidiaconatus et aliorum reddituum vacancium in ecclesia Eboracensi quos archiepiscopus suus non dederat in fixum Latranensis concilii terminum, set officiales Eboracensis archiepiscopi, scilicet magister Gyrardus de Rouuelle et magister Honorius appellaverunt contra privilegium illud et appellacionem quam dominus eorum archiepiscopus in recessu suo fecerat pro statu ecclesie sue renovaverunt coram legato et toto concilio, et quamvis in privilegio illo continebatur remota appellacione, tamen legatus detulit appellacioni officialium Eboracensis archiepiscopi.[3]

---

[a] ipse ... celebravit Hb; celebravit concilium Hc.   [b] *om.* subscripta Hc. [c] Hc *omits this paragraph.*   [d] ipsis; episcopis HbS.

[1] C. of Lateran III, c. 8.   [2] JL 17127, W. i.503-4. [3] For the troubles in the chapter of York see Stubbs's introduction to Hoveden, iv, pp. xxxiv-lxxvii; C.T. Clay in *Yorks. Archaeol. Journal*, xxxvi; M.B. Lovatt, 'The Career and Administration of Archbishop Geoffrey of York (? 1151-1212)' (Cambridge Ph.D. thesis 1974-5).

IV. *Canons of the council*

For manuscripts and editions see above, pp. 1043-4.

Decreta Huberti Cantuariensis archiepiscopi apostolice
sedis legati.

[1] Cum inter cetera ecclesie sacramenta hostia salutaris pre-
mineat, tanto impensior circa eam debet existere devocio sacerdotum ut cum humilitate conficiatur, cum timore sumatur,[a] cum
reverencia dispensetur; et minister altaris sit certus quod
panis et vinum et aqua in sacrificio[b] ponantur; nec sine ministro literato celebretur. Provideat[c] eciam ut in pixide munda
et honesta hostia reservetur, singulisque dominicis diebus
renovetur.

[2] Quociens autem communio exhibenda est infirmis, sacerdos
in propria persona hostiam in habitu clericali tanto sacramento
convenienti deferat, lumine precedente, nisi aeris intemperies
vel viarum difficultas vel alia racio prepediat.[d]

[3] Quia secretum misse frequenter invenitur aut scriptorum
falsitate aut librorum vetustate corruptum, ita ut legi distincte non possit, archidiaconorum sollicitudo provideat ut in
singulis ecclesiis ad verum et probatum exemplar canon misse
cum omni diligencia corrigatur.

[4] Prohibemus eciam ne sacerdos laico ad penitenciam venienti
optentu cupiditatis iniungat ut missas faciat celebrari. Et
illud eciam decrevimus prohibendum ne sacerdos aliquis pro cele-
bracione missarum precio constituto pactum ineat, set hoc dum-
taxat quod offeretur[e] in missa recipiat.

[5] Statuimus ne in baptismate plures quam tres suscipiant
puerum de sacro fonte, masculum duo mares et una mulier, femi-

---

[a] *corr. from* consummatur Hb.   [b] sacrificium Hc.   [c] Provideatur S.
[d] impediat L.   [e] offertur L.

nam unus mas et due femine.[a] Ubi autem puer cuius baptisma
ignoratur reperitur expositus, sive cum sale sive sine sale
reperiatur, baptizetur, cum non intelligatur iteratum quod
nescitur fuisse collatum.

[6] Decrevimus eciam ut non nisi summa et gravi urgente necessitate diaconus baptizet vel corpus Christi cuiquam eroget vel
penitenciam confitenti imponat, cum[b] iuxta paternorum tenorem
canonum hec ordini sacerdotali proprie convenire decernat anti-
quitas.[1] Sub eodem tenore constitucionis adicimus ut quociens
sacerdos ad puerum baptizandum vel infirmum communicandum invi-
tatur, moras innectere non presumat.[c]

[7] Cum in domo oracionis que domus Dei nuncupatur[2] nichil
debeat esse indecens, nichil inordinatum, precipimus ut persone
et vicarii ecclesiarum studeant providere secundum competentes
eis pensiones,[d] prout racio dictat et consuetudo approbata
expostulat, quatinus ecclesie que reparacione indigent reparen-
tur et cum ornamentis ministerio congruis ministretur, et cum
calice argenteo ubi facultas suppetit sacramentum eucharistie
conficiatur. Huic ordinacioni terminum prefiximus ab inicio
nostre legacionis in annum. Quod si hec medio tempore execucioni
mandata non fuerint, decrevimus ut post elapsum terminum de
ecclesiarum redditibus disposicio nostra plenum sorciatur effectum.

[8] Statuimus eciam ut clerici qui ab episcopo coronam susceperunt tonsuram habeant et coronam, quam si habere contempserint,
ad hoc beneficiorum si que habent privacione cogantur. Qui vero
beneficia non habent per archidiaconum[e] vel decanos tondeantur
inviti.[3]

---

[a]unus ... femine: *reading* mulieres *for* fem. HcL; due ... mas S, *marked
for transp.* Hb.   [b]cum L; ut HbHcS.   [c]*corr. from* presumpmat Hb.   [d]por-
ciones L.   [e]archidiaconos L.

---

[1]*Decretum,* D. 93 c. 13.   [2]Mat. 21, 13, etc.
[3]Cf. C. of Westminster (1175), c. 4.

[9] Precipimus eciam ut sacerdotes non in cappis manicatis incedant set in vestibus suo ordini congruis, ut sicut ceteris dignitate preeminent, sic plenius formam et exemplum exhibeant[a] honestatis.

[10] [fo. 153^v] Cum scriptura beatum eum esse testetur qui manus suas excutit[b] ab omni munere,[1] diligenti studio[c] providendum est ut gratis exhibeatur iusticia, nec pro ea in causis ecclesiasticis facienda vel adimenda sive acceleranda vel differenda quisquam precium[d] presumat[e] accipere, ut ei fructum iusticie sue tempore oportuno retribuat iustus iudex.

[11] Cum decime sint tributa egencium animarum[2] et ex precepto Domini dari debeant, non est reddentis eas diminuere. Statuimus itaque ut de his que renovantur per annum cum omni integritate decime debite et consuete offerantur,[f] ita ut inprimis decime absque ulla diminucione ecclesie dentur. Postmodum de novem partibus[g] mercedes messorum et aliorum servientum pro arbitrio solventis tribuantur.

[12] Exigit professio religiose sanctitatis ut monachi et canonici regulares et moniales religiose et regulariter conversentur.[h] Ut ergo eis adimatur oportunitas evagandi, prohibemus ne redditus quos obediencias vocant ad firmam teneant, nec iter peregrinationis arripiant, nec extra monasteria sine certa et racionabili causa nec absque societate cuius certa sit honestas et indubitata proficiscantur. De monialibus autem id specialiter adicimus ut absque societate abbatisse vel priorisse ambitum monasterii non egrediantur. Nec ecclesiarum augeant pensiones, cum in Lateranensi concilio sit statutum ut nec episcopis nec abbatibus liceat veteres census augere vel novas imponere.[i3] Adicimus eciam prohibentes ne laicus aliquis ecclesiam

---

[a]exemplar prebeant L.   [b]excuit Hb; exuit S.   [c]cura L.   [d]quicquam precii HbHcS.   [e]presumat Hb, *corr. from* presumpmat.   [f]offerantur L; conferantur HbHcS,   [g]*om.* de novem partibus L.   [h]conversentur L; conserventur HbHcS.   [i]Nec ec. ... imponere L; *om.* HbHcS.

[1]Isa. 33, 15.   [2]*Decretum,* C. 16 q. 1 c. 66.
[3]Cf. C. of Lateran III c. 7.

vel decimas ad firmam recipiat, sive solus sive clerico socia-
tus.[1]

[13] Ut calumpniatorum improbitas et temere iurancium malicia
timore celestis iudicii retundatur,[a] precipimus ut quilibet
sacerdos decetero ter in anno sollempniter, accensis candelis
pulsatisque campanis, eos excommunicet qui in recognicionibus
aliisve testimoniis scienter et sponte peierabunt, et eos qui
maliciose alios facient peierare, eosque singulis dominicis
diebus excommunicatos denunciet ut crebra maledicccionis itera-
cio eos a sua iniquitate retrahat quos accusacio proprie con-
sciencie non deterret. Si vero de periurio peniteant, ad
archiepiscopum vel episcopum vel generalem[b] diocesis confessorem
absente archiepiscopo vel episcopo transmittantur, ab eo penitenciam suscepturi.[c] In extremis vero laborantibus insinuanda
non imponenda est penitencia, eisque firmiter iniungatur ut si
vixerint archiepiscopum vel episcopum vel generalem diocesis
confessorem absente archiepiscopo vel episcopo[d] adeant, ut eis
penitencia competens imponatur.

[14] Quia sermo Domini est: sacerdos meus si deliquerit delin-
quere faciet populum meum,[2] et ruina populi sacerdos nequam,
exigit tanti ordinis excellencia ut a publicis potacionibus et
tabernis sacerdotes abstineant, et qui voto continencie sunt
astricti nequaquam ad actus turpitudinis se relaxent. Prohibemus igitur ne focarias habeant in domibus suis, nec ad eiectas
in nostre constitucionis fraudem accessum in domibus alienis.
Si vero in turpitudine sua perstiterint et hoc decani dissimu-
lantes ad noticiam prelatorum suorum non detulerint, ab officio
suspendantur. Qui vero zelo Dei accensi prelatis nunciaverint
excessus eorum, divine benedictionis graciam consequantur. Pena
autem eorum qui publice focarias tenent hec erit, ut tamquam
infames ab aliorum accusacione et a testimonio repellantur. Si

---

[a]recondatur L.   [b]add sue L.   [c]ab ... suscepturi HbHcS; accepturi L.
[d]om. vel gen. ... episcopo L.

---

[1]Cf. Council of Westminster (1175), c. 10.   [2]Levit. 4, 3.

vero nec huius pene metu resipuerint ab officio et beneficio se
noverint suspendendos.

[15] Suspectus de crimine per famam communem vel verisimilia
indicia per decanum loci admoneatur familiariter semel, secundo,
et tercio, ut se corrigat. Quod si non fecerit, decanus adiunctis sibi duobus vel tribus penes quos eius fama laborat eum
corripiat. Si nec sic videatur corrigi, dicatur ecclesie,[1]
scilicet arguatur in capitulo [fo. 154] ut convictus vel confessus canonice puniatur. Inficianti[a] si convinci non poterit,
canonica purgacio indicatur, ita quod numerum duodenarium non
excedat, infra quem[b] numerum plures paucioresve poterint recipi
secundum statum persone et quantitatem[c] sive qualitatem infamie[d]
pro arbitrio iudicantis, et statim primo die quo paratus est
is qui infamia laborat se purgare, purgacio admittatur, ne metu
vexacionis ex dilacionibus contingentis pecunia extorqueatur.[e]
Hoc[f] et supradicta statuimus salva in omnibus sacrosancte
Romane sedis auctoritate et dignitate.

181

7 DECEMBER 1197. COUNCIL OF OXFORD (?)

In December 1197 Archbishop Hubert Walter, acting as justiciar,
gathered the English magnates to ask for military aid to the
king in France. This was the celebrated occasion when (St.) Hugh,
bishop of Lincoln, and Herbert Poore, bishop of Salisbury, objected to the request so strenuously that the project was abandoned.[2] Gervase alone, writing in the context of the dispute

---

[a]Inficianti LS; inficienti HbHc.   [b]om. quem HbS.   [c]quantitem Hb.
[d]sive qualitatem infamie HbHcS; culpe L.   [e]L ends here.   [f]Hoc HbS; Hec
Hb[1]Hc.

---

[1]Mat. 18, 17.
[2]*Magna Vita S. Hugonis*, ed. D.L. Douie and Hugh Farmer (NMT, 1961-2), i,
pp. xlii-xlv, ii.98-100; cf. Hoveden, iv.40 (s.a. 1198); Giraldus, *Opera*,
vii.103-4. On this council see Cheney, *Hubert Walter*, pp. 94-5; J.H. Round,
Feudal England (London, 1895), pp. 528-38; H.M. Chew, *The English ecclesiastical tenants-in-chief and knight service* ... (London, 1932), pp. 39-43.

between Archbishop Hubert and the monks of Christ Church, Canterbury, describes a meeting of bishops,[1] which may possibly have been a brief provincial council held at the same time as the justiciar's council.

Gervase of Canterbury, Chronica, s.a. 1197

> From Gervase, mss. Ga, fo. 213, and Gc, fo. 177 (see pp. 771, 973 n.); ed. Stubbs, i.549.

VIIo idus Decembris convenerunt apud Oxenefordiam ad[a] archiepiscopum episcopi Anglie; et abbates, comites quoque,[b] barones et monachi Cant(uariam) reversi sunt. Conventus autem assiduis precibus Deum et sanctos ecclesie patronos exorabant ut eos eriperent ab inimicis.

182
MAY 1199? COUNCIL OF WESTMINSTER

In the *Magna Vita Sancti Hugonis*, v. 17 (see below), there is a reference to a council at Westminster late in the life of St. Hugh, bishop of Lincoln, presided over by the king and the archbishop: it tells how St. Hugh renewed the anathema he had already laid on any who tried to misappropriate the bequests made in his will, and had this converted into a general excommunication against those who abused bequests in legal wills. This happened *in concilio generali*, which could well have been a royal council at which the bishops present were permitted to utter an anathema. It may, however, have been an ecclesiastical council in the king's presence.[2] Richard I was out of the

---

[a]Oxen. ad *om.* Ga.   [b]Gc *adds* et.

[1]The sentence runs oddly, and may have been meant to read '... et barones; et monachi' - i.e. to describe the magnates gathered for the justiciar's council. On the dispute between archbishop and chapter, see Cheney, *Hubert Walter*, chap. 7.

[2]The editors of the NMT edition translate 'concilio' in the last sentence 'a council', which would imply that the royal assent was given at another council following the 'general council' in which the anathema was made; but it seems more natural to take it as the same meeting, and render it 'the council'.

country from May 1194 until his death, and it seems impossible
to find a suitable occasion for such a council at which he and
Hubert Walter could have presided; in any case the implication
of the passage is that it was towards the end of Hugh's life,
and he died on 16 November 1200. The only possible occasions in
John's reign when king and archbishop could have presided together at a council in Westminster are in May-June 1199 and
March-April 1200. There was a great concourse of bishops for
the consecration of William of Ste-Mère-Église as bishop of
London on 23 May 1199 and the coronation of King John on 27
May, and this seems a possible occasion for the council. The
consecration took place in St. Catherine's chapel in Westminster
abbey on the Sunday in the presence of the archbishop, and the
bishops of Rochester, Norwich, Lincoln, Ely, Winchester, Exeter,
Chichester, Coventry, Bath, Salisbury, Durham, St. Andrew's,
and Llandaff, and the archbishops of Dublin and Ragusa -
gathered in Westminster for the king's coronation.[1]

Magna Vita Sancti Hugonis

> From *Magna Vita Sancti Hugonis*, ii, ed. D.L. Douie and
> H. Farmer (NMT, 1962), p. 205; ed. J.F. Dimock (RS, 1864),
> p. 351.

... Et summas post regem regni potestates ita sepe artaverat
gladio Spiritus Sancti [sc. Hugo] ut prone vestigiis eius pro-
volverentur, ea que legatariis tulerant restituere festinantes.
Quorum insidias a rerum quas ipse legaverat contrectatione
funesta cupiens arcere, proprio instinctu vinculo primum

---

[1]Hoveden, iv.89-90; Diceto, ii.166; Gervase, ii.410; cf. W. Stubbs,
Registrum sacrum Anglicanum (2nd edn., Oxford, 1897), p. 53. It is perhaps
significant that Hubert Walter received royal confirmation of his will on
30 Aug. 1199 (Rymer, i, i (1816), 78); on Hugh's precautions, see *Magna
Vita*, v. 16 (NMT, ii.186-7, 188); Hoveden, iv.141. Taken in isolation, the
passages in the *Magna Vita* might suggest that Hugh first made his will on
his deathbed, and had his anathema confirmed while he was still in his final
illness in London (NMT, ii.186-7, 205); and Dimock (p. 351 n.) supposed the
council to be that of Sept. 1200. By then, however, the king was abroad;
and if the text quoted above has any substance in it, it must refer to an
earlier occasion and perhaps to an earlier version of his will (cf. Theobald's will, JS, *Letters*, i, no. 134).

anathematis, ut supradictum est, illos innodavit qui tale quid
vi sive fraude in ipsis rebus presumerent attemptare. Optinuit
quoque tempore consequenti ut in concilio generali, quod eo
vivente adhuc apud Westmonasterium celebratum est, sollempnis
innovaretur sententia anathematis, non solum in sui testamenti,
immo et in cuiuslibet fraudatores legittimi testatoris. Huic
sententie rex ipse assensum suum, concilio cum archiepiscopo
presidens, favorabiliter acclamando dedit ...

183

19-23 (?) SEPTEMBER 1200. COUNCIL OF THE PROVINCE OF CANTER-
BURY AT WESTMINSTER; WITH AN APPENDIX OF DIOCESAN STATUTES

The council assembled by Archbishop Hubert Walter in 1200 (commonly known as the Council of London) was the first council of
the province of Canterbury to utter legislation since the
council, also held at Westminster, in 1175. Few of the contemporary annals and chronicles record the council, apart from the
four quoted below. It is noted briefly in the *Annales Wintoni-
enses* (*Ann. Mon.* ii.74). See *EHR* l (1935), 388-9 and C.R. Cheney,
Hubert Walter, pp. 53, 64-8. It has sometimes been treated as
a legatine council; but Hubert had ceased to be papal legate in
1198. The words of the dean of St. Paul's (below, no. I), re-
peating as they do his comment on the Council of Westminster,
1175, suggest that a tradition of primatial authority over all
England lingered in twelfth-century Canterbury, but it can have
had no practical result. We have no trace of summons to northern
prelates or of any attendance from the north. To judge by
Diceto's account, the council was composed of the archbishop of
Canterbury and ten of his suffragans with numerous monastic
prelates. This was enough to constitute, in Hoveden's eyes, a
generale concilium, but it is difficult to assign any exact significance to this term in the twelfth and thirteenth centuries.[1]

The duration of the council is uncertain. If Diceto is correct and if Gervase rightly says that the consecration of the

_____
[1] Cf. *EHR* l.197-8 and *Councils*, ii.100 n. 1, 240-1, and 1415a (index).

bishops occurred on the morrow of the council, then the business which Gervase describes must have occupied from Tuesday
19 September until Saturday, with the consecration ceremony on
the following day, Sunday the 24th. Hoveden's statement that
the council was celebrated 'against the prohibition of the
justiciar' is hard to interpret. The justiciar (Geoffrey Fitz-
Peter, who was intimate with the archbishop) may have lodged a
formal protest against the holding of a council while the king
was overseas - King John returned from Normandy early in October - or he may have forbidden, as happened in later times, any
action in derogation of the royal dignity.[1] In particular, the
prelates may have been told not to discuss the pope's recent
demand for a Crusading tax, as happened in 1207.[2]

The canons of the council show much dependence on the Lateran
Council of 1179 and draw on recent decretal letters and on the
provincial council of Rouen, 1190. Like the York canons of 1195
they have more details about the administration of the sacra-
ments and clerical behaviour than earlier laws, in this respect
foreshadowing the statutes of thirteenth-century English bishops
for their dioceses. Direct borrowing from the canons of Westminster has been noted in the statutes of Archbishop Stephen
Langton, 1213 x 1214, and in statutes for an unknown diocese,
1222 x 1225.[3] The canons are found in two texts of Hoveden's
chronicle and in one other manuscript:

Hb. Bodleian ms. Laud Misc. 582 (Hoveden), fos. 186^V-189.
  Written in 1201 or soon after. The main text used by
  Stubbs in his edition of Hoveden, iv.128-37 (cf. above,
  p. 1043).
Hc. BL ms. Arundel 150 (Hoveden), fos. 122^V-124 (cf. above,
  p. 1043).
R. BL ms. Royal 7. C. vii, fos. 53^V-55. This text occurs in
  a 13th-cent. miscellany, which belonged to the Austin
  Canons of St. Bartholomew's, Smithfield (cf. *EHR* 1.389).

---

[1] *Councils*, ii.10, 157, and 1415b (index, s.v. Councils, national or
provincial).
[2] For the king's action in 1207 see ibid. ii.10.
[3] Ibid. ii.23-36, 139-54.

Despite corrupt readings, the text sometimes shows greater
fidelity than does Hoveden to the source of the canons
and sometimes resembles derivatives more closely. Its
arrangement is different from Hoveden's: here Hoveden's
cc. 10-13 follow Hoveden's 14-16. The rubrics are usually
different and a few are inserted at different points. The
concluding chapter (Hoveden's c. 13) is followed by other
material, for which see the Appendix below.

Printed by Henry Savile (1596), fos. 458^V-461 in his edition of Hoveden from Hb or a derivative, perhaps with
corrections from another manuscript (cf. Stubbs, ii,
pp. xv-xix); whence Sp. ii.123-8 and W. i.505-8. Printed
from Hb and Hc by Stubbs, Hoveden, iv.128-37. Printed here
from Hb, collated with R. The rubrics are those of Hb.
Selected readings of Hc and S (= Savile) are noted where
they depart from Hb.

The Appendix. In R the final chapter (= Hb c. 13) is followed
by seven new chapters (fo. 55^{r-v}). This addition differs from
the canons which precede in being independent of the Third
Lateran Council (quoted extensively in eight places in cc. 1-
16). Moreover, there are reminiscences in Appendix c. 2 of Westminster c. 5, and Appendix cc. 3-4 repeat verbatim parts of
Westminster cc. 9-10 and elaborate them. Finally, three of the
chapters contain phrases which suggest the commands of a diocesan bishop rather than a metropolitan ('cum speciali auctoritate nostra et conscientia', 'per episcopatum nostrum', 'nisi
nobis prius fuerit presentatus'). We may infer that these chapters formed no part of the proceedings of the Council of Westminster, 1200, and there is no reason to attribute them to the
archbishop of Canterbury. It is noteworthy that they are unlike
the Westminster canons in leaving very little trace in later
diocesan statutes.[1] Yet their connection is fairly close. The
text ends with the saving clause which appears at the end of

---

[1] There may be a trace of c. 2 in the statutes of Canterbury I, c. 20
(ibid. ii.29), if this is not due to a common source.

all chapters of Westminster except the last, in Hoveden's text.
There is no trace of either the Fourth Lateran Council or the
Council of Oxford, 1222; and while the argument *ex silentio* is
not decisive, these statutes would be unique among English diocesan statutes in this respect if they were later than these
councils. Survival in a manuscript of London provenance suggests
that they may have emanated from a bishop of London; but this
hypothesis has not much to commend it. We are only justified in
saying that they probably are the work of an English bishop,
intended as a local appendix to the Council of Westminster,
issued before 1215. Even with this imperfect ascription they
deserve attention, for they are one of the first evidences of
statute-making for an English diocese.

I. *Ralph de Diceto, Ymagines historiarum, s.a. 1200*

From Dublin, Trinity Coll. ms. E. 4. 24 (508), fo. 141^v;
ed. Stubbs, ii.169.

Celebratum est consilium apud Westmonasterium xiii kalendas
Octobris, presidente H(uberto) Cantuariensi archiepiscopo,
presentibus episcopis W(illelmo) Lundoniensi, G(ileberto)
Rofensi, H(ereberto) Saresbiriensi, I(ohanne)[a] Exoniensi,[b]
E(ustacio) Elyensi, G(aufrido) Coventrensi, R(oberto) Bangor-
nensi, episcopo Landavensi, R(einero) de Sancto Asaph, G.[c]
electo Herefordensi, cum abbatibus et prioribus diversi ordinis,
qui ad vocationem domini Cantuariensis eo convenerant ut de
causis ecclesiasticis tractarent. G(aufridus) prior Cantuariensis sedit ex opposito contra dominum archiepiscopum a latere
episcopi Roffensis. Archiepiscopus Eboracensis concilio non
interfuit, cum esset in Anglia, nec[d] qui eius allegaret absentiam, cum iuxta priscorum consuetudinem ad vocationes Cantuariensis concilio teneretur interesse vel iustam absentie sue
causam allegare.[1] Dominus Lincolniensis a Roma rediens gravi

---

[a]*Recte* H(enrico).   [b]Oxoniensi ms.   [c]*For* E(gidio).   [d]ne ms.

---

[1]Cf. this sentence with the corresponding passage in Diceto's account
of Westminster, 1175 (above, p. 982).

tactus[a] infirmitate tunc temporis apud Vetus Templum Lundoniis
lecto decubuit. Dominus Wintoniensis et dominus Cisestrensis
corporis sui infirmitatem pretendentes litteratorie se excusaverunt. Vacabat tunc sedes Norwicensis. Dominica sequenti,
scilicet viii kalendas Octobris, consecratus est in episcopum
Herefordensem Gilo de Brause, et in episcopum Norwicensem
Iohannes de Grai, domesticus clericus regis, in capella sancte
Katerine a domino H(uberto) Cantuariensi archiepiscopo presentibus pluribus eius suffraganeis.[1]

II. *Gervase of Canterbury, Actus pontificum*

   From Cambridge, Corpus Christi Coll. ms. 438, p. 495.
   Ed. Stubbs, ii.410.

Archiepiscopus interea concilium apud Westmonasterium celebravit, ubi post sermonem decenter completum, post varias discus-
siones causarum, capitula promulgavit, et in crastino duos
sacravit episcopos, Egidium scilicet Herefordensem et Iohannem
Norwicensem.

III. *Annals of Dunstable, s.a. 1200*

   From BL ms. Cotton Tib. A. x, fo. 11; ed. H.R. Luard,
   Ann. Mon. iii.28.

Eodem anno Hubertus Cantuariensis apud Wemust' concilium celebravit, et Lateranum concilium iussit firmiter observari.

IV. *Roger of Hoveden, Chronica, s.a. 1200*

   From Bodleian ms. Laud Misc. 582, fo. 186[v] (= Hb); ed.
   Stubbs, iv.128.

Eodem anno Hubertus Cantuariensis archiepiscopus generale

---

[a]tactu ms.

[1]The professions of obedience to the church of Canterbury made upon consecration by these bishops are preserved at Canterbury. That of Giles de
Braose is endorsed: 'Anno mcc facta est hec professio apud Westmonasterium
capella sancte Katerine viii kal. Octobris contra appelacionem a monachis
Cantuariensibus super hoc factam.' *Canterbury Professions,* no. 142.

celebravit concilium Lundoniis apud Uestmonasterium contra
prohibitionem Gaufridi filii Petri comitis de Essex[a] tunc temporis summi[b] iusticiarii Anglie. In quo concilio idem archiepiscopus subscripta promulgavit decreta, statuens ea a suis
subiectis inviolabiliter observari.

V. *Canons of the council*

For manuscripts and editions see introduction above.

Decreta Huberti Cantuariensis archiepiscopi.[c]

[1] Cum in divinis officiis non sine periculo corporum et animarum erretur, salubri provisione concilii prospeximus ut a
quolibet sacerdote[d] celebrante verba canonis in missa[e] rotunde
dicantur et distincte, nec ex festinatione retracta nec ex
diuturnitate nimis protracta. Non est enim ibi diu immorandum
propter insurgentes cogitaciones, quia musce morientes perdunt
suavitatem unguenti.[1] Similiter et omnes hore et omnia officia
aperte et distincte dicantur, ita quod ex festinacione nimia non
precidantur vel sincopentur.[f] Quod si observatum non fuerit,
sacerdotes hoc non observantes post trinam admonicionem usque
ad condingnam satisfactionem suspendantur.[g] Salvo in omnibus
sacrosancte Romane ecclesie honore et privilegio.[2]

[2] Quod non liceat presbitero bis in die celebrare nisi necessitate cogente.[h]

Non liceat presbitero bis in die celebrare,[3] nisi necessitate
urgente; et tunc idem, quando in die bis celebrat, post primam
celebracionem et sanguinis sumptionem nil infundatur calici set

---

[a]Essex Hc; Essexe S; Exexe Hb.   [b]summu Hb.   [c]Decreta ... archiep.
HbS; Constitutiones archiep. Hc; Non [*sic*] regni regis Iohannis secundo
celebratum est concilium apud Westmonasterium a domino Huberto Waltero tunc
Cantuariensi archiepiscopo ubi promulgabantur hec decreta R.   [d]*add* missam R.   [e]in missa R (*cf. Canterbury I, c. 19*), *om.* HbHcS.   [f]vel sincopentur (cinco- Hc) HbHcS; nec sincopizentur R.   [g]suspendatur Hb.   [h]*om.*
nisi ... cogente HcRS.

---

[1]Eccle. 10, 1.   [2]Cf. C. of York (1195), c. 15 *ad fin.*
[3]Cf. *Decretum, De cons.* D. 1 c. 53.

post tantum secundam celebracionem.[a] Sane post primam celebracionem diligentissime absorbeantur stillule[b] de calice et digiti sugantur vel lingua lambantur, et laventur, reservata lotura in vase mundo ad id specialiter deputato, que lotura sumatur post secundam celebracionem. Hec ita se habeant nisi in prima celebratione assit diaconus vel alius minister honestus qui loturam sumere possit.

Hiis adicimus[1] ut reponatur eucaristia in pixide munda et honesta, et in pixide munda et honesta deferatur ad egrum,[c] lintheo mundo superposito et lucerna precedente ac cruce, nisi eger valde remotus fuerit. Renovetur quoque hostia ipsa singulis dominicis diebus, habeaturque certitudo circa ipsam eucaristiam, ita quod non sumatur non consecrata[d] pro consecrata.

Hiis adiciendum decrevimus ut secreto non detur communio eucaristie impenitenti,[e] set publice et instanter petenti danda est, nisi publicum sit eius delictum. Salvo in omnibus, etc.

[3] De baptismate vel confirmatione si dubitetur.[2]

De baptismate vel confirmatione si dubitetur, sacrorum canonum statuta sequentes,[3] statuimus ut conferatur, quia non dicitur iteratum quod nescitur [fo. 187] fuisse[f] collatum. Ideoque baptizentur expositi, de quorum baptismo dubitatur, sive inveniantur[g] cum sale sive sine sale.

Adicimus eciam ut nullus teneatur ad confirmationem a patre vel matre vel victrico vel noverca, et[4] ut non liceat diaconibus baptizare vel penitencias dare nisi duplici necessitate, videlicet quia sacerdos non potest vel absens est[h] vel stulte non vult, et mors iminet puero vel egro.[i] Si vero in necessitate puer baptizetur a laico, quod[j] fieri potest a patre vel a

---

[a]set ... celebracionem R (*cf. Canterbury I, c. 16*), *om.* HbHcS.   [b]stille R (*cf. Canterbury I, c. 16*).   [c]add vel consimili Hc.   [d]sumatur non consecrata R; sumat non consecratam HbHcS.   [e]impenitenti HcR; impetenti HbS.   [f]nescitur esse R; non scitur fuisse HbHcS.   [g]inveniatur Hb.   [h]est HcR; *om.* HbS.   [i]egro HbHcS; egroto R (*cf. Canterbury I, c. 28*).   [j]add si R.

---

[1]Cf. C. of York (1195), cc. 1, 2.
[2]Ibid., c. 5.
[3]*Decretum, De cons.* D. 4 c. 113 and *Comp. II* (in *Quinque compilationes antiquae* ..., ed. E. Friedberg, Leipzig, 1882), 5, 20, 2.
[4]Cf. C. of York (1195), c. 6.

matre absque matrimonii preiudicio, sequentia immersionem, non precedencia, per sacerdotem expleantur. Salvo in omnibus, etc.

[4] De penitencia.

Cum in penitencia,[a] que est secunda tabula post naufragium,[1] tanto maior adhibenda sit circumspectio quanto magis est necessaria post lapsum reparatio, nos sacrorum canonum statuta sequentes,[2] precipimus ut sacerdotes in penitencia diligenter attendant circumstancias: qualitatem[b] scilicet persone et quantitatem delicti, tempus, locum, causam, moram[c] in peccato factam, devocionem animi penitentis; et ut penitencia talis iniungatur uxori unde[d] non reddatur marito suo suspecta de aliquo occulto et enormi peccato vel crimine;[e] idem de marito observetur.[f] Nullus eciam sacerdos post lapsum, antequam confiteatur, ad altare presumat accedere celebraturus. Id adicimus[3] ad sacerdotum cupiditatem resecandam, ut misse non iniungantur in penitencia hiis qui non fuerint sacerdotes. Salvo in omnibus, etc.

[5] Quomodo archiepiscopus et episcopus et eorum officiales debeant hospitari cum subiectis.

Cum inter ea que statuta sunt a modernis patribus Latranense concilium celeberrimum[g] sit et omnimoda observacione[h] dignissimum, nos ipsius instituta humiliter ac devote sequentes[4] decernimus ut archiepiscopus parochias visitans quadragesimum vel quinquagesimum evectionis numerum, episcopi[i] vicesimum vel tricesimum nequaquam excedant; archidiaconi[j] vero quinque aut septem, decani constituti sub ipsis[k] duobus equis contenti

---

[a] in penitencia HcR; _om._ in Hb; penitencie HbS.   [b] qualitatem HcR; quantitatem HbS.   [c] morem Hb.   [d] unde HbRS; ut Hb¹Hc.   [e] peccato vel crimine HbHc; crimine R; peccato S.   [f] observetur R; conservetur HbHcS.   [g] celeberrimum HbHcS; saluberimum R.   [h] observatione R; conservatione HbS; conversatione Hc.   [i] episcopi R; episcopus HbHcS.   [j] archidiaconi R; archidiaconus HbHcS.   [k] ipsis R; episcopis HbHcS.

---

[1] _Decretum, De pen._ D. 3 c. 72 (Jerome), and P. Lombard, _Sent._ lib. 4 dist 14.
[2] _Decretum, De pen._ D. 5 c. 1 (Augustine), and more closely D. 1 c. 19 (= _Digest,_ 48, 19, 16).   [3] Cf. C. of York (1195), c. 4.
[4] C. of Lateran III (1179), c. 4 (largely verbatim).

existant. Nec cum canibus venatoriis aut avibus proficiscantur
set ita procedant ut non que sua sunt set que Iesu Christi
querere videantur.[1] Prohibemus eciam ne subditos suos talliis
et exaccionibus episcopi gravare presumant. Sustinemus autem,
pro multis necessitatibus que aliquociens superveniunt, ut si
manifesta et racionabilis causa extiterit, cum caritate moderatum[a] ab eis valeant auxilium postulare. Cum enim dicat[b] apostolus:[2] Non debent filii thesaurizare parentibus set parentes
filiis, multum[c] longe a paterna pietate videtur si prepositi
subditis suis graves existant, quos in cuntis necessitatibus
pastoris more debent fovere. Archidiaconi autem sive[d] decani
nullas exactiones vel taillias in presbiteros seu clericos exercere presumant. Sane quod de predicto[e] numero evectionis secundum toleranciam dictum est, in illis locis poterit observari in
quibus ampliores sunt redditus et ecclesiastice facultates. In
pauperibus autem locis tantam volumus teneri mensuram ut ex
accessu maiorum minores non debeant gravari, ne sub tali indulgentia illi, qui paucioribus equis uti solebant actenus, plurium[f]
sibi credant potestatem indultam.

Spectat autem ad visitatoris[g] officium ea inprimis que ad
salutem animarum pertinent cum omni diligencia procurare, et ut
unaqueque ecclesia habeat calicem argenteum et vestimenta sacer-
dotalia sufficiencia et honesta et libros necessarios et utensilia et cetera que spectant ad cultum et reverentiam sacramenti. Sane ad precidendum tam avaricie quam negligencie vitium,
auctoritate Toletani concilii[3] subnixi precipimus ut[h] visitator
[fo. 187[v]] ab ecclesia, in qua visitacionis officium debito modo
non exercet, procurationem aut procurationis redemptionem exigere non presumat. Salvo in omnibus, etc.

[a] moderatum R; modicum HbHcS.   [b] dicat R; dicit HbHcS.   [c] multum R;
multo HbHcS.   [d] autem sive R; aut sui HbHcS.   [e] predicto R; supradicto
HbHcS.   [f] plurium R; plurimum HbHc; plurimam S.   [g] visitatoris R; visitationis HbHcS.   [h] add archidiaconus R.

[1] Cf. Phil. 2, 21.   [2] II Cor. 12, 14.
[3] Decretum, C. 10 q. 1 c. 9.

[6] Ne quis ordinetur sine certo titulo.

Illud eciam iuxta tenorem Lateranensis concilii[1] firmiter observari precipimus ut si episcopus aliquem sine certo titulo, de quo vite[a] necessaria percipiat,[b] in diaconum vel presbiterum ordinaverit, tamdiu ei necessaria[c] subministret donec ei in aliqua ecclesia convenientia stipendia milicie clericali assingnet; nisi forte talis qui ordinatur extiterit qui de sua vel paterna hereditate subsidium[d] vite possit habere. Idem in subdiaconi ordinatione statuimus,[2] adiungentes ut si archidiaconus citra speciale mandatum episcopi sui aliquem predictorum ordinacioni[e] presentaverit, et is ad eius presentacionem ordinatus fuerit, predicte pene subiaceat. Salvo in omnibus, etc.

[7] Quod non liceat prelatis suspensionis vel excommunicationis sentenciam proferre in subiectos, nisi canonica commonicio precedat.

Rursus Lateranensis concilii statuta sequentes,[3] precipimus ut nec prelati, nisi canonica commonitione premissa, suspensionis vel excommunicationis sentenciam proferant in subiectos, nisi forte talis sit culpa que[f] ipso genere suo excommunicationis penam inducat, nec subiecti contra disciplinam ecclesiasticam ante ingressum cause in vocem appellationis prorumpant. Si vero quisquam pro sua necessitate crediderit appellandum, competens ei ad prosequendam appellationem terminus prefigatur, infra quem, si prosequi forte neglexerit, libere tunc episcopus auctoritate sua utatur. Si autem in quocunque negocio aliquis appellaverit, et eo qui appellatus fuerit veniente qui appellaverit venire neglexerit, si proprium quid habuerit, competentem illi recompensacionem faciat expensarum, ut hoc saltem timore perterritus in gravamen alterius non facile quis appellet.

---

[a]vite (*Lateran c.* 5); iure R.   [b]de quo ... percipiat R; *om.* HbHcS.
[c]necessaria R; *om.* HbHcS.   [d]subsidium R; subsidia HbHcS.   [e]ordinacioni HbHcS; taliter ordinandum R.   [f]*add* in HbHcS.

---

[1]C. of Lateran III, c. 5 (largely verbatim).
[2]Cf. *PL* ccxiv.68 (3 April 1198), 'Cum secundum apostolum', to the bishop of Zamorra (*Comp. III* (see p. 1061 n. 3), 3, 5, 1, *Extra,* 3, 5, 16) and *Sel. letters of Innocent III*, ed. C.R. Cheney and W.H. Semple, p. 35.
[3]C. of Lateran III, c. 6 (largely verbatim).

Precipue vero in locis religiosis[a] hoc volumus observari, ne
monachi sive quicunque religiosi, cum pro aliquo excessu fuerint
corrigendi, contra regularem prelati sui et capituli disciplinam appellare presumant, set humiliter ac devote suscipiant
quod pro salute sua eis fuerit iniunctum.

Ad reprimendam eciam multorum maliciam hiis duximus adnecten-
dum ut singulis annis in genere sollempniter excommunicentur
sorciarii, periuri super sacrosancta,[b] incendiarii,[c] fures
atrociores, raptores, ita ut qui scienter in dispendium cuiuslibet peieraverint[d] non absolvantur,[1] nec eis penitencia ab
aliquo iniungatur, nisi ab episcopo diocesano vel eius auctoritate, preterquam in articulo mortis; et tunc eis iniungatur
quod ex quo convaluerint episcopum adeant, ab eo vel eius
auctoritate penitenciam suscepturi. Salvo in omnibus, etc.

[8] Prohibetur ne aliquid exigatur pro sacramentis ecclesie.

Sicut in Lateranensi concilio salubriter a sanctis patribus
est provisum,[2] inhibemus ne pro[e] personis ecclesiasticis dedu-
cendis ad sedem, vel sacerdotibus vel aliis clericis instituen-
dis, aut sepeliendis mortuis, aut benedicendis nubentibus, seu
pro crismate, seu quibuslibet aliis sacramentis, aliquid exigatur. Si quis autem contra hoc venire presumpserit, porcionem
cum Giezi se noverit habiturum, cuius factum exaccione turpi
muneris imitatur.

Hiis adicimus ne pro licencia celebrandi divina a sacerdotibus, vel docendi a magistris, aliquid exigatur,[f] et si solutum
fuerit, repetatur.[3]

De eiusdem eciam auctoritate concilii[2] prohibemus ne novi
census ab episcopis vel abbatibus[g] aliisve prelatis imponantur
ecclesiis nec veteres augeantur, nec partem reddituum [fo. 188]

---

[a]religiosis RS; *om.* HbHc.   [b]super sacrosancta R; supra sacramenta HbS;
super sacramenta Hc.   [c]*add* usurarii R (*cf. Councils, ii.33, 150, 192*).
[d]peieraverint S; peioraverint HbHc; deierantur R.   [e]pro R; a HbHcS.
[f]requiratur R.   [g]ab abatibus Hb.

---

[1]Cf. C. of York (1195), c. 13.
[2]C. of Lateran III, c. 7 (largely verbatim).
[3]Ibid., c. 18 and *Appendix Conc. Lat.* (see pp. 969 n. 2, 1013), 2, 17 (*Extra,*
5, 5, 2).

suis usibus appropriare[a] presumant; set libertatem quam maiores
sibi conservari desiderant, minoribus quoque suis bona voluntate conservent. Si quis autem aliter egerit, irritum quod
fecerit habeatur.

Nulla[1] insuper ecclesiastica ministeria seu eciam beneficia
vel ecclesie alicui tribuantur vel promittantur antequam vacent,
ne desiderare quis proximi sui mortem videatur in cuius locum
et[b] beneficium se credit successurum. Cum enim id eciam[c] in
ipsis[d] gentilium legibus inveniatur prohibitum, turpe nimis est
et divini plenum animadversione iudicii si in[e] ecclesia Dei
future successionis expectacio locum habeat, quam et condemp-
nare ipsi gentiles homines curaverunt. Salvo in omnibus, etc.

[9] Ne decima minuatur occasione mercedis servientum vel messorum.[2]

Cum decimas Deo et sacerdotibus Dei[f] dandas Abraham factis
et Iacob promissis insinuent, et auctoritas veteris et novi
testamenti necnon et sanctorum patrum statuta declarent[3] decimas de omnibus que per annum renovantur prestandas, id inviolabiliter decernimus[g] observandum, ita quod occasione mercedis
servientum vel messorum decima pars non minuatur set potius
integre persolvatur. Habeant eciam presbiteri potestatem ante
autumpnum excommunicandi omnes fraudatores decimarum suarum et
eosdem secundum formam ecclesiasticam absolvendi. Huic adicimus
sancioni ut de terris noviter excultis non aliis[h] dentur decime
quam ecclesiis parochialibus infra quarum limites terre ille, de
quibus decime proveniunt, excoluntur. Detentores vero decimarum
iuxta Rothomagensis concilii constitutum,[4] si semel, secundo,
et tercio commoniti, excessum suum non emendaverint, usque ad

---

[a]appropriare R; applicare HbHcS.   [b]et R; vel HbHcS.   [c]id eciam
(*Lateran c. 8*); id et R; et HbHcS.   [d]*add* locis HbHcS.   [e]in RS; *om.* HbHc.
[f]decimas ... Dei R; Deo et sac. Dei decimas HbHcS.   [g]decrevimus R.
[h]aliis R; alias HbHcS.

---

[1]C. of Lateran III, c. 8 (largely verbatim).
[2]Cf. C. of York (1195), c. 11.
[3]Cf. *Decretum*, C. 16 q. 7 c. 6.
[4]C. of Westminster (1175), c. 13, which quotes C. of Rouen (650) from
Decretum, C. 16 q. 7 c. 5, and C. of Rouen (1190), c. 23.

satisfacionem congruam[a] anathematis vinculo feriantur.[b] Salvo in omnibus, etc.[c]

[10] Statuimus ut in ecclesia cuius redditus annuus quantitatem trium marcharum non excedit nullus instituatur nisi qui in propria persona ibidem voluerit deservire.

Ne clerici in sacris ordinibus constituti focarias habeant.[d]

Statuta eciam Lateranensis concilii reverenter amplectentes,[1] decernimus ut clerici in sacris ordinibus constituti, si mulierculas in domibus suis sub incontinencie nota[e] tenuerint, aut abiciant eas et continenter vivant aut ab officio et beneficio ecclesiastico fiant alieni.

Hiis eciam adnectimus ut clerici non intersint tabernis et publicis potacionibus.[2] Hinc etenim accidunt contenciones et rixe, adeo quod laici quandoque clericos verberantes incidant in canonem,[3] qui cum ad papam mittantur non est equum ut clerici, qui culpa sua quodammodo causam[f] dedere delicto,[g] maneant impuniti. Clerici eciam omnes habitum habeant clericalem et tonsuram canonicam. Archidiaconi autem et alii in dignitatibus constituti et presbiteri cappis manicatis non utantur. Salvo in omnibus, etc.

[11] Quales persone debeant contrahere matrimonium.

Vir non contrahat cum aliqua consanguinea olim uxoris sue, similiter nec uxor cum aliquo consanguineo quondam viri sui. Et susceptus in baptismo non contrahat cum filia baptizantis vel suscipientis, ante vel post genita. Nec contrahatur[h] aliquod matrimonium sine trina denunciatione publica in ecclesia, neque si fuerint persone incognite. Set nec copulentur alique persone matrimonio, nisi publice[i] in facie ecclesie et presente sacerdote; et si secus factum fuerit, non admittantur alicubi in

---

[a]congruam R; condignam HbHcS.   [b]feriatur Hb.   [c]c. 14 follows in R.
[d]Rubric misplaced, above at Statuimus HbHcS; Quod clerici non habeant uxores R.   [e]nota R (Lateran c. 11); vota HbHc; voto S.   [f]causam R; tamen HbHcS.
[g]delicto R; delictum HbHcS.   [h]contrahant R.   [i]add et R.

[1]C. of Lateran III, c. 11 (largely verbatim).
[2]Cf. C. of Westminster (1175), c. 2 and C. of York (1195), c. 14.
[3]Decretum, C. 17 q. 4 c. 29.

ecclesia, nisi speciali auctoritate episcopi.

Nulli eciam coniugatorum[a] liceat iter remote peregrinationis arripere, nisi[b] mutuo consensu publicato. Salvo in omnibus, etc.

[12] Diffamatis publica fama indicatur purgacio.[1]

Diffamati fama publica vel verisimilibus indiciis super crimine de quo convinci[c] non possunt, commoneantur semel, secundo, et tercio ut confiteantur et satisfaciant. Si vero incorrecti[d] in negatione perstiterint, indicatur eis [fo. 188ᵛ] purgatio, et non occasione pecunie captande differatur de die in diem, set statim primo die si parata fuerit suscipiatur et canonicum numerum non excedat. Salvo, etc.

[13] Ut leprosi cimiterium et proprium habeant capellanum.

Affectu pietatis inducti, concilii Lateranensis eciam insti-tucione suffulti,[2] decernimus ut ubicunque tot leprosi simul fuerint congregati, qui ecclesiam cum cimiterio sibi construere et proprio valeant gaudere presbitero, sine contradictione aliqua habere permittantur. Caveant tamen ut iniuriosi veteri-bus ecclesiis non existant. Quod enim eis pro pietate concedi-tur ad aliorum iniuriam nolumus redundare. Statuimus eciam ut de ortis et nutrimentis animalium suorum decimas tribuere non cogantur. Salvo in omnibus, etc.

[14] Ne aliquis sine episcopali auctoritate ecclesiastica bene-ficia de manu laica recipiat.

Lateranensis concilii tenore perpenso,[3] decernimus ne fratres Templi vel Hospitalis sive quicunque alii religiosi ecclesias vel decimas vel alia beneficia ecclesiastica sine episcopali auctoritate de manu laica recipiant, dimissis eciam quas contra tenorem istum moderno tempore receperunt. Excommunicatos et nominatim interdictos tam ab illis quam[e] ab omnibus aliis, iuxta

---

[a]coniugato R.   [b]sine R.   [c]convinci R; vinci HbHcS.   [d]incorrepti R.
[e]tam ... quam (*Lateran c. 9*); tam ab aliis quam R; tamquam HbHcS.

---

[1]Cf. C. of York (1195), c. 15.
[2]C. of Lateran III, c. 23 (largely verbatim).
[3]Ibid., c. 9 (largely verbatim).

sentenciam episcoporum statuimus evitandos. In ecclesiis suis,
que ad eos pleno iure non pertinent, instituendos presbiteros
episcopis presentent,[a] ut eis quidem de plebis[b] cura respon-
deant ipsis vero pro rebus temporalibus rationem exibeant
competentem. Institutos autem, inconsultis episcopis, non
audeant removere. Si vero Templarii sive Hospitalarii ad ecclesiam interdictam venerint, non nisi semel in anno ad ecclesiasticum admittantur officium, nec tunc ibi corpora sepeliant[c] defunctorum interdictorum. De fraternitatibus autem hoc[d] constituimus ut, si non se predictis fratribus omnino reddiderint set
in proprietatibus suis duxerint remanendum, propter hoc ab
episcoporum sentencia nullatenus eximantur set potestatem suam
in eos[e] sicut in alios parochianos suos exerceant, cum pro[f]
excessibus suis fuerint corrigendi. Quod autem de predictis
fratribus dictum est, ab aliis quoque religiosis, qui presump-
tione sua episcoporum iura preripiunt et contra canonicas eorum
sentencias et tenorem privilegiorum suorum venire presumunt,[g]
precipimus observari. Si autem contra hoc statutum venerint, et
ecclesie in quibus ista presumpserint subiaceant[h] interdicto,
et quod egerint eiusdem auctoritate concilii[i] irritum habeatur
et vacuum.

[15] Monachi[1] eciam sub precio non recipiantur in monasterio,
non peculium habere permittantur, non singuli per villas et
opida sive quascunque parochiales ponantur ecclesias, set in
maiore conventu aut cum aliquibus fratribus maneant, nec soli
inter seculares homines spiritualium hostium conflictum[j] expec-
tent, Salomone dicente:[2] 'Ve soli! quia si ceciderit, non
habebit sublevantem.' Si quis autem exactus pro sua receptione
aliquid dederit, ad sacros[k] ordines non ascendat;[l] is[m] autem

---

[a] representent R.   [b] plebit Hb.   [c] sepeliant R; sepelient HbHcS.
[d] hoc R; hec HbHcS.   [e] suam in eos (*Lateran c. 9*); suam HbHcS; in eos R.
[f] pro R; de HbHcS.   [g] presumant HbS.   [h] subiaceant R; subiciant HbHc; subij-
ciantur S.   [i] egerint ... concilii HbHcS; egerunt ut R.   [j] conflictum R;
afflictum HbHcS.   [k] sacros R; canonicos HbHcS.   [l] ascendat R; acendat Hb;
accendet Hc; accedat S.   [m] is (*Lateran c. 10*); his HbS; hiis HcR.

---

[1] Ibid., c. 10 (largely verbatim).   [2] Eccle. 4, 10.

qui acceperit,[a] officii sui privacione multetur. Si vero peculium habuerit, nisi ei ab abbate fuerit pro iniuncta administracione permissum, a communione removeatur altaris, et qui in
extremis cum peculio inventus fuerit, nec oblatio pro eo fiat
nec inter fratres recipiat sepulturam; quod eciam de diversis
religiosis precipimus observari. Abbas autem[b] qui diligenter
ista non curaverit, officii sui iacturam se noverit incursurum.
Prioratus quoque seu [fo. 189] obedientie precii dacione nulli
tradantur, alioquin et dantes et accipientes a ministerio fiant
ecclesiastico alieni. Priores vero, cum in conventualibus ecclesiis fuerint constituti, nisi pro manifesta causa et racionabili
non mutentur, videlicet si delapidatores fuerint, si inconti-
nenter vixerint, aut tale aliquid[c] egerint pro quo amovendi
merito videantur, aut si eciam pro maioris necessitate officii
fuerint transferendi.

[16] Et[d] illud preterea dignum adiectione[e] videtur, ne monachi
aut canonici nigri vel moniales nigre cappis coloratis utantur,
set tantum nigris. Nec utantur coopertoriis nisi nigris vel
albis, cum pellibus agninis vel catinis vel vulpinis. Monachi
eciam aut alii religiosi pileis non utantur, nec optentu[f] peregrinationis claustrum egrediantur.

Decernimus eciam ut in qualibet ecclesia monachorum vel
quorumlibet religiosorum suis usibus canonice appropriata
vicarius instituatur provisione episcopi honestam et sufficientem sustentacionem de bonis ecclesie percepturus.

VI. *Appendix of diocesan statutes*

        Printed here from BL ms. Royal 7. C. vii, fo. 55[r-v] (= R).

[1] Qualiter populus instruendus est.

    Precipimus etiam ut sacerdotes populum sibi commissum cum
omni diligentia, verbo pariter et exemplo, instruant. Doceantque frequenter in lingua materna orationem dominicam: scilicet

---

[a]acceperit R; accepit HbHc; accipit S.   [b]autem (*Lateran c. 10*); *add* et
HbS; etiam R.   [c]aliquid HcRS; aliquod Hb.   [d]Et HbS; *om.* HcR.   [e]adiec-
tionem R; abiectione HbHc; adiectione S.   [f]optemptu Hb.

Pater noster, et symbolum apostolorum: scilicet Credo in Deum,
et confessionem generalem: scilicet Confiteor. Instruantque eos
sollicite quod sine firma articulorum fide et futurorum bonorum
spe necnon et caritate, que est dilectio Dei et proximi, salus
provenire non potest. Doceantque[a] eos quante sit auctoritatis
confirmationis sacramentum. Licet enim sine eo salus proveniat
parvulo post perceptam baptismi graciam morituro, valde tamen
necessaria est confirmatio in hac vita victuro et cum spirituali-
bus nequitiis incessanter pugnaturo; ideoque instruantur ut par-
vulos suos offerant episcopo cum oportunitatem habuerint, ut cum
debita reverentia et summa devotione suscipiatur tantum sacramentum, quod non nisi per manus episcopi ministratur.

[2] De ornamentis ecclesie.

Precipimus etiam ut singule ecclesie calicem argenteum
habeant, pallas quoque altaris et vestes sacerdotales honestas,
vasa quoque et utensilia competentia, que[b] omnia postquam
fuerint sacris usibus deputata ad humanos usus extrinsecus
minime resumantur. Sed cum attrita[c] fuerint vel confracta, com-
burentur vel conflentur et cineres seorsum in loco sacro recon-
dantur. In libris quoque necessariis et ad divinum officium
competenter sufficientibus prospiciatur[d] cuilibet ecclesie, et
hii cum ceteris ornamentis non vendantur nec pignori obligentur
nec aliquo alienationis titulo ab ecclesia ammoveantur cum semel
fuerint deputata, nisi in casibus a canone concessis,[1] et hoc
cum speciali auctoritate nostra et conscientia.[e]

[3] De prestatione decimarum et potestate sacerdotum.

[fo. 55ᵛ] Quia sine decimarum prestatione salus omnino pervenire non potest, utriusque testamenti auctoritate subnixi
precipimus[2] ut decime de[f] omnibus que per annum renovantur
matrici ecclesie cum debita integritate solvantur, nisi forsan
alique fuerint ab integritate matricis ecclesie auctoritate

---

[a]Doceanque R.   [b]omnes *expunged* R.   [c]atria R.   [d]perspiciatur R.
[e]concientia R.   [f]*om.* de R.

---

[1]*Decretum*, C. 12 q. 2 c. 70.   [2]Cf. c. 9 above.

episcopali separate; ita quidem ut occasione mercedis servientum[a] vel messorum decima pars non minuatur. Habeant etiam presbiteri potestatem excommunicandi omnes fraudatores decimarum
suarum in genere et eosdem secundum formam ecclesiasticam absolvendi, si privatim ad satisfactionem venerint. Si vero publica-
tum[b] fuerit eorum delictum non absolvantur nisi ab episcopo vel
archidiacono. Quia vero nonnulli clerici decimas sibi ad
pauperum sustentaciones concessas in laico consueverint feodo
collocare, et multiplex ob hoc ipsum a laicis potestatibus
ecclesie et clericalibus[c] personis irrogari consueverit[d] iactura,
districte precipimus ut omnes per episcopatum nostrum decime in
libero[e] ecclesie tenemento collocentur, et si que forsitan per
clericorum nostrorum negligentiam vel malitiam fuerint in laicis
possessionibus adunate, nisi ad admonitionem per decanum loci[f]
ex parte nostra faciendam fuerint infra competentem terminum
ad ecclesiasticum tenementum delate, si per clericos nostros
steterit, in ipsos competenter animadvertemus; sin vero per
laicos, terram illam in qua decime[g] fuerint violenter detente,
usque ad competentem satisfactionem iubemus sub interdicto concludi.

[4] Antiqua etiam canonum statuta sequentes,[1] decernimus ut
clerici in sacris ordinibus constituti, si mulierculas in domibus suis sub incontinentie nota tenuerint,[h] aut abiciant eas et
continenter vivant[i] aut ab officio et benefitio ecclesiastico
fiant penitus alieni. In minoribus vero ordinibus clerici constituti, si inventi fuerint concubinarii, quia ipsis libertatem
ab apostolo concessam[2] auferre nolumus nec valemus, per censuram ecclesiasticam, interdicti scilicet et excommunicationis,
compellantur ad alterutrum, videlicet vel concubinas penitus
abiciant vel cum ipsis in facie ecclesie publice ac[j] sollempniter contrahant.

---

    [a]*om.* servientum R.   [b]publicato R.   [c]clerici R.   [d]consueverint R.
[e]libro R.   [f]leti R.   [g]decimam R.   [h]continuerint R.   [i]*add* et R.
[j]hac R.

---

   [1]Ibid., c. 10.   [2]I Cor. 7, 2.

[5] De clericali habitu.[a]

His[b] etiam adnectimus[1] ut sacerdotes et clerici cuiusque
ordinis habitum habeant clericalem et tonsuram canonicam. Si
quis vero inventus fuerit comam nutriens[c] et quasi sus ad volu-
tabrum luti et canis ad vomitum reversus,[2] ab eo quem semel
assumpsit, si archidiaconi commonitione[d] tonsuram non resump-
serit, si benefitiatus fuerit ab officio et benefitio ecclesiastico suspendatur.

[6] His adnectimus ut clerici abstineant a turpibus spectaculis,
ab his maxime in quibus sanguis humanus effunditur, adeo ut nec
torneamentis nec duellis de cetero interesse presumant, sed nec
tabernis nec publicis intersint potationibus. Prohibemus etiam
ne sacerdotes vel reliqui clerici usuris vel negociationibus
vel lucris turpibus invigilent. Fenerari[e] quidem omnibus indistincte prohibetur; negotiari vero, cum sit laicis ubicunque
permissum, clericis tamen omnibus est in antiquis canonibus
usque quaque prohibitum.[3] Si quis autem post hanc nostram in-
hibitionem clericus fuerit inventus et negotiator, in ipsum
noverit iuxta canonum statuta severissime iudicandum.

[7] Quod sacerdotes non admittantur.

Dum simus debitores, iuxta verbum apostoli,[4] pro commisso
nobis grege ante Christi tribunal respondere, grave quidem
gerimus quod sacerdotes annui[f] absque nostra conscientia[g] ad
animarum curam gerendam inutiles interdum admittuntur et indigni.
Et cum fuerint admissi, nobis insciis[h] et inconsultis, pro
libitu clericorum, cum parochianorum[i] suorum secreta didicerint,
indistincte ammoverentur et alii in eorum locum, pro ut levius
ac vilius sicut aliquod vile mancipium conduci possunt, in grave
discrimen animarum substituuntur. Eapropter precipimus ne quis

---

[a]*Rubric misplaced before* Antiqua etiam, *above* R.   [b]Hii R.   [c]nutries R.
[d]communitione R.   [e]Fenerarii R.   [f]animi R.   [g]concsientia R.   [h]inciis
R.   [i]parochinorum R.

---

[1]Cf. c. 10 above.   [2]II Pet. 2, 22.
[3]Cf. *Decretum*, D. 46 cc. 9-10, C. 14 q. 4, C. 21 q. 3.
[4]Not an exact citation: cf. Heb. 13, 17 and II Cor. 5, 10.

de cetero capellanus vel annuus vel perpetuus ad curam animarum
admittatur, nisi nobis prius fuerit presentatus, et cum fuerit
admissus non nisi nobis consultis ammoveatur. Salvo, etc.[a]

184

1200-4. PAPAL NUNCIOS AND VISITORS

In April 1200 Master Philip, a papal subdeacon and notary, came
to England, sent by the pope to raise money for the Crusade;
he was able to arm himself with a royal letter of recommenda-
tion, toured the country instructing the bishops how to raise
the tax, and also raising money to pay his expenses and as gifts
to the pope. Complaints were made that he gathered substantial
sums for himself and the pope, and there is some evidence to
confirm this. The tax for the crusade was the fortieth of ecclesiastical revenues demanded in a papal encyclical of December
1199. In a mandate of 5 May 1201 the pope renewed his order;
but he was never satisfied with the funds received from England,
and complaints and discussion of it rumbled on for many years.[1]

In 1201 John of Salerno, cardinal priest of S. Stefano in
Monte Celio, legate to Scotland and Ireland, passed through
England. At Canterbury he gave help to St. Augustine's abbey
against some royal officials; in London he was received in
solemn procession at St. Paul's (late August); at York he tried
to take action in the dispute between Archbishop Geoffrey and
his chapter - Geoffrey alleged that he ordered the chapter and
the bishop of Durham to withhold obedience from himself.[2] His

---

[a]*Cf. above, Westminster (1200) c. 1 ad fin.*

---

[1]For all this see C.R. Cheney, in *EHR* lxiii (1948), 342-50; id., *Innocent III and England*, pp. 243-6; and see ibid., pp. 247-8 for a fortieth
granted by the king in 1201-2. As in 1188 it was the fruit of joint initiative by the kings of England and France, although there is no evidence that
Philip II collected it. Collections were made in England and at least
attempted in Normandy; their destiny is unknown.
[2]Cheney, *Innocent III and England*, p. 38 n. 55; Tillmann, p. 90; London,
Public Record Office, E164/27, fo. 102 (cited Cheney, loc. cit.); Thorne,
col. 1854. On Archbishop Geoffrey's complaint see M.B. Lovatt, 'The Career
and Administration of Archbishop Geoffrey of York' (unpubl. Cambridge Ph.D.
thesis, 1974-5), pp. 334-7; Hoveden, iv.174-5.

visit to London may have been the occasion of a council. He was
received at St. Paul's on 31 August, and meanwhile on 24 August
Archbishop Hubert, at Westminster,

> praecepit universis suffraganeis suis in virtute obedientiae
> et ex parte domini papae ut ipsi, facta diligenti inquisi-
> tione per suas dioceses, compellerent, si quos invenissent
> viros qui crucis religionem abiecerant, cruces resumere, et
> iter peregrinationis suae arripere,

giving them to St. Martin next (11 November) to resume the
cross, and to the Purification (2 February) as 'terminum motio-
nis'.[1] It was probably late in August that the cardinal
attached his seal to the settlement of the great dispute about
Lambeth between the archbishop and the monks of Christ Church
Canterbury.[2] The settlement was made by judges delegate on 6
November 1200 and ratified by the pope on 31 May 1201;[3] but the
sealing must have taken place during the legate's visit. Sixteen
seals were attached, the first that of the chapter of St. Paul's,
which suggests that the ceremony took place during the legate's
reception there. The other seals confirm the impression that a
council took place during this period: they are of Henry bishop
of Llandaff, Roger dean of Lincoln, Samson abbot of St. Edmund's
(Bury), bishops John of Norwich, Eustace of Ely, William of
London, Archbishop Hubert, Cardinal John, bishops Godfrey of
Winchester, Gilbert of Rochester, Henry of Exeter, Robert of
Bangor, Mauger of Worcester, Giles of Hereford, and the Hospital
of St. John of Jerusalem at London.

Another papal envoy, Gerald, abbot of Casamari, while acting
as nuncio in France with the task of making peace between Philip
II and John of England, may have visited England early in 1204

---

[1]Diceto, ii.173; Hoveden, iv.173.
[2]Canterbury, Cathedral Archives Chartae antiquae, L 130 (formerly L 344);
C.R. Cheney in *English Episcopal Acta, Canterbury, 1193-1205*, no. 383 and n.;
Ep. Cant., pp. 512-14; for the case ibid. and Cheney, *Hubert Walter*, chap. 7.
The legate's seal makes it clear that the sealing cannot belong to November
1200.
[3]*Letters of Pope Innocent III concerning England and Wales*, ed. C.R. and
M.G. Cheney, no. 322.

and perhaps attended a royal council in March 1204.[1]

Pope 'Innocent III did not renew Hubert's legation, which lapsed with Celestine's death. So long as Hubert lived he gave him important commissions, administrative and diplomatic, and he sent no legate'.[2]

185

? 1203. DEMANDS BY THE ARCHBISHOP OF CANTERBURY FOR ALMS, AID, ETC.

Two mandates of Archbishop Hubert Walter refer in similar, but far from identical, terms to a special demand for alms, which may possibly be dated to 1203, and arise from a meeting of bishops, or even from a provincial council, otherwise unrecorded. They are discussed by C.R. Cheney in 'Levies on the English clergy in 1203, for the poor and for the king', *EHR*, xcvi (1981), forthcoming.

1. One mandate, known only from the reply of the bishop of Salisbury (Canterbury Cathedral Archives, Christ Church Letters II, no. 225; printed in *HMCR, Report on Various Collections*, i.234) was probably addressed to all the archbishop's suffragans. It requested alms for the poor from the diocesan clergy, both resident and non-resident, and also ordered the bishop to summon and induce them to pay an aid to the king. In his reply the bishop of Salisbury complained that barely a tenth of the parochial clergy, mostly annual vicars with few rectors or perpetual vicars, responded to his summons to chapters, and requested instructions for dealing with absentees. The demand for an aid may be connected with a royal levy in 1203: Wendover states that Hubert Walter was instructed to organize a levy on the clergy: cf. S.K. Mitchell, *Studies in taxation under John and Henry III*, pp. 62-3.[3]

---

[1]Cheney, *Innocent III and England*, pp. 41, 287-91; he shows at p. 289 n. 58 how slight is the evidence that he came to England; on his mission see also Tillmann, pp. 90-2.

[2]Cheney, *Innocent III and England*, pp. 37-8; cf. id., *Hubert Walter*, chap. 6.

[3]For further evidence on the date and significance of these documents, see Cheney, art. cit.

2. The second mandate, not certainly authentic, is only known in a late text addressed to Geoffrey (de Muschamp), bishop of Coventry. It is to put into effect in his diocese the provision made by the archbishop, with the advice and assent of his fellow bishops, to meet the evils of the time. The clergy of each diocese are to be exhorted and, if need be, compelled to help the poor in their parishes lest they die of starvation. Non-resident clergy are to be obliged to give a quarter of their revenues in alms. There are also provisions for prayers and processions (Durham Cathedral Lib., ms. C. IV.24, fo. 101). References in the letter, e.g. to the famine, would fit 1203 or shortly after;[1] and it is possible that the meeting of bishops lay behind both these mandates. But the differences between them make this far from certain.

---

[1] See p. 1076 n. 3.

Note: Ecclesiastical dignitaries are indexed under their Christian names, with cross-references from the names of churches etc. or the titles of their offices; and the names are usually noted even if they are not named in the text. Medieval persons are indexed by Christian name; those who lived between *c.*1500 and *c.*1800 under surnames; names after *c.*1800 are omitted. For both personal and place-names, medieval forms not identified on the same page are given in the index with cross-references. English place-names are given their traditional shires. More than one reference on a single page has not been separately noted.

Abbreviations include:

abb.	abbot		card.	cardinal
abp.	archbishop		dioc.	diocese
archd.	archdeacon		el.	elect(ed)
archdry	archdeaconry		mk.	monk
bp.	bishop		pr.	prior
C.	Council			

637 n., 658, 669 n., 674
Alexander II, Pope, 448 n., 563-4,
572, 588, 590, 627, 668, 681;
letter to Lanfranc, 577, 616;
letter from Lanfranc to, 585-6,
591, 597-601; transfer of see to
Lincoln, 566; legates, 563-5;
death, 586; his relations in Normandy, 590 n.
Alexander III, Pope, formerly Card.
Roland, papal chancellor, el. and
recognition, 835-41; (and legation
of Theobald, 1160-1), 806 n., 820;
(C. Montpellier, 1162), 845; (C.
Tours, 1163), 845-7, 850 n.; and
Const. Clarendon (1164 and later),
855-7, 861-7, 869-71, 878-83, 893;
(1164), 855, 894, 909-10, 913-14;
(and Becket's exile and events of
1164-70), 864-5, 914-20, 929;
(1165 and crusade), 1023; (1169),
927, 931, 933-4, 936-7, 939;
(1170), 940, 942; (1171), 941;
(1172), 943-50, 953, bull of, 955-
6; (1173-4), 944, 959-60, 1003,
1009; (and precepts and decretals
related to C. Westminster, c.1175),
968-70, 975, 983, 986, 987 n., 988,
990; (1176), 996, 998-1002; (III
Lateran, 1179), 1011-14, 1047;
Vita Alex. III, 945, 950; other
refs., xxxix n., 877, 905, 976,
992
Alexander, bp. Lincoln, Lincol(n)i-
ensis, 745, 753, 765, 784, 794,
808, 812
Alexander of Canterbury, 656-7
Alexander Walensis, 903-4
Alexandria, 273; bp. (patriarch) of,
see Athanasius, St.
Alfred, king of Wessex (West Saxons,
and Angles and Saxons, 17), vi,
17; and Abingdon, 187 n.; his version of *Cura pastoralis*, vii, 16,
170 n.; gift of Exeter to Asser,
171 n.; his Laws, 14-35, 49 n.,
468 n., 470; and Laws of 'Edward
and Guthrum', 302, 304; letter to,
4, 6-13; and Peter's pence ('Rome
money'), 62 n.; and scholars, 7,
13; his brother, 186 n.; his daughter, see Ælfthryth
Alfred, bp. (dioc. unknown), 82 n.
Alfred, bp. Sherborne, 82 n.
Alfred of Beverley, 795 n.
Alfricus, see Ælfric

Alfwold, abb. Winchcombe, 190
Alfwold, bp. Crediton, 189; will of,
382-6
Alfwold, bp. Crediton *or* Sherborne,
132
Alfwold the monk, 385-6
Alfwold, thegn, brother of Æthelwine,
ealdorman of E. Anglia, 162-4
Alice de Valognes, 815
All Martyrs, feast of, 59
All Saints, feast of, 34, 59
alms, almsgiving, 70, 74, 76, 228,
380-1, 773; by guild, 517; for bps.'
souls, 403, 405; distribution of,
332-3; as duty for bps., 415; for
clergy, 268; before election, 773;
on feastdays, 330; in *Reg. Concordia*, 136; for security of nation,
374, 378, 606; tithes as alms for
the poor, 210, 391; (1009), 376;
(1027), 507; (1188, for Holy Land
and poor), 1029; (?1203), 1076-
7; *and see* poor
Alps, 84, 647, 757
Alricus, see Æthelric
altars, 328-9; to be consecrated,
324, 456, and of stone, 575; fur-
nishing, cloths, 208, 292-3, 325,
328-9
Alton, treaty of (1101), 668
Alured, Master, 720
Aluricus, see Ælfric
Alwinus, see Ælfwine
Amalarius, *De regula canonicorum*,
135, 137 n., 195, 216 n., 348 n.;
De eccl. offic., 134
Ambrose, St., 69
Amesbury (Wilts.), C. in, 157; abbey,
947
Amiens, bp. of, see Theobald
ampulla, 1041
Anacletus II, anti-pope, as Peter
Pierleoni, card. priest S. Maria
in Trastevere, legate to France,
England and perhaps Ireland, Scot-
land, etc., 723-5, 731, 754; as
anti-pope, 754-5, 766
Anagni, xxxix n., 959
Ananias and Sapphira, 126
Anastasius, St., 199 n.
Anastasius IV, Pope, 806 n., 827
Anathoth, Anathot, 851
Andegavia, see Angers, Anjou
Andover (Hants), 95, 97, 107
Andrew, St., 300
Andrew, bp. Caithness, 997

717-19, 724; (1125-7), 731, 742,
744; (1163), 846, 848, 873 n.;
(1175), 976 n.; (1176), 994-6,
998-1000; privileges, documents,
forgeries, 35-6, 82, 89, 165, 587,
591 n., 600, 655, 724, 727, 730;
professions, 81-4, 599, 604-5, 715,
719, 1059 n.; provincial councils,
see Councils; relation of bp.
Rochester to abp., 1030; of Theobald and Henry of Blois, 780, 805,
810; and Welsh church, 813-14;
  archd., 454 n., and see Geoffrey
(Ridel), Helewise, Herbert, John,
William;
  cathedral, Christ Church, as
'mater ecclesia', 589; fire at
(1067), 599-600; (1070), 585, 588;
and Anselm's pallium, 646; consecration of bps., in, 601, 705,
714, 1033; 'misera Cant. ecclesia',
1041; purgation after Becket's
murder (1171), 941 n.; priory,
conversion from clerks to mks.,
238; archives and mss., (archives),
531 n., 565 n., 592-3, 610, 698,
(mss.), 246, 354 n., 390 n.,
535 n., 711 n., 735, 744, 820,
974; ASC at, 155 n.; catalogue of
mss., 247 n.; mss. of C. Clermont,
648; I Lateran, 729-30; Const.
Clarendon, 872-3, 875-6; Gospel
book, 444, 447; letter collections
of Anselm, 659 n., 671, 696; and
see decretals; scribes, 6 n.;
legacy to, 239; mks. of, (1095),
646; (1100), 655; (1143), 808-10;
(1191), 1024; dispute with abp.
settled (1201), 1075; and see this
entry above, under election; see
also Eadvius, Warner; precentor,
1024; prior, 708, and see Alan,
Ernulf, Geoffrey, Henry (of Eastry),
J., Jeremiah, Odo; priory as
prison, 625;
  St. Augustine's abbey, 595, 696;
case against Abp. Theobald, 804-
10; abb., see Ælfsige, Clarembald,
Hugh, Scollandus, Wulfric; archives,
592; ms. from 646; chronicles, 805,
807-10; Life of St. Dunstan revised at, 86; papal privileges for,
808; vacancies at, 644, 653 n.;
  St. Gregory's priory, 1033
Cantia, see Kent
capital crime, 493-4; punishment,
342, 346, 614

Capua, siege of, 645
care of souls, see cure
Carlisle (Cumberland), Carleolensis,
Kardullia, Karlel, 767-8; bp. of,
see Adelold, Bernard; bishopric,
see, 1043; pr. of, 757
Carolingian capitularies, 195
carpet, tapeta, 739, 775
Carthage, C. of (348), 985-6; (397),
984
Carthusian Order, mks. of, 917, and
see Engelbert, Simon
Casamari, abb. of, see Gerald
Cashel-Lismore, C. of (1172), xl n.
castles, of bps. (1139), 782, 785-6;
castle works etc. (1143), 803;
(1151), 823
Cathars, in England, 920-5; bishops,
920; called Publicani, 923
cathedral chapters, constitutions of,
x
Ceadwalla, king of Wessex, 187
Cedd, bp. East Saxons, 78 n.
Celericus, thegn (? for Ælric), 526,
532 n.
Celestine II, Pope, 806 n.
Celestine III, Pope, 1029, 1035,
1038, 1041-2; letter to, 1036-7;
and chapter of York, 1045-7; death,
1076
celibacy, for clergy, and clerical
incontinence, (Fulk of Rheims), 13;
(IV Edgar), 108; (Ælfric), 196-201
passim, 204, 277-81, 289-90, 299 n.;
(Wulfstan and Cnut), 432; (1049),
522, (1070), 576; (1076), 616-17,
619; and Bp. Wulfstan, 617; (1096),
649; (1102), 617, 675; (1108), 695,
698, 700-3; (1125), 740; (1127),
747-8; (1129), 751-4; (1175), 967,
984;
  concubines and wives condemned,
13, 289-90, 299 n., 668 n., 685,
698, 748, 776, 833, 979, 1051,
1067, 1072; in NPL, 459; see also
concubines; hereditary benefices
and prebends, 685, 739, 775, 967,
969, 979, 984;
  married archds., 688, 752 n.;
bp., see Leofwine; canons, 685,
688, 740, 747-8; other clergy,
(1005 × 8), 337; (1008), 343, 365;
(1076), 616-17; (1102), 670, 675,
679, 688; (1108), 700; (1125), 732;
(1127), 745; (1129), 751-4; (1175),
979, 984; in 11th cent. Normandy,
616-17; see also bishops, clergy;

celibacy (*cont.*)
  masses of married priests, 680;
  twice married or bigamous clergy,
  290, 343, 459
Celtic names, *see* Kenstec
Celwerdus, etc., *see* Æthelweard
cemetery, graveyard, 98, 390 n.,
  795 n., 799, 986; and excommuni-
  cates, 801, 803; and lepers, 1068;
  and see burial, sanctuary
Cenomannum, *see* Le Mans
Centwine, king of Wessex, 632
Cenwold, 385
Cenwulf, bp. Dorchester, 169
Cenwulf, bp. Winchester, 260 n.
Cenwulf, king of Mercia, 18 n.
Ceolnoth, abp. Canterbury, 171 n.
Ceolric, 240-1
Ceolweard, 240
ceorl, 31, 33; marriage of, 438;
  punishment for magic etc., 462;
  slave of, 30
Cerisy, de Cerasis, abb. of, 962,
  and see Martin
Cerne (Dorset), abbey, 186 n., 193,
  653 n., 811; abb., *see* Bernard,
  Edward, Hamo
Certesei, Certisei, *see* Chertsey
Cestria, Cestrum, *see* Chester
Chaise-Dieu, La, abbey of, 655
Chalcedon, C. of (451), 215, 274 n.,
  275, 985-6
chalice(s), 208, 224, 1041; in
  Theodred's will, 77, 80-1; in
  Alfwold's will, 386; to be of
  metal, 292 (or glass), 327-8; to
  be of silver, 1049, 1063, 1071;
  not of 'wax' (for brass), 576;
  wooden, 456, 576 n.; stolen, 860
Chalon-sur-Saône, bp., *see* Engelbert
chamberlain, *see* William Mauduit
Channel, English, 643, 656, 691
chapel, royal, 708; as place for
  episcopal consecrations, 714; for
  elections, 868 n., 869, 882, 890;
  royal free, *see* Gloucester, St.
  Oswald; other chapels, 676, 777,
  802; castle chapels, 825
chaplains, *see* priests
Charité-sur-Loire, La, prior and convent, 841-2; mk. of, *see* Adam
charters, vi, x, 119-33, 525-33;
  charters of liberties, ix, (Henry
  I), 652-5; (Stephen), 762-6;
  (Henry II), 828-9
Chartres, bp. of, 756, *and see* Fulbert, Ivo, John of Salisbury;

synod at (1124), 731
chastity, 62, 196-7, 199-200, 204,
  264-9, 276-81, 287, 290, 365, 663,
  675, 683, 685; life of, for married
  couples, 466-7; for clergy, 264,
  348, 576, 675, 688; (in C. 1108),
  699-700; for canons, and mks., 348;
  and see celibacy
chasuble(s), 77, 81
Chaumont-en-Vexin, 721, 941
Chelsea, synod of, 77 n., 403
Chertsey (Surrey), Certesei, Certisei,
  etc., abbey, mks. introduced, 114;
  privilege for, 543-4; vacancies,
  644 n., 653 n.; abb. of, 403, *and*
  see Hugh, Lyfing, Ordbyrht, Wulf-
  wold
Chester, Cestrensis, etc., St. Wer-
  burga's abbey, 640; abb., *see*
  William
Chester, al. Coventry, bp., *see* Geoffrey (de Muschamp), Gerard Pucelle,
  Hugh (of Nonant), Peter, Richard
  (Peche), Robert (de Limesey), Roger
  (de Clinton); bishopric, see, moved
  to Chester, 613; to Coventry, 657;
  and abp. York, 590; vacancy, 572,
  753; *and see* Coventry, Lichfield
Chester, earl of, *see* Hugh (of Avranches), Ranulf, Richard; Franciscan convent, library of, 780 n.
Chester-le-Street (Durham), bp. of,
  see Wigred; see of, 443
Chichester (Sussex), Cicestrum,
  Cisestrensis, etc., Sussex, archd.
  of, *officiales* of, 816, *and see*
  Jordan; bp., *see* Hilary, John (of
  Greenfield), Ralph, Seffrid I, II,
  Stigand; see of Selsey, transferred
  to Chichester, 609, 613, *and see*
  Stigand; deans and deaneries in,
  816-17; town, 'Pallant' in, 816 n.
Chickering (Suffolk), 78
Chinon, 1025
chirograph, in St. Albans case, 835;
  of Const. of Clarendon, 852 n.,
  854, 871, 875, 886-93
Cholsey (Berks.), abbey, 237 n.,
  240; abb., *see* Germanus
chrism, and holy oil, 205 n., 210,
  306 n., 454, 605, 809, 1033; blessing of, 250, 258, 306; payment for,
  244, 254, 738, 774, 979, 986, 1065;
  and excommunicates, 800-1
Christian, bp. Galloway, 997
Christianus, queen's clerk, 791
Christina, princess, 661 n.

clothing, dress, 321; in Roman
times, 3; decree on (1102), 680,
683; 'scarlet' in sumptuary legislation (1188), 1028; of bps., 679;
of clergy, 219, 296, 300, 321 n.,
329, 676, 680; of nuns, 749, *and
see* furs

Cluny, abbey, 645, 655-6, 755, 810
n.; abb., *see* Peter (the Venerable); mk., 688-9, *and see* Alberic,
Imar, Peter the Chamberlain; Order,
755

cniht(as), 515

Cnut, king of England, Denmark and
Norway, charter for Glastonbury,
632 n.; *Consiliatio Cnuti*, 303,
468; *Instituta Cnuti*, 452, 468;
Laws, early draft, 431-4; selec-
tions from I and II Cnut, 468-
506; Text of I (ecclesiastical
ordinance), 471-86; from II (secular ord.), 486-506; 12th-cent.
ms., 962; other refs., 194, 339-
41 *passim*, 343, 359 n., 428, 435,
450-1; drafting of, *see* Wulfstan;
Letters from, (of 1019 × 20),
303, 435-41; (of 1027, and visit
to Rome), 469 n., 506-13; visit
to Rome, 506-10; letters to, from
Fulbert, 94 n.; from Wulfstan,
444, 447-9; writ addressed to,
447-9;
(in 1019), 469; visit to Denmark (1019), 435; (1020), 435;
(1027), 445; visits to Denmark
(1027), 506, 511; Cnut as witness,
428; and Bp. Ælfric, 514; coun-
cillor of, 227 n.; housecarl, *see*
Urki; his wife, *see* Ælfgifu

Coenlaf, Keonolaf, 41

Coenræd, Conrat, Konrat, 41, 43

Coenwald, bp. Worcester, Keonowald,
Keonwad, 40-3, 87

Coenwulf, abb. Peterborough, Kenulf,
190

Coenwulf, king of Mercia, 186, 186-
7 n.

Coenwynn, Kenuun, Kenvun, 41-3

coins, money, 343, 357, 432, 450;
in Æthelred II's laws, 341; in
Cnut's laws, 470; gold, 514, 515;
mancuses (gold and silver), 76,
79, 240, 384-6; moneyers' frauds,
371, 735; moneyer at Bury, 561

Colchester (Essex), abb. of, *see*
Gilbert

Collections, in IV Books, 735; in
IX Books, 658 n., 660 n.; in Ten
Parts, 651 n.; in XIII Books, 729 n.;
in XVII Books, 734; *and see* Anselm
of Lucca, Deusdedit, Lanfranc, law
(canon), decretals, Pseudo-Isidore

Cologne, 1012

Columbanus, Bp. (suffragan of York),
444

comet (975), 156, 158-9

commendatory letters for clerks and
mks. travelling, etc., 68, 575,
606, 613, 619, 776, 825, 980, 985-6

communion, payment for, forbidden,
738, 774, 979, 986; *and see*
eucharist, mass, sick

Comoere, Cemoyre, Comuyre, priest and
bp. of Cornwall, possibly = Wulfsige, 172 n., *and see* Wulfsige

compensations, *see* wergild; 19-20,
26-9 *passim*, 50, 65, 312, 354-5,
396, 399, 458-63 *passim*, 480, 490-
7 *passim*, 500; by priest, 458-61;
for bridal offences, 431; for offences against clerks, 492, 494,
497; for crimes in Lent, 496; for
heathen practices, 462; for incest,
497; for offences against Sundays
and feast days, 494; for perjury,
490; for breach of sanctuary,
388-9, 456, 463; for slaying a
priest, 457-8; for sureties, 500

Compostella, C. of (1056), 567

compurgation, 31, 57, 394-5, 397,
492-8, 701; compurgators, 462, *and
see* oath-helpers

Conan, bp. Cornwall, Cunune, 171-2

Conan, count of Brittany, 878

concubines, 321 n., 466 n., 499;
concubinage in *NPL*, 459; for clerical concubines, *see* celibacy

confession, 23, 214-15, 225, 295, 308,
319, 355, 370, 683; and penance,
65; and condemned man, 494; (in
1009), 375, 379; in *NPL*, 454; to
sodomy, 678; confessors, 380, 421,
481, 484; confessor of diocese,
1051; text on, 313, 491 n., 501 n.

confirmation, 205, 284, 424 n., 484,
1051-2; and godparents, 322; payment for, 244; for sick, 335; teaching on, 1071; priest's duty to un-
confirmed, 319

confraternities, 1069

Congresbury (Somerset), 546-7

Cono, card. bp. Palestrina, papal

COUNCILS AND SYNODS (*cont.*)
670-1; G Clermont, 647-9, 651 n.,
670, 672; R Rockingham, 644, 646;
(1096), N Rouen, 648, 795 n.;
(1098), G Bari, 645, 650-2, 671;
(1099), G Rome, 649-52, 671;
(1100), L Poitiers, 565 n.; E
Lambeth, 661-7; (1102), E Westminster, xi, 657, 659, 668-88,
695, 755; canons and decisions,
668, 670, 672-3, 674-80, 686-7;
aftermath, 695, 699-700; (1105),
G Rome, 659; (1106), Guastalla,
690 n.; (1107), Troyes, 690 n.,
691; R Westminster, 689-94; (1108),
?Winchester, 698; London, R 694;
E 694-704; canons, 695-7, 700-3,
745; (1115), R Westminster, 709-
16; L Châlons-sur-Marne, 710;
(1116), R Salisbury, 717; (1119),
G Rheims, xi, 718-21; Toulouse,
735; (1120), Naples, 670 n.; L
Beauvais, 723; (1121), R, 723;
(1123), G I Lateran, 728-30, 735,
826 n., 862; R Gloucester, 725;
(1124), Chartres, 731; (1125), L
Westminster, 720 n., 721, 733-41,
769; canons, 738-41, 744-5, 795;
(1127), R London, 743; L Westminster, 721, 743-9; canons, 746-
9; (1128), N Rouen, 750 n.; (1129),
L London, 750-4; (1130), Clermont,
Würzburg, 755; (1131), G Rheims,
754, 757-8; (1132), R London,
757-61; (1135), G Pisa, 776 n.;
(1138), L Westminster, 735, 766,
768-79, 794 n., 795, 796 n.;
canons, 774-8; (1139), L Winchester, 781-7, 790, 794; G II Lateran,
779-81, 862; (1141), L Winchester,
788-92; L Westminster, 792-4;
(1143), March, L London, 735, 769,
771, 782, 794-804; canons, 800-4,
820, 822; *c*.Sept., L Winchester,
804-5, 808-9; Nov., L London,
804-10; (1145), L London, 811-13;
(1145 × 8), 812; P London, 814;
(1148), G Rheims, 796, 814, 817-
20, 862; (1151), L London, xi,
796, 821-6; canons, 823-6; (1152),
L London, 826-8; (1154 × 61), M
London, 815; (1156), R, 859; London, 829-35; (1160), Pavia (im-
perial), 836; E London, 835-6;
N Neufmarché, 837; (1161), Canterbury, 841-2; (1162), RN 848 n.;

(1163), G Tours, 845-7, 862, 974;
R Westminster, 848-52, 860; (1164),
Jan., Clarendon, 852-93, *and see*
Clarendon; October, R Northampton,
ix, 853-4, 894-914; (1166), R and
E(?) Oxford, 918, 920-5; (1166-7),
M, at Northampton and elsewhere,
918-20; (1172), L Avranches, 944;
(1173), April, June, M London,
957-65; (1175), P Westminster,
viii-ix, xii, 847, 965-93, 1043,
1055; letter of summons, 967, 977-
8; provincial status, esp. 966 n.;
mss., 970-5; canons, 967, 973, 983-
91; preliminary propositions, 967-
70, 978-81; (1176), R Northampton,
996-8; L Westminster, 994, 997-1003;
(1179), G III Lateran, 1011-14; (use
in C. 1195), 1047, 1050, 1056-7;
(use in C. 1200), 1059, 1062, 1064-
5, 1067-9; (1184), M Windsor, London, 1015-22; (1188), R Le Mans,
1024; R Geddington, 1024, 1029 n.;
(1190), N Rouen, 1056; (1190), L
Westminster, 1029-31; (1191), M
Westminster and Canterbury, 1031-4;
P York, 1035; (1193), P London,
1037-41; (1195), L York, 1042-52;
canons, 1043-4, 1048-52, 1056;
(1197), R and ?P Oxford, 1052-3;
(?1199), R or P Westminster, 1053-
4; (1200), P Westminster, 1055-70;
canons, 1057, 1060-70; (1203), ?P,
1076; (1204), R, 1076; (1215), G
IV Lateran, 1058; (1222), P Oxford,
1058; (1261), Lambeth, 697;
other references: *conventus*, 73;
papal and general Cs., x, 215-16,
982; attendance at, 862; *generale*,
regionale et universale, 982; legatine, 743; (1139-41), ix; royal,
ix, 400, 623; secular, local, 163,
164 n.; English, pre-conquest,
xii-xiii; (12th cent.), xii; provincial, 814-15; list in annals of
Margam, 668; collection of English
and Norman Cs., 568, 596; precedence and procedure in, 612-14;
seating, 1029-30; *and see* synods
courts, church, 809, 866-7; William
I's ordinance on, ix, 620-4; *and
see* abp.'s, archd.'s, bp.'s courts,
Rome
courts, lay and royal, and advowsons,
856-7; and churches, 824; and
criminous clerks, 857-61; and
frankalmoign, 866

England, English (*cont.*)
309 n., 486; custom (kiss of peace), 897; *and see* Clarendon; fines under, 305-6, 308-11 *passim*, 390, 465 n., 495-7; ordeal under, 359-60; English money, 306, 310; Norman Conquest of, 563, 909; English people, and Gregory I, 353 n.; Cnut's letters to, 435-41, 506-13
Enham, King's (Hants), *see* Æthelred II, Laws
Eotkarus, *see* Edgar, bp. Hereford
Ephesus, C. of (431), 274 n., 275
Episcopus, *see* bishop(s), Wulfstar
Eraclius, patriarch of Jerusalem, 1023
Erdulf, 42
Erfastus, *see* Herfast
Ermenfrid, bp. Sion, papal legate, 563-4, 566, 567 n., 569, 577-9 *passim*, 582-3, 585
Ernald, Abb., St. Bernard's biographer, 756
Ernald de Bosco, 1002
Ernulf, pr. Christ Church Canterbury, abb. Peterborough (later bp. Rochester), 691, 694
Esau, 300 n.
Esgar the staller, 542
Essen-Verden, bishopric, 678 n.
Essex, 623; ealdorman of, *see* Byrhtnoth; earl of, *see* Geoffrey (de Mandeville, FitzPeter); sheriff of, *see* Ralph Bainard, Robert FitzWymarc, Swein
Étampes, 755
Ethelbert, St., king of East Anglia, 78 n.
Ethelbert, king of Kent, 78 n.
Etherius, abp. Lyons (wrongly called Arles by Bede), 446
Étienne of Rouen, *Draco Normannicus*, 846
Eu, count of, *see* John
eucharist, 203-5, 220-4, 269, 285, 981, 990; doctrines of, 534; and Good Friday, 219; and heretics, 924; neglect of, 456; reservation and use of reserved sacrament, 222, 251, 326, 774-5, 1048, 1061; *and see* communion, mass
Eudo Martel, pincerna, 766
Eugenius III, pope, 531 n., 811, 813-14, 820, 823, 826; and C. of Rheims (1148), 795, 818-20; nephew of, *see* Gratian

eunuch, 248, 279-80
Europe, 'Europe fines', 712
Eustace, bp. Ely, 1054, 1075
Eustace, Count, son of King Stephen, 819
Eutyches, 274 n., 275
Everard, Ebrardus, Eoverardus, bp. Norwich, 745, 753, 765, 770, 812
Everton (Hunts.), 814
Evesham (Worcs.), abb. of (Æthelwig), 403; *and see* Adam, Ælfweard, Æthelwig, Kenod, Manni, Reginald (Foliot)
Évreux, Ebroicensis, Ebroycensis, bp. of, *see* Audoen, Gilbert, John, Rotrou
Ewenny (Glamorgan), priory, dependency of Gloucester abbey, 811
exceptio spolii, 832
Excerptiones Pseudo-Ecgberti, 245-6, 314
Exchequer, 898
excommunication, 22, 458, 470, 522, 606, 658-60, 688, 701, 710, 713, 869 n., 905, 919, 1072; not to be pronounced lightly, 412; of Arius, 273; for attacks on clergy, 457 n., 794 n., 798-9; of apostate clerks and mks., 576, 680; of clerks and mks. engaging in business, 987; in C. Westminster (1102), 672, 674; (1125), 740; (1138), 774, 776-8; C. London (1143), 800-1; (1151), 824-6; C. Westminster (1175), 969, 979, 985, 987-9; of emperor by pope, 626 n.; of Gilbert Foliot, 916, 927, 940; of heretics, 925; for incest, 466 n.; of Jocelin, bp. Salisbury, 916, 940; of king, decision not to excomm. Stephen, 787, Henry II, 876 n.; of king's subject, 927; of criminous laymen, 619-20; for magic, 614; for marriage offences, 466 n.; for minor offences, 863, 867, 879, 884; for murder, 232; and outlawry, 372, 401, 440, 493, 496, 500-1; of peace-breakers (1188), 1029 n.; of rebels in York chapter (1195), 1046; for simony, 614, 987; of royal officials, 864; for selling into slavery, 345; for sodomy, 678-9, 681, 683, 687; of tenants-in-chief, 864-5, 880, 884-5, 888, 928, 937; for theft from churches, 458 n.; and tithes, 64, 979, 988-9, 1072; of violators of papal privileges,

forgery (*cont.*)
  Canterbury, primacy, privileges,
  Crowland, Pseudo-Ingulf, Westminster
Formosus, Pope, 12; letter of, 35-
  8; and division of West Saxon
  sees, 165-73
fornication, 1, 8, 29, 307, 371,
  472, 484, 496-8, 584, 688
forsteal, obstructing the law, 360
fortress work, 341
fosterlean, 428-9
Fountains, abb. of, *see* Henry Murdac,
  Richard; chronicle of, 770
France, Gallia, 906; French bps.,
  995; canonists (1102), 657 n.;
  Cathars, 920, 923; church, Galli-
  cana ecclesia, 923; crusading
  taxes in, 1023-4; kings (French),
  see Louis, Philip; court of, 784-
  5; (English, in France), 625,
  721-3, 828, 956, 1023, *and see*
  Henry, William; *see also* Normandy;
    French mss., 780 n., 795; mona-
  steries, 175-6; France and the
  papacy, 626, 918, 1075-6; and
  Innocent II, 755-7; *see also* Anacletus II, Cono, Rome, papal
  legates
Francia, Frantia, 41; Frankish kingdom, tithes in, 45 n.; Frankish
  people, conversion by St. Rémi,
  8
Frankalmoign tenure, and lay fee, in
  Const. Clarendon, 866-7, 880-1,
  884
Frascati, Tusculanum, Tusculum, 956,
  and see Tusculum
fratricide, 234-6
Frederick, Fredericus, abb. St.
  Albans, 579 n., 604, 615
Frederick I, Barbarossa, western
  emperor, 836, 917, 1011
Fréteval, 918
Friday, Good, 219, 221
Friday, observance on, 54
Fridegod, and his Life of St. Wil-
  frid, 93 n.
Frideric, Fritheric, priest of St.
  Helen's Worcester, 637
Fridolef (Fritholef) 43
Frithestan, bp. Winchester, Frido-
  sten, 42, 168-71, 185 n.
Fulbert, bp. Chartres, letter of,
  94 n.
Fulham (Middlesex), 80

Fulk, abp. Rheims, letters from,
  6-14, 16, 17
Fulk, count of Anjou, and his daughter, 731
funeral feast (guild regulations),
  58; *and see* burial
furs, beaver, ermine, gris, marten,
  sable, vair, forbidden to nuns
  (1138), 778; gris, sable, vair in
  sumptuary legislation (1188), 1028;
  furs forbidden to monks, canons,
  nuns (1200), 1070; *and see* clothing
fyrdwite, 521

G., bp. (unidentified), 664 n.
Galannus, abb. Winchcombe, 615
Galloway, Galveia, *see* Whithorn
Gandersheim, Gospel Book at, 38 n.
Gascony, Gasconia, 923
Gaul, Gallia, churches of (and
  monastic customs), 137; legate for,
  see John
Geddington (Northants.), C. of (1188),
  1024, 1029 n.
Gehazi, Giezi, 1065
Gelasius I, pope, 626, 870 n.
Gelasius II, pope, 719
Genoa, 755
Geoffrey, abb. St. Albans, 771, 779 n.,
  812
Geoffrey, Goisfridus, abb. Westminster,
  604
Geoffrey (Brito), abp. Rouen, 709,
  716, 719
Geoffrey (Plantagenet), abp. York,
  son of Henry II: as archd. Lincoln,
  958; as bp.-el. of Lincoln, 958-60,
  962, 966; as abp., 960, 1035, 1041,
  1043-4, 1047, 1058, 1074
Geoffrey, archd. Nottingham (dioc.
  York), 818 n.
Geoffrey (de Muschamp), bp. Chester-
  Coventry; as archd. Cleveland (dioc.
  York), 1046; as bp., 1054, 1058,
  1077
Geoffrey (de Montbray, Mowbray), bp.
  Coutances, 603, 608, 615
Geoffrey (Rufus), bp. Durham: as
  royal chancellor, 749; as bp., 770
Geoffrey (Ridel), bp. Ely; as archd.
  Canterbury 926-7, 930, and bp.-el.,
  958-9, 962; as bp., 983, 999
Geoffrey, count of Anjou, 909
Geoffrey, pr. Christ Church Canter-
  bury, 1037, 1039-40, 1058

Keondrud, 41-3
Keonolaf, 42
Keonowald, Keonwad, see Coenwald
Kettering (Northants.), 164 n.
killing, homicide, 299, 360, 372 n.,
  395; in church, 388; of kings, 18,
  68; by priests, 396; of relatives,
  236-7; of son, 235; penance for
  (1067 × 70), 583-4
king, authority of (as Christ's
  deputy), 125, 128, 388; (in *NPL*),
  468; and bishops, 70-1, 412;
  chapel, royal, 591, *and see*
  chapel; church, protection of, 351;
  and church dues and tithe, 392-3,
  476; compensations to, 307, 312,
  494, 501, 503, *and see* wergild;
  and councils, ix; counsellors,
  see witan;
    court, king's, 591; co-operation
  with church courts, 869, 882; and
  criminals, 470 n.; and criminous
  clerks, 879, 884, 887; and debt,
  869; and frankalmoign tenure, 866,
  881; *and see* Henry I, II, William
  I, II;
    election of, 68; and excommuni-
  cated persons, 359, 372; hospitality to, 187, 467 n.; killing of,
  18, 68, attempted, 359; kingship
  in Edgar's charter, 128-9; kingship and 'legitimate succession',
  789, *see also* Matilda, Stephen;
    and laws, 450; *see also* Æthel-
  red II, Alfred, Athelstan, Cnut,
  Edgar, Ine, etc.
    loyalty to, 344 n., 362-3, 375,
  402, 434, 450 n., 471, 500;
  mass(es) for (1009), 377, (1072),
  606; and military service, 358,
  372; payments to, 357 n.; and perjury, 490; prayers for, 54, 206,
  338 n.; priests, king's, *see*
  clergy; protection by, 70, 305,
  312, 399, 471-3 *passim*, 492, 494;
  reeve, king's, *see* reeve; residence, royal, 32; resistance to,
  360; and role in monastic affairs,
  140, protection of monks, 129,
  royal assent to election of abbs.
  etc., 139, *see also Regularis
  Concordia*; and sanctuary, 56,
  387-9, 463; surety, 500; treason
  against, 470 n., 606; and widows,
  355; *and see vicarius Christi*
Kingsbury, *see* St. Albans

King's Enham (Hants), *see* Æthelred
  II
Kingston (Dorset), 185 n.
King's Worthy (Hants), *see* Worthy
Kirtlington, C. of (977), 156-7,
  160
knights, 643; dubbing of, 676, 680
Konrat (Conrat, Coenred), 42

lahslit, laxelit, etc., fine in the
  Danelaw (p. 305 n. 3), 100 n.,
  305-11 *passim*, 360, 452, 457,
  462-3, 465 n., 495-7 *passim*, 618,
  620
Laigle, 661, 689, 690 n.
laity, *see* lay, laymen; *see also*
  church(es)
Lambard, William, 14 n., 15, 43 n.,
  44
Lambert of Arras, 651 n.
Lambeth (Surrey), *see* London
lamps, in monasteries, 613
Lanalet Pontifical, 407 n., 408 n.
land, purchase of, 467
Landavensis, *see* Llandaff
Landberht, priest, 527-8
Landuuithan, *see* Lawhitton
Lanfranc, abp. Canterbury: as mk.
  and pr. Bec, abb. Caen, 585, 588;
  as abp., 579 n., 587, 603, 607,
  614, 812, 859; 'Brittanie primas',
  619; 'totius Britannice insule
  primas', 612; 'totius Britannice
  regionis primas', 592 n.; as
  'novus Anglus', etc., 573, 589;
  (1070 and el.), 582, 585-6, 588;
  two pallia, 448 n., 569, 587, 590,
  601; (1070-1), 572-3; his *Intravit*,
  588-91; his dispute with York,
  586-91, 601-3; (1072), 578, 591-
  607 *passim*; (1074 × 5), 607-14
  passim; (1076), 616-19; (1077/8),
  xxxv n., 624; (1080-1), 627-31
  passim; (1085), 632-3; (1089 and
  death), 596, 640;
    and anti-pope, 634; and Bury, 668;
  and bp. Chichester, 580; and Canterbury lands, 643; and celibacy, 616-
  17; and consecration of the bp.
  Orkney, 630; and nuns, 663-4; professions to, 565, 572-3, 574 n.;
  and St. Albans, 830;
    his *Acta, see Acta*; his *Life, see*
  Milo Crispin; his works: Lanfranc's
  Collection, abbreviated Pseudo-
  Isidore, 608, 617, 729-30, 735,

priests, mass-priests, priestly
order (*cont.*)
219 n., 245, 296-9 *passim*, 329,
336, 398, 459; attacks on, 457;
authority of, 418, 421; and bap-
tism, 455, 1049, 1061; as bp.'s
counsellors, 460; and books,
291-2, 334;
   and celibacy, 277-81, 299 n.,
264, 336-7, 343, 349, 422, 459,
619, 688, 699-703, 776, *and see*
celibacy; hereditary, 679; twice
married, 290, 349 n.;
   and chalice, 292; as chaplains,
802-3; and chrism and oil, 455,
800-1; church, not to abandon,
458; compurgation of, 394-5, 701;
and confirmation, 370, 1049; and
costume, 296, 1050, 1067; crimes,
see clergy; deans to be, 739,
747; disobedient, 684; in Edgar's
laws, 109; expulsion of, 457, 740;
and festivals, 306, 441; and fishing, 300; and gambling, 334;
guild of, 318, 450, 461; and
homage, 648; household of, 316 n.;
and hunting, 300, 334-5; institu-
tion to benefices, 606; and interdict, 803, 825; killing by, 29-
30, 396, 492, *and see* criminous
clerks; killing of, 457, 491; and
lepers, 1068;
   and marriage, 991, 1067; and
mass, rules for, etc., 324-7, 376,
426-7, 455-6, 1060; and ordeal,
50, 334, 395, 460; pastoral letters for, viii, *and see* Ælfric;
and penitents, 581, 1048; and perjury, 490 n., 1051; not to be
reeves or hold farms, 244, 296,
682-3, 748, 803; and reserved
sacrament, 326, 775; and shaving,
459; son of, impediment to orders,
587; and sureties, 453;
   and taverns and drink, 210-11,
296, 324, 333, 335, 416, 460,
675-6, 679, 979, 984, 1051, 1067,
1073; and teaching, 293-4, 331,
1070-1; and title for ordination,
740; not to be traders, 210, 296,
319; not to transfer from one
church or diocese to another, 210,
301, 317; and vestments, 292;
   wergild and status of thegn,
336, 349, 397; *and see* clergy,
commendatory letters, *NPL*,

ordination;
   king's priests, 32, 542
primacy, *see* Canterbury, York
primitiae, *see* church dues
prioratus, 138; *secularium prioratus*,
140
prison, imprisonment of clerics,
800; for simony, 452 n.
privileges, papal, 543-5, 548-52,
and see John XII, Rome
privilegium canonis, 861; *fori*, 861-
2
proctors, 744, 746
procuration for consecrating a
church, 775; *and see* hospitality
professions, of bps., 81-2, 715,
1059 n.; of Remigius of Dorchester-
Lincoln, 573-4; of Thomas I of
York, 586, 588-91, 604-5; of
Gerard, 691-2; of Thomas II, 705-6;
and primacy issue, 706; of Giles of
Hereford, 1059 n.; *and see* Athulf,
Osbern.
Protheus, 684
psalter, 54 n., 186, 381, 606; for
soul, 58, 403; for bp., 427
Pseudo-Ingulf, chronicle of, xxxvi n.,
592 n., 634 n., 677 n.
Pseudo-Isidore, collection of canons,
xi, 195 n., 248 n., 860 n., *and
see* Lanfranc, Lanfranc's collection
Publicani, *see* Cathars
pulpit, 556
punishment, 487; 'life-sparing',
346; *and see* death penalty, excommunication, mutilation, penance
purgation, canonical, 1052; of public
notoriety, 1068
pyx, 1048, 1061

Quadrilogus (lives of Thomas Becket),
(1495) 876; *and see* Elias of Evesham, Roger of Crowland
Quadripartitus (*Quad.*), 654, 669;
extract from, 682-3; Latin versions
of AS laws in, 15, 44, 47, 53, 55-6,
61, 302, 373, 375, 418, 427, 451,
468, 512 n.; and Abp. Gerard, 697

R., 841
Radbod, pr. St. Samson, Dol, letter
of, 38-40
Ræinbaldus, Reginbald, etc., priest,
531
Ragusa (Dubrovnik), abp. of, 'Slavo-
nia', *see* Bernard